MULTICULTURAL APPROACHES IN CARING FOR CHILDREN, YOUTH, AND THEIR FAMILIES

Edited by

NEIL A. COHEN
California State University, Los Angeles

THANH V. TRAN
Boston College

SIYON Y. RHEE
California State University, Los Angeles

Boston ■ New York ■ San Francisco
Mexico City ■ Montreal ■ Toronto ■ London ■ Madrid ■ Munich ■ Paris
Hong Kong ■ Singapore ■ Tokyo ■ Cape Town ■ Sydney

Senior Series Editor: Patricia Quinlin
Series Editorial Assistant: Sara Holliday
Marketing Manager: Laura Lee Manley
Production Editor: Susan McNally
Editorial Production Service: Integra
Composition Buyer: Linda Cox
Manufacturing Buyer: JoAnne Sweeney
Electronic Composition: Integra
Cover Administrator: Kristina Mose-Libon

Library of Congress Cataloging-in-Publication Data
Multicultural approaches in caring for children, youth, and their families /edited
by Neil A. Cohen, Thanh V. Tran, Siyon Y. Rhee.
   p. cm.
Includes bibliographical references and index.
ISBN 0-205-42028-1
1. Child welfare—United States. 2. Children of minorities—Services
for—United States. 3. Social work with minorities—United States.
4. Multiculturalism—United States. I. Cohen, Neil A. II. Tran, Thanh V.
III. Rhee, Siyon Y.

HV741.M813 2007
362.7089'00973—dc22

2006005418

Printed in the United States of America

10 9 8 7 6 5 4 3 2 1   10 09 08 07 06

Photo Credits: Pages 1, UPI/Corbis/Bettmann; 37, Bob Mahoney/The Image
Works; 80, Studio M/The Stock Connection; 122, Lawrence Migdale/Pix; 158,
Andrew M. Levine/Photo Researchers; 215, Getty Images; 261, Stockbyte; 295,
AP Wide World Photos; 345, Michael Newman/PhotoEdit.

CONTENTS

CHAPTER THREE
Child Welfare Perspectives and Approaches with African American Children, Youth, and Families   75

Marlene E. Coach

CHAPTER FOUR
American Indian and Alaska Native Children: A Legacy of Suffering, Survival, and Strength   114

Rita Ledesma

CHAPTER FIVE

Child Welfare Practice with Asian and Pacific Islander
American Children, Youth, and Families   148

Siyon Y. Rhee and Anh-Luu T. Huynh-Hohnbaum

CHAPTER SIX

Multicultural Child Welfare Practice with Latino Children,
Youth, and Families   196

Lirio K. Negroni-Rodríguez and Gloria DeLa Cruz-Quiróz

CHAPTER SEVEN
Social Services Among White Ethnic and Middle Eastern Children, Youth, and Families   238

Tanya R. Fitzpatrick, Gordon Limb, and Suzanne Bushfield

CHAPTER EIGHT
Transcultural Approaches in Working with Traumatized Refugee and Asylum-Seeking Children, Youth, and Their Families   269

S. Megan Berthold

CHAPTER NINE

Administrative Issues in Diversity   312

Eileen Mayers Pasztor, Paul Abels, Teresa DeCrescenzo, and Vernon McFarland-Brown

CHAPTER TEN

Summary and Closing Remarks   350

Neil A. Cohen, Thanh V. Tran, and Siyon Y. Rhee

PREFACE

This book will provide students and practitioners of child welfare with theory and practice knowledge that is relevant, important, and timely for effective and successful interventions with communities, child welfare organizations, children, youth, and families. It will use a multicultural focus that will include different racial, ethnic, religious, gender, economic, and structural backgrounds. This book, based on generalist, strengths, and empowerment perspectives, will also discuss the commonalties found among all families, irrespective of class, race, ethnicity, age, language, gender, religion, sexual orientation, and family structure.

In a nation as wealthy and powerful as the United States, we continue to discover poverty amidst affluence. According to the U.S. Census Bureau there were 35.9 million Americans (12.5 percent) who lived in poverty in 2003, up by 1.3 million from 2002 (U.S. Census Bureau, 2004a). Children accounted for more than half of the increase in this number, with an addition of 700,000 children under 18 living below the poverty line. This has driven the total to 12,900,000 children. There were 11.4 percent of all children, or 8.4 million children in the United States who were without any form of health insurance in 2003 (U.S. Census Bureau, 2004b). Particularly, lack of health coverage is one of the most critical issues facing minority children and their families in the United States. Poverty is the major stressor and variable most closely associated with children being served by the child welfare system. The vast majority of children in out-of-home care and who have languished in the system awaiting adoption are poor children, especially poor children of color. Census 2000 (U.S. Census Bureau, 2001) also revealed the United States to be more ethnically and racially diverse than at any time in its history, as a result of increased immigration, refugee resettlement, and the mobility of families.

"Child welfare systems need to undergo constant change as they struggle to provide culturally competent and appropriate services to families and communities" (Velasquez, McPhatter, and Yang, 2003, p. 101). These factors pose further challenges to child welfare systems that are stretched to the near breaking point. The U.S. child welfare system receives about 2 million reports of child abuse and neglect each year involving about 3 million children. Nearly a million of these children are found to be maltreated, with more than half of them being victims of neglect.

Over 500,000 children are in out-of-home care in this country, many languishing far too long in a variety of settings. Child maltreatment is on the increase with too many children dying under the care of public child welfare systems' supervision. Emancipated minors are seen to continue to have poor outcomes. There is certainly a pressing need to strengthen our child welfare systems' care for the children, youth, and families in the United States. The Pew Commission on Children in Foster Care provides five guiding principles for child welfare system including (1) "Children must be physically and emotionally safe and must be protected wherever they live," (2) "Children must have their needs met in a timely manner at every stage of their development and every stage of public decision making about their future," (3) "Children must have continuity and consistency in care giving and relationships, including healthy ties to siblings and extended family," (4) "Children must have equal protection and care, including attention to meeting children's needs in the context of their community and culture," and (5) "Children and their families must have an informed voice in decisions that are made about their lives" (Pew Commission on Children in Foster Care, 2003). Although this book does not organize around these guiding principles, it endeavors to clearly frame the child welfare issues, offer culturally competent intervention modalities, and provide increased knowledge, skills, and understanding for the student and the practitioner.

The authors come from different backgrounds with a wealth of knowledge and experience in child welfare. Each selected chapter offers interested readers and students an in-depth analysis of critical and well-timed issues in the area. For the most parts, readers and students will find the chapters covering theoretical frameworks, practice paradigms, recent research findings, and case studies illustrating various aspects of practice in child welfare. This book has nine key chapters. We devote three chapters for special topics including "The Boundaries of Child Welfare" by Dale Weaver; "Fairness and Multicultural Competence in the Child Welfare System" by Sherrill Clark and Elizabeth Gilman; and "Administrative Issues in Diversity" by Eileen M. Pasztor, Paul Abels, Teresa DeCrescenzo, and Vernon McFarland-Brown. These three chapters offer the readers and students an overview of the field of child welfare, how to handle fairness and becoming culturally competent in the child welfare system, and an introduction of administrative matters within the child welfare system. The remaining six chapters address demographic and cultural background, and therapeutic interventions in selected minority populations including "Child Welfare Perspectives and Approaches with African American Children, Youth and Families" by Marlene E. Coach; "American Indian and Alaska Native Children: A Legacy of Suffering, Survival and Strength" by Rita Ledesma; "Child Welfare Practice with Asian and Pacific Islander American Children, Youth and Families" by Siyon Rhee and Anh-Luu Huynh-Hohnbaum; "Multicultural Child Welfare Practice With Latino Children, Youth And Families" by Lirio K. Negroni-Rodríguez and Gloria DeLa Cruz-Quiróz; "Social Services Among White Ethnic and Middle Eastern Children, Youth and Families" by Tanya R. Fitzpatrick, Gordon Limb, and Suzanne Bushfield; and "Transcultural Approaches in Working with Traumatized Refugee and Asylum Seeking Children, Youth and Their Families by S. Megan Berthold.

ACKNOWLEDGMENTS

The three editors would like to extend special thanks to their families and to all the families of the authors who have provided support, encouragement, and understanding over the many, many months of preparation of this book. Most importantly, all the contributors deserve special acknowledgment and recognition for their expertise and contributions to expanding our knowledge and skills in working with diverse children, youth, and families.

We thank the following reviewers for their comments on the manuscript: Susan Bowers, Northern Illinois University; Fay Wilson Hobbs, University of Alabama; Jill C. Keogh, University of Missouri, Columbia; Rosilyn Meisel, Ohio State University; Maureen Scalera, Rutgers School of Social Work; Sharon C. Wetterau, Ohio State University. The field of child welfare is extremely dynamic, multifaceted, and complex.

Additionally, we would like to thank many other professionals who reviewed this book at various stages. We are also deeply appreciative to Patricia Quinlin and Sara Holliday at Allyn and Bacon and to Satishna Gokuldas, Sendil Mourougane, and entire staff of Integra Software Services for their thorough guidance and dedicated work throughout the development of this book. Dr. Weaver also gratefully acknowledges the assistance of Jim Mamer in writing Chapter One "The Boundaries of Child Welfare."

Finally, we would like to respectfully acknowledge the support of the following persons who have been very supportive and instrumental as proofreaders and technical assistants: Glorianne Mar, Indira Velasquez, Melinda Vasquez, Carla Galvan, and Flavio Argueta.

It is difficult and almost unrealistic to address all issues and aspects of this field in one book. Nevertheless, we hope our readers and students will find the book informative and useful in working with children and their families from multicultural backgrounds.

NEIL A. COHEN
THANH V. TRAN
SIYON Y. RHEE

REFERENCES

The Pew Commission on Children in Foster Care. (2003). Fostering the future: Safety, permanence and well-being for children in foster care, executive summary. Retrieved August 15, 2005, from www.pewfostercare.org.

Velasquez, J., McPhatter, A.R., and Yang, K.Y. (2003). Preface. *Child Welfare, 82*(2), 101–102.

U.S. Census Bureau. (2001). *All Cross the U.S.A.: Population Distribution and Composition, 2000.* Retrieved September 8, 2004, from www.census.gov/population/pop-profile/2000/chap02.pdf.

U.S. Census Bureau. (2004a). *Income, Poverty, and Health Insurance Coverage in the United States: 2003.* Retrieved September 8, 2004, from www.census.gov/prod/2004pubs/p60-226.pdf.

U.S. Census Bureau. (2004b). *Health Insurance Coverage, 2003.* Retrieved September 8, 2004, from www.census.gov/hhes/hlthins/hlthin03/hlth03asc.html.

CHAPTER ONE

THE BOUNDARIES
OF CHILD WELFARE

DALE WEAVER, PH.D.
School of Social Work, California State University, Los Angeles

■ ■ ■ ■ ■
Minor children working at a sweat shop.

OVERVIEW

Child welfare is an established field of social work practice, but the boundaries and definitions of this field are by no means settled. This is because the issues of child welfare reflect the most fundamental controversies in our society. The basic value underlying the field of child welfare is the value that we put on childhood.

In contemporary Western society, the value of children is sentimental, not instrumental. Parents carry the burden of protecting and nurturing our valuable children, but there is controversy over who qualifies as a parent. More fundamental are the rights and obligations of the state to intervene when parents appear to fail to meet their responsibilities.

Policies guiding the implementation of child welfare services are overt expressions of society's best current efforts to achieve a balance between the rights of children, parents, and the state. Actual services reflect the ambivalence in these compromises, understood best as the distinction between residual and developmental services.

The persistent failure of a residual approach to services has resulted in an expansion and growth in the boundaries of child welfare. Over the course of American history, there has been an expansion of attention paid to the problems of children, an expansion of the types of problems that count as part of child welfare, an expansion of the range of child welfare practices, and an expansion of the breadth and extent of both private and public institutions. This trend toward a more developmental approach to child welfare has not been linear. The Progressive Era, the Depression and the 1970s were periods of major expansion, each followed by a conservative return to limiting the role of the government in public life.

We cannot adequately consider the boundaries of child welfare without accounting for the role of poverty in driving the underlying social problems. And we know that status and wealth are not distributed evenly in American society, so historical changes encompass changes in the relative power and affluence of economic classes, gender, and ethnic and cultural groups.

INTRODUCTION

When we think of child welfare, usually we think first about child protection—the work the state does to protect children after something has gone wrong in their families. However, the field of child welfare is much broader and more complex than the responses of public child protection agencies. If we define child welfare services as activities that enhance the well-being of children, it is apparent that this includes a very wide array of services. Child welfare programs range from broad-based services such as education, community development, and housing to narrow specialized services such as residential care for emotionally disturbed children; from long-term prevention programs such as vaccinations and product safety regulations to short-term crisis response services such as child protection; and from services focused directly on children, such as tutoring or play therapy, to services for families, such as substance abuse counseling and parent education, to advocacy services to promote new legislation and case law to protect children. Child welfare services are intended to reach all children, from the most affluent to homeless families; long-time citizens and recent immigrants; traditional two-parent families, single-parent families, extended families, and gay and lesbian families; and children and families from all of the cultural and ethnic groups that make up American society today. Social work is uniquely able to encompass this array of problems and services, but child welfare services are provided by professionals from nearly every profession—teachers, doctors, psychologists, recreational therapists, probation officers, attorneys, and others. This vast and unwieldy complex of services is intended ultimately to achieve specific goals, and the effectiveness of services should always be measured against these goals. Pecora et al. (2000, p. 9) describe these goals as protecting children from harm, preserving existing families, and promoting children's development into healthy and contributing adult citizens.

The nature and extent of the array of child welfare services that are available at any particular time and place, however, varies greatly, and is always a reflection of wider forces in the social, economic, and political context. The content of child welfare services varies over time, depending on demographic and economic changes. Differing political climates, conservative or liberal, lead to different types of child welfare services. And, because the well-being of children is so important to all of us individually, and to the community as a whole, the quality and quantity of child welfare services always reflect deep society values. "When we examine how a society cares for its children, especially its disadvantaged children, we are peering into the heart of a nation" (Lindsey, 2004, p. 1).

The boundaries of the field of child welfare are not clearly defined, and these boundaries are in fact controversial and fiercely contested in real-world politics and practice. In American civil society, including public welfare and social services, political decisions regarding the proper allocation of funds and legitimacy are always outcomes of interest group struggles. In the social services, professions, institutions, practices, and populations compete for the limited attention and resources of the public and of the political establishment.

For this reason, as an introduction to the field of child welfare, we will carefully consider these disputed boundaries. In doing so, we will move toward answers about how to define the essential characteristics of the field of child welfare and the boundaries that separate it from other fields of practice. This discussion will provide guidance to the value, historical, political, and institutional issues that will inform the consideration of specific child welfare topics for specific populations in the subsequent chapters of this book.

In this chapter, we will consider the pressing underlying issues that structure our understanding of the details, strengths, and weaknesses of the field. How are clients valued? How are their problems and strengths defined? To what extent are the presenting problems embedded in larger issues of poverty and society's neglect? Who represents the best interests of clients? What is the best array of services to meet those interests? Who should provide those services? How have these issues changed over time? And, most important for the present book, how does each of these issues vary for different ethnic and cultural groups? We begin by briefly relating the historical framework that informs contemporary child welfare practice.

CHILD WELFARE AND HISTORY

The Importance of History

The present is an extension of the past, so an examination of the past is essential for understanding the present and for shaping the future. The issues of the boundaries of child welfare addressed in this chapter cannot be fully understood outside of a historical context. The exploration of history and its application to the present is valuable because we come to understand how firmly the present is rooted in the past. The persistence and continuity of social issues and interventions becomes evident. The important issues of child welfare, and frequently the ways in which these issues have been resolved, persist over the history of American child welfare. For example, the contemporary division of labor between public and private child welfare agencies can only be understood in terms of the historical response of different sectors of society to social problems.

At the same time as we explore the persistence of social problems and society's various ways of addressing these problems, we achieve a sense of possibility for the present. Present circumstances could be drastically different if events had gone just slightly differently at times in the past. For example, Nixon's Family Assistance Plan—an extensive program proposed by a conservative administration to ensure the economic viability of all families—is likely too extreme to be considered viable during the 2000s. Nevertheless, it was defeated in part by liberal politicians who were more concerned about the low levels of support than about the opportunity to put in place a new precedent (Handler and Hasenfeld, 1991).

Thus, we take two seemingly contradictory lessons from history: "There is nothing new under the sun," and, "Everything is possible." These principles lead us to both a practical understanding of the reasons for current circumstances, given the past, and also an appreciation for the possibilities of change. For post-modern students of the past, ". . . the world's past is not seen as a unified developmental story or as a set of standardized sequences. Instead, it is understood that groups or organizations have chosen, or stumbled into, varying paths in the past. Earlier 'choices,' in turn, both limit and open up alternative possibilities for further change, leading toward no predetermined end" (Skocpol, 1989, p. 2). The following historical framework of the American field of child welfare examines factors from the past that persist into the present, as well as those that have varied over history. These factors define the contemporary boundaries of possible changes within the field of child welfare.

The Historical Expansion of Services

The field of American history in recent decades has been transformed by historians that investigate the lives of ordinary, marginalized, and oppressed citizens rather than only the lives of the elite (e.g., Gordon, 1994; Jones, 1992), and by institutional historians (Skocpol, 1992) who study the social and political past for factors that have become institutionalized over time in such a way as to structure contemporary circumstances. There is an ebb and flow to this historical story, as institutions slowly build up over time but then are suddenly and unpredictably shaken, transformed, or destroyed. Thus, we examine both the general flow over American history of the institutions and policies of child welfare, and the times in which that flow has been stopped or diverted. American history, which encompasses a relatively brief period of time, has not experienced a transforming revolution, but rather occasional periods of reform that have shaken the existing political structure without completely transforming it.

Building on this view, American history since the Revolution is described here in terms of an increasing centralization, rationalization, and bureaucratization of political and economic institutions (Scott and Meyer, 1994). This parallels, and is driven by, the development of increasingly sophisticated technologies. As American society moved from the agrarian social system of the Colonial Era through the Industrial Revolution, and into the computer age, methods of communication, manufacturing, and transportation transformed the social structures of society. As our world has expanded from rural farms and towns to urban cities in an industrialized nation, and currently into a global system, larger, more differentiated, and more impersonal economic, social, and political structures have evolved.

This process is as true of social services, and the field of child welfare, as of society as a whole. A look back at the history of American child welfare services reveals a persistent expansion and growth in the boundaries of child welfare. There has been an expansion of attention paid to the problems of children, an expansion of the types of problems that count as part of child welfare, an expansion of the range of child welfare practices, and an expansion of the breadth and extent of both private and public institutions. The boundaries of responsibility for the welfare of children have gradually moved from parents to the state. This responsibility has over time moved up the hierarchy of American government from local towns to the federal government. The boundary-defining role of the judicial system, both criminal and constitutional, has expanded greatly over time. Professions have emerged, thrived, and done a great deal to define and expand the boundaries of child welfare. Through all of this expansion, a vast system of laws, regulations, professions, agencies, and government bureaucracies has developed to govern the welfare of children.

These efforts tend to fall short over time because the economic and the demographic conditions underlying children's problems change rapidly and unpredictably, and because political efforts inevitably reflect contradictory value beliefs about the meaning of children and their role in society (Sealander, 2003). The persistent shortcomings of local and family efforts to ensure the welfare of children lead to the development of broader and more complex efforts. In this way, the history of child welfare has been one of expansion, centralization, and bureaucratization, fueled by the persistent inadequacies of contemporary efforts.

This is not to say that this expansion has been steady or predictable, either in its pace or in its nature. Rather, the process has been one of occasional periods of expansion, followed by periods of some retrenchment; two steps forward, followed by one step backward, so to speak. This expansion and contraction of child welfare services is part of larger processes in American society as a whole (Campbell and Trilling, 1980; Kolko, 1984). The Progressive Era, the New Deal, and the 1960s to 1970s were such periods of expansion of services and the role of government. These periods were followed by conservative periods of retrenchment, in which efforts were made to shift responsibility down the government hierarchy and back to the state or local level, or to the private sector. Through a gross oversimplification, an underlying pattern of unregulated business expansion, overproduction, depression, social service expansion, then contraction can be perceived in U.S. history. The following historical framework of the development of child welfare services illustrates how these services have grown over time in the context of these larger historical patterns. Many simplifications and generalities, especially the designation of historical periods, are inevitable in such a brief history.

The Colonial Era: From Colonization to Civil War (1700–1860)

The economic context in early America was agrarian. Daily life occurred in the context of family farms. A community consisted of a number of farms surrounding a small township. The extent of isolation and self-sufficiency of life in those days is unfathomable today. News traveled by individuals on horseback—it could take months to learn of crucial developments in the capital of the country. Goods moved by horseback or boat—though few goods moved, as families were nearly self-sufficient, producing not only their own food but also their own clothes, shelter, and utensils, not to mention entertainment. The unit of society was truly the family, as there was not the differentiation within the family we take for granted today. There were no breadwinning fathers or stay-at-home mothers. Though there was differentiation of labor within the family, the family thrived or failed as a unit. Everyone worked, certainly including the children. An analogous situation can be seen in the role of animals on those farms. While today we have pets in our homes that accomplish nothing practical, cats and dogs in colonial America had very specific tasks to carry out, and were not tolerated if unable to complete those tasks. In the same way, we need to understand children in terms of their economic value in the context of agrarian families. They were workers, indispensable cogs in the family farming machine; the more children you had, the more workers you had. It is also important that the persistence of family farms over generations required male children as heirs.

As we move through this period of time, of course, the move away from farming, toward industrialization and centralization of the state was underway, especially as methods of communication and transportation improved. Increasingly, household goods were produced in shops for sale to farming families, and these families began to produce agricultural products for cash sale, not just for home consumption. So towns increased in size and usefulness, while interactions between towns and farms increased (Brogan, 1999; Johnson, 1997).

In these self-sufficient families, there was little perceived need for the state to intervene to ensure the welfare of children. Education and health care were provided within the family or, later, possibly within the local community. No intervention to prevent cruelty was contemplated. Why would parents threaten the economic usefulness of their children through neglect or disability, even more than they would diminish the economic usefulness of their farm animals? If harsh measures were sometimes necessary to ensure the continued hard work of children or animals, then certainly these measures were justified.

If we look at the development of child welfare services as residual, that is, the state steps in when families are unable to cope, circumstances in which child welfare services would be required for such self-sufficient families would be rare. In case of death or disability of the parents, and if children no longer had a family to care for them, the local township authorities stepped in and placed the children with other families or with craftsmen. The resolution of the problem of the absent parents was to place children in a context that restored their economic usefulness and reinforced their development as useful members of society.

A more difficult problem was the presence of inadequate parents who through laziness, disability, or criminality were unable or unwilling to provide the desired family setting for children. The state, in this case the local township authorities, was, as it remains to this day, reluctant to take away from parents their duties and responsibilities to their children. Even at this early stage, a court decision was required for authorities to remove children from their parents, in recognition of the gravity of the action and out of concern for the potential for state abuse of its power to remove children. Courts were early recognized as necessary mediators between the rights of parents and the obligations of the state.

During these years, there was the development of the two major streams of services in American social work, and also in child welfare. There was some outdoor relief, that is, families received funds, or charity, directly to help them over tough times. This relief allowed some families to resume caring responsibly for their children without further community intervention. The other stream was institutional care, as entire families were put in poor houses if they were chronically unable to fulfill their societal obligations as productive citizens. In these cases, children simply were institutionalized along with their parents or, if orphans, without their parents. In both cases, parental inadequacy was defined in those days as the inability to instruct children in industriousness; idleness was the defined problem of child welfare (Day, 2003, Ch. 5).

This general historical outline describes the lives of white Americans. As always, minority ethnic groups experienced a very different history (Zinn, 2003). African American children were enslaved in the South, or completely segregated in the North. They did not have access to even the rudimentary services available for white children. This situation resulted in the development of parallel service structures for black children. These services in content mirrored the mainstream white services, though always comparatively scarce and poor. And this lack of adequate formal services resulted in the development of enduring institutions of informal care, most particularly the black churches and the black extended families that continue to play important roles in African American communities (Billingsley and Giovannoni, 1972).

Native Americans, as indigenous people, have always presented a special problem for the white political structure. The first policy toward Native Americans, if not always explicit, was extermination. A more enlightened policy of removal began with the Indian Removal Act of 1830, which arranged for the removal of Indians to territory beyond the Mississippi River, the assumption being that there would be no future need of that territory for the whites. This removal and resettlement was accompanied by a network of treaties and obligations that formally recognized tribes as sovereign political entities (Deloria and Lytle, 1983). Though there was never equality and mutual respect between white and Indian nations necessary for a fair and reasonable implementation of these treaties, this network of laws, regulations, and institutions, in particular the strong role of the federal government, continues to inform Indian child welfare (Mannes, 1995).

The Gilded Age: Civil War to the Progressive Era (1860–1900)

With the onset of the urbanization and immigration of the Industrial Revolution, farming declined in importance economically, though of course never disappeared as an important segment of the American economic and social structure. As we shift attention to urban America during this period of time, there are very different economic activities, and therefore very different family structures and roles of children. In manufacturing settings, the key unit of labor was no longer the family, but the individual factory worker. All family members, including women and children, continued to work, but they no longer worked at home as a unit, and they no longer produced products for their own use. Workers worked for cash and purchased food and other necessities (Brogan, 1999; Johnson, 1997).

Children as workers in industrialized settings were important. They were hard working, yet not so troublesome as adults, and frequently, as in mining, their small size was a considerable advantage. In addition, children could engage in additional economic activity such as begging or selling newspapers on the street. The income of children was essential to the survival of families. In these early days of the Industrial Revolution, wages from all family members were necessary for survival.

Gradually over this period of time, children came to be seen by interested observers as victims, rather than mere participants, of the factory system. The first reason may be increased visibility. In urban settings, the lives of children were being lived in the streets and the factories of the city, rather than in the seclusion of farm families. Also, the role of the family had diminished. Urban exploitation of children was being carried out by impersonal managers and capitalists, not by family members. In fact, the factory system was seen as destroying the ability of families to stay together and care for their own. Children were increasingly on their own without the support and protection of barely surviving families. During the same period, perhaps as a reaction to the burdens of industrialization, children came to be seen as having needs distinct from those of adults. In particular, for their appropriate development children needed emotional and religious nurturing, as well as leisure time in which to cultivate personal and moral attributes other than industriousness.

In the economic and social environment of the 1800s, religious reformers began to take an interest in the welfare of children. This was a continuation of an earlier trend (Day, 2003, Ch. 6), which expanded in earnest after the Civil War. These reformers saw their role as rescuing children from the vice, crime, and poverty of the industrialized cities. Many of our current mainstream private child welfare agencies began during these times. In the 1860s, Boys' Clubs were established in major cities. They provided sports and social activities deemed appropriate for children as an alternative to the rigors of urban life. In 1874 in New York City, the Society for Prevention of Cruelty to Animals was called on to intervene in a family abuse case. This led to the establishment of the New York Society for the Prevention of Cruelty to Children (SPCC), a type of organization that soon spread to other major cities. Though a private agency, the SPCC was the first organization given responsibility to intervene in abuse cases (Day, 2003, Ch. 7).

This concept of rescuing children had perhaps its fullest expression in the system of orphan trains, beginning with the Children's Aid Society in New York in 1853, and peaking in 1875 with a number of similar agencies. Children in need of rescue were put on trains from cities to farms and shops in the country. In this approach to child welfare, we can see reflected many of the values of that time, as well as a number of program innovations (Cook, 1996). The belief in the wholesomeness of the countryside reflected concerns about the benefits of modernization. Work continued to be the main activity for children and families, but the work of the farm was considered to be better for children than the work of the city. Some casework was necessary to carry out these transplantations. Successful placements were threatened by difficult or unsuitable children, by insincere or exploitive destination families, and by ethnic, religious, or other types of mismatch between children and families. To prevent these problems required investigation, follow-up, and judgments regarding the suitability of children, new parents, and communities. Religious and ethnic controversies were pervasive, and presaged later ethnic child welfare controversies (Gordon, 1999). The Catholic Church objected to the rescuing and placement of Catholic children with Protestant families, seeing this practice as stealing their children. Over time, major religious and ethnic groups developed their own parallel systems of child rescuing.

Though child placement and removal was, as always, cheaper than institutionalizing, there was also an increase in orphanages during this period. The poorhouses of a century ago had developed separate sections in which to shelter children away from the adults. In time, these evolved from separate wings of poorhouses into orphanages. The increase in institutionalization stemmed from the same child-rescuing impulses as the orphan trains.

While this period of time was characterized by the establishment and development of private charitable agencies, toward the end of this period there was increased state involvement in child welfare. Local governments were able to provide coordination of services and the provision of specialized services such as reform schools.

After the Civil War, the Freedmen's Bureau was established to provide services and money to African American families. This was a revolutionary development because it was the first provision of federal money for direct aid, but it was short-lived as Southern reaction to Reconstruction led to the establishment of the Ku Klux Klan and the long-lasting Jim Crow era in the South (Foner, 1988). This period of time also saw a migration of African American families to Northern cities, contributing to the general population move from rural to urban America. In both the South and the North, social services were completely closed to blacks, and the establishment and development of parallel service systems continued. The late 1800s saw the development of numerous self-help group services, clubs, schools, and so on in the black community (Billingsley and Giovannoni, 1972).

The geographical solution continued to be enforced for Native Americans, though it eventually was replaced by a policy of cultural assimilation. In 1879, the first Indian boarding school was established away from the reservation. The intent of this policy was to educate young Native Americans in such a way that they would abandon their native culture, families, and tribes, and become assimilated into the mainstream white culture (Deloria and Lytle, 1983).

The Progressive Era: Beginning of Twentieth Century

The Gilded Age of rampant economic expansion and industrialization ended with the depression of 1893. After that, the period from the beginning of the last century until World War I saw the first major expansion of the state, in particular the federal government, into the business of protecting children. The view of children from the Gilded Age—as victims in need of protection from the rigors of industrialization and urbanization—was carried forward into this period. What changed was the institutionalization and expansion of this view through the recognition that the state had a legitimate and crucial role in ensuring that protection. The focus of attention was the poor, mostly immigrant, families that had accumulated in urban areas as labor pools for factories and shops.

Also, the perils of children in this system increasingly came to be seen as a result of the destruction by that same system of the family as the provider of essential needs for children. As the family ceased to be the basis of economic activity, it also lost its ability to nurture and care for its children amid the vice and poverty of the city. From these perceptions by child welfare providers and advocates came the realization that the family can and should be the focus of support. Rather than simply removing children from suffering families, either to place them with better families or into institutions, attention turned toward directly enhancing the capacities for families to provide for the health, recreation, mental health, and other needs of their children. Another consequence of this new focus on the value of family and home life was the effort, when children did have to be removed, to make their new homes, whether foster families or orphanages, as home-like as possible. This appreciation for the primacy of family and home in nurturing and protecting children became a cornerstone for child welfare services.

The new and rapidly developing field of psychology provided the scientific framework in which to understand these social developments. In particular, a life development model became pervasive, a model that differentiated childhood and adolescence as distinct phases of life, qualitatively different from the stages of adulthood. It became seen as important that children successfully negotiate these phases, each with its own set of tasks and demands, in order to become fully realized adults. Here we see the theoretical underpinnings for such political demands as ending child labor and preserving families.

Accompanying and fueling this shift of focus from rescuing children to supporting families was the development of social work as a profession (Lubove, 1965). This development was led by well-educated affluent white women, who found themselves in a transitional period in terms of the integration of women into the economic and political system. At this time, white women of means had access to education and to the social and cultural advantages of society, while still blocked from professional careers (Reisch and Andrews, 2002). Jane Addams, who first considered a career in medicine, is the prototype of these women who found themselves with education, intelligence, connections, and energy, but few professional opportunities (Davis, 2000).

The development of social work took two simultaneous paths, a split in the profession that remains in social work to this day (Lubove, 1965). Through the Charity Organization Societies, casework was developed as a new and effective way to provide necessary services directly to families in their homes. Mary Richmond wrote the casework texts that remain the basis for much of child welfare practice. Casework was defined by the progress through diagnosis, plan, and intervention. This period also saw the development of the settlement house movement, where social workers established and lived in centers in poor communities. Both streams of social work focused on supporting and preserving families in order to provide the best context for childhood, but the settlement house social workers focused their attention on ameliorating the conditions—poverty, crime, lack of education and health care, lack of services such as socialization and translation, and unsanitary homes and neighborhoods—impeding families from achieving the strengths needed to properly care for their children. In addition, settlement house social workers, by living in the neighborhoods in which they worked, sought to minimize the class and ethnic differences between themselves and their clients. Though this effort met with limited success, the focus on civic and political issues did lead to the development from the ranks of settlement house workers of articulate and committed advocates on the national stage for the well-being of children. Julia Lathrop, for example, became the first director of the Children's Bureau. Also of great importance in the expansion of federal involvement and legislation was the research done by these settlement houses on the conditions faced by their clients. The rigorous house-to-house and neighborhood-to-neighborhood studies undertaken by these social science researchers for the first time were able to document the demographic, linguistic, physical, educational, and health status of the mostly immigrant residents of these neighborhoods. In 1909, for example, Hull House established the Juvenile Psychopathic Institute to explore causes of delinquency. These studies were of great value in educating the general public and in making the case for federal services and legislation.

The formal move of the federal government into the protection of children began with the 1909 White House Conference on Children. No federal funding was to be made available for services, but the federal government recognized its unique ability to coordinate local efforts and to disseminate relevant scientific and professional information nationwide. Annual White House Conferences resulted in the 1912 establishment of the Children's Bureau, which remains to this day a crucial source in the dissemination of information regarding the well-being of children. One of the tasks of the Children's Bureau was to identify areas for federal legislation and provide the background information for those efforts (Day, 2003, Ch. 8).

Federal legislative intrusion into the welfare of children had begun earlier with the 1904 National Child Labor Committee, the intent of which was to reduce the extent and burden of child labor. Only the federal government could effectively take on a nationwide problem like child labor, as no local jurisdiction could handicap itself economically by limiting local labor. This began a period of momentous and unprecedented movement by the federal government into areas that had previously been considered the province of local government, if not of families. Interestingly, the reduction of child labor was a controversial issue, and even many progressives were skeptical about it. This effort was first of all an intrusion of the government into family decisions; more pressing, however, was that it threatened the economic livelihoods of these families. How were they to survive without income from all able-bodied family members?

In the 1920s, there were a series of compulsory education laws. The balance between the economic needs of families and the developmental needs of children continued to be negotiated through these laws. There were exceptions to mandatory school attendance for situations where children needed to work to support their families. This issue continues to be negotiated up to the present, as we consider how much and under what circumstances high-school students should be allowed to work.

The Progressive Era phase of government expansion peaked with the 1920 Shepherd-Towne Act. Based on research from the Children's Bureau, this Act provided, for the first time, direct federal aid through the establishment of maternal and child health centers. Its passage was extremely controversial, given the unprecedented expansion of the federal government into family affairs, and it was repealed shortly after passage, as the onset of World War I began a period of conservative retrenchment (Reisch and Andrews, 2002).

The Progressive Era also saw, at the state level, the emergence of a juvenile justice system. In 1899 the first Juvenile Court was established in Illinois. The intent was to use the legal leverage of the courts to encourage and enforce the protection of children. Though not criminal courts, these courts adjudicated delinquent behavior as well as family shortcomings, with the intent of representing the best interests of the children. Juveniles had no rights of due process in these early courts (Platt, 1977).

Though the expansion of government involvement seems to be the signature development of the Progressive Era, there was also an expansion of the system of private child welfare agencies that had begun in the earlier century. Our current complex network of public and private agencies took on its basic character during this period of time, as niches were established and working relationships maintained between and among the public and the private sectors. In 1919, the American Association for Organizing Family Social Work, later the Family Service Association of America, was founded, followed by the founding in 1920 of the Child Welfare League of America. The advent of psychology as a profession led to the establishment of private child guidance clinics.

The plight of immigrants was the backdrop for the political advances of the Progressive Era. Urban industrialization was fueled by massive immigration, mostly from Southern and Eastern Europe, between 1890 and 1900 (Zinn, 2003, Ch. 11). For the most part these immigrants over time became part of the mainstream culture, but the class and ethnic distinctions during this period between Northern European long-time citizens and recently arrived Southern Europeans was considerable. Though Chinese and Japanese had immigrated to the United States after the Civil War, often against their will, for the most part they were excluded from this wave of immigration. Hispanic immigration into the West and Southwest, driven by the constant need for agricultural workers, expanded during this period along with the economy (Day, 2003, Ch. 8). Though these Northern cities contained a large number of black workers, little progress was made for African Americans or Native Americans during the Progressive Era. Though reformers like Jane Addams were acutely aware of, and deplored, the conditions of African Americans, there were no political possibilities for the advancement of equality during a time when the great struggle for advancement was to obtain the vote for white women. The general climate of reform, however, led to an increased awareness nationally of the injustices of segregation, and there was considerable contact between white settlement workers and their counterparts in the black community (Davis, 2000, p. 129).

Depression and War (1920–1960)

The advancements of the Progressive Era ended with World War I, which ushered in a period of conservative retrenchment, one giant step backward (Reisch and Andrews, 2002). The red-baiting backlash against social workers and progressive reformers was intense and bitter. Jane Addams overnight went from being the most admired woman in America to being one of the most reviled, as her egalitarian principles evolved in a time of war into a universal pacifism (Davis, 2000).

As with the Gilded Age, a great depression ended a period of unregulated industrial growth and conservative politics in the 1920s and began another era of expansion of federal services. Poor economic times in which large numbers of employable people live with uncertainty lead many to conclude that social problems stem from structural inequalities of the capitalist system, not simply from individual deficiencies. With the Rank and File Movement, social work took on the task of confronting these structural inequalities (Reisch and Andrews, 2002). Clinically, beginning in the 1920s, this period of time was marked by the emergence of psychoanalysis, as the perennial split in the social work profession between micro and macro interventions took the form of both intensified personal introspection and intensified radical involvement in labor movements. The psychoanalytic view of child development served to further emphasize the inherent value of childhood, as it came to be believed that events of childhood were directly responsible for the emotions and behaviors of adults.

The New Deal focused on poverty as a background to social problems, changing the climate in favor of providing cash support and services to populations in need, and changing the fiscal and administration relationships between the federal and the state governments. The picture of poverty in the 1930s was one of widows suffering from malnutrition and exposure, and one of able-bodied men unable to find work to support their families. As a result, the great interventions of the New Deal focused on the problems of the elderly and the unemployed. Aid to Dependent Children (ADC), the first direct provision of federal government financial support to families, was part of the 1935 Social Security Act, but as the plight of children was not foremost in the minds of reformers the structure and funding of ADC fell short of the advancements of Social Security benefits for the elderly. The administration of ADC was primarily left to local governments, and grant levels were not high. Federal policy interventions continued, with legislation such as the 1938 Fair Labor Standards Act, which further restricted the labor of children (Day, 2003, Ch. 9).

As with World War I, World War II was followed by a period of relative affluence, conservatism, and backlash against the advancements of the New Deal. The activist stream of social work practice—agitating for the advancement of children and families through social change—was nearly destroyed by the extremes of McCarthyism (Reisch and Andrews, 2002). For clinical psychology and social work, during the 1950s Bowlby's attachment theory had a profound influence on the development of child welfare services. This understanding of the importance of attachment between infant and mother reinforced the value of family, and led to further reforms of both family and institutional placements of children to ensure that children received the individual attention necessary. The negative effects of orphanages were recognized and the prevalence of these institutions for placement waned.

In the1950s, with the Bureau of Indian Affairs Relocation Act, the federal government embarked on another attempt to smother the Native American culture, this time by encouraging the movement of Indians into urban areas. Together with the earlier boarding school movement, these efforts were unfortunately quite successful, as tribes today struggle to reclaim their cultures, accompanied by the development of pan-Indian urban cultures (Olson and Wilson, 1984). During this period African American children continued to be excluded from formal service systems. However, the 1950s did see the development of important advocacy groups, such as the National Association for the Advancement of Colored People (NAACP) and Urban League, as the African American community embarked on a new phase in its struggle for equality through confrontation with the legal system, culminating in the 1954 Supreme Court decision desegregating local schools (Billingsley and Giovannoni, 1972).

The Age of Aquarius: 1970s

The 1960s and 1970s saw another major expansion of child welfare and other social services, this time not accompanied by an economic depression. This was a time of affluence, coupled with the emergence of liberation politics. The civil rights movement set the stage for this period, followed by the feminist movement, and movements of sexual liberation. It was a time of greater social problems, or at least greater recognition of social problems, together with considerable confidence in the ability and obligation of the state to address these problems. There was a strong movement toward understanding government services as an entitlement rather than a stigma. This period of time saw the emergence of the welfare rights movement, for example. The traditional family underwent some changes during this period as the only source of stability for children. There was an increase in teenage pregnancies, single mothers, and absent fathers, accompanied by an expansion of drug and alcohol abuse. While there was an increased recognition of the feminization of poverty, which allowed for the possibility of women uniting across color lines, the public face of welfare shifted from a rural white family to that of an urban black single-mother family. At the same time, increased opportunity and good economic times led to the development of a black professional middle class.

This was a paradoxical time, with the development of seemingly incompatible social and political developments. The federal government was recognized simultaneously as an oppressor of disenfranchised people both abroad and within the country, and as the only institution powerful enough to reduce this oppression. There was a centralization of power through the expansion of existing federal services, with a simultaneous decentralization of services through local community empowerment initiatives. The need for professionals increased along with the expansion of services, while at the same time the importance of community-based para-professionals was acknowledged. There was an emphasis on individual rights, coupled with a reliance on the federal government to articulate and enforce those rights.

Rather than a restructuring of the existing network of multilevel public and private services, the 1970s saw an expansion in the size and scope of existing services. Welfare roles expanded. In child welfare, there was a steady increase in services, placements, and adoptions, accompanied by increased regulation and bureaucratization. The potential for the state to meet the social needs of citizens seemed limitless. The 1960s saw the establishment of Project Head Start, the culmination of the developmental view of children. In 1975, federal law mandated the equal education of children with disabilities (Day, 2003, Ch. 10).

In the private sector, there was a corresponding decentralization of services, with a return to local community action, frequently defined by gender and ethnic issues. The women's movement led to the development of certain kinds of services, such as battered women's shelters and support groups, along with advancements in the egalitarian management of these agencies. This period of recognition of gender and ethnic differences led to the development of ethnic-based community service and advocacy efforts (Iglehart and Becerra, 1995). Together with the emergence of self-help groups, such as Alcoholics Anonymous (AA), many of these small-scale developments de-emphasized the role of professionals and increased the participation of para-professionals that were seen to be closer to the communities, and recovered victims that were seen to be better able to communicate the secrets of success. On a national scale, while the child welfare service agencies continued to provide valuable service, there developed more assertive public and legislative advocacy groups. The Children's Defense Fund, for example, was founded in 1973.

Social work as a profession reflected these changes. This period saw the development of family, ecological, and systems models, approaches that extended the incorporation of environmental elements into the understanding and amelioration of the problems of individuals. Recognition of the importance of para-professionals came with the beginning of Bachelor of Arts in Social Work (BASW) programs in 1969. In 1972, the National Association of Black Social Workers controversially came out against cross-cultural adoptions, referring to the practice as cultural genocide. The obligation of the social work profession to participate in efforts to overcome social and economic justice was codified in the 1976 Code of Ethics. The ability of the profession to comfortably straddle both the professional and the nonprofessional modes of service for both individuals and communities was, and continues to be, a difficulty (Reisch and Andrews, 2002).

For a hundred years, the issue of child abuse and neglect had remained for the most part out of the view of the state and the public. The contemporary era of systematic child abuse recognition and prevention began in the 1960s as emergency room doctors, equipped with new X-ray machines, began to notice unexplainable, sometimes long-standing, injuries in children. Through communication among these physicians emerged the new concept of the battered child syndrome. The apparent scope and brutality of physical abuse among the general population shocked the public and the legislators (Nelson, 1984). In 1972 the National Center for the Prevention of Child Abuse was established by Congress, then the 1974 Child Abuse Prevention and Treatment Act for the first time mandated the reporting of suspected child abuse. The emphasis of this act was on child protection, that is, the prompt identification of abuse and the removal of children from abusive families.

The 1960s and 1970s were periods of legislative liberation for Native Americans. The 1972 Indian Education Act finally put an end to the boarding school system, ceding educational control of Indian children to the tribes. The 1975 Indian Self-Determination and Educational Assistance Act encouraged tribal cultural, political, and economic self-reliance (Olson and Wilson, 1984). Finally, in 1978, the Indian Child Welfare Act was passed. This Act, the operative Indian child welfare legislation to this day, empowers tribes to maintain their own child protection systems, and prevents the placement of Indian children outside of the tribes (Weaver and White, 1999).

Another Step Backward: 1980—the Twenty-first Century

Since the service expansion of the 1970s, we have been in a period of retrenchment. Just as the 1970s expansion did not significantly change the structure of the system of social services, this period of retrenchment has not seen the political bitterness and hostility of the 1920s and the 1950s. The persistence of social problems such as racism, poverty, and child abuse in spite of the progressive steps of the 1970s led to a questioning of the limits of government and its ability to finally address these problems. Social service budgets had increased enormously, and with the Reagan realignment, the increasingly successful welfare backlash, and the troubled economy of the 1980s, the usefulness of these expenditures began to be questioned. Typical of these periods of retrenchment, there were successful efforts to reduce expenditures, to shift funds and decision making to lower levels of government, and to shift funds and responsibilities from the public to the private sector. In public child welfare, this period of time was devoted to refining and improving the effectiveness of the existing child protection system, without expanding the system or significantly changing its structure.

In general, as part of the temporal cycle of solutions becoming problems, the services expanded during the 1970s began to be perceived as problems rather than as solutions. Most notably, the provision of cash welfare came to be seen as creating dependence on the welfare system and reducing the motivation to work among poor people. Thus, welfare reform efforts have focused on reducing welfare roles, rather than reducing poverty. A similar dynamic developed in the field of child protection, as the problems of the foster care system itself became the focus of child welfare legislation. What was intended as a temporary solution to house abused children until either their parents became ready to accept them back into the home or an alternate home could be found became a de facto permanent placement system, one with a number of problems. Alleviating the problems associated with this foster care drift—children remaining at times indefinitely in the foster care system—was the intent of most public child welfare legislation since the 1980s. In addition to its obvious negative effects on rapidly developing children in need of a nurturing home, the system requires extensive monitoring to prevent its own child abuses, foster care is expensive, and foster parents are difficult to recruit and train.

The 1980 Adoptions Assistance and Child Welfare Reform Act was the first federal attempt to move children out of the system more quickly by encouraging early permanency planning at both ends of the system. On one hand, there was funding for services to families to keep children at home when possible. On the other hand, the legislation mandated and funded state adoption programs. There were additional funds for special needs children. The 1986 Independent Living Initiative, and the 1999 Foster Care Independence Act addressed the issue of foster care youth leaving the system by mandating and funding independent living services.

These efforts were not entirely effective in addressing the problems of foster care drift, and the 1993 Family Preservation and Support Services was the next major effort to address the problems of children at risk without removing them from their families. Funding was provided for the establishment of separate programs designed to provide families with the support and services necessary to prevent removal of their children. Many of these programs were contracted out to private agencies. The system was again streamlined somewhat in 1997 with the Adoption and Safe Families Act, which put specific limits on the amount of time children could spend in each phase of the system, as well as on the amount of time families had to prove their ability to reunite with their children.

The contentious issue of ethnic matching between children and foster or adoptive parents was clarified in the 1994 Multiethnic Placement Act and the following 1996 Interethnic Adoption Placement Amendment. This legislation, while acknowledging the importance of ethnic and cultural match in making placement decisions, asserts that the desirability of doing this is outweighed by the need for timely placement and adoption. These laws do not apply to Native Americans. The 1978 Indian Child Welfare Act was updated and clarified with the 1991 Indian Child Protection and Family Violence Act.

In terms of professional involvement, recent decades have seen an increased medicalization of child welfare problems. This is most evident in the increased diagnosis and treatment of attention deficit hyperactivity disorder (ADHD) and depression among children. In child protection, there is increased attention and funding addressing the issues of placing and adopting physically and mentally handicapped children.

THE MEANING OF CHILDHOOD

"Child and family welfare services reflect society's organized conviction about the worth of the child and the family, and the child's rights as a developing person and future citizen" (Downs et al., 2004). The first sentence in this standard child welfare text captures the heart of the matter. The boundaries of child welfare services are distinguished by the value and meaning of children as unique and separate from adults. The extent and nature of child welfare services are determined by society's conception of the meaning of childhood, a socially constructed meaning that varies over time and circumstances. The important postmodern insight that childhood is a socially constructed historically variable concept originates with the work of Philippe Aries (1962). The scope of much of the subsequent work in this tradition includes the transformations of childhood and family life from European medieval times, through the Enlightenment and the Industrial Revolution, to the modern era (Cunningham, 1995; Heywood, 2001).

The scope of American history is considerably smaller, yet understanding the historical and contemporary socially constructed meaning of childhood is essential to understanding the development of American child welfare services. Though there is historical evidence (often inadequate) of the social and economic roles of children in the past, "meaning" is primarily an untraceable internal matter of consciousness. Our ability to understand and articulate how past generations felt and thought about their children is severely limited, and we must guard against the present-centric temptation to judge other eras by our own standards. We should not conclude that we love our children more than parents did at other times. Rather we must keep in mind that we cannot know the hearts and minds of people in the past, that what changes over time is the content of meaning, not its inherent quality, and that meanings are socially constructed in ways that are appropriate and necessary given the realities of a time period.

We can describe the current American view of children as sentimental. The role of children in contemporary American social life is essentially emotional and social, rather than economic. Though underlying this sentimental value may be relief about the carrying forward of our family name and traditions, and at times we may even consider the ways in which our children may be able to provide economic support for us in our old age, these more instrumental notions of childhood are overwhelmed by the joy we take in beholding our children. Regarding children as objects of sentiment has emphasized the vulnerability of children and the need to protect them from the rigors of adult life. Thus, the shift in the social meaning of childhood in American history can be seen as a shift from viewing children instrumentally as part of an economic unit to viewing children sentimentally as an essential part of the emotional lives of families. Like so much in the development of modern child welfare, this transition occurred during the Progressive Era. Zelizer (1985) describes in detail the American shift from viewing children as economically essential to "economically worthless but emotionally priceless" (p. 5).

We have seen above how demographic and economic shifts in American society have been accompanied by shifts in how society views children and their economic and sentimental roles, and by corresponding shifts in the institutional arrangements that arise to ensure the well-being of children. " . . . the birth of a child in eighteenth-century rural America was welcomed as the arrival of a future laborer and as security for parents in later life" (Zelizer, 1985, p. 5). During Colonial times, arrangements for the protection of children reflected the reality that they were integral parts of the family economic unit. Later industrial advances and excesses separated children from their families, exposing them as occupiers of unique developmental stages that required protection from the burdens of urban industrialization. The great shift in the first part of the last century was to remove children almost entirely from the economic realm, resulting over time in smaller families and the contemporary sentimental roles of children. We have seen how theoretical and institutional developments in the professions have both reflected and fueled this shift—first developmental psychology, then Freudian psychoanalysis and attachment theory, and finally family and ecological social work models.

It is important to note that the socially constructed meaning of childhood is always unavoidably intertwined with socially constructed meanings of the importance of families, and the desirable role of women in society. In value, political, and economic terms, children always come accompanied by mothers, and efforts to define the place of children always reflect efforts to define the place of women. In providing for the well-being of children, this confluence between the needs of children and the needs of mothers has been the most problematic in the area of ameliorating poverty (Abramovitz, 1996).

These value shifts are never smooth or final. Rather, at any point in time we observe struggles between competing values, resulting in controversial situations. The movement of children in the Progressive Era from workers to elementary school students was protracted, controversial, and bitterly contested. Currently in child welfare we are witnessing a value contradiction between the belief on the one hand that poor mothers should work rather than remain at home with their children and the belief on the other hand that the government should have no role in providing child care for these working mothers.

In contemporary society, racist and ethnocentric views prevent many Americans from regarding children of other ethnic and cultural backgrounds as sentimentally valuable as their own children. This is evident in that access to quality services still varies in this country by class and by ethnicity. At the same time, social pressures in contemporary society are leading children to become adolescents at younger ages, and then becoming adults at older ages. Children from poor single-parent families are often pressed prematurely into adult roles as friends to their mothers, or as contributors to family income, while children from affluent families find themselves increasingly pressured to succeed academically, with their time increasingly structured and focused on achievement. All American children are subject to the early sexualization and commodification of childhood and adolescence pervasive in the advertising that drives our consumer society. For young adults, the postponing of marriage and child-bearing and the difficulties in becoming economically self-sufficient result in a prolonged adolescence and late assumption of full adult responsibilities.

RIGHTS AND RESPONSIBILITIES

Children, Parents, and the State

Essential to understanding the boundaries of child welfare is to consider rights and responsibilities as they are contested among children, their parents, and the state. Contemporary American children are seen as vulnerable and in need of protection from the threats of family, institutional, and social life. They are seen as occupying stages of childhood and adolescence that are necessary for development into adult citizens, each stage requiring nurturing and protection to preserve its unique needs and features. Given this need for protection, the question arises as to who is responsible for providing this protection, for ensuring the well-being of children. The first and obvious answer to that question is parents. Families are the fundamental social units of contemporary American life, with the well-being of children inseparable from the well-being of parents. It is the duty of parents, or substitute parent figures, to ensure the safety and health of children in their care.

However, the ability of the state to overrule the decisions of parents is nearly absolute, and the intervention of the state in parents' raising of their children has steadily increased over the decades. At the same time, parents' decisions are being increasingly challenged by their children, as they grow older sooner and demand to be heard. We can understand the situation as three spheres of responsibility (Archard, 2003), with parents increasingly being squeezed between children's rights on one side and the obligations and intrusions of the state on the other side.

Though it is the boundaries among the spheres of children, parents, and the state that are most contentious, the definition of each sphere is also contentious. First, who counts as a child, where controversies mostly have to do with age? At the earliest age, there is bitter controversy over when childhood begins, and what rights pertain at what early age. As children approach adulthood, again there is controversy over the point at which they can and should be making decisions for themselves.

Second, who can be a parent? For the most part, biological parenthood equals responsibility, but often that principle does not resolve dilemmas. Fathers must demonstrate significant personal relationships with their children to have any say as parents, in addition to their biological status. What say do grandparents have in making decisions about children? Same sex partners? This issue of who can be a parent becomes evident in the juvenile court system, as courts assign parental responsibility to competing adults, and in the child protection system, as agencies choose who is eligible to be foster parents, and then who is eligible to be adoptive parents. There continues to be controversies about the fitness for parenthood of single mothers, older parents, parents of other ethnic groups, and gay and lesbian parents (Archard, 2003).

Finally, what institutions constitute the state? The U.S. federal system is a complicated network of federal, state, county, city, and regulatory courts and agencies. The first issue is the relative importance of the level of government in mandating, regulating, and funding child welfare services. As we have seen, while over time increased federal involvement has led to increased regulation and bureaucratization, these issues are constantly being negotiated and adjusted. At a local level, what are the related roles and responsibilities of child protection, education, law enforcement, health, mental health, housing, and other agencies and bureaus to protect children?

Achieving a Balance

The judicial system, ultimately the U.S. Supreme Court, mediates these relationships among children, parents, and the state, ensuring that solutions are consistent with the U.S. Constitution. This kind of change through the judicial system is slow because the Supreme Court reacts to cases that come to it through the judicial system, rather than initiating the consideration of issues that seem to be of constitutional importance. Nonetheless, one turns to a series of Supreme Court decisions to observe and understand how these disputes are resolved at any point in time. Case law, like legislative law, builds up over time, so the system of laws, mandates, and legislation has grown larger, more pervasive, more intrusive, and more complex over time (Stein, 1991, Ch. 1).

There are important differences between rights and responsibilities. To have rights means that one's ability to carry out some behavior cannot be limited, if one desires to engage in that action. Responsibility, in contrast, means that one is obligated to engage in some action. Thus, having a right to do something entails choice, while having responsibility limits choice. Children increasingly have some rights, but few legal responsibilities, due to their limited capacity. Parents have not only more rights than children, but also considerable responsibilities. The state has the responsibility to ensure that children receive proper care from parents or others, though the force of this responsibility is constantly being politically negotiated. At the same time, the state has almost absolute rights to intervene, including the use of police powers. The concept of the best interests of the child is used as a guide through this maze of conflicting rights and responsibilities (Archard, 2003).

Rights imply a choice to behave that should not be abridged, but carry no implications about resources. One may have the right to do something, but lack the ability. Responsibilities, by contrast, are obligations to act or to provide, and so do require resources. The meeting of responsibility is limited by the availability of resources. Thus, the state is required to protect children, but this can be accomplished only to the extent that resources are made available. To protect every child from harm would require almost infinite resources, and so is not expected of the state, beyond a reasonable effort. More to the point, the primary responsibility (with limited rights) for protecting children lies with parents, but often our society does not provide parents with the resources to do so. Parents are required to provide medical care, when no affordable care is available; to provide for children's nutrition when fresh food is not available in their neighborhoods.

Which of these sectors—children, parents, the state—is making which decisions about the welfare of children is constantly under negotiation, and, as we have seen, over time the authority and role of the state has substantially increased. At the same time, the rights and abilities of children have increased over time, though not to the same degree (Pardeck, 2002). Areas of controversy today between parents and children include the reproductive rights of children and the circumstances of commitment to residential treatment. The contested territory between the rights of children and the responsibilities of the state includes issues of independence and emancipation, but historically has been preoccupied with the rights of juvenile criminals. From the beginning, in contrast to adult criminal courts, juvenile courts were nominally concerned primarily with the best interests of the children. Judges determined the fate of children, both abused and delinquent, by choosing a path intended to result in the protection or rehabilitation of children. This process did not include the same rights to due process that, were required for adult criminals (Platt, 1977). This paternalistic approach to juvenile justice ended with the *Gault* case in 1967, in which juvenile defendants were guaranteed the due process rights of adults, though with some provisions that ensure their protection as children (Day, 2003, Ch. 10).

The state imposes considerable constraints on the ability of parents to make decisions about their children through the established authority of *parens patriae* (Stein, 1991, Ch. 2). Children must be educated, and should not work. They must receive the type of health care mandated by the state. At the point that parents are not adequately complying with these mandates, the state will step in and compel compliance under threat of removing the children. Parents are increasingly squeezed between the demands of the state and the demands of their own children, without being able to count on having the resources to meet their responsibilities. The boundaries between the rights and responsibilities of parents, and those of the state are being contested in such areas as the type and length of education, necessity for vaccinations, and commitment to institutions.

CHILD WELFARE AND POVERTY

Poverty among Children

A case can be made that the boundaries for child welfare services are determined by rates of poverty. Though a lack of resources in and of itself is not sufficient grounds for child removal, poverty, especially as associated with single parenthood, is the primary predictor of children being removed from their homes. Nationally, 75 percent of children in foster care are from non-self-sufficient families. In Los Angeles County, 95 percent of children in foster care live in poverty (Lindsey, 2004). As we have seen in the above discussion of urban poverty in the Industrial Age, the close relationship between poverty and problems of child welfare has not changed over history.

According to the U.S. Census Bureau (2003), in 2002, 34.6 million Americans—12 percent of the population—had incomes below the official poverty line. Twelve million of those in poverty were children, almost 17 percent of American children. Comparatively, the poverty rate for adults and for seniors was about 10.5 percent. For children, poverty is related to family structure, as 26.5 percent of female-headed single-parent families were in poverty, compared with 5.3 percent of two-parent families. Anti-poverty efforts beginning with the New Deal and continuing through the 1970s, together with unprecedented post-war prosperity, brought childhood poverty rates to a low of less than 15 percent in the late 1960s. Recent highs of almost 23 percent were reached between the mid-1980s and the mid-1990s, with a more recent decrease from 1993 to the 2002 rate of 16.7 percent. There are large regional differences, with overall poverty rates varying from 5.6 percent in New Hampshire to 18.0 percent in Arkansas. As always, poverty rates vary by ethnicity. In 2002, 32.3 percent of African American children, 28.6 percent of Hispanic children, 13.6 percent of white children and 11.7 percent of Asian children lived in families with incomes below the official poverty line (U.S. Census Bureau, 2003). Because poverty rates vary by ethnicity, and poverty is closely associated with coming to the attention of child protection services, the preponderance of children of color in the public child welfare system is one of the most challenging of contemporary child welfare problems (Roberts, 2002). (This is discussed more fully in Chapter 2.)

If poverty were eliminated, how much of the problems of children would remain? Clearly, some problems not directly due to poverty, such as mental and physical disabilities, and accidents, would remain. In looking specifically at child abuse, it is clear that a great deal of child neglect would disappear, along with much physical abuse, which seems to be provoked in part by the stressors of poverty, while the role of poverty in sexual abuse in such areas of crowded housing may be less pronounced. However, it is indisputable that satisfactory nutrition and education, safe and clean neighborhoods, and consistent preventive medical care would drastically increase the well-being of children and reduce the necessity of the state to intervene.

In any case, the relationship between the welfare of children and poverty is another instance of blurred boundaries. It is clear that a consideration of the problems of children cannot exclude a discussion of the problems of poverty, and that assuring the welfare of children requires ameliorating the effects of poverty. Poverty among children is actually the poverty of parents, and so the issue of child poverty becomes entangled in the political and ideological struggles in our society over how to address issues of poverty. Just as the meaning and values assigned to women are inextricably bound up with the meaning and values associated with children, the problem of the poverty of children has shifted to the current problem of the poverty of mothers. The entire discourse over poverty issues in this county moves forward at times without mentioning the interests of children, as if welfare programs were not for children. The 1996 Personal Responsibility and Work Opportunity Reconciliation Act (PRWORA) is considered a success because it has drastically reduced welfare roles, but it is not primarily responsible for recent modest reductions in poverty. The discussions of the merits of the legislation seldom include the possible benefits of mothers remaining at home with their children rather than entering the workforce (Besharov, 2003).

Welfare Policy

The question of what elements of society should receive direct cash payments for support takes the form of controversies over the deservingness (Katz, 1986) of different groups of people. It was the great achievement of the New Deal to establish that senior citizens deserve sufficient cash support if they or their spouses worked. Social

Security, administered exclusively by the federal government, is the most universal and generous of cash support programs. At the other end of the deservingness scale are able-bodied single adults, who receive severely means-tested and skimpy General Assistance payments, administered at the most local government level. The closer a defined social group is to the top of the scale of deservingness, the more generous the payments, the less means-testing, and the higher the level of government involved. More or less deserving groups include veterans, the temporary unemployed, and the disabled (with controversy over whether mental illness or substance abuse are disabilities). In considering the plight of families with children, our society considers the relative deservingness of parents, almost always mothers, rather than of children. Though welfare is nominally for children, its relative generosity, degree of means-testing, and location in the government system depend on society's evolving value of women, motherhood, and employment. Welfare payments barely bring families to self-sufficiency, and never above the poverty line; other income is immediately deducted from payments; mothers are required to work; and the program is administered through complicated arrangements among federal, state, and county agencies. In times of retrenchment in the generosity of cash payments to families with children, as in the 1990s and 2000s, decision making is devolved from the federal to the local level.

The history of the state's attempts to address family poverty revolves around controversial issues of class (Piven and Cloward, 1971), race (Quadagno, 1994), the American work ethic (Handler and Hasenfeld, 1991), and especially the role of mothers in society (Abramovitz, 1996). Direct cash support to mothers began as widows' pensions, the first in 1911. These were local efforts based on the recognition that compensating for the absence of a breadwinning male was both a humane and a cost-effective manner of maintaining the sanctity of family. The goal of these programs was to ensure that deserving women would not have to enter the work force and could remain at home caring for their children. Those eligible for these pensions included only white nonworking women who had been married to industrious hardworking men who died through no fault of their own. These widow's pensions spread across states over the next century. The New Deal saw the first federal codification of cash support to families, with the development of ADC as part of the Social Support Act of 1935. Not until 1950 was cash for mothers added to the program. In 1961, the inclusion of fathers was allowed, and in 1988 was required. In 1962, the program became Aid to Families with Dependent Children (AFDC).

In the 1970s, the problem of poverty became viewed as an urban African American phenomenon, and welfare rolls increased considerably. At the same time, over the decades, the perceived desired role of women changed dramatically. Women's liberation provided the opportunity for women to enter the work force, and economic hardship provided the necessity for women to work. So, in the 1980s, as we saw above, welfare dependence became viewed as the problem, rather than as the solution (Abramovitz, 1996). Work requirements for women receiving AFDC were added with the Family Support Act of 1988, and dramatically expanded with the 1996 PRWORA. The PRWORA changed the name to Temporary Assistance to Needy Families (TANF), required welfare recipients to work, provided a maximum 5-year lifetime welfare stay, and shifted much administrative responsibility from the federal to the state governments. Programs to reduce poverty go beyond TANF, and include Food Stamps, Women, Infant and Children (WIC) food program, worker's compensation, and the Earned Income Tax Credit (EITC).

Personal Responsibility and Work Opportunity Reconciliation Act reduced the welfare rolls considerably without doing much to reduce the problem of poverty among children (Besharov, 2003). So the problem of poverty among children persists. Lindsey (2004) proposes enforced paternal child support and a universal children's allowance, which would acknowledge children as a separate class worthy of support regardless of the behavior of their parents, as ambitious methods for eliminating child poverty. More modest efforts to address the needs of children by alleviating the poverty of their parents, given that welfare amounts and tenures are not likely to rise soon, are in the area of making work pay by expansion of the EITC and increasing the minimum wage. Another important way to relieve the burden of poverty for working families is to address broad developmental issues such as medical care, housing, and transportation—expenditures that currently account for too much of the limited income of poor families.

CHILD WELFARE POLICY

Policy—legislative and judicial mandates coded in laws and regulations—is the bridge between the values of the society and the specific practices used to address social problems. The understanding of a social problem embodied in policy leads to the implementation of certain interventions. As seen in the above historical discussion, large-scale change is often marked by legislation. The passing of legislation is not the beginning of social change. Rather, the changing economic circumstances and values of a society generate perceptions about the need to address social problems, which in turn results in the passage of legislation and the establishment of policy. Then the legislation serves as the template for the actual interventions (Kahn, 1979). The link between legislation and the specifics of its implementation is notoriously loose. The prescriptions of policies are frequently left vague to accommodate both conflicting values and goals informing the policy, and local preferences for implementation. To understand the nature of practice in child welfare settings requires a close look at local economic, political, ideological, institutional, and professional factors. Nonetheless, legislated policy provides both a general template for social service interventions and a marker for large-scale changes in political attitudes toward social problems.

The 1974 Child Abuse Prevention and Treatment Act, the first major federal legislation directed toward preventing child abuse, was a reflection of the then 20-year increase in the public awareness of the horrors of child abuse, and the failures of state and federal information-sharing efforts to address the problem. The Act mandated for the first time child abuse reporting by social workers and others, thus having an enormous impact on the practice of child protection. In turn, the 1980 Adoptions Assistance and Child Welfare Reform Act and, later, the Family Preservation and Support Services Act of 1993 reformed the practice of child protection by shifting resources and focus from removing children to supporting families. These changes were driven both by expensive practical problems in the system, and by the enduring American value that children are always better off with their parents if possible. Another example of policy both reflecting values and effecting practice is the requirement that children removed from their families always receive treatment in the least restrictive environment possible.

CHILD WELFARE SERVICES

The Range of Problems and Services

The range of problems to be addressed in the field of child welfare has expanded relentlessly over the decades, driven by the persistent failure to achieve basic child well-being. The persistence of poverty, the reluctance to fully fund preventive programs, the expansion of government institutions, and the innovations and developments of the helping professions all result in the discovery and incorporation into the social service system of new social, educational, and medical problems.

In looking briefly over the history of the expansion of American child welfare, we have seen the steady expansion in the definitions of child welfare problems, how these definitions stem from economic and political problems of the times, and how new social service practices have arisen to address these problems. In the Colonial Era, the problem of child welfare was that of idleness, and occasional intervention by local civic authorities, with the early development of institutional services, was about the extent of child welfare practices. Even education and medical services were sparse and local.

In the second half of the nineteenth century, in the context of urban industrialization, exploitation through overwork was seen as the problem of child welfare. Social, educational, recreational, and religious interventions were added to the mix of child welfare practices. The child rescue movement, epitomized by the orphan trains, required the initial development of foster placements and rudimentary casework to ensure the success of these placements, as institutional care became more sophisticated.

The Progressive Era saw the development of the two streams of professional social work. Perhaps ultimately the most significant practice development for child welfare was social casework, which remains the primary practice intervention for working directly with families in their homes to both respond to and prevent childhood problems. At the same time, the settlement house movement expanded the social, educational, and recreational services of the previous century and proved the effectiveness of new methods of community interventions. Advocacy for children, families, and communities, initiated by social work leaders from the settlement houses, became an important avenue for change at all levels of community and government, but especially with the newly energized federal government. The implementation of compulsory education put elementary education at the very heart of child welfare, where it remains today.

The New Deal institutionalized direct economic support as an essential aspect of child welfare. Insights of psychology led to the development of mental health services for children. It was the medical profession in the 1950s that brought child abuse to the national attention, and the legislation of the 1970s that mandated the structure of child protection services that still exists, including casework, crisis intervention, foster placement, adoptions, and institutional care.

The end of the twentieth century has seen contemporary variations of centuries-old problems for children, such as poverty, homelessness, child care, truancy, and delinquency. Expansion of services during the conservative period of the end of the twentieth century and the beginning of a new century has not occurred at the macrolevel of legislative or structural changes; rather the expansion, refinement, and increasing sophistication of the helping professions, especially psychology and medicine, have resulted in the increased medicalization and specialization of childhood problems at the individual level. Services have become increasingly specialized by the type of problem, such as behavior problems, emotional disabilities, and various types of physical disabilities. New medical and mental health problems such as HIV-AIDS, asthma, fetal alcohol syndrome, and attention deficit disorder further lead to specialized and professionalized services. The development of the Internet has led to new ways of exploiting children, and necessitated new ways of combating that exploitation.

The list of social services and other interventions that contribute to the welfare of children is impossibly long and inclusive. We can add to the above list substance abuse services for children and their parents, self-help groups of various types, parent-education classes, community crime prevention, and product safety innovations.

Professions

We have seen how professions such as social work, psychology, and medicine have contributed to the development of child welfare services over time. A glance at the wide range of services that are crucial parts of the network of child welfare services shows that there is room for an equally wide range of professions—not only child psychologists, pediatricians, and teachers, but also public health nurses, child development workers, police officers, substance abuse counselors, recreation therapists, and attorneys. The involvement with children's problems of so many professionals with diverse professional assumptions, working with so many agencies and bureaus inevitably leads to all of the usual turf and ideological conflicts among professions. One example is the ongoing efforts between child protection caseworkers and police officers to coordinate their efforts and to understand each other's mission and philosophy.

A related contemporary policy issue is the degree of professionalization required for child welfare practice (Pecora et al., 2000, pp. 439–447). This controversy appears in many child welfare areas of practice. Residential treatment programs and other institutional settings hire nonprofessional or para-professional staff to cover evening and night shifts, as well as to provide basic and recreational services for residents. Frequently, the less professional the staff, the more time they actually spend with residents. In foster care, there is gradual movement toward professionalization of foster parents, especially in settings that care for children with special needs. In both of these examples, frequent and high-quality training is the key to ensure effective service delivery.

The biggest controversy, however, is in the area of child protection. Traditionally, across the country, educational qualifications have been quite low for entry-level child protection workers. In many agencies, an Associate Arts degree is sufficient; in most public agencies a BA in any field is accepted. There is an effort to increase the professionalization of child protection workers with the use of federal funds to provide a Master's in Social Work to prospective child welfare workers. The success of this effort depends on the degree to which child protection agencies are able to use the increased professionalism of their staff.

Services for Children

With many child welfare services, it is difficult to distinguish between those addressing the lives of only children and those intended to improve the lives of all members of the community. The entire community benefits from crime prevention, parks, well-lit streets, and public health efforts. Some areas of service that are also applicable to the adult population require specializations for children. Health care, mental health care, and education have developed specializations that require training and regulations to meet the special needs of children. At the same time, there are services applicable only to children such as child protection services, product protection, and so on, just as there are services such as Social Security that target only adults.

So we see that the social and economic status of children in our society requires the establishment of services specifically targeted to children, as well as specializations within professions, while children also are beneficiaries of more broad-based services. As resources are always limited, there is inevitably political and social conflict between and among these age-based sectors. Frequently, because of their vulnerability and sentimental value, children are seen as having a claim to priority in services, even if at the expense of adults. Recent efforts to increase the number of citizens with health insurance target children while not necessarily including their parents. Homeless families and runaway teens, rather than single substance-abusing adults, are priorities for shelter services. While it is possible to provide medical insurance to only some members of a family, it is more difficult to provide cash aid to children while bypassing their parents. The TANF is a special case of controversial child welfare services, as the underlying problem has been shifted from the poverty of children to the welfare dependency of adults.

Residual and Developmental Services

A more useful distinction among services than the age-based differences is captured by the distinction between developmental and residual services, originally from Wilensky and Lebeaux (1965). This distinction reflects deep-seated value and political controversies about the role of government in private life. Developmental services are broad-based services that seek to improve the lives of everyone by supporting communities and families. The underlying philosophy is a communal one, the view that all families are interconnected through their communities, that all families at times require and can always benefit from basic support, and that the state can and should play a role in providing that support. This approach is intended to build on the strengths of existing natural family and community support networks. In addition to enhancing the quality of life for all citizens, a goal is to prevent problems with children and families from developing. Some developmental child welfare services such as parks, universal education, and vaccinations have become firmly established, but others remain controversial. While TANF may be the most controversial, there continues to be conflicts about such services as community economic development and sex education for teens.

A residual approach to social services, including child welfare services, is more prevalent. This approach rests on the political philosophical view that families and communities are naturally self-sufficient, or should be, and that the state should not intervene until these natural systems have failed. Rather than a preventive approach, the residual approach represents a responsive, therapeutic, individual, disease model of intervention. This is a safety net approach, in which services are available only after need becomes evident and pressing. In child welfare services, the issue becomes how the state defines failure, and who has failed. For the most part, it is parents that fail to provide state-mandated minimum standards of care for their children, though conflict naturally continues about the point at which state intervention is most effective.

Because of its targeted methods, a residual approach usually is the most efficient use of resources, and the need for this approach is evident. There are always individual, family, and community failures that require immediate attention to save lives and to relieve the most pressing misery. No matter how extensive a developmental system is established, this will always remain the case to a certain extent.

The developmental approach, in contrast, is less efficient and its effectiveness is difficult to demonstrate. However, it has the potential to reduce or eliminate reliance on emergency and responsive services. On one hand, a residual approach targets resources where they are needed most, while developmental approaches encompass everyone, diluting the benefit for particular individuals, and including many that may not require or desire services. On the other hand, a fully implemented developmental approach would drastically reduce the need for residual services. This idea is enormously attractive for social workers and other professionals, and the case is often made for the long-term effectiveness of preventive services. However, the long-term effectiveness of prevention services is difficult to demonstrate through formal studies, and is less likely to be directly experienced by providers or by the public than the short-term benefits of residual services.

The press of immediate and severe problems, the effectiveness of targeting resources to the most in need, and the uncertain future promise of developmental approaches, all in the context of American beliefs about the limited role of government, mean that the U.S. system of social services is inherently a residual one. Though the field of child welfare potentially encompasses an almost unlimited array of services, for the state and for the field of social work, attention becomes focused on child protection rather than on more developmental issues such as reducing poverty and supporting communities. Because of the immediate and pressing nature of the residual approach, the field of child welfare has come to be associated first and foremost with the purely reactive activities of child protection.

As described above, the concepts of residual and developmental services can be applied at a macrolevel to the history of child welfare services. Our starting point, the state of child welfare services in the Colonial Era, was purely a residual approach. The economic and social assumption was that families can and should care for their own. The general expansion of child welfare social services in America since the Colonial Era has been driven by the failure of this residual approach. Over the broad scope of American history, a developmental approach to child welfare services has gradually developed as residual approaches have consistently fallen short of adequately solving the social problems of children (Epstein, 1999; Golden, 1997).

So the scope of child welfare services, both contemporaneously and over time, is driven first by a reaction to pressing problems, followed by the buildup of developmental services in efforts to go beyond responding only to immediate problems. In this way, the American system of child welfare services is primarily of a residual nature, with the gradual establishment over time of more developmental services in response to the shortcomings of limited residual services.

Level of Intervention

While the competing merits of residual versus developmental approaches to social services is an ongoing underlying conflict in the provision of social services, a related tension about the most appropriate level of intervention is also played out in the field of child welfare. How do we best sustain, protect and nurture children? By working directly with the children to build their capacities and to overcome their traumas? By working with families to improve their abilities to accomplish these things with their children? With communities and tribes to increase the availability of the resources—recreation, education, health, safety—necessary for parents to do their jobs? Or at the level of the legislative process, by passing legislation ensuring that children, parents and communities will have the opportunity to provide the context for the positive development of children? The actual mix of these services varies over time. As described above, we have seen how the relative importance of macrointerventions in social work has increased during progressive periods and decreased during conservative periods of retrenchment, while approaches at the individual level have expanded during conservative times.

The overwhelming inclination, however, in child welfare services is to address interventions toward parents. There is a value consensus in contemporary American society that the family, however it is constituted, is the best social context for raising children and ensuring their well-being. The less that outside interventions are needed to substitute for the care that children should naturally receive from their parents, the better. Therefore, services that address parental obstacles to child-rearing are considered the most effective way to ensure the well-being of children. This approach is also efficient as it builds on the strengths of existing social structures, rather than seeking to replace them. Family preservation programs, whether targeted toward families whose children are about to be removed, or to families who volunteer for supportive services, are the prototype of family-directed services.

Still, direct services for children are frequently necessary. Except for such broad-based services as elementary education and vaccinations, these are generally reactive therapeutic services. In addition, increasingly, services intended to strengthen community supports for families have come to be seen as legitimate child welfare services. Midnight basketball, after-school programs, community fairs, and street lighting are examples of community-based services intended to enhance the quality of life for all the community's children, as well as ultimately to reduce the incidence of child abuse. Class and legislative advocacy continue to be crucial areas of intervention as well.

CHILD WELFARE AND ETHNICITY

The extent and nature of the problems of children vary by ethnicity. These differences come, first, from the different histories of these groups. We have seen how slavery and segregation have led to the development of parallel formal and informal institutions among African Americans, and how centuries of efforts to wipe out Native American culture have led to current policies intended to preserve that culture. The immigration histories of all ethnic groups must be considered (see Chapter 8), including both the traumas they bring with them and the difficulties they experience on arrival (see Chapter 9). Second, the problems of children are closely tied to the prevalence of poverty, and poverty rates vary greatly among ethnic groups, as do problems that stem from poverty. African Americans have had high rates of child neglect (Chapter 4), and Native Americans high rates of substance abuse and suicide (Chapter 7). Thus, just as it is difficult to separate out the role of family income in child welfare, it is difficult to separate out the relationship between ethnicity and poverty in understanding child welfare problems across ethnic groups. Third, there are cultural differences that underlie different views of child-rearing, child abuse, family structure, and the role of women across ethnic groups. The boundaries of child welfare are constantly being negotiated between ethnic, cultural, and religious groups, and the dominant culture. Some Hispanic families rely on the use of traditional folk medicine, the effects of which can be suspect to mainstream child protection workers (see Chapter 6). Korean immigrants show high rates of physical abuse of children because of their traditional use of corporal punishment (see Chapter 5). Fourth, services are not equally available for different ethnic groups, as well as for different classes. Historically, ethnic minorities have been under-served and poorly served by services that do not respect cultural differences (see Chapter 2).

These differences in types of problems and the views on different types of solutions raise the question of the extent to which child welfare services should be structured around ethnic and cultural groups. On one hand, it is clear that services must be culturally appropriate, at the very minimum to the extent that individuals are not excluded. Services must be available in the language of clients to even begin an intervention. Further, service providers must understand the family and interpersonal dynamics among the presenting cultural group in order to engage clients and to work toward solutions. For example, the Native American Community-Based Family Resource and Support Program has been established by the Southern California

Indian Center to serve the unique needs of urban Indians (Children's Bureau, 2004). In addition, ethnic-specific services are able to target resources toward specific problems of particular groups. For example, the One Church/One Child program focuses on the recruitment and training of African American foster and adoptive families (Veronico, 1983).

On the other hand, there are factors mitigating against the effectiveness of ethnic-specific services. Often, as among Los Angeles' Latino and Asian communities, there are many subgroups that are as culturally distinct among themselves as between ethnic groups. It is difficult for agencies to develop the cultural and language specificity to meet the cultural needs of all of these groups. Members of ethnic or cultural groups are often geographically dispersed, so that members of a cultural group are faced with the choice of going to a culturally specific service a great distance away, or to a mainstream service nearby. There is always tension between tendencies toward assimilation among members of minority groups, and desires to preserve and extend cultural identities. Some members of a cultural group may value assimilation more than cultural maintenance, preferring the use of mainstream services. In particular, this may reflect generational differences among cultural groups, whereby second- or third-generation immigrants prefer culturally dominant services, while culturally specific services are more appropriate for their parents and grandparents.

In any case, no matter what the local demographic, cultural, or institutional differences are, it is essential to account for cultural differences in the provision of child welfare services, in a manner that accounts for these local differences (Hogan and Siu, 1988; McPhatter, 1997; National Association of Social Workers, 2001).

GENERALIST SOCIAL WORK

Given the wide range of problems of contemporary youth and children, the cultural and ethnic diversity among American children, the expanse of specialized services available, the need to operate on both microlevel and macrolevel and the need to simultaneously address crises and provide preventive services, where is a social worker to start? What problems are to be addressed first? What skills are most important? Consistent with a generalist social work orientation, care is needed in properly matching the level of intervention with the presenting problem, matching worker skills and training with the problem, and maintaining a proper balance between levels of intervention. Social work is uniquely situated with a broad understanding of the entire field of child welfare, an understanding that allows for assessing and maintaining balances between all of these demands.

Within the conceptual framework for child welfare presented in this chapter, we advocate for the importance of a generalist social work perspective. While specialists are always needed to address specifically diagnosed individual, family, and community problems, the broad range of child welfare services requires a generalist to take an overview and to structure treatment planning that can take effective advantage of the array of available services. We have seen that child welfare services do, and should, include both crisis and preventive services; problems with child and adult individuals, families, and communities; and clients from diverse ethnic, cultural, and class backgrounds. Effective child welfare practice requires an understanding of the demographic, economic, and institutional realities of diverse children and families, and an appreciation of the importance of class and legislative advocacy.

SUMMARY

Child welfare is an established field of social work practice, but the boundaries and definitions of this field are by no means settled. What counts as child welfare is often ill-defined, and always controversial. This is because the issues of child welfare reflect the most fundamental controversies in our society: What does it mean to be a child? A family? What are the correct power relations among children, parents, and the state? The fundamental value underlying the field of child welfare is the value that we put on childhood. In contemporary Western society, the value of children is sentimental, not instrumental. The nature and boundaries of sentiment are impossible to quantify and specify. They vary by class, gender, and ethnicity, and so they are controversial by nature, and always will be.

Parents carry the burden of protecting and nurturing our valuable children. Of that, there is little doubt in current American society, but who qualifies as a parent—gay and lesbian couples, single parents, or older adults—evolves over time and remains controversial. More fundamental are the rights and obligations of the state to intervene when parents appear to fail to meet their responsibilities. This issue reflects ongoing fundamental conflicts about the sanctity of family, the individual rights of parents, and the role of the state in public life.

Policies guiding the implementation of child welfare services are overt expressions of society's best current efforts to achieve a balance between the rights of children, parents, and the state. Actual services reflect the ambivalence in these compromises, understood best as the distinction between residual and developmental services. Broad-based developmental services seek to improve the lives of all citizens by supporting communities and families. The underlying philosophy is communal and preventive, emphasizing community over individual rights, and often emphasizing government over private intervention. The residual approach rests on the views that families are self-sufficient by nature, and that government services should be available only as a last resort, and only for those who have demonstrated incapacity for self-sufficiency. Other areas of boundary disputes in child welfare are reflected in the competition among professions to provide services to children, and in the issue of the best level of service intervention—individual, family, community, or policy.

To understand the present circumstances of these boundaries, we need to consider the history of the field of child welfare. The persistent failure of a residual approach to services has resulted in a persistent expansion and growth in the boundaries of child welfare. Over the course of American history, there has been an expansion of attention paid to the problems of children, an expansion of the types of problems that count as part of child welfare, an expansion of the range of child welfare practices, and an expansion of the breadth and extent of both private and public institutions. The responsibility for the welfare of children has moved from parents to the state. This responsibility has moved up the hierarchy of American government from local towns to the federal government, and the role of the judicial system has expanded greatly over time. Professions have emerged, thrived, and done a great deal to define and expand the boundaries of child welfare.

This trend toward a more developmental approach to child welfare has not been linear. Rather, there have been periods of expansion followed by periods of retrenchment. The Progressive Era, the Depression, and the 1970s were periods of major expansion, each followed by a conservative return to limiting the role of the government in public life. The 2000s are dominated by efforts to increase the decision-making power of parents and families, and to devolve power from the federal government to the states and other local governments.

These historical changes of course reflect large-scale economic and demographic changes. Thus, the economic fate of children, always connected to the status and wealth of their parents and affected to varying degrees over time by government intervention, is a persistent theme in the field of child welfare. We cannot adequately consider the boundaries of child welfare without accounting for the role of poverty in driving the underlying social problems. And we know that status and wealth are not distributed evenly in American society, so these historical changes encompass changes in the relative power and affluence of economic classes, gender, and ethnic and cultural groups.

CHAPTER TWO

FAIRNESS AND MULTICULTURAL COMPETENCE IN THE CHILD WELFARE SYSTEM

SHERRILL CLARK, PH.D.
California Social Work Education Center, University of California, Berkeley

ELIZABETH GILMAN, M.A., J.D.
School of Social Welfare, University of California, Berkeley

Multicultural human service setting.

OVERVIEW

This chapter addresses how race, culture, language, life experiences, and power status shape our understanding of fairness as a value in child welfare practice. One's own beliefs about fairness influence social work practice. These beliefs have been developed

35

and transmitted by our families of origin, the communities in which we live, and by our status in society. They have been shaped further by personal life experiences.

As social workers it is important to understand and to be respectful of different groups' views about fairness. To have this awareness in child welfare practice, the decision-making process must be thoroughly understood in order to anticipate when fairness could be an issue, to help other child welfare professional team members understand those issues, and to advocate for remedies to unfair allocation of resources for families.

This chapter offers a social exchange/distributive justice framework for examining the concept of fairness and describes how different groups conceptualize fairness in different ways. Using examples from recent research about the overrepresentation of children of color in the child welfare system, divergent ideas about fairness are illustrated by examining the decision points in the course of a child welfare case. Using the decision points as a framework, strategies are outlined for preventing or significantly reducing inequities of treatment and intervention that produce and perpetuate system overrepresentation. Finally, knowledge, values, and skills required for ethical, culturally competent social work in the child welfare context are described.

INTRODUCTION

This chapter will address how race, culture, language, life experiences, and power status shape our understanding of fairness as a value in child welfare practice. We raise the issue of fairness in a book on multicultural child welfare practice because persons from different cultural and racial groups hold different conceptions about what constitutes fair treatment. Consequently these competing views often clash or create misunderstandings in a diverse society. There is evidence that families and children of color are treated unfairly throughout the child welfare system.

One's own beliefs about fairness influence social work practice. These beliefs have been developed by our families of origin, the communities in which we live, and by our status in society. They have been reinforced by our life experiences. As social workers it is important for us to understand and to be respectful of different groups' views about fairness. To have this awareness in child welfare practice, we need to know enough about the decision-making process to anticipate when fairness could be an issue in child welfare, to help other child welfare professional team members understand those issues, and to advocate for remedies to unfair allocation of resources for families.

The consideration of fairness affects individual social worker relationships with clients, organizations, and communities. Fairness enters the public policy arena when decisions are made as to how and when to distribute resources to families to help them provide safe and healthy environments for their children. Inevitably, social work practice is influenced by the concepts of fairness embedded in public policy. Organizational rules about service eligibility or appropriate levels of service affect fairness. Organizational rules interact and may even conflict with views of fairness held by individual social work practitioners. Even though public policy makers may strive to create systems that treat persons fairly overall, fair and equitable outcomes for individual families may not always result. When social workers work with families, we make decisions about distributing resources according to our assessment of the need and the availability of resources. As with organizational rules, our own informal personal rules influence social work practice with colleagues and families.

■ ■ ■ ■ ■

CASE STUDY 1 THE DECISION TO PLACE A CHILD IN OUT-OF-HOME CARE

Tina, a child protective services worker, has been called to take a report on Charles, an 8-year-old boy, who came to school with extensive bruises on his arms and legs. Charles lives with his parents in a very poor part of town which is also a high-crime neighborhood. Tina decides to place Charles in foster care. She calls her office from the school to find out where there are foster home vacancies. She finds three vacancies, two of which are in Charles' neighborhood, but Tina decides that neighborhood is too dangerous and places Charles in the third foster home on the other side of town. She then calls Charles' mother.

Discussion Question: Under what circumstances should a social worker make the decision to remove and place a child in foster care before talking to the family?

This chapter will address how fairness and child welfare practice interact. First we will present a framework for examining the concept of fairness and its many meanings. The framework will then be applied to examples of multicultural child welfare social work practice. Using examples from recent research about the overrepresentation of children of color in the child welfare system, we will discuss how fairness affects the course of a child welfare case at different decision points.

It is extremely important to remember that at each decision point, child safety, risk of reabuse, and the protective capacity of the parents *must be fairly* assessed, using appropriate assessment tools (see Figure 2.1). It is the fairness of the assessments that we focus on in this chapter.

After examining the decision points, we will outline strategies for preventing or significantly reducing the inequities that result from such overrepresentation. Finally, we will describe the knowledge, values, and skills necessary for practicing in the field of child welfare in the context of ethical standards for culturally competent social work.

THREE RELATED FRAMEWORKS FOR FAIRNESS

Social Exchange

Social work practice focuses on the interaction between a client and his or her environment. When a family is referred or voluntarily comes to a social agency for help, the social worker and the agency he or she represents become important aspects of the family's environment, and the family, worker, and agency interact to affect each other.

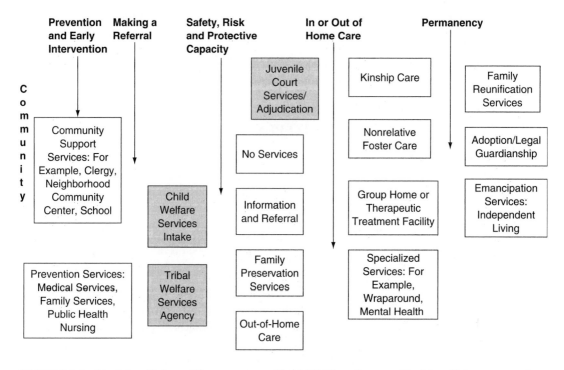

FIGURE 2.1   Decision Points: Elements in a Child Welfare System. Decision Points occur when transitioning from one state (represented by the boxes) to another. Assessments precede all decision points.

Social exchange theory focuses on the interaction itself, not necessarily on the actors. From varying perspectives, other psychosocial theories tend to address the following question: "Does the individual influence the group or does the group influence the individual?" Social exchange, by focusing on the interaction, conceives of influence as a two-way, reciprocal process, with the individual and the group influencing each other. The extent to which each has the power to influence the other affects the value of the social exchange.

The main propositions of social exchange theory are

1. Social behavior is an exchange of material and nonmaterial goods.
2. People behave purposively in ways that cause beneficial exchanges to happen and will repeat this behavior if it is rewarding. Cultural background may influence what is held materially and symbolically valuable for groups and individuals.
3. Benefits received in an exchange are contingent on benefits perceived as given, and people try to maximize their gains in any exchange. There is a satiation factor when maximum utility is achieved.

With its concepts of costs and rewards, social exchange is similar to an economic exchange. However, unlike an economic exchange, which can be a one-time occurrence, a social exchange depends on an ongoing relationship (Emerson in Rosenberg and Turner, 1981). Fairness comes into social exchange when one takes into account the value of the items or resources exchanged.

■ ■ ■ ■ ■

CASE STUDY 1   Continued

Tina's telephone call to Charles' mother, Sylvia Brown, did not go well. It started off all right; in fact, Mrs. Brown sounded relieved that Charles was safe. She said the bruises had been inflicted by her striking Charles with a belt, but she was only trying to keep him from hanging out with "the bad kids down the block." Mrs. Brown was deferential and polite to Tina. She repeatedly, but respectfully, asked when she could see Charles. But when Tina told Mrs. Brown that Charles was placed in a foster home across town, Mrs. Brown got angry. Mrs. Brown wondered why Charles' grandmother or the neighbor on the next block who is a foster mother was not contacted. "It would be much easier for me to visit him there and he has stayed there before. I have to take three buses to get to and from work and now you are making me take three in the opposite direction to see my son! What about his school? That isn't fair!" She was very upset and demanded to see Charles "now." Discussion question: In the example above what happened to change Mrs. Brown's approach to Tina? Who holds the power in this exchange? As long as Mrs. Brown felt she could see Charles easily, she was polite but she seemed to come to the end of her rope. Why? When did the exchange stop being mutual?

The sociologist, George Homans, developed the theory of social behavior as social exchange. He noted that social equilibrium among individuals is primarily concerned with the relationship between reward and cost. When reward and cost are balanced, he called this relationship "equity." However in comparing the behavior of cooperative subgroups in a society toward each other, their objective "should tend toward equality. The less-advantaged group will at least try to attain greater equality" (Homans, 1958, p. 604). He called this tendency to move toward equality among comparable groups "distributive justice." Distributive justice has been conceptualized in several different ways involving the achievement of equilibrium among groups of people in a society.

When the usual or normative expectations for resource allocation are not met and a condition of injustice or inequality is identified, the result is pressure to change the distribution system. Different justice norms are preferred under different conditions. Within society in the United States, apparent tolerance for different norms of justice can be explained by differential consideration of the social, political, and economic realms of life. For example, there is little support in our society for a ceiling principle limiting the amount of money one person can make or for the redistribution of wealth, especially in the economic domain (Hochschild, 1981). However, there is support for the principle of equality in the political domain (one person, one vote).

■ ■ ■ ■ ■

WHAT IS JUSTICE?

For what is justice? It is to fulfill the fair expectations of man. Thus, American justice is a very special thing. For, from the first, this has been a land of towering expectations. It was to be a nation where each man could be ruled by the common consent of all—enshrined in law, given life by institutions, guided by men themselves subject to its rule. And all—all of every station and origin—would be touched equally in obligation and in liberty. Lyndon Baines Johnson, Howard University commencement address, June 4, 1965 (Johnson, 1965).

Distributive Justice

Distributive justice is often used in the macrocontext of group social exchange, but it applies to individual exchanges as well. In individual relationships (social exchanges), microdistributive justice principles apply. Examples are *need, equity, merit, contribution, desert, entitlement, retribution, and rank inequality* (Rescher, 1966). *Need* is a principle of subjective equality, defined by a person. *Need* appears to be a straightforward principle, but depending on who is defining the need, it can be controversial. For example in health care, a doctor defines "medical need" for certain treatments, while a patient may feel quite differently. The opinion of a managed care company representative may differ from the doctor's definition.

Equity can be defined as relative equality or a two-way transfer of resources for mutual benefit (Adams, 1965; Cook and Hegvedt, 1983). *Merit, contribution, entitlement*, and *desert* are related to *equity* in that they represent a type of equality that depends on an individual's relative input into a social exchange. They are all relative equality principles: A person gets what he or she deserves or merits by measuring the extent of his or her contribution. The difficult part is the equation of value, which is subjective. *Rank inequality* results from the assumption that some persons require unequal rewards according to their relative rank or class. An example is reserved parking places close to building entrances for the disabled and assessing fines on those who use them illegally.

A form of social exchange theory closely related to rank inequality is called "status value theory" (Berger et al., 1972). Status refers to a person's standing in a group, community, or society. Status value theory can be used to explain why new immigrants have less social power than those who have been in a country long enough to establish group membership and political influence. Within different ethnic groups, high status may be conferred on one who has lived in this country for 20 years and can speak English and low status may be conferred on one who has recently immigrated and does not speak English. Similarly, the value of an exchange with a person of high status is greater than the value of an exchange with a person of low status. In child welfare, an example could be that while both a child and a prospective foster family may be Hispanic, placing a child of a new immigrant with a family who are second-generation Hispanic may create a power imbalance and thus an uncomfortable situation for both families.

On a macrolevel, social exchange creates obligations among members of different groups. Members of one group will benefit from exchanges with other groups, but when exchanges are unequal, people incur obligations to one another. In some communities, the custom of giving dowry to a bridegroom's family provides an example of this type of exchange. Social interaction is often considered the glue that holds societies together. Public policy derived from the principles governing social interaction is distributive justice (Homans, 1958).

- - - - -

GIFT-GIVING AS SOCIAL EXCHANGE

In preindustrial societies, the gift incurred reciprocal obligations. Some societies are known for holding ceremonies in which the rich and powerful give food, beverages, and other gifts in exchange for loyalty. The Northwest Coast American Indians held potlatch ceremonies (Boas, 1967) in which goods would be given away or destroyed. The intent was that valuable gifts, such as elaborately carved art and canoes, eventually would be returned for in-kind value as loyalty to the chief of the tribe. Gift-giving also had mystical meanings and was intended to remind people of their ancestral heritage and past obligations to each other.

In German the word *Gift* means both gift and poison: The *Rhinegold* extracts a very high price from the person who dares to take it from its natural state in the river bed and forge it into a ring of power.

In medieval Europe the poor were often seen as sacred or favored by God and to be revered. It was the obligation of those more fortunate in this world to give to the poor who were seen as giving up their claim on this world for the next.

Examples of macrosocial exchange or macrodistributive justice are the principles of *Equality, equal opportunity*, and *equal results*. The microprinciples of *equity, need*, and *desert* are the individual-level precursors to the macroprinciples. For example, one person's *need* may be seen as representative of the needs of others in the same group and as a call for *equality* for all the individuals in the group. In 1955, Rosa Parks' refusal to give up her seat on the bus, which led to the boycott of Montgomery Alabama buses by the African American community, is a good example.

In the child welfare context, if some children receive in-home family preservation services as the first choice of intervention, why are not all children entitled to equal consideration under the same conditions?

- - - - -

CASE STUDY 2   THE DECISION TO PROVIDE IN-HOME SERVICES

Connie, a child protective services worker assigned to work with the local hospitals, is called to take a referral on Jae-Sung Kim who was born 4 weeks prematurely and who shows signs of being an "irritable baby." He currently is in the neonatal intensive care nursery. His mother, who went home 48 hours after the birth, is a young, unmarried Korean woman who only visits him late at night and some of the nurses think she is "high"

(continued)

■ ■ ■ ■ ■

CASE STUDY 2   Continued

when she visits. The nursery staff, including the resident on call, are very concerned about whether the baby's mother can take care of him at home and want him placed in a foster home directly from the hospital.

While Connie is visiting, Ms. Kim comes to visit her baby and they realize that there is a language barrier. Connie informs the nursery staff that Ms. Kim is highly fearful of the hospital because her father died in a hospital last year, but she has agreed to go with Connie to the mental health clinic to speak with a Korean-speaking intake worker. There is no Korean translator on duty at the moment. When Connie returns, she informs the staff that Ms. Kim is very worried about her ability to care for a sick baby and has welcomed the suggestion that several visits with the public health nurse to prepare to take Jae-Sung home would be beneficial, even as he remains in the hospital.

She states she has no plans to remove Jae-Sung to a foster home at this time. The charge nurse shakes her head and tells Connie, "I don't know why we call child protective services. You people never do anything."

Discussion Question: What happened? How should Connie handle this?

While social exchange considers the value of the resource exchanged, it, unlike an economic exchange, does not end after one transaction. Because the relationship or interaction is not complete after one instance, each actor in the exchange incurs certain obligations toward the other. Such obligations create differences in status between people: Conventionally, creditors (those who are owed) hold power over those who owe. Those who owe are dependent on those who have resources to distribute. However, the person who is owed may in reality depend on the power to reciprocate and may rely further on the continuance of the relationship for his livelihood. Hence, social exchange is a "theory of mutual interdependence" (Thibaut and Kelley, 1959).

One person's reliance on another person is a potential source of power. Social exchange creates a power-and-dependence relationship. For example, a child welfare worker may be more powerful than parents because he or she can remove their child from them with the state's authority.

■ ■ ■ ■ ■

CASE STUDY 1   Continued

Tina's perception of Charles' neighborhood as dangerous affects her decision-making about first making a foster care placement, and then where that placement should be. She is satisfied that Charles is safe for now and is baffled by Mrs. Brown's response to her decision.

Most parents in this situation feel powerless; parents with low status may feel even more powerless relative to most parents. Once the child has been removed, the social worker holds even more power: the power to decide when to return the child and under what conditions. It is important to keep in mind that some parents, especially refugees and asylees, have had negative experiences of powerlessness with any government intervention in their lives.

■ ■ ■ ■ ■

CASE STUDY 2   Continued

Connie, recognizing that the anxious Ms. Kim does not speak English well, meets with her and an appropriate translator before making a decision to place Jae-Sung, but now her relationship with the hospital nursery team needs repair.

Procedural Justice: How Is Fairness Decided?

The decision making does not end when the principles of fairness are determined. How the decisions are made is another consideration. This is called "procedural justice."

Political philosopher John Rawls (1971) devised a "thought experiment" as a way to illuminate a society's decision making about resource distribution. This experiment's primary condition was that no one person knew his or her status as decisions were being about how to distribute resources in a new society. The idea was that by not knowing one's own status (how each would wind up), each decider would be more likely to apply fair procedures.

In the United States the avowed purpose of public social policy is to "limit arbitrary distinction among individuals or groups" (Purtilo and Cassel, 1981). However, achieving a fair distribution of society's benefits or the *right* to such distribution does not mean that individuals will be treated fairly (procedural justice). For many impoverished children, for example, the right to a public education does not guarantee their receiving the same quality of education as their more affluent neighbors. Procedural justice is the set of rules for the application of distributive justice principles. By isolating certain groups of persons who are not perceived as part of the social majority, the society as a whole may not apply majority-group fairness standards to these individuals.

These three constructs—social exchange, distributive justice, and procedural justice—are perhaps the most frequently noted when theories of fairness are discussed. What the theories do not tell us is how people decide how to attribute value to an exchange. Nor do they tell us the extent to which different groups value different things. As ethical social work practitioners, however, it is our job to learn how different people value different things, especially regarding the family. It is essential to keep in mind that most cultures regard their children as their most important and valuable contribution to the society.

The social exchange/distributive justice framework gives us tools with which to analyze decision making within the child welfare system. There is compelling evidence *that even when cultural considerations are not taken into account*, the child welfare system has operated unfairly with regard to families of color and has created inequitable situations for those families. The next section of this chapter will be devoted to applying principles of social exchange and distributive justice in the context of the child welfare system and looking at how children and families of color are disadvantaged. As a further application of this framework, we will then examine the roles and tasks of child welfare social workers and the development of competencies to foster equitable practice.

CHILDREN OF COLOR ARE OVERREPRESENTED IN THE CHILD WELFARE SERVICES SYSTEM

Children in the United States

How do we know there is a problem? According to the 2003 updates to the 2000 census, the United States had an estimated total population of 290,809,777 persons. There were an estimated 70.6 million children under the age of 18 who make up 24.3 percent of the total population. Of these children, 27 percent have low income, defined as below 200 percent of the federal poverty level. To what extent does the child welfare system reflect these numbers?

Children in the Child Welfare System

According to reports from Child Trends Databank and the Adoption and Foster Care Analysis Reporting System (AFCARS) in 2001, African American and American Indian/Alaska Native children were overrepresented in the foster care system nationwide based on their proportion in the U.S. general child population. In other words, more African American and Native American children appeared in the child welfare service population than we would have predicted, given their numbers in the general population of children.

Among the children in the child welfare system, there are also disparities among different groups with respect to the proportions in out-of-home care. Because federal funding for children in the child welfare system is derived primarily from Title IV-E of the Social Security Act, which pays for out-of-home care, we might expect that most children in the child welfare system would be in out-of-home care rather than other parts of the child welfare system, such as in family maintenance, emergency response or early intervention. However, among children in out-of-home care, there are higher proportions of children of color.

There were 542,000 children in foster care nationwide during the 2000–2001 federal fiscal year that ended on September 30, 2001. Table 2.1 shows the percentages of children who entered and left foster care during fiscal year 2001 and compares these percentages to the estimates of the population of children by race or ethnic group.

According to Table 2.1, among children in out-of-home care, 2 percent were American Indian/Alaskan Native children, compared to 1 percent American Indian/Alaskan Native children in the population. Further, 38 percent of the children in out-of-home care were black, non-Hispanic, as compared to the 15 percent of the general child population occupied by this subgroup in 2001.

TABLE 2.1 Race/Ethnicity of the United States Foster Care Population as of September 30, 2001, Compared to Estimated Population of Children under 18

	PERCENTAGE OF RACE/ETHNICITY OF CHILDREN IN FOSTER CARE (NUMBER)	PERCENTAGE OF RACE/ETHNICITY OF CHILDREN WHO ENTERED FOSTER CARE (NUMBER)	PERCENTAGE OF RACE/ETHNICITY OF CHILDREN WHO LEFT FOSTER CARE (NUMBER)	PERCENTAGE OF ESTIMATED UNITED STATES POPULATION OF CHILDREN UNDER 18?
American Indian/Alaskan Native	2% (10,106)	3% (7,364)	2% (6,544)	1%
Asian/Hawaiian/Pacific Islander/non-Hispanic	1% (5,200)	1.4% (4050)	1.4% (3,735)	4%
Black non-Hispanic	38% (204,973)	28% (81,118)	30% (79,308)	15%
Hispanic	17% (89,785)	16% (46,574)	15% (40,346)	18%
White non-Hispanic	37% (203,222)	46% (134,773)	45% (117,377)	62%
Unknown/unable to determine	3% (17,235)	3% (9,079)	4% (9,602)	—
Two or more races/non-Hispanic	2% (11,479)	2% (7,042)	2% (6,087)	—
Total	100% (542,000)	99.4% (290,000)	99.4% (262,999)	100% (72,600,000)

Sources: U.S. Department of Health and Human Services, Administration for Children and Families, Administration on Children, Youth, and Families, Children's Bureau. Population: U.S. Census Bureau Population Division, Table US-EST2001-ASRO-01-National Population Estimates-Characteristics.

Children in Poverty

Demographic information compiled from the Census Bureau by the National Center for Children in Poverty shows the proportion of children of color who live in poverty. The federal poverty level is $18,400 annual income for a family of four. Low-income families have less than $36,800 per year of income or are below 200 percent of the poverty level. In 2001,

- 62 percent of Hispanic children lived in low-income families
- 29 percent of white children lived in low-income families
- 58 percent of black children lived in low-income families.

Research shows that family structure is associated with family poverty. Children living in families with single mothers tend to be poorer than those who live with two parents or with grandparents. Again, information from the National Center for Children in Poverty shows that

- 54 percent (6,633,961) of low-income families are headed by a single parent.
- 18 percent (4,571,058) of all other families are headed by a single parent.

The proportion of children of color who live in families where poverty co-occurs is greater than the proportion of children with white parents. It may be that poverty and family structure interact with race and ethnicity to bring children of color into the child welfare system at greater rates than their white counterparts. However, it is important to note here that the presence of poverty, although a factor among single-parent families and a contributor to the lack of available resources in communities, does not explain why the child welfare system treats families of color differently than majority families (Roberts, 2002).

CASE STUDY 1   Continued

When Tina talks to Charles' mother, she only has time to tell her about the placement, ask that she come to the office, tentatively ask about what happened, and to gather basic information about the immediate family. She finds the mother overwhelmed with work and caring for Charles' two younger sisters. Mr. Brown has moved out of town to try to find work and will be gone for at least 6 months. Tina does not find out that Mr. Brown's married sister lives nearby and may be a resource for the family. Tina does not ask about any other relatives.

For his part, Charles says he misses his family. This week he will miss a field trip to the natural history museum because he is not at home and his foster parents cannot find transportation to take him across town to school. The foster parent reports that after his mother visits, Charles becomes weepy and will not eat.

Discussion Question: Tina does not ask about other relatives because she believes that "the apple doesn't fall very far from the tree." How does this affect her decision making from now on, since Charles is already in foster care?

CHILD WELFARE SYSTEM DECISION POINTS

To improve child welfare services, we need to examine where key decisions are made in existing systems to determine whether practice reflects the values of fairness and equal opportunity. We need to do this on a local, community basis and resist relying on aggregate national or even statewide data. Recent studies have examined the role of a host of independent variables in child abuse incidence, looking for possible factors in bias. These include child's race, type of abuse and type of reporter, substantiation rate, victimization determination, parental characteristics, abuser characteristics, and child welfare system differences. In this section, we will systematically look at the decision points in a child welfare case and review what research shows about each area. We will also introduce skills and knowledge necessary for fair child welfare practice, and we will present strategies for avoiding unfair or potentially unfair results.

Prevention and Early Intervention

In some communities, formal agency resources are available to help families prevent problems. Specific examples of *formal* programs for families and children are

- Public health nursing visits for first-time mothers
- Early Head Start programs for very young disadvantaged children
- Health insurance through the state children's health insurance program
- Early Periodic Screening Detection and Treatment (EPSDT) through Medicaid to detect preventable learning and health conditions and to direct children and their families to treatment and after-school programs.

In addition, school social workers or counselors may offer referral and other counseling services to students. Informal services also act as supports and prevention agents to families in many communities. Examples of *informal* services include

- Family members unofficially caring for children while parent is working away from home, in prison or under residential treatment, or otherwise unavailable
- Neighbors providing informal supervision after school
- Church or other faith-based organization members offering food or voluntary childcare services. Some church communities keep up-to-date lists of formal and informal local resources for parents who need help with specific problems, such as childcare availability.

One important service gateway for poor families is through the Temporary Assistance for Needy Families (TANF) public program that replaced Aid to Families with Dependent Children (AFDC) in 1996 under the rubric of welfare reform. Workers in this program used to be called "eligibility workers" because they primarily determined whether families were eligible for cash assistance, according to federal policies. Now these workers can be called "employment counselors" or "intake workers." This program is designed to support poor families with cash grants as long as the parent (usually a single mother) is willing to look for work or to get training for work. The focus of the TANF program has been employment development, but several counties and states, El Paso County in Colorado, for example, have assigned workers to the TANF program to provide services to address the needs of families with working parents (Berns and Drake, 1999). The county director in El Paso County has conceptualized the poverty program to be the primary prevention program for child welfare services (Berns, 2001). Not only this is done in order to support the work effort and help the parent succeed in becoming economically self-sufficient, but it also serves the purpose of assessing a family for potential problems and offers preventive services.

Although these formal and informal supports exist in many communities, all community members, particularly those who are impoverished and socially isolated, do not have equal access. Children of color, in particular, do not always have equal opportunity to access culturally competent prevention and early intervention services (see Johnson, 1965). Additionally, children whose families speak English as a second language, or who do not speak English at all, are disadvantaged by the lack of proficient, culturally knowledgeable service providers. The culturally specific strengths and customs of some families may be misinterpreted by child welfare workers unfamiliar with the culture in question, sometimes with serious detrimental results.

Strategies

At the prevention and early intervention stages, strategies for addressing fairness concerns can include public services in ethnic communities such as child abuse prevention and new parent education, early childhood health screening, and child safety outreach campaigns. Child welfare agencies can collaborate to develop minority-defined and minority-based models of early intervention and family preservation. Policies can be developed that expand the definition of "relative" care to include nonmajority-based definitions of who is part of the family. The community of service providers can be encouraged to participate in intercultural communication training. The various professionals who constitute the multidisciplinary response team could benefit from the same, as well as training on how to work effectively as a team. Child welfare services agency staff could be located or outstationed in the community they serve with other members of the multidisciplinary team; for example, the TANF workers, mental health practitioners, domestic violence counselors, substance abuse counselors, and public health nurses.

In addition, new options for service could be offered at the paraprofessional level such as teaching homemakers, substance abuse aides, and community home visitors. Through focused, on-the-job training, social workers and other decision makers could develop greater expertise in engaging, assessing, and motivating parents. Communities could develop their own child safety plans with support from community and public agencies. Poverty-targeted intervention and support programs could be codeveloped by the agency and community members. To heighten effectiveness and a sense of "ownership," agencies could assign certain community resource development tasks to specific social workers.

■ ■ ■ ■ ■ ▬▬▬▬▬▬▬▬▬▬▬▬▬▬▬▬▬▬▬▬▬▬▬▬▬▬▬

CREATIVE FIELD PLACEMENT

A student who had been a former county employee who had returned to school to obtain her Master's degree in social work wanted to do "something different" for her second-year internship. Working with the field instructor and the school, she developed as a special project a community-based center for grandmothers who were taking care of their grandchildren with child welfare system involvement. The center was such a success that upon graduation, the county not only continued the project, but made her the project manager. Her goal was to expand services to grandmothers who were informally taking care of their grandchildren as a prevention service.

Reporting Suspected Child Abuse and Neglect—Bias at the Beginning?

A report of suspected child abuse is obviously the result of a decision-making process on the part of the reporter. In that moment of decision, bias may play a role. Many professionals are mandated reporters of suspected child abuse and neglect. Every state has laws about mandated child abuse and neglect reporting. These can be social workers, teachers, domestic violence counselors, police officers, doctors, and public health nurses. When a mandated reporter or other concerned person calls to make a report of suspected child abuse or neglect, the first point of contact is generally the Hotline or Emergency Response line. Once that occurs, the recipient of the call (who may be a social worker, a social work aide, or a clerk) gives the information to a decision maker about the risk to the child or children based on the caller's information. Sometimes there is very little information available. Based on the caller information about the child's or children's safety or risk of harm, the Hotline worker's decision options are (1) to offer referrals to community services, (2) to refer to the emergency response workers, or (3) to do nothing.

There is some research to support the assertion that reporting may be biased from the first point of contact. The timing and act of reporting is one of several points in the child welfare process in which biased judgment may enter. Bias may indirectly enter the equation in several contexts such as:

- *Service availability:* In affluent areas, there may be fewer calls to the Hotline because of a higher awareness of prevention services and the greater presence and greater accessibility of services in such areas.
- *Screening practices:* County public hospitals may routinely screen every newborn for drugs, but private suburban hospitals may only screen teenaged parents. In most communities, teenaged parents are more likely to be persons of color and/or poor.

Looking at state level data on investigation and victimization, Fluke et al. (2003) found that African American children were overrepresented and white children consistently underrepresented at the "decision to investigate" stage in a five-state study. At the point of victimization determination, little disproportionality was found statewide, but differences remained from county to county. This may mean that the disproportionality occurs when African American children are initially referred to the child welfare agency (Fluke et al., 2003). In addition, it may mean that aggregated state information may mask certain types of disproportionality.

If the call is referred to the emergency response worker, once that worker has assessed the situation for safety and risk, he or she must make a decision about whether to offer child welfare services. In one study done in California, 80 percent of the calls to the Hotline resulted in no services. Only 8 percent were opened in the child welfare system. Of those 8 percent, however, 40 percent of the cases opened had an additional report made in the next year (De Panfilis, 2002).

Based on the social worker's knowledge of the community, the first decision may be to substantiate child abuse and/or neglect, and the first intervention may be to remove the child from the home and place him or her in out-of-home care. Judgments are made by social workers and the court legal dependency system about viable alternatives to out-of-home care, such as the fitness of relatives, the location of the relatives' neighborhoods, and the character of the community. In the flow of a child welfare case, does the family have community or other resources on which to rely? The greater the availability of community ties and resources, the less often crisis will occur and the less likely government intervention becomes. However, what if a family doesn't have any or doesn't know of any resources, and they are poor? What if they are new to this country? What if there is no source of relative care nearby? In a more perfect world, a family's dependence on public resources has many alternatives and is only necessary as a last resort.

Increasingly, as more multicultural data become available from child welfare agencies required to demonstrate the efficacy of their services, the discrepancy between outcomes for the children of culturally diverse families and outcomes for white children grows. Minority children are more likely than white children to be removed from their homes for child abuse and neglect, receive fewer services within the child welfare system, remain in foster care for longer periods, and are more likely to come back into foster care again after they return to their families (Courtney et al., 1996). As we examine various aspects of the child welfare process, we can see elements of this disturbing pattern as it takes shape.

Substantiation and Victimization Rates

Substantiation is the point at which an investigator or a social worker determines that child abuse or neglect has occurred and can be substantiated with facts. There is some evidence to indicate that cases involving children of color are substantiated more frequently than those involving white children. However, the victimization rate, the rate at which children of various backgrounds are harmed or injured, does not show the same discrepancies. In an earlier study, the authors reached the conclusion that African American children are not at greater risk for abuse and neglect than white children, but they are reported and investigated more often (Ards and Harrell, 1993; Ards et al., 1998).

A Minnesota study comparing substantiation rates among American Indian and African American children revealed that the children of color were not treated the same way as white children. Researchers Ards and colleagues examined data from counties with large minority populations ("study counties") and compared this data with data from nonstudy counties and with statewide aggregated data (Ards et al., 2003). Ards and colleagues found that disparities in the treatment of children of color "could not be explained fully by characteristics of victims, offenders, counties, reporters, and the types of alleged maltreatment." When the Minnesota group could not explain the variance between groups after accounting for all variables noted above, they concluded that the differences resulted from discrimination.

Safety and Risk Assessment

Safety assessment occurs at the initial referral for the first time and subsequently along the case planning and treatment process. Risk assessment often happens when a child has been referred to out-of-home care and the risk of going home to his or her family must be calculated. Researchers who have developed actuarial tools for assessing risk in child abuse and neglect report that bias exists in risk assessment screening when clinical judgment is used (Baird et al., 1999), as opposed to seemingly more objective risk assessment tools. Child welfare researchers, practitioners, and policy makers continue to debate the potential for predicting abuse using clinical judgment versus actuarially developed risk assessment tools. On their side of the debate, actuarial tool designers are able to present research evidence of fair decision making in rerisk assessment. These actuarial tools, however, assess risk in situations where abuse and neglect have already occurred; consequently these instruments assess the possibility or *reabuse* rather than initial abuse or neglect (Baird et al., 1999).

On the other side of the coin, risk assessment is an area in which clinical judgment and the effort to be fair have resulted in some incorrect assessments. In an effort to attend to cultural issues (and to be fair) some safety considerations may be missed, especially in an effort to be fair to families who present with different values than those held by the social worker (Baird et al., 1999). Baird found this to be true for social workers who were trying to be culturally aware, but who did not really understand the culture of the family with whom they were working. The social workers were often reluctant to act when a situation was neglectful because they did not want to appear to single out the parent because of his or her cultural values. One strategy to address this potential problem is to insure that professionals are able to interpret and correctly assess abuse and neglect in terms of both more universal child development stages, and a "prudent parent"[1] standard that exists for families in a given community.

CASE STUDY 1   Continued

Tina is writing a court report to request that Charles remain in foster care for now. Her supervisor asks her what her reasons are for continuing to keep Charles in foster care. Tina states that the community is unsafe and therefore it is likely that Charles will be abused again if he goes home.

Discussion Question: If you were the supervisor what would you ask Tina now?

Foster Care

As noted previously, significantly more children of color are placed in foster care than their numbers in the child population would indicate. Several factors appear to combine to create this situation. At a stage when placement might be prevented, African American families are offered access to family preservation services at lower rates than other families (Denby et al., 1998). Children of color tend to be offered out-of-home care in lieu of in-home services at the front end of service provision more often than majority children. Thus they enter foster care at higher rates than white children, although their characteristics may be the same or similar. Their families are offered fewer services to keep families together before the option to place a child in out-of-home care is used (Denby et al., 1998); consequently they are found in out-of-home care more often than other children and in greater proportions.

The fact that placement is used, an action that must be supported by legal intervention, may prejudice the type of service subsequently provided. By the time the situation is such that the child gets to court, there are few other alternatives or resources available. This makes the court very powerful. It is generally understood

[1]Some states have legal definitions of prudent parent. The concept refers to parental liability due to negligence. A prudent parent is one who exercises good judgment and common sense in matters affecting the well-being of his or her child.

that the child welfare legal dependency system overrelies on out-of-home care as the intervention of choice because of the way child welfare services are funded by public policy (Pew Report, 2004).

Personal and residential characteristics of families may conflict with those of the social worker or court officer, resulting in stereotyped thinking and decision-maker bias toward using out-of-home care, rather than in-home services. Stereotyping may occur on the basis of ethnicity, neighborhood, economic level, culture, age, substance abuse history, sexual orientation, or single-parent status. The worker may regard kin or the neighborhood of kin as unsafe. There may also be a bias against using kin because of fear of collusion with family members or outmoded thinking: "the apple doesn't fall far from the tree." The child may be placed out of the neighborhood because the worker may be afraid to go into the neighborhood. The worker may not speak the family's language and translators may be unavailable. Choosing placement may be not so much an assessment decision. Rather, it may reflect a lack of confidence in one's assessment tools and skills or a way to avoid making the wrong decision. These biases are not limited to social workers. There may be a local judicial culture biased in favor of out-of-home care and against teenaged single parents, for example. Judges and court systems, court-appointed clinicians, police, and school personnel often exhibit the same or similar conflicts and issues with regard to family characteristics as social workers. In its efforts to rebuild foster care and establish broad community support for local foster care networks, the Annie E. Casey Foundation's (2001) Family to Family Program is attempting to ameliorate this situation.

Through removing children to a safer neighborhood, with more financially secure parents or with a two-parent family, or by placing children in culturally different neighborhoods, social workers and other professionals often intend to improve the child's life chances. Despite being well-intended in many cases, these decisions may create unfair and even emotionally destructive situations for families and children. Perhaps the most prominent and extreme example of such placement was the forced separation of thousands of Native American children from their parents in the nineteenth century to attend "Indian Schools" far from home (Lomawaima, 1994; Trennert, 1988). As noted in a recent study, foster care placement itself can have a traumatic effect on children, giving children a sense of loss, fear, abandonment, isolation, helplessness, and confusion (Finkelstein et al., 2002). Not surprisingly, it appears that a combination of preplacement and placement trauma leads to negative effects on both academic performance and school behavior in foster children (Geroski and Knauss, 2000).

Nevertheless, when the decision maker is an individual social worker with many cases, or a law enforcement officer responding to an emergency call, there is a greater possibility that the error will be in favor of out-of-home placement as the more conservative choice for the child's safety. If, as it appears, families of color are offered in-home services less often than white families, then this practice creates further unfairness in the system. What are some of the factors that result in unfair distribution of resources? Do workers intend to be unfair? This is not likely. Moreover, the placement system is constrained by legal time limits, for example, that call for permanency planning for children who have spent 15 of the last 22 months in out-of-home care.[2] Sometimes the most convenient placement is made instead of the best one. The initial decision to place based on child safety may wind up being more permanent even in light of new information. Placing a child across town with a foster family may seem to be less complicated and expensive when compared to placing him or her with an aunt who lives 2000 miles away.

The Timing of Family Reunification

In some child welfare systems, there is now an option of differential response to child abuse and neglect. In differential response systems, it is readily acknowledged that one service does not fit all families. However, at the point of determining which response to take to a family, placement, or in-home services, are there some assessments biased by who is more cooperative and who is more resistant, rather than safety and risk? Do those groups of persons who are seen as more resistant wind up going to court more often than those who are seen as cooperative and who can generate a case plan without going to court? The social worker must have skills in assessing, engaging, and motivating parents to participate in the child protection and service planning processes. Further, it may be the social worker's role to motivate other team members to do the same. Unfairness in the child welfare decision-making process results when service availability determines decisions rather than needs. To compound the problem, needs are often decided without parental input, especially when workers have difficulty communicating with families. This kind of unilateral process does not encourage social exchange and cooperation.

Harris and Courtney (2003) report finding a significant interaction between race, ethnicity, and family structure with respect to family reunification. Specifically, they found that being a single-parent family and being African American put a family at a disadvantage for reunification. In two-parent families, being Hispanic conferred a reunification advantage on both African American and Caucasian families. A child of an African American single parent, however, is more likely to experience longer periods of foster care than the children of other single parents. Once children of an African American single parent have been placed in out-of-home care, they are reunified at a slower rate than two-parent Hispanic or white children.

The researchers also found that child health problems slowed reunification, as did being in out-of-home care with kin. Children who were removed because of neglect were reunified more slowly. Neglect may be a sign of poverty or of the presence of substance abuse in the family. Hence, it could be argued that substance use by parents is another factor in slower reunification, but this study did not indicate the presence of substance abuse among the population of families.

Once African American and Native American children are in the child welfare system, they tend to stay longer. Biases not only come into play at the time of the decision to place a child in out-of-home care, but they also affect the offering and provision of family reunification services when the time comes to decide where the

---

[2]See the *Adoptions and Safe Families Act of 1997* (Public Law 105–87).

child should live after out-of-home care. Reunification may depend on equal access to services for different groups. Availability of services in one's neighborhood can influence reunification rates positively.

When services are not available, children's legal rights may not be equally enforced. In case planning, a core issue is that needed services are unavailable or are limited in poor neighborhoods.

■ ■ ■ ■ ■

CASE STUDY 1   Continued

Tina has developed a treatment plan for Charles and his family which has been approved by the juvenile court judge. This plan indicates the mother's need for improving her parenting skills and managing her anger. Mrs. Brown has to take three buses to the family services agency across town after work because there are no anger management classes during the day nearby in her neighborhood. As a result, she misses every other class because her childcare is unreliable. Her missing classes are characterized as resistance or noncooperation to the juvenile court judge, and reunification is delayed. What would a better strategy have been? A better strategy might have been to explore the single-parent self-help group that has been developed by the pastor of the church in Mrs. Brown's neighborhood. Although she is not single, since Mr. Brown has been out of town for so long, the pastor feels Mrs. Brown could benefit from participating in this group. This arrangement would permit the mother to participate in the services and also make it easier for her to carry out the treatment plan without having to take three buses.

Mental Health Service Use among Children in Foster Care

Multiple variables affect mental health services use: Older, male children who are not in kinship care, who have been sexually or physically abused, and those with greater emotional and behavioral problems receive more mental health services than other children. In a study of foster youth, however, even when controlling for the level of need, one report showed that a court referred Caucasian youth more often than African American and Latino youth, 71 percent, 46 percent, and 61 percent respectively (Garland et al., 2003).

System level factors may interact with family/cultural factors to complicate the study of racial/ethnic bias in mental health services use. For example, Latino youth are referred to mental health services less often than Caucasian youth, and numerous studies have shown that Latino families have been found to use formal mental health services less often than others and to rely more on traditional healers. Caseworkers may make assumptions about family preferences, culturally appropriate services availability, or the efficacy of such services, and not refer to formal mental health services. When this kind of biased thinking occurs, families are not given the opportunity to choose whether they want traditional healing or are willing to try Western medicine or both.

In addition, families may feel more comfortable when the service treatment planning process includes them and community traditional healers who can provide support and connection to their community (Jackson, 2003).

Strategies for Addressing Fairness at the Point of Foster Care Entrance

As a standard matter of assessment, identifying Native American children and complying with the Indian Child Welfare Act (ICWA) (P.L. 95–608) is essential at the start of intervention and prior to a foster placement decision. Signed into law in 1978, the ICWA was drafted to prevent the breakdown of Indian families and tribes. As a federal statute, the ICWA takes precedence over state laws and reaffirms tribal jurisdiction in custody cases involving Native American children. In terms of supporting individual child welfare worker's efforts to employ fairness, collaborative supervision to identify and address individual assumptions is crucial. For supervision, the expectation that families are to be included in case planning is a must, in order to put the treatment in the context of the family's values. A team approach to case planning should include more than one professional in addition to the family. Although usually seen as a more mesotask or macrotask, the individual worker can also work with community leaders to identify resources that may be needed by many families, thus including the community in the solution to child abuse and neglect. Most urban planning and architecture schools know how to design buildings to be family friendly and these professionals can help to design or to renovate existing buildings to make them more "welcoming" and approachable to the community.

Developing standardized safety assessment tools with community members and applying them fairly can be an important strategy for staying in touch with the community and for supporting social workers. Since safety is not an one-time activity, safety guidelines may have to be reestablished at many decision points along the way. Parents will have to understand the components of safety assessment and should be helped to develop plans for when situations become unsafe. If local resources are not available, then the community and agency can develop them together. This is another area in which local community resources that are nearby and *culturally consonant* with the families are very important.

Training should be multidisciplinary whenever possible to ensure that professionals, paraprofessionals, and community members understand their common goals—as well as their different focus and language. Learning something new together is an important social exchange activity that can level the power playing field and encourage team communication. Training, when agency-based and inclusive of the community, can also serve as a venue for clarifying shared and individual responsibilities within an agency environment and a community. Training that includes mandated reporters of child abuse and neglect can help in a number of ways. First, it can address the community's assumptions about child abuse and neglect and the expectations of the child welfare agency and the community.

In terms of the organization and the system, neighborhood-based services or family resource centers located in communities encourage cross communication and accessibility. Co-locating different professionals in one community-based office creates team membership and encourages the community to approach and participate in helping families and children.

Adoption

Children of color who are legally available for adoption remain in the child welfare system longer than white children (Needell et al., 2003). Some are not placed at all. According to the AFCARS Report using 2001 data, 22 percent (116,653) of children in foster care have the case goal of adoption, up from 19 percent in 1999. Among the 126,000 children who are waiting to be adopted, including children not in foster care, 45 percent (56,306) are African American children, up from 42 percent (53,340) in 1999, 2 percent (2,146) are American Indian/Alaskan Native children waiting to be adopted.[3] Among the 50,000 children who were adopted in 2001, 35 percent were African American (17,500); 1 percent (715) were American Indian/Alaskan Native (U.S.H. & H.S., 2002, 2003).

The Adoption and Safe Families Act (1997) and the Safe and Stable Families Act (2000) call for concurrent planning when children go into foster care. This means that the child welfare worker must plan for two contingencies at the same time: safety and permanency. If after a certain amount of time in the child welfare system the conclusion is that a child cannot be made safe within his or her own family, then alternative permanent arrangements are supposed to be implemented. The preliminary work and the investigation of these permanent arrangements are required to be done at the outset.

As part of the California Long Range Adoption Study (C.L.A.S.), researchers found about one-third of prospective white adoptive parents willing to adopt African American children reported being discouraged from doing so by their social workers. Among those prospective parents who actualized their adoption, only 12 percent of those who were willing to adopt an African American child actually adopted one. The same study also showed that among those prospective parents who were not willing to adopt African American children, very few of them could be convinced to change their minds (Brooks and James, 2003).

To conduct concurrent planning calls for special kinds of foster parents: those who might be willing to adopt children as well as temporarily foster them. To identify such parents, special local agency efforts can be made to recruit in local communities, and special training can be provided.

Older children, children of color, and children with behavior or anger problems are less likely to be seen as adoptable by their workers, as well as more likely to be perceived as costly to care for by prospective adoptive parents. These factors may lead to serious disadvantages for these children in the permanency decision-making process.

---

[3]Waiting children are children who have a goal of adoption and/or whose parental rights have been terminated. Those children who are 16 or older and who have "emancipation" as their goal have been excluded from this figure.

In addition, there are financial disincentives for families to leave the child welfare system, through either adoption or other means. Strategies to encourage the adoption of children of color include support of kin adoption and nonrelative legal guardianship or guardianship within extended families. The concept of "extended family" needs to be broadened to more closely reflect the definition held by the local community. Many families of color have a broader definition of "family" than do majority families, but laws may not support this broader definition.

Strategies for Encouraging Permanency

Again training is an important strategy to address permanency issues. Workers need to be aware of their biases regarding the adoptability of all children: older children, children of color, and special needs children. They also must be taught about out-of-state adoptions and placements with single/working/gay/lesbian parents. In some states, placement with gay or lesbian parents is discouraged or not supported. Multicultural training consisting of racial awareness, multicultural planning (directed at a family's shaping their status as multicultural family), and survival skills (for the child to cope with institutional racism) is helpful for parents considering transracial adoption (Vonk, 2001).

We also know about the factors that lead to adoption disruption. One factor is having some negative feelings about the adopted child. Social workers need to carefully assess prospective adoptive parents' attitudes toward child characteristics such as race and ethnicity. Those parents who are willing to consider adopting children with special needs are more likely to adopt African American children (Brooks and James, 2003).

■ ■ ■ ■ ■

SIDEBAR

The adoptive parent of eight special needs children told me, "Once you've been through the home study process you think you're supposed to be perfect. When problems surface with the child, you don't want to talk about it, because you're supposed to be perfect. It must be your fault!" *Postadoption wraparound services* have been developed and can assist adoptive families in adjusting to their new circumstances and avoid adoption disruption.

Teenagers in the Child Welfare System and Beyond

Another point in the course of a child welfare case is occupied by foster youth. Too often the way out of the child welfare system for foster youth, especially adolescent boys of color, is through the juvenile justice system. In fact, some have theorized that the child welfare system is the cause of many youth going into the juvenile justice system (Finkelstein et al., 2002; Lowenthal, 1999). Many services available to children in the child welfare system are not available to youth in the juvenile justice system. Strategies for addressing these issues are collaboration with juvenile justice probation officers and others (e.g., substance abuse treatment personnel), and training for social workers and foster parents to help youth avoid being expelled from or "blowing" placements.

Independent Living Programs and resources for former foster youth after the age of 18 such as the John Chafee Foster Care Services Program (created by the Foster Care Independence Act of 1999, P.L. 106–169) offer resources for independent living to all former foster youth between the ages of 18 and 21. The Foster Care Independence Act also enabled the states to offer Medicaid to former foster youth.

Although he was speaking about what it would take to remedy institutional racism on a societal scale, President Johnson's words apply to foster children who "age out" of the child welfare system:

> But freedom is not enough. You do not wipe away the scars of centuries by saying: "Now you are free to go where you want, and do as you desire, and choose the leaders you please."
>
> You do not take a person who, for years, has been hobbled by chains and liberate him, bring him up to the starting line of a race and then say, "you are free to compete with all the others," and still justly believe that you have been completely fair.
>
> Thus it is not enough just to open the gates of opportunity. All our citizens must have the ability to walk through those gates.
>
> This is the next and the more profound stage of the battle for civil rights. We seek not just freedom but opportunity. We seek not just legal equity but human ability, not just equality as a right and a theory but equality as a fact and equality as a result . . . .
>
> To this end equal opportunity is essential, but not enough, not enough. Men and women of all races are born with the same range of abilities. But ability is not just the product of birth. Ability is stretched or stunted by the family that you live with, and the neighborhood you live in—by the school you go to and the poverty or the richness of your surroundings. It is the product of a hundred unseen forces playing upon the little infant, the child, and finally the man. (Lyndon Baines Johnson, Howard University commencement address, June 4, 1965)

The Voting Rights Act of 1965 was approved by the president on August 6, 1965.

PREPARATION AND SUPPORT FOR THE WORKFORCE

Given the very substantial multicultural challenges faced by child welfare service workers at each point along the service continuum, an effective and thorough system of education and training is essential for us to reach the goals of equity and fair treatment for all families. The culturally effective child welfare organization would be one that promotes a learning environment in which assumptions can be questioned and treatment models can be examined for fairness. In this environment, outcomes would be examined, not to sanction but to identify and remedy unsuccessful models and to develop better workers and best practices. This requires an organizational environment that sees fair treatment as a parallel process from client to worker to supervisor, program manager, and administrators.

If families have difficulties establishing relationships with helpers, especially helpers whose ethnic and cultural backgrounds differ from their own, hiring workers whose ethnicities reflect those vulnerable populations might positively affect the entries and lengths of stay of children in the child welfare system. The research on counselor–client racial matching is somewhat equivocal about these empirical outcomes. Perhaps more importantly, however, a more culturally diverse workforce is likely to affect positively the *experience* of the child or family in dealing with a helping agency, the experience of potentially being heard and understood and appreciated on one's own terms.

Seeing cultural diversity as a source of strength, both for the clients themselves and for the agencies that serve them, is an important step. Using a strengths-based practice approach with regard to clients requires the capacity to *perceive* the strengths of clients and families—and this capacity is nurtured by hiring individuals who reflect the client base and also by staff development programs that encourage greater understanding of different cultures and world views. The workforce needs support for ongoing education and training, good supervision by culturally aware and diverse supervisors, and supportive work environments, which themselves model ways that diverse individuals can work cooperatively and effectively together.

Ethnic and Cultural Diversity among Workers and Supervisors

Working sensitively with diverse persons both as clients and as coworkers will enhance the worker–supervisor system and help us achieve deeper understanding of different groups (and probably ourselves), but these relationships may also be a source of misunderstanding and tension. Even the routine training of social workers in the postindustrial West may prove a stumbling block, when the students are from another culture. In a study of Arab social workers who attended Western universities, researchers discovered that the students experienced discomfort, conflict, and other undesirable reactions when their own cultural values came into conflict with the values they encountered while performing their field work (Haj-Yahia, 1997).

A key factor in establishing a meaningful cross-cultural exchange in the relationships between client and worker, supervisor and supervisee, and between coworkers appears to be a willingness and openness to discussing cultural variables, at all levels. For example, although wide acceptance and support appears to exist for bringing multiculturalism into the supervisory relationship, in practice these discussions may be very limited, possibly due to the discomfort of the individuals involved, lack of knowledge, or even lack of time.

A recent article examining cultural variables in supervision revealed that when discussions of cultural issues did take place between counseling supervisors and supervisees, those supervised reported greater satisfaction with their supervision and the ability to forge a stronger working alliance (Gatmon et al., 2001). Further, the researchers found that a supervisor's being able to provide an atmosphere of safety, depth of dialogue, and frequent opportunities to discuss cultural variables contributed significantly to working alliances and to satisfaction with supervision. These findings suggest that more training may be needed to increase supervisor competence in discussing cultural issues. The researchers concluded that it is not entirely the cultural match between the supervisor and the supervisee that is important, but rather the existence and the quality of the discussions that take place regarding cultural difference and similarity.

Inadequate access to supervisors and mentors who have had multicultural training or who are from culturally diverse backgrounds continues to be a problem among counselors and therapists, as is the gap of understanding between more recently trained staff who have had some form of multicultural education and supervisors who lack such training (Tummala-Narra, 2004). Undoubtedly the same challenges exist in social work. An additional, important reason to impart cross-cultural competencies and communication skills to supervisors is to ensure they are able to model these capacities for their supervisees (Garrett et al., 2001). When multicultural perspectives and education are not woven into every aspect of practice, especially supervision, the resulting divisiveness, alienation, and power imbalances are likely to impair agency–staff and worker–client relationships and prevent the agency from serving families effectively.

Education and training that strengthen the capacity of individuals and helping institutions to work respectfully and fairly with diverse families and staff members are essential if the goal of equal treatment is ever to be met. It is just as clear that equity goals must pervade all levels of an institution or agency, from administrators to clerical staff. Yet a mere recitation of the need for fairness, sensitivity, and understanding is not enough. The mechanics of inequality are far too long-standing and far too subtle and far-reaching to disassemble so easily, even when the force of law has repeatedly been applied. The challenge for the field of child welfare and all other human services fields is to understand what equal practice really should look like, and to devise ways of achieving it, in very practical terms. In the next sections, we will examine some historical and legal context, and begin looking at ways to fashion the kind of child welfare system we need to create for the future, one in which all children and families have equal access to the resources they require.

REACHING THE GOAL OF EQUAL PRACTICE

Translating the intent to render fair and equitable treatment into the attitudes and practice that result in such treatment is a complex and challenging task. Since the passage of the Civil Rights Act of 1964, many systems within the society have struggled both to define the meaning of fairness and to make fair treatment a reality. These systems include not only the field of child welfare, but also several major components of society's infrastructure: education, the election system, medicine, the labor and housing markets, and the fields of civil and criminal justice. Possibly the most telling lesson in how far the society has come and also how far it has yet to go is the famous court decision in *Brown* v. *Board of Education*,[4] which reached its 50th anniversary in 2004. Although many of the most blatant trappings of racial discrimination have faded since Brown, educational and other forms of equity have not been achieved in most communities of the country. Specific instances and policies that constitute discrimination, or at least inequity, have become more subtle and difficult to examine, confounded as they often are with economic factors and unacknowledged forms of unequal treatment.

As discussed earlier in the chapter, the kind of continuing racial and ethnic placement, overrepresentation, and service disproportionalities we have seen in child

---

[4]*Brown* v. *Board of Education*, 347 U.S. 483 (1954).

welfare cannot be the result of chance; some more insidious process must be at work to reproduce or sustain mechanisms of injustice. Even when prescribed conduct and policies have changed, significant numbers of individuals may be so enmeshed in their own cultures and long-held beliefs that they continue to discriminate, some intentionally and some when they are not fully aware of the discriminatory and potentially harmful character of their behavior towards others.

Despite the best efforts of many individuals seeking to create fair policies over the 40 years since the Civil Rights Act, unequal treatment and inequities similar to those cited earlier in the chapter continue to pervade many aspects of life. We still have a substantial gap between the level of equal treatment shown in daily child welfare practice and the multicultural understanding required to bring about true equity in the major systems of society. Although "diversity" and "multicultural" terminology have entered the mainstream, and most acknowledge the need to better serve multicultural human services clients, for many the dominant European white culture remains the standard and the "other" cultures the exceptions (see Hird et al., 2001).

As noted earlier, we must be clear about what we mean by "equity" in terms of treatment by agencies and individuals. Equity in operational terms does not mean the *same* treatment for all, or even the same treatment accorded to the members of the majority. This principle should be especially clear in the case of a society like this one in which constitutional provisions are expressly intended to prevent the majority from dominating the rights of the individual. Rather, equity requires *treatment as an equal*, which is the right, as legal philosopher Ronald Dworkin framed it, not to receive the same distribution of a burden or benefit, but to be treated with the same respect and concern as anyone else (Dworkin, 1978).

Regarding the US Supreme Court case of DeFunis,[5] a reverse discrimination action in which a white law school applicant challenged a school's affirmative admissions policy, Ronald Dworkin observed:

> We must try to define the central concept on which [the plaintiff's claim] turns, which is the concept of an individual right to equality made a constitutional right by the Equal Protection Clause. What rights to equality do citizens have as individuals which might defeat programs aimed at important economic and social policies, including the social policy of improving equality overall? There are two different sorts of rights they might be said to have. The first is the right to *equal treatment*, which is the right to an equal distribution of some opportunity or resource or burden . . . The second is the right to *treatment as an equal*, which is the right, not to receive the same distribution of some burden or benefit, but to be treated with the same respect or concern as anyone else. If I have two children, and one is dying of a disease that is making the other one uncomfortable, I do not show equal concern if I flip a coin to decide which should have the remaining dose of a drug.

(Ronald Dworkin (1978), *Taking Rights Seriously*, Boston: Harvard University Press, p. 227)

[5] *Defunis v. Odegaard*, 416 U.S. 312 (1974).

SETTING STANDARDS FOR PRACTICE

To bring practice more in line with aspiration and insure that all are served fairly by society's institutions, many professions have created frameworks and standards of conduct for their practitioners. Increasingly, as many job descriptions become more service oriented, flexible, and multidimensional, many human services, medical, educational, and corporate entities are using competency frameworks to establish and maintain practice standards within their organizations (McLagan, 1997). These frameworks attempt to analyze even complex occupations and break them down into units, not only into the individual tasks and behaviors that make up the job, but also into the internal attributes, the value, and orientation important to a good performance.

Although competencies and the values in which they are embedded may be specific to a given field of work, typically, the framework includes the knowledge, skills, and attitudes considered desirable for effective work. If the goal is equitable practice in a given profession, it is clear that all three are essential. Knowledge of cultural differences is important, as are the skills to put this knowledge into practice. But these two attributes alone will not make an effective practitioner, if the attitudes and values needed to practice well in a multicultural environment are absent. Although attitudes and values are harder to observe and to measure than objective knowledge and demonstrable skills, these make up an important part of any competency framework. It could easily be argued that values and attitudes are central, because in most human services frameworks they underlie the kind of openness of mind, even-handedness, sensitivity, and flexibility necessary to understand another person's culture and another person's world. In child welfare services, family members *outside of* the dominant, mainstream culture are doubly vulnerable; not only may they face allegations of abuse or neglect, but they are also likely to be unfamiliar with the culture of the person investigating such allegations.

CULTURALLY APPROPRIATE SERVICES: HEALTH CARE

Before moving to a discussion of social work competency frameworks, it may be valuable to do a little cross-cultural comparison by examining the development of competencies from another professional culture: health care. Especially in the public health field, health care has several common features with social work: it must deal with a highly diverse population; it must often render an important service to a vulnerable, sometimes unwilling or reluctant group of clients; and it must prepare its professional staff to bridge communications gaps between cultures. Just as failures of understanding and communication in child welfare may place children at risk of harm, in medicine, the failure to communicate well with patients of other cultures may lead to the failure to diagnose and treat disorders successfully.

Health care, though grounded in science, has many elements of a counseling relationship. Trust, open communication, and understanding between care provider and patient is important, even essential, to successful treatment. When these elements are lacking, recovery may not be as rapid or treatment may fail completely. As in child welfare when cross-cultural communication is impaired, many problems can arise—the diagnosis may be wrong for lack of adequate information exchanged by doctor and patient or patient's family; the patient may not follow the treatment regimen because he did not understand the doctor or nurse or pharmacist; the patient may not receive his or her medication because a family member preferred to use folk remedies—and some of these problems are due to barriers between cultures.

Possibly the most compelling account of this kind of cross-cultural misunderstanding is Anne Fadiman's (1997) report of the course of treatment of a young Hmong child in Merced, California, who eventually was diagnosed with severe epilepsy. In this harrowing example, the child's parents, members of a Hmong family from Laos, struggle both to heal their daughter through traditional remedies and to comprehend treatment offered by Western doctors, and the doctors struggle equally hard to communicate with the family and to insure their own regimen is followed. In the middle of the struggles were social workers, nurses, and other hospital staff, few of whom were able to successfully open and sustain a channel of communication. Though one social worker valiantly grew close to the family and learned much about their culture, she was unable to bridge the gap between the parents and the medical staff. When the child lost her life, it was a sorrow borne by people on both sides of the cultural rift, each of whom arguably did their best to protect and save the child.

In health care, language and communication barriers are common and, as noted above, can lead to patient dissatisfaction, poor comprehension, and adherence to provider instructions, as well as lower care quality (Center on an Aging Society, 2004). Just as minority families often have less access to in-home supportive child welfare services, many racial and ethnic minority individuals and their children are more likely to be uninsured and to have lower access to health care services than whites (Child Welfare League, 2000). In addition, racial and ethnic minorities have higher incidence of and mortality from chronic diseases (Center on Aging Society, 2004). The health services provided to racial and ethnic minority clients are often inferior, and the mental health care provided is often inappropriate and antagonistic to the cultural values and life experiences of populations of color (Sue, 2003).

Growing challenges in achieving equity in health care and mental health services have led to the development of the National Standards on Culturally and Linguistically Appropriate Services (CLAS)[6] by the Office of Minority Health of the Department of Health and Human Services (U.S. Department of Health and Human Services, 2001). Implementation of several of the more concrete among these fourteen standards is mandatory for organizations receiving federal funds. Other standards remain at the "recommended" or "suggested" level for different kinds of educational or health care organizations (U.S. Department of Health and Human Services, 2001). Private practitioners are encouraged to adopt practices consistent with the standards.

[6]CLAS is to be distinguished from the California Long-Range Adoption Study (C.L.A.S.) noted earlier in the text.

In enacting the CLAS standards, the Office of Minority Health commented as follows:

> The following national standards . . . respond to the need to ensure that people entering the health care system receive equitable and effective treatment in a culturally and linguistically appropriate manner. These standards for culturally and linguistically appropriate services (CLAS) are proposed as a means to correct inequities that currently exist in the provision of health services and to make these services more responsive to the individual needs of all patients/consumers. The standards are intended to be inclusive of all cultures and not limited to any particular population group or set of groups; however, they are especially designed to address the needs of racial, ethnic, and linguistic population groups that experience unequal access to health services. Ultimately, the aim of the standards is to contribute to the elimination of racial and ethnic disparities and to improve the health of all Americans. (U.S. Department of Health and Human Services, 2001)

The standards are significant because they are national in scope and are the product of a multiyear deliberative process involving numerous health professionals within and outside of the Office of Minority Health, as well as members of the public who attended regional meetings and contributed written comments. They are truly *national* standards, which can be applied to any regional organization, and, unlike many human service practice frameworks, they are potentially enforceable at least among institutions receiving federal dollars.

NATIONAL CULTURALLY AND LINGUISTICALLY APPROPRIATE STANDARDS FOR HEALTH CARE

1. *Standard 1.* Health care organizations should ensure that patients/consumers receive from all staff members effective, understandable, and respectful care that is provided in a manner compatible with their cultural health beliefs and practices and preferred language.

2. *Standard 2.* Health care organizations should implement strategies to recruit, retain, and promote at all levels of the organization a diverse staff and leadership that are representative of the demographic characteristics of the service area.

3. *Standard 3.* Health care organizations should ensure that staff at all levels and across all disciplines receive ongoing education and training in culturally and linguistically appropriate service delivery.

4. *Standard 4.* Health care organizations must offer and provide language assistance services, including bilingual staff and interpreter services, at no cost to each patient/customer with limited English proficiency at all points of contact, in a timely manner during all hours of operation.

5. *Standard 5.* Health care organizations must provide to patients/consumers in their preferred language both verbal offers and written notices informing them of their right to receive language assistance services.

6. *Standard 6.* Health care organizations must assure the competence of language assistance provided to limited English proficient patients/consumers by interpreters and bilingual staff. Family and friends should not be used to provide interpretations services (except on request of the patient/consumer).

7. *Standard 7.* Health care organizations must make available easily understood patient-related materials and post signage in the languages of the commonly-encountered groups and/or groups represented in the service area.

8. *Standard 8.* Health care organizations should develop, implement, and promote a written strategic plan that outlines clear goals, policies, operational plans, and management accountability/oversight mechanisms to provide culturally and linguistically appropriate services.

9. *Standard 9.* Health care organizations should conduct initial and ongoing organizational self-assessments of CLAS-related activities and are encouraged to integrate cultural and linguistic competence-related measures into their internal audits, performance improvement plans, and patient satisfaction assessments, and outcomes-based evaluations.

10. *Standard 10.* Health care organizations should ensure that data on the individual's/consumer's race, ethnicity, and spoken and written language are collected in health records, integrated into the organization's management information systems and periodically updated.

11. *Standard 11.* Health care organizations should maintain a current demographic, cultural, and epidemiological profile of the community as well as the needs assessment to accurately plan for and implement services that respond to the cultural and linguistic characteristics of the service area.

12. *Standard 12.* Health care organizations should develop participatory, collaborative partnerships with communities and utilize a variety of formal and informal mechanisms to facilitate community and patient/consumer involvement in designing and implementing CLAS-related activities.

13. *Standard 13.* Health care organizations should ensure that conflict and grievance resolution processes are culturally and linguistically sensitive and capable of identifying, preventing, and resolving cross-cultural conflicts or complaints by patients/consumers.

14. *Standard 14.* Health care organizations are encouraged to regularly make available to the public information about their progress and successful innovations in implementing the CLAS standards and to provide public notice in their communities about the availability of this information.

Standards 4, 5, 6, and 7 are current requirements for receiving federal funds.

The Office of Minority Health recommends Standards 1, 2, 3, 8, 9, 10, 11, 12 and 13 for adoption as mandates for Federal, State and national accrediting agencies.

These standards have the advantage of being both very comprehensive and concrete in the way they may be applied within an organization. The standards operate on several levels, each layer building on the prior standards to achieve a systematic, structural approach to integrating the principles and actions of culturally competent practice into every aspect of the organization's functioning. For these reasons, the CLAS standards may be considered a potential foundation on which to build other human service frameworks for multicultural competence.

CONSTRUCTING SOCIAL WORK COMPETENCIES FOR EQUAL PRACTICE

In tailoring competencies for multicultural practice in social work, we first need to think about what is meant by the construct of cultural competence; second, we must consider the roles and tasks a social worker will be performing and how principles of multicultural practice can be applied in those contexts. Although there exist many statements of what constitutes cultural competence, the following definition of cultural competence appears to capture the many aspects of its meaning:

> Cultural and linguistic competence is a set of congruent behaviors, attitudes, and policies that come together in a system, agency, or among professionals that enables effective work in cross-cultural situations. "Culture" refers to integrated patterns of human behaviors that include the language, thoughts, communications, actions, customs, beliefs, values and institutions of racial, ethnic, religious, or social groups. "Competence" implies having the capacity to function effectively as an individual and an organization within the context of the cultural beliefs, behaviors, and needs presented by consumers and their communities. (See Cross et al., 1989)

International Perspective

The importance of cultural sensitivity in working with children and families from a culture other than the social worker's home culture cannot be overemphasized. This is particularly the case in child welfare, when the balance of power is heavily weighted towards the social worker, who both wields the power of the state and is also in helping relationship with a client. As Hardy-Desmond and colleagues put it, too often the prevailing view is that "culture is the icing when in fact it is the cake" (2001, p. 151). Culture is not merely "world-view"; in many ways people from distinctly contrasting cultures may reasonably be said to inhabit different worlds (Berger and Luckmann, 1966). Clearly the meanings of many seemingly sound and "universal" values and constructs blur when we take an international perspective.

As Garland and Escobar (1988) pointed out, not only do values differ across cultures, but professional social work values also vary from one country to another. In one study they cited dealing with international professional values taught in social work schools, no value or ethnic issue was stressed in as many as 50 percent of the schools studied (Yelaja, 1984). The kind of individualism, self-determination, and rationalism that are held as desirable attributes by mainstream American culture may be unacceptable personal flaws in a culture that encourages cooperation and self-denial. In formulating competencies for cultural competence, an obvious but important first step is for the social worker to acknowledge the presence and power of one's own cultural background, as well as its nonuniversal character. Given that this cultural limitation will hold for all or most of us equally—clients and social workers alike—flexibility and openness will serve well as multicultural tools.

Among key characteristics noted as essential building blocks of cultural competence are

1. Awareness and acceptance of difference
2. Awareness of one's own cultural values
3. Understanding the dynamics of difference
4. Development of cultural knowledge
5. Ability to adapt practice to the cultural context of the client. (Cross et al., 1989)

In addition to knowledge, flexibility, self-awareness, and an attitude of respect and acceptance regarding other cultures, it is important to be aware of the subtleties of language and artistic expression, through which much cultural information is conveyed. This information may help a social worker understand a culture's accepted coping mechanisms, manner of accepting help, and mutual assistance styles (Lum, 1999). All of these aspects of culture, if close attention is paid, will enhance understanding of family and group roles, and deepen the social worker's capacity to foster child and family well-being.

Roles, Tasks, and Responsibilities of the Social Worker

As noted earlier, integrating cultural competence awareness and the behaviors that flow from this awareness is challenging for any human service activity. This challenge is especially demanding when the perceived mission and mode of operation of that service activity or organization conflict with the traditions of the people served, or when power differences exist, either real or perceived. The social worker, in keeping with social work traditions, is likely to be cast in the role of helper or facilitator, but if he or she is also working in a hospital, school, or agency setting, the social worker is charged with working within or even enforcing the rules of the organization. Inhabiting this dual role is the special challenge of the child welfare social worker, who may be called on to investigate allegations of abuse or neglect, decide whether or not to remove children from their home, and then work with the family members for reunification.

In all of these roles, however, the culturally competent social worker is responsible for *mediating* the mores, values, and regulations of the dominant, mainstream culture for those clients who may not be assimilated into that culture or who may be members of a distinct subgroup. By learning as much as possible about the client's culture and by paying sensitive, respectful attention to the client and the client's family and associates, the social worker is then capable of interpreting the dominant culture for the client while striving to enhance client well-being. To be culturally competent is, at the very least, to be capable of serving as a useful bridge between cultures. Such a role is fully compatible with a strengths-based approach. The culturally sensitive social worker finds creative ways to establish mutual understanding and common ground with a member of another culture, while seeking out and utilizing the client's unique strengths and those present in the social environment to accomplish service goals.

National Association of Social Workers (NASW) Standards for Practice

The preamble to the NASW Code of Ethics states that the primary mission of the social work profession is "to enhance human well being and help meet the basic human needs and empowerment of people who are vulnerable, oppressed, and living in poverty" (National Association of Social Workers, 2000). Increasing numbers of the service population are also members of other cultures. Recognizing that cultural diversity is not limited to racial and ethnic groups, NASW has expanded its idea of multiculturalism to include cultural experiences of people of different genders, social classes, sexual orientations, ages, spiritual beliefs, and physical and mental abilities. Thus NASW's concept of cultural competence has a very broad reach: cultural competence in social work practice implies a heightened consciousness of how clients experience their uniqueness and deal with their differences and similarities within a larger social context (NASW, 2001).

As revealed in previous sections of the chapter, especially in the section dealing with the standards for health care practice, rendering the many systems of large service organizations more culturally competent is extremely difficult. The NASW has set forth five essential components to help a system move in that direction. We have seen some of these elements in operational form in the National Standards for Culturally and Linguistically Appropriate Services CLAS in Health Care (2001):

ESSENTIAL ELEMENTS FOR A SYSTEM TO BECOME MORE CULTURALLY COMPETENT

The system should:

1. Value Diversity
2. Have the capacity for cultural self-assessment
3. Be conscious of the dynamics inherent when cultures interact
4. Institutionalize cultural knowledge
5. Develop programs and services that reflect an understanding of diversity between and within cultures.

(NASW, 2001)

Regrettably, child welfare agencies and social work education programs do not have the resources or necessary influence within the society to make certain that the kinds of standards mandated for health care are mandated similarly for child welfare. If the mandatory CLAS Standards dealing with client primary language, bilingual staff and interpreters, written materials and notices, and signage were practiced in the daily operations of child welfare agencies nationwide, and if the recommended standards were nationally disseminated, we might be further along the road to equity. Attitudinal change regarding equitable treatment of all individuals takes place slowly, but as we have seen in the years since the Civil Rights Act and *Brown* v. *Board*, the presence of mandate can be a significant spur to change.

With a view toward establishing a generalist's guide for culturally competent practice, NASW approved ten standards in 2001. These standards contain within them the idea that achieving cultural competence is not stagnant but an ongoing process. The presence of various cultures within the society is constantly changing and the society itself adapting; to practice effectively, the social worker must continue to grow and learn in response to this dynamic process. Also prominent in these standards is the idea of advocacy: for a more diverse professional workforce, for more culturally sensitive services and programs, for better social policies affecting multicultural clients, and for more language and linguistically appropriate services for clients. Significantly, some of these elements are mandated in the CLAS Standards, notably those dealing with signage, materials, information, and interpreters provided in the client's language.

NASW STANDARDS FOR CULTURAL COMPETENCE IN SOCIAL WORK PRACTICE

1. *Standard 1. Ethics and Values* Social workers shall function in accordance with the values, ethics, and standards of the profession, recognizing how personal and professional values may conflict with or accommodate the needs of diverse clients.

2. *Standard 2. Self-Awareness* Social workers shall seek to develop an understanding of their own personal, cultural values and beliefs as one way of appreciating the importance of multicultural identities in the lives of people.

3. *Standard 3. Cross-Cultural Knowledge* Social workers shall have and continue to develop specialized knowledge and understanding about the history, traditions, values, family systems, and artistic expressions of major client groups that they serve.

4. *Standard 4. Cross-Cultural Skills* Social workers shall use appropriate methodological approaches, skills, and techniques that reflect the workers' understanding of the role of culture in the helping process.

5. *Standard 5. Service Delivery* Social workers shall be knowledgeable about and skillful in the use of services available in the community and broader society and be able to make appropriate referrals for their diverse clients.

6. *Standard 6. Empowerment and Advocacy* Social workers shall be aware of the effect of social policies and programs on diverse client populations, advocating for and with clients whenever appropriate.

(continued)

■ ■ ■ ■ ■

Continued

7. *Standard 7. Diverse Workforce*   Social workers shall support and advocate for recruitment, admissions and hiring, and retention efforts in social work programs and agencies that ensure diversity within the profession.

8. *Standard 8. Professional Education*   Social workers shall advocate for and participate in educational and training programs that help advance cultural competence within the profession.

9. *Standard 9. Language Diversity*   Social workers shall seek to provide or advocate for the language appropriate to the client, which may include use of interpreters.

10. *Standard 10. Cross-Cultural Leadership*   Social workers shall be able to communicate information about diverse client groups to other professionals.

NASW Standards for Cultural Competence in Social Work Practice can be found at www.socialworkers.org/sections/credentials/culturalcomp.asp.

Competencies for Public Child Welfare in California

In moving from the NASW Standards for Cultural Competence in Social Work Practice to the multicultural practice section of the Curriculum Competencies for Public Child Welfare in California, we are obviously taking our examination of competency frameworks from the general to the more specific. The California competencies are promulgated by the California Social Work Education Center (CalSWEC), a partnership among California schools of social work, public human service agencies, and professional organizations dedicated to integrating child welfare social work education and practice in the state to insure effective, culturally competent service delivery. The CalSWEC competencies, the basis of a public child welfare curriculum in California, were initially adopted in 1992 after a statewide collaborative drafting effort involving school faculty, agency personnel, and other stakeholders. The goal was to develop a competency-based curriculum to meet the needs of both graduate social work education and professional child welfare services (Clark and McCormick, 2000).

The CalSWEC competencies as a whole are revised every 4 or 5 years to reflect current practice. The most recent revision, adopted in 2002, was the culmination of an inclusive process involving human services stakeholders and educators throughout the state. In crafting the final revision, a curriculum modification workgroup strived to integrate its efforts with the educational guidelines and accreditation standards set forth by the Council on Social Work Education. The structure divides the competencies into Foundation and Advanced categories, which roughly correspond to the first and second years of the MSW program. As with the very first version, the elements are competencies that capable graduate social work specialists in child welfare are expected to know and be able to do (Clark and McCormick, 2000).

ETHNIC SENSITIVE AND MULTICULTURAL PRACTICE (FIRST YEAR)

A working knowledge of and sensitivity to the dynamics of ethnic and cultural differences are at the core of child welfare services. Culturally competent practice acknowledges that an individual's culture is an integral part of overall development and selfhood and strives to use concepts of culture in a manner that enhances individual and family functioning. Given the diverse service population, cultural competency and understanding of the cultural norms of major ethnic groups should be a criterion for competent performance throughout the curriculum. This section includes foundation knowledge, values, and skills for culturally competent child welfare practice.

1.1 Student demonstrates sensitivity to clients' differences in culture, ethnicity, and sexual orientation.

1.2 Student demonstrates the ability to conduct an ethnically and culturally sensitive assessment of a child and family and to develop an appropriate intervention plan.

1.3 Student understands the importance of a client's primary language and supports its use in providing child welfare assessment and intervention services.

1.4 Student understands the influence and value of traditional, culturally based childrearing practices and uses this knowledge in working with families.

1.5 Student demonstrates the ability to collaborate with individuals, groups, community-based organizations, and government agencies to advocate for equitable access to culturally sensitive resources and services.

CULTURALLY COMPETENT CHILD WELFARE PRACTICE (SECOND YEAR)

This section builds upon the skills developed towards cultural competence in the foundation. A comprehensive understanding of the cultural norms and values of California's major ethnic, cultural, and immigrant groups is critical in order to make appropriate assessments and to work effectively with members of these groups. Advanced culturally competent practice requires knowledge of the specific challenges faced by different ethnic and cultural populations and the ability to apply that knowledge in legal, social, and psychosocial contexts.

5.1 Student demonstrates knowledge of legal, socioeconomic, and psychosocial issues facing immigrants and refugees and is able to devise sensitive and appropriate interventions.

5.2 Student is able to critically evaluate the relevance of intervention models to be applied with diverse ethnic and cultural populations.

(continued)

■ ■ ■ ■ ■

Continued

5.3 Student demonstrates knowledge of the requirements of the Indian Child Welfare Act and is able to apply its provisions in working with tribal representatives.

5.4 Student demonstrates knowledge of and the ability to apply the Multi-ethnic Placement Act.

Like the NASW standards, the CalSWEC multicultural practice competencies acknowledge the need to broaden the reach of "diversity" to embrace individuals of different sexual orientations as well as different ethnic and racial backgrounds. The importance of a client's language, the effects of psychosocial issues and the need to advocate for equitable access to resources are also stressed. But a close comparison of the NASW and the CalSWEC formulations, which are certainly compatible if not fully congruent, reveals that the CalSWEC competencies include an emphasis on practice skills.

While it is not practical or even desirable to include an inventory of every specific skill needed for multicultural practice, the CalSWEC competencies include specific requirements for actual decision points along the child welfare service continuum, beginning with the ability to conduct an "ethnically and culturally sensitive assessment" at Competency 1.2 for the first year of study. The more advanced second-year competencies include, at numbers 5.3 and 5.4, knowledge of the requirements of placement acts regarding Native American and multi-ethnic children.

Significantly, competency 5.2 implies within its text the knowledge that not all intervention models used with families of the dominant culture have application or relevance to all kinds of families. The competency CalSWEC member schools and agencies aspire to instill in master's level social work graduates is the capacity to "critically evaluate the relevance" of these models. This capacity is clearly an advanced skill, one requiring a depth of self-knowledge, objectivity, and analytic power possessed by few professionals. The challenge is all the greater in the present context in which we have few reliable multicultural intervention models and fewer tools to measure the efficacy of the models we do have. All the more skill, judgment, creativity, and respect for cultural differences are then required of the practitioner.

The competencies as written are not "finished" in any sense; they will be modified as needed to adapt to anticipated advances in practice and structural changes in California's child welfare services system. Nevertheless we can see the trend toward greater specificity and application—how the policy language of multiculturalism is gradually being translated into the attitudinal and action steps a professional needs to take to accomplish the reality of culturally appropriate, equitable child welfare practice.

SUMMARY

Although four decades have passed since the Civil Rights Act, traces of cultural and racial bias continue to operate in American society and its institutions. Despite the legal and moral imperative to offer services fairly and to limit arbitrary distinctions among people served, such bias is evident in current child welfare practice. Bias is revealed most clearly by the significant overrepresentation of children of color in the child welfare system and by the differential treatment certain groups of children and their families are likely to receive. Without increased awareness of these cultural deficits in practice and meaningful strategies to correct them, the child welfare system is in danger of inflicting further injury on the children and families it is designed to protect.

In this chapter we have suggested a framework for examining the idea of fairness and its meanings in the child welfare context. By using a construct of fairness derived from the concepts of social exchange and of distributive and procedural justice, we are able to analyze how the child welfare system can fail to operate fairly with multicultural families and also how to approach and remedy many of these problems. At each decision point in the child welfare services continuum, there is an opportunity to intervene in a culturally appropriate way. At each of these points, beginning with the initial report and assessment, and ending potentially with adolescent services, the social worker can learn to respond sensitively to the family's individual strengths and needs. Consequently we have taken a systematic look at these stages and introduced skills, knowledge, and strategies for effective practice.

Clearly more than intent is required to effect cultural change within a social institution. Over the years, we have seen intent supported by legal action and we have seen the systems of education, health care, social work, and other human services entities adopt policies designed to alleviate bias. Many professional fields have established a system of multicultural "competencies" to help guide their practitioners to more sensitive practice. In some fields, like health care, certain practices are mandatory.

It is useful for the child welfare field to compare across disciplines to examine the cultural competencies we hold in common and those areas in which we differ. In this chapter we have looked at the structure of national health care competencies, as well as those for the NASW and for the child welfare–specific competencies of the CalSWEC. These codified values, skills, and attitudes are valuable tools to foster the kind of equitable practice which the field as a whole must adopt. As knowledge and understanding deepen, along with particular practice skills, we would expect further refinements in our competency frameworks. Nevertheless, broad, comprehensive, and consistent systems of education and training, as well as support within the workforce, are required to reach the goals of fair treatment and equal practice. External measures and regulations will not be effective in the absence of the kind of internal multicultural understanding that can only be achieved through informed communication and through formal and continuing education.

STATE EXAMPLE OF DISPROPORTIONALITY

California has a more diverse population than many other states. The following table describes the proportion of races and ethnicities of all children in California compared to the proportion of each race among (1) children with substantiated cases of abuse and/or neglect and (2) children under the jurisdiction of the California public child welfare system, starting in 2001.

(continued)

Continued

	CALIFORNIA'S POPULATION OF CHILDREN (AMONG 9,249,829 CHILDREN UNDER THE AGE OF 18 IN CALIFORNIA) (%)	CHILDREN IN CALIFORNIA WITH SUBSTANTIATED CASES OF ABUSE AND/OR NEGLECT (%)	CHILDREN UNDER THE JURISDICTION OF THE CALIFORNIA PUBLIC CHILD WELFARE SYSTEM (BEGINNING OF 2001) (%)
African American	7.1	15.7	31
Native American	0.5	1.0	1.2
Asian American/ Pacific Islander	9.6	9.3	2.8
Latino	43.8	40	33.4
Caucasian	34	33	30.6
Other or some other single race alone	4.3	Not defined	Not defined
	99.3	99	99

More than twice as many African American children are among those with cases of substantiated abuse and/or neglect and more than four times as many among those who are under the jurisdiction of the California child welfare system. There are 2.4 times more Native American/American Indian children under the jurisdiction of the child welfare system than there are in the total population of California children.

CHILD WELFARE PERSPECTIVES AND APPROACHES WITH AFRICAN AMERICAN CHILDREN, YOUTH, AND FAMILIES

MARLENE E. COACH, ED.D., QCSW, LSW

Hawaii Pacific University

African American family.

OVERVIEW

This chapter provides an overview on African American families, children, youth as it pertains to child welfare and intervention strategies. It gives a historical, socio-political, and economic perspective leading to a factor that impacts African

The author of this chapter is grateful for the initial work done by Emily Bruce.

American families. The chapter reviews the child welfare system in relation to issues that result in the overrepresentation of African American children and youth within the system. It addresses policy implications and workers' bias in working with African American families. The chapter also includes vignettes, discussion questions, and some intervention strategies for working with African American families.

This chapter will focus on African American families, children, and youth as it pertains to child welfare and intervention strategies. The student will be given an overview of issues and policies that impact African American families. Students will be provided with a social services framework characterized by discussions and vignettes that will allow assessments using a strengths perspective.

By no means is this chapter meant to lump "the black experience" into one. Nor is it intended to minimize the experiences of black families who have different life challenges and/or experiences.

OVERVIEW OF DEMOGRAPHIC AND CULTURAL CHARACTERISTICS

Families exist in the context of events and relationships between individuals; relationships with other individuals within each family; and relationships between families, their communities, and the overall environment within which families live. This chapter focuses on reviewing the systems that interact with African American families, particularly when they are experiencing difficulties. The terms "African Americans" and "blacks" will be used interchangeably when referring to the populations I will be discussing. People of African descent who are citizens of the United States may be considered, by definition, African Americans; nonetheless, black people in the United States are a very diverse group. However, there are many people with different cultural backgrounds who are U.S. citizens of African descent: specifically, immigrants from the Caribbean Islands (i.e., the Bahamas, Jamaica, the Virgin Islands, Haiti, the Dominican Republic, etc.), people from Cuba, Puerto Rico; immigrants from nations in Africa (i.e., Eritrea, Ethiopia, Nigeria, Senegal, Zaire, etc.), those from Europe (i.e., Britain, France, Germany, etc.), as well as those whose ancestors were brought to the United States as slaves. As a result of the African Diaspora, people of African descent can be found all over the globe. However, when we refer to U.S. citizens of African descent, we specifically are referring to those individuals whose ancestors faced forced immigration to the part of North America now known as the United States; who experienced the socio-cultural-political experiences of slavery in the United States, the subsequent war between northern and southern United States, the movement for civil rights beginning with the abolitionist movement before the Civil War and continuing to its zenith during the 1960s and throughout the 1970s, and the ongoing residual socio-economic and political circumstances of those events.

IDENTIFYING FACTORS OF THE AFRICAN AMERICAN EXPERIENCE

Central in the consideration of working with black families and children, who are potentially in need of services, is the history of black families in the United States. While an individual may not experience a daily confrontation with the history of slavery in the United States and the concomitant effects of racism in his/her everyday life, those issues and effects permeate the daily fabric of an African American's life in the United States. While political sensibilities have evolved somewhat, the legacy of considering an African American as less than a white person continues to resonate in African Americans' experience of racism and continues to resonate for many in the dominant culture. As Pinderhughes (1982) suggests, for African Americans there is a circular negative feedback mechanism that facilitates the difficulties that African American families face in attempting to negotiate their way in a world that confirms their perceptions and expectations regarding racism. That negative feedback loop functions in such a way that

> barriers to opportunity and education limit the chance for achievement, employment and attainment of skills. This limitation can, in turn, lead to poverty or stress in relationships, which interferes with adequate performance of family roles. Strains in family roles cause problems in individual growth and development and limit the opportunity of families to meet their own needs . . . (Pinderhughes, 1982, p. 109)

Observations of inequities in the environment and/or in individual experience facilitate this negative feedback loop, which then becomes even more reinforced.

While the socio-economic and political experiences regarding race have shaped the development and social evolution for all citizens of the United States, the specific events regarding the legacy of slavery have had the most profound impact on those of African descent, who had relatives who were alive less than 100 years ago and who were born into this country when the ownership of people of African descent by white people was legal. Changes in the socio-economic and political conditions of this country as a result of the end of slavery, the primary method of economic prosperity in the south, and as a result of the "Reconstruction" period have had a profound effect on families of African descent right up to the present. In general, for some whites, the demise of slavery has resulted in their continued aggregate attempts to maintain economic and political dominance (Hope and Moss, 2000; Takaki, 1993). Across the United States, methods used to reinforce the social, economic, and political dominance over people of African descent have included marginalization, disenfranchisement, exclusion through harassment, terror, or just plain disregard.

The response of the descendants of those Africans who survived (1) the crossing in slave ships from Africa to what would become the United States and (2) the indignity and horror of slavery was to fight, literally and figuratively, against these attempts by those whites who wanted to reinforce their economic and political power. Yet there have been significant losses for African American families in the process of engaging in that struggle: loss of community structures, for some the loss of the integrity of family structure, and ultimately the loss of individual lives for others. In the context of systems theory, when a set of reinforcers are lost or rendered ineffective, other reinforcers are employed in order to maintain homeostasis. To the best of their abilities African American families have consistently found other sets of supports to withstand losses that threaten the individual's demise, the demise of families, or the demise of communities. Consequently, when families lose the infrastructure of the systems that hold them together, they seek other sources of support. Sometimes where supportive infrastructure has been lost, those attempts to establish some semblance of social structure have been seen by mainstream society, as it currently exists, to be less than effective. There is an amorphous experience of "African-American-ness" in the United States, which is further heightened by the identification of the similarities and differences between African Americans and other racial groups in the United States.

The extended family in most nondominant groups is a primary source of support compared to the dominant culture where emphasis is focused on the nuclear or the primary family unit. When looking at family structure and roles, Mexican American families appear to have close ties with extended family and are closely connected to the community and the church. Palacios and Franco (1986 as stated in Canino and Spurlock, 1994, p. 58) wrote, "For traditional Mexican American families, the family structure is characterized by formalized kinship relations to the godparent system and by loyalty to the family. Often the extended family takes priority over other social institutions." In this instance, families have more to say about expected behaviors, traditions, beliefs, and values. Family obligations often take priority over external commitments.

When looking at American Indian families, once again we find strong ties with extended family members. According to Red Horse (1983, as cited in Canino and Spurlock, 1994, p. 58) "American Indian families usually include parents, children, aunts, uncles, cousins, and grandparents in an active kinship system. This lateral extension to include multiple households may be further broadened to incorporate unrelated individuals. For example, a person significant to the family be inducted into the family system by formal rituals and would then assume a family role within that system." From this perspective, the American Indian family is even more inclusive. Queralt (1996) describes an American Indian family member as an extension of their clan, where they take every one into consideration when making a decision and one does not make decisions independently.

For the most part, in Asian American families (including Pacific Islander, Japanese, Chinese, Korean, Vietnamese, Cambodians, Laotians, Filipinos, and Asian Indians) the family unit is valued more than the individual. Each individual is seen as a product of all the generations that make up his or her family. Since this is the belief, one's personal actions reflect not only on the individual but also on the extended family as a whole. Therefore, in order not to bring shame on the family, societal expectations and proper behavior are enforced (Diller, 2004).

The extended family for African American families is equally important. A more in-depth look will provide a foundation for beginning to understand the family system. Being African American does not give one carte blanche to speak for all African Americans. However, most African Americans share a common ancestral history. With that history came slavery and centuries of customs, beliefs, values, knowledge, and oral history that were handed down from one generation to another. According to Queralt (1996) the later are known as "culture." McCray (1994) refers to culture as "the totality of the ways of life of a people and include the basic conditions of existence, behavior, style of life, values, preferences, and the creative expressions that emanate from work and play." McCray describes the family in the African American culture as being resilient, adaptable, and strong (in terms of surviving in an unfriendly environment). There is internal strength in individuals and families that is strongly connected with the church as a religious foundation and community.

Research reported that both male- and female-headed black households were more likely to live in extended family situations than whites and that black children and grandparents were also more likely to reside in extended family households. The fact that older black family members reside with their families explains why there are fewer blacks in nursing homes (Pollard, 1996).

Works by historians such as Coontz, 1992, Katz, 1993 and Trotter, 1993 (as cited by Hill, 1998) reveal how female-headed families evolved, why a black underclass exists and the importance of the extended families. Hill (1998) notes that anthropologists such as Sudarkasa, 1975, 1980; Valentine, 1971; and Aschebrenner, 1975 wrote about the importance of understanding the link between African cultural heritage and black family life. Sudarkasa (as cited by Hill, 1998) stressed that roots of the African marriage are not centered on the "nuclear family" as the term is used in the Euro-American culture. He stated:

> Although Africans recognize the mother-child dyad as primary social and affective unit . . . . it is erroneous to characterize this unit as a separate "nuclear family" within the African extended family. Such a formation has not explanatory value since none of the normal functions of a family were traditionally performed by this unit in isolation. It was not a unit of socialization in and of itself, it was not a unit of economic production or consumption in and of itself; it was not an isolated unit of emotional support or mutual aid; it obviously was not a procreative unit. Why then term it a "nuclear family?" (Hill, 1998, p. 16)

Hill (1998) ventured on to say that even in the instance where there is a husband, wife, and child in Africa, they do not provide for the needs of their unit alone, but everything is provided by the extended family. According to Hill, Sudarkasa found that if a family was isolated and headed by a female that was formerly married or never married and had children, the family would become part of a larger household of male kin.

As we look at African American families, it is imperative that the African concept of family be considered. From that perspective, it is clear why generations of family members reside under the same roof and why it is not uncommon to see nonblood-related people residing together as family. Hill identifies the "African American family as the equivalent to the 'extended family,' networks of functionally related individuals who reside in different households. In addition, we characterize related individuals who reside in the same household as an 'immediate family,' even if they contain three or more generations."

Billingsley (1990, as cited in Devore and Schlesinger, 1999) describe African American families as "an intimate association of persons of African decent living in America, who are related to each other by a variety of means which include blood, marriage, formal and informal adoption, or appropriation; sustained by a history of common residences; and are deeply imbedded in a network of social structures internal and external to themselves" (p. 86).

Hill (1971) talks about five attributes that are important to the survival, stability, and advancement of black families. These attributes are strong achievement orienta-tion, strong work orientation, flexible family roles, strong kinship bonds, and strong religious orientation. We realize that these attributes are not exclusive to the African American family but they link African American families to their history, which tightens the bonds. When examining these attributes, one must consider societal, community, family, and individual factors that assist or interfere with the family strengths.

In terms of family strengths, Hill writes:

> We consider family strengths to be African-based cultural assets that are handed down from generation to generation, and are not merely adaptations or coping responses to racial or economic oppression (Slaughter and McWorter, 1985; Mcdaniel, 1990). We operationally define as family strengths those traits that facilitate the ability of the fam-ily to meet the needs of its members and the demands made upon it by systems outside the family unit. They are necessary for the survival and maintenance of effective family networks. Moreover, a family's strength is not determined by its ability to function in only one area, but in all domains of the family. (1998, p. 19)

Exploring the African American family from this perspective, one can clearly see how diversity in roles and responsibilities factors into the functioning of the family unit.

Hurd, Moore, and Rodgers (1995, as cited in Devore and Schlesinger, 1999) identified the following themes and trends in African American families: substantial parental involvement, support from external caregivers, and considerable male involvement. Themes that surfaced were connection with family, emphasis on achievement, respect for others, spirituality, self-reliance, education, teaching coping skills, self-respect, and racial pride. These themes and trends differ from what is usually identified as characteristics attributed to African American families. The truth of the matter is that male role models are present and often provide a positive image for children. African American parents historically and currently teach the importance of values and responsible behaviors to their children.

In an article entitled " Race, Class and the Dilemmas of Upward Mobility for African Americans" by Cole and Omari (2003), a reflection of the history of the African American culture reveals how class is emphasized. The article describes the upper class, the middle class, the working class, and the underclass. Most of the emphasis is placed on the middle and the working class as they were seen as the black Americans who would struggle for upward mobility and freedom from restriction imposed by the larger society because of racism. Cole and Omari (2003) cite in their article that Gains (1996) stated, "At the end of the 19th century, many black leaders, educated and from elite backgrounds, embarked on a political project for the improvement of the race based on the idea of 'uplift' (p. 778). Uplift ideology held that Black Americans would progress as a race when they adopted the culture and values of the White middle class." As a result of this ideology, there was a push in the African American community for black to become educated and trained in vocations.

During this time the black community identified themselves as middle class based on values and behaviors that were respectful to family and community (i.e., pursuing education, going to church, and participating in cultural events). Cousins (1999), as cited in Cole and Omari (2003), contends that class is "complexly relational and cultural" meaning it is shaped by different practices that are related to time and situation; students are taught to identify class and behaviors related to different levels of class. The interesting thing about the class divisions is, despite the increase of the black middle class, African Americans continue to enjoy less economic privilege than white middle-class Americans. According to Conley (1999, as cited in Cole and Omari, 2003) "black families who would be classified as middle class according to traditional measures of educational attainment and income lag far behind their White counterparts in terms of accumulated wealth" (p. 789).

Cole and Omari (2003) discuss two ideologies of class within the African American culture:

> First, within African American culture, there has been a great emphasis on self-improvement and the importance of striving for achievement, both as an individual value, and as a strategy for advancing the race as a collective, both historically and in the present. African Americans have viewed education as the most respected and most effective mechanism for accomplishing the goal of upward mobility, the achievement of which challenges race- and and class-based oppression. At the same time, African Americans have protected and preserved their consciousness of their race as a socially and economically oppressed group: in part, this reflects the on-going experiences of discrimination faced by African Americans (Feagin, 1991; Feagin & Sikes, 1994), but it is also a strategy for individual and group coping. (p. 790)

This statement suggests that there is an internal struggle to balance moving up and living up to the values and expectations of the dominant group while still holding on to one's own roots, values, and traditions.

As we continue to look at the African American family it should be noted that upward mobility has been impacted along all strata. An overall examination of the economic status and the educational levels of many urban black families suggest that disparities exist and systemic limitations are placed on resources. These disparities are a result of institutional discrimination.

AUTHORS' PERSPECTIVE

One of the particular issues that African American families have faced and continue to face in the United States is the issue of poverty. There is broad diversity in the nature of economic security for African American children and families. Many African American families continue to face severe economic hardship; in 1999 nearly 2 million African American families (approximately 22 percent of all African American families in the United States) were living below the poverty line (U.S. Census Bureau, 2001). Further, nearly 4 million African American children (one-third of all African American children in 1999) were living below the poverty line (U.S. Census Bureau, 2001). Our perspective is that over the past 200 years the fight for civil rights has also been a fight to ensure economic self-sufficiency. The notion of poverty has been a central theme for many African American families:

1. how to escape poverty
2. how to attain economic self-sufficiency
3. how to maintain economic self-sufficiency, and for a select few (based on U.S. Census data [2001] this appears to apply to fewer than 15 percent of the black population in the United States)
4. how to maintain and grow inherited wealth.

Many of the issues covered in this chapter (i.e., education, housing, substance abuse, family violence, health care, delinquency, and mental health) are all critically influenced by economic self-sufficiency. It is within this context that the author addresses those issues and how they affect African American families.

Specifically, the attention to economic self-sufficiency as a focus of people's energies is borne out in a number of ways for African Americans. Early in this country's history, education was legally denied systematically to African Americans. Consequently, education was seen as the door to economic self-sufficiency. This was the primary point of view well into the 1960s. However, with the cultural shifts brought about during the 1960s and the experimentation with integration in schools, some young people concluded that even with education, the economic opportunities for African Americans were still severely limited. Education was a promise unfulfilled for many as integrated public schools and institutions failed young African American children. Young people have found other means to economic self-sufficiency; underground economies with violence and substance abuse support these economies. As one can see, there are spiraling effects of economic disadvantage that have negative implications for African American children and their families.

Tied into obtaining alternative means of economic self-sufficiency (illegally) is the threat of imprisonment. It is obvious that poor people did not bring drugs and uzis into the black communities on their own, but these communities have become the haven for breaking up African American families and destroying the black community; at the same time, supplying warm bodies for the prison industrial complex. For individuals in this type of environment things may truly appear to be hopeless.

Saundefur et al. (1998, as cited in Lott and Bullock, 2001) write, "the U.S. poverty range has been defined in the same way since 1965." Taking what the Department of Agriculture determines to be the cost of a minimally adequate diet and multiplying that figure by three calculates the range. "This formula is based on the assumption that families spend one-third of their cash income on food, one-third on shelter, and one-third on clothing. Poor families are expected to pay nothing for child care, transportation, laundry, phone service, pharmacy items, entertainment, health care, or taxes" (p. 3).

Devore and Schlesinger (1999) reported "Although two-thirds of all poor people are White, the chances of being poor are much greater for African Americans." Female-headed households make up a large percentage of the poor families. Devore and Schlesinger (1999) further stated, "a child's risk of poverty in a female-headed household is one in three." According to the Children's Defense Fund (2003), the U.S. Census Bureau's 2001 report revealed that almost one million black children live in extreme poverty, where the family's after-tax income was below half of the poverty line (which was $7,064 a year for a three-person family). These figures are startling especially since it appears that this sharp increase occurred as a result of the passing of the 1996 welfare reform law, even though prior to the passing of the law 8 out of 10 black children were already living in poverty.

Poverty is one of the things that attack the black family's strengths. It can leave families with a sense of helplessness. So the prospect of upward mobility may entail just being able to provide for the needs of the family. Anything else may appear to be unattainable to many African American families.

The National Center for Children in Poverty (2003) reports that approximately 27 million (37 percent) children live in low-income households. With 80 percent of the children living in households where at least one parent is working and 65 percent where both parents are working. The report noted that the poverty rate among African Americans is the highest (30 percent) and among Latinos (28 percent) is the second highest.

CHILD WELFARE ISSUES AND PROBLEMS WITHIN AND ACROSS SUBGROUPS

Close examination of population dynamics of African American children over time provide a context of the historical perspective of the community of African American children and their families in the United States.

Historically, more often than not, mainstream systems were not available to provide assistance to African American families when they were faced with situations that left them unable to provide for their children. Consequently, African American families looked to each other for assistance; and generally found some assistance provided (Billingsley and Giovannoni, 1972). Over time there is evidence that mainstream systems reversed their posture of disregarding African American children, to a posture of "rescuing" African American children in the 1960s, near the time of the

War on Poverty. That trend has continued and escalated over the course of the past 40 years to the point that it has become perverse (Roberts, 2002).

Further in this chapter we will be examining education, employment housing, family violence, health care, delinquency, and mental health on African American children and families. Specifically, there have continued to be inequities in education, employment, social service utilization, and health care. With disproportionate difficulties in these areas there are the concomitant difficulties with substance abuse and family violence. What has indeed changed, however, has been a reversal of African Americans' absence from social systems that had initially been voluntary to overrepresentation in systems that have become mandatory.

Exploring the themes of inequity in education, employment, housing, and health care as a result of overt racism and its cousin the less observable institutional racism provides the platform for understanding how African American children and families experience the mandatory systems that are ostensibly established to provide service, yet are experienced as punitive. For those who seek to work with African American children and families these themes may provide some additional insights about how people may perceive your efforts. Consequently, it is imperative that while these observations are true in general experience, each individual's experience is specific and not general, so that making assumptions about individuals based on the information in this chapter could easily be incorrect (Lum, 2003).

Education

In the United States the outcome measures of success in the educational setting include the numbers of children who successfully complete high school, and subsequently the numbers of children who complete various levels of postsecondary education (i.e., vocational education certificate, junior college degree, 4-year college degree, postgraduate degree). Alternately, measures of failure include the numbers of those who fail to complete high school and, more difficult to measure, the competencies of those who do complete high school. The institution of slavery denied education for African American children, and with the demise of slavery less than adequate schools for African American children was the norm well into the middle of the twentieth century. While the civil rights court decisions and legislation of the 1960s and 1970s made changes in how localities provided for schools that serve African American children, 30 years later there continue to be institutional disparities in education for African American children. Currently, African American students in general attend schools that have less to offer students, in terms of skilled teachers, and current books and other materials, while attending facilities that are overwhelmingly in disrepair.

Subsequently, African American children who do succeed, those from poor schools as well as those who have more resourced experiences, are expected to participate successfully in academic competition with students whose educational experience has spared no expense. Subsequently, when the African American children do not measure up in the comparison, they are seen to be less than capable (Bowen and Bok, 1998).

While these educational limitations appear to ensure poor outcomes for African American children in general, that is not at all the case. As in many instances, when faced with chronic and acute pressures to fail, many African American children refuse to capitulate and in defiance of expectations succeed against unreasonable odds, and in some cases succeed on their own terms. It is critical that the factors that facilitate that success for individuals be identified and implemented.

The National Assessment of Educational Progress (NAEP) conducts surveys on the reading, science, and math (major subject areas) progress of children aged 9, 13, and 17 in the United States. The 1999 surveys revealed there was a large gap between the scores of African American children and their white peers. The low reading scores among African American children is especially disturbing because if a person has difficulty reading they often have problems in other areas of learning (Washington, 2003). The survey further suggested that few attempts have been made to correct the deficiency or close the gap in educational achievement levels between ethnic groups at the major subject areas.

In the literature on education of children in the United States, a lot of attention has been on students and their reading levels. It has been noted that poor children, African American children, Hispanic children, and children attending urban schools have lower reading levels than middle-class, European American and suburban children (National Research Council, 1998, as cited in Washington, 2003). Washington (2003) explores three reasons why students may fail to achieve grade-level reading. The first is child-based, the second is home-based and the third is instruction-based.

The child-based explanation is that African American children are not exposed to the same knowledge base as their white counterparts (lack of world knowledge), therefore their language skills are different as is their dialect. So the differences between the language spoken in the classroom and the language of the student in their cultural environment are different. This is similar to students who are immigrants and for whom English is their second language. The differences in linguistics make it difficult for African American students to excel academically (Washington, 2003).

Home-based explanations concern poverty, low parental education, and home literacy practices. Both poverty and low socioeconomic status (LSES) are known risk factors for reading and other learning problems. Duncan, Brooks-Gunn, and Klebanov (1994), Baumann and Thomas (1997) (as cited in Washington, 2003, p. 4) stated "census figures indicate that African American children are 2–3 times more likely to be raised in poverty than their white peers." This statement suggests that more African American children will be negatively impacted in the area of education because of their limited exposure to information outside of their culture, community, and family. Most African American children who live in poverty have parents who have low educational levels. In the home of poor children the educational practices may not be enforced as much as in middle-class homes. "A study of home literacy practices indicate that less than half of the children in poverty are read to everyday compared to 61 percent of their middle income peers and they are read to much less frequently than white children" (Federal Interagency Forum on Child and Family Statistics, 2000, as cited in Washington, 2003). Looking at this from one perspective, one could speculate that there is apathy on the part of poor African American parents. Studies on poverty suggest that poor parents (many times headed by single females) struggle to make ends meet and work hard at providing for the basic needs of their children. From another perspective, availability of educational resources in poor communities are deficient making it literally impossible for parents to adequately work with their children.

Instruction-based explanations involve the ways in which the teacher presents the lessons to the students. Often the teachers of poor African American students have low expectations of the students. The teachers' attitude toward these students will greatly impact their level of enthusiasm, motivation, and self-esteem regarding their academic abilities.

In an effort to enhance school performance, the Bush administration implemented "The No Child Left Behind Act" (U.S. Department of Education, 2003). The act is meant to increase educational opportunities for underprivileged children. The act requires the United States to assess students' knowledge, teachers' performance, and schools' scores holding each district accountable for the quality of education in their area; parents are allowed to transfer their children to better-performing schools if their children are failing because of the poor quality of the education they are receiving in their child's current school; the federal government will expand funding to charter schools; reading in early grades will be emphasized; and students limited in English proficiency will be tested after attending school in the United States for 3 years. The purpose of the act is to shorten the gap between the quality of education of privileged and underprivileged children and to ensure that all children receive the education resources they need. In an ideal situation, the act would prove to be beneficial; however, if schools do not meet the criteria for testing, they risk losing funding from the federal government. This would place schools already in need in an even worse position and in the long run the children still suffer.

"The interesting point in all of this is, three years after the act was passed, Bush did not keep his promise to provide federal support for education. In the two years since the he signed the No Child Left Behind (NCLB) Act, none of his budgets have come close to meeting the level of funding authorized in the Act. The FY 2004 budget submitted by President Bush fell $9 billion short of the amount authorized for 2004 and his FY 2003 budget fell $7.2 billion short of approved funding.

Important programs for comprehensive school reform, rural education, dropout prevention, school counseling, training teachers to use technology and a program to provide resources to reduce class size were all eliminated from Bush's FY 2004 budget. Each program was part of Bush's own No Child Left Behind Act" (www.democrats.org; Office of Democratic Leader Nancy Pelosi, 6/9/03, Associated Press, 2/24/03).

Butler (2003) reports that more than 35 percent of African Americans children under the age of 18 live in poverty. Keeping this in mind, the majority of these children are affected by multiple environmental factors (i.e., crime, unemployment, violence, and drugs), which labels them as "at risk youth." With a label such as this, they are seen by teachers as destined to fail academically. Since a large percentage of urban African American children fall within the category of being poor, they are the ones impacted the most by any amount of funding cuts from the federal government. It is common knowledge that an educational gap exists between African American and

European American students so funding cuts in education to poor African American students will perpetuate this trend.

According to Tucker et al. (2000), "Ogbu (1991, 1995) theorizing from an extra familial perspective, believes that many African American students learn that education is not a vehicle for opportunities of social mobility and, thus, develop negative attitudes toward schooling" (p. 205). For the majority of the time, the adults the students come in contact and interact with on a daily basis and who are in positions of power and authority are people who do not look like them. African American students don't have many positive role models who are in positions of power and authority, but do have role models who are entertainers, models, and sports celebrities. When they are in school, teachers normally don't encourage or support them to setting their sights high. Often times in the classroom, teachers will avoid calling on African American students even if they raise their hand.

In an article by Harvey and Hill (2004) they discuss how the African American male is "under siege." They report that African American youth are detained, suspended, expelled, and placed in special education classes at a higher rate than any other ethnic group. The classroom setting and pedagogy of the teacher does not lend itself to creativity and flexibility. Accountability for different learning styles is not readily explored and does not encourage a student to feel empowered.

It appears that teachers need more cultural awareness and sensitivity when it comes to working with African American students. Most teachers that poor black students come into contact with are Caucasian and do not always take culture, family, and tradition into consideration when working with them.

Housing

According to Taylor, Chatters, and Celious (2003), the availability and affordability of housing correlates with living arrangements in terms of who lives in a household. This is significant for blacks, whites, and Hispanics when one considers what the data imply about extended family members and who can afford to live in middle-class neighborhoods. Since data reveal there is a disproportionate representation of African Americans among the ranks of the poor, it is safe to say that blacks are also impacted by the lack of affordable housing.

The National Low Income Housing Coalition (2003) reported that the cost of housing has surpassed income. "Wages have not kept pace with sharply rising housing costs. After rising somewhat at the end of the 1990s, real median earnings have fallen throughout much of 2002 and 2003 as earnings growth has declined. Throughout this period, and since 1997, the federal minimum wage has remained at $5.15" (p. 2). As a result, families are spending from 30 to 50 percent of their income on housing. There is not enough affordable housing so families have a difficult time leaving the welfare system to go to work. And, too many working people in United States cannot afford safe, decent rental housing for themselves and their families.

It is estimated that there has been a 90 percent reduction in the amount of federal funding allotted for low-income housing. In 2002 the total budget allocation for the Department of Housing and Urban Development (HUD) was less than half the amount allocated in the late 1970s. Families searching for Section 8 housing often have a difficult time finding adequate housing. Not many families in the inner city are fortunate enough to find an apartment in a two-family home that is safe and comfortable. The majority of poor families are clustered in inner-city housing developments. And an increasing numbers of poor young families are homeless, forced to live on the streets or periodically in shelters for the homeless. Those living in housing developments must often deal with a high incidence of crime. Drug dealing and prostitution are common.

Families in poverty are extremely stressed and often very angry. Violence, both within the family and outside the home, is frequent. Attempting to create a good home environment in poor inner-city neighborhoods is difficult. Children have difficulty sleeping through the night due to late-night drug activity. They often have limited or no safe place to play outside. Allowing kids the freedom to explore their environment and to learn from their mistakes is unrealistic in such an unsafe environment. Parents must choose between overprotecting their young and risking rebellion or giving them some freedom and hoping they can make the right choices in an environment saturated with crime.

Because families live so close together, privacy is rare. Friendships become strained, as individuals know too much about each other. Working together for change can be difficult when not everyone is concerned with what is going on in the community especially when their focus is to survive. Tenants are often fearful of becoming homeless and are careful not to complain too often. Sometimes they view advocacy groups as potentially harmful to their security. Some landlords use this powerlessness to their advantage, allowing apartments to degenerate, ignoring drug dealers who hang out, raising rents arbitrarily, and, in general, maintaining an unsafe, unpredictable environment.

To measure housing hardship, the National Survey of American Families (NSAF, 1999, as cited by Zedlewski, 2000) asked adults whether they had been unable to pay their rent, mortgage, or utility bills at some point during the previous year. Nationwide, the housing hardship rate for nonelderly persons remained unchanged at 13 percent between 1997 and 1999. Families' ability to afford housing may have stayed the same despite the economic boom because housing prices rose faster than incomes (Zedlewski, 2000). An analysis of housing hardship by race and ethnicity reveals that while whites were better able to afford housing in 1999 than in 1997, blacks were more likely to encounter difficulties paying for housing than before. As a result, the disparity between blacks and whites in 1997 (ibid.) widened during the 2-year period. Housing hardship for Hispanics remained steady at 19 percent from 1997 to 1999.

The lack of affordable housing and the increases in rent mean that some families may have to move more often. Moving in and of itself is a stressful event. Compounding it with adjusting to another environment will affect the emotional stability of the whole family. A change in environment may also require a change in schools for the children. Frequent changes in schools weaken the emotional stamina of any child and when coupled with being black and poor, children are placed at a real disadvantage.

Substance Abuse/Alcohol and Drug Abuse

Drug and alcohol abuse is one of the most controversial topics being discussed in our society. The drug war has been the longest war fought on American soil and the most costly. At the federal level, the first (and most effective) law targeted toward recreational substances (and other drugs) was the Food and Drugs Act of 1906 (which began as a grassroots movement in the 1870s). This act did not create prohibitions, what it did do was ensure that products met standards of purity, and were honestly labeled.

At the turn of the twentieth century the attitude toward prohibition increased throughout the United States. In the early 1900s several states banned the use of alcohol and other drugs. In 1914 the Harrison Narcotics Control Act was passed. It was the first drug policy legislation that was passed to regulate the sale of certain narcotics (opium, heroin, cocaine). This laid the foundation for the enforcement of the modern drug war.

In 1917 the congress approved the eighteenth amendment to the constitution, which the necessary states ratified, becoming law in 1920. This brought a nationwide prohibition of alcohol. Initially alcohol consumption dropped, but in a few short years organized crime gangs filled the demand for alcohol. Violence and crime flourished, funded by the ill-gotten gains of the illegal alcohol black market. Alcohol use steadily rose to exceed preprohibition levels.

The crime and other social problems associated with prohibition were clear for all to see, and in 1933 the twenty first amendment to the constitution was ratified, repealing the eighteenth amendment and ending national alcohol prohibition. The laws relating to other drugs, however, remained in place.

In 1937 another tax act was introduced, this one targeting Marijuana (which up to this time was legal, and in fact a commonly used drug in the U.S. pharmacies). In 1965 the Drug Abuse Control Amendments were passed, creating the Bureau of Drug Abuse Control. (It's interesting to note that from 1965 forward, the national homicide rate began a sharp increase, as did drug use among 12–17-year-olds.)

In 1969 President Nixon declared a war on drugs and crime. In 1970, the modern "War On Drugs" came to the forefront in the name of the "Comprehensive Drug Abuse Prevention and Control Act." Title II (the "Controlled Substances Act" or "CSA") established five "schedules" of substances, with schedule "one" prohibiting substances even from medical use. (Marijuana was placed in schedule one, despite the recommendations of the task force that marijuana not be criminalized.) The CSA affects an absolute prohibition on many substances, and allowed federal law enforcement to act even on an intrastate level.

In 1973 Nixon reorganized the drug law enforcement agencies into the Drug Enforcement Agency, or DEA. In 1986 Nancy Reagan started the "Just Say No" campaign. Initially there was a decline in drug use but there was a sharp increase within a few years after her campaign. In 1988 the Office Of National Drug Control Policy (office of the "Drug Czar") was formed. The first Drug Czar was William Bennett (who ironically is a smoker, drinker, and compulsive gambler).

In 1994 and 1997, The RAND Corporation released reports revealing that drug treatment and education was seven times more cost-effective than incarcerations. This is interesting when you look at our prisons system and the numbers of prisoners there because of nonviolent low-level drug offenses.

Research and data show that African American males between the ages of 18 and 29 make up a large percentage of the inmate population. And most are there as a result of drug activity. The majority of the prisoners are drug users who could benefit from treatment.

The drug war has been a costly war. It has broken families up, left children without parents, taken lives, incarcerated more people than any other Western civilized country, and turned the prison system into a corporation. According to Belenko et al. (1998), between 1980 and 1996, the number of prisoners in state, federal, and local institutions increased from 501,886 to 1,700,661, which was a 239 percent increase. Another interesting aspect of incarceration is that even though most of the inmates were in prison for drug offenses, while they were in prison, little or no attempt was made to treat their drug problem.

Belenko et al. (1998) noted, "in 1996, white non-Hispanics comprised 76 percent of the U.S. adult population, but only 35 percent of state, 38 percent of federal and 39 percent of jail inmates. Black non-Hispanics comprised 11 percent of the adult population, but 46 percent of state, 30 percent of federal and 42 percent of jail inmates. Hispanics comprised 8 percent of the adult population, but 16 percent of state, 28 percent of federal and 17 percent of jail inmates" (p. 3). They further reported that blacks make up half the prison population in all state prisons and Hispanics make up 26 percent. With this disproportionate representation in the prison population, African American and Hispanics are the most affected by not receiving treatment or ancillary services while they are incarcerated.

Belenko et al. (1998) related that in state and federal prisons, there is a huge gap between available substance abuse treatment and inmate participation, and the need for treatment and participation is enormous and widening. Government spending on treatment programs for inmates with drug and alcohol problems has been small compared to the cost of housing the same inmates. The Center on Addiction and Substance Abuse (CASA) 1999 reported "on average, states spend 5 percent of their prison budget on drug and alcohol treatment. In 1997 the Federal Bureau of Prisons spent $25 million on drug treatment which was on 0.9 percent of the federal prison budget."

Gil, Vega, and Turner (2002) conducted a study to examine the risk factors for alcohol and marijuana dependence and abuse for African American adolescence and European American adolescence. They found that African Americans who are alcohol and drug dependent have a great chance of getting certain health conditions connected with the use of alcohol and drugs. This is because most African Americans who are dependent on alcohol and/or other drugs are poor and therefore have fewer resources. However, one finding that was not expected was that African American adolescents used alcohol and other drugs at a much lower rate than European Americans.

Brunswick (1999), as cited in De La Rosa, Segal, and Lopez, discusses the interlinking of "social structural, institutional and interpersonal networks" from an ecological perspective when considering the drug pattern use within the African

American community. She further adds, "drug involvement differences are best explained by heterogeneity in degrees of success in and attachment to mainstream social institutions (family, church, schools, workplace)" (p. 5).

As a result of the circumstances under which most African American's ancestors arrived in this country, living in a stressful and often hostile environment is constant for most poor to middle-class blacks. Age, gender, geographical location, and socio-economic status are also important factors when exploring substance abuse and use in the African American community. In areas where there is high unemployment, a decline in working-class jobs and an absence of middle-class or other stable African American role models, youth may turn to alternative means of acquiring income, which is often easiest done by selling drugs. One can speculate that once exposed to drugs on a regular basis, youth may go from selling it to using it. The cycle of being trapped in an environment that offers fewer opportunities for decent legal wages, health care, childcare, and job opportunities impact African American families and communities in a devastating way.

If one reflects on our society and the richness of our country, it would appear that rehabilitation and treatment of drug offenders would be a benefit that would be valued. Treating inmates would reduce stress on the taxpayer's dollar by allowing them to become productive citizens. The money used to house prisoners could be invested in our educational system.

DOMESTIC VIOLENCE/CHILD MALTREATMENT

Family violence is a nonspecific reference to a multitude of situations in which many families find themselves. In the context of this chapter, the term "family violence" is used to refer to (1) the issues of domestic violence and (2) the issues of child maltreatment, and their consequences. The two distinct types of violence, domestic violence and child maltreatment, have severe, related, and negative consequences for children and their families, and specifically for African American children and families. While these two types of violence often co-occur in families, it may be best to explore them separately, and then in summary to review their corelated implications for African American children and families.

Domestic Violence

Generally, domestic violence is considered to include those acts of violence that occur between two adults involved in an intimate relationship. Theoretical considerations posit that while domestic violence is an act of aggression, the focus of that aggression and violence is control and dominance of one person in the relationship by the other individual in the relationship. There are at least four couple combinations for adults involved in intimate relationships; so, there could be four couple combinations for those involved in intimate partner abuse: (1) male perpetrator/female victim, (2) male perpetrator/male victim, (3) female perpetrator/male victim, and (4) female perpetrator/female victim. For African Americans, the usual victims of domestic violence are women and the usual perpetrators are men, which is not the only configuration of this type of assault. Intimate partner abuse includes types of physical assault (i.e., ". . . punching, kicking, biting, choking, eating up, and threatening with or using a knife or gun," Browne and Bassuk, 1997, p. 262), intimidation (i.e., causing fear of physical assault or fear of economic deprivation; failure to provide economic support), and/or threats to cause physical injury or emotional injury to the victim or to individuals close to the victim (i.e., children or other loved ones) in order to control the behavior of the victim.

The rate of domestic violence for African Americans has been reported to be higher than the rates of domestic violence for other ethnic groups (Cazenave and Straus, 1979; Tjaden and Thoenns, 1998, 2000; Wolfner and Gelles, 1993). However, it is simplistic to conclude that race is a sole factor in contributing to the high rates of domestic violence among African Americans.

Economics is a significant factor in domestic violence for both African Americans and whites, with higher rates of domestic violence occurring in poorer families in comparison to the rates of domestic violence occurring in well-off families. In fact, to some degree economic self-sufficiency mitigates against the occurrence of domestic violence. Economic self-sufficiency provides individuals with options that are not available to people who are extremely disadvantaged. Consequently, one finds that families that tend to be dealing with the stress of poverty as a result of poorly paid employment, inconsistent employment, or no employment opportunities at all are more likely to experience intimate partner abuse. Research has shown that factors which contribute to domestic violence include economic insufficiency and the resultant stress of not having the economic resources to provide for one's needs, the needs of one's family, or the resources to just effect change in one's own life. Economic stress and limited resources are factors African American men and women may experience, which contribute to the higher rates of domestic violence for African American families. Another factor that contributes to domestic violence is substance abuse; alcohol and/or drugs reduce inhibitions regarding behaviors that would otherwise not be tolerated. Substance abuse, the lack of economic resources and/or personal efficacy, and the resulting stress combine for a devastating set of circumstances for African American families. "Factors such as the breakdown of families, unemployment and underemployment, poor schools, inadequate vocational skills and training, bad housing, the influence and use of drugs, and the density of liquor stores in the inner city contribute to the problem of domestic violence" (Pryor, 1999). All of these factors may compound and erupt into domestic violence.

Ultimately, domestic violence is primarily an act of control. Consequently, one can find evidence of domestic violence in well-off African American families where the woman is employed, as well as other well-off families. Domestic violence is primarily as a function of control, particularly when the victim has no access to a source of income.

For women who are victims of domestic violence and unemployed, becoming employed serves to (1) reduce isolation which in turn reduces the probability of victimization, and (2) reduce dependency and provide the opportunity for economic self-sufficiency, which in turn reduces economic and emotional dependence. This is not to say that African American women seek employment to only escape abuse. Unfortunately, as women victims' economic self-sufficiency increases, the ability of their partners to control the women's behavior decreases. This reduction in control threatens those who feel a need to control, resulting in an increase in some women's risk of severe victimization. The ultimate consequence of domestic violence can be homicide, either as a result of self-defense or as the result of a perpetrator's extreme attempt to control the behavior of the other in the relationship.

The higher rates of employment and education for African American women in comparison to African American men give rise to concerns about black women in violent relationships attempting to increase their economic self-sufficiency. Yet without becoming economically independent, the abuse can continue. In general, as a matter of historical necessity, independence is a long-time characteristic of African American women. Given the value of family to African Americans, a woman may feel extremely conflicted about having to choose between continuing to risk violence in their relationship and keeping their family intact. Browne and Bassuk (1997) report nearly two-thirds (67 percent) of women victims of intimate partner abuse; during their childhood, these women had been victims of maltreatment by a caretaker. Further, a preponderance of women who were victims of violent relationships were also victims of physical and/or sexual abuse as children. So there is a cycling effect of violence occurring in these families.

Adults who feel the need to dominate and control another person through threats of physical violence and through intimidation do not stop at just abusing the object of their attention and focus. Often times for families dealing with intimate partner abuse there is also evidence of child maltreatment. In these cases, children are hurt (1) trying to protect a parent, (2) by getting in the way between two abusive adults, or (3) just by being the targets of abuse by the victim or the perpetrator of abuse, or by another care provider who feels the need to dominate someone who cannot defend themselves.

Child Maltreatment

Similar to incidents of domestic violence, maltreatment of children is an occurrence that is more observed in families experiencing economic disadvantage. Despite the fact that child maltreatment can result from the frustrations of poverty, it is also an expression of power and control for those who exert little power or control over their own lives.

While stranger abuse of children does occur, more often children are abused by a parent or an adult caretaker. Child maltreatment specifically includes the following types of behaviors: physical abuse (i.e., hitting, slapping, punching, pushing, choking, burning, and the like), emotional abuse (i.e., harassing and terrorizing a child verbally or psychologically), and neglect (i.e., not providing for a child's needs for food, clothing, or housing, medical neglect, and/or educational neglect) (*Encyclopedia of Social Work*, 1997).

The sexual abuse of children is most similar to the issues involved in domestic violence. The similarity between the two behaviors rests primarily in the fact that they both are acts of domination and control over someone who has less power. Ultimately, the abuse of children in all its permutations also functions as a behavior that attempts to control the behavior of children by adult caretakers.

In 2002 a little more than one quarter (26.1 percent) of the near 900,000 children who were abused were African American (McDonald and Associates/American Humane, 2004). From the data compiled by the National Child Abuse and Neglect Data System, the authors concluded that African Americans have the second highest rate of child maltreatment—20.2 children for every 1,000 children (McDonald and Associates/American Humane, 2004). There is indeed a relationship between intimate partner abuse and child abuse. Many African American families may feel that they are absolutely disregarded as a result of their experiences struggling in a public and social environment that is openly hostile to them. As parents, they try to control their situations with fewer resources and less assistance than parents in other ethnic groups. They may become less effective in their roles as parents to their children, and in their roles as partners to each other. As a consequence of not having much assistance in this struggle, many African American parents have lost control over the circumstances they face and have become more frequently than other ethnic groups likely to lose care and custody of their children. In 1997 the U.S. population of African American children was only 17 percent, yet 39 percent of the children are in out-of-home care (Roberts, 2002).

Foster Family Care

Initially, in the early nineteenth century at the inception of public and private child welfare services in the United States, African Americans were not well served by any of these systems. In fact, those services were exclusively developed for white children alone (Hacsi, 1997). Billingsley and Giovannoni (1972) outlined that the criteria used in the nineteenth century to determine whether systems designed to care for those who were dependent were rarely designed to include African Americans. Specifically, black children should not be provided any more assistance than the poorest white children. Given that context, the framework was set to establish inequities in institutional infrastructures.

However, from a historical perspective, African American communities have traditionally always taken care of their children whether it was kinship or nonkinship. Children were also left with relatives and sometimes given to them to raise (informal adoption) if the parent(s) was unable to take care of a child. Ironically, slavery was the impetus for this type of child welfare. It was, in fact, the first method of child welfare for African American children. Since children were not the legal responsibility of their parents, the parents had no rights. The children were the property of their slave owners and could be sold at the drop of a hat (Lacy, 1972; McRoy, 1990). If a child were separated from his or her family of origin, he or she would become a child of the slave community and would be parented by the adult slaves. According to Gutman (1976), this would be in keeping with the African culture.

During the 1960s War on Poverty the attempts to "rescue poor Black children resulted in a transition from a lack of service provision to mandatory systems designed to 'rescue' children from their damaging/abusive families" (Billingsley and Giovannoni, 1972). Currently, the concern for many African American families who are experiencing problems managing their lives is that there are now severe consequences for becoming involved in the public child welfare system. While this system suggests that it provides services, the experience of many African American families involved with public child welfare programs is that they do not receive any assistance at all. Rather, their experiences are that the system entraps people into situations from which there is extreme difficulty of finding a suitable exit. Currently, as a group, African American children represent the largest proportion of children in out-of-home care in this country (Smith and Devore, 2004).

The Third National Incidence Study of Child Abuse and Neglect [NIS-3] (U.S. DHHS, 1996) reported that low income was the primary common factor for those children who were victims of child abuse and neglect, rather than race. However if that is indeed the case, ". . . higher reporting rates for African American children must result from systemic bias" (Roberts, 2002, p. 6). National Study of Protective, Preventive and Reunification Services to Children and Their Families (U.S. DHHS, 1997b) provides further evidence of the fact that services to prevent out-of-home placement are less often provided to African American children and families in comparison to white children and families. Specifically, in-home child welfare services (U.S. DHHS, 1997a) and family preservation services (Denby, Curtis, and Alford, 1998; Stehno, 1990) are disproportionately not provided to African American children and their families, particularly when you consider the numbers of African American children involved in public child welfare services.

Once African American children have come to the attention of the public child welfare system, the more likely they are to be placed in out-of-home care (Courtney and Wong, 1996). Further, once African American children come into out-of-home care, they are not likely to be reunified with their families of origin, but to remain in out-of-home-care (Berrick, Barth, and Needell, 1994).

Child welfare researchers have suggested that the low rate of family reunification for African American children has primarily been a function of the numbers of children being placed with relatives in kinship care. Berrick et al. (1998) openly suggest that the public child welfare system is a preferred alternative source of economic support for African American families. What is clear is that if African American families were provided minimum levels of governmental support (i.e., health care, housing assistance, more generous tax supports for low income families) instead of the tax benefits for the most well-off families then perhaps there would not be African American children in the public child welfare system.

Kinship Care

According to the U.S. Department of Health and Human Services (U.S. DHHS, 2000), in 1998 there were approximately 2.13 million children in this country that were living in some type of kinship care arrangement. In 1997 approximately 200,000 children were in public kinship care. This is well below 1 percent of all U.S. children but 29 percent of all foster children. Public kinship care has increased substantially during the late 1980s and 1990s. Three main factors have contributed to this growth. First, the number of nonkin foster parents has not kept pace with the number of children requiring placement, which resulted in a shortage of foster caregivers. Second, child welfare agencies have developed a more positive attitude toward the use of kin as foster parents. Today, extended family members are usually given first priority when children require placement. Third, a number of federal and state court rulings have recognized the rights of relatives to act as foster parents and to be compensated financially for doing so (Hegar and Scannapieco, 1995; U.S. DHHS, 2000).

As stated earlier, traditionally in African American families, the extended family has long played a role in caring for children whose parents were unable to do so. Over the last decade, child welfare agencies have increasingly relied on extended family members to act as foster parents for children who have been abused or neglected. However, very little information is available on the extent to which kins serve as foster parents and how this practice varies across states. In addition, it has been difficult for federal and state policy makers, as well as advocates and practitioners, to evaluate how well kinship care ensures children's safety, promotes permanency in their living situations, and enhances their well-being, which are three basic goals of the child welfare system. Nonetheless, both federal and state governments continue to implement kinship care policies, both explicitly and implicitly. Recognizing the need for more information on the policy implications of using kin as foster parents, Congress directed the DHHS, in the Adoption and Safe Families Act (ASFA) of 1997 (P.L. 105-89), to "convene [an] advisory panel and prepare and submit to the advisory panel an initial report on the extent to which children in foster care are placed in the care of a relative."

Federal child welfare policy historically overlooked the role of kinship caregivers and if states provided assistance to kin they did so through income assistance programs, effectively keeping them out of the child welfare system. As states began to rely on relatives to serve as foster parents, they often applied existing federal foster-care licensing, supervision, and permanency planning requirements (designed for nonkin foster parents) to kin caregivers. More recent federal policies have acknowledged the unique circumstances of kinship care and have encouraged states to consider giving preference to relatives when placing a child in foster care.

Kinship care families differ from nonkin foster families in several ways (U.S. DHHS, 2000). Kinship caregivers usually receive little, if any, preparation for their new role. Public and private kinship providers are older, more likely to be single, more likely to be African American, and more likely to have less education and lower incomes. For the most part, kinship providers are more likely to receive public benefits and less likely to report being in good health.

Children in private kinship care appear to be older than children in nonkin foster care and much more likely to be African American and appear to have fewer physical and mental health problems than children in nonkin foster care.

One relative resource that has not been approached is the fathers of the children in the child welfare system. O'Donnell (1999) conducted a study involving a secondary data analysis looking at casework practices in kinship foster care. The study revealed that caseworkers initiated very little, if any, contact with the fathers of African

American children on their caseloads even if they knew how to reach them. The study also revealed that the fathers did not trust the child welfare system and since no help was offered when they informed the caseworker of some of their problems they would avoid having contact with the worker. Their level of mistrust interfered with them participating in intervention strategies on behalf of their children.

The fact that there are so many African American children in the child welfare system, it is essential that caseworkers look at all the resources available to them. The practice of focusing primarily on maternal kin needs to be reassessed.

Group Home Care

One of the aspects of concern has been the out-of-home placement of young children in group care. Research has shown that the group care of young children is not the most efficacious placement option for this population (Berrick et al., 1998). Consequently, placements have trended toward removing group care as an option for young children. An interesting development is that as the group home placement options for young children have diminished, agencies have pushed for the establishment of foster family home options for young children and the foster family home options for older children have diminished. Families are less willing to provide substitute care for adolescents (Pardeck, 1984; Smith et al., 2001). Nearly 40 percent of the children and youth in out-of-home care are of African decent (U.S. DHHS, 2004). In fact, in the United States the average age for a child in out-of-home care is 10.2 years (U.S. DHHS, 2004). While there is no report of the average age for youth living in group care, many of the children in group care are older children. Often the reason they may be in group care is that it may be easier to secure family-setting placements for children who are of elementary school age (National Research Council, 1993); older children are often considered to be more challenging to authority. Further, there is no governmental data indicating the race/ethnicity of children and youth in different types of placements; however, for African American children and youth, placement in group care would serve to even further distance them from their families of origin.

The majority of the literature suggests that group homes are usually the placement of choice for youth with emotional problems or who have a history of delinquent behavior. More than likely, these youth are older (adolescents). Finding a foster family willing to take an older child is usually difficult.

Although the foster care system is supposed to protect children and adolescents, there are times that vulnerable children and adolescents are impacted by their inter-action with their peers. The peer interaction sometimes results in negative peer influences especially if they are placed into and experiencing group foster care. One can project that if a child with no history of delinquency is placed into a group home with youth who have a history, the odds of the youth being influenced by his or her peers is heightened.

According to the Administration for Children and Families (2003), nearly 20 percent of the youth in foster care live in group homes or institutions. Of that 20 percent, half range in ages from 11 to 18 years. The irony of this is that the child welfare system seems to be lacking in the area that it is supposed to be protecting the children from.

If group homes do not deliver the services that the youth need, they may only be a holding place until the youth is emancipated. After emancipation, their next home may be jail.

Adoptions

When it comes to adoption of African American children, there is reportedly a lack of adoptive homes for black children. African American child welfare providers would argue that adoption service providers have failed to consider and/or approve African American families for adoption. Early in the practice of formalized adoption proceedings, African American families rarely met the income criteria to become adoptive parents, leaving white families as those primarily eligible for adoptive consideration. With the Transracial Adoption (TRA) Movement many black children were transracially adopted ("the joining of racially different parents and children together in adoptive families," Silverman, 1993).

The TRA Movement started in the mid-1960s and continued to the early 1970s when nearly 15,000 African American children were placed in white adoptive homes (Davis, 1991). By 1971, 1 out of every 3 African American children in the Child Welfare System who was adopted was done so by white parents (Ladner, 1978).

In 1972 the National Association of Black Social Workers (NABSW) issued a position statement on their stand against African American children being adopted by Caucasian couples (Bremner et al., 1974). This statement came as a result of a number (2,500) of African American Children being placed into Caucasian families in 1971 (Fenster, 2002). The NABSW called the practice a form of "cultural genocide." Their position was that black children should be placed in black homes. They believe that only a black family can prepare a black child how to survive in a racist society and that the socialization process occurs early in the child's development. The organization (NABSW) also rejected the claim that "black will not adopt" (Bremner et al., 1974).

The research literature has historically represented that transracial adoption has been of great benefit in providing permanent homes for African American children in out-of-home care. The average response to transracial adoption by African American child welfare providers was that the practice should be curtailed (Curtis, 1996). Further African American child welfare professionals made demands that the criteria for being considered as an adoptive family reflect the realities of African American children (Hairston and Williams, 1989). African American families began to be targeted for adoption consideration. Yet, despite these adaptations, the number of African American children in need of adoption has outstripped the number of African American families studied and approved for adoption. Further, the Congress passed the Multi-Ethnic Placement Act (MEPA) of 1994, which states:

> Organizations and agencies that receive federal funds could not "categorically deny to any person the opportunity to become an adoptive or foster parent solely on the basis of the race, color, or national origin of the adoptive or foster parent, or child involved.

In 1996 Congress passed The Small Business Job Protection Act, which included Section 1808, "Removal of Barriers to Interethnic Adoption." This new law,

Interethnic Adoption Provision (IEP), decreased the length of time children had to wait to be adopted and amended the MEPA. It prohibited agencies from denying or delaying placement of a child for adoption on the basis of race or national origin. Federal funds would be withheld if any agency was found to be in violation of the Act (Kaplan, 1997).

The ASFA of 1997 made African American children more susceptible to being permanently removed from their families of origin at even faster rates than under the policy direction of the Adoption Assistance and Child Welfare Act of 1981.

At the end of the day, the U.S. Children's Bureau has responded to the concern regarding the disproportionate numbers of African American children in out-of-home care by hearing from those in providing child welfare services: child welfare workers, agency providers, and other service providers.

A summary of the findings of the report from child welfare service providers indicated that culturally sensitive service provisions that is effective for all children and families, and in particular services to African American children and families need to be tailored to the concerns and issues presented by those families. And finally, the administrative and political need should be found to allocate sufficient resources to implement these changes not only for African American children and families, but also for all ethnic children of color and their families.

Health and Mental Health Care

When examining health care for African American children and their families, a striking finding is that access and utilization to health care is problematic. Historically, African American children and their families initially had no access to health care beyond what was provided by charity until African Americans had opportunities to formally acquire health care skills. In the early nineteenth century there were very few formally trained medical practitioners of any ethnic background. Most health care provided was provided to African Americans by African American elders who had developed skills and knowledge from observation over the years. In the early twentieth century, few African Americans were formally trained as doctors. Further, these black doctors, while few and far in between, often exclusively served black patients, because generally African Americans with health problems generally were not served by white doctors or white hospitals. Changes occurred very slowly during the early twentieth century so that into the 1950s it was not an impossibility to find a white doctor who would provide services to African American patients on a fee for service basis. However, there are stories of African Americans who were refused medical treatment well into the 1950s and 1960s because the white medical establishment would not make its doctors or hospitals available to assist African Americans.

Change proceeded with great speed upon the implementation of the War on Poverty, the Civil Rights Act of 1968, and Titles 18 and 19 of the Social Security Act, Medicare and Medicaid respectively. These policies fundamentally altered the medical services landscape by cutting medical practitioners out of the public funding loop altogether, unless services were offered to everyone, regardless of race, culture, and/or ethnic background (Quadagno, 1994). As union jobs became increasingly available to

African American workers, employer-sponsored health insurance further provided increased access to health care services for African Americans. Often these were secure jobs that people could acquire with only a high-school diploma. These jobs most often were in heaving manufacturing. However, as manufacturing declined in the United States, African Americans were among the first to lose their jobs and ultimately lose access to health care.

At the time of writing, nearly 12 million of the more than 72 million children under the age of 18 years in the United States were African American, approximately 15 percent of the children in the United States under the age of 18 years (Table 3.1). The Annie E. Casey Foundation reports that 12 percent of all children in the United States have no health insurance. Applying those proportions, approximately nearly 1 million African American children have no health insurance, further decreasing their access to health care.

Along with the concern about the lack of access to medical health care, there exist concerns about access and utilization of mental health services. Again, health insurance has a major contribution to both access and utilization of mental health services.

The prevalence of mental health disorders for African American children is difficult to ascertain. This uncertainty regarding prevalence is in part due to questions about access to mental health services and questions about utilization. There is significant distrust of institutional health providers, which has contributed to lower rates of mental health utilization for African Americans. Further, for African Americans there is little confidence in mental health services.

In particular, many have preferred to use other types of intervention, such as churches or personal confidants, to address personal problems rather than seeking mental health services. There has traditionally been some stigma for African Americans using mental health services regardless of whether those services were provided by private or public providers.

In addition to the historical stigma, distrust, and lack of confidence affecting utilization, there has been a very real lack of access for those African Americans who were inclined to seek services. Historically, the costs of mental health services were beyond the means of many African Americans, and chiefly seen as superfluous in comparison to other matters of family survival demanded by the bulk of a family's

TABLE 3.1   Rates of Children Without Health Insurance by Race

	ALL CHILDREN		APPROX NO. OF CHILDREN WITHOUT HEALTH INSURANCE	
	F	*%*	*F*	*% OF TOTAL*
All races	72,894,000	100	8,747,280	12
African American	11,976,000	15	1,312,092	1.8
White	43,835,000	60	5,248,368	7.2

Sources: Adapted from U.S. Census Bureau (2004) and The Annie E. Casey Foundation (2004).

economic resources (i.e., rent/mortgages, food, clothes, transportation to jobs, utilities, and the like). In addition to the costs for services, health insurance is not widely provided by employers even for those with secure sources of employment. And if health insurance is provided by employers, only recently have mental health services been required to be included in the health insurance packages.

SEXUAL ORIENTATION AND YOUTH IN THE CHILD WELFARE SYSTEM

For the most part very little attention has been given to youth who are questioning their sexual orientation or who identify themselves as gay or lesbian. Most youth in the system are not identified nor is there a support system in place for them. Issues of safety, discrimination, and harassment are of particular concern for any youth. But for African American gay and lesbian youth it is a double-edged sword. In the child welfare system the ramifications of being homosexual leave very little hope for permanency outside of emancipation. However, on September 6, 2003, AB 458, the Foster Care Non-Discrimination Act was signed into law and went into effect on January 1, 2004.

According to the National Center for Lesbian Rights, "AB 458 prohibits discrimination in the foster care system on the basis of actual or perceived race, ethnic group identification, ancestry, national origin, color, religion, sex, sexual orientation, gender identity, mental or physical disability, or HIV status." The law requires training for service providers on an ongoing basis. This includes group home administrators, foster parents, department licensing personnel, and community college districts that provide orientation and training to relative caregivers. It is also important that social workers receive training to reinforce the importance of equal access to all services available to children and adults in the system.

JUVENILE JUSTICE SYSTEM

African Americans comprise 12 percent of the U.S. population and nearly half (47.3 percent) of the state's prison population. According to the Children's Defense Fund (2002) the rate of violence and crime committed by all youth was declining and especially black youth. "Between 1996 and 2000, the number of juveniles arrested for violent crime declined 23 percent." Violent crime by juveniles reach their highest point between 3 and 6 o'clock, which correlates with the time where there is a lot of idle time.

The Child Welfare League of America (2002) provided fact and figures that indicated that in the year 2000, 79 percent of the juvenile population were white and 16 percent were black. However, 42 percent of the youth arrested for violent crime were black. They were also overrepresented in property crime arrest at 27 percent.

Court intervention with children, youth, and families has been challenged and undergone criticism. Most of the criticism is centered on differences over the correct purpose, focus, and procedures of the juvenile court (Downs et al., 2004). According to Downs et al. (2004), the first juvenile court in the United States came into existence in April 2, 1899, in the state of Illinois as a result of a cooperative effort on the part of social workers, lawyers, and civic leaders from various organizations in the community. The legislation that was the initial piece served as a model for other states. It was entitled "An Act to Regulate the Treatment and Control of Dependent, Neglected, and Delinquent Children."

In 1914 Cincinnati, Ohio, established the first family court. This court has jurisdiction over issues involving children and families. The issues the court has jurisdiction over include "divorce, child support, custody and visitation, paternity establishment, child abuse and neglect, including termination of parental rights, juvenile delinquency, guardianship, emancipation, and emergency medical and mental health treatment authorization" (Downs et al., 2004, p. 189).

Juvenile delinquency occurs once a juvenile violates a federal or state law or a municipal ordinance. The data published on juvenile crime in 1999 revealed, "The youths at the time of arrest for all crimes were as follows: 23 percent were 17 years of age, 68 percent were 13 through 16 years of age, and 9 percent were less than 13 years of age. The racial composition was 69 percent White, 28 percent Black, 1 percent Native American, and 2 percent Asian. Males make up about 73 percent of all delinquency arrest" (Snyder, 2000, as cited in Downs et al., 2004, p. 412).

A majority of the literature agrees that there is an overrepresentation of African American youth in the juvenile justice system. Research shows that African American youth are more likely to be arrested and less likely to be released while they are waiting to go to trial than Caucasian youth (Downs et al., 2004). The American Bar Association (1993) wrote, "Florida courts were three times as likely to transfer an African American or Native American charged with delinquency to adult court than they were to transfer his or her white counterpart. The impact on African Americans was particularly disproportionate, and they were far more likely to be sentenced to detention by a juvenile court" (Downs et al., 2004, p. 428).

An in-depth look at our legal system and the practices of police in patrolling and targeting low-income areas indicate that there is a higher incidence of arrest. African American youth are highly suspected of committing offenses because of their LSES. They are stopped, arrested, and held more often and longer than their white peers.

Juszkiewics and Schindler (2001) wrote, "a comprehensive national report prepared by the National Council on Crime and Delinquency titled '*And Justice for Some: Differential Treatment of Minority Youth in the Justice System,*' which found that minority youth received more severe treatment than Caucasian youth at every decision point throughout the justice system, even when charged with the same offenses" (p. 102). African American youth were also overrepresented when it came to felony charges filed in adult courts and was most evident in charges for drug and public order offenses. Since the majority of these youth are poor, they are probably represented by a public defender. Having a public defender increases their chances of being convicted since most public defenders are overworked, are often assigned to the youth at the last minute, and have high caseloads. Poor representation is similar to having no representation.

Downs et al. (2004) theorize that effective intervention occurs when the practitioner takes a holistic view of the family unit. They reported the following:

> The November, 2002, Amendments to the Juvenile Justice and Delinquency Prevention Act recognizes the interconnection between the child welfare and the juvenile justice systems. States are required to implement policies across systems to ensure sharing of case information necessary for treatment planning and services, and require case plans and review policies and procedures for federally funded (Title IV-E) delinquency cases similar to those required for abuse and neglect under Title IV-E. (p. 433)

This statement implies that the Juvenile Justice System will implement policies that will improve the services provided for the youth who are trapped in the system. The policies and procedures will emulate that of child welfare, neglect, and abuse under Title IV-E. The interest in this approach is how effective the policies and procedures will be once programs are implemented and services are up and operating.

Organizational/Administrative Responses

On an organizational level (Macro), it important for agencies to ensure that the goals and objectives are congruent with their mission and that a strategic plan is implemented to change deficiencies. Agencies and organizations periodically conduct surveys and program evaluations to improve the functioning of the organization. In most instances, when problems or issues arise, most agencies attempt to correct the imbalance. From a systems perspective, if one part of the organization is malfunctioning, the entire system is affected.

An example of the way in which deficiencies are corrected is the way in which the juvenile justice system is working on change. In 1974 the federal Department of Justice created the Juvenile Justice and Delinquency Prevention Act (Ellis and Sowers, 2001) and the act have been amended several times since then to change policies that were not effective. As a result of the 1974 act, the Office of Juvenile Justice and Delinquency Prevention (OJJDP) was established. The Office of Justice Programs (OJP), the National Criminal Justice Association (NCJA), and RAND (a not-for-profit organization that conducts research and disseminates information on several topics) work in corroboration with the OJJDP where they establish policies, obtain funding, develop programs, conduct research, and disseminate information about effective practice to individuals and organizations throughout the country. Dissemination of information is normally done in the form of publications that are sent to the target population's institutions.

On a more local level, an organization that provides services to poor ethnic families may have connections with resources in the community and may receive funding through private donations, grants, and federal subsidies. These organizations can develop policies and procedures that encourage and support cultural understanding and cultural competence in the provision of services.

The generalist model for social work practice for undergraduate and first-year masters students allows for the opportunity to explore working with micro level, mezzolevel and macrolevels which includes practice with organizations and communities (Devore and Schlesinger, 1999). Traditionally, white administrators and staff have operated agencies serving communities of color. With communities becoming increasingly diverse (i.e., race, gender, age, people with disabilities, religion, and sexual orientation) agencies are developing and establishing training to heighten awareness of cultural sensitivity.

Hyde (2004) describes the "Multicultural organizational development and agency transformation (MCOD)" as complex organizational change process where the focus is to reduce the patterns of racism and sexism as well as other forms of oppression that is dominant in most organizations and institutions in this country. The change is a long and slow one that is accomplished through a fundamental transformation of the organization's culture. "In the ideal, MCOD would result in an organization that embraces full social and cultural representation of all levels; the elimination of sexism, racism and other forms of oppression; in full inclusion and valuing of differences; and the redistribution of power and influence among all stakeholders (Jackson and Holvino, 1988, as cited by Hyde, 2004, p. 8).

The MCOD model is inclusive in the sense that most of the areas of concern are addressed. However, it shows itself as a utopia and will not be respected or accepted by those who are not flexible in their thinking or practices.

Individual and Family

Working with African American families on a micro level requires an understanding of the African American experience. This includes remembering their history of slavery along with continuous episodes of racism and discrimination. Historically, African Americans have not sought help from outsiders. Because of their history of trauma, racism, discrimination, and oppression, there is a general mistrust of the system and people who represent the system that oppresses them.

Cultural beliefs are that personal and family business is kept within the family. A strong philosophy that exists is "God and prayer" will get one through the tough times. And going to church, being a good Christian, having faith, and relying on the power of God is an important custom for African Americans when there is a need to seek help. Quotes from the Bible such as "God help those who help themselves" is literally believed and practiced in the culture. A good strategy to use when working with African American families is to recognize, acknowledge, and respect their strong spiritual beliefs, and draw on those same beliefs using a strengths-based perspective.

Stewart (2004) talks about working with African American families from an Afrocentric perspective. She says, "Afrocentric thinkers take a pluralist approach to human services and acknowledge that no one world view can explain the actions of all people across all cultures. Nor should one world view's assumption about human behavior be used to develop interventions for those from various cultures" (p. 221). She further talks about the embodiment of the total person in terms of the mind, body, and soul from the Afrocentric perspective. In her article, Stewart introduces

"The Seven Principles (Nguzo Saba)" which is the work of Dr. Maulana Karenga (1988) and is seen as a guide to Afrocentric thought and behavior Dr. Katenga writes:

> Umoja translates to unity of interconnectedness which strives to maintain unity in the family, community, nation and race; Kujichagulia means self-determination where we define ourselves, name ourselves, and speak for ourselves; Ujima means collective work and responsibility to build and maintain our community together and to make our brothers' and sisters' problems our problems and solve them together; Ujamaa translates to cooperative economics to build our own stores, shops and other businesses and to profit from them; Nia means purpose to take as our collective vocation the building and developing of our community to restore our people to their traditional greatness; Kuumba is creativity to always do as much as we can, in the way we can, to restore our people to their traditional greatness; Imani means faith to believe in our parents, our teachers, our leaders, our people, and ourselves and in the righteousness and victory of our struggle. (p. 221)

According to Diller (2004), researchers who have made adaptations in their approaches to working with African American families noted that the following three elements are essential: "understanding the cultural context of the family; viewing differences in family dynamics as adaptive mechanisms and strengths; and developing practices that take into account the needs, cultural dynamics, and style of African American culture" (p. 198). It is also important to develop interventions that will work well within the existing family structures instead of trying to model them after white families. Emphasis placed on the family unit as a support system should be acknowledged as a strength, with the understanding that each family is unique. Family members should be included or consulted regarding the plan of intervention of an African American client whenever possible. Be aware that traditional forms of intervention may not be appropriate or even effective for black families.

Manning, Cornelius and Okundaye (2004) theorize, "Empowerment theory, an Afrocentric perspective, and ego psychology can individually offer a positive framework for assisting African Americans" (p. 233). Integrating the three as an approach would strengthen the framework in which to work with the client. The rationale behind this theory is to work with the African American client from a holistic perspective (using history, culture, race, communalism, spirituality, and resilience) as a way of reaffirming and acknowledging his or her strength at the same time understanding that internal and external forces are always prevalent.

It is essential that practitioners honor and respect the cultural values of black clients and avoid trying to change them. Being willing to learn more about their client's culture and taking the time to learn will help in establishing a good rapport with the client and the family. The fact that black families many not trust members of the Euro-American culture, practitioners must be aware of how they communicate with the client. Black families are sensitive to both verbal and nonverbal communication and are watchful of the practitioner for clues regarding sincerity, openness, respectfulness, friendliness, and warmth (Ellis and Sowers, 2001).

Harvey (1997) suggests working with African American Juvenile offenders using an Afrocentric approach through the use of groups as a viable way of connecting them with their heritage while enabling them to develop a strong sense of self and allowing them to create a positive relationship with their peers.

For the most part, African American youth are faced with negative stereotypes; oppression, discrimination, and poverty; lack of employment opportunities; poor education; crime, violence, and pressure from gangs. They usually know very little about African culture or their roots. Utilizing an Afrocentric approach will instill a sense of pride and help them to discover their inner strength. This approach can also allow them to explore their aspirations and build on their strengths so they will be empowered to make socially responsible decisions. Having a support system, feeling connected to others, and being respected by adults who can impact their lives are important variables while working with this population of youth.

Locke and Ciechalski (1995) encourage practitioners and counselors to have African American youth talk about themselves, their families, and their life experiences. These stories will provide the practitioner with valuable information about culture, values, and the things they have experienced in life. The stories can also shed light on the strengths of the family and the adolescent. Social workers need to be curious and ask questions about things they are not familiar with instead of making assumptions. Showing respect for the culture, being open, honest, and participating in community activities will enhance the relationship between the worker, the youth, and the family.

Community

The ecosystem theory at the community level has to do with location and the interaction of people within that location. A community is the place where significant events happen to people and where life chances and quality of life opportunities emerge (MacNair, as cited in Kilpatrick and Holland, 1999).

From an ecological perspective, the African American community is one where an interrelatedness and interconnectedness exist. People in the community share a common language, values, beliefs, experiences, history, traditions, spirituality, and ancestry. In these communities, families often turn to the church for consultation and help when in need. In an effort to get to know the African American community, social workers and other agency representatives should form alliances with faith-based organizations in providing services to them. Getting familiar with the resources and strengths in the community will educate the social worker on the needs of the community.

Black churches have a reputation for providing multiple services to families in the community. Without the assistance of the church many families in the community would be without services. Mays and Nicholson (as cited in Taylor et al., 2000) noted "that churches sponsored a diverse array of community outreach programs, including programs to feed unemployed people, free health clinics, recreational activities, and child care programs. These activities reflect a longstanding tradition of providing for those in need in their communities" (p. 73).

According to Appleby, Colon, and Hamilton (2001), in most cases, the client who lives in the community has limited knowledge (which is primarily obtained through word of mouth). So, educating the community and the people who live in it is an important intervention strategy. Education can come in the form of organizing the community to build alliances with other oppressed groups and developing their own leadership will empower them to advocate for themselves.

The capacity of the social worker to develop cultural competence in working with African American communities may require internal changes within the worker's own organization. Kretzmann and McKnight (as cited in Kirst-Ashman, 2000) talk about building on the strengths of the families, community organizations, and social institutions. From a strengths perspective it would be easier to know what resources are available in order to work on developing a stronger foundation for needed changes.

Building communities to fight problems in poor black neighborhoods is essential in empowering the members of the community to become proactive. Naparstek and Dooley (cited in Kirst-Ashman, 2000) discuss four principles that go into building communities. They say it is important for social workers to help community resource systems to work together in forming new alliances with agencies within the community and external to the community to bring additional resources; to target neighborhoods whose residents have strong connections with local institutions will increase the chances of making positive changes; and to building on neighborhood strengths which requires residents to come together to advocate for resources that will improve conditions in their neighborhoods.

INTERVENTION STRATEGIES: IDENTIFY, DISCUSS, APPLY PRACTICE COMPETENCIES

Pinderhughes (1997) notes the increasing number of African American children in out-of-home care and states that they are in a system that is "insensitive, ineffective, fragmented and remote" (p. 19). She asserts that social workers need to incorporate cultural competence into their intervention. Cultural competence will require the worker to look at themselves and how they deal with and value diversity. Pinderhughes (1997, p. 20) mentions the need for the following:

- knowledge of values, beliefs, and cultural practices of particular clients
- the ability to respect and appreciate the values, beliefs, and practices of all clients, including those who are culturally different
- the ability to be comfortable with differences in others
- the ability to control and even change one's own false beliefs, assumptions, and stereotypes
- the ability to think and behave flexibly.

Dillion (1994) on the other hand believes that cultural competence should be done at the assessment phase of the intervention and emphasize spiritual, intellectual growth, cultural identity, ethnicity, and social class in placement consideration. During the assessment phase the following requirements would assist the worker in being more competent:

- skills in thinking cross-culturally, considering differences within ethnic groups
- the ability to operate from a knowledge base grounded in reality, which addresses the array of ideas, values, and lifestyles of the families' group
- an accurate assessment of the beliefs, virtues, and attitudes of the African American community
- assumption of an Afrocentric perspective which looks at the clients' view of the world and their situation in it.

There are common themes one can identify when working with African American children and their families. However, we encourage all who are interested in the helping profession to be careful to make no assumptions when working with a family of any racial and/or ethnic background (Lum, 2003). That is most certainly essential advice when working with African American children and their families.

When intervening with any family, that family as an entity must be approached with respect and humility. This is not because the family has done or has not done anything specific to deserve respect. This approach is warranted because it is a privilege to come into someone else's home and to be allowed to discuss issues that if not considered to be intimate, may at least be considered private. Specifically, in social work practice the approach widely encourages the examination of the family concerns in the context of the strengths the family brings to address their own concerns. Often those involved in the helping profession focus on the problems of an individual, the consequential problems that individuals create for his or her family, and the overall difficulties the family faces in the context of the environment. However, beginning with the identification of the family's resources and the resources that individual members of the family bring to a problem situation can provide the framework from which effective services can be provided. This process requires attentiveness so hurrying through the process may reduce one's effectiveness and efficiency. Finally, the author suggests that each family's situation represent itself with a set of unique challenges and resources. Because the constellation of individual circumstances, resources, and challenges is myriad, it is unrealistic, ineffective, and inefficient to provide children and their families with boilerplate solutions to the issues they face. Problem-solving and solution development must be tailored to the experiences and needs of families.

In review, when working with African American children and their families it is essential to (1) make no assumptions, (2) to treat individual family members and the family as a whole with respect, (3) to recognize the strengths and resources a family brings to the helping process, (4) to tailor helping efforts to meet the needs of a specific family, and (5) to speak with confidence and authority, and with humility. Adopting this perspective is not the only way to effectively work with African American families; however, using this perspective should insure effective interactions with any child and/or their family.

■ ■ ■ ■ ■ ▬▬▬▬▬▬▬▬▬▬▬▬▬▬▬▬▬▬▬▬▬▬▬▬▬

CASE STUDY 1

Geraldine Gleason was a third-grade teacher at Genius Elementary School and Robert Gleason was a supervisor in the housekeeping department at Cureall General Hospital. They had been married for 10 years and had two daughters Kari, aged 9 and Halie, aged 7 and a son, Jamal, aged 4. They owned their home in a quiet neighborhood with modest homes.

During Thanksgiving Holiday the family was returning home from having dinner with Roberts' parents, when an oncoming car driven by a drunk driver crossed into their lane and ran into their car. The impact of the accident left Robert with a broken back, internal injuries, and paralysis on his right side. Geraldine sustained a broken arm, two broken ribs, and minor cuts and bruises. Jamal was crushed in his seat and was in critical condition in the hospital on life supports. Halie had a few cuts and bruises and Kari sustained broken ribs, a concussion, and some cuts and bruises. Robert and Jamal remained in the hospital for several weeks. Both of their injuries were so bad that they required intensive treatment and rehabilitation.

Since both Geraldine and Robert had health coverage they were not concerned about the cost of their medical bills. But because of the nature of Roberts' injuries he would not be able to return to work anytime in the near future. The longer he was off from work the less sick time he had until it was all exhausted. The family then had to depend on Geraldine's salary alone to support them. But with all of the health problems and limited financial resources Geraldine and Robert had a hard time paying their bill. They fell behind in their mortgage and lost their home.

They then had to move into an apartment that was affordable. Geraldine was concerned about the safety of the area they moved into but knew that this was all they could afford. The bills continued to come in. Roberts' health insurance dropped him stating he was no longer eligible for the policy since he was not working at the hospital anymore. So the medical bills started coming in. Geraldine was having a difficult time trying to manage everything alone and she was unable to make ends meet. Robert tried to get disability compensation but kept getting rejected. Family members helped as much as they could but had limited resources themselves.

Geraldine got a second job which required her to work long hours after teaching. She became so exhausted and stressed that she was on the verge of a nervous breakdown. She and Robert had problems communicating with each other because of his aphasia and his chronic pain. She became frustrated and started to feel as if she were the only adult with four children instead of three.

To help her to relax she started taking Valium. Then she started missing days at school because she could not get herself up and ready. There were times she felt depressed and hopeless. Geraldine would go to church every Sunday and pray that things would get better.

Jamal was recovering well but still needed special medical services. The girls started fighting, arguing more than usual, and their grades in school declined. Geraldine decided to seek help at the county social services agency.

(continued)

CASE STUDY 1   Continued

DISCUSSION GUIDE

- From a strengths perspective, what would be the best approach to use in working with the Gleason family?
- Assess the needs of the family.
- What additional information would be useful for the social worker that would be working with the family?

INTERVENTION STRATEGIES

- Be supportive of Geraldine and assist her in identifying what her needs are.
- Set up referral mechanism.

CASE STUDY 2

Lolita is a 15-year-old biracial (Panamanian/German) female who has been in the foster care system off and on for the last 5 years. She is currently in a group home because of her frequent running away from her foster home and truancy from school. She has been sexually active with boys since she was 13 years old but states that she doesn't really enjoy sex. She does it just to be doing something and to have boys like her. Since being in the group home, Lolita has been hanging out with Betty, who is a 17-year-old Caucasian female. Lolita finds herself really attracted to Betty and has kissed her on several occasions, with the last kiss resulting in sexual intercourse. Lolita never thought of herself as liking girls, but finds that she is more attracted to Betty than boys. Betty has had previous sexual relations with other girls and none with boys. She has come out as a lesbian. Lolita is not sure if she is a lesbian or bisexual but she does know that she wants to be in a relationship with Betty.

Some of the group home staff and residents have ostracized Lolita and Betty causing them to rebel and not follow house rules. You are the social worker assigned to work with the staff, the residents, and Lolita and Betty to assess the situation and to resolve the conflict.

DISCUSSION GUIDE

- What strategy would be best to use at approaching this situation?
- What supports should be in place for adolescents who are questioning their sexual orientation?
- What, if any position, does the Social Work Code of Ethics take in matters of sexual orientation?
- What rights, if any, do Lolita and Betty have?

INTERVENTION STRATEGIES

- Act as a mediator
- Meet with Lolita and Betty separately
- Meet with staff
- Have a group meeting
- Discuss the issue of sexual orientation in an overall group meeting.

CASE STUDY 3

Annette and Roy were a Caucasian couple and had been married for 8 years. They had no children of their own but love children and decided to become foster parents. They went through the application and licensing process and attended the foster parent training. They were open to having any child in their home but preferred to have a young child. The first child they received was an infant by the name of Kalani, who was biracial (the mother was African American and the father was Caucasian). Annette and Roy instantly fell in love with the baby even though he was a premature baby and had some respiratory problems. Kalanis' mother ran away from home when she discovered that she was pregnant and stayed with Kalanis' dad. They broke up right before she gave birth and so she was essentially homeless and unable to care for her baby. She felt she had no choice but to place him in temporary care until she could get her life on the right track.

Initially, Kalanis' mom came to visit him on a regular basis but she had a difficult time keeping a job and finding a place to stay. She stayed with friends and relatives for short periods of time but no one was willing to help her with the responsibilities of an infant. Eventually the visits became more infrequent until she was no longer visiting him. Kalani grew healthier even though he still had respiratory problems.

When he was 2 years old, Kalanis' mother lost her parental rights and he was free for adoption. His foster parents had the first right to adopt because he had bonded with them. However, the social worker was concerned that the foster parents did not live in or near a diverse community and wondered how Kalani would be exposed to the ethnic heritage and how he would be prepared to step out into the real world of racism and discrimination as a young adult.

DISCUSSION GUIDE

- What factors should be considered in transracial adoptions?
- What efforts should be made, if any, to locate another placement?
- Should African American infants be placed in Caucasian foster homes?
- Discuss the position taken by the NABSW on transracial adoption.
- What factors should be taken into consideration when placing African American Children in Caucasian homes?

(continued)

■ ■ ■ ■ ■

CASE STUDY 3   Continued

INTERVENTION STRATEGIES

- Assess what is in the best interest of the child.
- Know the policy regarding transracial adoption in your state.
- Educate the foster parents on issues regarding transracial adoption.

■ ■ ■ ■ ■

CASE STUDY 4

Margaret is a 67-year-old African American widow who has the responsibility of caring for her four grandchildren aged 4, 5, 7, and 10. Margaret is diabetic and her glucose levels are out of control. In addition, she has hypertension and has recently been experiencing shortness of breath. Her son, who is the father of the children, and their mother died in a house fire leaving Margaret as the sole surviving relative of the children.

Margaret is on a fixed income but fought to have her grandchildren placed in her custody instead of going to a nonkin foster home. Margaret went through the foster licensing process and finally received her license to have her grandchildren in her care. She receives some financial assistance but it is limited. The children have been living with her for 6 months and Margaret is finding it difficult to meet the needs of all of the grandchildren. She loves her grandchildren and they love and are very attached to her. Margaret is a religious woman and believes that God will give her the strength to see them through these hard times.

Margaret is very insightful and knows that the children are mourning the loss of their parents but they do not talk much about them. Seven-year-old Galya cries a lot and keeps her 4- and 5-year-old siblings close by her side. Ten-year-old Greg isolates and gets into fights at school and with children in the neighborhood.

You are the social worker assigned to work with this family. What strategies would you use to intervene with this family?

DISCUSSION GUIDE

- What are the prevailing issues in this case and what course of action should be taken?
- Discuss ways in which Margaret's spiritual beliefs should be addressed.
- In terms of "in the best interest of the child," what are the factors that should be taken into consideration?
- Discuss ways in which the social worker can work with the family to assist them to become more self-sufficient.
- Discuss the strengths and weaknesses of the case.
- Discuss whether this is a case where the children should be removed from kinship care.

INTERVENTION STRATEGIES

- Assess the family situation for risk factors
- Identify strengths
- Identify support systems
- Identify what Margaret wants
- Assess the physical and mental health needs of the family
- Identify resources.

SUMMARY OF KEY ISSUES AND CONCEPTS

Working with African American children, youth, and their families can be a challenge to any practitioner if the black experience is incorporated into the method of intervention. Poverty, racism, discrimination, and oppression have plagued African Americans throughout history. It is evident if we review the literature which repeatedly suggest that African American children, youth, and their families have higher rates of poverty, unemployment, incarcerations, children in out-of-home placements, less health care, less child care, and more reports of substance use.

Cultural knowledge, sensitivity, and using a strengths-based approach are important when working with black families. Acknowledging that each family is different and the intervention should be tailored to a family's specific needs is essential. Drawing on the strength and support of community, church, and extended family, the practitioner will help the family to become empowered.

AMERICAN INDIAN AND ALASKA NATIVE CHILDREN: A LEGACY OF SUFFERING, SURVIVAL, AND STRENGTH

RITA LEDESMA, PH.D., LCSW

School of Social Work, California State University, Los Angeles

Alaska native family.

OVERVIEW

The contemporary circumstance of American Indians and Alaska Native (AI/AN) children and families reflects histories of contact, colonialism, and conflict. The unique legal and political relationships that exist between American Indian and Alaska Native communities and the U.S. governments indicate the obligations of the federal government to American Indian and Alaska Native tribal nations. The demography of the community is notable for a host of challenges that undermine the capacities of American Indian and Alaska Native communities. Despite a legacy and the present circumstance that is marked by exposure to horrendous trauma and multiple loss experiences, American Indian and Alaska Native nations persevere. The enduring nature of the profound commitment to traditional cultural values, beliefs, behaviors, and practices is a fundamental strength and resource for tribal nations. Although there is much diversity within American Indian and Alaska Native communities, children and family relationships are highly valued across tribal nations. Cultural values, beliefs, and behaviors have contributed to the survival of the American Indian and Alaska Native nations in the face of generational traumatic challenges and losses. Attachments to traditional cultural values, beliefs, and practices contribute to a legacy of survival and strength that bodes well for the future.

INTRODUCTION

> My parents belonged to that great plains tribe which is now called the Sioux. But before the white man came, we called ourselves the Lakotas. The first white men to come to this country thought they had discovered India, a land they had been searching for, so they named the people they found here Indians. Through the mistake of these first white settlers, we have been called Indians ever since.
>
> (Luther Standing Bear, *My Indian Boyhood*, 1988, p. 1)

My great granduncle, Luther Standing Bear begins his book, *My Indian Boyhood*, with this passage. In this brief passage, he asserts his tribal and family affiliation, and he notes the origins of the strengths, conflict, contradictions, and challenges that characterize the American Indian and Alaska Native experience. Luther Standing Bear wrote quite eloquently and humbly of the transformations that occurred during his lifetime. The traditional Lakota way of life was profoundly altered as the Lakota nation was conquered and colonized. Children were removed from their families and sent hundreds of miles away to Carlisle Indian School in Pennsylvania. Luther Standing Bear entered Carlisle in 1879, and he described how he selected his name by bravely pointing at a name on a list "as if I were about to touch an enemy" (Standing Bear, *My People the Sioux*, 1975, p. 137). He discussed the pain of separation from family and place, the challenges associated with adapting to a foreign environment and new expectations, the strength of spirit and intellect required for survival in a hostile institution and foreign environment, the sorrow that permeated the Lakota nation as children died and were buried far from home, and the sense of mastery that he experienced as he demonstrated resilient capacities and developed skills that promoted adjustment, accommodation, and survival. With simple and humble prose, he described the transformation of the Lakota Nation, which resulted as a consequence of contact with non-Indians, military conquest, and colonization.

His story and the experiences of his family and descendents are not unique in Indian Country, where countless families and nations adjusted, resisted, and accommodated to the multiple changes that transpired after contact with Europeans and representatives of the U.S. government. These experiences are transferred across generations in family and tribal stories, oral histories, letters, books, art, and song and dance. These experiences have informed my social work practice and scholarship as a clinician and educator in the urban community of Los Angeles. For the Lakota people and many other American Indian and Alaska Native tribal communities, contact with nonnatives and the military conquest of American Indian nations culminated in a legacy of suffering, survival, and strength that continues to influence American Indian and Alaska Native children and families in contemporary society.

Individuals, families, and nations were challenged to respond to and make sense of a wide range of cultural, spiritual, political, and material conditions that forever shifted the trajectories of family and tribal life. Luther Standing Bear offers an analysis of these conditions before and after colonization. His struggles to adjust to life outside his home and tribal community and his experiences at Carlisle Indian School predict and parallel the experiences of American Indian and Alaska Native generations that followed. In Luther Standing Bear's analysis, factors that demonstrate the resilient capacities and strengths of American Indian and Alaska Native people are illustrated: the significance of cultural material is made visible, the importance of storytelling and witnessing is illustrated, and the centrality of cultural and tribal identity is underscored. The story that Luther Standing Bear reveals is both specific and general; it reflects his specific experience and historical epoch, while capturing the elements that are common to the wider American Indian and Alaska Native experience and the shared legacy and consequences that followed contact.

Practice in American Indian and Alaska Native communities requires that social workers and allied human services professionals develop knowledge about the specific and diverse nature of these communities, including the cultural values, beliefs, and productions associated with the tribal community; the social and political history; the precolonial, postcolonial, and neocolonial experiences; and the material conditions that illuminate the shared history of suffering, survival, and strength. It is critical to develop appreciation for the degree to which cultural material is embedded in the fiber of individual and community life and obscured by social and political context. Culture mediates and influences all life experiences, informing relationship protocols and social expectations, identifying the boundaries of the physical world, and organizing social and political structures. The influence of culture on these processes is not immediately visible to those outside of the community, so practitioners must develop a theoretical orientation and skill set that promotes understanding of cultural differences, knowledge about the specific story, history, and conditions associated with consumer populations, and respect for diversity and the self-reflective capacities required for effective practice.

Strengths-based, culturally focused, narrative, and ethnographic theoretical orientations have great efficacy for constructing analyses of social and personal conditions that do not pathologize American Indian and Alaska Native communities nor confuse American Indian and Alaska Native culture with pathology. Additionally, these approaches promote understanding of resilient capacities found within families and communities. Attachment theory advances our capacities to interpret the nature of bonds and affiliation with family, community, place, and nation and to examine exposure to loss and trauma and to interpret the intergenerational manifestations of loss experiences. The strengths perspective has great utility for increasing knowledge about the specific issues of concern to American Indian and Alaska Native clients, and the narrative approach is useful for eliciting the perspective of the client and constructing, deconstructing, and reconstructing the client experiences and life events. Strengths-based and narrative approaches support investigation of the influence of cultural material, information about the tenacity or fragility of cultural bonds, and engagement with clients from a collaborative stance. Ethnographic interviewing techniques significantly enhance the skill set of practitioners by supporting the ability to learn from the client and elicit the client's story and experience, to practice cross-culturally and sensitively, to explore and enter the "world" of the client, and to acknowledge that the client possesses expertise and knowledge that are the foundations upon which interventions build. Professionals working within the American Indian and Alaska Native community are encouraged to develop skills and self-reflective capacities that support the intentional use of self in order to interact with clients in ways that respect difference, that promote collaborative relationships between client and worker, and in order to ensure that interpretations of client experiences reflect the client's perspective and not the worker's experience.

This chapter will present information that advances the capacities of social workers and allied human services providers to effectively engage with American Indian and Alaska Native communities. The chapter includes an overview of historical, demographic, and cultural characteristics, an analysis of issues associated with the healthy and productive development of children and families, and a discussion of considerations in the design and development of assessment and interventions for children and families. The discussion is supplemented by the voices of selected American Indian service providers who work in the Los Angeles urban community.

HISTORICAL CONSIDERATIONS

> We are colonized and any time a people are colonized, there is much unrest. Colonialism leaves such a bitter taste with the people, and they continue to fight. They might even end up fighting one another. If we can truly understand what colonialism does, what it has meant in our lives, then we might better understand why we should not fight one another anymore. Colonialism makes us fight; it creates confusion, separation, unease and unrest. And then, we become sick; our Indian people are sick when we start fighting among each other.

The demography of American Indian and Alaska Native nations cannot be discussed independent of historical context. The experience of American Indians and Alaska Natives differs dramatically from the experiences of other minority populations in the United States. Historical and contemporary relationships between the federal government and the American Indian and Alaska Native people reflect their unique status as sovereign nations within the United States. In 1832, Chief Justice John Marshall delivered the landmark decision (*Worcester v. Georgia*) that recognized Indian tribes as sovereign, domestic, dependent nations and affirmed that the Constitution gave Congress the right to wage war, establish peace, regulate trade, and enter into treaties with American Indian tribes (Price, 1973, pp. 17, 40–45). These long-standing legal and political relationships between the American Indian and Alaska Native nations and the federal government influence every dimension of life. Treaties, compacts, judicial opinions, and federal regulations and policies have each influenced the resources, opportunities, challenges, and struggles that unfold within American Indian and Alaska Native communities and reflect the history of contact between American Indian and Alaska Native communities and nonnatives.

Western Europeans first explored the continent from the east, while Asians explored the far northwest of the continent. As each entered the "New World," they found a continent inhabited by many indigenous tribes and nations. For this indigenous population, daily life was shaped by the relationships that existed between the people and the place they inhabited. The cultural, social, spiritual, and political structures that developed reflected these relationships. The food, clothing, homes, stories, ceremonies, songs, and dances that evolved in each tribal community were influenced by the physical ecology and illustrated the nature of the attachment that the people experienced with the environment. Social and political organizations, spiritual and cultural belief systems, and social roles and expectations demonstrated reciprocity and mutuality with the physical environment. The ecological diversity of the continent resulted in cultural diversity amongst the many groups and nations that populated the continent. Similarities in cultural values across tribal groups evolved, as evidenced in the origin stories and spiritual practices that have passed down through the generations and that have influenced daily life in contemporary communities. Despite the diversity of tribal nations, indigenous communities have shared a history of loss and suffering as a consequence of colonization and the oppressive conditions that characterized the postcolonial experience.

Disease-decimated tribal communities, and colonization resulted in numerous massacres of warriors, children, women and elders, military conquest, and the destruction of many tribal nations. The postcolonial experience of the last 200 years traumatized traditional communities through federal policies and practices. American settlers gained access to natural resources and were encouraged to exploit these resources for personal gain when the U.S. government institutionalized removal policies. American Indians were removed from traditional homelands by force and deprived of homelands through fraud and policy initiatives. The "Trail of Tears" was one of the most well known examples of the removal policies of the United States and has been rightly described as a death march, because it resulted in the deaths of hundreds of Cherokee children and adults. Federal policies supported the conversion and Americanization of native children by removing children from families and placing them in boarding schools. These efforts resulted in the abuse and victimization of children at the hands of government-funded caregivers and promoted the destruction of nations and cultures as children were separated from tribal communities. In many communities, the boarding school experience was so traumatic that there have been profound generational consequences manifesting as unresolved grief, violence, diminished parenting capacities, substance abuse, and high rates of suicide. Federal and state adoption and foster-care policies actively promoted the removal and out-of-home placement of Indian children, until the passage of the Indian Child Welfare Act (ICWA) (PL 95–608) in 1978.

Federal policies and legislation also banned traditional spiritual practices and political structures, further eroding the integrity of traditional nations. American Indians did not receive citizenship and the right to vote until 1924. Yet, American Indian men served valiantly in World War I, World War II, and every subsequent conflict. The contributions made by "code talkers" in each of the World Wars have only recently received public attention. The "code talkers" provided significant support to the U.S. war efforts by using their native languages to communicate sensitive information for the military command. While many Americans are familiar with the contributions of Navajo soldiers, soldiers from other American Indian nations also participated in these efforts. In the 1950s, young adults and families were relocated from tribal communities to urban communities in efforts to promote assimilation, and federal recognition of many tribal nations was terminated. Both of these initiatives (relocation and termination) represented policies designed to end the federal obligation to provide services to Indian nations, despite guarantees provided in federal treaties and statutes.

The history of interactions between American Indian/Alaska Native communities and nonnatives is a history of contact, conflict, resistance, suffering, survival, and strength. The colonial and postcolonial experiences, including the policies of removal from traditional homelands and the establishment of the reservation system resulted in death, dependence, and the disorganization of social and cultural institutions. The intentional and unintentional introduction of diseases for which native people had no immunities resulted in the deaths of thousands. Dependence was promoted as tribal communities were separated from the physical environment that sustained life and when traditional, cultural, and spiritual practices were banned. Disorganization resulted as traditional cultural, political, and social structures were undermined by federal policies, and American Indians were required to emulate the sociopolitical structures of the conqueror and the colonizer.

American Indians and Alaska Natives have never been silent about the injustices visited upon traditional communities. The issues confronting American Indian and Alaska Native children and families in contemporary society must be understood in context. Many current problems are related to the postcolonial legacy of loss, trauma, grief, and suffering. Yet, in each generation, there have been individuals or movements that sought to resist, renew, and revitalize the community. For example, Crazy Horse was an Oglala Lakota warrior and leader who actively resisted incursions of the U.S. government. He stated his opposition as follows:

> We did not ask you white men to come here. The Great Spirit gave us this country as a home. You had yours. We did not interfere with you. The Great Spirit gave us plenty of land to live on, and buffalo, deer, antelope and other game. But you have

come here; you are taking my land from me; you are killing off our game, so it is hard for us to live. Now, you tell us to work for a living, but the Great Spirit did not make us to work, but to live by hunting. You white men can work if you want to. We do not interfere with you, and again you say, why do you not become civilized? We do not want your civilization! We would live as our fathers did, and their fathers before them. (McLuhan, 1971, p. 67)

Although he never surrendered, he was assassinated while in federal custody in 1877. His body was retrieved from Fort Robinson Nebraska by his parents, who carried their son home to the "Paha Sapa," Black Hills of South Dakota and the ancestral birthplace of the Lakota. The courage of his parents who carried their son home and buried him in a secret location illuminates incredible strength in the midst of overwhelming sorrow. The legacy of Crazy Horse lies in the strength of his convictions, his commitment to his nation, and his sacrifice on behalf of his people. The resistance of Crazy Horse in only one example in a long and complex history of resistance associated with American Indian and Alaska Native nations.

It is critical to develop knowledge about the relationship between historical context and the issues that plague American Indian and Alaska Native children and families in contemporary society. Many current problems are related to the postcolonial legacy of loss, trauma, grief, and suffering. American Indian and Alaska Native communities have experienced multiple losses as a consequence of contact: the loss of autonomy and independence; the loss of ancestral homelands and social-political organizations; the deaths of tribal members in battle and as a result of military conquest, through starvation and disease; the rape of women; the pillaging of natural resources; the forced removal and coerced separation of children from families and tribal communities; the violations of rights guaranteed by treaties; the destruction of cultural structures; a health status which is notable for premature mortality and biomedical vulnerabilities; and the grueling toll of poverty across generations and the subsequent social and psychological dependence.

This legacy of grief, loss, and suffering is transferred across generations through stories, family/community interactions, and sociopolitical relationships. Multiple losses have "piled-up" across generations, creating stress and disrupting the homeostatic balance of tribal nations, communities, and families. Exposure to loss across generations has fueled a range of healthy and unhealthy responses that led to accommodation and adaptation to the changed circumstances. Efforts to restore a healthy homeostatic balance and to integrate loss experiences within nations, communities, and families are supported by traditional culturally based behaviors and beliefs. The enduring nature of cultural values, beliefs, and practices and the commitment to this cultural material present in contemporary American Indian and Alaska Native communities illuminates the resilient capacities of tribal nations and promotes survival and strength. Despite multitudes of losses over hundreds of years, American Indian and Alaska Native tribal nations survive and continue to actively addressing the profound problems that confront traditional communities by drawing on the capacities that have supported survival and that build on cultural strengths.

DEMOGRAPHIC CONSIDERATIONS

American Indian and Alaska Native communities are notable for their heterogeneity, despite similarities in cultural values, beliefs, and practices and a shared history of contact with the U.S. Government. There are 562 federally recognized tribal nations and Alaska Native villages, and several more tribal nations that are actively seeking recognition and/or restoration of their tribal status. There are many dimensions of diversity within these 562 American Indian and Alaska Native communities including: tribal affiliation, language, land base, social and political history, and access to resources. Characterizations of the community in the popular culture often obscure the nuances of difference. Members of the American Indian and Alaska Native communities are often pathologized as alcoholic and dysfunctional, or mythologized as saviors of the environment or as spiritual guides for "New Age" philosophers. Each characterization promotes the invisibility of the community, because the community is narrowly interpreted from the perspective of those outside. The diversity and the specificity of tribal experiences are diminished when the interpretation of experience does not emanate from within the community. Tribal nations are perceived as a monolithic group, instead of many vibrant, diverse, and specific tribal communities that participate in unique legal and political relationships with the U.S. government, which hold in common a broad set of traditional and culturally based values and which share a legacy of sorrow, strength, and survival.

The most recent census data indicates that there are 4.1 million American Indians and Alaska Natives in the United States, which represents about 1.5% of the total U.S. population (Ogunwole, 2002). The American Indian and Alaska Native population is young and growth in the population is forecasted (Pollard and O'Hare, 1999). Census 2000 questions on race allowed respondents to indicate race "alone" or race "in combination;" the "in combination" reporting process recognizes the multiracial heritage of many members of the community and promoted a more accurate count. The figure cited above reflects the category of "American Indian and Alaska Native alone or in combination with one or more other races." Of the total number of respondents (4,119,301) in this category, 2,475,956 individuals were identified as "American Indian and Alaska Native alone." For the "alone" and "in combination" data, Census 2000 indicates that:

- the largest concentration of American Indians are found in the Western United States;
- the ten states with the largest population are (in order) California, Oklahoma, Arizona, Texas, New Mexico, New York, Washington, North Carolina, Michigan, and Alaska;
- the population is becoming urbanized with New York (87,241) and Los Angeles (53,092) having the largest communities, followed by Chicago, Houston, Philadelphia, Phoenix, San Diego, Dallas, San Antonio, and Detroit;
- approximately 51 percent of the population reside in metropolitan areas with the remainder of the population residing on reservations or in rural areas;

- the Cherokee, Navajo, Choctaw, Sioux, and Chippewa nations each had 100,000 or more respondents indicating tribal affiliation; and
- Eskimo were the largest Alaska Native community, followed by Tlingit-Haida, Alaska Athabascan, and Aleut. (Ogunwole, 2002)

The increased presence of American Indians and Alaska Natives in metropolitan communities presents some specific challenges, because they are frequently disconnected from reservation-based social, educational, and health service delivery systems as well as reservation-based cultural and spiritual resources. Their issues and concerns are often obscured by the needs and issues of other populations in the region, and there may not be a specific geographic or residential community of urban American Indians. For example, adjusted census numbers indicate that Los Angeles County has the largest urban American Indian and Alaska Native population and that many members of the American Indian and Alaska Native community are poor and that American Indian and Alaska Native "children face persistent economic and educational hardships" (Ong, Sung, and Heintz-Mackoff, 2004, p. 6). The community is dispersed across the greater Los Angeles metropolitan area, which makes regional planning for service delivery systems that can address the multiple needs of the community difficult. Further, the complex and pressing needs of American Indians and Alaska Natives in the region are eclipsed by the needs of other communities, because the American Indian and Alaska Native population is relatively small when compared to the Latino, Asian Pacific Islander, and African American communities that dominate the region.

Data released by the U.S. Department of Commerce in 1995 provides an important snapshot of housing conditions on reservations and indicates that:

- 20 percent of American Indian households on reservations lacked complete indoor plumbing;
- many of these household rely on outhouses, chemical toilets, and facilities away from the main residence;
- many of these homes are overcrowded;
- 18 percent of American Indian households on reservations lack complete kitchen facilities;
- 52 percent of homes on reservations do not have telephones; and
- wood is the most common home heating fuel.

This snapshot and the persistent poverty that plagues American Indian and Alaska Native communities illustrate the failure of the historical federal obligation to provide assistance and restitution. Far too many American Indian children on reservations live in circumstances that undermine healthy growth and development. Indian Country is notable for numerous psychosocial and health problems that undermine the well-being of American Indian and Alaska Native children and families and that are the consequences of contact with non-Indians. American Indians and Alaska Natives are overrepresented on every social and demographic marker (low educational attainment, poverty, substance abuse, unemployment, under employment, inadequate housing, high mortality rates, poor health status) that is a risk factor for compromising the growth, development, and well-being of American Indian children and families. The urban environment, which is home to a very large sector of the American Indian and Alaska Native community, offers few protections from these problems, and in many cases, it appears that the urban environment promotes additional stress and exacerbates existing conditions.

The *Kids Count Data Book 2000* published by The Annie E. Casey Foundation provides information about ten key indicators of child well-being culled from data obtained in 2001, 2002, and 2003. On nine of the ten indicators, the data indicate the severity of the challenges experienced by American Indian and Alaska Native children in comparison to the total population of children in the United States (Table 4.1). The data is summarized below:

These findings indicate that American Indian and Alaska Native children are at greater risk to experience social, educational, and health problems that are related to historical, social, and environmental conditions. Fetal Alcohol Syndrome is the leading cause of birth defects among Southwestern Plains groups (Dorris, 1989; May, 1988; McShane, 1988). Dorris (1989) believes that alcohol abuse is the most pressing problem affecting American Indians, impinging on the development of future generations and pervasively affecting the development of afflicted children.

TABLE 4.1 Indicators of Child Well-Being

INDICATOR	TOTAL	AMERICAN INDIAN
% of low-birthweight babies	7.8	7.2
Infant mortality rate (deaths per 1,000 live births)	6.8	9.7
Child death rate (deaths per 100,000 children ages 1–14)	22	29
Rate of teen deaths by accident, homicide & suicide (deaths per 100,000 teens ages 15–19)	50	92
Teen birth rate (births per 1,000 females ages 15–17)	23	31
% of teens who are high-school dropouts (ages 16–19)	8	10
% of teens not attending school and not working (ages 16–19)	9	18
% of children living in families where no parent has full-time year-round employment	25	43
% of children in poverty	17	35
% of families with children headed by a single parent	28	49

The Indian Health Service reports that American Indians and Alaska Natives are five times more likely to die of alcohol-related causes than whites, which creates vulnerability for children whose caregivers are actively substance abusing (Indian Health Service, 1997). LaFromboise and Bigfoot (1988), May (1988), McShane (1988), and Moncher and colleagues (1990) examine adolescent substance abuse and report that American Indian children initiate use earlier and abuse a variety of substances, including alcohol, drugs, hair spray, gasoline, spray paint, tobacco, and snuff. The patterns of use differ and use clearly represents a threat to physical, emotional, and spiritual well-being. Methamphetamine abuse is beginning to surface on reservation communities, and American Indians and Alaska Natives in urban environments are often at high risk for substance abuse problems. There is a need for more data about the presentation of mental disorders in American Indian and Alaska Native children. The high rates of suicide in this population raise concerns about depression and mood disorders, specifically because children appear more likely to externalize depressive symptoms. Given the demographic profile of American Indian and Alaska Native children, it appears that male children and young adolescents are a particularly vulnerable group for experiencing psychological distress.

Data from U.S. census reports, the Bureau of Indian Affairs, and the Indian Health service indicate that American Indian and Alaska Native communities experience multiple challenges:

- overcrowded and inadequate housing;
- persistent and pervasive poverty;
- high rates of substance abuse, accidents, injuries, suicide, delinquency, incarcerations, and interpersonal violence, including child maltreatment; and
- economic development and community infrastructures that are inadequate to sustain healthy communities, because there are extraordinary rates of unemployment, limited public transportation and roads in poor conditions, and multiple access barriers to health care, educational, and social services.

For many American Indian and Alaska Native communities, this state of affairs has existed for generations and reflects the institutionalized oppressive conditions that are characteristic of the postcolonial experience. A colleague offered an analysis of the relationship between poverty and conditions that erode the fiber of the community:

> Poverty is the most overwhelming cause of illness, and not only in our community. I see this society becoming more and more ill, because of poverty. I truly believe that the social disruptions and unrest comes from the unequal distribution of wealth. And, this is because of the public policy decisions we have made. And, poverty masks itself in other ways besides economically, so we have poverty of the spirit, poverty of the soul and when that happens people have a tendency to despair, to give up and to get violent.

The relationship between persistent poverty and the conditions of life for American Indian children and families must be understood. These conditions undermine the capacities of *some* American Indian and Alaska Native parents and illustrate the failure of the federal government to adequately meet its historic obligation to tribal communities.

Despite the presence of multiple challenges, members of American Indian and Alaska Native communities continue to actively advocate on behalf of the communities' children and families and to actively engage in efforts to design and implement culturally focused services to meet the many needs of community members. These efforts are supported by attachment and commitment to the tribal community, understanding of the causal factors of social problems, and appreciation for the strengths and resilient capacities of community members. Anecdotal reports from colleagues who work in Los Angeles and on the Pine Ridge and Navajo reservations and my own practice experience with vulnerable children and families in the urban Los Angeles community offer ample evidence that children and families can emerge strengthened and renewed despite the fact that they have weathered tremendous adversities. It is also clear that cultural material plays a significant role in these processes. As one colleague noted:

> We have seen families that entered the system, with multiple problems, with horrendous histories, and then, they have been really traumatized by their experiences with the courts, with other social workers, with other professionals on top of whatever brought them into the system. Yet, lots of them really hang on to their values and their sense of themselves, despite the way that they are treated and in spite of how hard it is to make their life, because of the poverty, the lack of resources, the lack of transportation, the isolation. And, when we approach them in a respectful way, when we let them know that we aren't sitting in judgment, and we're clear about what is needed, and what we can offer, and when we're willing to sit with them and listen to their stories and their struggles, and we're willing to re-parent them, we see how committed they are to their kids, to their family, to their beliefs and how responsive they are to things that make sense to them.

CULTURAL CONSIDERATIONS

The effectiveness of human services professionals in working cross-culturally is enhanced by a capacity to appreciate, respect, and bridge cultural differences. This capacity promotes the creation of collaborative working relationships across cultures, because the worker is attentive to their own culture and actively seeks knowledge about the client's culture. Social work practice with its person-in-environment focus acknowledges that cultural differences exist and that the social environment (composed of social, historical, economic, political, and legal dimensions) significantly influences individual and community development (Schriver, 1995; Zastrow and Kirst-Ashman, 1994). In order to attend sensitively, respectfully, and appropriately to the "person-in-environment" focus, social workers develop knowledge about cultural differences. The Council on Social Work Education Curriculum Policy Statements (Schriver, 1995, pp. 6–7) supports this orientation in discussion of the profession's values and acknowledges the impact of diversity. The fields of psychology, medicine, public health, and the human services have each embraced appreciation for culture in the last 15 years. However, the fundamental values that influence our theoretical understanding of human development, the human condition, social problems, and problem-solving interventions tend to articulate the values and beliefs associated with Western knowledge, reflect a Eurocentric and male-centered analysis of human relations and human development, and focus on the identification and analysis of pathology. Therefore, knowledge of cultural material associated with specific client populations must be developed in order to expand the theoretical paradigms associated with the helping disciplines.

Cultural diversity is evident across a wide range of cultural beliefs, values, productions, and practices. Cultural values and beliefs generate cultural practices and productions. It is important to develop an orientation that supports examination of cultural material and that acknowledges the relationship between culture and multiple dimensions of the daily life experiences. Culture is an internal and intimate experience; it resides within each individual and influences how one feels, thinks, and behaves. It provides structure and meaning for all life experiences and influences identity, beliefs, values, social behavior, expressions of distress, help-seeking behaviors, and treatment expectations. Culture mediates communication patterns, interpersonal relationships, time orientation, relationship protocols, and conversational currency. This constellation of beliefs and behaviors, about how one should engage and behave, form a recognizable pattern that is transferred from generation to generation through culturally based religious, healing, linguistic, artistic, educational, and organizational practices that are indigenous to the group. Evidence of the process is visible within American Indian and Alaska Native communities in the cultural values, belief systems, oral histories, stories, dances, family traditions, and relational styles of members of the community.

Cultural values and beliefs identify aspects of the "worldview" that are significant to the group and influence the development of identity. Culture specifies what is important and what is unimportant. For example, despite the diversity of American Indian and Alaska Native nations, nearly all hold beliefs about the importance of family relationships and children to the nation. The narrative that follows is an exemplar of how one American Indian program manager considers this issue:

> As Indian people we all have the same values—family, generosity, honesty, respect for people, our sacred colors. Some values overlap, some are a little different, but the only things that make us different are the outward things, like the art, the jewelry, the songs, but under that, the basic fundamental values are the same from tribe to tribe. Like children, children are the most important people traditionally. We call them sacred in some tribes. And the circle, the circle is the basis of life, the cycles in life, or the idea that the total person is made up of the intellectual, spiritual, cultural and physical and that each one of these areas must be nourished independently; the idea that the earth is important, the creation stories of the earth, the stars, and the moon and all relationships.

A discussion of child- and family-focused concerns in American Indian and Alaska Native communities must acknowledge the significant role of traditional cultural material on these communities. As noted, cultural diversity is evident across a wide range of cultural beliefs, values, productions, and practices in American Indian and Alaska Native communities. Blanchard (1983), Duran and Duran (1995), (1998), Green (1999), Guilmet and Whited (1989), LaFromboise and BigFoot (1988), Locust (1988), Red Horse (1983), Sage (1991), and Tafoya (1989) describe the traditional values and beliefs that appear universal to American Indian and Alaska Native communities:

- humans are multidimensional, composed of spirit, mind, and body;
- plants, animals, and nature share equal status with humans;
- a supreme "Creator" is acknowledged as a giver and sustainer of life; additional spirit helpers exist who model appropriate relational styles and provide support and guidance;
- individuals are responsible for their behavior; and
- harmony and balance are necessary for sustaining life.

Values flowing from this traditional orientation include interdependence, a collective orientation, respect, equality, generosity/sharing, honesty, patience, courtesy, autonomy, personal responsibility, cooperation, veneration of elders, mutuality, modesty, discipline, tranquility, orientation to the present, allegiance to kin (immediate, extended and tribal), and respect for the environment. Cultural values and beliefs influence relational styles and culturally sanctioned behaviors. These include developing observational and listening skills, maintaining delineated divisions of labor and social responsibilities, and teaching through modeling and by example, noninterference and a nonjudgmental stance. A fundamental characteristic organizing this set of culturally based values, beliefs, and behaviors is the familial and collective orientation that is characteristic of traditional tribal communities. Guilmet and Whited (1989), state that "the extended family support system is of ultimate importance" and quote Primeaux (1977, p. 92) in stating that "To be really poor in the Indian world is to be without relatives."

Family appears as a core value within American Indian and Alaska Native communities. Family attachments—through blood relationships and networks of kin, clan, and tribe—shape individual and group identity, identify responsibilities, offer support, sustenance and comfort, reduce isolation, and link the present and the past. Family is the building block for every life experience and the cornerstone of the spiritual, psychological, and material support systems that promote healthy growth and development. Family is the linchpin that drives, supports, and organizes other values, beliefs, practices, and behaviors. An American Indian social worker stated:

> Family is a central value; family meaning your own kin, the tribe and the community. And, generosity is evident within the community, in that we are always giving to our family, to our extended family. We are sharing meals or giving somebody gas money or using your gas to pick someone up. These are just examples of that on-going giving. Also, respect comes with family. Respect is best exemplified by respect for all people, especially for people who are older than me, and lot of our learning comes from people who have lived longer, who have more experience.

The significance of values such as respect, interdependence, and the collective orientation are illustrated in the concept of the "Seventh Generation" that is described by Oren Lyons. He discusses the reciprocal and interdependent nature of responsibility and obligation across generations (1990; 1991; 1997). He notes that all actions and decisions made by the present generation of American Indians must consider and protect the interests of the Seventh Generation to follow in order to assure that contemporary resources are available for succeeding generations. The concept of the "Seventh Generation" is one that endures across generations and demonstrates the protective capacities and strength of traditional culture. It is articulated across American Indian and Alaska Native tribal communities and functions as a reminder of the communities' obligations to the children yet unborn and of the historical obligations to the children of the current generation. The concept of the "Seventh Generation" illustrates the nature of the attachment that tribal communities have to the children of their community and to the generations that will follow.

In most American Indian and Alaska Native traditional communities the creation and origin stories are the fundamental source of knowledge. The creation story is another common denominator that promotes attachment to the tribal nation. The history of the people, values, beliefs, moral prescriptions, and guidelines for living are embedded in the origin story, and the creation story is the foundation for the tribal belief system and tribal spirituality. The creation stories can be understood to set forth prescriptions for personal behavior and to identify roles and responsibilities within circles of reciprocal and harmonious relationships. For example, a colleague notes:

> My tribe's story is simple; others are more ritualistic and complicated. Ours is simple, not complicated, but it lets me know who I am as an Indian person, what I should follow. It tells us how to behave, it tells about the beginning of humans and the beginning of my tribe. In it, I can see how culture and religion are tied together. The creation story for every tribe is the foundation of their beliefs.

Commitment to values such as family, respect, generosity, honesty, truthfulness, discipline, patience, courtesy, and the behaviors through which values are operationalized (giving, nurturing, caring, sharing, listening, learning through observation, silence, passivity) reflect the bond that links the traditional and the spiritual orientations characteristic of American Indian and Alaska Native communities. Traditional values can function as a significant resource on reservation and in urban communities. These values demonstrate longevity, durability, and practicality; they can buffer the stressors associated with life in contemporary American Indian and Alaska Native communities.

The ability to speak the tribal language is highly valued, and many American Indian and Alaska Native are non-English speakers. Knowledge of the tribal language also facilitates participation in traditional practices. Language allows one to engage with elders, to participate in ceremonies, and to experience the world from the "tribal point of view." Language promotes understanding of history and of the stories that recount the experience of the people and offer guidance for daily life. Language is critical for maintaining the oral traditions of the people and for learning the "old ways from those who know how it should be" and for participation in ceremony. Ceremony is the central structure for expressing cultural beliefs, for giving thanks, for prayer, and for participation in actions that mark life transitions and elicit support and remedy during times of distress. The ability to engage in specific ceremonial practices and to be exposed to tribal language may be limited in urban communities. Some members of reservation and urban communities lost knowledge of the tribal language as a consequence of the boarding school experience, because until the 1970s most schools forbade and punished children for speaking the native language.

It is critical to remember that not every member of any community can be expected to rigidly adhere to any given set of values and beliefs. There exists cultural diversity within American Indian and Alaska Native communities, because culture is always dynamic and evolving over time. The nature of affiliation with and knowledge of traditional values varies within the group, as members of the group have specific experiences that influence how cultural material is transferred across generations. The process of accommodating to non-Indian political, social, and cultural structures is a reflection of the specific tribal history, culture, values, and political history. This process creates a cultural continuum on which are located behaviors that range from traditional to nontraditional and which promotes cultural dominance, cultural preferences, and bicultural socialization. The bicultural individual is one who possesses the necessary skills and knowledge for adaptive functioning in both the home and the external culture. The nature of attachment to core values reflects individual and familial processes of accommodation and adjustment to postcolonial experiences, exposure to trauma, and capacities to integrate and manage loss and individual decision making. Attachment to traditional culture may be tenuous for those members of the community who have had greater difficulty adjusting to and coping with the losses associated with the postcolonial experience and a hostile social environment. Poverty, internalized oppression, depression, and the stressors associated with conditions on reservations and in urban environments undermine the capacities of community members to construct life on the bedrock of traditional values and beliefs. As noted previously, every dimension of American Indian and Alaska Native life is influenced in some way by the history of contact and the legal and political relationships that exist between tribal communities and federal and state entities.

Many of the social and economic problems that exist in tribal communities are the legacy of these historical relationships. The traumas that resulted as a consequence of genocide and military conquest, the loss of traditional territories and the traditional way of life, the removal of children from family and tribal communities, the widespread physical, psychological, and sexual abuse that occurred in boarding schools, the termination of rights, the relocation of community members to urban environments, and the grueling poverty that is a feature of life in many native communities fueled loss experiences. Exposure to trauma and the loss and grief experiences that ensued have undermined the integrity of cultural material, eroded the care-giving capacities of families and communities, contributed to the rise in substance abuse and interpersonal violence, and inhibited capacities to draw on cultural material in managing these conditions. Practitioners working within this community must appreciate that despite this painful and problematic legacy, cultural material continues to influence how individuals and families construct life, address problems, and engage with others outside the community, although the influence of cultural material may not be readily apparent. Further, the traditional cultural inheritance is widely perceived to be the foundation on which the health of the community can be restored, the sorrows of the community can be resolved, and the healing of wounded communities can be facilitated and sustained. Practitioners can promote this process integrating knowledge of tribal and community, social and political history in the assessment of individual and family functioning and the etiology of problems and by drawing on the rich legacy of survival and strength that are characteristic of American Indian and Alaska Native communities. A colleague, who works in the urban community, provided the following insights:

> Many of the issues that we see with our families are related to a parent being raised in the Boarding School, where the emphasis was on structure and rules, and less on passing on the skills needed to raise children in the traditional way. It doesn't matter what tribe, the being exposed to Boarding School, leaves the same kind of impact. On the reservation and in this community, for the families who don't have ceremony and a positive support system to help them, then, there's the alcohol, the depression, and then, we see kids who are being abused or not properly exposed to their traditions. But, once we start talking about the experiences and the stories that the parents or grandparents remember from their childhood, or we start talking about how it should be between a parent and a child, it all comes together. But, the pace of the work is really slow, so you have to have a lot of patience, and you have to offer a lot of support, cause here in the city, so many of our Indian families are isolated from one another and from home.

These comments illustrate the intersection of the history of contact with the development of social and interpersonal problems and indicate the efficacy of drawing on cultural material in the intervention process.

When information about cultural beliefs, values, and practices is elicited and interpreted from the point of view of the individuals and communities who are members of a particular cultural "world," our understanding of the issues (from their perspective) is enhanced. Therefore, efforts must be made to assure that analysis of social issues and social polices consider the influence of "difference." Cautious evaluation and reflection on these issues can balance the Euro-centric tendencies of many theories of intervention and promote the design and delivery of services that are strengths based and culturally focused. The strength of the American Indian and Alaska Native cultural inheritance lies in its capacity to offer guidance, solace, and stability in the face of the pressures associated with modern life. A traditional orientation promotes health and well-being and enhances capacities to cope with the vicissitudes of daily life. A colleague has noted, "These values give a centeredness, a strength, a knowledge of who you are, who you should be, where you come from, who you can become." Social workers who are able to develop knowledge of the specific cultural values, beliefs, and traditions associated with client populations and demonstrate respect for cultural material can deepen capacities to establish meaningful, collaborative relationships with clients and to identify client resources and client needs.

PRACTICE CONSIDERATIONS

Effective practice in American Indian and Alaska Native communities requires knowledge of the cultural traditions, sociopolitical history, and social conditions that have influenced the development of the client and their family. It is critical that any practitioner who engages with the American Indian and Alaska Native clients develop knowledge about historical and cultural material, as well as social and political considerations. These issues affect the development of the "problem" which brings the client to the attention of professionals, help-seeking behaviors, treatment expectations, and possible solutions. Knowledge about the history and provisions of the ICWA (P.L. 95-608) must be developed if one is providing child- and family-focused services in American Indian and Alaska Native communities. The strengths perspective associated with social work practice facilitates the capacity of workers to attend to cultural material. Attachment theory supports analysis of the quality of the client's relationship to family, community, and culture. Attachment theory also promotes the assessment of individual, family, and tribal loss experiences and unresolved grief. Basic understanding of the consequences of exposure to trauma and of the processes associated with negotiating grief and loss experiences is required for developing comprehensive assessments and complex intervention strategies. Strong foundational knowledge about the biopsychosocial dimensions of child and family development is required. Ethnographic interviewing techniques advance capacities to develop cultural knowledge as these techniques encourage professionals to approach clients as cultural guides who possess expertise about their own lives.

Workers who engage in self-reflective practice develop abilities to understand the influence of personal history, cultural material, and sociopolitical history on their practice and to develop insights about these processes. The culture of worker and client "meet" as the helping relationship unfolds and influences the development of the relationship and the therapeutic process. Knowledge of culture can assist in the process of assessing history, functioning, problems, interventions, and solutions. The establishment of the professional helping relationship between worker and client is essential to practice in the human services. Cultural values associated with traditional American Indian and Alaska Native communities support the development of therapeutic relationships. Rapport is promoted through kind, courteous, genuine, and honest interactions. The ability to engage with clients from a shared values perspective establishes the worker's credibility and legitimacy and authenticates the connection between both.

The Indian Child Welfare Act was passed in 1978 and the legislation was intended to address the problem of the out-of-home placement of thousands of Indian children in non-Indian homes. The ICWA "provides that an Indian tribe will have exclusive jurisdiction over child custody proceedings where the Indian child is residing or domiciled on the reservation, unless federal law has vested jurisdiction in the state" (Champagne, 1994, p. 419). The law represents federal efforts to preserve the cultural and family relationships of American Indian and Alaska Native children and to assign decision-making authority on placement (foster care, preadoption, and adoption) and custody (termination of parental rights) issues to tribal authorities for children living on and off reservations. Federal and state governments have long colluded in the separation and removal of children from their families and tribal communities. Before the passage of ICWA, congressional hearings found that 25–35 percent of American Indian and Alaska Native children were removed from their families and placed in foster care, adoptive homes, or institutions (Champagne, 1994, p. 420). Children were often removed simply because their families were poor or parents engaged in traditional child-rearing practices. The ICWA attempted to address these issues by recognizing tribal sovereignty, restoring tribal authority in custody proceedings, establishing standards for placement, and providing funds for the development of child and family services and training activities. The ICWA represented a significant departure from policies that actively undermined family relationships and tribal communities. It promoted respect for tribal sovereignty and the integrity of tribal cultures and communities. In both urban and reservation communities, the provisions of ICWA should be invoked for every family where American Indian heritage is noted. However, it is clear that the protective services delivery systems outside of reservation communities do not always have efficient and consistent mechanisms in place for identifying children and families for whom ICWA applies.

Social work practice is advanced as professionals adopt perspectives that support the strengths and capacities of clients through the analysis of wellness and health and attention to the social environment. The strengths perspective promotes the empowerment of individuals and families. Dennis Saleebey (2002) notes that this perspective develops as an alternative to the disease- and deficit-oriented models of practice and analysis of client conditions, and he articulates the orientation and core assumptions associated with this perspective:

- Every individual, group, family, and community has strengths;
- Trauma and abuse, illness and struggle may be injurious, but they may also be sources of challenge, opportunity, and mastery;
- Assume that you do not know the upper limits of the capacity to grow and change and take individual, group, and community aspirations seriously;
- Clients are best served when we collaborate with them; and
- Every environment is full of resources.

This perspective acknowledges the resilient and empowered capacities of clients and the human needs for affiliation, belonging, healing, dialog and collaboration. It promotes understanding of the role of attachment experiences and supports the integration of cultural material in the helping relationship, thereby enhancing the effectiveness of therapeutic relationships.

Attachment theory addresses the quality of the relationship that exists between infant and caregiver(s) and examines the influence of early relationships on development. John Bowlby and others typically examine human relationships and interactions in the analysis of personality and emotional development as issues of attachment and loss are negotiated in infancy and across the lifespan. It is possible to utilize concepts associated with attachment theory to understand the nature of the attachment that exists between traditional cultural material and American Indians and Alaska Natives.

Bowlby (1983) concluded that there is a biological mechanism that mobilizes attachment behaviors, because the infant's physical survival depends on adult caregivers who respond to basic needs. This system evolves as the infant protests separation and seeks closeness with the caregiver who provides physical and emotional sustenance/nourishment. He also concluded that the infant was emotionally nourished as the caregiver responded; the quality of the caregiver's response can result in the development of secure, insecure, or ambivalent attachment behaviors. The infant protests separation and seeks reunification with the caregiver when distressed, but the infant can despair and withdraw when attachment efforts are frustrated. Bowlby determined that attachment behavior is also activated during times of threat and stress, as the individual seeks to maintain or establish closeness to an attachment figure. Although he studied attachment primarily in the mother–infant dyad, many authors (see Cassidy and Shaver, 1999) have indicated that attachment experiences are important across the life course, that early experiences influence personality development and adult intimacy and that supportive relationships promote capacities to overcome adversity. In addition to informing our ideas about attachment, Bowlby influences conceptualizations about loss, grief, bereavement, and trauma, and his work can inform conceptualizations about resilience and strengths. Trauma and loss experiences are human experiences engendering grief or sorrow. Survival and strength result as one integrates loss experiences into the life narrative, and attachment behaviors influence these processes.

Attachment theory has utility for advancing knowledge about the generational transmission of loss within American Indian and Alaska Native communities. Attachment theory supports capacities to interpret the losses of children who are removed from home. It also supports understanding about the nature of the losses that tribal nations experienced as they were separated from culturally based caregiving systems that sustained and nourished the group. The attachment that the infant establishes with a caregiver is similar to the attachment that tribal communities maintained with cultural structures—values, beliefs, behaviors, and ceremonies. Responsive caregivers promote the infant's capacity to experience trust and security. Within American Indian and Alaska Native communities, culturally based beliefs and behaviors often reference attachment to the ecological environment that sustains and nourishes the community. The attachment that tribal nations feel for homelands and traditional culture appears as profound as the attachment that the infant feels for the loving and caring caregiver. Indeed, in many ceremonies, songs, and stories, the earth is referenced as "mother." The losses that accompanied the postcolonial experience destroyed and disrupted tribal attachment systems. These losses include illness, genocide, removal from traditional homelands, confinement on reservations, prohibition of traditional practices and language, development of boarding/mission schools, and the out-of-home placement and adoption of scores of children. Communities protested losses, but when protestations were squelched by military might and oppressive and abusive conditions, depression and despair ensued with generational consequences for children and families. Parenting capacities were compromised, and alcoholism, substance abuse, and violence manifested in reaction to the suffering that accompanied losses. The strength of the attachment to traditional cultural values, beliefs, and behaviors promoted the survival of American Indians and Alaska Natives despite exposure to multiple adversities across generations.

Ethnographic interviewing techniques demonstrate great utility for exploration of attachment experiences, cultural material, individual, family and community development, and the identification of client issues and strengths. According to Green (1995) and Leigh (1998), ethnographic interviewing techniques:

- acknowledge that cultural material influences the resolution of human problems;
- recognize that the diversity of cultures results in diverse modes of identifying and solving problems;
- examine the influence of cultural material on the client's life and situation;
- recognize the capacities of the client to act as a "cultural guide," who can provide knowledge and insight about his/her world and circumstance;
- appreciate that the client possesses insight and knowledge about his/her experience; and
- seek to discover how language organizes and brings meaning to the client's experience.

The ethnographic interview consists of four elements, and each element helps the worker become more immersed in the client's world. The process increases the worker's understanding of the client's narrative or life story and enhances the possibilities for attending to culture, building on strengths, and developing collaborative and productive relationships.

It is important to integrate cultural material in designing and delivering services to American Indian and Alaska Native communities. Culture is recognized as a resource in addressing the profound and complex problems that confront the community. Organizations which offer a broad array of services (legal, educational, health, psychological, spiritual, social, and residential) and which introduce and promote cultural practices are recognized for making significant contributions in both reservation and urban Indian communities. Many existing intervention programs addressing problems of substance abuse, child maltreatment, family violence, malnutrition, health, literacy, education, and unemployment have philosophies for services that articulate traditional cultural values and practices. Typically, these services also provide clients with the opportunity to engage and affiliate with other American Indians, and the social isolation that often accompanies social problems is reduced.

Personal responsibility, sharing, respect, and commitment to children, families, and tribal communities are endorsed when traditional cultural values, behaviors, and practices are integrated in the intervention process and social/health services delivery systems. Interventions and social service programs, which are infused with cultural material, become vehicles for modeling, mentoring, and practicing culturally appropriate behaviors. For example, programs for elders can reinforce the valued role of elders within the community and model respectful interactions and reciprocity across generations. Programs for children and families present opportunities to demonstrate and teach nurturing and care-giving behaviors, to illustrate levels of interdependency, and to model methods for the management of conflicting needs within families. Culturally based service delivery systems can promote attachments to traditional values and beliefs by creating opportunities to examine loss experiences, to uncover sources of suffering, and to harness strengths that have facilitated survival. Although there is a great need for strengths-based and culturally based programs, such programs can be labor and cost intensive. However, the benefits of continuing to promote culturally based interventions can substantially shift generational legacies of trauma and suffering. A colleague who is a director of a social services program stated:

> As an Indian agency, we are charged with a responsibility to the whole community; there's community involvement and opportunities to participate in traditional activities. Granted, it may be inter-tribal and based on the Plains, but at least there's that family and doing it as traditionally as possible. We have a responsibility and we try to act accordingly in providing for the children and the elders . . . and we are doing it with attention to cultural issues.

The development of American Indian and Alaska Native children is supported with exposure to culturally based beliefs and behaviors, strong connections to extended/tribal family, and the opportunity to affiliate with healthy and productive adults. Traditional values provide children with the opportunity to understand their "place" and their role within a network of supportive and caring relationships and reinforce attachment to the American Indian community. The core values associated with traditional culture promote the possibility that children can experience respectful, disciplined, responsible, and nurturing interactions, which will strengthen identity, self-confidence, and self-esteem. Knowledge of cultural traditions and values becomes critical in support of the healthy growth of American Indian children, especially those who are raised in the nontraditional environments, because it provides the bedrock foundation and context for individual and familial development. As one colleague notes:

> Values are passed on by showing this is the way that we do it; it is a matter of observation, of seeing adults live and act in a certain way that is important. When children see that you are connected to family, when they see demonstrations of love—kindness—sharing—friendliness—respect, they learn what is important. But, they also learn that they are important to be treated in such a way, they can feel good about themselves and their family, and this is such a help in this environment, where so much is hostile to them as Indians.

American Indian and Alaska Native children and families can overcome legacies of trauma, sorrow, and suffering and demonstrate resilient and survival capacities by building on the strengths that result from attachment to tribal communities and culture.

Practice Applications

Effective practice in American Indian and Alaska Native communities is dependent on the worker's abilities to demonstrate genuine and authentic interest in the client's situation and to establish a meaningful relationship with the client and the client's significant others. The worker must also possess knowledge of the contextual variables that influence client/community development and the etiology of social and psychological problems. Practitioners will draw on knowledge associated with cultural values, intervention theories, normative individual and family development, the resolution of the psychosocial tasks associated with productive functioning in this society, and community resources in the assessment and intervention processes. It is crucial to understand how social policies may intersect the helping process. Strengths-based, culturally focused, solution-focused narrative modalities and ethnographic interviewing techniques demonstrate great utility for developing collaborative relationships with clients.

The ability to access and integrate cultural material in the helping relationship can assist in the process of developing assessments and modifying practice theories to meet client concerns and needs. The professional relationship is enhanced when workers engage with clients in culturally sanctioned ways. Workers can thereby demonstrate awareness of traditional values and signify their respect for the roles, rules, relationships, and communication patterns that exist within client families and communities. From this stance, workers can observe, listen, and express deference for elders and for culturally based values and behaviors. The core values associated with many American Indian and Alaska Native communities, such as autonomy, honesty, respect, fairness, and confidentiality can promote worker–client relationships that are marked by patient, solicitous, and attentive interactions. Professional demonstrations of concern and warmth are crucial to relationship building, because for many in the community, the route to treatment is circuitous. There are multiple access barriers and limited resources available to meet the community's needs. Integrating cultural knowledge with conventional practice modalities adds depth and complexity to the helping relationship and bridges cultural differences between worker and client.

From this perspective, a traditional cultural orientation and the opportunity to affiliate and engage with healthy and productive American Indians and Alaska Native role models would enhance the capacities of clients to draw on indigenous strengths and cultural resources. These capacities promote empowerment, reflections on loss experiences, the meaning-making processes invoked in examining exposure to loss and trauma, and the survival of the Indian community. Although much of American social policy is reactive, the American Indian and Alaska Native communities (as well as other vulnerable communities) would benefit if strengths-based and culturally focused primary prevention efforts targeting specific problems (educational attainment, substance abuse, interpersonal violence, job readiness, etc.) were expanded. Practitioners must always be mindful that there are no "recipes" for working within American Indian and Alaska Native (or any other) communities. It is critical to prepare oneself for practice by learning about the community setting and sociohistorical context and the prevailing values, strengths, and struggles that are embedded in the individual and reflected in the community.

As noted previously, cultural values and practices inform expectations and responsibilities of community members, delineate relationships, and authenticate the role of children within the community. Children are appreciated as the most vital resource for the American Indian and Alaska Native communities, and this resource must be protected and nurtured. There is an interdependent and reciprocal structure of relationships and obligations that exist between community, family, and child that is informed by cultural material. Cultural values, beliefs, and behaviors have contributed to the survival of the American Indian and Alaska Native community in the face of significant challenges and traumatic losses and function as the major supports for ameliorating vexing social problems.

Attachment theory promotes knowledge about the significance of culture within American Indian and Alaska Native communities. Narrative and ethnographic approaches can advance the practitioner's understandings about the present circumstances of clients and elicit perspectives about tribal and community history of American Indians from the point of view of the client/consumer. Narrative approaches help the practitioner to elicit the client's story in efforts to determine how experiences are constructed and interpreted and to explore exceptions and alternative explanations for problems and experiences. Narrative approaches support strengths-based orientations by externalizing problems and investigating how interactions with relevant systems impinge on and support productive functioning. The cultural values that resonate across tribal communities indicate that family is conceptualized broadly to include immediate, extended, and tribal members, that "family" drives and organizes the core/bedrock cultural values, and that children are highly regarded as the community's "most precious resource." Within tribal communities, a group and collective orientation characterizes interactions, and the significance of values such as respect, responsibility, interdependence, and generosity cannot be underestimated. Invoking this knowledge in the helping process promotes appreciation for the characteristics associated with traditional life, which includes affinity for core values, the ability to speak the native language, knowledge of traditional practices, a disciplined lifestyle, and knowledge of self and tribe. Knowledge about the community is enhanced through the use of narrative and ethnographic techniques as clients/consumers explain how the presence of unresolved losses across generations, exposure to trauma, the pressures of acculturation, the stressors associated with reservation, rural and urban life, sociopolitical history, and isolation can contribute to the development of social, psychological, and behavioral problems and undermine the productive expression of traditional values. Despite the presence of multiple problems and hazards that confront American Indian and Alaska Native children and families, it appears that the rich cultural inheritance of tribal nations is a resource for addressing problems in many tribal communities for many practitioners. Evidence of this orientation to provide services from a cultural base is seen in the numerous social services and health maintenance programs that have developed in the last 15 years across Indian Country.

Cultural knowledge, values, and behaviors foster the establishment of collaborative and strengths-focused relationships between client and practitioner. The prevailing practice paradigms can be modified and adapted in consideration of the influence of cultural material, exposure to loss, and the social, political, and historical context of a specific client or community. Practitioners are encouraged to seek supervision and consult with colleagues in order to advance self-reflective capacities. Self-reflective capacities include the development of awareness about personal biases and capacities, as well as increase insight by evaluating interactions with clients, and examining transference and countertransference material. The expansion of this awareness supports the practitioner's abilities to engage in a more intentional, directive, and proactive collaboration with clients and supports practice that integrates narrative and ethnographic approaches. The self-reflective and intentional stance can enhance abilities to practice across cultures and to develop bicultural practice paradigms that are more active, directive, engaged, and involved than the conventional models that espouse objectivity, neutrality, and distance and exclude attention to social, political, and historical material. The efficacy and effectiveness of cross-cultural and bicultural paradigms are demonstrated in direct practice with clients/constituents.

The following case examples provide the opportunity to reflect on these issues and to consider how interpretations of client material are informed by the culture of both the worker and the client.

CASE STUDY 1   CHRISTINA

Christina is a 17-year-old high-school student who has been in foster placement for the last 9 years. She and her 16-year-old sister, Nancy, have been in the current placement, a group home, for the last 3 years. Before the current placement, there were multiple placements with relatives and foster parents. Christina and five siblings were removed from the home of parents as a result of mother's ongoing substance abuse and neglect. The children have verified Indian heritage through their father, Leonard. Leonard was killed in a car accident 5 years ago. The tribe decided to leave jurisdiction with the County, because there was an initial plan for reunification with mother and father. Father was separated from mother, had completed a substance abuse treatment program and job-training program, and had rented a home in anticipation of the children's return to his custody and the start of family preservation services at the time of his death. The tribe was not contacted following the death of Leonard. Christina is taking "Independent Living" classes in preparation for emancipation and "graduation" from the group home in four months when she graduates from high school and turns 18. Christina appears depressed; she worries about her siblings and wishes to be reunited with them. She recalls her father's instructions to "always look after" her siblings and the stories he shared about how he and his siblings "looked out for each other" in boarding school. She does not know the whereabouts of the youngest sibling who was "freed" for adoption following father's death, and she is unable to visit with two brothers who are placed in a residential treatment facility. She writes to her brothers, sends "care" packages, and reminds them that she will prepare a home for them.

CASE STUDY 2   MARY

Mary is a 37-year-old single parent, who resides with her boyfriend, her three children from a previous relationship, her mother, father, and maternal aunt on the Rosebud Reservation. She presented for family counseling, because her 17-year-old daughter, Mayanne, was arrested for possession of marijuana. Mayanne has been sentenced to a substance abuse treatment program, and Mary is ordered to participate in family counseling. Mary does not have a car, but she has managed to either borrow a car or arrange a ride to the center for family therapy meetings. She has not missed an appointment in the six weeks that Mayanne has been detained. Mary is attending tribal college and training for a career as a radiology technician. She is employed as a clerk in the admitting office of the local hospital. Mary acknowledges a history of substance abuse, but notes that she has been "in recovery" for 3 years. She believes that Mayanne has used drugs recreationally and that Mayanne's acting-out behavior in the last year is related to changes in the family's circumstances and her age.

CASE STUDY 3   JOHN

John is 15-year-old, who resides with his four siblings and maternal grandparents in a small trailer on the Navajo Reservation. His mother is serving a 5-year sentence on drug-related charges; his father's whereabouts are unknown. He is doing well in school and spends his time caring for his younger siblings or playing basketball. He is on the high-school basketball team. He functions as the family intermediary with governmental entities, because his grandparents' fluency in English is limited. His grandfather is well known on the reservation as a medicine man, and John accompanies and assists his grandfather with ceremonial activities. John assists his grandmother with laundry, cooking, and cleaning, because her arthritis and diabetes often make it difficult for her to perform family tasks. His homeroom teacher is concerned, because John is very quiet, passive, and reserved. John states that he does not feel burdened by his responsibilities at home, noting that all the siblings have chores and that Grandmother supervises their work. His interactions with the social worker are polite and courteous and he is uncertain why he was referred to speak with the social worker.

CASE STUDY 4   RUBY

Ruby is a 57-year-old woman who resides with her husband, adult daughter, and three grandchildren in an urban community. Her husband is employed, her daughter is disabled as a result of a car accident, and her three grandchildren are, in her words, "running wild." She acknowledges that her husband is a functioning alcoholic and that the marriage is very conflicted. She wishes to return home to her reservation, because her siblings would be available to help her and she had a home built for her family. She believes that the reservation would

(continued)

■ ■ ■ ■ ■

CASE STUDY 4   Continued

offer her grandchildren and family safety and stability, and she worries that she will lose her house if she doesn't take ownership within the next 6 months. However, her grandchildren resist the idea, and she is concerned that her husband might not be able to find employment. She left the reservation over 25 years ago and although she longs to go home, she is not sure where her home is anymore. She regrets relocating to the city, and she notes that she spent her childhood and adolescence in a boarding school. She states that she feels guilty and sad, because she couldn't return "home" when her mother became ill and subsequently died, due to her daughter's accident. She indicates that she feels isolated and unable to mobilize herself, but she believes that her circumstances would be different if she were back on the reservation.

■ ■ ■ ■ ■

CASE STUDY 5   RAYMOND

Raymond is a 67-year-old man, in good health, who retired from the military after 30 years of service. He followed his military service by working as a mechanic on a local military base for 15 more years. He was raised on a reservation in North Dakota, spent most of his adolescence in boarding school and entered the military immediately after graduation from high school. He traveled widely when he was in the service, married a woman from England, and ultimately settled in Washington state, adjacent to the base where he was last stationed. He has four children and ten grandchildren. His children have done well, are college educated, and are gainfully employed. His wife recently died of breast cancer after a long illness. Raymond wants to return to his reservation to live out his retirement. He has a land allotment; he has five siblings still alive who live on the reservation and numerous nieces and nephews. His children do not have a strong affilia-tion with the reservation, although they visited frequently when they were younger. His children do not understand his desire to return to his home reservation and do not support his decision. Raymond feels very conflicted, although he longs to return to the "traditional" life he had in his youth.

DISCUSSION

The traditional models of social work practice encourage neutrality, objectivity, and distance and discourage examination of cultural material. Generally, the prevailing practice paradigms articulate a deficit orientation and assume that the causes of prob-lems are located within the individual and reflect individual pathology or the absence of effective interpersonal and problem-solving skills. If this stance were adopted in any of the cases cited, it is unlikely that collaborative relationship would be fostered. A strengths and cultural perspective can be fused with traditional models of practice in order to examine client issues in the context of family, community, and tribal history. For each of the cases noted above, attention must focus on individual, family, and community strengths and assets and examine the influence of loss experiences on the current situation.

As one begins to prepare for engagement with each case, it is important to reflect on initial reactions and perceptions about each case. Social workers are encouraged to "begin where the client is"; however, in order to accurately locate the client in the helping relationship, the practitioner must begin by locating *herself* or *himself* in the process. The practitioner is encouraged to identify "where she/he is" with reference to the client, the client's individual, family, and community history and the client's cultural affiliations and attachments and to examine initial constructions and assumptions about the client's condition and story. It is equally important for the worker to possess insight about personal assumptions, experiences, and values, to examine initial reactions to client data/information and to reflect on how these factors intersect the interpretation of client material and capacities to explore alternative explanations. This process helps the practitioner to identify and appropriately contain biases, values, assumptions, and preconceptions and promotes capacities to establish efficient and permeable boundaries that support an inquisitive learning stance.

In each of the case studies, the clients present with multiple strengths that are challenged by multiple losses. The nature of the attachment to cultural material associated with traditional American Indian and Alaska Native communities is not obvious. Bicultural socialization, the skills that promote abilities to negotiate traditional and dominant cultures, is not explicitly clear. The histories of attachment experiences are obscure and must be examined in greater detail. Finally, the client's assessment of concerns is obscured by the case study format; whose story has been presented? As the practitioner begins the process of engaging with the client and initiating a therapeutic relationship, it is critical to begin with a stance that allows the practitioner to divulge what is known and to elicit the client's elaboration and clarification of history and concerns. Narrative approaches and ethnographic interviewing skills have demonstrated utility for exploring the issues and eliciting the client's perspective.

The assessment process must integrate attention to the issues identified above as well as investigate normative developmental processes. One must be mindful to identify client strengths and capacities and to investigate the presence of loss experiences and normative and maladaptive grief processes. It is also imperative to examine exposure to trauma and loss and to investigate processes associated with interpreting loss experiences The following questions should be examined as one begins to develop a multidimensional assessment and to develop a comprehensive inventory of client strengths and challenges.

- How has the client negotiated the normative developmental tasks that are associated with productive functioning in the dominant society?
- Have developmental tasks been resolved in a manner that supports the client's optimal growth and functioning?
- Have the social and educational skills associated with the stated age of the client been successfully mastered?
- What strengths are evident in the client's functioning and story?

- What capacities has the client demonstrated that indicate courage, perseverance, bravery, insight, sound judgment, effective problem solving, and/or tenacity?
- Has the client experienced any losses? If so, how have the losses intersected normative development?
- What external supports have been available to assist the client in management of loss experiences?
- Have any loss experiences been triggered by social, political, historical, or cultural considerations?
- Why has the client chosen to persevere in spite of the absence of social supports or despite exposure to trauma or loss?
- What "meaning" has the client assigned to the loss experiences?

Capacities to cope with exposure to trauma and loss are influenced by the quality of attachment experiences and by the depth and substance of relationships, therefore it is important to examine the nature of attachments throughout the life course as well as the nature of attachment to culturally based care-giving and care-receiving systems. In order to elaborate the assessment and intervention process it is critical to examine a range of attachment experiences. The following questions can be useful in helping to illuminate attachment experiences.

- What is the nature of the client's attachment experiences?
- Has there been the presence of consistent, reliable, and supportive attachment objects across the life course?
- How do social, political, historical, and cultural considerations intersect attachment experiences?
- What values, beliefs, and behaviors are important to the client and why?
- What lessons were learned early in life?
- What relevance do these lessons hold for the present circumstance?
- Despite the suffering and sorrow that has been experienced, when has the client experienced a sense of efficacy?
- What events or experiences in the client's life provide evidence of mastery and/or challenge the prevailing themes in life narrative and roles?
- How do capacities for self-efficacy promote insight and motivate the desire to persevere?

The investigation of these issues seeks to uncover the logic that drives client behavior, to locate behavior in a particular cultural and sociohistorical context, and to promote the social worker's ability to apprehend the client's experiences more complexly and from the client's point of view. Further, this data can inform the development of interpretations of the client's narrative and can inform the development of intervention plans that meet the often complex and multiple needs of clients and families.

These questions are not posed in a rote manner to the client. Rather, the practitioner adopts an inquisitive stance and initiates a collaborative dialog with the client in an effort to ascertain how the client constructs and experiences the world. The responses that flow from this dialog may illuminate strengths and promote a relationship wherein the client is appreciated for possessing expertise about their own life circumstances and capacities for addressing personal issues. The practitioner is interested in uncovering not only the story of the distress and conflict, but also the exceptions to the story and the alternative explanation or unanticipated outcomes associated with the prevailing story. Under which circumstances did the client not experience sorrow, depression, conflict, isolation, suffering, and confusion? Despite the presence of challenges, why does each client consent to discuss concerns? Each of the clients in the case studies possesses multiple strengths, although each also appears to struggle with the sorrows that emanate in loss experiences. Christina, Mary, John, Ruby, and Raymond have demonstrated resilient capacities and strengths. Christina recalls attachment experiences with care-giving parents and actively engages in efforts to reunite with her siblings and reenact the values of her father. Mary demonstrates abilities to overcome multiple barriers in order to participate in counseling appointments, in addition to working full time and attending school. John demonstrates capacities to manage multiple responsibilities in spite of his youth and appears to have a strong sense of obligation to his family. Ruby demonstrates insight about her circumstances, verbalizes concerns about family issues, and recognizes her limits. Raymond has a history replete with examples of his capacities to meet obligations and responsibilities.

Each case study is also notable for the presence of obvious loss experiences and loss experiences that are implied and less obvious. Losses associated with the absence of social and cultural supports, resources, and opportunities can significantly influence developmental processes and influence capacities to address and integrate the more obvious manifestations of loss. Christina has experienced multiple losses at an early age. The practitioner can adopt a questioning stance and explore how Christina was informed of loss events, who was available to comfort her in the immediate crisis and who provided consistent and caring support across time that assisted in the "meaning-making" process of each loss event. It appears that Christina's early attachment experiences with her parents provided a strong foundation for trust, hope, and optimism. However, she has struggled because after removal from her parents, the quality, consistency, and availability of nurturing and caring adults has been erratic. She is ill prepared for independent life, despite being touted as an "exemplar" of emancipation and independent living skills programs. She indicates that she relies on mental representations of her parents to help her during times of distress, and she frequently recites a traditional prayer that her father told her would bring her courage. She is burdened by the loss of the youngest sibling; she is resentful that county social workers could not keep the siblings together and that care providers and social workers assumed that her father's car accident was caused by substance abuse.

Narrative practices and ethnographic interviewing techniques can support exploration of the details and nuances of each client's life condition and investigate alternative explanations and unanticipated outcomes. Mary might be encouraged to elaborate and specify how she learned of her daughter's arrest and how each family member reacted. John could be asked to "paint a picture" with words of a typical day in his family before he lived with his grandparents and now. Ruby could be asked to specify and provide examples of what is meant by "running wild." The nature of Raymond's relationship with his wife, her illness and demise, and his grief can be explored by invoking these methods. In each case, the practitioner has the objective of constructing the client's perspective about their individual specific circumstance and of promoting opportunities for the practitioner to gain entry into the client's world.

It is critical to assess the nature of attachments to family, community, and cultural values and beliefs and to evaluate bicultural functioning. The social worker would examine the supportive qualities of relationships that are significant to the client, the quality of transactions with community networks, the depth of affiliation to cultural material, and the capacities of client and family members to negotiate Indian and non-Indian worlds. The nature of the attachment to the cultural inheritance is not always readily apparent, because cultural material is often embedded in memory and in the history of transactions with significant others across the life course. The influence of this material on current functioning may be unexamined by the client. Therefore, the practitioner is encouraged to adopt a stance that supports examination of this material in a collaborative and supportive dialog with the client as follows. What are the circumstances and conditions that motivate Christina's efforts to pray? What resources are available in the family and community environment to support Mary's desire to reclaim her daughter? What conditions in the family and community undermine these capacities?

As the concerns of the teacher for John are explored, additional data must be elicited to assess whether John's behavior is cause for concern and evidence of paren-tified behavior or psychological distress. Is it possible that John is not burdened and that his behavior offers evidence of a very traditional orientation to the world? On further examination, it is concluded that the family adheres to a traditional orientation and that grandparents have promoted an environment that has promoted resolution of loss experiences and enhanced capacities to integrate cultural material for all family members. Attachment experiences, cultural orientation, and the presence of unresolved losses might influence problem identification, help-seeking behaviors, treatment, and problem-solving expectations. The practitioner would be interested in Ruby's history of attachment, her experiences as a care-recipient and caregiver and would investigate the possibility that she may be grieving for relationships and a network of supports that is unavailable in her current environment.

It is important to be guided by the client; each client possesses valuable knowl-edge and expertise about their life experiences and the present circumstances. Raymond's desire to return home is misunderstood by his children and grandchildren who believe that he is "running away" from his grief for his wife. In fact, dialog with Raymond indicates that his mourning for his wife evoked additional layers of grief for the life he knew as a child, for his siblings, and for the comfort of his tribal commu-nity. He indicates that he initially intended to return home after first tour of duty, but the commitment to marital and family obligations motivated the desire to remain in the military and in Washington in order to ensure that his children were firmly established. He notes that his wife was aware of his longing to return home. Indeed, as an immigrant herself, she often experienced similar feelings. Before her illness, they intended to divide time between their home in Washington and the reservation.

His conflict about returning home is rooted in his desire to avoid causing pain to his children and grandchildren. Social workers must suspend personal explanations for client behavior in order to uncover how the client perceives and explains his or her experience. Professionals must often adapt interviewing techniques, modify intervention modalities, balance the needs of the human services organization with the client's needs, and engage in practice that is collaborative, active, directive, and involved.

The development of comprehensive assessments of client experiences and concerns is an important dimension of work with American Indian and Alaska Native clients. Individual/family assessments and traditional fact-gathering techniques (such as genograms and eco-maps) can be modified in order to explore additional information that is specific to the American Indian and Alaska Native experience. Genograms and eco-maps can be used to construct family, clan, or tribal history, to document relationships across generations, to map the location of individual, family, and tribal members, to map resident patterns, to reconstruct boarding school or out-of-home placement experiences (location, duration, return), and to chart trauma exposure and loss experiences. Assessment protocols can also be expanded to explore the following issues:

- extended family and tribal history;
- individual, family, and community strengths and assets;
- attachment, care-giving, and care-receiving experiences;
- loss experiences and exposure to trauma;
- the presence of historical or unresolved grief;
- boarding school and/or placement experiences across generations;
- substance abuse history within the family;
- health status and concerns within family;
- healthy and productive opportunities to affiliate with other American Indians;
- relocation experiences and length of time in urban community;
- losses associated with urban life and nature of contact with reservation or homeland community;
- cultural dominance and preferences and fluency in native language;
- educational and employment history; and
- quality and accessibility of support networks.

Interventions with clients should be attentive to policy concerns and be designed to include multiple levels of service such as counseling, advocacy, psychological education, grief and bereavement work, and modeling and mentoring activities. The clients might need advice and instruction with regard to negotiating relationships with other systems or accessing needed resources. Workers may be called on to interpret and reframe client experiences and interactions with other institutions or systems and to advocate on client's behalf. Case management, outreach activities, and crisis intervention services may be required. Workers must ensure that basic needs for food, shelter, and clothing are met and must understand the influence of poverty on daily life and client concerns. Complex, confounding, and complicated issues bring American Indian and Alaska Native clients to the attention of human services organizations. These issues are most effectively addressed by utilizing strengths-based and culturally focused approaches and by examining the quality of attachment to family and community.

Practitioners may advocate for the development and implementation of policies which promote self-determination and empowerment in the American Indian and Alaska Native community and which build on the bedrock values of the community. Policy and advocacy efforts must support and protect the legal rights and entitlement of American Indian and Alaska Native people on reservations and in urban and rural communities. In light of the profound problems confronting the community, social welfare policies should strive to protect the legal and political rights of American Indians and Alaska Natives off the reservation and should ensure that the reservation service delivery system is replicated in the rural and urban communities.

Despite the renewed interest and popularity of "family values," social welfare policies implicitly assume that all families and all values are the same. Within American Indian and Alaska Native communities, "family" is constructed in consideration of relationships to relatives, community, and tribe and with appreciation for the responsibilities and obligations that organize relationships. Traditional cultural values and behaviors that inform the social construction of life, and the rich cultural inheritance associated with tribal communities can function as a resource for addressing problems and promoting the healthy growth and development of community members. Social policy must acknowledge the significance of culture in substantive ways by fostering self-determination and by recognizing the strengths and expertise of individuals and groups situated within the community. Since policy informs practice, it is vital that policy reflect the lived realities and concerns of children, families, and groups affected by policy.

Policy can support the design of a centralized and comprehensive culturally based service delivery systems that could be available to families for both preventive and healing activities. Policy can promote and support bicultural approaches that address the problems experienced by families in reservation, rural, and urban environments by encouraging the design of programs offering opportunities for American Indians to engage with other Indians around a wide range of services, such as language, health education, parenting, dance, beadwork, literacy classes, mentoring, nutritional, counseling, legal, housing, social services, and socialization. Policy can promote the development of human services training and practice curricula addressing these issues. Significant practice issues can be addressed through policy; issues with regard to access barriers, fragmentation of services, and competition for funding can be addressed through policy. Finally, policy can advance the development of the culturally based comprehensive and coordinated multiservice centers which are indicated for promoting the health and well-being of American Indian and Alaska Native children and families.

This chapter offers multiple implications for human services practice by encouraging appreciation for the social, political, and cultural history of tribal nations, by emphasizing the relationship between current conditions and the history of contact with nonnatives and through discussion about the nature of the legacy of suffering, survival, and strength that characterizes indigenous communities. Culture influences the development of behavior and creates the context for the social construction of life. Effective practitioners must develop the skills for interpreting culture and evaluating its impact on functioning and relationships. Cultural variables and the sociopolitical history of children and families must be integrated in the development of individual and family assessments and in the treatment-planning and treatment-evaluation process. Community organizing, outreach, and educational activities must attend to cultural issues if they are to prove relevant and useful to the targeted community. The case studies illustrate that cultural variables will influence: problem identification; help-seeking behaviors; treatment expectations; relationship protocols; communication patterns; family roles, rules, and relationships; issues regarding self-disclosure; and the process of establishing collaborative working relationships between worker and client.

The development of cross-cultural practice skills and the creation of culturally appropriate interventions are directly correlated with the ability of practitioners to appreciate and respect cultural values, beliefs and practices, and cultural differences. American Indian and Alaskan Native children and families will very likely seek assistance from non-Indian providers, who must develop knowledge and skill in cross-cultural practice if they are to effectively meet the needs of this client population.

SUMMARY

The contemporary circumstance of American Indian and Alaska Native children and families reflects histories of contact, colonialism, and conflict. The unique legal and political relationships that exist between American Indian and Alaska Native communities and the U.S. government define and articulate the historic obligations of the federal government to American Indian and Alaska Native tribal nations. The demography of the community is an indicator of the complex challenges that confront the community and the capacities of American Indian and Alaska Native communities to survive in spite of exposure to horrendous trauma and multiple loss experiences. The enduring nature of the profound commitment to traditional cultural values, beliefs, behaviors, and practices is a fundamental strength and resource for tribal nations. Cultural values and practices inform expectations and responsibilities for members of the community and are the basis of evaluation for those who enter the community. Although there is much diversity within American Indian and Alaska Native communities, children and family relationships are highly valued across tribal nations. Children are appreciated as the most vital resource for the American Indian community, and they should be protected, nurtured, and respected. Cultural values, beliefs, and behaviors have contributed to the survival of the American Indian and Alaska Native nations in the face of generational traumatic challenges and losses. Attachments to traditional cultural values, beliefs, and practices may be as significant and vital as the attachments the infant establishes with a caregiver. There is much work to be done to address the legacy of sorrow that is present in the community. However, there is a legacy of survival and strength that bodes well for the future.

CHILD WELFARE PRACTICE WITH ASIAN AND PACIFIC ISLANDER AMERICAN CHILDREN, YOUTH, AND FAMILIES

SIYON Y. RHEE, PH.D.
School of Social Work, California State University, Los Angeles

ANH-LUU T. HUYNH-HOHNBAUM, PH.D.
School of Social Work, California State University, Los Angeles

Asian American family.

OVERVIEW

The number of children living in poverty in the United States is much greater when compared to any other industrialized countries. Furthermore, there are numerous culturally distinct ethnic groups, which hold different sets of norms, ideologies, and child-rearing practices. In such a socioeconomically diverse multiethnic environment, child welfare services are confronted with the continued challenge of providing ethnic-sensitive services to minority children and families in order to be responsive to their unique social realities and life experience.

Asian Americans are often lumped together as a single unit by policy makers and social service systems. However, contrary to the general belief that Asians are all similar and homogeneous, Asians are characterized by extreme diversity in terms of national origin, language, generation, educational attainment, income, and religious preference. This chapter provides an overview of Asian Pacific American immigration history, diverse socioeconomic backgrounds, cultural values, and child-rearing practices as underlying factors influencing the experiences of Asian Pacific Islander (API) children and their families. Attention is given to some of the key issues facing Asian Pacific American children, youth, and families as it pertains to child welfare and child welfare practice strategies. Those central issues include language barrier among immigrant parents, intergenerational conflict due to differential rates of acculturation between U.S.-born children and immigrant parents, high rates of domestic violence, risk for child physical maltreatment, delinquent behavior as opposed to the general stereotypical image of a model minority, and the systemic issues of racial discrimination and prejudice.

In order to effectively practice culturally competent services, this chapter highlights the selected perspectives (generalist, strengths, and empowerment) that lend themselves well to being applied to the API population. The psychosocial approach is selected as a relevant treatment model for work with Asian Pacific American children and families. It includes several cases child welfare workers may encounter as well as culturally competent intervention guidelines for working with Asian Pacific American children and their families. The chapter concludes with current issues and directions for the future.

INTRODUCTION

One of the most important human resources is our children. As Crosson-Tower (1998) expressed, certainly, it is through our children that we are connected to the future. Although primary responsibility for the care of children is assigned to the family, every society is required to nurture children collectively and insure their optimal well-being and healthy growth. The number of children living in poverty in the United States, ironically, is much greater when compared to any other industrialized countries (Children's Defense Fund, 2004; Lindsey, 1994). Furthermore, there are numerous culturally distinct ethnic groups which hold different sets of norms, ideologies, and child-rearing practices. In such a socioeconomically diverse multiethnic environment, enhancing the psychosocial functioning of children and their families continues to pose a challenge to the profession of social work as well as child welfare services today. Particularly, child welfare workers face the challenge of providing ethnic-sensitive services to minority children and families in order to be responsive to their unique social realities and life experiences (Prater, 2000). As the size of ethnic minority populations grows in the United States from 34 million in 1970 to 69.8 million in 2000 mainly through a massive influx of immigrants from Asia and Latin America (U.S. Census Bureau, 2003a), more and more children and their families with minority backgrounds have been brought to the attention of the child welfare system. Cross-cultural competency and child welfare workers' in-depth understanding of their clients' cultural differences and social-class backgrounds are prerequisite to child welfare practice with minority children and their families (Baumrind, 1994; Hong and Hong, 1991).

Asian American families are often viewed as stable and free from serious family problems or child welfare issues. Such a "model minority" image of the Asian Americans distorts the actual diverse realities they experience. Contrary to their general stereotype of an intact family, immigrant API families were reported to experience a variety of problems ranging from domestic violence to divorce, parent–child conflict, substance abuse, juvenile delinquency, unemployment, and discrimination, all of which have a significant bearing on API children's psychological well-being. Kitano and Nakaoka (2001) briefly summarized the socioeconomic situation faced by many Asian Americans:

> Socioeconomic indicators for Asian Americans in the latter half of the twentieth century show that certain segments of some [Asian] ethnic groups have made considerable strides, while the other groups still face an uphill battle. We must also remember that even those who are on the "upper" ends of the socioeconomic scale still face issues such as the "glass ceiling," underemployment, unequal returns on their education, blatant discrimination, and hate crimes. (p. 16)

The API children with immigrant backgrounds often report feelings of confusion, anger, and frustration attributable to relationship difficulties with their traditional parents (Ho, 1992; Lee, 1997). They are expected to value and maintain their heritage culture through socialization with immigrant parents and members of their ethnic community. At the same time, they are expected to learn quickly the language and certain behavioral patterns of the host society as part of their successful psychosocial adjustment to the new social environment. More specifically, immigrant Asian parents tend to emphasize obedience and conformity with parental expectations and yet, paradoxically, to recognize the importance of individual autonomy and self-assertion for the academic and social success of their children in the host society (Rhee, 1996). Furthermore, the perception and experience of racial discrimination are also likely to undermine API adolescents' ethnic pride, which may contribute to their psychological distress such as feelings of social isolation, inferiority, and inadequacy (Uba, 1994). It is not uncommon to find many API youth in counseling expressing their negative emotions and extreme psychological pain.

BACKGROUND

Asian immigration in significant numbers started in the mid-nineteenth century when the California Gold Rush required a steady supply of cheap labor from Asian countries. A large number of Chinese workers, the first Asian group to immigrate to the United States, were brought to California for mining and railroad construction. Subsequently, other Asian groups including Japanese, Filipino, Korean, and Asian Indian laborers were brought mainly to Hawaii and California by plantation and farm owners after the Chinese Exclusion Act of 1882, which legally barred the Chinese from entry into the United States. Several discriminatory immigration policies passed in the 1920s prevented Asian nationals from entering the U.S. territory for over four decades. Those early Asian immigrants were mostly unskilled workers and illiterate farmers who were unfamiliar with urban life settings. There was little immigration from Asia from then until the late 1960s, and in the 1960s Asians were mostly invisible to the general public (Kitano and Daniels, 2001; Min, 1995).

The Immigration Act of 1965, known to be the most liberalized immigration law to date and taken into full effect in 1968, allowed a massive influx of Asian immigrants from various Asian countries favoring family reunion. One of the major effects of this law was a shift in the major source of immigrants from European to non-European countries (Min, 1995). Approximately 200,000 new Asian immigrants have arrived in the United States annually since the 1970s, and consequently the Asian community has experienced a phenomenal growth in size over the past three decades. In 1970 there were fewer than 1.5 million Asians in the United States, accounting for only 0.7 percent of the total U.S. population. In March 2002, there were as many as 12.5 million API Americans, comprising 4.4 percent of the population. The Asian population consisted of Chinese, Filipino, Asian Indian, Vietnamese, Korean, Japanese, Cambodian, Hmong, Loatian, and other Asian groups. Notably, the 2000 Census, for the first time, began to classify Native Hawaiians and other Pacific Islanders (NHPI) into a separate ethnic category. Of the 12.5 million APIs, slightly less than 1 million (935,600) identified themselves as a member of the NHPI community (U.S. Census Bureau, 2003b). Approximately 2 million API immigrants were admitted to the United States during the 1990s, and among those about one-third settled down in California, and most of the rest chose New York, Texas, Illinois, Washington, New Jersey, and Florida (in this order) as their final destinations for living (Modarres, 2003).

Asian Americans are often lumped together as a single unit by policy makers and social service systems. However, contrary to the general belief that Asians are all similar and homogeneous, Asians are characterized by extreme diversity in terms of national origin, language, generation, educational attainment, income, and religious preference. According to the 2000 U.S. Census, for example, Asians consisted of over twenty-five distinct ethnic groups. As shown in Table 5.1, among these groups, the largest proportions of Asians were non-Taiwanese Chinese (2,314,537), Filipino (1,850,314), and Asian Indian (1,678,765) followed by Vietnamese (1,122,528), Korean (1,076,872), Japanese (796,700), Cambodian (171,937), and Hmong (169,428) (U.S. Census Bureau, February 2002).

TABLE 5.1   Population of the United States by Asian/Pacific Ethnicity, 1970–2000

	1970	1980	1990	2000
Total U.S.	203,211,926	226,545,805	248,709,873	281,421,906
Total Asian/Pacific	1,429,562	3,446,421	7,273,662	10,019,405
Chinese	436,062	812,178	1,645,472	2,432,585
Filipino	343,060	781,894	1,406,770	1,850,314
Asian Indian	—	387,223	815,447	1,678,765
Vietnamese	245,025	245,025	614,547	1,122,528
Korean	69,150	357,393	798,849	1,076,872
Japanese	591,290	716,331	847,562	796,700
Cambodian	—	—	—	171,937
Hmong	—	—	—	169,428
Native Hawaiian	—	166,814	211,014	401,162
Samoan		41,948	62,964	133,281
Guamanian		32,158	49,345	92,611

Sources: The 2000 figures for Asian Pacific Americans in this table are from U.S. Census Bureau, February, 2002. The 1970, 1980, and 1990 numbers are from Kitano and Nakaoka (2001): U.S. Census Bureau (1973a, 1981, 1993a, 1995).

Of the 12.5 million API, about 88 percent are either foreign-born themselves or have at least one foreign-born parent. More precisely, 8.3 million API (66.4 percent) were foreign-born residents, comprising one-fourth of the nation's foreign-born population. Table 5.2 shows the percent of seven major Asian ethnic groups' population that was foreign-born. The five largest contributors to the nation's foreign-born population from Asia are China, the Philippines, India, Vietnam, and Korea (U.S. Census Bureau, August, 2002). As shown in Table 5.2, there have been rapid increases in foreign-born Asian populations since the 1960 census primarily due to post-1965 immigration (Kitano and Nakaoka, 2001).

TABLE 5.2   Percent of Foreign-Born Asians, 1970–2000

	1960	1970	1980	1990	2000
Chinese	39.5	47.1	63.3	69.3	57.2
Filipino	48.9	53.1	64.7	64.4	66.1
Asian Indian		—	70.4	75.4	60.0
Vietnamese		—	90.5	79.9	76.9
Korean		—	81.9	72.7	64.8
Japanese	21.5	20.9	28.4	32.4	30.2
Cambodian		—	—	—	71.3

Sources: The 2000 figures for Asian Americans in this table were obtained by dividing the total ethnic Asian population by the number of foreign-born Asians (U.S. Census Bureau, August, 2002). The 1970, 1980, and 1990 numbers are from Kitano and Nakaoka (2001): U.S. Census Bureau (1973b, 1981, 1993b).

The API population is relatively young compared to other ethnic groups. The proportion of the Asian population 18 years of age and under was 26 percent, whereas the age-matched proportion of the non-Hispanic white group was 23 percent in 2000 (U.S. Census Bureau, 2003b). More specifically, in Los Angeles County, Hmong, Tongans, Samoans, and Cambodians had the youngest median ages of 19, 20, 21, and 24 years respectively, while Los Angeles County's overall median age in 2000 was 32 years (Asian Pacific American Legal Center of Southern California, 2004). Most of the Asian immigrants typically came as adults and brought their elderly parents and young children with them. The overwhelming majority of new Asian immigrants have settled in metropolitan areas including Los Angeles, New York, San Francisco, Honolulu, Houston, and Chicago. As of July 2001, nearly all APIs (96 percent) live in metropolitan areas (U.S. Census Bureau, 2003b).

In 2000, the annual median family income of API households was $53,635, compared to the national average of $50,046 (U.S. Census Bureau, 2003b). This figure represents the highest among the nation's major racial groups. While paradoxically API Americans appear to do well in terms of median income, they actually earned significantly less than non-Hispanic whites in terms of per capita income, because the API households on average were much larger than white households. Additionally, the proportion of API families who lived below the poverty thresholds in 2001 was much higher (10.2 percent) than the rate for non-Hispanic whites (7.8 percent) (U.S. Census Bureau, September 2002). These statistics indicate that there are a significant number of API families who are experiencing economic hardships and difficulties as they struggle with day-to-day survival in the new environment. Although race-based census data provide useful information about the overall picture of the group, they tend to ignore the within-group diversity. Nishioka (2003) puts:

> The API community is highly diverse population, arguably more so than any other racial group. While some families have been in the United States for five generations or longer, many more are recent immigrants. From the Indian high-tech worker to the village farmer from Laos, they come to this country with varying degrees of education, skills, and financial resources. (p. 34)

For example, there were significant differences among ethnic API groups in income and the poverty rates. There were significant differences in the amount of median family income between the more established groups and recent Southeast refugee groups. Similarly the poverty rate from one group to another within the API community varied widely. Specifically, in 1990, 14 percent of Chinese, 6.4 percent of Filipinos, 9.7 percent of Asian Indians, and 13.7 percent of Koreans lived below the poverty line, while the poverty rates for Vietnamese, Cambodians, and Hmong were consistently much higher than other API groups, 25.7 percent, 47.0 percent, 67.1 percent respectively (Kitano and Nakaoka, 2001; Lai and Arguelles, 2003). Furthermore, more than a quarter of Tongans, Samoans, and Bangladeshis live below the poverty line in Los Angeles County (Asian Pacific American Legal Center of Southern California, 2004).

ASIAN AMERICAN COMMUNITY PROFILE

Chinese

The 2000 U.S. census reveals that, among diverse ethnic groups of Asian ancestry, Chinese Americans are the largest and the fastest growing group in the United States. Over 40 percent of all Chinese Americans are concentrated in one state, California. Unlike early immigrants who were primarily farmers and unskilled laborers, the post-1965 Chinese immigrants are characterized by much more intragroup diversity in terms of places of origin, spoken languages, socioeconomic backgrounds, and types of social mobility. Recent Chinese immigrants have arrived from various places including Hong Kong, Taiwan, Mainland China, Vietnam, Cambodia, Malaysia, and Central American countries. Although there is only one written Chinese language, they speak so many different regional dialects that outsiders cannot understand easily. Many of those recent immigrants had completed college education before coming to the United States, and held managerial and professional occupations, while others were migrating from impoverished regions of Southeast Asian countries with minimal to no education and few job skills (Zhou, 2003). Data in Table 5.2 suggest that the Chinese community is in transition from a predominantly immigrant community in the 1970s to a community of a mixture of more assimilated U.S.-born Chinese Americans and first-generation immigrants.

While overall median family income and years of education for Chinese Americans are above the national average, the trend of diversity and polarization of the community is noteworthy, especially between immigrants from Taiwan and Hong Kong on one side and immigrants from the mainland and Southeast Asian countries on the other. Recent immigrant Chinese families often retreat to ethnic enclaves such as Chinatowns in San Francisco and Monterey Park in Los Angeles County due to language and cultural barriers. Despite their prosperity in ethnic entrepreneurship and technical/professional specialty job categories, racial discrimination, underemployment, especially for Chinese-Vietnamese refugees, and cultural shock characterize their multifaceted life in the United States. Takaki states (1989):

> Many of the young Chinese are high educational achievers. But there are others, especially the children of the "Downtown Chinese," who do not find promising futures ahead of them. Many are alienated and angry. Facing an English-language barrier and prospects of low-wage work in restaurants and laundries, they turn to gangs. . . . (p. 431)

Filipinos

The Philippines is the leading Asian country that sends the largest number of immigrants to the United States today. For the past two decades, over 50,000 Filipino immigrants have been admitted legally to the United States a year. The Filipino population, including hapas of part-Filipino ancestry, accounts for nearly 1 percent of the U.S. population in 2000. The largest proportion of Filipinos is concentrated in California (46.4 percent), followed by Hawaii (11.7 percent), New York (4.0 percent),

New Jersey (4.0 percent), and Washington state (3.9 percent) (U.S. Census Bureau, 2000). The major segment of this population grew from the U.S. military bases in the Philippines that heavily recruited Filipinos for enlisted army positions and civilian employments.

Most enlisted Filipinos were relocated to various naval bases in the United States, and subsequently developed cohesive ethnic communities around such cities as San Diego, Long Beach, Honolulu, and Norfolk. The majority of recent foreign-born post-1965 Filipino immigrants tend to settle primarily in those areas where Filipino ethnic enclaves are firmly established (Dela Cruz and Agbayani-Siewert, 2003). With regard to the current socioeconomic structure of the Filipino community, Dela Cruz and Agbayani-Siewert (2003) state:

> In times of crisis, the United States has relied on the surplus of Filipino workers, particularly women, to fill jobs considered "unwanted" by natives. In the last thirty years, many large American cities have recruited Filipino nurses to meet shortages in their hospitals. Recently, Filipino school teachers are also in demand, due to the colonial, English-speaking schools set up when the Philippines was a U.S. territory. . . . Many Filipinos occupy low-wage and middle-wage sector jobs that offer very little opportunity to advance up a higher-paying career ladder. As more second and third generation Filipinos earn better educations, hopefully the move towards greater economic mobility can be accomplished. (p. 50)

In regard to Filipino Americans' socioeconomic characteristics, foreign-born Filipino immigrants are more highly educated than other major Asian groups. However, U.S.-born Filipino Americans are behind in education, compared to other major Asian American groups. For example, Filipino Americans are slightly higher in the rate of college enrollment than their white American counterparts, but significantly lower than other major Asian ethnic groups. Furthermore, college dropout rates among second-generation Filipino college students are much higher than the rates of other Asian groups, and their socioeconomic achievements are significantly lower than those of Chinese, Japanese, and Koreans. Traditionally, Asian immigrants including first-generation Filipino Americans tend to consider education as the key to success, and place their first priority on children's education. However, perhaps, monolingual English-speaking second-generation Filipinos who have minimal or no ties with the Philippines seem to view education as less important than their parents (Agbayani-Siewert and Revilla, 1995).

Asian Indians

Similar to other Asian groups, significant immigration of Asian Indians did not take place until 1968. According to the latest census data, the Asian Indian community is one of the fastest growing ethnic minorities in the United States primarily due to the influx of new immigrants. The growth in the number of Asian Indians was further accelerated by the employment-based immigration category created for the first time in 1990. More recently, many young, well-educated immigrants from India were recruited to the high-tech industrial sector under the temporary worker program. Asian Indians are predominantly concentrated in East and West Coast cities including the San Francisco Bay area and New York.

Asian Indians in the United States are economically well adjusted to the host society. "According to the 1990 Census, Indians had the highest median household income, family income, per capita income and annual median income ($40,625) of any foreign-born group" (Rao, 2003). However, it is very likely that relative earnings achieved by the Asian Indian households are significantly lower than those of the white families, when the larger average household size is taken into account. Nonmixed Asian Indians are relatively young compared to the white population. According to the 2000 Census, the median age of this population is 30.0 years and 8.5 percent are children below 15 years of age. In general, the Asian Indian population is characterized by a high level of education and a strong commitment to their traditional family values and practices (Kitano and Daniels, 2001). For example, arranged marriage is still highly valued in the Indian community, and bringing one's spouse from their home country is not uncommon.

Asian Indian families are known to be remarkably stable (Kitano and Daniels, 2001). For example, the majority of Asian Indian children under 18 years of age live in a two-parent household. With regard to their psychosocial adjustment, divorce and separation rates among Asian Indian Americans are lower than those for other Asian groups, and significantly lower than those of the general public. In 2000, only 2.8 percent identified themselves as either divorced or separated, while over 10 percent of the total population selected such marital categories (Rao, 2003).

Vietnamese

Nearly 40 percent of the entire Vietnamese population in the United States was residing in California in 2000 (U.S. Census Bureau, February, 2002). While this demonstrates the largest concentration of the Vietnamese population in just one state, it actually reflects a decrease from 47 percent of the total Vietnamese population found in California in 1990. Among the entire Vietnamese population in California, almost half of them (233,573) were concentrated in the Los Angeles and Orange County area. The next largest number of Vietnamese was found in San Francisco and San Jose (146,613) (Pfeifer, 2001).

Since the end of the Vietnamese War in the spring of 1975, unprecedented numbers of Indochinese refugees have entered the United States. Unlike other voluntary Asian immigrant groups, Vietnamese refugees were forced to leave their home country. Many of the Vietnamese refugees had little or no time to prepare for their hasty escape into a foreign country due to their fear of retaliation by the Communist regime that had triumphed over the South Vietnamese government (Do, 2002; Strand and Jones, 1985).

The Vietnamese influx to the United States occurred in five major waves. The first wave was triggered by the events of April 1975, when South Vietnam fell to the Communists from the North. New political upheavals and a deteriorating economy accelerated the second and more massive exodus of Vietnamese refugees. Starting from 1978 the second wave refugees fled to neighboring countries through the sea (boat people) or across the jungle (land people), often risking attacks from pirates, starvation, and death. Passage of the Amerasian Homecoming Act in 1987 brought on the third wave children of U.S. military or civilian personnel and Vietnamese women born during the years of the Vietnam War. Most of these Vietnamese Amerasians were born out of wedlock and stigmatized for their mixed racial heritage in Vietnam (McKelvey and Webb, 1995). Over 75,000 Vietnamese Amerasians and their immediate family members were resettled in the United States during the late 1980s and early 1990s. The fourth wave Vietnamese, mostly former soldiers, political prisoners, and their families who had been persecuted under Communist reeducation programs, were admitted to the United States through the Humanitarian Operations Program. Finally, through the establishment of the Resettlement Opportunities for Vietnamese Returnees program, thousands of Vietnamese who were unable to prove their refugee status in Southeast Asian camps and subsequently returned to Vietnam were given another chance for resettlement in the United States (Chuong and Ta, 2003).

The first wave of Vietnamese refugees consisted of individuals who had a predominantly middle-class background with a high level of educational attainment in South Vietnam. Several characteristics distinguish the later wave refugees from the first wave. The second wave cohorts were generally younger, less educated, and much less able to speak English than the first wave. A large percentage of the nonfirst wave refugees were farmers and fishermen in their homelands. Unlike the first cohort, most of the second and subsequent groups of Vietnamese refugees came from rural backgrounds, and their levels of education, literacy, and transferable job skill were significantly low (Strand and Jones, 1985). Despite various U.S. resettlement programs designed to promote speedy economic self-sufficiency for Vietnamese refugees, they have experienced significant difficulties adjusting to life in the competitive, fast-paced, and high-technology environment of the United States. The extremely hazardous and degrading experiences of the most later migrating Vietnamese refugees increased their risk for developing mental health problems such as posttraumatic stress disorder, major depression, and adjustment disorder as well as various other psychosomatic ailments such as general fatigue and weakness, stomach pain, and headaches (Montero, 1979; Segal, 2000).

Koreans

Similar to other East Asian groups, Koreans are heavily concentrated in the Western region of the United States. Nearly one-third of the total Korean population were settled in California both in 1990 and in 2000. The second and third most populous states for Koreans in 2000 were New York and New Jersey respectively (Yu, Choe, and Han, 2002). With regard to their socioeconomic status, Koreans, like other immigrant Asians, demonstrate higher levels of educational attainment when compared to the national average. Nearly 50 percent of Korean immigrant males have received some college education in their home country and more than 70 percent of them held professional and white-collar occupations before coming to America (Hurh and Kim, 1990; Min, 1995).

After immigration, however, a major source of living for Korean immigrants is the entrepreneurship of small business. Among many different adjustment problems, Korean immigrants tend to identify an inability to speak English and difficulty in learning the new language as the most difficult and stressful problem. Due to language difficulties and lack of adequate job opportunities, many well-educated Korean immigrants work as unskilled menial laborers. After a few years of hard work in areas of blue-collar jobs, about one-third of Korean immigrant households nationwide engage in a self-employed labor-intensive small business such as garment factories, liquor stores, restaurants, and dry cleaners in high-risk inner city neighborhoods. In addition, a significant proportion of this population is employed in low-paying unskilled service sector occupations. For example, Min (1998) found that 45 percent of Korean immigrants in Los Angeles were self-employed, and additional 30 percent of Korean immigrants worked for Korean-owned businesses. Economic and social conditions have improved substantially in South Korea over the past 10 years. Subsequently, in the 1990s many newcomers started businesses shortly after arriving partly due to the strong economy in Korea and their liberalization of foreign exchange policies. The mean family income for Koreans in 2000 was $72,600, which was slightly over the national average of $66,000. However, the mean individual income for Koreans aged between 25 and 64 was $32,807 as compared with the national average of $35,017 (Yu, choe, and Han, 2002).

Nearly 75 percent of Korean immigrants attend ethnic Korean churches regularly every week where services are rendered in the Korean language (Hurh and Kim, 1990; Min, 1995). Lack of language capacity, deprivation of suitable job opportunities, and extended work hours generally contribute to the high level of stress and uncertainty in life. This may explain in part why the overwhelming majority of Koreans in the United States turn to religion and have become Christian, mostly Protestant. For immigrant Koreans, churches have now become the most important integral part of the community structure throughout the nation. Ethnic Korean churches serve as places for exchanging social interactions, maintaining traditional activities, and sharing mutual support. As Min (1995) indicates, for foreign-born first-generation Koreans, cultural homogeneity and cohesiveness, high affiliation with immigrant churches, and concentration in small businesses have contributed to their strong sense of ethnic attachment and ethnic solidarity, suggesting a low level of assimilation, a low level of tolerance for cultural differences, and a high level of resistance toward American customs and practices.

Japanese

With regard to immigration patterns, the Japanese migrated to the United States in two historical periods—before and after World War II. About 450,000 Japanese came to this county during the first eight decades before the World War II. Since 1946, about one quarter million Japanese have immigrated to the United States (Kitano and Daniels, 2001; Toji, 2003). Table 5.1 presents that the Japanese population in the United States has decreased from 847,562 in 1990 to 796,700 in 2000. "The explanations given for the apparent decrease included low birth rates, high rates of outmarriage and assimilation, and low levels of immigration" (Toji, 2003, p. 73). However, as Toji (2003) pointed out, according to the 2000 Census, there were additional 1.15 million Americans who identified partial Japanese ancestry. The size of post-1965 Japanese immigration is relatively small when compared to other major Asian immigrant groups. Table 5.2 shows that only about one-third of all Japanese Americans were foreign-born (30.2 percent) and two-thirds named the Unites States as their place of birth (69.8 percent), according to the 2000 Census. Thus, the Japanese community has the highest proportion of U.S.-born Asians of Japanese ancestry among all API groups in the United States. In terms of settlement patterns, Japanese Americans continue to remain concentrated in the west coast. Over 70 percent of this population reside in the following four states—California (34 percent), Hawaii (26 percent), and Washington and Oregon (13 percent).

One of the salient characteristics of the Japanese American population is a very high rate of intermarriage between Japanese Americans and non-Japanese. Shinagawa and Pang (1996) report in their demographic study that about three-quarters of U.S.-born Japanese American young adults were married to non-Japanese in 1990 and that this trend is likely to continue. It is noteworthy that Japanese American women outmarried at much higher rates than men. More specifically, over two-thirds of all Japanese intermarriages were rendered between Japanese American female and non-Japanese males. In the 1960s and 1970s intermarriages were predominantly between Japanese American women and white American men. However, since the 1980s, the Japanese community has experienced a remarkable shift from interracial marriages to pan-Asian interethnic marriages. In 1990, marriages between Japanese Americans and other Asians became the dominant intermarriage pattern. The rapidly increasing number of intermarriages is primarily responsible for the emergence of a large proportion of mixed-ancestry Japanese (Toji, 2003). One of the implications for high intermarriage rates for Japanese Americans is that divorce rates are higher among the intermarried. Fugita and O'Brien (1991), in their survey of second- and third-generation Japanese males who were married to non-Japanese women, found that the divorce rate among outmarried Japanese American males was significantly higher than that of inmarried males.

Native Hawaiians and Pacific Islanders (NHPI)

The 2000 Census identified Native Hawaiians and other Pacific Islander Americans separately from the Asian American racial category. Discernible cultural, ethnic, political, and socioeconomic backgrounds of NHPI groups could convincingly justify separate racial categorization by the Census Bureau. The Native Hawaiian people are generally referred to as descendants of the native inhabitants of the Hawaiian Islands. On the other hand, 23 Polynesian, Micronesian, and Melanesian subgroups identified in the 2000 Census represent the other Pacific Islander groups. Among these diverse subpopulations, Samoans (Polynesian), Tongans (Polynesian), Guamanians (Micronesian), and Fijians (Melanesian) are considered as the four major Pacific Islander subgroups (Moy, 2003).

Ever since indigenous Native Hawaiians had initial contact with the West in 1778, they "have undergone a long history of decline both in number and in socioeconomic status with a recovery only evident in recent decades" (Ong and Leung, 2003, p. 14).

> Despite a high rate of interracial marriage, Native Hawaiians are not fully or equally incorporated into the dominant society. Socioeconomic statistics show that they are below parity with the dominant groups in Hawaii. Native Hawaiians have been marginalized by a territorial and state educational system that has failed to provide an adequate education. There are signs of positive changes that can redress some of the historical wrongs, but the future remains uncertain.

As the above quote indicates, the Native Hawaiian population is characterized by a high rate of outmarriage with Asians and whites, alienation from the mainstream society, lower educational attainment, high rates of unemployment, increased welfare dependency, and substantially lower overall socioeconomic status compared to Caucasians, Japanese, and Chinese in Hawaii. Although there is a growing trend that many older part Native Hawaiians tend to identify themselves as full Native Hawaiians, the majority of the youth population have racially mixed heritage. For example, only 5 percent of Native Hawaiians aged 18 or under were classified as full Native Hawaiians in 2000. The level of educational attainment among both full and part Native Hawaiians is much lower than that of other ethnic groups in Hawaii. Only 16 percent of Native Hawaiians aged between 25 and 39 had some college education, while almost 50 percent of Japanese American and over 40 percent of Anglo American counterparts had attained this level of education in 2000 (McGregor, 2003; Ong and Leung, 2003).

Although the NHPI population is found in almost all states, the majority reside in the Western region. Particularly 58 percent of NHPIs lived in two states—Hawaii and California in 2000; and Washington, Texas, New York, Nevada, Florida, and Utah also have a substantial number of these populations (Moy, 2003). Currently, the Polynesian islands of Samoa in the South Pacific consist of two geographical parts—American Samoa and neighboring Western Samoa. American Samoa is the United States' southern-most territory, whereas Western Samoa remains as an independent nation. American Samoa became an unorganized U.S. territory over a century ago in 1900. However, traditional Samoan culture has survived outside influences relatively well, although the Western missionaries had a great religious influence on its inhabitants. At the time of writing, according to the World FactBook (2004), almost all American Samoans were Christians (roughly 50 percent Congregationalist, 20 percent Roman Catholic, and 30 percent Protestant and other).

Many American Samoans have relocated to the mainland for a variety of reasons, but most notably for improved economic opportunities. At the time of writing, like Native Hawaiians, a disproportionate percentage of Pacific Islanders including Samoans and Guamanians were economically impoverished, had lower education, and need public assistance compared to whites and some Asian Americans. "The model minority myth surrounding Asian Americans, which obscures problems with disadvantaged members of the group, was hurting NHIPs, too" (Moy, 2003, p. 91). For example, in 1999, the median earnings for NHPI full-time workers aged 16 years or older were $28,457, while the overall median earnings for the U.S. general population were $32,098 (Moy, 2003).

Other South East Asians: Cambodians and the Hmong

Unlike other Asian groups, such as Chinese, Filipinos, Koreans, who voluntarily immigrated to the United States, most Cambodians and Hmong immigrants were forced to leave their homelands and subsequently arrived in the United States as political refugees in the late 1970s and thereafter. About one-third of the Hmong, an ethnic minority from the rural highlanders of the remote forested regions of Laos, who carried out U.S. military operations, have escaped their homes in fear of revenges by the communist Pathet Lao since the fall of Vietnam (Takaki, 1995). Many Hmong refugees settled in St. Paul, Minnesota, where they established the largest urban Hmong enclave in the world. According to the 2000 Census, about 40 percent (70,232) of immigrant Cambodians were concentrated in California, and over half of the California Cambodian population (36,233) found their permanent homes in the Los Angeles area, especially in the city of Long Beach. At the time of writing, the Cambodian population in California was decreasing, while Cambodian communities throughout the nation were expanding significantly in the states of Washington, Pennsylvania, and Minnesota. Among California's Cambodians in 2000, 41 percent were minor children under the age of 18 years (Hmong Studies Internet Resource Center, 2004).

From 1975 through 1979 Khmer Rouge leader Pol Pot took power, which marked one of the bloodiest rules of the twentieth century. This communist regime brutally carried out deurbanization policies and torture techniques in an attempt to bring about a total change in their traditional socioeconomic structure and restore the peasantry base by forcing the population into labor camps in the countryside (Tenhula, 1991). It is estimated that approximately 1 to 3 million people, or as many as a quarter of its people, were massacred during the 4 years of Khmer Rouge rule. Thousands of Cambodian survivors of the Pol Pot labor camps fled to refugee camps in Thailand that have been established since 1975. These journeys were dangerous as they went through jungles. Many died of malnutrition, starvation, and exposure to many diseases. Broken families and loss of human dignity became a central legacy of the Cambodian people's tragic past. Their horrific experiences during both the war in Cambodia and their flight as a refugee resulted in a wide range of psychological symptoms, such as posttraumatic stress disorder (PTSD) and survival guilt, among the Cambodian American refugees (Hopkins, 1996). The majority of adult Cambodian refugees in the Unites States had little or no education. Many of them struggled with finding employment and adjusting to life in America.

CULTURAL VALUES AND PARENTAL EXPECTATIONS

As indicated previously, API Americans are extremely diverse groups of people in terms of ethnic background, socioeconomic status, generation, length of residence in the United States, and English proficiency, along with cultural norms and values governing the family (Kitano and Daniels, 2001; Min, 1995; Yee, Huang, and Lew, 1998). Cultural values and beliefs held by the API population may vary from one subgroup to another. Furthermore, most immigrants experience a gradual change in their values, beliefs, and expectations, as they interact with people in the American mainstream over the years. Despite significant diversity among API subgroups, however, many Asian American families, especially immigrant Chinese, Korean, Japanese, and Vietnamese families, share relatively similar cultural backgrounds that originated from the common philosophical principles of Confucianism. The Confucian-based fundamental belief system tends to remain relatively unchanged for many immigrants who have been in this country for decades. The salient cultural values and issues that child welfare professionals should know to promote effective practice with API families and children include a strong tradition of mutual support and interdependence rather than self-reliance among immediate and extended family members, emphasis on parental authority, rigid sex role and male dominance, family reciprocity and filial piety, harmonious relationship among family members, strong parent–child bond, negation of personal needs, modesty, and self-control.

Interdependence

"A critical strength of API communities is strong family and social ties that buffer many API individuals from the devastating consequences of life crises" (Yee, Huang, and Lew, 1998, p. 83). The APIs tend to emphasize a collective sense of the self and reliance on the family in comparison to the American model of individual autonomy. For example, Samoans have strong communal ties, with less emphasis on individualistic orientations and strong, assertive personalities (Furuto, 1991; Kitano, 1997). Family needs and interdependence take precedence over the individual want and independence. Consequently, conflicts and confrontations that disrupt group harmony are generally discouraged in API culture, whereas family loyalty is highly stressed (Weaver, 2005).

Hierarchical Family Structure

Asian culture places a great emphasis on the maintenance of hierarchical social order, respect for authority, male dominance, and obedience to rules and authority (Rhee, 1996). Age- and gender-based family roles and responsibilities are much more rigid in the Asian American cultures than the mainstream culture. One of the most prominent characteristics of immigrant Asian families is the husband's or father's traditional definition of man as an authority figure. Traditional API families tend to be highly male-dominant and expect wives and children subservient to patriarchal authority. Traditionally, the father was the unquestioned head of the family who was deeply involved in his children's lives (Lee, 1997; Uba, 1994). Children are taught to show unconditional obedience to their parents' needs and wishes and never to talk back to them. Furthermore, younger siblings are expected to show appropriate respect toward older siblings, especially the eldest. Family exercises firm control over children's behavior including peer selection, dating, and marriage. Thus, the societal structure in API families tends to be vertical in nature, rather than horizontal in relationships. Therefore, the rank and status and submissive attitude toward authority are highly stressed. An important practice implication includes that child welfare workers should recognize the importance of the critical issue of the status of fathers in API families. "Since the concept of egalitarian roles is unfamiliar to Asian families, the child welfare worker needs to be sensitive to how difficult it can be for the male head of the family if his wife can find a job more easily than he can, or his children can speak English and therefore are able to negotiate with public officials and service providers more effective than he can" (Mass and Geaga-Rosenthal, 2000, p. 151).

Family Reciprocity/Filial Piety

Parents care for minor children, and, reciprocally, it is the children's responsibility to take care of their elderly parents. This sense of family reciprocity is reflected on the concept of filial piety and obligations of child to parent. Especially, the eldest son has distinct responsibilities and obligations to his parents as they age. Filial piety, which is considered as the cornerstone of morality in many Asian cultures, involves not only providing economic and emotional support, comfort, and affection, but also bringing honor to the parent by performing well in educational and occupational activities. Filial piety "is deeply ingrained in the Chinese culture and has served as the moral foundation of interpersonal relationships in China for centuries" (Lin and Liu, 1999, p. 236). When family obligations are not fulfilled, parents, relatives, and other significant others tend to engender feelings of shame and guilt in their children.

Indirect Communication Pattern/Inconspicuousness

The APIs are generally socialized to be indirect and subtle in communicating with others, especially with seniors. Assertive attitudes are considered rude, poorly disciplined, and self-indulging or self-propagating. This pattern of communication may be a result of the cultural value of harmony and priority of group over individual's desires. Asian parents teach their children to be less direct and less confrontational, and to behave for group unity (Kitano and Daniels, 2001). Additionally, "experiences with racist segments of American society further convinced Asian immigrants of the need for and value of silence and inconspicuousness" (Ho, 1992, p. 38). In the area of mental health, many API American adolescents' verbal passivity is often misconstrued as indicators of emotional dysfunctioning and/or resistance by some social service providers. It is crucial to understand that the subtle nature of communication pattern and less confrontational attitudes among API youths and adolescents reflect their integral cultural value, which can promote the welfare of the group.

Modesty/Middle Position

The virtue of the middle position is another important value emphasized by many API parents. "The Asian American emphasis on middle position brings an individual in step with others instead of ahead or behind other" (Ho, 1992, p. 37). It is believed that the practice of middle position in daily interactions with family members and outsiders can strengthen the individual's sense of harmony and togetherness. The value of modesty (*enryo* or *gaman* in Japanese; *joong-yong* in Korean) also guides API children's behaviors toward the goal of intrafamilial stability and harmonious interpersonal relationships. "The value *enryo* requires that an individual maintain modesty in his or her behavior, be humble in expectations, and show appropriate hesitation and unwillingness to intrude on another's time, energy, or resources" (Green, 1982, p. 137). Blatant self-promoting behaviors and a display of arrogant attitudes are generally considered as signs of personal weakness and noncompliance of the socially prescribed body of behavioral codes. One child welfare practice implication of this value is that, sometimes, helping professionals from mainstream culture tend to take this at the face value and misinterpret it as exaggerated politeness or lack of self-pride. Child welfare workers need to understand that API children's nonassertive behavior is not necessarily an expression of lack of motivation or self-efficacy.

Emphasis on Children's Education

One of the main reasons for immigrating to America in the API population is undoubtedly better education for children. Despite some noticeable variations among API subgroups, API parents are highly committed to their children's education and extracurricular activities regardless of their socioeconomic differences (Chen and Stevenson, 1995; Lee and Zane, 1998; Sue and Okazaki, 1990). It is not unusual to encounter API parents taking their children to private tutors after school or on weekends to ensure their academic and/or career success. As such, API parents generally have high expectations for their children's academic success. Distinction in academic performance and extracurricular activities may enhance API children's personal efficacy and self-esteem and prevent a variety of maladaptive behaviors. However, it should be noted that the highly stressful competitions for overall excellence can also have heavy psychological costs and adversely contribute to significant emotional distress for some API children and youths as a result of the tremendous amount of pressures from their families and significant others (Lee, 1994).

STATUS OF PSYCHOSOCIAL ADJUSTMENT

Both immigrant API parents and their U.S.-raised children increasingly experience a variety of psychosocial problems and distress such as adjustment difficulties and intergenerational tension, which may contribute to high rates of criminal and gang activities, running away, and substance abuse among API youths and adolescents (Furuto and Murase, 1992; Segal, 2000). Immigrant API parents tend to retain their own native language, traditional values and lifestyles, and child-rearing practices, while their children speak English more fluently and absorb mainstream cultural beliefs and behavioral patterns at a much faster rate than their parents. Differences in values due to acculturation disparity between immigrant parents and their children often result in greater miscommunications and intergenerational conflicts (Farver, Narang, and Bhadha, 2002; Fu, 2002; Ying et al., 2001). The typical generation gap resulting from these acculturation differences has become a common issue facing many immigrant API families (Chae, 1990; Lee et al., 2000; Ying, 1998). For optimal treatment outcomes, it is essential for child welfare workers who have direct encounters with API families to acquire cross-cultural sensitivity toward the overall psychosocial experiences of API children and youths in the context of their family and surrounding social environment.

Language Barrier among Parents

For many Asian immigrants, English remains as an almost impossible language to master, due to the vast linguistic differences between the two languages. Lack of work experience in America and insufficient English skills make white-collor jobs far less accessible to Asian immigrants despite their advanced educational backgrounds. This explains why Asian immigrants turn to highly competitive family-run small businesses which require husband and wife working more than 12 hours a day, 7 days a week. A critical issue facing API immigrants, especially the male head of the household, is the high level of stress and low self-esteem resulting from status inconsistency and extended working hours without having vacations for many years. Apparently, communication difficulties due to the differences in English proficiency and cultural values between parents and children have become a common feature among many immigrant API families throughout the nation (Rhee, Chang, and Rhee, 2003). A recent study suggests that immigrant parents' language proficiency correlates significantly with indicators of intergenerational conflict and adolescent psychological well-being in immigrant Chinese American families (Lim, 2002).

Parenting Practices and Parent–Child Relationships

A strong preference for male children has persisted for centuries in many parts of Asia and Pacific Islands. The main motivation for marriage in traditional API families was to continue the patrilineal family line through sons, and to obtain a daughter-in-law to serve the parents. The formation of well-defined parent–child subsystems was regarded more important than husband–wife relationships in many patriarchal API families.

Parenting style, in general, has a critical impact on child's psychosocial development (Baumrind, 1991). Immigrant API parents tend to impose their traditional expectations on children's daily activities, and make decisions for children with a belief that it is one of the most important parental obligations toward the child's well-being. Studies suggest that immigrant Asian parents including Chinese, Indians, Vietnamese, and Koreans place greater emphasis on parental involvement in children's overall achievement, and are more likely to rely on physical punishment than Caucasian parents in general (Rhee and Chang, 2004; Yee, Huang, and Lew, 1998). Studies focusing on Baumrinds's conceptual framework of parenting styles among API families reveal that Asian American youth were predominantly raised by authoritarian, authoritative, or inconsistent parents. On the other hand, extremely few API adolescents consider their parents as being permissive when compared to their Caucasian counterparts (Kim, 2004; Park, 2002).

Asian American children who are influenced strongly by the mainstream American culture often experience alienation from their parents due to considerable differences in role expectations and value systems. Foreign-born immigrant API parents and their U.S.-born children often experience conflicts and misunderstanding in values, role expectations, and behavioral norms. Conflicts can arise as children perceive the sharp differences between the views of the mainstream culture and those of their parents. "Out of helplessness and frustration, parents might increase discipline as a reaction to restore traditional family roles" (Yee, Huang, and Lew, 1998, p. 89), and this could contribute to the potential risk for child maltreatment. Studies of immigrant Asian families describe that some of the most serious difficulties Asian American children experience include unrealistic parental expectations in academic and career achievements; parental overinvolvement in their children's lives; parents' overall tendency to exclude their children in the decision-making process; and negative remarks and attitudes toward their children's over-Westernized behavior and lifestyles (Lee, 1997; Stevensen and Lee, 1990; Uba, 1994; Way and Chen, 2000). Ying (1994) also found that U.S.-born Chinese adolescents felt less understood by their mothers and had less physical contact than foreign-born Chinese.

Domestic Violence

Contrary to their general stereotype of a model minority, immigrant API families were reported to experience high rates of spousal abuse among various ethnic groups throughout the nation (Furuto, 1991; Rhee, 1997; Sue, 2005). For example, the Korean American Family Service Center (2004) in Los Angeles reported that domestic violence was one of the leading reasons to seek help from the agency among immigrant Korean families. Samoan adults and Native Hawaiian men were overrepresented as perpetrators of child maltreatment and spouse abuse respectively in Hawaii in proportion to the total population size (Furuto, 1991). A recent study shows a high level of verbal aggression perpetrated by Chinese men toward their spouse or intimate partners, implying that Asian men do not necessarily view marital violence as a violation of a woman's right (Yick, Shibusawa, and Agbayani-Siewert, 2003). Another study, which examined wife abuse attitudes among immigrant Cambodian, Chinese, Korean, and Vietnamese adults living in the United States, demonstrates that as high as 24–36 percent of the sample agreed that violence is justified in certain situations such as a wife's sexual infidelity, her nagging, or her refusal to cook or clean (Yoshioka, Dinoia, and Ullah, 2001).

Child Maltreatment

Parenting styles in API cultures differ significantly from the American norm. Physical punishment is generally permitted and considered necessary by many API parents as a way to educate and discipline children. Many API parents still believe "spare the rod and spoil the child"—"*mae ga yak ida*" in Korean. The Vietnamese old saying that states "When we love our children we give them a beating; when we hate our children, we give them sweet words" (Freeman, 1989, p. 28) also reflects the strong tradition of corporal punishment for child discipline among Vietnamese refugee families. In fact, physically disciplining children is widely practiced and favored as an intrinsic part of child rearing in many Asian countries and Pacific Islands. Immigrant API parents consistently tend to define only extremely harmful physical punishment such as skull fractures and severe burn cases as child abuse. Because of this acceptance of physical punishment, the potential for overall child maltreatment is relatively high among traditional immigrant API families. Child welfare workers need to be aware that the concept of child abuse within the family and public intervention in private family matters for the sake of child protection are still foreign and unacceptable to many API parents.

Ima and Hohm (1991), in their study of child maltreatment among API refugees and immigrants in San Diego, found the following distinctive characteristics of API maltreatment—"greater proportions of female victims, younger child victims, physical abuse rather than other forms of abuse, and a greater likelihood of parents being charged as abusers individually rather than jointly" (p. 276). Segal's (2000) exploratory study of child abuse among Vietnamese refugee families in the United States demonstrates that 71.4 percent of the parents reported to use aggressive forms of discipline such as shouting and screaming, 64.3 percent threatened to spank or hit, and 57.1 percent reported actually hitting their children on the bottom with a bare hand. A study of abuse among Vietnamese Amerasians also indicates a high rate of physical and sexual abuse in this population (McKelvey and Webb, 1995). This study reveals that 22 percent of male and 18 percent of female Amerasians reported a history of physical and/or sexual abuse, and that abused male Amerasians had significantly high levels of psychological distress than their nonabused male counterparts. Some other studies examined the characteristics and patterns of child abuse among immigrant Asian families in Los Angeles County (Chang, Rhee, and Weaver, in press; Rhee & Chang, 2004). Some of the major findings from these studies include (1) immigrant Asian families are more likely to be charged with physical abuse and far less likely to be charged with neglect or sexual abuse in comparison with their counterparts in Los Angeles County; (2) the circumstance under which physical abuse occurred most frequently was corporal punishment used by Asian parents with an intention to discipline their children; and (3) the context under which emotional abuse occurred was likely to be children's witnessing domestic violence.

Ethnic Identity and Self-Esteem

Adolescence is considered as a critical developmental stage during which young people explore who they are and what they want regardless of ethno-cultural and generational differences. They are likely to experiment with a variety of roles and activities in search of their secure sense of identity (Erikson, 1963). However, for ethnic minority adolescents, identification with their own culture and people is an additional burden in the process of general identity development (Lee and Zane, 1998; Phinney and Alipuria, 1990). It has been well documented in the research literature that more API adolescents than other ethnic minority youths tend to display their preference for a Caucasian group membership if possible for a variety of reasons (Lee and Zane, 1998; Phinney, 1989). Some API children and youths erroneously believe that they are not physically as attractive as their white peers in terms of height, skin color, and body posture, suggesting a profound influence of Eurocentric orientation on their belief system. This negative perception toward their own body image may clearly have unfavorable effects on the development of ethnic identity. It appears that higher levels of ethnic identity are likely to have a positive impact on the overall psychological outcome, while feelings of role confusion and alienation resulting from ethnic identity conflicts can lead to psychological as well as behavioral problems for API adolescents (Shrake and Rhee, 2004).

Studies show that self-concepts or self-esteem among API children and youths are influenced by the length of residence in the United State, generation, age, socioeconomic status, and ethnicity. However, existing studies of self-esteem among API adolescents present contrasting views regarding its determining factors. For example, Chen and Yang (1986) found that second-generation Chinese American adolescents and those who came to United States at an early age scored higher on the Harter Self-Perception Scale, while recent immigrant Chinese adolescents had lower self-concept scores. On the other hand, Florsheim's (1997) research, contrary to the general expectation, shows that Chinese adolescents who preferred English to Chinese, indicating an advanced level of acculturation, reported more social adjustment difficulties. The researcher's explanation for this finding is that English-speaking Chinese youth are less identified with Chinese culture and more isolated from their Chinese peers. Rhee and colleagues (2003) examined self-esteem in two ethnic groups—Asian and Caucasian American adolescents who grew up in the same neighborhood. Their findings provide evidence of significant ethnic differences in behavioral patterns, peer networks, family contexts, and levels of self-esteem. In general, Asian adolescents expressed more difficulty discussing problems with their parents when compared to their Caucasian counterparts. Further, self-esteem was found to be significantly lower among Asians than Caucasians.

Psychological Adjustment Problems

Foreign-born Asian Americans have been found to have more psychological adjustment problems and a greater number of stressful life events than U.S.-born Asian Americans (Abe and Zane, 1990; Padilla, Wagatsuma, and Lindholm, 1985). Nguyen and Peterson (1993) found that with foreign-born Vietnamese American college students, acculturation was positively associated with increased depressive symptoms and greater number of stressful life events. These psychological maladjustments are closely related to the interpersonal stress associated with emigration and immigration. In addition to the stress and grief of leaving one's homeland, there is the stress of learning and adjusting to a new culture and oftentimes learning a new language. Acculturation is also related to high-risk behaviors, such as substance abuse in adults (Erickson D'Avanzo, 1997) and adolescents (Hahm, Lahiff, and Guterman, 2003).

Delinquent Behavior

With the 'model minority' stereotype holding up one end of the spectrum, the opposite end is represented by the API delinquency that has been on the rise (Kim and Goto, 2000). Adolescence is a period where fitting in with peers is of particular importance.

The family background of many API adolescents may place them at increased risk for delinquent behavior. Parental supervision reduces the likelihood that adolescents will commit delinquent acts (Smith and Krohn, 1995); however, in many API families, both parents are in the workforce, leaving little to no supervision at home (Toy, 1992). And, in situations where a grandparent is at home, adolescents may not feel that the grandparent has any authority over them and opportunities for intergenerational conflict are amplified. Due to these intergenerational differences with parents and grandparents, the peer relationships can serve as a substitute for family for API adolescents, serving as a source of support and guidance (Spencer and Dornbusch, 1990). This alliance is exemplified in participation in gangs; reasons for gang membership range from a sense of alliance and group membership to protection from adversaries (Toy, 1992). Hence, involvement with delinquent peers is one of the most robust and consistent predictors that the individual adolescent will become delinquent (Thornberry et al., 1994; Warr and Stafford, 1991). Moreover, because of the traditional collectivist value of Asian groups, API adolescents may be more susceptible to group influence and be more inclined to succumb to peer pressure than mainstream adolescents (e.g., European American) (Kim and Goto, 2000). Kim and Goto (2000) suggest that it is because of those collectivist ties that API adolescents place more emphasis on their peer networks and are more likely to succumb to peer influence. Thus, when API adolescents become involved with delinquent peers, they are more likely than not to become delinquent themselves.

Effects of Prejudice and Discrimination

Development of a positive self-concept and a secure sense of ethnic identity is also influenced by the quality of interactions between adolescents and their larger social environment (Pinderhughes, 1982; Schaefer, 2002). As members of ethnic minority groups, API children and youths are often confronted with a systemic issue of racial discrimination and unfair treatment, which may negatively influence their psychological and behavioral development. API Adolescents' perception of their ethnic/racial status in the larger society and awareness of prejudice and discrimination against their ethnic groups are likely to undermine their ethnic pride, which may contribute to their psychological distress such as feelings of social isolation, inferiority, and inadequacy (Phinney and Kohatsu, 1997; Uba, 1994). More specifically, Asaman and Berry (1987), in their study of Japanese American college students, found that those who perceived more racial prejudice against them were more likely to have a lower self-esteem than those who perceived less racial prejudice. Additionally, a recent study shows that API adolescents' perceptions of racial discrimination are a significant risk factor for developing deviant behavioral problems in this population (Shrake and Rhee, 2004).

Those API adolescents who were involved in behavioral problems including substance abuse and youth crimes may have experienced multiple accounts of discrimination and developed a strong sense of anger and frustration toward our multiethnic environment at an early age. Many API adolescents in probation often described their embarrassment and frustration when they were pulled over by police with no specific reason except that they were of Asian descent, or when they were mistreated or stereotyped by school teachers and non-Asian peers (Shrake and Rhee, 2004).

UNDERUTILIZATION OF FORMAL SERVICES

It has been well documented that APIs tend to underutilize mental health services in proportion to their population size (Bui and Takeuchi, 1992; Chen et al., 2003; Cheung and Snowden, 1990; Sue et al., 1991; Uba and Sue, 1991; Zhang, Snowden, and Sue, 1998). In their assessment of national utilization rates, Matsuoka, Breaux and Ryujin (1997) found that Asian Americans were three times less likely to utilize mental health services than their European American counterparts. The same can also be said of other types of services, including public agencies and social services. According to the Center for Mental Health Services (1999), in their comparison of child protective agencies in forty states, Asian Americans were underrepresented among the cases of all types of reported abuse (e.g., physical, neglect, sexual, and emotional maltreatment). This underutilization of service should not lead to the false assumption that there is not a need for services among the API American population. For example, APIs are often found to have lower rates of reported child sexual abuse but, this may be related to the underlying unwillingness to report child sexual abuse for fear of blame or rejection by the API community than actual prevalence (Ima and Hohm, 1991; Wong, 1987). Sue and Morishima (1982) caution that these low utilization rates often have more to do with the lack of appropriate services and barriers to service than the lack of service need (Sue and Morishima, 1982). There are four broad categories of barrier to Asian Americans seeking and maintaining services—cognitive, affective, value orientation, and physical and structural (Leong and Lau, 2001)—and while there is a great deal of overlap, it helps to provide a distinction between the various barriers.

Cognitive Barriers

The first barrier is cognitive and refers to the culturally informed conception of psychosocial and mental health (Leong and Lau, 2001). This conception relates to how APIs view the nature of their problem, reason for causation, and the cure. These etiological explanations affect identification of psychosocial and mental heath problems and help-seeking behaviors. These culturally informed conceptions are manifested in two Confucian themes: (a) an orientation toward others and (b) a sense of holism among body, mind, and spirit (Torsch and Xueqin Ma, 2000). In Shin's (2002) study of Korean immigrants, participants perceived a healthy state of well-being as when the self is in harmony in one's relationships as well as within oneself. It is important to understand these cultural conceptions as they provide an explanatory model as to how the problem arose, the meaning of any symptoms, what solution has previously been effective, and who is seen as an appropriate source of help (Green, 1999).

There is an emphasis on external factors as a source of stress, rather than intrapsychic factors (Lin, 1985; Uba, 1994). Because of the Asian cultural value that stresses harmonious relationships and collectivism, interpersonal conflicts are often seen as the cause of distress; thus, with a rejection of any signs of assertiveness, individuals seek relief through working on relationship with others rather than focusing on themselves (Lin, 1985; Suan and Tyler, 1990). For example, if a child and his classmate are not getting along, rather than separating the two, an API parent will advise the child that it is up to him to initiate and improve the relationship. The maintenance of smooth interpersonal relationships is believed to be the means to acquiring and sustaining good personal health, mental and physical.

Another etiological explanation has to do with belief in karma and social retribution. For example, as an explanation to their child's mental illness, Vietnamese parents believed that mental illness was due to a spiritual imbalance or an actual karmic punishment inflicted by the gods because of some misdeed in the current or past life (McKelvey et al., 1999). And, because of the considerable emphasis on family, there is also the tenet that the sins of the father will be visited upon by the son (Ito and Maramba, 2002). Therefore, there is greater acceptance of the problem and attempt to endure as the individual does not have a great a deal of control in preventing or changing misfortune. When causal attributions are metaphysical, Asian Americans may rely on alternative healers, such as herbalists or acupuncturists, spiritual/religious leaders, or indigenous healers (Abe-kim, Takeuchi, and Hwang, 2002; Herrick and Brown, 1998; Lin et al., 1982; Sue and Morishima, 1982).

The nature of the problem affects which people are seen as the appropriate sources of help. As physical illness is much more culturally acceptable than mental illness, seeking physical treatment from a physician is more suitable than psychological treatment from a mental health professional (Atkinson and Gim, 1989; Sue and Morishima, 1982; Uba and Sue, 1991; Ying, 1990). This is congruent with the more culturally appropriate manifestation of emotional distress as somatic complaints, which are physical in nature (Sue and Morishima, 1982; Uba, 1994; Zhang, Snowden, and Sue, 1998). For example, a Japanese American woman who is grieving the death of her husband will express her sorrow through continuous headaches and stomachaches. She does not need to seek treatment for her emotional state; instead she can focus on her physical complaints. Common somatizations are headaches, backaches, and gastrointestinal complaints, such as poor appetite and indigestion. Somatization is related to the holistic view of the mind and body that is common to many Asian cultures; there is the underlying belief that the emotional and physical distress is from the same underlying disorder (Akutsu, 1997; Sue and Morishima, 1982; Uba, 1994). There is also the possibility of receiving or accessing mental health services at medical facilities (Akutsu, 1997). And while physicians are able to refer individuals for mental health services, this overreliance on the medical profession makes it particularly difficult for professional to detect mental health problems. Chung and Colleagues (2003) found that though the rates were comparable, physicians were less likely to be able to identify psychiatric distress in Asian American patients than Latino patients. They also state that many Asian American physicians will not inquire about any psychiatric symptoms for fear of stigmatizing the patient. Therefore, the underutilization among Asian Americans may also be associated with this pattern of under-recognition.

Another acceptable source of help is school counselors, as academic and vocational problems are seen as both more important and socially acceptable than personal problems (Atkinson, Lowe, and Matthews, 1995; Tracey, Leong, and Glidden, 1986). Not only accepting help for academic concerns is more compatible with Asian values of educational achievement, but the manner in which the help, which includes assessment test and interest inventories, is provided is more compatible as it does not require much self-disclosure, which reduces the likelihood of any shame or guilt. Moreover, API students may view receiving academic counseling as one integral part of their educational process. In their comparison of Asian American and European American college students, Tracey, Leong, and Glidden (1986) found that the endorsement of the importance of problems were reversed for European American and Asian American students, with the latter more likely to over-endorse academic problems (e.g., vocational choice, occupational information, and academic motivation) and under-endorse inter-personal and intrapersonal problems. Tracey, Leong, and Glidden (1986) explicate this difference by examining the attribution of problems. When Asian Americans feel stressed, they seek help for areas they believe are most central to their well-being, which are more often academic in nature. Placed in similar situations of feeling isolated and doing poor academically, European American students may focus on the loneliness and seek help for emotional distress, while Asian American students will more likely focus on the grades and seek academic counseling (Tracey, Leong, and Glidden, 1986).

Affective Barriers

The affective barriers refer to the expression of and response to psychosocial and mental health problems. While cognition deals with the acceptance of distress, the willingness to express and report problems is related to the affective response (Leong and Lau, 2001). One of the most prominent reasons why APIs do not report problems and seek services is due to the shame and stigma, which are distinct though related concepts, attached to having any types of distress. In the study of culturally competent therapists, one mental health professional elucidated the difference: that is, shame as being a judgment from within and oftentimes governed by the culture of the family values whereas stigma is from the outside and the culture of the societal values (Ito and Maramba, 2002). They go on to discuss that the culture of the immediate family is often more important than the culture of the society; therefore, getting the family to support the individual seeking services is crucial. Consequently, when the individual does seek treatment, involvement of family members, particularly key immediate members, is more persistent and intensive in Asian Americans (Lin et al., 1982). Moreover, Asian Americans are more likely to seek services based on referrals from family and friends than self-referred (Akutsu, Snowden, and Organista, 1996).

In addition to reasons of shame and stigma, Asian Americans have been culturally trained to endure signs of distress longer and as a result do not seek help (Narikiyo and Kameoka, 1992; Sue and Zane, 1985). Some feel that overcoming any emotional distress is based on their willpower and that they are capable of relieving distress by themselves (Shin, 2002). In Shin's (2002) study of Korean immigrants suffering from depression, this woman stayed home when she was having problems at work:

> Because I thought I needed to take care of my own problems, I didn't ask for help when I was really low. When something happens, I avoid interaction with people until I resolve the issue alone. I do not want to make trouble. My mother always said, "Even between parents and children, there are some things that are better not to discuss. Don't say everything on your mind. It's better to try to resolve it alone. (p. 465)

Narikiyo and Kameoka (1992) found Japanese American college students to report not only that they were more likely to keep their problems to themselves and rely on themselves to deal with those problems, but that this was also one of the causes of distress. The pressure of keeping problems to oneself is compounded by the cultural value of suppression of emotions, both positive and negative (Hsu, 1983; Kim, Atkinson, and Yang, 1999; Uba, 1994). In fact, an overt display of emotion is often seen as a weakness. This is true for both anger and physical affection. For example, Asian American parents do not convey their love for their children through affectionate acts, such as hugs and kisses, but rather through the fulfillment of more physical needs, such as buying school books and favorite foods (Hsu, 1983; Tang, 1997). Tang (1997) tells of her experience when sharing with a Chinese friend about a European American father who was proud of his son's ability to pay for his own skateboard; the Chinese friend is appalled that a parent would expect or allow a child to pay for this is how Chinese parents express their love for their children. The expectation of roles for the parent is to physically provide for the child in exchange for compliance and respect.

Corresponding to the collectivist nature of APIs, the previously mentioned shame and stigma is also associated with the cultural values that stress not sharing personal problems outside of the family (Atkinson and Gim, 1989; Dhooper and Moore, 2001). Due to the interdependent nature of APIs, what affects one individual ultimately affects all others associated with the person. Thus, individuals are reluctant to admit to the need for social services or any outside help, saving the family from shame and embarrassment. Many times, unless the problems are causing overt problems, the family will minimize or deny its existence (Ho, 1992). For example, James, Kim, and Moore (1997) found that in API families with substance-abusing adolescents were inclined to deny any problems and seek help until it became a serious drug problem. Moreover, in cases of child sexual abuse, many times API children will recant their allegations on account of filial piety and the pressure to sacrifice individual need for the needs of the family, which include saving family integrity (Okamura, Heras, and Wong-Kerberg, 1995). Both of these findings are consistent with trends that APIs delay treatment and the low rates of service utilization.

With respect to interpersonal relationships, admitting to having problems is seen as a disgrace as having harmonious relationships is a key Asian cultural value; this is particularly true for parent–child relationships where respect and deference are core values (Ho, 1992). Paradoxically, Abe-Kim, Takeuchi, and Hwang (2002) found that family conflict often precipitated seeking mental health services; in other words, a primary reason why individuals sought mental health services was due to family conflict. This contradiction highlights the extreme weight placed on the role of family, serving as a great source of both strength and strain. The roles and expectations within the family often place a strain on the individual, specifically when differing levels of acculturation are taken into consideration (Dhooper and Moore, 2001). Due to the important role of the family and wanting to keep problems within the family, many APIs will seek help from family members and close friends before turning to formal services (Dhooper, 1997; Ito and Maramba, 2002; Narikiyo and Kameoka, 1992; Ying, 1990; Zhang, Snowden, and Sue, 1998).

Fatalism, which is the acceptance of one's situation, is another reason why APIs do not voice their need for services and seek help. It is seen as an admirable trait to be able to endure one's suffering, seen as the path to maturity (Masaki and Wong, 1997). In addition to the value of preserving, there is the belief that the individual is powerless and not the agent of change; rather it is up to karmic fate (Dhooper and Moore, 2001). This is typically the rationale used to condone family violence, including domestic violence, in API families (Ho, 1990; Masaki and Wong, 1997). Consequently, the belief in fatalism acts as a disincentive to seeking help and changing the situation; rather, it leads to acceptance of the situation.

Barriers of Value Orientation

Differences in value orientation of services are the third barrier. The primary collectivist value orientation of APIs conflicts directly with the individualist value of American culture. As mentioned earlier, APIs traditionally hold collectivistic values and the emphasis is on the interests of the group, even if this means self-sacrifice of personal goals and interest (Green, 1999). The API family, not the individual, is viewed as the basic unit (Dhooper and Moore, 2001). This is in sharp contrast to Western culture, and much of Western therapy, which focuses on individualism and autonomy.

Another value difference is the level of expressiveness and communication expected in therapeutic relationships. While traditional therapeutic orientations place a high value of verbal communication, this can be difficult for APIs who are more verbally inhibited and tend to rely more on nonverbal cues to convey their thoughts and feelings (Uba, 1994). The APIs often are not comfortable straightforwardly stating their problems; therefore, will only hint at it or bring it up indirectly (Dhooper and Moore, 2001). Rather than directly stating that the person is uncomfortable with a topic, an individual may look down to the floor and not respond. This can be misinterpreted as a language barrier, and thus, the social worker may simply repeat the question, rather than recognize what the individual is trying to communicate. Not wanting to dominate the conversation is another reason for the lack of verbal expressiveness (Uba, 1994); this can be especially problematic in group counseling sessions where APIs do not want to contribute in fear of preventing another member from speaking. Finally, this lack of verbal communication may also be related to the value placed on deference to authority; there is an effort to be deferential and respectful to the mental health professional (Uba, 1994).

Physical and Structural Barriers

Physical and structural barriers are related to social class, such as lack of awareness of services and inaccessibility of services. Socioeconomic factors are not limited to APIs alone, as they affect many individuals within the lower classes. Factors range from not being able to get to services due to lack of child care, transportation, or not having the time off from work, to not being able to afford services and lack adequate insurance coverage (Abe-Kim, Takeuchi and Hwang, 2002; Leong and Lau, 2001).

Many APIs do not feel comfortable with the American social service system. Much of the lack of information about available services is due to the lack of culturally appropriate outreach to API communities, such as limited outreach programs through appropriate avenues (e.g., ethnic papers and television shows) (Uba, 1994).

Language barriers and lack of proficiency in the English language compound this underutilization (Sue and Morishima, 1982; Uba, 1994). Language difficulties extend beyond accessing services, such as learning about services and correctly filling out necessary forms. Leong and Lau (2001) caution that individuals may appear to be more withdrawn or disturbed when unable to communicate in their native language. Asian Americans stay in services longer and believe it is more effective when the counselor and the client speak the same language (Leong, 1986; Sue and Morishima, 1982). With respect to Asian American parents endorsing mental health services for their children, language difficulties present as a barrier in seeking services for their children (Yeh et al., 2003). This was true even after controlling for level of parent's acculturation, suggesting that older adults feel less comfortable with the English language, regardless of the number of years in the States.

In addition to the structural barriers, there is a general mistrust of social services and law enforcement within the API community (Cheung and Snowden, 1990; Ho, 1990). This is particularly true for refugees who have a deep distrust of government officials due to experiences they had in their native land where there was a great degree of corruption (Dhooper and Moore, 2001). Immigrants must also deal with their immigration status and those consequences. There is fear of discrimination and lack of confidentiality, which may lead to their deportation (Uba, 1994). In their study of abused Asian immigrant women, Bauer and Colleagues (2000) found that one of the pertinent barriers to seeking help at a local community-based organization was the fear of discrimination and deportation. The women believed that if they sought assistance, they would be reported to immigration authorities; therefore, they felt trapped in their abusive relationships. Additionally, issues of social isolation and language difficulties were identified as barriers to seeking help, both related to the lack of knowledge about social services, not only where to go but what services are offered.

Finally, utilization rates are often measured through demographic studies, and unfortunately, APIs are often ignored or collapsed with other minority groups as "other" in large national surveys (e.g., National Institute on Drug Abuse), thus their utilization and treatment numbers are not accurately represented (Ja and Yuen, 1997). And, as there is an unfortunate absence of Asian Americans epidemiological studies, Asian American utilization rates may be underrepresented (Abe-Kim, Takeuchi, and Hwang, 2002; Herrick and Brown, 1998; Uba, 1994).

IMPACT OF ACCULTURATION ON SERVICE UTILIZATION

Similar to the ethnic diversity within the Asian American population, the differences in level of acculturation must be taken into consideration. Typical problems that arise at the individual and family levels may be due to differences in acculturation. Acculturation refers to changes in an individual's or group's cultural attitudes, values, and behaviors that result from contact between two distinct cultures (i.e., Asian and American cultures) (Berry, Trimble, and Olmedo, 1986). While acculturation is a two-way process, as both the minority and the majority group may change over time, it typically refers to the ethnic minority group adapting to the majority group's culture (Graves, 1967). Acculturation has a unique role in mental health services as it is related to both the receptivity of seeking mental health services and the reason for seeking mental health services.

Acculturation is one of the major influences determining how receptive Asian Americans will be to mental health services. As the level of acculturation increases, so does the level of amenability to seeking mainstream mental health services and tolerance to the stigma of those services (Leong, Wagner, and Kim, 1995; Suinn, Ahuna, and Khoo, 1992; Suinn et al., 1987; Ying and Miller, 1992; Zhang and Dixon, 2003). Narikiyo and Kameoka (1992) found that as Asian Americans became more acculturated, there were less pronounced differences in help-seeking behaviors and attitudes from their European American counterparts. Sociodemographic factors (e.g., education and income) which are correlated with the individual's level of acculturation, are also associated with help-seeking behaviors (Abe-Kim, Takeuchi, and Hwang, 2002). Individuals with higher socioeconomic status are more likely to be able to afford services and/or have adequate insurance coverage. However, even after controlling sociodemographic factors, Kim & Omizo (2003) found that the weaker adherence there was to Asian cultural values, the more likely Asian Americans will seek mental health services. In other words, while sociodemographic factors may be an important consideration in help-seeking behaviors, more important are the cultural values towards seeking mental health services. However, complete dismissal of Asian cultural values is not necessary to be receptive to services. Leong, Wagner, and Kim (1995) found that of the four modes of Berry's (1980) bi-dimensional acculturation model, Asian Americans who were integrationists were most likely to believe in mental health services. Integration, as opposed to assimilation, separation, or marginalization, refers to the maintenance of an individual's own cultural heritage while also adopting the views of the mainstream culture. Assimilation is the sole adoption of mainstream culture while relinquishing the heritage culture. Separation is the maintenance of only the heritage culture and remaining segregated from the mainstream culture. And, marginalization occurs when the individual is not connected with either the heritage culture or the mainstream society.

As lack of knowledge about the services is one reason for underutilization, Ying and Miller (1992) reported that level of acculturation was correlated to seeking and understanding the purpose of mental health services; Chinese Americans who were less acculturated were the most in need of education about the utility of mental health services. Acculturation is also related to the likelihood of recognizing the personal need for professional mental health help. Once in therapy, acculturation is positively associated with being more open to discussing problems with a therapist (Atkinson and Gim, 1989) and having greater confidence in the mental health practitioner (Gim, Atkinson, and Kim, 1991; Zhang and Dixon, 2003).

Acculturation also affects help-seeking behaviors. For less acculturated API Americans, the help-seeking process can typically be delineated into four stages (Shin, 2002; Zhang, Snowden, and Sue, 1998). The first stage is characterized by self-reliance (Narikiyo and Kameoka, 1992), and then if that does not work, they seek help from family and friends (Akutsu, Snowden, and Organista, 1996). The third stage includes informal service providers, such as spiritual healers or religious leaders (Sue and Morishima, 1982). And then finally, Asian Americans turn to formal service providers, first medical professionals and then finally mental health professionals (Shin, 2002).

ISSUES OF CULTURAL COMPETENCE

Prior to discussing which specific interventions are culturally appropriate and ethnic sensitive for the API population, it is necessary to define cultural competence and the importance of its application. While there are many working definitions of cultural competence, it generally involves three interrelated areas: cultural awareness, knowledge acquisition, and skill development (Green, 1999; Lum, 2003; Miley, O'Melia, and DuBois, 2004). Cultural awareness involves not only self-awareness on behalf of the social worker, including recognition of individual racism and prejudices, but the awareness of the cultures of others. The knowledge of other cultures and their values may be systematically acquired through practice experience and discussions with multicultural clients, as well as through literature reviews and textbook learning. Another way of gaining culturally appropriate knowledge could include the consultation of "gatekeepers," who often have the power to grant access to key individuals such as community leaders, spiritual leaders, or indigenous healers (Green, 1999; Herrick and Brown, 1998). Possessing knowledge of another culture goes beyond factual information, such as the group's demographics and sociohistorical context; it includes the understanding expression of tone and affect, such as demeanor and facial expressions, and the predetermined roles of various individuals (Green, 1999). Skill development is the process of enhancing the culturally sensitive and appropriate interventions that match the identified cultural values of the group (Lum, 2003). The culturally competent social worker is engaged in continuous and lifelong learning of all three areas.

Green (1999) warns against the misconception that working with a particular community for a lengthy period of time makes one a self-prescribed expert on the culture and a participating member of the client community. Many professionals may spend years working with a community that they do not truly understand and "their longevity is sometimes used as justification for flawed judgments and even obvious prejudices" (Green, 1999, p. 99). Rather than being able to achieve a final state of cultural competence, learning about another culture is a lifelong process with the continual awareness of one's partial understanding of another culture being the goal (Dean, 2001). There is a necessary paradoxical combination of "being informed and not knowing simultaneously" in order to acquire and maintain cultural competence (ibid., p. 628).

Culturally Competent Practice with API Children and Families

When applying the term "cultural competence" to working with API Americans, Fong (2003) adds the knowledge of indigenous interventions and a critique of Western interventions that contradict or detract from the traditional cultural values. Atkinson and Gim (1989) clarify that while underutilization of services is related to conflict between Asian cultural values and the psychotherapy process, premature termination is related to the inadequacies of how the services are provided. Most services inadequately meet the needs of the population by not being consistent with many of the aforementioned Asian values (Cheung and Snowden, 1990; Cho, 1998; Uba, 1994). Conflict may occur when there are discrepancies between the workers' and the clients' expectations of the treatment and function of involved parties. For example, deeply ingrained in the Eastern culture is the significance of the family, which goes against the individualism of Western culture. Whereas Western professionals may view a family's involvement as unnecessary, intrusive, and even pathological, exclusion of the family can pose an even larger problem for APIs (Lin and Cheung, 1999). In fact, family members frequently assume that it is their responsibility to remain with the individual when meeting with mental health professionals (Lin and Cheung, 1999). This often goes against concerns of confidentiality with Western mental health professionals. When working with children, it is important to be sensitive to the child's fear of isolation from the family and to treat API children with their families. Futa, Hsu, and Hansen (2001) highlight the complications and contradictions in treatment that the importance of the family role may present. As mentioned earlier, due to the probability of children recanting their allegations of sexual abuse, particularly when the perpetrator is a family member, having a family member present may increase the likelihood that recanting may occur. However, having a family member there may also help alleviate fears of rejection from the family and will serve to encourage the child's decision to seek help.

The gap between clients' needs and clients' services can be alleviated by developing and training social workers of culturally sensitive interventions. Culturally sensitive practice, which is the union of theory and action, is achieved through the application of cultural competent knowledge and skills to interventions that are specific to and appropriate for a circumscribed group. Culturally sensitive practice involves an understanding of the group's philosophical, contextual, and experiential domains (James and Prilleltensky, 2001). This may include an understanding of the sociopolitical history of the group's immigration. For example, the Chinese history of immigration dates back to the Gold Rush of 1849 as sojourners with the intention of returning to China, whereas Cambodians are a recent group who in the mid-1980s came to the United States as refugees from a war-torn country with no possibility of return (Kitano and Daniels, 2001).

Not only do the various Asian ethnic groups share common values, they share the unique experience of being a minority in the United States where there is some universal discrimination and prejudice. Goto, Gee, and Takeuchi (2002) found one in five Chinese Americans experienced discrimination based on race, ethnicity, language, or accent and that 43 percent of that occurred within the past year. Additionally, Asian Americans face issues of social and institutional racism that are unique to them. Due to their physical appearance, lifestyles, and values, Asian Americans are frequently perceived as "perpetual foreigners" (Dhooper and Moore, 2001; Goto, Gee, and Takeuchi, 2002). In addition to U.S.-born Asian often being told they "speak English so well," they are frequently asked where they are *really* from (when answering "Where is your family from?" with "Los Angeles," they are asked again "No, where is your family really/originally from?"). Omi (1993) argues that Asian Americans are not only targets of institutional racism, but are often scapegoats of discrimination by other minority groups. In their study of high-school students, Rosenbloom and Way (2004) reported that because the teachers preferred Asian American students to African American and Latino adolescents, the latter groups resented that teacher bias and thus harassed the Asian American students. This preference was based on "model minority" beliefs, which portrays Asian Americans as "well-behaved, diligent high achievers who persevere and are educationally successful despite socioeconomic and linguistic obstacles" (Hune and Chan, 1997, p. 44). Labeled as the "model minority," Asian Americans are often resented for the educational and economic success the groups have achieved and there is less tolerance when Asian Americans do experience discrimination (Delucchi and Do, 1996). Furthermore, as the "model minority," Asian Americans are expected to remain resilient and immune from emotional breakdown and behavioral problems and thus no treatment is necessary, let alone culturally sensitive treatment (Lin and Cheung, 1999; Sue and Morishima, 1982). However, there is evidence that Asian Americans have comparable, if not higher, rates of mental health problems (Uba, 1994). And the rates of high risk behaviors, such as suicide, school dropout, juvenile delinquency, and gang involvement, have been increasing at an alarming rate for API adolescents (Ja and Yuen, 1997; Liu et al., 1990). Mercado (2000) reports from the Asian American Residential Recovery Services survey that there is a growing trend of substance abuse among APIs, with cocaine use rising from 20.2 to 70.3 percent. The rates are compounded by the fact that APIs often delay treatment (Lin et al., 1982; Shin, 2002) thus, by the time they do enter treatment, they have a greater degree of disturbance, including a more severe diagnosis, lower rating of functioning, and greater presence of psychotic features (Akutsu, Snowden, and Organista, 1996; Durvasula and Sue, 1996) and require longer hospitalization or outpatient care (Lin and Cheung, 1999).

ETHNIC-SPECIFIC PROGRAMS

One way of achieving culturally sensitive interventions is to utilize an ethnic-specific program, in which the providers are members of a similar ethnic group to the clients (Takeuchi, Sue, and Yeh, 1995). The rationale for this matching goes beyond speaking the same language; there is the belief that the staff and client will have shared similar cultural values and interpersonal communication skills. Ethnic-specific programs—which serve to reduce the abovementioned four barriers: cognitive, affective, value-orientation, and physical and structural—also offer other benefits that make the individual feel more comfortable, such as being located within the ethnic community and having announcements written in the ethnic language. Murase (1977) identified structural and organizational characteristics that facilitate the development of an ethnic-specific program for the API community: (1) location of delivery site within the community itself; (2) involvement of broad cross-section of community in decision making about service programs; (3) employment of bilingual and bicultural staff; (4) cultivation and utilization of existing indigenous formal and informal community support systems; and (5) development of innovative intervention methods. Ethnic-specific programs serve to provide a stronger fit with the sociocultural and community life context of the ethnic clients. For example, some clients may use the agency as a central meeting place even when they do not have an appointment and may celebrate certain Asian festivals, such as the Chinese Moon Festival (Ito and Maramba, 2002).

These ethnic-specific programs have been shown to not only increase utilization and retention rates, but to improve service outcomes (Takeuchi, Sue, and Yeh, 1995; Yeh, Takeuchi and Sue, 1994). Asian Americans who entered ethnic-specific programs were nearly fifteen times more likely to return after the first session than those in mainstream programs (Takeuchi, Sue, and Yeh, 1995). However, both Takeuchi, Sue, and Yeh (1995) and Yeh, Takeuchi, and Sue (1994) reported that clients entering ethnic-specific programs had higher scores of functioning on the Global Assessment Scale upon entering treatment; thus, it is possible that Asian Americans and their families may be more receptive to seeking services early from ethnic-specific programs, as compared to mainstream programs, where there may be numerous barriers preventing Asian Americans from entering services until there is a greater degree of disturbance. This is consistent with previous findings that Asian Americans often delay treatment (Lin et al., 1982; Shin, 2002) and that by the time they do enter treatment, they have a more severe diagnosis, lower rating of functioning, and greater presence of psychotic features (Akutsu, Snowden, and Organista, 1996; Durvasula and Sue, 1996). Then again, even after controlling for pretreatment severity and diagnosis, Lau and Zane (2000) found a better treatment outcome for Asian Americans enrolled in ethnic-specific programs as compared to those in mainstream programs. Nonetheless, those clients in ethnic-specific programs used significantly less crisis intervention services than those in mainstream programs and were more likely to use individual therapy, suggesting again that Asian Americans were more comfortable going to ethnic-specific programs and not delay treatment.

Ito and Maramba (2002) argue that ethnic-specific programs are more than a simple bilingual/bicultural matching of client and counselor and that previous studies, while do measure outcomes, fail to identify what specific therapeutic elements distinguish ethnic-specific programs from their mainstream counterparts. Ito and Maramba (2002) delineate three areas germane to increasing cultural competency with the Asian American population: baseline cultural match, beliefs about treatment, and the therapeutic relationship. The baseline cultural match refers to the structural and organizational characteristics mentioned above; matching of culture, including the provision of a comfortable cultural environment, and language, verbal and nonverbal communication. Beliefs about treatment refer to treatment modifications that must be made in order to accommodate clients' beliefs about the rationale behind and goals of treatment. There needs to be a constant negotiation of goals and the types of services provided (Ito and Maramba, 2002). For instance, due to the shame and stigma associated with a mental illness, rather than insist on the client admit to a mental illness, one avenue is to reframe the problem by emphasizing the social and practical aspects. These accommodations, which are based on the cultural values of the client and client's family, help foster the therapeutic relationship and incur a deeper level of trust. Finally, regarding the therapeutic relationship, there is also a unique negotiation that mental health professionals must have with their Asian American clients. Deviating from the conventional Western view of the therapeutic relationship with clear boundaries, in addition to viewing mental health professionals as authority figures, Asian Americans will often try to form friendly relationships with their therapists, inviting them to family and even asking for their home telephone number (ibid.). Seemingly contradictory, this is a complementary relationship in that within the social hierarchy of Asian Americans, authority figures are often treated like family. Hence, many counselors must consider the level of formality within the therapeutic relationship and find an interpersonal and professional balance. More than an enumeration of specific characteristics, ethnic-specific programs provide culturally competent services by managing the constant negotiation between client and mental health professional and the type of services expected and provided.

OVERARCHING INTERVENTION PERSPECTIVES

In order to effectively practice culturally competent services, it is important to link culturally competent knowledge with theoretical perspectives in order to build the partnership between knowledge and practice. Theoretical perspectives help provide a backbone to assess and determine behavior and which practice experience can build upon. This holistic approach of integrating the educational process with practice experience also helps the connection between the two become clearer. There are numerous perspectives that are prevalent in the field of child welfare when working with children and their families; however, this chapter serves to highlight the selected perspectives (generalist, strengths, and empowerment) that lend themselves well to being applied to the API population.

Generalist Perspective

The generalist perspective focuses on the interaction between the multiple systems with multiple interventions. The interventions span the individual, family, group, organizational, community, and societal level. The generalist perspective "reflects the evolutionary response over the past century to societal concerns and needs and to events and thinking" (Johnson, 1992, p. 33) as it is grounded in social systems theory and then later influenced by the ecological approach. Developed in the 1970s, it was a response to the realization that clients had complex problems and needed an integrated solution, rather than the current singular intervention at the individual, group, or community level (Johnson, 1992). The generalist has a wide range of knowledge and skills that will target the intervention at the microlevel, mezzolevel, and macrolevel; it is the usage of multiple integrated methods at multiple levels (Devore and Schlesinger, 1999).

The cornerstone of the generalist perspective is the systems/ecological framework, which involves determining the fit between the individuals and their environment (Ambrosino et al., 2001). This systems/ecological framework is useful in looking at how an intervention may be formed at the various levels by identifying the different issues at those levels. Generalist practice involves working with multiple individual and systemic demands. A social worker has been working with Sue, a middle-school student, and comes to learn that Sue's parents are in the middle of a divorce and her dad is suicidal. Sue's attendance at school is becoming poor and her grades are dropping rapidly. The generalist social worker would respond to Sue's needs with an intervention(s) that takes into consideration her family situation, including extended family support, friends, the school system, and other formal institutional systems, such as medical services for dad. Generalist practice often requires directing simultaneous attention to different needs and systems. The generalist framework is concerned not only with the individual problems, but also with identifying the social problems that may play a contributing role to those problems. Thus, it is possible for the generalist approach to be used in various settings.

The client is looked at as a multidimensional system consisting of the client, the family and friends, and local and global community (Derezotes, 2000). And, the social worker is also considered in a system of the agency and the community. When looking at the social environment, acknowledging the unique issues that may face a person due to being a racial minority is essential to applying cross-cultural sensitivity to the generalist model. Asian Americans still face a great deal of discrimination and often suffer from institutional racism (Dhooper and Moore, 2001). This inequity is compounded by the fact that many Asian Americans do not trust the police and government officials; this is true for refugees (i.e., Vietnamese) as well as those who have been Americans for generations, but whose families who may have been in the United States for several generations but have a poor history with the American government (i.e., internment of the Japanese Americans during World War I) (Kitano and Daniels, 2001). And to further complicate matters, it may not be uncommon for Asian Americans to use denial as a defense mechanism against the fact that they have experienced any racism (Dhooper and Moore, 2001).

Strengths Perspective

Though the strengths perspective is one that today appears synonymous with the field of social work, it is a dramatic departure from the conventional foundation of social work practice (Saleeby, 2002). The charity organizations in the mid-nineteenth century marked the beginning of social work practice, the focus was on how to make the individual fit better into the environment. Friendly visitors were used as role models to guide and rehabilitate people in need, usually immigrants, and problems were viewed as personal weaknesses, such as laziness and other moral deficiencies (Ambrosino et al., 2001). In sharp contrast, the strengths perspective is predicated on identifying the individual's strengths in order to maximize the fit between the person and the environment. And unlike the earlier hierarchical relationship between client and friendly visitor, the relationship between social worker and client depends on collaboration, in which both work together to identify the client's strengths and resources. There is a systematic assessment of the client's skills, knowledge, and resources in order to help the client achieve his goals.

A related concept linked to the strengths perspective is the concept of empowerment. Empowerment, which is both a process and a goal, involves helping clients discover their resources, both personal and environmental, to better serve them and become self-sufficient. In the process of empowering a client, a social worker may help the client with the decision-making process rather than make those decisions. There is inherent belief that clients are their own agents of change and are capable of making the right decisions for themselves; hence, the role of the social worker is to nurture and promote those capabilities (Cowger and Snively, 1999).

Another one of the key terms in discussing the strengths perspective is resilience. Resilience refers to the ability to respond to adversity by recovering quickly and completely to misfortunes and challenges (Kahn and Juster, 2002). While there is the aptitude to rebound from barriers or stressful experiences, this is not a naïve or cheerful disregard of traumatic life experiences. Resilience, like empowerment, is a process that includes adapting to the environmental stressors through continued growth and articulation of abilities (Saleeby, 2002).

There are several guiding principles to the strengths perspective, each focusing on encouraging the client to recognize and develop his own strengths, and building off the two key terms of "empowerment" and "resilience." The first is to realize that every client system, whether it is the individual, family, group, or community possesses strengths and it is a dangerous assumption for social workers to believe they know the parameters of their client's abilities (ibid.). In order to identify these strengths and aspirations, it is essential that the social worker listen to the client's stories and interpretations of life events. Only the clients truly understand how they have to preserve in their life and manage to survive their circumstances and they deserve the worker's acknowledgement and respect.

In addition to the individual client's strengths, the environment offers many resources to draw upon. Saleeby (2002) warns that though the strengths perspective appears simple in theory, it is much harder in practice. Social workers are not immune to looking at clients from a disease- and disorder-based perspective since clients become clients when they are in need of some sort of assistance and their weaknesses— whether they are behavioral, emotional, or physical—are emphasized. Furthermore, it is often easier to look at individual deficiencies as there is the misguided belief that by identifying the cause for any disorder, the solution to the problem simply follows. In other words, in working with a client who is at the risk of getting fired since she consistently shows up late, identification of her weaknesses or lack of resources includes lack of dependable childcare. By seeking out why she does not have dependable childcare, lack of family support and financial means may come up; however, neither of these leads to an appropriate solution to her problem.

A strengths perspective provides opportunities where individuals can display strengths, learn from past experiences, and display new strengths (Early and GlenMaye, 2000). One way of identifying strengths is to do a 'strengths assessment.' Early and GlenMaye (2000) have applied this 'strengths assessment' to families in the recognition that the family is the primary environment for the child.

Empowerment Perspective

The empowerment perspective views the connection between personal and public issues and is simultaneously concerned for individuals and their environment (Devore and Schlesinger, 1999). This approach builds upon the previously mentioned strengths perspective by incorporating all the individual's strengths while considering the environmental constraints. It aims to reduce the powerlessness that is created by those constraints and negative evaluations of certain groups (Solomon, 1976). Guided by the unifying principle that there is a two-way relationship between personal and political levels of empowerment, it is the linking of individual strengths to proactive behavior that will lead to not only individual change, but social change as well (Zimmerman and Rappaport, 1988). An equally important component to empowerment is that of psychological empowerment, wherein individuals believe in their ability to take control of their lives and actively participate in their environment (Zimmerman and Rappaport, 1988).

The empowerment approach is grounded in the ecological perspective, which focuses on the interdependence and reciprocal transactions of living and nonliving systems (Lee, 1996). (The ecological perspective: Bronfenbrenner's ecological model.) One of the considerations is the "goodness of fit" between individuals and their environments. "Goodness of fit" refers to the match between the person and the environment, how well the individual functions in his environment. "By definition, poor people and oppressed groups seldom have this 'fit,' as injustice stifles human potential" (Lee, 1996, p. 220). Therefore, the empowerment approach focuses on altering that power structure to rectify that injustice.

Simon (1994) identified five elements to the empowerment approach: (1) construction of collaborative partnerships with clients; (2) the emphasis on their strengths; (3) focus on both individuals and their physical and social environment; (4) recognition of their rights, responsibilities, and needs, and (5) the direction of professional energies toward helping disempowered individuals and groups. The empowerment model has two primary objectives: to achieve a more equitable distribution of resources and to enable people to achieve a sense of power through self-respect, confidence, knowledge, and skills.

Lee (1996) describes five perspectives that need to be taken into consideration when applying the empowerment approach to practice. The first is the historical perspective which is learning about the group's history of oppression, including looking at related social policy. The second is the ecological perspective and identifying individuals' coping strategies and how they function in their environment. The next two perspectives are related as they refer to considering minority status: ethclass and feminist perspectives. Both identify how ethnicity, race, class, and gender dictate "ceilings and lowering floors" and how these affect the individual's fit with the environment (Lee, 1996, p. 220). Finally, the critical perspective lends the lens of analyzing the status quo.

The empowered community is made up of individuals and organizations that unify their skills and resources together to provide support for one another through a mutually dependent relationship (Israel et al., 1994). Thus, one of the most central concepts related to the empowerment approach is the recognition of the community and the importance of both individual and collective empowerment. Too often there is an emphasis on individual autonomy without reference to the important role of the community (Riger, 1993). This concept goes alongside the ecological model in which the person must be taken into consideration with the environment.

Querimit and Conner (2003) argue that while most empowerment models promote well-being at the individual, psychological, and community levels, there is rarely a consideration of race and how to apply the empowerment model specifically with youth of color. They propose that through the incorporation and validation of race issues, empowerment will be fostered and the assets of youth can be built and strengthened. There is a need to confront and educate clients about issues of racism and ethnocentrism that they may face at an individual and a community level, including racist remarks and institutionalized racism. In other words, clients may need assistance in recognizing the strengths they possess despite the racism that they face. In addition to the education, child welfare professionals, who often serve as role models, must perform appropriate acts of individual and community activism by speaking out against such discrimination. While recognizing strengths, it is essential that those strengths are socially and culturally compatible.

RELEVANT TREATMENT MODELS

Psychosocial Approach

Social work is most commonly aligned with the psychosocial approach and its concepts. The psychosocial approach integrates the idea that individuals are both psychological and sociological beings (Devore and Schlesinger, 1999). That individuals are self-contained entities that are not impacted by other forces is false, rather individuals are influenced by not only internal processes but also external processes. Furthermore, there is a bidirectional relationship between the two. There is an emphasis on the influence of biological factors, internal psychological processes, external social and physical conditions, and the relationship between these factors. The focus is on the intrapersonal, interpersonal, and intersystem and the historical issues that may help to shape these current dynamics (Turner, 1974). Thus, all individuals have the ability to shape their own lives and it is through their relationships with their families, friends, and community that they reach their potential.

Psychosocial treatment and intervention are not always aimed at the "pathological" or "dysfunctional" aspects of the individual's life, but rather are focused on aspects that are most accessible and capable of change (Woods and Robinson, 1996). Similar to the systems approach, the belief is that change in one part of the individual's life will inevitably bring subsequent change to another aspect, as the systems interact with one another. For example, a father who is unhappy at work may bring his troubles home through his relationship with his children. Thus, he can possibly reduce this family tension by focusing on alleviating what is wrong at work. However, in comparison to the systems approach, the emphasis in the psychosocial approach is that individuals are governed by their past.

Typically, Asian Americans do not seek psychotherapy; they have a difficult time with traditional psychodynamic therapies because of the conflict in values between the Asian culture and Western values that are typically present in psychotherapy, such as self-disclosure, seeking help from those outside the family, and verbal catharsis

(Atkinson and Gim, 1989; Sue and Sue, 1990). One of the core concepts of Western psychotherapy is the concept of expression of emotion (verbal catharsis). The individual must be able to accurately identify and express any felt emotions. Many Asian Americans, however, find verbal catharsis to be not only socially unacceptable, but counterproductive for they believe it actually creates disharmony. Psychotherapy also focuses on internal sources of distress and psychological understanding of behavior. Asian Americans typically have a difficult time with the psychiatric dynamics and psychological explanations of human behavior (Dhooper and Moore, 2001). There is a preference to therapies that focus on external sources of stress and immediate techniques that manage practical problems, rather than comprehensive and exhaustive discussions of the problem (Uba, 1994).

Since much of the traditional psychosocial approach runs counter to Asian values, it is important to adapt it to make this approach culturally sensitive. An important point to begin with is educating the client about the psychosocial approach and the nature of therapy, while also taking into consideration the specific values of the group. The psychosocial approach is dependent on the relationship between the worker and the client. This involves an agreement of the problems and its source and the client's goals and motivations; and from this agreement, an intervention is planned. The emphasis of the relationship is on collaboration. However, as mentioned earlier, Asian culture promotes hierarchical relationships and Asian American clients feel better if the therapist has an authoritative position, rather than one of egalitarianism. There is the capability to maintaining a position of authority that is nonhierarchical that is a middle ground between being directive and supporting the individual's autonomy (Diaz, 2002). Correspondingly, a key value of the psychosocial approach is that of self-determination. This value runs counter to that of Asian Americans, in which there is respect for the authority figure and expectation that the person in a higher status takes the lead. It is, therefore, important to explain to Asian American clients that there is some expectation of clients making their own decisions and that the less the worker does to direct their actions, the more likely these autonomous decisions will make the person feel more competent and independent (Woods and Robinson, 1996). It is equally important that the social worker understand the client's position and thus a culturally sensitive approach may include the worker guiding the client in making the decisions. It is possible to guide the client in an uncontrolling and nonjudgmental manner and explain to the client that active involvement in the treatment process will increase the likelihood that the change will not only occur, but endure. As the client begins to understand the treatment process and becomes more active, the social worker may alter the process to accommodate the client's values and needs. Ito and Maramba (2002) found that when culturally competent therapists attempted to educate their clients about the therapeutic process, it was actually the therapists who adjusted their practices to the clients and their families. This aided in building trust between the therapists and the clients and establishing a long-term working alliance.

In addition to looking at the role of the therapist, another point of consideration is the role of the family. For many Asian Americans, the family plays a significant role in decision making and should be included in the treatment process (Ito and Maramba, 2002). Whereas the Western culture focuses on independence and autonomy, the Eastern culture focuses on goals of interdependence (Markus and Kitayama, 1991).

This is important as this can easily be misconstrued as overly dependent on the family by the Western culture, especially if the client is an adult. However, in the Eastern culture, understanding the impact of one's decision on the family and taking the family into consideration is seen as a sign of maturity.

CULTURE-SPECIFIC CHILD WELFARE PRACTICE GUIDELINES

Ho (1992) emphasizes that competent service to ethnic minority children should be (1) multidimensional, that is, working with individuals, families, groups, organizations, and the larger community in the child's environment; (2) multidisciplinary, involving professionals and community leaders from a variety of fields and disciplines; and (3) multimodal, providing a combination of both individual, family, and group treatments and macrolevel interventions seeking changes in child welfare programs and policies. The following cases selected from various API subgroups illustrate a wide range of psychosocial issues and problems experienced by API children and families. Specific practice guidelines for use in multidisciplinary child welfare settings are presented within an overarching framework of generalist, empowerment, and strengths perspectives with a special emphasis on the client's problem-solving process.

CASE STUDY 1   JI-HOON K. (KOREAN AMERICAN)

Ji-Hoon, a 16-year-old Korean American male student who came to America at the age of 5 with his parents, was referred to an Asian American counseling center because of his aggressive behaviors toward his peers, frequent truancy, and rapid deterioration in school performance. Ji-Hoon's recent involvement in physical fights after school was the catalyst for the referral. The school psychologist who made the initial contact to his parents had difficulty reaching them due to their long work schedules. Another challenge for the school psychologist in her attempt to communicate with his parents was their lack of fluency in English.

At the initial assessment, his therapist has learned that on occasion, Ji-Hoon's father has been physically and verbally aggressive toward his son. Recently, Ji-Hoon had difficulty concentrating on his study at school and began to lose interest in both academic and extracurricular activities. Ji-Hoon began to lie to his parents about his school performance for fear of disappointing his parents regarding his underachievement and being shamed by his parents, his father in particular. Eventually, his parents discovered that Ji-Hoon, former straight A student, was getting mostly Bs, Cs, and even a couple of Ds. It was found that Ji-Hoon's declining academic performance greatly concerned his parents. This contradicts his father's wish for Ji-Hoon to be admitted to a prestigious university to become a future neurosurgeon. In order to accomplish that goal, Ji-Hoon's father required complete devotion to his studies in addition to developing esoteric interests such as practicing the violin at least 15 hours per week in order to improve his

(continued)

■ ■ ■ ■ ■

CASE STUDY 1   Continued

chances to gain acceptance at a first-rated college. Ji-Hoon finds himself floundering under his father's unrealistic expectations and overly strict parenting style, in which children should be seen but not heard. Ji-Hoon currently feels very depressed, worthless, and confused about who he is and what he really wants.

PRACTICE GUIDELINES

■ Individual counseling for Ji-Hoon to address his current difficulties in conjunction with treatment for the entire family may be an appropriate form of intervention for problems arising from unrealistic parental expectations, authoritarian parental attitudes, and subsequent intergenerational conflicts (Rhee, 1996). When individual therapy is provided to Ji-Hoon who reacted to an extremely distressing situation with feelings of helplessness, anger, anxiety, depression, and confusion about himself because of his parents' domineering attitudes and use of excessive shaming to reinforce their expectations, the child welfare practitioner should consider the following tasks as his primary treatment goals: (a) Relieving Ji-Hoon's overwhelming emotions by grasping his evident as well as underlying emotions accurately and empathically getting in touch with his feelings and their meanings to him. This goal will assist Ji-Hoon, who has been socialized not to discuss personal feelings or family problems with outsiders, to unburden himself of painful emotions significantly. (b) Restoring his impaired self-esteem by empowering his strengths and positive attributes as a separate individual who deserves respect and recognition. In so doing, the worker can clearly enhance his motivation and hope for the future. (c) Facilitating a process of bicultural identity development, as suggested by de Anda (1984) and Feliciano (2001). It is necessary to clarify which values Ji-Hoon feels comfortable between the two cultures, the Korean and the majority culture. The worker can assist Ji-Hoon to draw resources from both cultures to function more adaptively as an Asian American, while retaining the basic values of the Korean culture. Additionally, helping Ji-Hoon to have pride in his bicultural identity is crucial for his smooth adjustment and positive mental health (Rhee, 1996; Rhee, Chang, and Rhee, 2003).

■ It is imperative to involve Ji-Hoon and his parents together in family therapy to address the issue of a breakdown in meaningful parent–child relationships. It appears that a rigid form of patriarchal attitudes held by Ji-Hoon's father and his vertical communication styles lacking openness, combined with the father's lack of English skills, might have further exacerbated communication difficulties and family conflicts. The worker needs to guide Ji-Hoon's parents to realize that such interpersonal difficulties experienced by adolescents often undermine their positive psychosocial functioning. As mentioned previously, "openness in communication with parents" is a significant predictor of self-esteem for both Asian and Caucasian American youth (Rhee, Chang, and Rhee, 2003). As such, it is crucial for the worker to assist his parents to gain insight into the importance of the quality of communication between parents and children in promoting their son's self-esteem. Ji-Hoon's parents must learn to allow him to express his opinions and inner feelings more freely, while family treatment ultimately assists them to build more nurturing relationships without negating their cultural heritage.

■ Another task for the worker is to help this family recognize the need for adequate interpersonal boundaries, as emphasized by Minuchin (1974) in his structural model, in order for Ji-Hoon to differentiate more adaptively and to achieve an increased sense of autonomy. It is critical to help Ji-Hoon's parents better understand that overemphasis on their son's academic achievements, strict adherence to traditional values and norms, and inflexible communication styles can have damaging consequences for their son's healthy psychosocial development and success (Rhee, 1996; Rhee, Chang and Rhee, 2003).

The following case example demonstrates that child welfare practitioners should assess children's difficulties more holistically and plan generalist intervention strategies involving both microsystems and macrosystems such as individuals, families, institutions, and communities:

CASE STUDY 2   SIA A. (SAMOAN AMERICAN)

Sia, a 13-Year-old U.S.-born Samoan female, was referred to a child guidance clinic by her 7th grade school teacher, who was concerned about Sia's excessive absences, withdrawn behavior accompanied by feelings of worthlessness, occasional impulsive reactions, and a poor relationship with peers. The teacher was puzzled because Sia used to be a well-behaved student who rarely missed school assignments or activities. It was noticed recently that Sia was extremely reluctant to interact with the rest of the class or teachers.

During the initial interview, the therapist at the clinic found that Sia was much taller and well-developed than other girls in her age group. At first, Sia looked uncomfortable and was reluctant to disclose her feelings to the therapist. After a few moments when the therapist showed her genuine interest in Sia's well-being and helpful intent with an aim to establish a trust-based working relationship, Sia's response became much more spontaneous.

The therapist explored her recent changes in behavior at school and academic performance. It was found that she was greatly concerned about her physical appearance including her dark skin and strong physicality that does not conform to conventional Western standards of female beauty. Further discussion revealed that her classmates including boys often teased her with the comment that she might be an ideal candidate for the boys' football team at their middle school. Her classmates also taunted about her ethnic Samoan food that her mother prepared for her lunch. Sia felt that these ethnically charged comments were very humiliating and hurtful to her self-pride. Sia feared the stereotype that athletes were unintelligent, especially those with strong physical appearances. She was also fearful of the common stereotype that athletes of dark complexion were only suitable for rigorous contact sports such as football.

Her feelings of alienation were compounded by the fact that her foreign-educated parents were not interested in listening to her concerns and did not understand her present challenges. Lately, she was often scolded by her parents for her poor school performance. Occasionally, her mother was physically aggressive toward her.

(continued)

■ ■ ■ ■ ■

CASE STUDY 2   **Continued**

PRACTICE GUIDELINES

- It has been reported that many API children and youth tend to unfavorably compare their physical appearance with preferred Anglo norms. A cognitive therapy (CT) model emphasizes that dysfunctional thought patterns, misinformation, and mistaken beliefs are some of the major factors that contribute to adolescents' emotional difficulties (Schrodt and Fitzgerald, 1987; Weisz et al., 1987). Cognitive therapy is particularly useful in working with API children and adolescents whose personal functioning is impaired by their distorted perceptions of self-identity. In assessing an API adolescent's level of psychosocial development and functioning, a child welfare practitioner should explore the child's subjective evaluation of his/her ethnic heritage and physical appearance and its impact on the client's overall psychological adjustment. Subsequent to the multidimensional assessment based on a systems framework, if the child is found to have negative attitudes toward his/her cultural background and the way he/she looks, as portrayed in Sia's case, the worker should be proactive in helping the adolescent client gain awareness of misconceptions and self-defeating thoughts about his/her ethnicity. For example, Sia's misconceptions of her API background, which appear to have influenced her withdrawn behavior and depression, should be replaced with more realistic and functional beliefs and behaviors through appropriate cognitive restructuring interventions;
- As mentioned previously, API adolescents generally have greater difficulty in communicating with their first-generation immigrant parents than their Caucasian peers. Many of them believe that their parents are not good listeners, while immigrant parents tend to believe that their American-raised children are too insensitive to their parents' cultural expectations. Therefore, in addition to individual treatment with the adolescent alone, it is essential to see parents and children together in family therapy in order to enhance positive feedback and mutual understanding. In working with Sia's difficulties, first and foremost, it is vital to encourage Sia's parents to allow their daughter to voice her daily concerns, life experiences, and peer relationships more openly. Although children's free exchange of feelings and opinions and confrontation are discouraged in API culture, it is necessary to assist Sia's parents to understand that the open expression to a certain extent and parental encouragement and approval in return promote the growth of their children's psychosocial functioning;
- As Ho (1992) suggested, a practitioner should recognize the importance of school as a major social institution where latency-aged children and adolescents are socialized and "minority children first experience cultural conflict and behavioral adjustment problems" (p. 20). Adolescents' perceptions of racial discrimination are significant risk factors for developing psychological as well as behavioral problems such as juvenile delinquency and aggressive behaviors in this population. School settings in collaboration with community child welfare agencies need to provide a variety of programs and opportunities for cultural exposure and increased interactions among ethnically diverse students to foster tolerance and understanding of different cultures (Shrake and Rhee, 2004). In addition, it is important to consider a zero tolerance for racism and discrimination in the educational setting as a step toward a cultural diversity.

The following case example serves to illustrate using an empowerment framework to work with a Chinese American family dealing with domestic violence.

■ ■ ■ ■ ■ ▬▬▬▬▬▬▬▬▬▬▬▬▬▬▬▬▬▬▬▬▬▬▬▬▬▬▬▬▬▬▬▬▬▬▬▬▬▬▬

CASE STUDY 3   PATRICK L. (CHINESE-AMERICAN)

Patrick L., an 8-year-old, first-generation Chinese American boy, was referred to the child guidance clinic due to behavioral problems. Patrick's teacher, who made the referral, reported that Patrick, who is typically very easygoing and laid-back, has been more aggressive and short-tempered with his classmates. When his teacher tried to talk to Patrick, he denied that there were any problems at home or school and quickly changed the subject.

Patrick has an older 10-year-old brother, Michael. Both parents work full-time, and their maternal grandmother, who speaks limited English, watches the boys after school. When asked if Patrick was having problems at home, Mrs. L. did report that he was having some nightmares, but attributed it to him having academic problems at school. While meeting with the social worker, Patrick was very quiet and looked very uncomfortable, but finally Patrick disclosed that there have been instances where his father has hit both him and his mother. When asked about these allegations, Mrs. L. starting crying and said that her husband has beaten her in the past, but has not abused her or the children lately.

PRACTICE GUIDELINES

- Experiences of isolation, low self-esteem, lack of resources, and self blame are exacerbated for API women who are influenced by cultural factors that affect their experience and their relationships with others. In addition to family dynamics, API women are often more secluded from social and structural support systems as they may have less knowledge about services and furthermore, their limited English skills may also prevent them from adequately receiving services when programs have been identified (Krishnan et al., 1998; Masaki and Wong, 1997). This extreme powerlessness makes the empowerment perspective especially useful in cases of domestic and family violence.
- The empowerment perspective puts forward concrete and specific ways in which battered API women and their children can overcome their oppressive situations. The primary goals of this approach are to increase self-efficacy and develop critical consciousness into one's situation, which is related to reducing self-blame (Gutierrez, 1990). One of the most important steps is accepting the client's definition of the problem. Understanding Mrs. Liu's and John's definition of their situation and the cultural factors that must be taken into consideration is crucial in providing culturally competent services. For example, an important feature in API families is patriarchy; there is often the belief that as the head of the household, it is the husband's responsibility to discipline, which may take the form of battering (Masaki and Wong, 1997). This is underscored by the traditional views of placing the family and community before oneself. As domestic

(continued)

■ ■ ■ ■ ■

CASE STUDY 3   Continued

violence is considered shameful to the entire family, in order to preserve family honor, many API families pressure the woman to keep the abuse a secret or deny its existence (Masaki and Wong, 1997). The woman is typically blamed for precipitating family problems, and because divorce is an unacceptable phenomenon in API families, leaving is usually not an option; if she does initiates a divorce, she may be considered a 'bad mother' for the risk of leaving the children behind (Yick, 2001). These factors are important in understanding how the woman defines the situation and how it may impact her children. Many times the woman may believe that she is protecting her children by remaining in the marriage; this way the children are financially taken care of and have the benefits of a two-parent household. These factors are also important in understanding how the children view the situation. John may be struggling with the conflicting views of patriarchy and the effects of abuse, both witnessing his mother being abused and his own abuse. As both Mrs. Liu and John begin articulating their situation, they will also begin to define their goals and needs.

■ Another important step is identifying and building upon existing strengths and mobilizing additional resources (Gutierrez, 1990). This is one of the most effective techniques to get the clients involved in the process. By helping clients understand those strengths that may have helped them endure the situation, such as the steps that Mrs. Liu has taken in protecting her children from abuse, they may begin to understand their ability to make their own decisions and initiate change. She may also draw upon her strong relationship with her mother, who provides her emotional and physical support; this relationship may provide her with encouragement to seek help for her and her children. And, through resource mobilization, the client may see that the larger social structure may provide resources for the client. By meeting other women in similar situations, Mrs. Liu may form a support group and gain new "life skills," such as parenting and self-defense, and interpersonal skills, such as assertiveness and self-advocacy (Mercado, 2000). And, by using the importance of the family systems, Mrs. L. may encourage Mr. L. to seek family counseling. The empowerment framework aims to move individuals from feelings of hopelessness and helplessness to those of active change. By recognizing the strengths that they have, they will also be able to recognize that they have the ability to change their situation.

■ ■ ■ ■ ■

CASE STUDY 4   BORA VING

Bora Ving is a 15-year-old Cambodian male. The school social worker has been trying to contact his parents because of his failing grades and repeated truancy, but has not been able to reach them. Mr. Ving recently got a job as a cross-country truck driver and is frequently out of town working, leaving Bora alone with his step-mother, Mrs. Ving.

Bora often spends nights at a friend's home to avoid his stepmother, who he does not get along with.

Mr. Ving and Bora arrived to the United States 5 years ago, after spending 2 years in a refugee camp in Thailand. Bora's mother died of pneumonia in the refugee camps and Mr. Ving remarried 3 years ago. Mr. and Mrs. Ving, who spoke limited English, told the social worker that they were very frustrated with Bora. They said that Bora often disobeyed them and they blamed the American culture for Bora's delinquent behavior; they also suspected that he might be in a gang and abusing drugs.

Bora spoke openly with the social worker and said that he felt that his parents were too strict and did not understand him. He did not think that meeting with a social worker would be effective as he did not believe his parents would change.

PRACTICE GUIDELINES

- The systems approach can be very effective with the API population given the importance of the family. The systems approach identifies the individual being part of and shaped by larger systems. These systems extend beyond looking at the intergenerational relationships within the API family and assessing the adolescent's role in the family to the identification of other integral systems, such as at the peer and school systems. All of the system members are integral parts of treatment, especially the family members. While the social worker may help guide, it is chiefly up to the clients to effect change. This may be particularly effective with API families who may acknowledge the social worker as an authority figure, but feel uncomfortable seeking help from outsiders. This allows the authority figure to help provide insight into the situation, but it is ultimately dependent on the relationship between system members. Due to beliefs in filial piety and respect for elders, Mr. and Mrs. Ving may not perceive they play an integral role in Bora's actions; moreover, they assume that Bora is unilaterally responsible for achieving and maintaining harmony in the parent–child relationship. Perhaps discussion of Bora's mother will help him come to terms with his stepmother. Due to the limited expression of emotion common in API families, Bora may feel that his father never grieved the loss of his mother and remarried too quickly. The systems approach may help clients understand the perspectives of others in the systems. Bora may come to realize that his father feels obligated to support his family and does not enjoy being on the road constantly, but because of Mr. Ving's limited English, there are not many employment options. Another avenue that the systems approach may explore is the exploration of why Bora is having problems in school. Rather than assume that Bora is simply missing school to be with his friends, looking at the school system may shed some light on his problems. It turns out that Bora is too embarrassed to ask for tutoring and would rather miss class than go and feel frustrated with not understanding the material. The systems approach provides concrete interventions and shows not only how individuals are accountable for their own actions, but also how those actions may influence or be influenced by others. With this emphasis on interconnectedness and the API cultural value of interdependence, the systems approach can be very effective with this population.

CURRENT ISSUES AND DIRECTIONS
FOR THE FUTURE

The APIs represent one of the fastest growing minority groups in the United States (U.S. Census Bureau, 2003a). And, the needs of the population equal the diversity in the population itself. According to the 2000 U.S. Census, there are over twenty-five distinct ethnic Asian groups and over three-fourths (88 percent) are either foreign born themselves or have at least one foreign-born parent (U.S. Census Bureau, August, 2002). Extending beyond the differences in ethnic groups, APIs differ in their immigration status, level of acculturation, and socio-economic status. Thus, needs of the group may range from more concrete public welfare needs to the psychosocial needs of individuals and families. This chapter presented an overview of the API experience, which is highly complex and goes beyond the simple model minority stereotype. Immigrant and U.S.-born API families experience various problems, ranging from within the home, such as domestic violence, to outside of the home, such as unemployment and discrimination, all of which have a significant bearing on API children's psychological well-being. In addition to key issues, necessary cultural values and theoretical approaches have been provided.

While there is great diversity in the population and their difficulties, many Asian American families, especially immigrant Chinese, Korean, Japanese, and Vietnamese families, share relatively similar cultural backgrounds that originated from the common philosophical principles of Confucianism. There is a strong tradition of mutual support and interdependence rather than self-reliance among immediate and extended family members, emphasis on parental authority, rigid sex role and male dominance, and individual modesty and self-control. Childcare professionals should understand that many of the difficulties that API parents and their U.S.-raised children encounter are related to the adjustment difficulties and intergenerational tension, which may contribute to high rates of criminal and gang activities, running away, and substance abuse among API youths and adolescents (Furuto and Murase, 1992; Segal, 2000).

Another difficulty facing those who work with this population is the widespread underutilization of mental health and social services (Bui and Takeuchi, 1992; Chen et al., 2003; Cheung and Snowden, 1990; Sue et al., 1991; Uba and Sue, 1991; Zhang, Snowden, and Sue, 1998). However, this underutilization of services should not lead to the false assumption that there is not a need for services among the API population. Rather, we often have more to do with the lack of appropriate services and barriers to service than the lack of service need (Sue and Morishima, 1982). The four broad barriers to Asian Americans seeking and maintaining services include cognitive, affective, value orientation, and physical and structural (Leong and Lau, 2001). Therefore, one of the challenges of this population requires practitioners to work on encouraging APIs to seek services when needed by understanding and eliminating the aforementioned barriers.

Building the partnership between knowledge and practice occurs by linking culturally competent knowledge with theoretical perspectives to develop culturally sensitive interventions. This will help fill the gap between clients' needs and client services. This chapter presented three theoretical perspectives (generalist, strengths, and empowerment) and treatment models prevalent for working with children and their families and applied them specifically to the API population. As traditional theoretical approaches and interventions incorporate culturally competent knowledge, new approaches and interventions need further development to anticipate further changes as current API youth adapt to American culture and additional Asian groups immigrate to the United States.

As these changes continue to take place, there are future directions which individuals, child welfare practitioners and researchers who work with the API population need to consider. As this chapter notes the many varieties of individuals with Asian ancestry, the continual disaggregation of Asian Americans is important. The differences in national origin, historical time of immigration, age of immigration, settlement patterns, and socioeconomic status have an impact on the distinctive identity that individuals may form. This identity then has impact on the particular difficulties faced and how the individuals respond to those difficulties. In addition to examining these issues in the individual context, it is especially important to understand these issues in the context of the API family and the dynamic relationship between the two.

CHAPTER SIX

MULTICULTURAL CHILD WELFARE PRACTICE WITH LATINO CHILDREN, YOUTH, AND FAMILIES

LIRIO K. NEGRONI-RODRÍGUEZ, PH.D.
School of Social Work, University of Connecticut

GLORIA DELA CRUZ-QUIRÓZ, PH.D.
School of Social Work, California State University, Los Angeles

Latino children and their family.

OVERVIEW

Latino children and adolescents are a heterogeneous group. Some are born to immigrant or migrants and refugees and were brought to the United States and others were born and raised here and their connections to the Latino culture and history is through the previous generations. Most Latino children and youth live in different cultures and are challenged to learn how to negotiate the demands and expectations of their family's and communities' different cultural values and lifestyles. Their experiences of migration or immigration and acculturation, the different stressors confronted by their families of origin, play a vital role in how they develop intrapersonally and interpersonally and must be taken into consideration when conducting assessments and planning interventions. Different social, psychological, economic, educational, and cultural barriers threat the well-being of Latino children and youth and lead them and their families to become involved with the welfare system. Data shows that the welfare system has been unresponsive to Latino children, youth, and their families because it lacks the necessary understanding of the specific needs, pays limited attention to those needs, and has provided limited opportunities and services for them. In serving this population the use of a generalist approach can be quite helpful. Interventions must be multisystemic and multimethod and must consist of an ecological, strength-based, and culturally focused approach. This chapter provides an overview of the demographic and cultural characteristics of Latino children, youth, and their families in the United States, highlights their welfare needs and problems, and proposes multicultural interventions that promote their emotional, physical, social, and spiritual well-being and prevent them from entering or remaining for too long in the child welfare system.

INTRODUCTION

This chapter provides an overview of the demographic and cultural characteristics of Latino children, youth, and their families in the United States, highlights their welfare needs and problems, and proposes multicultural interventions that promote their emotional, physical, social, and spiritual well-being and prevent them from entering the child welfare system. For the purpose of the chapter children are individuals from birth to 18 years old.

DIVERSITY AMONG LATINOS

Latino children and adolescents are a heterogeneous population. They can be associated with Caribbean nations such as *Puerto Rico, Cuba, and the Dominican Republic,* Central American countries like *Mexico, Nicaragua, Costa Rica, Guatemala, El Salvador, Honduras,* and *Panama* and South American countries like *Venezuela, Colombia, Ecuador, Peru, Bolivia, Chile, Argentina, Paraguay, Uruguay, and Brazil.* There are different groups of Latino children and youth in the United States: for instance, those who are born to immigrant/migrants and refugees and were brought here at their early stages of life and those who have been born and raised here and their connections to the Latino culture and history is through the previous generations. Most Latino children and youth live in different cultures and are challenged to learn how to negotiate the demands and expectations of their family's and communities' different cultural values and lifestyles. Although most youth are Mexicans, Cubans, and Puerto Ricans, there is an increasing presence and participation of Latino children and youth from most Central and South American countries.

In order to understand Latino children and adolescents it is crucial to recognize the uniqueness of each of the nations they come from and/or connect with. Latinos in general share a history of Spanish colonization, similarities in their connection and adaptation to the Catholic Church, the dominance of the Spanish language, and ethnic and/or racial mixtures. Because of the above factors, they also share similar cultural values, beliefs, and traditions. However, they differ in geography, topography, specific customs, and racial and ethnic mixtures (Negroni-Rodríguez and Morales, 2002). They have different sociopolitical histories and historical ties to the United States which have affected their entrance and acceptance in this country and have created resentment, distrust, and competition among the groups (García-Prieto, 1996). Latinos' experiences of migration, immigration, and acculturation are also different. Those differences are subtle which facilitates that the groups coexist. However, the differences are too complex to be fairly and appropriately presented in any discussion without analyzing, comparing, and defining the sociopolitical context in which the cultures have evolved (García-Prieto, 1996). Latino children and adolescents may not usually see themselves as Latinos and may prefer to be identified by the national group they or their family belong to or by the group they specifically identify with. It is within such diversified reality that Latino children and adolescents are to be understood and cared for.

For decades, education and research on Latino children and youth focused on Mexicans, Cubans, and Puerto Ricans. There was little attention to other Latino groups perhaps because of their small numbers and their invisibility due to lack of economic and political power of the Latin American nations they represent. Generalizations about Latinos were made constantly without acknowledging their differences and the role that their differences played in the different issues under study. Such generalizations were also extended to children and adolescents. Experts now recognize that combining Latino groups is not appropriate and reporting research findings in the aggregate diminishes important distinctions among Latino children (Ortega, 2000).

DEMOGRAPHIC AND CULTURAL CHARACTERISTICS

Demographics

The 2002 U.S. Survey of the Population identified 37.4 million Latinos representing 13.3 percent of the total U.S. population. Mexicans accounted for 66.9 percent of the U.S. nation's Latino population followed by Central and South Americans (14.3 percent),

Puerto Ricans (8.6 percent), other Latinos (6.5 percent), and Cubans (3.7 percent) (Ramírez and De La Cruz, 2003). Puerto Ricans were not included on this count. There are approximately 4,000,000 Puerto Ricans living in Puerto Rico. Census projections indicate that by 2050 Latinos will increase to 97 million, constituting nearly one-fourth of the U.S. population (U.S. Department of Health and Human Services, 2001b).

Most Latinos reside in the West and South areas of the nation. Latinos of Mexican origin are more likely to live in the West and South while Puerto Ricans are more likely to live in the Northeast, and Cubans in the South. Dominicans are mostly concentrated in New York and New Jersey; Nicaraguans in Florida; Salvadorians and Guatemalans in California, Washington, DC, and Texas; Hondurans and Costa Ricans in the New York–New Jersey areas; Columbians, Peruvians, Ecuadorians, and Panamanians in New York and California; Argentineans more likely concentrate in the Northeast (García-Prieto, 1996); and Chileans in California.

Latinos are more geographically concentrated and more likely to live in metropolitan areas (Ramírez and De La Cruz, 2003). Latino groups are divided between U.S.-born Latinos and Latino immigrants and migrants. The term "migrant" is used to refer to Puerto Ricans who, because of ascribed U.S. citizenship, do not abide by U.S. Immigration laws. Later in the chapter the term will be used to refer to the immigrant people who work in the camps and have been traditionally called "migrant workers." By the year 2002, 40.2 percent of Latinos were foreign born and among those more than half (52.1 percent) entered the United States between 1990 and 2002 (Ramírez and De La Cruz, 2003).

In 2002 there were 12,342,259 Latino children in the United States compared to 10,885,696 African American children and 44,027,087 non-Latino white children. Latino children represented 34.4 percent of the Latino population while non-Latino white children represented only 22.8 percent of the non-Latino white population (Ramírez and De La Cruz, 2003). Most Latino children lived in the following states: California (4,050,825 or 36.9 percent of the state's Latino population), Illinois (552,310 or 36 percent of the state's Latino population), Texas (2,386,765 or 35.7 percent of the state's Latino population), Arizona (493,143 or 38 percent of the state's Latino population), New York (893,032 or 31.1 percent of the state's Latino population), and Florida (702,539 or 26.1 percent of the state's Latino population) (Annie E. Casey Foundation, 2003). With the increase of Latino children and youth it is predicted that one-third of those under 19 years of age will be Latinos by 2050 (U.S. Department of Health and Human Services, 2001b). The Latino population is very young. Latino children are now the second largest group of children in United States. They are more likely to live in large families and have extended networks (Suleiman, 2003).

Characteristics of Different Latino Groups

Mexicans. Mexico is a country that enjoys diverse geography and topographies. Mexicans are a mixed of different ethnic groups: Mayans, Aztecs, Hopis, Spaniards, and Caucasians. Part of what today is U.S. territory once belonged to Mexico. Mexicans have been in the United States since the 1600s and 1700s (García-Prieto, 1996). They have had the longest U.S. residency than any other Latino subgroup as many Mexicans remained in the United States after the United States took over large Mexican territories from Texas to California (U.S. Department of Health and Human Services, 2001b). Mexicans came in large number in the early 1900s escaping from Mexico's economic depression and the Mexican Revolution. In the early 1800s the U.S. attempted to occupy the territory known as Texas leading to the Mexican War which lasted from 1846 to 1848 and ended with Mexico loosing the territories of present-day Texas, Arizona, New Mexico, and California to the United States.

Mexican-Americans' fights on behalf of their civil rights have ended in their increased political power in many regions of the United States. There is a constant movement across the Mexican border despite the stronger protections and the lessening of job opportunities (García-Prieto, 1996). This proximity has allowed for Mexicans to make frequent visits to their country including weekend trips which is quiet common among those who live in California or Texas. The significance of this is in the preservation of one's culture and in strengthening of their family ties.

Chicanos. The Chicano generation rose out of the Mexican-American population which became a voice protesting the cruelty and injustice to Mexicans in this county, Chicanos rejected the negative stereotypes and "burst forth from the campuses and the *barrios* [neighborhoods] to stamp their presence on society by creating organizations, political movements, service centers, and artistic expression, to present a bilingual, bicultural face to the world that their parents avoided" (Hayes-Bautista, 2004, p. 7). Chicanos were a group who did not identify with the American societies' definitions of who they were and also found themselves too American to identify with Mexicans from Mexico. They have become a significant group in the history of the Mexican-American experience as they were responsible for developing this new identity as Chicanos. They became the political voice for their parents who could not voice their claims of Mexican culture out of fears, intimidations, and fears of the past history and treatment of Mexicans.

Puerto Ricans. Puerto Ricans are a racial mix of native Taínos, African slaves, and white Europeans, mostly Spaniards. Their recorded history began with its invasion in 1493 by the Spaniards who became attracted by its gold, fertile soil, and strategic location. The Spaniards severely exploited, overpowered, and finally exterminated the native population and, to maintain their colonization, imported African slaves whom they forced to work under inhuman conditions in the gold mines and farms (Wagenheim and Jiménez, 1994). The "Guerra Hispanoamericana" (Spanish American War) changed the historic trajectory of Puerto Rico. In 1898 the Treaty of Paris gave Cuba, Puerto Rico, the Philippines, and Guam to the United States. Soon the United States established a military government in the island followed by a colonial one.

The Jones Bill of 1917, which coincided with World War I, instituted a more representative government and granted U.S. citizenship to Puerto Ricans. They have citizenship but are not acknowledged as citizens. Migration to the United States began after the war and the Great Depression as Puerto Rican society itself continued to be challenged by problems of unemployment, poverty, criminality, drug abuse, political corruption, and crises in the educational system.

More than 3 million Puerto Ricans now live in the United States. There is a constant movement back and forth and a cross-pollination of customs and attitudes. The island continues to grow more urban and more technological and the culture gap with the United States is narrowing. However, Puerto Ricans still resist surrendering their culture and language.

Cubans.   Cubans are also a racial mix of native Taínos, African slaves, and Spaniards. They began to arrive to the United States after Fidel Castro won the revolution of 1959. Massive numbers of Cubans entered as refugees and were granted the privileges and benefits of such legal status. The first waves of Cubans who came to the United States were mainly white, middle class, highly educated, and business oriented. Most settled in Miami and saw themselves as "exiles waiting to return when the revolution was over" (García-Prieto, 1996, p. 148). They were able to adjust and prosper. Later waves of Cubans represented other lower socioeconomic backgrounds and were more racially mixed. Different from the first waves, the last waves of Cubans encountered the effect of racism, classism, and prejudice and have identified more with other Latino groups than with the earlier group of Cubans who "identified themselves with the Spaniards and the elite classes." (García-Prieto, 1996, p. 148)

Dominicans.   The Dominican Republic has a long history of poverty and economic devastation. It occupies two-thirds of the island of Hispaniola. It was the first colony settled by the Spaniards who soon neglected it after occupying Mexico and Cuba. The French took over the west side of Hispaniola and brought massive numbers of slaves to work in the land. The slaves eventually rebelled and proclaimed their independence. Haiti emerged as a new country. In 1844, Dominicans proclaimed their territory a republic after wining a war against the Haitians who tried to take over. Most of the population is mulatto, a mixture of black and white races. However, blacks and descendants of African slaves are subject to discrimination by the government while policies favor the island's Spanish roots (Novas, 1994 cited in García-Prieto, 1996).

Central Americans.   Many Central Americans immigrated into the United States because of their countries' civil wars and authoritarian governments. Like the Cubans, many Central Americans entered as refugees fleeing their war-torn countries. However, the aid and welcoming that they received from the U.S. government was quite different to what Cubans received since they are not recognized as political refugees which meant they were not provided with the same support services that other refugees received in spite of the civil wars they were fleeing. Many Central Americans began to arrive in the United States during the 1970s, the height of their countries' civil unrest. A majority of them arrived in this country with symptoms of post-traumatic stress disorder, due to the exposure of political terror, the witnessing of numerous atrocities, torture, and systematic killings and consequently suffering with severe war-related trauma. Many children and their families were seen in mental health clinics with multiple problems and diagnosis originating from profound traumatic experiences.

South Americans.   In relation to South Americans, García-Prieto (1996) notes that South America's geography, climate, and diversity of races and groups of peoples create a "complexity of cultures" (p. 150). Countries like Colombia and Venezuela have more in common with Central American and Caribbean countries than with Argentina and Uruguay. For instance the food, the rhythms, and some linguistic colloquialisms are similar. Ecuador, Bolivia, and Perú have large indigenous populations while Chile, Argentina, and Uruguay tend to be more European. African slaves were also brought to these countries after the indigenous populations were exploited and killed. Many South American immigrants in the United States were Jews who established in South America after they emigrated from Europe. Ecuador, Bolivia, and Peru have been at war with each other mostly because of territorial demarcations. Interestingly, in the United States, the differences among Latino groups are less noted as they come to share similar experiences of racism and oppression.

MIGRATION AND IMMIGRATION EXPERIENCES

For many Latino children and adolescents immigration and migration play a vital role in how they develop intrapersonally and interpersonally. Those whose parents are migrants or immigrants may have been exposed to a series of events and developmental changes including premigration, the migration per se, and encounters with cultural transitions. Latino groups deal with such stages under different conditions. For example, Puerto Ricans are considered migrants because they are U.S. citizens and their movement to and from Puerto Rico is considered part of the internal migration of Americans. They do not need visas or passports to move back and forth between the Continental U.S. and Puerto Rico. Children and adolescents from these Puerto Rican families can maintain more communication and stronger connections with their island counterparts and can be more connected with the geography and culture because traveling to United States is less expensive than traveling to Mexico, Central, and South America; for other Latino children and adolescents coming to the United States may require their families years of planning, saving and many efforts to obtain a visa. Many Latinos end up entering the mainland with undocumented status. Being undocumented limits their opportunities, fair treatment, and quality of life while placing them at high risks of discrimination, oppression, and abuse. Once they arrive to the United States it proves expensive and more difficult to return to the country of origin. Usually, many of the families of Latino children and adolescents, whether documented or undocumented, are primary providers for both their families in the United States and back home.

There are Latino children and adolescents whose families did not immigrate or migrate to the United States. These are families, primarily of Mexican origin, in which generations were born and raised in the United States and do not identify themselves as migrants or immigrants. Furthermore, they do not necessarily relate to the challenges and difficulties experienced by immigrant/migrant Latinos because they are not directly impacted by the challenges posited by the immigration/migration journey. The realities for children and adolescents coming from these families may differ.

For migrant and immigrant families the process seems to be a major source of stress placing members at risk of physical, emotional and family difficulties. It also allows them to learn about their resiliency and strengths. Generally migrants and immigrants enter the economic and social systems at the lower rungs of the ladder. Both adults and children can experience a cultural shock that posits a threat to their sense of self. For other migrants or immigrants, particularly those who can enter with a legal status and can enjoy better economic conditions, the experience can be less uprooting allowing them to transition and adapt faster and more successfully.

ACCULTURATION

Acculturation can be viewed as both a process and an outcome. As a process it refers to the changes in values, beliefs, and behaviors as a result of contact with other cultural groups. As an outcome it is tied with *cultural identification* or the level of connection that the individual maintains with a given culture. Acculturation is multidimensional and can have either positive or negative impacts on individuals and families.

Acculturation is a powerful factor responsible for differences among Latinos. Once in the United States, Latinos' level of identification with their traditional values may change and evolve. For some Latinos the process could be faster depending on the needs and pressures to acculturate and the degree of exposure to the Anglo culture combined with the demands to remain identified with the original values and behaviors. There are different degrees of acceptance and observance of these values even within a family group. Moreover, many Latinos attain a level of acculturation in which they alternate their behaviors and practices according to the culture in which they may find themselves interacting (Falicov, 1998).

Acculturation requires an adjustment of the individual to the new society in which he or she has come to live. Language, values, behaviors, and worldviews are challenged during this time of adaptation. It is important to assess and facilitate this process for newly arrived immigrants and migrants living here for some time. The reasons for migration or immigration may have a major effect on the person's adaptation and adjustment including effects on health and mental health. For instance if an individual is forced to leave his or her country for reasons of life or death the acculturation process may complicate their adjustment in a different way from that for an individual who decides and plans how and when he or she will leave his or her country. Issues of "loss" are significant in the adjustment and the levels of acculturation. The impact of the loss of oneself affects one's sense of being and can have consequences to the mental health of an individual resulting in depression and or anxiety including the self medication of alcohol and substance abuse. It is important for individuals to have an opportunity to tell their stories of their losses and their journey to the United States. It is in the telling of the story that one can properly grieve if he or she has not had the opportunity to do so. The loss includes that of the cultural and environmental landscapes that contains, sustains, and organizes children and their families internally and externally. For many individuals these are the daily landscapes, routines, and rituals that provide them with a meaning that have fortified their existence. In traumatic separations and abrupt immigrations these containing and meaningful experiences may lead to adjustment and adaptation problems complicated with mourning and pining for what has been lost.

RACE

For Latinos, *race* is a continuum of skin colors. They are used to mixed skin colors within a same family and do not necessarily establish the race distinctions as people do in the United States. Racism exists both among and within Latino groups. Sometimes it is subtle and noticed only when race is experienced as a threat to family's skin and related to social-class differences. Adults, children, and adolescents may experience that their skin color may be a cause of dramatic change in social status when treated by the racial standard of people in the United States.

EDUCATION AND SOCIAL CLASS

Latinos who come to the United States can be of any educational level and social class. There are differences among Latino groups in terms of how much their education is validated and their social class retained. Sometimes, Latino professionals' access to job opportunities similar to the ones enjoyed in their country of origin may be limited or none. As a result they may experience a decrease in social status that is likely to impact them individually as well as their families. Education and job opportunities as well as decrease in social class may vary among Latino groups. For example, most educational institutions in Puerto Rico are accredited by U.S. accreditation organisms. Therefore, Puerto Ricans who come to the United States with an associate degree in nursing or a bachelor degree in psychology will be able to have their degrees validated when they apply for jobs. That will not be the case of someone from any other part of Latin America. Access to employment opportunities will be very limited or salaries may be much lower given that their education and degrees are not validated in this country.

RELIGION

Latinos in general are religious and value spirituality. Catholicism is the primary religion in all Latin American countries. Also, there are other belief systems and those can be more prevalent among some Latino groups and subgroups than in others. Cubans, Puerto Ricans, and Dominicans have been strongly influenced by African folk beliefs and practices and in addition to their Catholic identification they may believe and practice *santeria or espiritismo*.

The power of religion and spirituality cannot be overlooked among Latino families. Religion serves as a powerful institution of bonding and socialization. Many families turn to their faith and traditions before, during, and after a family situation of pain and grief and in gratitude for joyous events. Children are socialized through religious and spiritual events, functions, ceremonies and teachings. Religion and spirituality can hold children and their families together and assist them in finding strength in accepting and organizing sorrow, hurt, negative experiences, trauma, and loss.

In stressful events Latinos may seek help from a family member, a friend, priest, spiritualist, herbalist, physician, *curandero*, and/or a *sobador*. This person represents an authority with significant power attributed to him or her and consequently is held in high esteem and sought out for consultation and advice. This power may be greater than that of a service provider or therapist. DeLaCruz-Quiroz, working in several cities with significant Latino populations (Detroit, Michigan, Denver and Boulder, Colorado and Los Angeles, California), has found similar beliefs and responses to the power of the clergy, its importance in the assessment, intervention, and helping process and the need to collaborate with these members when appropriate. Service providers need to understand the impact that traditions have on coping mechanisms and the solace that faith brings to Latinos, and pay attention and respect to the impact that these beliefs may have on helping outcomes, and on how the person is sustained and contained.

CULTURAL SIMILARITIES AMONG LATINOS

Familismo, respeto, dignidad, confianza, and *personalismo* are core values shared by Latino groups. Most Latino children and adolescents grow within these core values and are expected to identify or at least respect and honor them. The concept of *familismo* stresses family unity, loyalty, and interdependence. The needs of the family override the needs of the individual. Intimate relationships with the kinship family are a source of pride and safety (Badillo-Ghali cited in Lecca, Quervalú, Nunes, and González, 1998). Individuals turn to family in times of stress and often consult them before seeking help from an outside source. This dynamic shapes individual's identity and it is not always understood by service providers.

Latinos have an extended-family system called "compadrazgo" which stresses the relationships between godparents (*compadres* and *comadres*), godchildren (*ahijados* and *ahijadas*), and the natural parents. Family also extends beyond extended relatives to friends and neighbors. When Latinos are connected and maintain strong attachments to the nuclear and extended family, the support and the collectivism can serve as a buffer against social and economical stresses. *Familismo* thus serves as a socialization function. Those individuals who identify with *familismo* values tend to develop social networks within the family that also serve as a source of comfort, communication, entertainment, and taking care of one another. It is this experience that for many adds to the "liveliness" of an individual and to the purpose of an individual within a family. The attachment and bonding to this group functions at a deeper level and gives individuals a sense of "belonging." It becomes a containing and organizing dynamic of the individual's internal life and psyche. This can fortify the individual's sense of identity and purpose in life. This is an important concept to understand in working with Latinos who may feel disconnected or lost, and/or depressed on not having contact with their family and even on having to make changes without family input.

Respeto "signifies proper attention to the order assumed in interpersonal relations, and acknowledgement of the other's unique soul, his/her individuality" (Díaz-Royo, 1983, p. 153). There are a series of *respeto* rules and those are inculcated since early childhood. Perhaps the meaning of *respeto* is no different for Latinos from that for other cultural groups. However, among Latino groups it is strongly emphasized and the development of any relationship is strongly based on the *respeto* that is experienced. Some experts note that for Latinos *respeto* connotes more emotional dependence and dutifulness that is conveyed by the English "respect" (Falicov, 1996). *Respeto* norms may be different when it relates to parent–child relationships. For instance, among traditional Mexicans and other Latino groups, parents' status is always higher and most parents do not expect or wish to be friends with their children.

Being respectful includes certain ceremonial requisites based on age, sex, socioeconomic position, and the particular context. For instance *respeto* towards those in position of authority has to be communicated. Authority is acknowledged based on the person's level of education, age, role, and family hierarchy. The elderly, for example, should be addressed as "don" (sir) or "Doña" (madam) followed by their first name and by using the formal "you" (usted). Self-respect means to respect both yourself and others.

More than a situational mistake, the lack of *respeto* is considered a character defect. In that sense it is closed to the value of *dignidad* (dignity). When a person is lacking in *respeto* his or her *dignidad* is also questioned. *Respeto* extends beyond the family to the property, the group conduct, and public and private gatherings. *Respeto* is seen when the woman and the children are submissive to the man (Laureano and Poliandro, 1991).

Personalismo stresses personal contact and social situations (Bernal and Shapiro, 1996). Latinos value personal relationships and the inner qualities that constitute a person's uniqueness. Cooperation is expected rather than competition. "*Confianza* (trust) is dependent upon *respeto* and implies that one's social self is placed in the realm of the other" (Díaz-Royo, 1983, p. 158). A relationship of *confianza* will develop if there is perceived mutual respect and acceptance. Children are expected to trust their parents, learn not to take advantage of other people's trust, and are taught to avoid those who are deemed distrustful. A relationship marked by *confianza* allows for closeness and intimacy.

CHILD REARING AND PARENTING STYLES

Child rearing is determined largely by cultural beliefs and socioeconomic conditions. Different levels of education and income, changes within the nuclear family, availability of work opportunities, and the disappearance of traditional community models supportive of child learning have brought significant new ways of thinking and living to Latino families in the United States. Latino families draw on their cultural values to manage their lives and the lives of their family. Managing obedience and respect from their children is particularly important. It is a way of keeping the family close and loyal. Children who misbehave or show *falta de respeto* (lack of respect) are usually disciplined immediately. Parents feel it is a reflection on their poor upbringing if they do not discipline their children for being out of control and/or acting out in a way that is dishonorable or disrespectful. Parents might use physical discipline that may be culturally syntonic for the family. It is important to keep this in mind when conducting assessments with a family who presents with problems of physical abuse. Many Latino parents feel insulted, intruded on, and infringed on their parental rights when charged with any physical abuse. Psychoeducation is useful and empowering to the parents who are confronted with this issue.

Studies suggest that Latino parents have similar knowledge of disciplinary practices as parents from other ethnic groups but may differ in their use (Zayas, 1994; Negroni-Rodríguez, 1998). Discipline varies according to the child's age. Parents use verbal approaches more likely with adolescents. Obedience is viewed as resulting from a combination of appealing to children through reason and controlling their misbehaviors by the use of punishments (Negroni-Rodríguez, 1998). More frequently parents believe in the use of verbal punishment and praise (Hesselbrock, Negroni-Rodríguez, and Grube-Chartier, 2003; Negroni-Rodríguez, 2003). Many Latino parents support mild physical punishment as a form to teaching children obedience and conformity (Rivera, 1995). The use of rewards and incentives is also common.

Latino children are central to the family. Children are perceived as extension of their own parents but are not allowed challenging or questioning their elders, neither do they have the right to voice their opinions (Juárez, 1985 cited by Green, 1999). Latino parents believe in the importance of spending time with their children, being familiar with their activities as well as whereabouts, and being committed to their education and emotional well-being (Hesselbrock, Negroni-Rodríguez, and Grube-Chartier, 2003). Extended family members (grandparents, uncles, aunts, cousins, godparents, and co-parents) are active participants in the children's rearing as they are acknowledged authority to discipline when parents are absent. When parental responsibilities fail, it is expected that the extended family will intervene in some way to protect the children. They will more likely prefer to make themselves available to care for the children before any stranger is paid by the system to do so because "*para eso es que* está la familia" (that is what family is for).

COMPARISON OF LATINOS AND OTHER ETHNIC GROUPS

Latinos and Anglos

Kluckhohn's value orientation model has been found useful to compare traditional Latinos and Anglos. Kluckhohn postulates that there is a series of human imperatives that are common to all cultures (Spiegel, 1982). These relate to (1) time, (2) human activity, (3) social relations, (4) person-nature, and (5) human nature. However, cultural groups differ in their orientation to these imperatives known as value orientations. Among traditional Anglo and Latino families several differences can be noted. Anglo families have a future orientation in relation to time in human affairs. In contrast, most Latino families maintain a present orientation and focus on the here-and-now issues (Nine, 1984). In terms of their emphasis on human activity, Anglos show a preference for autonomy and independence, doing and having. Most Latino groups, on the other hand, are oriented to the position of being, that is, tendencies towards spontaneous expression of feelings, improvisation, and informality. Being is more valued than doing and having. Inner qualities are the source of self-worth, regardless of worldly success or failure (García-Prieto, 1996).

Anglos have an individual orientation which holds that a person has primary responsibility for his or her own actions. Anglos value reward, independence, and autonomy (Sue and Sue, 1990). Latinos emphasize support, collectivism, and group affiliation, especially the family (collateral orientation). Anglos are guided by their mastery-over-nature orientation while traditional Latinos accept fate in their subjugated-to-nature orientation.

Anglo and Latino children are reared within differing cultural contexts. The value orientations that underlie their culture influence social networks which in turn influence values and beliefs about children's development and socialization and, thus, affect discipline repertoires and patterns as well as expectations and attributions of children's and parents' behaviors (Bornstein, 1991).

LATINOS AND AFRICAN-AMERICANS

Latinos have strong African roots. Africans were brought as slaves to the Caribbean, Mexico, Central, and South American colonies by the Spaniards, Portuguese, Dutch, French, and English to work in agriculture and mining. Most of them were brought from Eastern Nigeria, the Gold Coast, and the Congo Basin (Novas, 1991). Despite the odds they were able to preserve their religion and cultural traditions. They contributed to the cultural mix of most Latino countries, particularly those from the Caribbean. They also contributed with their religion, traditions, food, folklore, and language. Those strong connections between Latino and African cultures can facilitate the Latinos and African Americans in the United States to relate and connect. However, the situation is more complex.

Africans came to the United States by force and in fear and terror (Black, 1996). They outlived four centuries of slave trading and were able to preserve much of their heritage. Latinos in the United States and African Americans share a history of social, political, and economic oppression and their struggles against racism and discrimination. However, as Black (1996) explains, there are experiences that set black people apart from all other ethnic groups:

(1) the African legacy, rich in culture, custom and achievement; (2) the history of slavery, a deliberate attempt to destroy the core and soul of people while keeping their bodies in enforced servitude; (3) racism and discrimination, . . . and 4) the victim

system, a process by which individuals and communities are denied access . . . then blamed for their low levels of accomplishments . . . while their successes are treated as anomalies. (p. 59)

Those experiences are also part of the Latino reality in the United States and bring many Latinos and African Americans closer. Unfortunately, there have been situations when the racism of some Latino individuals, families, and communities has resulted in attitudes and treatments that resemble white racism. It is important to note that some Latino countries exhibit the influence of the European Western culture. Also, foreign-born Latinos are less likely to see themselves as minority than African Americans because they grew up in a context in which they were the majority (Black, 1996).

It is not surprising to find so many similarities in the value system of these two cultures. For instance, both Latinos and African Americans place great importance on the family, religion, and kinship groups (Black, 1996). However, contrary to many Latino parents, African American parents are more likely to encourage their children to be assertive, willful, and independent (Abney and Priest, 1995). Nevertheless, they seem to agree as to the use of more authoritarian child-rearing practices (Abney and Priest, 1995; Negroni-Rodríguez, 1998).

Latinos and Asian Americans (*Chinese, Japanese, and Filipino*)

To compare Asian Americans and Latinos is a challenging task because like Latinos, Asian Americans are a collective set of different populations. They differ among themselves in terms of migration history, population, language, religion, education level, occupation, degree of acculturation, and so on (Lee, 1996). However, there are traditional values that seem to parallel with Latino traditional values. For instance, family unit is highly valued and there is emphasis on interdependence. As in the Latino culture the family is the primary socializing unit for its children and family members. Child rearing can be shared with extended relatives, and in numerous families the older siblings are delegated childcare functions (Lee, 1996). Independent behavior is not always encouraged if it disrupts the structure and organization of the family in both Asian and Latino cultures. The Asian culture is concerned with family peace and harmony and therefore, restraint of potentially disruptive emotions is strongly emphasized in the development of the Asian culture (Sue, 1973). Within the Latino culture there is also a strong emphasis to keep the harmony within the family, and the concepts of *aguantar* (to endure) have been emphasized to contain one's emotion, *resignarse* (resign yourself) and finally to *sobreponerse* (overcome and accept fate). Shame and guilt are principal techniques that are instilled in both cultures as a way of controlling the behaviors of the individual and family members. The obligation to the family and the loyalty to the family are significant to the proper development of the child and reflective of good parenting in both cultures. A child who acts too independently without the parent or family consideration is considered selfish and not proper in both cultures.

THE IMPACT OF CULTURE ON LATINOS' RESILIENCY

Culture is a resource that provides internal and external structure. Latino children develop attachments to cultural values, traditions, and constructs that enhance and encourage their relationships and facilitate their ongoing growth and development. Thus, their culture helps to regulate and organize themselves. Culture speaks to the resiliencies of Latinos within the family and in their social environments. Values like *familismo* and *personalismo* play a role in Latinos' willingness to persevere and better their lives and help maintain important and necessary support networks. For that reason the cultural values and behaviors of Latino families should be seen as a wealth. Service providers and therapists should be cautious of not overlooking the cultural assets these children, youth, and families bring (cultural capital). In most instances the many stressors, difficulties, and limitations that Latino children and adolescents and their families encounter are not necessarily due to their cultural assets but due to the notion that their cultural capital has not been translated into a social capital that comprises different forms of resources and networks which allow for social and economic power and mobility (Zambrana and Zoppi, 2003).

CHILD WELFARE NEEDS, ISSUES, AND PROBLEMS

To safeguard the well-being of Latino children and youth it is essential to know their needs, and provide a nurturing, safe, and stimulating environment and opportunities for them to grow and develop (Pecora et al., 2000). Unfortunately for Latino children, youth and their families the barriers to attain good physical, mental, and social health and live under acceptable economic conditions are many.

Economic Insecurity and Instability

Poverty remains a serious problem among Latino children, youth, and their families in the United States. In 2003 the median income for Latino households was 32,997 while for non-Hispanic white households $48,000, for black households $30,000, and for Asian households $55,500. Latino households experienced a decline in median income of 2.6 percent between 2002 ($33,861) and 2003 ($32,997). Similarly the per capita income for Latinos declined by 2.2 percent from 13,796 in 2002 to 13,492 in 2003. In 2003 Latino' per capita income was lower than all of the other ethnic groups (De-Navas-Watts, Proctor, and Mills, 2004).

In 2002, 21.4 percent of Latinos were living in poverty compared to only 7.8 percent of non-Latino whites. Latinos represented 24.3 percent of the population living in poverty. The official poverty rate in 2003 was 12.5 percent, up from 12.1 percent in 2002 with 35.9 million people living in poverty, up from 1.3 million in 2002. Poverty rates remained unchanged for Latinos, non-Latino whites, and blacks, although it rose for whites and Asians. Among Latino, the poverty rate remained unchanged at

22.5 percent in 2003, although their number in poverty increased from 8.6 million in 2002 to 9.1 million in 2003 (De-Navas-Watts, Proctor, and Mills, 2004). In 2002, 26.3 percent of full-time year-round Latino workers had an income of 35,000 compared to 53.8 percent of non-Latino whites (De-Navas-Watts, Proctor, and Mills, 2004).

With Latino children being one of the fastest growing groups in the nation it is important to note that 33.6 percent of Latino children live in poverty compared to 10 percent of non-Latino white children with Puerto Rican and Mexican children representing the poorest subgroups among Latinos (Zambrana and Zoppi, 2003). While Latino children represented 17.7 percent of all children in the nation, they constituted 30.4 percent of all children living in poverty (Ramírez and De La Cruz, 2003). Although the poverty rate has declined in the last years (Delaker, 2001) the increase is not significant.

Poverty can be a correlate of many problems such as malnutrition, poor health, poor living conditions, and poor education. High levels of poverty have been associated with the lack of opportunities to educational attainment as well as to social mobility and intergenerational mobility (Zambrana and Zoppi, 2003). Poverty also limits the economic attainment of Latino immigrants (Zambrana and Zoppi, 2003).

There are ethnic differences in Latino children living in poverty and those need to be better understood. Experts claim that such differences cannot be explained geographically or by differences in family structure, education, language skills, immigrant or racial status, or the employment patterns of parents and other family members. For example, Landale and Litcher (1996) claimed that for Latina mothers the expectations of both working outside of the house and keeping a strong family does not necessarily lower child poverty. According to the National Council of La Raza (NCLR) (cited by Zambrana and Zoppi, 2003) Latinas will emerge to 40 percent in the workforce which will have a significant impact on their ability to work and attain higher paying jobs. If Latina women join the ranks of high-school "drop out" they will be left behind unable to compete for the higher paying job and continue the legacy of poverty. Their inability to move out of this cycle can affect the future of their children.

The needs of Latino children cannot be met effectively when their parents' access to job opportunities and appropriate job compensations is limited. Parents with limited financial resources may be less able to provide their children with enough learning resources and activities. Poverty has been associated with Latino children's lower academic achievement and lower educational attainment.

Housing

Latinos are more likely to be renters than homeowners. Latinos are more likely than other ethnic groups to experience discrimination in their housing search. Studies conducted by the Department of Housing and Urban Development (HUD) show that housing discrimination rates, both for looking to buy a home and for seeking to rent a unit, have gone down for Latinos since 1989 (Johansen, 2002) but still are the highest. In a study of 4,600 households 25 percent of the Latinos were victim of renters' discrimination and 27 percent were victims of sales discrimination (Johansen, 2002), compared to African Americans with 22 percent and 17 percent respectively.

Education

Education and responsibility are highly valued in the Latino community in spite of the statistics that reflect the contrary. However, the disparity and the failures of the institutions of higher learning along with the disparity in the appropriate educational opportunities create challenges for Latino children and adolescents. Those academic disparities originate at kindergarten and remains through age seventeen (Zambrana and Zoppi, 2003).

Although they are the second largest group of children in the nation's schools, Latino children are "less likely to participate in early childhood education and other enrichment programs such as Head Start, after-school programs, and rigorous academic courses. Less than two-thirds of Latinos (57 percent) graduate from high school compared to 88 percent of non-Latino Whites" (Therrien and Ramírez, 2000). A report by the President's Advisory Commission on Education Excellence for Latinos indicates that Latino children were more likely to enter school with less developed school-related skills than non-Latino children, and were more likely to be held back one to two grades during elementary education. "Latinos lagged behind all other racial and ethnic groups in terms of median years of education (10.3 years)" (Ortega, 2000, p. 6).

Studies show that Latino youth have higher dropout rates than white and African American youth, much lower high-school completion rates, and are more likely to be out of school or unemployed (Williams and Robinson, 2001). Many factors interfere with their academic achievement. Among those factors are many parental responsibilities, lack of children participation in preschool education, poor quality of elementary and high schools, limited neighborhood resources, and lack of presence of role models and gender role attitudes (Zambrana and Zoppi, 2003).

For many families there is no clear understanding of the role of the school and the role of the family in their children's education. Some families believe that the school is the authority and should be responsible for the education and training of their children. But the institutions of learning fail Latino youth and children with poor school environments and the crime that many times threatens Latino and all other children's safety. Many schools are ill equipped and poorly kept without proper sanitary conditions. There are instances when school personnel are not competent in engaging the cultural values and strengths of Latinos and thus the cultural wealth erodes as evidenced by disproportionate rates of suicide and higher stressors and with Latino students having the highest high-school dropout rate of all racial and ethnic groups (Zambrana and Zoppi, 2003).

The *No Child Left Behind Act* of 2001 (NCLB Act), a national policy that incorporates practices and programs to address the needs of America's children, appears to have flaws as it has a primary focus to have children memorize and pass tests. There are many Latino children that are experiencing trauma due to their life circumstances and are having major problems using their mind to focus and to memorize. These children are left behind emotionally if they are not given proper time and assistance to learn and develop their cognitive skills.

Developmental Delays and Learning Needs

Of the children in foster care, 40 percent are born prematurely or at low birth weight (Halfon, Berkowitz, and Klee, 1992). It is also estimated that more than half of these children "have developmental delays which includes motor development problems, hearing and vision problems, growth retardation and speech language delays four to five times the rate found among all other children" (Dicker and Gordon, 2002 cited by Lillas, Lester-Langer, and Drinane, 2004). Sometimes children suffering from learning disabilities are not assessed properly and consequently are not receiving the appropriate services.

The problems of being exposed to violence either by witnessing abuse of a parent, sibling, or relative, or being directly abused is in the complexity of internalizing this assault. This causes tremendous stress and keeps the child constantly assessing for safety and threats of danger. This is compromising the child's cognitive capacities, affecting his or her learning. These children are many times diagnosed with attention deficit hyperactivity disorder (ADHD) and are not being treated properly for their trauma-related experience. They are then lost to a misdiagnosis and a misunderstanding. They may in fact develop ADHD or symptoms that are trauma-related that look like ADHD. The failure to properly make an assessment and an intervention increases the mental health disparities for Latino children and their families.

PHYSICAL HEALTH

The health profiles of Latinos are unique: Puerto Ricans suffer disproportionately from asthma, HIV/AIDS, and infant mortality, while Mexican Americans suffer disproportionately from diabetes (Center for Disease Control and Prevention [CDCP], 2005). Factors that contribute to poor health outcomes among Latinos include language and cultural barriers, lack of access to preventive care, and lack of health insurance. In 2002 the ten leading causes of death in the United States for Latinos were (1) heart disease, (2) cancer, (3) unintentional injuries, (4) strokes, (5) diabetes, (6) chronic liver disease and cirrhosis, (7) homicide, (8) chronic lower respiratory diseases, (9) pneumonia and influenza, and (10) birth defects (CDCP, 2005). In addition, Latinos have disproportionately high prevalence of the following conditions and risk factors: Asthma, chronic obstructive pulmonary diseases, HIV/AIDS, obesity, suicide, teenage pregnancy, and tuberculosis (CDCP, 2005). Research suggests that Latino children have a high risk of asthma, diabetes, and obesity (Flores et al., 2002).

Reproductive Health

The Latino youth population is growing in this country, and consequently so are the risk factors as they engage in early sexual behaviors. Many Latino youth are engaging in unprotected sex as it is evident by the birth rate among young teens. Many Latinas do not use contraceptive methods due to religious beliefs that are associated with their cultural values (Kaiser Permanente, 2001). This also increases their risk for sexually transmitted diseases (STDs). The Latino population is younger and estimated to rise to 24 percent by 2025 (Driscoll et al., 2001). For that reason there is an increased need for establishing effective prevention efforts and culturally appropriate interventions (De Anda, 2002).

Of the Latinas in the United States who are younger and of child bearing age, 50.9 percent are between the ages of 15 and 44 (National Latina Health Network, 2005). In fact, they have a higher rate of teen pregnancy. While birth rates decreased for teens in general in 1998, Latinas had the highest birth rate between the ages of 15 and 19 (93.6 per 1,000 women), compared to 88.2 for African Americans and 35.2 for non-Latino white (Kaiser Permanente, 2001). In 2001 more than half of all the babies born in California were Latinos (National Latina Health Network, 2005).

Mental Health

Researchers have expressed that Latino children are at high risk of behavioral and developmental disorders but that there remain many unanswered questions about their mental health needs (Flores et al., 2002). Latino youth experience proportionately more anxiety-related behaviors and depression than non-Latino white youth (U.S. Department of Health and Human Services, 2001a). Latino adolescents report more suicidal ideation and attempts proportionally than non-Latino whites and blacks (U.S. Department of Health and Human Services, 2001a) and Latinas youth in comparison to white girls report more depression, attempts to suicide, and use of substances (National Alliance for Hispanic Health, 1999 cited by Zambrana and Zoppi, 2003).

Frequently Latino children's mental health problems are overlooked, unidentified, and ignored. Some of these children are so dampened down and unresponsive that they are misunderstood as not having problems when in fact they may be in a serious state of depression or anxiety. Sometimes their problems are indicative of severe posttraumatic stress disorder but pass unidentified.

Many child welfare workers lack proper training that helps them understand the cultural differences of the Latino populations and the implications of "trauma" as it relates to abuse, loss, attachment issues, and immigration. This leads to the "burnout" of these service workers and to the negative attitudes and experiences that occur with providers, families, and their children. Another limitation is that the screening and training of foster families on these issues is seriously lacking. Foster family members are not given sufficient information or training in child development, trauma from abuse and/or neglect, or even the culture of the child and the cultural issues which affect the child's language and coping skills. The lack of knowledge and training can revictimize these children and their families increasing their suspicions, heightening their anxiety, and increasing their risks of depression. Experts claim that the measures used to assess such symptoms are not validated enough to address within-group differences, and that the interpretations of the findings may be influenced by the assessor's ethnicity (Domínguez de Ramírez and Shapiro, 1998). Research findings suggest gender differences in mental health ratings. The conditions may be undertreated. Also, it is more common to treat only with stimulant medication while school-based services and mental health outpatient services are usually missing (Bauermeister et al., 2003).

Latino children suffering from separation anxiety may present symptoms expressed through somatization (Green, 1999). Somatization is strongly held among Latinos as a mean of expressing emotions. Symptoms of distress may be expressed "appropriately" through somatic type symptoms. It does not mean that the person is intentionally hiding something about herself or himself but that it will get initially displayed or known within the culture of behavior. It is sanctioned for female adults to have an "*ataque de nervios*" or "*nervios*" when they are reacting to a stressful event. An example of this is a woman who might feel overwhelmed after learning that her children have been injured or that her partner is going to leave her. It begins with a reaction as she is overwhelmed that is expressed through somatic-like behaviors. The reaction can lead to the family and/or friends to rally around her in support of what she is going through.

Health and Mental Health Care

Latinos in the United States are the least likely to have health insurance. In 2000 the rate of uninsured at 37 percent was twice that for non-Latino whites (U.S. Department of Health and Human Services, 2001b). In 2003 Latinos had the highest rate of people without health insurance of any ethnic group (Weinberg, 2004). Many Latinos are unable to seek medical care and/or medication. The majority will seek care from their primary health provider than from a mental health specialist (U.S. Department of Health and Human Services, 2001b). Latino children are less likely to have health insurance than children from other ethnic groups. In 1998, 70 percent of Latino children had health insurance compared to 86 percent of white children and 80 percent of black children (Williams and Robinson, 2001). In 2003, Latino children were more likely to be uninsured than Non-Latino whites, blacks, or Asian children (Weinberg, 2004).

Latinos in general and Latino children in particular are less likely than non-Latino whites to have regular access to health care services (Flores et al., 2002). Poor Latinos have lower access to special mental health care than poor non-Latino whites (Alegría et al., 2002). The most common reasons for this low use of services are lack of language fluency, cultural differences, lack of access to services, differences in recognition of mental health problems, and lower quality of mental health care (Alegría et al., 2002).

In general, rates of mental health service use are higher among children in foster care than children in the community. There are racial and ethnic disparities in reported mental health services utilization (Garland, Landsverk, and Lau, 2003) of minority children in foster care. Access to services is limited also due to lack of knowledge of available services; lack of transportation or financial resources; lack of confidence in services and previous negative experiences with service providers; lack of minority mental health providers; and cultural and language barriers such as beliefs about mental health, mental illness, and use of mental health services, biased assessment techniques, and biased referral patterns from "gateway" providers (Garland, Landsverk, and Lau, 2003).

Substance Use and Abuse

Cultural factors can help prevent use of substances among Latino children and youth. For instance Mexican-American adolescents with strong Mexican cultural identification are less likely than those with weaker identification to the regular uses of tobacco and more likely to believe that tobacco use is harmful (Marsiglia et al., 2003). Research findings suggest that school-age Latino children are aware of the risks of using alcohol and other drugs, have few friends who are using substances, and will be less likely to follow their friends' requests or imitate their friends' behaviors (Hesselbrock, Negroni-Rodríguez, and Grube-Chartier, 2003). Smoking cigarettes seems the most frequently reported substance, followed by alcohol and marijuana (Hesselbrock, Negroni-Rodríguez, and Grube-Chartier, 2003) in that age group. Data on older children is different. More Latino youth of ages 12–17 use illicit drugs than their white or black peers (Coalition for Juvenile Justice, 2005). Family bonding and school commitment are sources of resiliency for Latino children and youth and protect them from the risks of using and abusing substances (Hesselbrock, Negroni-Rodríguez, and Grube-Chartier, 2003; Marsiglia et al., 2003).

Gang Involvement

Gangs are clearly present in most large cities with large populations of Latino youth. They have become an alternative to the life experienced by many youths in their disruptive families. Poor homes, marginal and unstable economic conditions, and families headed by the mother with more siblings seem to be vulnerability factors for youth to be attracted to gangs (Green, 1999). For the youth the gang becomes their family and community, an opportunity to develop their identity and a sense of meaningfulness that they are not aware it is temporary. Gang life exposes the youth to risks like drugs and violence (Green, 1999).

Gang life has an effect on the developing mind of the child. For children living in this type of environment it can have abysmal consequences to their ongoing growth and development. For those who are exposed to violence early in life it can have profound effects on their personality development and their mental health. Children who are raised around violence have high rates of mood disorders including depression and anxiety. This exposure shapes their attitudes about life, their needs, and desires. Living with chronic violence can place them at risk of posttraumatic stress disorders as well as disassociative disorders.

Latino immigrant youth are especially at risk of gang recruitment if they are disillusioned in their schools and their homes. Immigrant Latino youth who have run away from home and are living in homes with domestic violence, substance abuse, and/or poverty are also easy recruits for gang life as they are vulnerable, looking for a home, and in need of "belonging."

Many immigrant youth from countries of civil unrest, who witnessed numerous atrocities including the maiming and murder of their significant others, joined gangs as a way of finding a home and as a way of feeling protected by the group. These youth are at the risk of losing their lives to death by gang warfare and at risk of serious physical and mental injuries. Many have lost limbs and abilities to walk and function including brain injuries incapacitating them. These youth might not have any health coverage and consequently are ineligible for physical health and mental health services.

Latino youth who join gangs come from the most impoverished families with either absent or unreliable fathers and single-parent mothers (Vigil, 2002). Gang membership and the proliferation of gangs have their roots in the marginalization of people living in poverty and institutional racism, fears of the authorities who have unjustly failed to protect the poor and the victims and who have also victimized this community as seen in the city of Los Angeles, California, with the rampart police scandal planting evidence on gang members. These actions lead to distrust, fear, and hatred of the authority that represents justice and protection.

Another failure of the social institution of law and order comes to perpetuate the need to protect your neighborhood, leading to gang proliferation. In California one of the responses to the gang proliferation has been to "just get rid of them!," which came to favor the recent passage of Proposition 21 lowering the age at which children may be tried as adults. Yet, despite all of the money that went into this policy, the crime rates have continued to rise and the prison populations increased dramatically (Vigil, 2002). Schools have been a negative experience for gang members who drop out by the age of 16 with the primary reasons of language problems, ethnic identity conflict, general malaise, and discrimination, and the point here is that "school problems generally precede and contribute to gang involvement" (Vigil, 2002, p. 41). Once again, instead of making the classroom and teachers bilingual, bicultural, culturally competent, and proficient, California has eliminated bilingual education and removed affirmative education from the universities (Vigil, 2002). The failures of the institution and the persistent poverty erode the families and their attachments to the institutions of care, education, law enforcement, and health, keeping young children and youth frustrated and hopeless, where gang life in their minds becomes the only answer to their tragic lives.

Involvement with the Justice System

There are different forms of delinquency behavior: Violent behaviors, violent thoughts, substance abuse, and general delinquency (Peacock, McClure, and Agars, 2003). Juvenile delinquency is considered to be caused by a combination of individual, familial, and sociocultural factors. Proximal variables such as attachment to parents and peers, and distal variables such as attitudes towards school, mobility, and exposure to community violence are considered to contribute to delinquency behavior (Peacock, McClure, and Agars, 2003).

The exact number of Latino youth in the juvenile system is unknown because available data fails to separate Latinos as a different ethnic group. Also, there is lack of uniform standards of what defines "Latino" and "Hispanic" (Coalition for Juvenile Justice, 2005; Villarruel and Walker, 2002). It has been noted that the means for collecting and accessing data appear to be inadequate. This inadequacy results in undercounting and inaccuracies of reports. The "absence of separate data makes them [Latino juvenile offenders] an invisible minority group for the purposes of planning and policy" (Talvi, 2002, p. 1). Findings from the first-ever national report on the prevalence of Latino youth in the juvenile justice system (Villarruel and Walker, 2002) revealed that Latino youth were overrepresented in the U.S. system and received harsher treatment than white youth even when charged with the same types of offenses. By 1993, Latino youth were three times more likely to be incarcerated than whites; were sent to detention and correctional facilities more often and for longer time periods than whites who had committed the same offenses; and were confined longer than white youth who committed the same offenses (Coalition for Juvenile Justice, 2005). This is another form of institutional racism that exists within the Juvenile Justice System and needs to be corrected in order to reduce the injustices to Latino children and their families. This adds to the apathy and suspicion of legal authorities, and increases hopelessness, anger, and attitudes of racism.

Studies on Latino youth suggest that exposure to community violence is the most important predictor of delinquent behavior (Peacock, McClure, and Agars, 2003). Thus a reduction in violent behaviors may be achieved as exposure to community violence is reduced.

Safety Issues

Safety should incorporate all children. But for many Latino children safety has become an unmet need. With a high rate of Latino poverty the majority of Latino children are likely to live in low-income communities that are lacking in resources and opportunities to keep children optimally involved and safe. Low income communities are fraught with crime and less police protection. In many of the schools in these and other communities security is problematic. Due to lack of adequate resources schools are not able to protect children from the risks of assaults, drug, and substance abuse. Such conditions increase children's vulnerability to develop depression and suicide. Depression and suicide attempts are a reflection of the stressful lives many Latino youth experience.

Safety is especially problematic for immigrant children who are faced with having to live with numerous people, sometimes strangers, and consequently may become victims of abuse and crime. They are extremely vulnerable as they are afraid to report for fear of being deported and/or separated from their family.

Child Abuse and Neglect

About 2.97 million children were allegedly maltreated in the United States in 1999, 28 percent of allegations were substantiated and of those substantiated reports 52 percent were female victims (U.S. Department of Health and Human Services, 2001a). African American children had the highest rate of victimization (25.2 per 1,000), followed by Latinos (12.6 per 1,000), whites (10.6 per 1,000), and Asian/Pacific Islanders (4.4 per 1,000) (U.S. Department of Health and Human Services, 2001a). In 2002 the trend changed. One half of the victims of child abuse and neglect were whites (54 percent), one quarter were African American (26 percent) while only one-tenth (11 percent) were Latinos (U.S. Department of Health and Human Services, 2004).

Although the previous findings suggest no disproportionate number of Latino children in the child welfare system due to allegations of abuse, still many Latino children and adolescents enter the child welfare system (Fluke et al., 2003). "Factors related to the involvement of children of color in the child welfare system are multiple and complex" (p. 521), and substance abuse, poverty, serious mental illness, domestic violence, and parental incarceration are among the common causes of child abuse, which in turn is the most common cause for children to enter the child welfare system (Hines et al., 2004).

Foster Care and Group Homes

According to data from the National Center on Child Abuse and Neglect (NCCAN, 2003), of the 542,000 children in foster care as of September of 2001, 17 percent were Latinos, an increase of 2 percent from 1998; of the 290,000 who entered foster care, 16 percent were Latinos; and of the 263,000 children who exited foster care that year, 15 percent were Latinos.

Foster care has become a common form of substitute and temporary care for children who are in need of protection due to their parents' inability to properly care for them. The number of children in out-of-home care has been alarming (Yancey, 1998). The situation is worrisome because studies show that children in out-of-home care, particularly those in group homes and institutional placement, are more likely to present a range of emotional disturbances and are at increased risk of problems such as pregnancy, educational underachievement, substance abuse, and juvenile delinquency (Yancey, 1998). The presence of Latino children and youth in foster care varies among states, and available data may undercount the number of Latino children in the system. Depending on the state, Latinos may have a large presence in the foster care population.

Many Latino children are unnecessarily removed from their homes for numerous reasons that at times relate to the system's lack of cultural sensitivity of Latino families. Such lack of sensitivity consequently adds to the stresses of families in crisis and/or in need of support services. The following are only some of the examples that reflect factors contributing to children removed from their homes unnecessarily:

- Lack of understanding of Latino parents' expectations and obligations of older siblings assuming care and responsibility for the care of their younger siblings.
- Lack of understanding of Latino family dynamics.
- Immigrant families' lack of understanding of accepted parental discipline and the rights of children and women in this country.
- Monolingual (Spanish-speaking) families confronted with the language barrier and the inability to understand the laws, requirements, follow-up appointments, and all the other requirements posited for them by the systems at large.
- Many immigrant parents who are fearful of deportation do not follow up with what is asked of them by a social worker, teacher, physician, and so on out of fears of deportation and try and remain unnoticed and consequently appear defiant and resistant.

- Many families especially immigrant families lacking affect out of fear, shock, or as a way of attempting to modulate the emotions and/or because they are not understanding what is being communicated (completely or partially) to them and as a result are assessed as parents with no remorse and uncaring.

Other problems that are of concern when working with Latino families are children who are separated from each other and placed in separate homes adding to their fears, anxieties, stress, and traumatic experiences. Many parents are told they need to seek treatment and are given referrals, yet on calling these agencies they are put on a waitlist and consequently are not called. Frequently they are told that because the waitlist is a year long the requested services can not be provided. The other hard fact and reality is the lack of available services. There is a lack of sufficient service agencies available to the families and children due to budget cuts and the low priority of children's services.

It is common for Latino children to be placed in homes that are located far away from parents and relatives. Thus, parental visitations become incredibly difficult. Sometimes the foster homes are not necessarily homes that are culturally syntonic and the distance becomes more than physical. The situation makes it more difficult for children to have access to their families. Because of the lack of awareness of these children's values, beliefs, language dominance, food preferences, and socialization experiences the quality of the care is limited. Many children already traumatized might not adjust to the notions of independence and competitiveness in a new foster home that might impose these values on them, as they might adhere to the values of interdependence and cooperation. These children, already challenged by the loss of their families, are particularly vulnerable to the accumulation of this type of stress and increased isolation when their collective values are not understood.

Other concerns with Latino children in foster care are directly related to the racial/ethnic disparities in mental health service utilization. Recent studies conducted in San Diego, California, report disparities in utilization of mental health and support services for children. In a particular study the findings showed that Caucasian American children in foster care were twenty-five times more likely to have received services than Latino American youth (Garland, Landsverk, and Lau, 2003). Other studies report that ethnic minority youth who have been identified by child protective services as maltreated are less likely to receive mental health than their Caucasian counterparts (Kolko, Selelyo, and Brown, 1999; Tingus et al., 1996). These studies indicate the disparities along the continuum of care for Latino youth. The inequality of service provision does not enhance the well-being and safety of the Latino child in the child welfare system.

Latino children and youth are almost twice likely to be in out-of-home care than non-Latino white children (Suleiman, 2003). It is not clear why a rate differential exists between white, Latino, and African American children. In the past 25 years the rate has remained consistent for white children but has doubled for Latino and African American children (Suleiman, 2003).

Kinship Care

Parents in general and Latino parents in particular prefer to have relatives to care for their children, specially their young children. For immigrant/migrant Latino parents, the option of relatives as care providers may be limited. For native-born Latino parents more family members may be available (Buriel and Hurtado, 1998).

Family Reunification or Adoption

The major goal of the Adoption and Safe Families Act (ASFA) of 1997 was to speed up permanency planning with a focus on child safety. For Latino children and adolescents, exiting foster care may be a more complicated process. The welfare policies resulted in "growing concerns about the decisions being made inappropriately while providing too little support to families throughout the process. Considering the limited availability and accessibility of bilingual services, the expedited process places an added burden on Latino families. . . . Latino families are at a disadvantage in meeting case plan requirements when bilingual resources are not available, accessible or adequate" (Suleiman, 2003, p. 5). The problems faced by Latino parents who are trying to comply with service plans place them at greater risk of termination of parental rights.

The interactions between race, ethnicity, and other characteristics of these children and their families such as family structure require a look. What are the strengths of different types of families that help them to resume care of their children? In Latino families by the year 2000 there were 60.4 percent of Latino children in married-couple families and 24.3 percent in single-parent families compared to 75.2 percent and 17.7 percent of non-Latino white children. About 64.8 percent of Latino children were in female-headed families with the mother in the labor force compared to 80.7 percent of the non-Latino white children (Annie E. Casey Foundation, 2003). Latino families that are two-parent headed are more likely to be reunified faster than African American and Caucasian families (Harris and Courtney, 2003). The similarities and differences in the experiences of different types of families, for example single parent versus two-parent families, affect both reunification and adoption. For instance, children and adolescents from single-mother households may require a different approach to reunification or adoption than those children or adolescents from two-parent families.

When children are placed in non-Latino homes or put for adoption, issues emerge around ethnic identity conflict: child forgetting Latino background, limited participation in cultural events, and the child not being taught skill to cope with racisms (Zambrana, 1999).

Little is known about the impact of ASFA on the Latino community despite the fact that in several large states and cities Latino children and youth represent a significant proportion (Suleiman, 2003). In 1995 the tragic death of a Latina child in New York city resulted in media and political attention and became a catalyst for change. It led Latino leaders and advocates to examine the many national and state level laws and policies affecting the well-being of Latino children.

Trans-Racial Adoptions

The intent of the Multi-Ethnic Placement Act (MEPA) of 1994 was to decrease the amount of time children waited to be adopted, eliminate discrimination in the placement of children, and enhance the identification and recruitment of foster and adoptive families that could meet the children's needs. The MEPA led to the creation of programs. A major concern experts have with this law is the risk of creating the impression that the search for families of the same national origin or cultural backgrounds would no longer be needed and conducted due to the pressure to place children more quickly.

Children of Seasonal Migrant Workers

The practice experience of one of the authors with children who belong to families that are seasonal migrant workers is addressed next. The families of these children live in nearby migrant camps with severely compromised housing conditions and surroundings. Many migrant camps do not meet the licensing requirements for standard living yet children and their families are provided with these substandard living arrangements by their employers. These deplorable conditions affect the morale of the children and their families with many of them suffering from depression. Latino children and youth are at risk of health hazards as many migrant camps are infested with rats, vermin, disease, dangerous farming equipment, and pesticides. Many children play in areas that are littered with garbage and drink water from large bins that contain rust. Latino children and their families are at risk for violent assaults from others living in the same settings. Latino youth are at risk of Methamphetamine (meth) use which has become easily accessible to Latino youth and their families in these migrant camps. It is used to anesthetize them from their plight and to produce higher levels of work performance for those working in the migrant fields. Meth use has major effects on the brain with detrimental effects that are irreversible. As these families migrate to work the land they are moving their children in and out of different schools. Latino families are enrolling their children into schools late and many times leaving school early, all related to the demands of this type of work. Latino migrant youth need special attention to their educational needs, housing, health, safety, and mental health. They are at risk of drug abuse and violent assaults with little protection from the authorities as they are isolated and with little support systems in tact.

Emancipation from Foster Care

Emancipation is like opening a door into adulthood and independence. For youth in foster care it is a time when new issues and struggles emerge. Some issues are common to all youth in transition: Poor health, homelessness, unemployment, welfare dependency, out-of-wedlock births, incarceration, and lack of education. The focus of preparation for emancipation has been on tangible self-sufficiency skills. However, experts claim that Latino youth also need help with the social and the emotional components of their transition. In their interviews with twenty-eight African Americans and Latino youth emancipating from foster care, Iglehart and Becerra (2003) found that emancipation preparation was a serious concern. The youth attributed the value of the independent living programs to the people in the programs and the relationships they had developed. At times those relationships were more important for the youth than even the skills development component of the program. Housing instability, work and school uncertainty, and family dysfunction were issues they were exposed to as they prepared to emancipation. For the Latino youth the socioemotional assistance was deemed as a crucial component to address. The authors also found that despite the hardships encountered Latino youth were attempting to cope.

Racism

Racial harassment is a serious problem that Latino children face in their schools and neighborhoods. Racism continues to be a major mental health problem for Latino children and adolescents because in effect racism imparts the mental health of the individual. It affects the person's sense of self and self-esteem and causes major stress on the daily life for the student at school and for the child or adolescents among peers and other adults. The stress factors can lead to an array of emotions and symptoms from vigilance, depression, fear, guarded behavior aggression, anger, and apathy, and posttraumatic symptoms. Racism can even lead to substance and alcohol abuse as a form of coping with this assault to one's sense of being. It can affect individuals' cognitive capacities as it compromises their desires with the constant threat to their dignity, integrity, and safety.

The lack of policies and guidelines in schools and communities that elaborate on no tolerance for racism is a concern. Latino children and adolescents, like all other children and adolescents, need to feel protected and their parents to be empowered to protect them. For children and parents to stand up against racism, the institutions of higher learning and the local and the state governments need to enact such protection for all children and families.

Children or adolescents who are in the United States without proper documentation are impacted by additional factors that need to be considered. Fears of being "found out" by the "migra" (immigration authorities) exacerbate their fears of separation and deportation of themselves and their parents. The fears of racism can reactivate their trauma keeping them at risk for developing serious mental health problems of anxiety, depression, and paranoia.

Gaps in the Child Welfare System

Child welfare services are many and extend from traditional services focused on family preservation, different types of foster care, reunification, adoption, and other permanent living arrangements to less traditional services such as childcare, in-school care programs, and parent education programs (Ortega, 2000). Many of these services may not be available for Latino children and youth. Some experts feel that the welfare system has been unresponsive to the needs of Latino children youth and their families. They claim that the system lacks the necessary understanding of the specific needs of Latino children, pays limited attention to those needs, and has provided limited opportunities and services for them (Ortega, 2000). There is no doubt that child welfare services in the United States have been expanded and improved but "little is known about the role child welfare services play in the lives of Latino children even at a time when Latino children represent the largest ethnic or racial population in the U.S." (Ortega, 2000, p. 5) and there are gaps that urgently need to be addressed (Ortega, 2000; Suleiman, 2003).

The welfare system's structure in itself is a concern. The system's process of considering and adapting to the cultural and linguistic characteristics of Latinos has been slow. There has been an inequitable distribution of resources for prevention and intervention services; system workers act as guardian instead of serving as facilitators to access the resources Latino youth and their families need; there is lack of involvement of Latino families in the planning process; and there is a differential treatment of poor Latino families as evidenced by parents not being provided adequate information. Interventions are usually driven by the deficits of the families rather than their strengths (Zambrana, 1999). Different ethnic groups receive differential treatment at "specific decision-making or key choice points in the system" (Hines et al., 2004, p. 523). African American and Latino families are less likely than Non-Latino whites to have specific service recommendations, and children of color [Latino] had fewer visits with their parents and siblings, fewer services overall, and less contact with caseworkers than white children (Zambrana, 1999).

There is limited awareness as to the process Latino children go through once they are in the Child Welfare Services (CWS), what happens to them and how decisions made within the system influence their trajectories in life. There is greater discrepancy between recommended and delivered services (Zambrana, 1999). Legislative efforts since 1980 to 1999 suggest that reform approaches have been inconsistently implemented (Zambrana, 1999). Also, there have been limited funds allocated for the recruitment and retention of qualified foster and adoptive parents from the same ethnic mix of children in care (Zambrana, 1999). Other concerns include "the lack of integrative services beyond child welfare to better address the complex and multiple needs of Latino children" (Ortega, Guillean, and Gutierrez-Najera, 1996, p. 2); and professionals' limited role, particularly Latino professionals, in influencing policy decision, program development, and practice implementation (Ortega, Guillean, and Gutierrez-Najera, 1996) on behalf of Latino children and youth.

Existing legislation does not provide options that promote family strengthening or protecting the children at risk. Moreover, persistent forms of discrimination "disfavor the strengthening of Latino families" (Zambrana, 1999, p. 9). Experts have raised concerns as to the racism of the welfare system, claiming that it is organized "of racialized public assistance attitudes, policy making and administrative practices" (Cazenave and Neubeck, 2001, p. 1) and alerting that such racism is hurting people in general and people of color in particular.

There are great gaps in research. Available research data on child welfare and Latino children, youth, and families is scarce. Census data has to be taken cautiously because it undercounted minority youth; as many as 20 percent of Latino youth (Armas, 2002). Child welfare studies do not differentiate Latino subgroups, therefore their findings are not as reliable (Ortega, 2000). Similarly many agencies fail to collect data on race and ethnicity making it impossible to develop a clear sense of the incidence of problems and needs which in turn limit the creation of appropriate program and the delivery of effective services.

Unmet Well-Being Indicators

The Child Welfare League of America (Culler, 2004) proposes that for any children to be healthy and safe the following five universal needs must be met: (1) *The Basics*: Equality, economic security and stability, nutrition, appropriate housing, health care, and education: (2) *Relationships*: Nurturing relationships with parents, kin, other adults, siblings, and peers; (3) *Opportunities*: Opportunities for affirmative connections to culture, traditions, and spiritual resources, development of talents and skills, and a positive transition to adulthood. (4) *Safety*: Protection from discrimination; accidental injury or death; environmental toxins; and abuse, neglect, and violence at home, school, the streets, and the media; and (5) *Healing*: Appropriate response to trauma by family, friends, and professionals; effective long-term support; and services that are comprehensive, needs-based interventions. Also inherent in the vision are a belief in strong communities and the need for more effective advocacy to ensure that appropriate resources are allocated to support family stability (Culler, 2004). After the previous discussion on welfare problems and needs of Latino children, youth, and their families the reader can note that for this population there are major deficits to address in most of the five need areas. Although many Latino families are managing to survive they are still experiencing great stress and limitations.

INTERVENTIONS

Overview

The characteristics, needs, and problems presented previously confirm to the reader that interventions to help Latino children, youth, and their families require a generalist perspective. Generalist practice has a multimethod and multilevel base and focuses on both individuals' problems and needs (private issues) and social problems with an emphasis on social justice (Landon, 1999). The generalist approach combines interventions to address Latino children's, youth's, and families' direct needs, problems and strengths, the realities, needs and strengths of their communities, and the socio economic and political conditions that permeate their daily lives. Devore and Schlesinger's (1996) ethnic-sensitive practice model is deemed appropriate when working with Latinos. Ethnic-sensitive generalist practice pays attention to the ethnic reality of people and the external and internal forces that sustain the role of social class and ethnicity, and views the helping process as a problem-solving endeavor. Attention is paid to both individual and systemic needs. The model allows for interventions to be based on an ecological, strengths-based, and culturally focused perspective.

Child welfare workers must be aware that many problems experienced by Latino children stem from external sources. For that reason they must explore the family's experiences of poverty, their lack of adequate resources, their immigration/migration experiences and levels of acculturation, their social class and experiences of racism, and the family's natural support systems. Oppression and discrimination may have affected these families, and their manifestations should be examined (Negroni-Rodríguez and Morales, 2002).

The strengths perspective—with its empowerment, membership, resilience, healing, dialogue, and collaboration and suspension of belief components (Saleebey, 2003)—offers these children and their families an opportunity to enhance their belief in family and community resources. They are seen as experts giving them an opportunity to be involved in the helping process and the community as resourceful. Power and respect are given to them as the belief is that all individuals have capacity and resource. The Latino culture's collectivist and interdependence approach and its contribution to the well-being of Latino children and youth need to be recognized, valued, and appreciated.

A culturally focused approach validates and acknowledges the children's and youths' culture and worldview as it relates to their perceptions through their cultural worldview. It has regard for the cultural material that is significant to their dynamics and state of mind and being. This perspective can keep child welfare workers culturally aware and expanding their knowledge of the clients' culture as well as developing their cultural proficiency.

The recommendations below address interventions at different levels: individual, family, community, and the society in general through the development and enhancement of policies and services. Both the recommendations and the vignettes propose the use of different methods of practice such as direct services, group work, community organizing, and policy development.

Individual and Family

Assessments and interventions of Latino children, youth, and their families must take into consideration their values, beliefs, and unique experiences. Lack of trust in service providers may be a result of their histories of being exploited and victimized by overt racism, and the impersonality and bureaucratic nature of the systems (Negroni-Rodríguez and Morales, 2002). Direct practice with these children and adolescents must assess the belief systems used by the Latino family to frame their problems and needs, and their help-seeking behaviors and coping mechanisms. When a worker lacks knowledge of the cultural values, beliefs and norms of the cultural group to which the child and his or her family belongs, there is the risk of defining certain child's or family's behaviors as problematic when they are functional within their cultural context (Negroni-Rodríguez and Morales, 2002).

It will be important that workers possess self-awareness, effective communication, engaging and relationship-building skills, and an understanding of the power dynamics involved in the helping process (Negroni-Rodríguez and Morales, 2002; Samantrai, 2004). Workers must receive ongoing training that addresses all of the issues of foster care and the problems that lead children in general, and Latino children and youth in particular, into foster care. They must also receive proper supervision with culturally competent supervisors who can facilitate their process of learning and their provision of proper services. Experts emphasize the need for education both for child welfare personnel and for foster families to address their attitudes and lack of knowledge with regard to different Latino groups (Garland, Landsverk, and Lau, 2003).

Because many child welfare workers are insufficiently trained to work in the field of child abuse, they should have a series of relevant intensive staff development training sessions before they are assigned cases. All social workers, including professionals with an MSW, need preparation and orientation to cope with the differences between clients who voluntarily seek help and those who are "forced" to accept it because the law requires it, as in the case of abusive mothers. Given the stressors and pressures caused by these cases, these professionals also need a supportive administration.

When working with Latino families it is important to utilize the support of kinship care which can consist of extended family members, nuclear family–blended family members, and/or *compadres/padrinos* (godfather) or *comadres/madrinas* (godmother). If these family members and friends are available it is useful to incorporate them into the helping process. These individuals can lessen the psychological and emotional trauma of loss and separation because they will continue for the most part in the same value system.

Many immigrant families have limited or no access to support systems as many of them are separated from their families whom they leave behind in their home country. These families may be at risk as they feel the vulnerability of being alone, without the proper support and at the mercy of the system. These are also the families that may have difficulties understanding all of the follow-up they need to tend and oblige with in order to reunite with their children.

The cultural wealth that Latino children and their families bring with them needs to be "known" and appreciated in the assessment process. It is a mistake to pathologize some practices because they may be part of the Latino family's cultural identity, and source of strength and resource. DeLa Cruz-Quiróz recalls an incident when her family was on vacation together and her niece's son appeared ill, crying, and was inconsolable. All family members took turns supporting him and his young mother in taking care of him. It was in the middle of the night and they were all worried and feeling alarmed as they were also out of town and had little knowledge of any facilities outside of looking for an emergency room in the yellow pages, which they could do immediately in the event that his situation escalated. Suddenly the author's mother said she wanted to cure him of the *susto* (freight) and so they hurried and got the old trusty egg out of the refrigerator and the mother began her ritual of rubbing the uncooked egg still in the shell over his body including eyes, forehead, chest, legs, stomach, and back and he was now sleeping. They then all sat around the kitchen table as the author's mother led them into prayer. They said the Rosary with her as she asked for the child's health. This ritual that has been performed by many Latino families was ever so soothing, containing and sustaining of the importance of caring for each other, bonding and attaching to the family members in ritual and traditions that seek to bind fears, anxiety, and symptomatic behaviors of health and mental health. It signifies the power of belief and the power of values, ritual, and tradition. For the family to engage in this ceremony for the health of the author's nephew was powerful and empowering. The child slept through the night and was fine the next morning.

When working with Latino children and their families, assessments need to be properly developed in order to capture the symptoms and behaviors that signify health and mental health for the culture of the Latino person. For many families and their children it is important to incorporate in the assessment how the child has been feeling physically or how the parent might have noticed bodily symptoms that indicate in their mind a suffering or a problem the child is having. It is important to ask what kinds of treatments or interventions were tried prior to seeking treatment. Asking these questions can also expand the service provider's understanding of the ways in which a cultural group thinks of health and mental health problems and the different methods of interventions that take place that are meaningful to a child and to the family.

Narrative therapies are useful and effective in helping Latinos explain their human condition. Oral histories have been part of the Latino culture and narratives are significant in helping to reconstruct their history and in telling their story. Attachment theories are useful in understanding the attachment process and how the Latino child or youth organizes and bonds to the significant others and the meaning of the extended family, attachments to the environmental landscapes, food, music, art, rituals, value systems, beliefs, and traditions.

Assessment of the family reunification situation is critical to providing proper services to these families. Children who are reunited with their families after having been separated from their parents due to migration to the United States for employment face many hurdles and challenges. Many times these children have been separated for many years and are strangers on reunification. Having been raised by other family members, they may have got attached to those significant others and once again find the separation from those who raised them traumatic and heart wrenching, to leave after having adjusted to life without their biological parents. There may be new siblings who were born and raised in the United States with their parents who are also strangers to them and who are attached to their parents which may become problematic for the new arrival children. There may be significant acting out as a way of protesting and mourning their losses and expressing their hurt and disappointment for being left behind only to be disrupted once again. The parents may also find themselves having difficulties attaching to their new arrival children and even resentful that they have sacrificed so much to bring their children to the United States and are not well received and not respected as parents. These parents may also feel guilty and lack knowledge as to how to manage the situation. They may find themselves unable to work through this situation in the best way they would want to. It is not uncommon for these new arrival children to find themselves unable to focus and having problems at school and may become easy prey to criminal behavior, and so on. These families need tremendous understanding and help in repairing the deep wounds of despair, rage, fears, and hopelessness.

Interventions to facilitate family reunification or adoption must take into consideration family structure and the different characteristics of the families. It is important to determine the nature of family reunification. Is this a reunification of a family that has been separated from each other prematurely due to the parents' relocation to the United States for work purposes? Or is this a reunification of a family that has been separated due to child abuse/neglect allegations?

Programs to help children cope with trauma must be able to address the issues of domestic violence and trauma to parents or caregivers. By incorporating these elements into future prevention and intervention programs and continuing to study effective strategies, practitioners can help break the cycle of violence by minimizing youth victimization and exposure to violence (Osofsky, 2001). Groups are an appropriate intervention when they combine supportive and empowering strategies and a focus on changes not only in these people's lives but also in the systems with which they interact on a daily basis, for example school (teachers, peers), family (foster parents, biological parents, siblings), protective system (social workers, probation officers, lawyer), and their communities.

Latino children placed in out-of-home care and foster care need to be provided with the same legal rights which ensure appropriate mental health, health, educational services, and any special services that are required of any child within a foster care and an out-of-home care placement. The Latino child's language in which he or she communicates is important to assess for proper placement. Placing a child in a home where his language is not understood adds to the trauma of separation, increasing his or her stress and impacting the child's sense of safety. The danger of placing a Latino monolingual child in a home where his language is not spoken or understood has to do with this child not being understood and unable to communicate with his caregivers. This can exasperate both child and caregiver, developing into negative experiences for both. Often Latino children who out of frustration, sadness, fear, and anxiety react with anger while in placement are misunderstood and diagnosed with disorders such as ADHD or other behavior disorders. Assessment of these behaviors is critical to the well-being of the Latino child to assure appropriate responses from caregiver and services and prevent unnecessary labels that take this child onto another path of incompetence on the part of the systems involved and a falling through the cracks of a child with needs that are never understood adding to his or her victimization.

It is imperative that Latino children be given a thorough assessment while in placement because they are at risk since they fall into the vulnerable category of children with major developmental delays. Latino children in foster care need to be given the proper emotional care to assist them in their process of adjusting to their new environment and in facilitating their unfortunate journey. The selection of placement for the Latino child needs to take into consideration:

- Any special needs of the child and the foster care provider's ability to comprehend and appreciate the child's emotional and developmental needs.
- The caregiver needs to be culturally proficient in order to address the cultural needs of the child.

- Temporary caregivers need to provide opportunities for Latino children to get attached to them in a proper way in order to help them during this traumatic time.

Community Interventions

Prevention is an essential community strategy. Community development and sustainability are considered the "best prevention strategy for family-well-being in Latino communities" (Suleiman, 2003, p. 21). Communities' infrastructures should be based on preventive practices that support, fortify, and strengthen families (Suleiman, 2003). Prevention should begin before Latino families enter the welfare system. Community-based multiservices agencies should provide a range of programs for families that include concrete services, recreational programs, activities for different age groups, and individual and group counseling (Suleiman, 2003).

Welfare services need to be more responsive to the multicultural reality of our nation. It has been the role of the state, as guardian of the community, to care and protect children suffering from neglect and abuse, homelessness, poverty, and danger of becoming delinquents (Samantrai, 2004). Laws have been created that establish welfare services for all children while a system of service delivery has been implemented that works together with public, private, and community-based organizations. The child welfare practice in the United States has been influenced primarily by the norms and standards of the Anglo-European culture. Those norms determined the definitions of a family and normal or healthy family functioning (Samantrai, 2004). In contrast, the majority of children involved in child welfare services have been of different ethnic backgrounds, and the imposition of Anglo-European cultural values on child rearing and, parenting on other cultural groups has caused problems and damage (Samantrai, 2004). It has not been until recently that the child welfare system began its journey into becoming culturally competent.

Cultural competence involves ways of thinking, feeling, and behaving. Cultural competence must be manifested in both effective organizational and individual worker cross-cultural work (Pecora et al., 2000). There is need for a cultural self-assessment process and the provision of opportunities for gaining and expanding cultural knowledge, understanding the dynamics generated by cultural differences, and adapting services to meet the unique needs of different cultural groups (Pecora et al., 2000). Cultural Competence requires that helping professionals "value" differences and that systems implement specific systems of care to effectively serve Latino children, youth, and their families. There is need for more culturally competent risk-assessment tools, family-centered services, neighborhood-based and family-centered foster care services, kinship care and efforts to keep siblings together. In its commitment to Latino and other children and youth of color both government and private agencies and organizations must seek adequate funding, pay attention to organizational and community barriers, and seek to eliminate institutional racism and inequities in income distribution (Pecora et al., 2000).

More culturally competent community-based organizations and neighborhood-based agencies are needed. These organizations and agencies should incorporate indigenous Latino leadership who can inspire and educate other Latinos and Latino children and youth as well. Pabón and Pabón (2004) have proposed to use natural cultural and community human supports called *facilitators* within neighborhoods to provide services to Latino at-risk youths and families. These facilitators supplement traditional juvenile services. They are responsible for surrounding at-risk families with a *circle of care* consisting of families and extra-family members, neighbors, and formal neighborhood representatives to assist the family and collaborate with the juvenile probation worker in providing supervision and services to the youth.

The use of a collectivistic approach that incorporates nonindividualistic intervention may be helpful. Communities must influence, secure, and maintain the power to change government and nongovernment structures in ways that facilitate their capacity to solve people's problems and meet people's specific needs. Applied to problems such as child abuse and neglect and juvenile delinquency, communities need to gain awareness of the scope of the problems in their own sectors, propose ideas and develop projects to eliminate and prevent the problem, and use their power to move the social system toward changes to achieve this goal. Prevention can be accomplished with efforts and programs directed toward parents, caregivers, and families and a focus on issues of violence within the family (Osofsky, 2001). Parents, teachers, principals, daycare providers, law enforcement officers, and juvenile justice system professionals can be trained to recognize "red flags" and identify risk factors for victimization early in the Latino child's life. More proactive laws and community-oriented policing that builds trust and relationships with both juveniles and family members are needed.

Social workers face the challenge of becoming skilled analysts of their social reality, learning to practice more social action and community organization, adopting a political activist role, and advocating for more prevention and community education.

Social Policies

Policies determine the type and amount of services available for populations in need. More policies are needed that focus on improving the well-being of the children's biological families; support the creation and evaluation of services tailored for Latino families; demand the provision of bilingual and culturally competent services; and increase incentives for the recruitment of Latino adoptive families (Suleiman, 2003).

In 1996 The National Latino Advocacy group published the findings of a study conducted in six states that explored the welfare needs of Latino children and their families. The following priorities were identified: (1) to make Latino children visible in data, (2) evaluate the inclusion of Latino child welfare experts, and (3) move the focus from child welfare to the welfare of Latino children (Ortega, Guillean, and Gutierrez-Najera, 1996).

In 2003 the Committee for Hispanic Children and Families, Inc. in New York proposed a welfare agenda that addresses issues of policy and practice on behalf of Latino children (Suleiman, 2003). The agenda was developed by attendees to the first national conference on issues affecting Latino families involved in the child welfare system.

The conference produced five strategic components that needed to be addressed: (1) Personnel and practice enhancements—recruitment of bilingual and culturally competent staff at every level of the field; (2) Planning and evaluation data—collection of accurate information that informs practice and policy decisions and advances the research agenda; (3) Policy—policies must be culturally responsive and should support the family and ensure equity; (4) Partnerships and positions of access—identify and develop working relationships with child welfare research, practice, and policy leadership and increase Latino presence and leadership in advisory groups and boards that design and implement research, practice, and policy; and (5) Public awareness—develop a media strategy to inform the broader community, replicate conferences that address child welfare needs and issues of Latinos, develop and disseminate conference proceedings, and conduct community forums on issues that affect Latinos (Suleiman, 2003).

Changes to support Latino families in the welfare system have to be systematic and have to address issues of race, class, and power. Latinos must be included in all child welfare policy discussions at all federal, state, and local levels; generating funding for research; and raising awareness in the community on how laws and legislation benefit or harm Latino children.

Policy makers and service providers must encourage funding and development of more culturally appropriate services (Garland, Landsverk, and Lau, 2003). More strategies are needed that fight welfare racism and that enhance education opportunities, research and monitoring, legal remedies, legislative policy action, and social protests and grassroots organization involvement (Cazenave and Neubeck, 2001). Data on many different issues is needed. For instance, research that examines the interactions between the individual, family, and community factors to propel children into the welfare system, and focuses on Latino children's, youth's, and their families' coping efforts and resiliency.

The ASFA needs to be revised in order to take into consideration the realities of Latinos. Experts in the field claim that reunification rather than adoption needs to become more of a priority. The fast-track approach to termination of parental rights needs to be revised. Factors like the ones already discussed in this chapter impede Latino families to comply with ASFA time frames (Suleiman, 2003). Practitioners and policy makers need to assess the best use of resources in order for these families to be able to meet those time frames. Moreover, research must be done to assess the impact that ASFA is having on Latino families (Suleiman, 2003).

CASE STUDY 1   DOMESTIC VIOLENCE

Felipe, Dalila and Isabel aged 3, 4 and 5 respectively are under the protection of the child welfare agency. They experience developmental delays directly related to an accumulation of traumatic events related to the violence between their parents. Mr. and Mrs. Ventura hail from Mexico but the children were born in the United States. The couple came to the United States because Mrs. Ventura's husband got an employment visa. Several years after their arrival they became legal residents. The children were temporarily placed in foster care after domestic violence and an incident of child physical abuse was substantiated.

In placing the children the protective worker explored first the kinship resources available in this family. The child welfare worker was aware of the importance of the extended family and knew that strengthening Mrs. Ventura's support system would help discourage risks for future domestic violence incidents or child neglect or abuse. Among traditional Latino families it is a function of the extended family to help in raising the children and to provide "consejos" (advise) in times of tension and difficulties. Bringing the family together would also impact positively Mrs. Ventura's self-confidence.

Among the services provided to this family was a referral to a group of battered women. One of the issues Mrs. Ventura was dealing with in the group was her ambivalence about what to do with her marriage and the weight her decision would have on her children's well-being. In a group meeting, and on returning from a visit to her hometown in Mexico, Mrs. Ventura reported to the group members about a meeting she had with her local parish priest whom she sought out after feeling anxious and "*con nervios.*" She told the priest how the man she had married had been beating her for several years and that her children were terrified of him as she was. She explained that she had left him and was worried because he was her husband and she had an obligation to him and the marriage as she had promised "*in sickness and in health.*" Mrs. Ventura was ambivalent about forgiving him. She felt that she could not get back with him, yet felt tormented by her decision to remain separate and move to a possible divorce. She felt scared, conflicted, and worried if she returned he would continue to inflict the violence on her and her entire family.

Surprisingly to Mrs. Ventura and to the other women in the group this priest told her she had made the right decision and that he would not support her returning to her husband. He reiterated he would be very disappointed and angry with her if she did so. She stated she felt truly sanctioned to leave this violent relationship feeling that she had his "*blessing.*" The blessing had a deeper meaning to her as she experienced this as a religious intervention, powerful and, most importantly, showing her she had the strength and internal resources to seek help. She acknowledged to the group how important they had been in helping her to call him for an appointment which was something she felt she could not do in the past. His words gave her the authority to do the right thing for her and her children.

The group facilitator showed appreciation of the deep loyalties and commitment to the representations of these authority figures and worked with Mrs. Ventura in a positive way to fortify her. Many Latinos do not speak about their religious beliefs to a provider because they do not want to be misunderstood. However, it is very common for clients to say in response to many things, including "I will see you next week;" "*Si Dios Quiere* (if God Willing)." The group worker was appreciative, understanding, and respectful of Mrs. Ventura's beliefs and attachments to her faith and religion and intervened in a supportive and empowering manner by using validation and encouraging her to validate herself and her decision-making process.

Mrs. Ventura is struggling with the decision of going back to school. The income she gets from her part-time job and the public assistance benefits are scarcely enough to care for her children. In addition, she has two elderly parents that she feels very committed to care for and a sibling with special needs. The child welfare worker is aware that in the mainstream culture the expectation would be that Mrs. Ventura thinks more in her and develops a plan that will allow her to become independent and self-sufficient. But the worker is aware that Mrs. Ventura's identity has been influenced by *familismo* values and understands Mrs. Ventura's refusal to focus on her needs and her independence because of her sense of responsibility to her family. If Mrs. Ventura's primary loyalty to her family

(continued)

- - - - -

CASE STUDY 1   Continued

is not understood and supported, her attempts to protect such loyalty may cause internal conflicts for her and will affect her relationship with the children and even with the welfare worker. The worker's appreciation of the meaning of this loyalty will help Mrs. Ventura with her internal struggle. This does not mean that Mrs. Ventura has individuation problems. It just means that in addition to individuation Mrs. Ventura also maintain close relations with her family and those areas need to be supported as part of the process of helping the children to be back.

The agency that is providing services to Mrs. Ventura and her family attributes great importance to the recruitment of Latino social workers and the training of culturally competent workers.

- - - - -

CASE STUDY 2   OUT-OF-HOME PLACEMENT

Mario is a Spanish-speaking Puerto Rican youth who came to the United States when he was 9 years old. He was raised by his elderly grandparents because his parents were incarcerated. Mario was always a bright student and his academic performance and behaviors were exceptional. However, at age 9 his behavior at school and home began to change. He became oppositional and rebellious. The grandparents decided to send him to the United States with their daughter Sylvia with the hopes that a change would help him and that their daughter would be more effective in controlling his behavior. When Mario came to the United States he had a difficult time adjusting. He was placed in a mainstream English-speaking program. He did not do well academically. After an evaluation was made he was diagnosed with learning and behavioral problems and placed in special education were he remained for years. Such evaluation had not been standardized for Puerto Ricans. The evaluator did not speak Spanish and had no knowledge and understanding of the Puerto Rican culture, nor of the impact of migration and acculturation on migrant or immigrant children. Mario was placed in a school environment that was not sensitive to who he was, nor to his specific educational, emotional, and social needs as a migrant child.

Mario's family was not supportive and nurturing enough. His aunt worked two shifts and her availability was very limited. Mario's cousins had been born and raised in the United States, did not speak Spanish and were busy with their own life and friends. Mario found himself quite lonely within his own family. At the age of 14 he joined a youth gang and started to try on substances. His academic progress was poor. Although his behavior had improved, Mario became a sad and quiet adolescent. The school had given up on him. In one occasion Mario and some other gang members were caught up stealing in a department store. As a result the juvenile system became involved. Counseling was offered with the goal of helping him with his "issues" and preventing further delinquent behaviors. Substance abuse education was another service provided to him. Unfortunately, Mario and the counselor never engaged successfully, which the counselor interpreted as resistance to change. He blamed Mario for his "unwillingness to cooperate" in helping himself. However, Mario did not feel he could communicate well with the counselor. Mario felt the counselor was not really interested in him. Mario could not trust him. The counselor's sole focus on changing Mario was not successful. The disciplinary team with which he consulted the case did not take into consideration Mario's attachment needs and the importance that family had for him. The strengths he brought as a Puerto Rican youth and a gang leader could have been reframed and utilized in the helping process as resources Mario could use differently. The mental health agency was not well equipped to serve this Latino adolescent. Mario became rebellious and aggressive. The fights between him and his cousins increased. He ran away once and when found his aunt decided he could not live with them any longer. Mario was placed in a group home.

The group home social worker conducted a thorough assessment of Mario's situation. Because of her knowledge of and exposure to the Puerto Rican culture and her appreciation of the impact of migration and acculturation stress in the emotional and social development of the youth, she was able to engage and connect with Mario and conceptualize Mario's problems in a different perspective. She referred the youth to culturally competent psychologists and educational counselors. When appropriate assessment tools were used to assess his intellectual and emotional functioning it was evident that Mario had much more intellectual strengths and potential than the ones identified in the past.

Therapeutic work was done to help Mario regain his confidence and empower him to use his strengths on his behalf. Services such as English, remedial classes, and mentoring were provided. In the group home Mario was treated with attention, consideration, respect, and appropriate boundaries and limit settings. Mario adjusted well. Soon after, his behavior and academic performance changed gradually. He developed attachments with the group home's social worker and other staff members, particularly a Latino recreational leader who ended up becoming a mentor and role model. Mario used to say that in the group home he found a *family*.

The director of the group made sure that appropriate policies were in place to provide a culturally competent home environment for Mario and youths from other ethnic groups. For instance, a policy safeguarded Mario's right to speak in his language of dominance; food menus included diverse ethnic dishes; and the different cultural traditions and celebrations the youth identified with were supported and celebrated. Also, the director supported staff and youth involvement in community events that celebrated the youths' identities and interests. Emphasis was also placed on strengthening his relationships with extended family members, parents, and other supportive adults who had been part of his life.

Mario completed his high-school diploma and enrolled in a college-preparatory program. In the meantime, he was prepared to learn independent living skills and provided tangible resources such as cash, household items, and a driver's license.

CASE STUDY 3   NON-LATINO FOSTER PLACEMENT

Jesse, a 6-years-old English-speaking Dominican, came into the attention of the child protection agency after physical abuse and neglect were substantiated. He was removed from his home and placed with the O'Neil's, a white foster family, after no Latino foster homes were found. When children are placed in non-Latino homes or put for adoption, issues emerge around ethnic identity conflict, child forgetting Latino background,

(continued)

■ ■ ■ ■ ■

CASE STUDY 3   Continued

limited participation in cultural events, and the child not being taught skills to cope with racism. The worker in this case was aware of the possible emerging issues and knew that part of her helping responsibility was to serve as liaison between the two worlds now involved in the child's life, protect the child's cultural identity, and prevent racism.

The protective agency had policies that included specific training for foster parents on parenting Latino children and on relating to Latino families. The training provided them with knowledge on the Latino culture and the impact if migration/immigration and acculturation on children and their families. The foster parents learned to think in terms of strengths and resiliencies and to interact with their foster children and their families using that approach. Part of the training also included addressing the impact of stereotyping and racism. The training included a component in which the O'Neil's had to examine and work with their attitudes, beliefs, and feelings about other ethnic groups, race, and social class. Nevertheless, the worker conducted an assessment of this foster family's readiness and willingness to have a Latino child.

Jesse was born and raised in the United States and spoke mostly English which helped him connect with the foster family. His parents were primarily Spanish speaking and strongly identified with traditional Dominican values and beliefs. In this case reunification was a possibility and the parents were allowed to have weekly visitations. The worker helped these two families to communicate by providing interpreters, having all documents in both languages, and connecting them with opportunities to learn each other's language. She helped the foster family to relate to Jesse and the biological parents in a way that would show appreciation of who they were culturally. The foster family learned about the country and once in a while cooked a Dominican or other Latino dish.

Jesse's separation and sense of loss was minimized by the caring and accepting attitude of the foster parents and their understanding of the child's cultural context. He was helped by the worker and the foster parents to understand that differences were good and that he brought strengths to the new family. The foster family made an effort to meet Jesse where he was and to accept him and help him through his transitions. To the best possible extent they provided space for Jesse to be in contact not only with his parents but with other family members, particularly his *padrino* and *madrina* (godparents).

Jesse had a dark skin color and the worker was aware that racism was a risk. In her interview of the foster family she addressed issues of racism. She kept regular contact with Jesse and constantly assessed how the child and the foster family were coping with their skin color differences.

■ ■ ■ ■ ■

CASE STUDY 4   CHILD ABUSE

Marisol is a 17-years-old adolescent who reunited with her mother Claudia 2 years ago. Claudia is second-generation and her daughter is third-generation Salvadorian. The reason for their initial separation was their many fights allegedly due to Marisol's disobedience and oppositional behaviors. In one occasion the fight ended up in both mother and daughter physically hitting each other. As a consequence, Claudia sent Marisol to

El Salvador to live with her father. The decision to bring Marisol back to the United States was influenced by the adolescent's many requests for another opportunity and Claudia's need for help in caring for her second daughter Nimia who is 3 years old. Nimia's father died very soon after Nimia was born. For the last year and a half Claudia has been in a new relationship with Wilbert. They have no children of their own.

Recently Marisol disclosed to a teacher that her mother's boyfriend attempted to "make love" with her and she was afraid to be back home. The youth reported that Wilbert threatened her if she would tell anybody and that he would make it sure nobody would believe her. After listening to the details the teacher suspected sexual abuse and made a referral to the child protective agency. The protective services worker came to the house and spoke with Claudia who reacted with anger and suspiciousness. Claudia refused to believe Marisol and saw her disclosure as a manipulation to get attention and to send Wilbert out of the house.

Marisol expressed to the protective services worker that she felt afraid to tell her mother because she had no "confianza" (trust) in her and was not sure her mother would believe her given their past problems. In the assessment process other issues came out, such as Marisol feeling like a stranger to her mother and her resentments for being treated differently from her little sister. Marisol was also protective of her mother. She worried that her disclosure would create problems to her mother whom she saw was so overwhelmed with two jobs and the responsibility of watching after her and her sister.

Marisol's case required the following multicultural practice considerations. First, the worker needed to be aware of the importance of family connections in this Latino family both for the mother and for the daughter. Services had to target both Marisol and her family.

SUMMARY OF KEY ISSUES AND CONCEPTS

Latino children and adolescents are a heterogeneous group. Their experiences of migration/immigration and acculturation, when applicable, as well as those of their family members must be taken into consideration when making decisions about safety and protection, placement, services provision, and mental health treatment. Unfortunately, many barriers threat the well-being of this ethnic group in the United States. The stressors confronted by these children and their families are many. In order to better serve and help them a generalist approach is recommended. Interventions must be multisystemic and multimethod and must consist of an ecological, strength-based, and culturally focused approach.

SOCIAL SERVICES AMONG WHITE ETHNIC AND MIDDLE EASTERN CHILDREN, YOUTH, AND FAMILIES

TANYA R. FITZPATRICK, PH.D., M.S.W., R.N.
Department of Social Work, Arizona State University

GORDON LIMB, PH.D.
School of Social Work, Brigham Young University

SUZANNE BUSHFIELD, PH.D.
Department of Social Work, Arizona State University

White ethnic children and family.

OVERVIEW

In light of the influx in the 1990s of Middle Easterners and other white ethnic groups to America, a greater need exists for culturally relevant information addressing the diversity within and among these groups. Although literature exists on social work practice with white ethnic groups, little attention has been focused on child welfare issues and practice. This chapter focuses on several European immigrant populations addressing demographic and historical information, theoretical perspectives, family values and beliefs, and child welfare issues. The ultimate goal is to consider and discuss therapeutic implications as they relate to social work practice. We specifically focus on the Irish, Italians, Russian Jews, Jewish and Palestinian immigrants, and Arab Americans. Along with demographic information, this chapter highlights theoretical perspectives as they relate to white ethnic groups and suggests additional theories, which are also relevant to children, youth, and families from all minority groups in this country. We present several case studies, which assist in providing examples of assessment, goals, and the treatment process for white ethnic families. Finally, we present questions for class discussion, exam questions, suggested readings based on theoretical perspectives, demographic and historical information, culturally competent child welfare practice, and PowerPoint presentation suggestions.

INTRODUCTION

The cultural diversity that is found within and among white ethnic groups in America brings a greater need for culturally relevant information. This will ultimately prepare social workers and child welfare practitioners to understand and appreciate the variety of values, norms, and family interactions to guide more appropriate services and interventions. Due to the influx of Middle Easterners and other white European groups in the 1990s, it would be misleading to clump all white ethnics into one society. Furthermore, it is misleading to compare white ethnic groups with the dominant white population as far as issues of poverty, domestic violence, foster family care, and adoptions are concerned. Although some literature exists on social work practice with European immigrant populations to the United States (Karger and Levine, 2000), little attention has been focused on child welfare issues and practice among these groups. In addition, very little is written as to who actually belongs in the group people refer to as "white" (Guadalupe and Lum, 2005).

This chapter focuses on several white ethnic groups addressing demographic information, family values and beliefs, theoretical perspectives, and child welfare issues with the ultimate goal of presenting therapeutic implications for culturally competent social work practice. Although we attempt to represent all categories of Eastern and Southern European and Middle Eastern immigrant groups, we highlight the Irish, Italians, Russian Jews from the Soviet Union, and

Jewish and Palestinian immigrants. The aims of the chapter will be addressed by focusing on:

Part   I. Demographic and theoretical perspectives
Part II. Child welfare issues and problems
Part III. Therapeutic interventions for social work practice
Part IV. Summary of key issues and concepts

We also include suggested readings and resources, recommended questions for discussion, questions for exams, and suggestions for PowerPoint presentations.

PART I: DEMOGRAPHIC BACKGROUND INFORMATION

An Overview: European Americans

It is difficult to describe white Americans as many can trace their ancestry to the following groups: English, German, Irish, French, Scottish, Polish, Dutch, Swedish, Norwegian, Russian, Czech, Slovakian, Hungarian, Welsh, Danish, and Portuguese (Karger and Levine, 2000). Assimilation into American society has occurred among most of the groups, yet diversity between and among the groups in their values and way of life has contributed to the uniqueness of our society. Therefore, the term "white ethnics" can be applied to a variety of groups from eastern and southern Europe in which migration to the United States began in 1900. This is in contrast to Irish immigration (northern Europeans), which began in the 1850s, and immigration from Germany, which peaked in the 1880s (Farley, 2000). European Americans form 80 percent of the American population. German Americans are the largest group (58 million), followed by the English (41 million) and Irish Americans (39 million) (Lum, 2003).

Farley uses the term "intermediate status" to describe the position and status of certain groups in the United States such as Asian Americans, Jewish, and other white ethnic Americans (2000, p. 256). Their status can be described as a minority group in terms of discrimination and exclusion from the "power elite" (p. 256), yet in other ways they are above the societal norm in terms of education and income. Most families from European American groups are multigenerational and have been in the Unites States for three or more generations (Giordano and McGoldrick, 1996). Some say that "cultural awareness of European roots has faded over time" (Lum, 2003, p. 79). However, religion and cultural values have prevailed in most groups.

The history of social welfare has been linked to the white English-American privileged class at the time. The Protestant work ethic was the leading force and social attitude toward welfare recipients. Discrimination and racism were directed towards Irish Catholics, American Indians, and gays and lesbians. Many European Americans are often ambivalent about their cultural identities as the desire to be accepted and be successful may be in conflict with their own particular family history and experiences.

Giordano and McGoldrick (1996) believe that it is difficult to build cultural awareness in European Americans, as ethnicity is perceived only in outward features unlike the Asian, African American, and American Indians where differences can be readily observed. A common perspective has been shared regarding issues of racial identity, affirmative action, busing, minority scholarships, and understanding of race-related events (Farley, 2000).

Nevertheless, a preference hierarchy was developed among the European American groups based on religion, the arrival times of the immigrants, and the region of origin in which the Protestants were the dominant group (i.e. ethnics from Northern and Western Europe such as the British). The amount of resistance encountered was usually associated with the degree of similarities to or differences from the dominant group (Healey, 1996). However, despite the lack of racial identity, which persisted among many white ethnic groups, many European people who immigrated during the early 1990s arrived with their own distinct culture.

Immigrants from the Middle East

Greater interest has been focused on the incorporation into the United States of persons of Muslim Middle Eastern origin since 9/11. Middle Easterners are one of the fastest growing immigrant groups in the United States with a population of nearly 1.5 million including both legal and illegal immigrants. These figures do not include 570,000 U.S.-born children (under 18) who have at least one parent born in the Middle East, or the grandchildren and great grandchildren. American citizenship rates are high (55 percent) and these numbers are expected to continue to increase to 950,000 by 2010 (Camarota, 2002). Children born in the United States to immigrants are by definition natives and this is one of the reasons for the tremendous increase in the population (Camarota, 2002).

Arab immigrants have been coming to the United States for over 100 years yet are most definitely not a homogenous group. At least 600,000 immigrants came to the United States from Iran, Iraq, Jordan, Lebanon, Egypt, Syria, and Turkey between 1971 and 1992 (U.S. Bureau of Census, 1994), and U.S.-born adults from the Middle East are descendants of Maronites, Armenians, and other Christian groups arriving in the late nineteenth century or the first half of the twentieth century (Camarota, 2002). Camarota's study defines the Middle Eastern groups as those from Pakistan, Bangladesh, Afghanistan, Turkey, the Levant, the Arabian Peninsula, and Arab North Africa. Cohen and Tyree (1994) state that over 30 percent of Israeli-born Americans are Palestinian-Arab natives of Israel, the West bank, and Gaza Strip.

Theoretical Perspectives

It is necessary to provide a foundation for understanding how theories that apply to ethnic and immigrant groups may help to explain the relationship between social work practice and child welfare issues that address the specific and unique needs of children from white ethnic and Middle Eastern families. Assimilation has been the major focus in the United States and a goal for immigrants and those from different ethnic backgrounds, in which former separate groups or cultures come together to melt into society and share elements from a variety of traditions. Assimilation theory views ethnicity and minority status as a temporary situation (Markides and Mindel, 1987).

After a period of time in the United States, one gradually rises up the socioeconomic ladder towards a middle-class position usually resulting in "loss of cultural distinctiveness" (Markides and Mindel, 1987, p. 38). The expectation is that everyone will become assimilated. In respect to family implications, children would lose their cultural traditions earlier and replace them with values and patterns from the dominant culture, which usually creates conflict among the older generations. However, some ethnic groups have been in the United States for generations and continue to follow ascribed cultural norms. In some cultures, younger family members are educated but remain active in family ceremonies and native religions such as the Native American tribes in the southwest.

"Cultural pluralism must be differentiated from assimilation. Assimilation occurs when two distinct groups merge and become one, in that the differences between the groups cease to exist. However, pluralism exists when each group observes its own unique identity and the groups remain separate despite the duration of time" (Fitzpatrick, 2001, p. 63; Healy, 1996). Acculturation on the other hand is a more subtle process. It takes place over a longer period of time and certainly relates to many of the European groups who have been in the United States, such as the Germans, the Irish, and Italians. Eastern European Jewish and Russian immigrants who have arrived more recently have experienced acculturation differently. Tran and colleagues (1996) state that English language acquisition is a major component in the process of acculturation. It includes basic elements in the individual's personal background and the host society in which language, education, familiarity with the host culture, and generational factors are all important.

Those of European descent make up the majority of cases within the child welfare system, yet for the most part, traditions of their specific cultures have been passed down through the generations. Depending on the time of arrival, the age, and length of stay in the United States, European immigrants and those from the Middle East have experienced assimilation, cultural pluralism, and acculturation at different rates and in different ways. It is important to recognize that although specific cultural and/or religious factors are important in all families, one should not assume that Caucasian or white ethnic families are not diverse (Mather and Lager, 2000). In what way will these factors affect the families coping mechanism and their utilization of appropriate services when needed?

Child welfare workers also need to be familiar with theories such as the "Person in Environment" (see Germain and Gitterman, 1980), the "Strength's Perspective" (see Saleebey, 1992), and the "Multiculturalism Perspective" (Mather and Lager, 2000). In general, social workers should familiarize themselves with these theories which can apply not only to immigrant populations but also to all other non-white ethnic minority groups. "Person in the Environment" (PIE) is a "classification system developed for the purpose of social work assessment. Assessment is based on four factors: social functioning problems, environmental problems, mental health problems, and physical health problems" (Hutchison, 1999, p. 469). These factors are transactional, yet never relay on classifying clients as normal or abnormal. This broad classification assures that most of the client's needs will be addressed. Germain (1994) in her work on Person in Environment states that social workers are more interested in seeking knowledge from both the environment and the personal factors. She also states that this recent trend is consistent with the multidimensional and transactional models. Germain and Gitterman (1980) have also paid particular attention to diverse persons in diverse populations.

The Strength Perspective is a humanistic approach for working with families (Saleebey, 1992). This approach can be defined as a way of understanding families and identifying how families have coped with challenges and difficulties in the past. Strengths that have been developed in the past are used to build towards needed change.

A multicultural viewpoint should be fundamental in the child welfare field. It should encompass an understanding of different ethnic and cultural characteristics, one's own beliefs and values of children and family systems, and how these may affect the nature of practice (Mather and Lager, 2000). As in different racial groups discussed in previous chapters, it as also critical in child welfare practice that social workers understand how theories of personality and child development provide a working knowledge of how different cultural and religious practices among these groups influence therapeutic interventions and service delivery.

In order to gather information to ensure adequate treatment and to address child and client needs, assessment must incorporate a broad understanding of theories, which will provide a means of organizing large amounts of family information. Samantrai (2004) provides a comprehensive summary of theories, which are basic to understanding children's developmental needs. (See pp. 38–82 for a full description of Psychoanalytic, Cognitive, and Psychosocial theories, and Attachment theory.) These theories view development through predetermined stages, which coincide with chronological age. When a child is not able to master the development task of the age and stage, difficulties can result in later stages that tend to slow down future age and stage tasks. Attachment theory (see Bowlby, 1969) on the other hand, rejects the stage model and is focused more on the relationship experiences the child develops with his parents, with those at school, and in the larger community (Samantrai, 2004). As described by Carlson and Harwood (2003), Bowlby's (1969) attachment theory suggests that "sensitive, responsive maternal care will lead to the development of secure attachment relationships and subsequent socio-economic consequences" (p. 54). Carlson and Harwood (2003) further stress the importance of exploring the role of culture in early relationship formation and child development among each cultural group.

Religious Diversity and Pluralism

The United States has a strong history of religious tolerance with over 1,500 religious bodies. It is estimated that 85 percent are Christian, 8 percent are nonreligious, and 6 percent are of other faiths. There is a long history of Jewish tradition, and Muslims number nearly 5 million (Schaefer, 2000). Schaefer states that despite religious tolerance, separate worship practices exist among many of the different groups, especially among blacks and whites. "Only 1 percent of Black Christians belong to White churches" (p. 139). Among Italians and Irish Americans, especially Irish immigrants and their families, the Catholic Church was and is considered to be the dominant religious center. However, opposition remains strong within the Catholic Church hierarchy to birth control, contraception, abortion, and gays and lesbians. Recently, pedophilia and the clergy sexual abuse crisis have taken center stage. Eleven thousand abuse cases have been reported across the country (Zoll, 2004). Yet, celibacy and participation in religious life remain central to Catholic ideology, but this trend has been continuously challenged over the past 50 years, especially among Italians, who are less likely to favor the priesthood for their sons as they favor the perpetuation of the family and children as the priority (McGoldrick, Pearce, and Giordano, 1982).

Many of the white ethnic groups share unique aspects of religious life, which may have a relationship to child welfare issues and the treatment of children in these families. While this chapter addresses several specific white ethnic groups in this country, there are certainly other white ethnic groups also having strong Catholic, Protestant, Jewish, Muslim, and religious traditions such as the Germans, Poles, Greeks, and various other Middle Eastern groups. Religious orientation will undoubtedly affect the lives and cultural traditions of the various groups as they attempt to assimilate into American society.

White ethnic groups, and especially Jewish Americans are difficult to identify because the census does not classify people according to religion. For example, the distinction is complicated and depends on whether one is classified as an active religious Jew or as a person from Jewish origin. The Jewish population has been estimated at 3.1–5.8 million; however, growth has been slow due to a relatively low birthrate and a 50 percent intermarriage rate (Farley, 2000). Muslim groups are said to be the fastest growing religious group in the United States and also in Canada. Similarly, Canada's Ethnic Diversity Survey reveals that two-thirds of Muslims regularly go to the mosque, pray or engage in other religious activities alone or in groups, which is said to be the highest of any religious group (Heinrich, 2004).

Russian immigrants of Jewish origin display ambivalence about their Jewish identity and religious orientation as the Bolshevik regime erased almost all cultural and religious customs. Only 15 percent are able to speak Yiddish and rarely go to the synagogue (Goldstein, 1979), yet the fist wave of Russian immigrants from the early 1970s from the Soviet Union are said to have a stronger sense of religious identity than those who immigrated to the United States in the 1990s.

Families and Children: Ideals and Values

Russian Immigrants.   Russian immigrants and family members are referred to as "Russian or Soviet Jews" as many immigrated before the decline and fall of the Soviet Union (see Alemán et al., 2001, for a detailed description). In 1991, two thirds of all Russian emigrants were Jewish. Gold (1991) states, however, that only estimates can be made of the number of Soviet Jews from Israel and other locations. The majority of

Russian Jews in the United States emigrated from the urban centers of central Russia and Ukraine and settled predominately in New York, Boston, Chicago, San Francisco, Cleveland, and Cincinnati. Unlike Italians and the Irish, Russian and Polish Jews immigrated with their entire families. Adult children usually initiated the move and brought with them not only their children but also elderly relatives to escape discrimination and persecution (Fitzpatrick, 2001). Their main connection was with their community and family and not their native land. However, in America, living conditions in tenement apartments were very different from what they expected and were often worse in terms of space, disease, and medical care. In many cases poor living conditions and extreme poverty was the norm for many newly arriving groups (Balgopal, 2000).

Thirty nine percent of Soviet Jews are of 50 years of age and over and are older than most immigrant groups, especially those who arrived in the United States between 1979 and 1989. Females tend to be older than males, yet male population tend to increase with age in contrast to the general population of the United States, the former Soviet Union, or other parts of the world (Fitzpatrick, 2001). Men and women are said to form more intense relationships with their friends than with their spouses as marriage is seen as a less significant institution. Although in most Eastern block countries, Russian families tended to consist of three generations living together in the same dwelling. In America, the goal of most resettlement agencies is to separate the generations into their own households. Russian Jewish immigrants highly value music, arts, sciences, and medicine, along with valuing strong and lasting family ties. Unlike American society where friendship is seen as less intrusive, Russian friendships include a total commitment to the needs of the other. In addition, the collectivism mentality values the whole or the consolidated rather than the needs of the individual, which is basically the opposite of American values.

Despite close and intimate friendships, marriage and fidelity are core values in Yiddish culture. The extended family and the growth and development of successful offspring are of paramount importance. Russian immigrants tend to have fewer children than other immigrant groups. The history of strong parental authority originates from the previous Russian political and economic system that was nevertheless a "cherished and unchallenged" value (Althausen, 1993). In return for grand parenting and financial contributions, adult children are expected to care not only for their young children, but also for their elder relatives. A recent article by Tyyaka (2002) focuses on parenting issues among groups of children from infancy to teens from Russian, Afghanistan, and the former Yugoslavian countries. Her research disputes the prevailing negative imagery marked by the traditional approach among immigrant's parents who settled in Toronto, Ottawa, and Kitchener-Waterloo Ontario. The results of the study identified a variety of approaches to parenting ranging from the traditional to the egalitarian/modern. The typical Russian Jewish family is close, the mother figure is revered, and domestic violence is uncommon. However, the close bonds between the generations have been challenged by the experience of immigration.

Russians are strong believers in the value of education, which has been a universal Jewish value in both Russia and other countries. Their median family income is almost

3000–4000$ higher than other white immigrant groups and this is due mainly to their employment as skilled physicians, engineers, economists, and technicians (Althausen, 1993). In contrast, from 1911 to 1920, Southern Italian immigrant children were less likely to make it into grade eight than their native peers. Italian immigrant high-school children were graduating at only 1/2 the rate of nonimmigrants (Rothstein, 2000). Rothstein reports that immigrant Jews perform less well than native whites but better than immigrant Italian children. Italian-born elementary-school children and Jewish and Irish students were held back more often in school than U.S.-born children. Jewish children seem to adapt more quickly to schools and learn English at a quicker rate than other immigrants groups, yet Italian children seem to adapt quicker than their Greek counterparts. Regarding health-seeking behavior, adolescent Russian immigrants are somewhat unique around birth control issues and pregnancy testing. They tend to come in groups and are skeptical, impatient, and not receptive to health education (Althausen, 1993).

Irish Americans.   Leaving their families behind, most of the Irish entered the United States between 1818 and 1870 and immigrated as peasants and unskilled laborers. They had lived in rural communities in Ireland and were escaping famine, terrorist groups, and increasing violence (McCaffrey, 1976). They settled mainly in the North Eastern United States and worked in the factories. As Catholics in America they were confronted with the values of the Protestant Anglo-Saxon society. Living conditions were poor and work opportunities were limited in many large urban cities. They experienced the breakdown of family relationships, and new challenges for survival took decades to overcome. Eventually, many, but not all, of the immigrant laborers began to rise out of the working class and today these immigrants have achieved equality as far as education, income, and occupational success are concerned (Healey, 1996).

Because of the country from which they immigrated, groups such as the Irish, Italians, French, and Polish were initially seen as non-whites, but are seen as whites today (Guadalupe and Lum, 2005). Yet, assimilation into the American society was easier and more achievable than for those who came from Asia and Mexico. Nevertheless, along with the Italians and Poles, the Irish faced bitter prejudice and discrimination (Healey, 1996). Although they dominated the American Catholic Church ladder, anti-Irish sentiment existed mainly due to their Catholic religion, and many employers refused to hire the Irish. The Anglo-American society feared the growth of Catholicism and feared that the Protestant religion would lose status. The Italian groups also faced hatred and discrimination and were often the victims of violent attacks. Irish Catholics still struggle to make sense out of the new and old rules and how these affect the meaning of their lives. However, the changes created by Vatican II have promoted more freedom for religious decisions, yet clear differences continue to exist between the generations as to old and new ways of viewing church values and authority (McGoldrick, 2005).

Some research has indicated that Irish American families display an emotional indirectness and have considerable difficulty in dealing with feelings, nevertheless the guilt and rigidity that plagued the Irish for many years is diminishing. They may designate a "good" child or a "bad" child and may tend to ignore behavior that does not fit into his or her designated role (McGoldrick, Pearce, and Giordano, 1982, p. 323). Discipline may be harsh and inconsistent and aspects of ridicule, belittling, and shame are used. The relationship between alcohol and dysfunctional behavior may contribute to a rise in aggressive or sexual acting-out behavior and incest. Child-rearing practices especially in the past were characterized by strictness, restraint, and harsh measures. Relationships between family members may lack closeness yet the mother–son tie is usually strong and idealistic placing the son in a double bind. The father–daughter relationship can be tense, which may be due to the "father's fear of repressed sexual impulses" (McGolderick, Pearce, and Giordano, 1982, p. 324). Other family members tend to form close relationships with the same sex and same generation. McGoldrick (2005) also states that in regard to sexuality, the Irish tend to be somewhat repressed, and may avoid tenderness, affection, and intimacy. When clinicians are working with Irish Americans in therapy, especially in a child-focused situation, referrals from the school or the court are mainly centered on behavioral problems. Parents are often embarrassed about their child's behavior and are not likely to initiate therapy. However, while Jewish families are most concerned about eating problems or underachievement in school, and Italian families are upset about disloyalty, rebellious or acting-out behavior is seen as humiliating for Irish American families.

The Irish Republican Army's (IRA) original mandate emerged in the 1970s due to anger against the British military presence in Northern Ireland. Since the 1970s, the IRA's largest financial supporters have been Irish Americans in the United States. To this day, Irish children are still faced with the stigma of alcoholism and violence stemming back from the early days of immigration and the incredible barriers their families faced around employment and seeking meaningful and decent-paying jobs. The Catholic Church in America continues to have an influence on the social and cultural training of Irish children (McGoldrick, 2005) especially through the parochial church. Yet, the Irish are truly an example for other immigrant populations. The loss of their identity is the sacrifice the Irish paid for escaping oppression and discrimination and succeeding in American culture and society (McCaffrey, 1976).

Italian Americans.   Italian immigrants and their families were peasants from Southern Italy and came to the United States to escape high rents, rising taxes, and other economic reasons, yet have maintained close ties with their homeland (Balgopal, 2000). Immigration began before the 1800s and similar to the Irish experience, the majority were landless peasants. However, Italians exhibit sharp cultural and economic distinctions as immigrants arrived from multiple geographic locations within Italy. The "padrone" system in the early years of immigration to the United States was the primary source of receiving employment through an ethnic labor contractor (Schaefer, 2000). Poor living conditions, manual labor, and the Catholic Church typified the Italian American experience in earlier days. Although the church was dominated by the Irish who arrived earlier, adjustment problems were eventually overcome with the establishment of ethnic parishes in which, eventually, Italians felt more a part of the community. Over 70 percent of Italians today identify themselves as Roman Catholics.

The extended family play an important role in all aspects of life, and even today many Italian families live in close proximity to each other. "La Familiga" (the family) was also the center of Italian immigrant life; however, the patriarchal image and cultural beliefs began to change as children who spoke English incorporated American values into their way of life. They married out of their Little Italy communities and many relocated elsewhere. Organized crime was another significant identifier among Italian Americans. Italians lived in crime- and poverty-ridden neighborhoods known as "Little Italies" and this image has continued among both Italian and Irish American groups. Schaefer (2000) describes what is known as "respectable bigotry among ethnic whites" in which crime has been linked with different ethnic groups due to the fear of "undesirables" (p. 149).

Despite their increasing need for becoming more educated, prejudice persisted. The Anglo-Protestant establishment imposed a serious educational barrier for advancement among Italian American children. In the earlier years of immigration, Italian children were poor and could not read or write and parents thought that children would be best educated at home. Children were viewed as an economic resource and were also expected to work and contribute to the family income. Older children, in particular, were expected to assist younger siblings and encourage them to complete their education. Eventually, children were forced to attend school until the age of 16; however, parents saw schooling as a barrier to their culture and household income. Fitzpatrick (1969) found that rates of juvenile delinquency in Italian communities was only one-seventh as great as in other areas or neighborhoods mainly due to intermediate structures such as the police, politicians, and other community links plus the strength of the group's strong ethnic identity.

There is a definite role distinction between sons and daughters in Italian families in which male children are taught to control their emotions as a means of protection against outsiders while girls are allowed greater freedom of expression. This contrasts with Irish or White Anglo-Saxon Protestant (WASP) children and males from these groups who tend to show a failure to express themselves due to embarrassment, privacy concerns, or inhibition. Italian children as a whole are more accepting of their ethnic background than other groups, in contrast to Jews and WASPs who feel anxious or guilty if they do not live up to their parent's expectations (McGoldrick, Pearce, and Giordano, 1982).

In summary, Italian Americans remain the seventh largest immigrant group and in 2000 the number of Italian Americans reached at least 16 million. Although they remain loyal to their native Italy, many have lost their close cultural ties and language (Schaefer, 2000). Yet, as so many Americans claim Italian ancestry, many of the colorful cultural values have remained an integral part of our society and life today. McGoldrick, Pearce, and Giordano (1982) describe striking distinctions that highlight the strengths of Italian families such as interpersonal characteristics, resourcefulness, and loyalty that provide much emotional support and assistance that other groups lack. In a recent article in *The Globe and Mail* (a Toronto, Ontario newspaper), Valpy (2003) describes the rich ethnic flavor of Italian families in which the evening meal is of central significance as a means of providing security and maintaining family values and traditions. "Love, intimacy and pleasure in each other's company" suitably fits the description (Valpy, 2003, p. 1). In the present political and cultural arena, Italians have showed considerable success and contributions as votes stem from close family and community ties and connections (U.S. Bureau of Census, 2000). However, in the commercial media including HBO's *The Sopranos*, a seductive blend of Italian American culture and pernicious propaganda has added a menacing distortion to the "500-year Italian legacy in America" (Italian Studies Institute, March 5, 2001). Children and adolescents have been exposed to the negative stereotypes and images of Italians as murders and thieves.

Arab Americans.   Arab Americans from Iran, Iraq, Jordan, Lebanon, Egypt, Syria, and Turkey have experienced acculturation as a different experience from most Islamic immigrants. Early statistics suggest that in 1970 approximately 15 percent of the Middle Eastern immigrants were Muslims, as most were Christians from Lebanon or Armenia. However, by 2000 an estimated 73 percent were Muslims (Camarota, 2002). Comparing Muslim and Christian religion in terms of life satisfaction in the United States, Muslims have reported less satisfaction with life and American cultural practices than the Christian group (Faragallah, Schumm, and Webb, 1997). Comparing language and gender roles, Muslims scored in the more traditional direction. Zeidner (1976) classifies Middle Eastern immigrants who settled in Utah into three groups: the Syro-Lebanese; the Armenians; and the post-World War II emigrants from Middle Eastern countries. The Syro-Lebanese had extensive interaction with Greek immigrants and established employment and businesses on the west side of Salt Lake City by Greek Town. The Armenians have a long history of oppression and bloody massacres. Later in 1897, a group of Armenian converts to the Mormon faith from Syria, Lebanon, and Egypt came to Utah because of their new religion. The University of Utah is also home to the nation's leading centers for the study of the Middle East. Since 1939, immigrants have come to Utah because of the higher education opportunities (Zeidner, 1976).

The ethnic diversity among and between Muslim and Christian Arab groups, however, continues to present challenges of adjustment for immigrant families, their children, the school system, and the community (Zaki, Sinno, and Johnson, 2001). Zaki, Sinno, and Johnson's (2001) project was directed towards the development of useful adjustment strategies and cultural educational programs for immigrant families of Lansing, Michigan. Schwartz (1999) reports that despite the increase in Arab American students in public schools and the development of new strategies and materials for integration, many schools have not yet acknowledged Arab culture and history or addressed Arab stereotyping and racism. Schwartz suggests that educators and practitioners need to focus their interventions on helping families cope with various levels of acculturation, language differences, and conformity to tradition to assist Arab students to develop a positive sense of identity. If students experience difficulties in school it is necessary for practitioners to determine if the problems stem from intergenerational issues within their family or from another source.

Bahira (1999) explored the role of Islamic values and beliefs in Muslim American families. She states that despite the contractual relationship under Islamic law in which women subjugate themselves to their husbands, Muslim American marriages have become more egalitarian and less restrictive towards women. She discusses the need for service professionals to address the role and expectations of children in these families and the unique and specific needs of these families. Following the 9/11, attacks on the World Trade Center, Abudabbeh (2001) describes the emotional reactions and fears of Arab American children and offers advice to parents on helping children to cope with possible harassment and blame by other adults and children at school. Children may experience isolation, slurs, and rejection from peers. A continued sense of stigma may persist, and families and educators need to be aware of possible negative consequences especially among teenagers who may tend to internalize these fears. Although, 2 years have passed since the crisis, parents, teachers, and professionals are advised to remain available and cognizant of delayed grief and stress reactions among Muslim children and teenagers and its effects on their home and school life.

Cohen and Tryee (1994) provide a rich description and comparison of demographic factors of Palestinian and Jewish Israeli-born immigrants in the United States. Both Jewish and Palestinian groups have high socioeconomic status, but Jews have higher education, have better jobs and income than their Arab counterparts. Over 30 percent of Israeli-born Americans are Palestinian-Arab natives of Israel, the West Bank, and Gaza strip. Actually the average born Jewish American enjoys a higher socioeconomic level than most European immigrant groups. Similar to other Middle Eastern groups but unlike European immigrants, most Jews and Arabs in the United States have more males than females and both groups have settled in urban areas. Jewish Israelis are mostly located in New York City and Los Angeles, while Arabs, both Muslims and Christians, have settled in cities such as Chicago, Detroit, Toledo, and the San Francisco Bay area. With the exception of Arab women, both groups are well educated and about 90 percent of the men were working based on the 1980 U.S. census. However, Jewish women are more likely to work than Arab women, as they tend to be better educated and have a good command of the English language. Furthermore, Arab men and women tend to work longer hours than their Jewish counterparts.

Most Muslims are dark skinned and are of Arab or South Asian descent, while most Christians are whites of European descent and are easily identifiable (Heinrich, 2004). Yet, we should question our assumptions about immigrants from the Middle East. "We seem to think that Europeans blend into the U.S. society without notice, whereas immigrants from the Middle East are kept apart" (Kulczycki, Aguirre, and Fernandez, 2002, p. 2). These authors state that intermarriage and childbearing are an important indicator of assimilation and identification. Persons of Arab descent become a part of the American society relatively quickly in a generation or two. Actually, these authors found that the majority of Arab children come from families where there is only one Arab parent. While they have advantages of becoming assimilated sooner, they have diminished Arab ethnic identity. Religion is also considered as effecting out-marriage among Arab Americans and findings indicate that Christian Arabs are more likely to intermarry than are Muslim Arab Americans. Heinrich (2004) reports that bigotry from the Catholic Church and the media remains prevalent despite the rising number of intermarriages between Muslims, Christians, and Jews.

PART II: CHILD WELFARE ISSUES AND PROBLEMS

When examining child welfare issues as they relate to white ethnics, it is important to realize that each white ethnic subgroup has its own unique cultural values and world-view. Just as there is enormous diversity in child welfare-related cultural content across communities of color, so too do white ethnics differ culturally from each other and from the so-called "mainstream" or majority culture. It is therefore erroneous to assume that white ethnics possess the same cultural patterns and values as majority whites, even though many bear, in many instances, a close physical resemblance. While some have assimilated so fully into the majority culture that they are culturally indistinguishable from other white majority clients, most still retain some cultural connection to the past. Further, although many white ethnics may be seen and treated as white by society at large, they do not necessarily perceive or identify themselves as members of the majority. More often than not, there is the sense that, "I am not white; I am Irish" (or Italian or Jewish or Middle Eastern) (Diller, 2004, p. 237).

Due to the diversity among and between white ethnic groups, the following section examines five child welfare-related areas as they relate to persons of Irish, Italian, Jewish, and Middle Eastern descent. First, the impact of family, extended family, and kinship care and how they differ from mainstream society are examined. Second, issues of cultural identity and inequality are discussed. Here focus is placed on the different meanings and interpetations of being "white" and its impact on white ethnics. Third, child maltreatment issues and child-rearing practices are detailed and the variability in perceptions of child maltreatment for white ethnic subgroups. Fourth, out-of-home care and adoption issues are examined. Emphasis is placed on the prominent role white ethnics have had in the historical development of out-of-home care and adoption policies in the United States. Finally, the importance of education and how white ethics were traditionally excluded from many educational opportunities are discussed, but at present there has been a shift in this focus.

Impact of Family, Extended Family, and Kinship Care

Traditionally, white ethnic families were characterized as male dominated with clearly delineated male/female roles. Husbands and fathers assumed more authoritative roles and were generally the breadwinners and responsible for things outside the home; mothers and wives, on the other hand, typically were responsible for things inside the home, including a more direct influence on the children (Hanson, 2004). While the central structure of white ethnic culture is the family, differences exist in how the family is defined and expressed. For example, Irish and Italian families typically have a child-centeredness emphasis were the focus is on the individual within the family. This often translates into active schedules for children, including after-school activities, in-home and out-of-home learning experiences, and an active social life that promotes and develops the child's individuality. Young children are often involved in early education activities, and preschool experiences generally are sought after. Given that many mothers are employed outside of the home (in 2004, over one-half were employed outside of the home), children are often placed in childcare and spend much of the time with caregivers other than their parents or extended family (Hanson, 2004).

In most Jewish and Middle Eastern cultures, the child's first and foremost loyalty is to his or her family, clan, or kin (Sharifzadeh, 2004). Here, emphasis is placed on the family as opposed to the individual, and there are strong pressures for children and youth to place the well-being of the family and the community before personal needs. For many within the Jewish and Middle Eastern culture, the development of an individual identity separate from that of the family or community is not valued or supported, and being asked to consider one's personal needs in a situation may cause confusion or guilt if they feel that doing so may betray or take precedent over their family (Diller, 2004). Many even consider family honor and status to be a central goal for each family member, and practicing conformity and placing family interests over individual ones are expected (Smith, 2004). Very high expectations are still placed on children to succeed and socialization is often accomplished through the threat of withdrawal of love and a feeling of guilt or of "letting the family down."

For white ethnic groups, the extended family networks have traditionally been a source of strength and a vital component in preserving the child's culture. For people of Jewish and Middle Eastern descent, it has often been the case that two or more generations would reside in the same household (Crosson-Tower, 2001). Other family members may live as close as a few houses or blocks away or as far away as another city. Physical remoteness, however, usually does not affect the loyalty and interaction of the extended family. Family dynamics, in turn, have traditionally been shaped by the religious rules and an extended family influence. Sharifzadeh (2004) states

> Religious rules provide the strongest guidelines in shaping the relationships within the family. This contrasts with many industrialized Western societies in which secular rules coming from formal institutions often govern the nature of interaction even within the family. The extended family performs important functions in the Middle Eastern societies. It provides many of the services that are performed by formal organizations in the West. For example, it is within the network of the extended family that the children, the elders, and those with disabilities are often nurtured and protected. (p. 389)

The prominence in much of the West of the nuclear family is not easily understood or appreciated by many people of Jewish and Middle Eastern descent. It is therefore difficult for many children and families to relate to the multitude of social organizations that are devised to replace the functions of the extended family. Even when the purpose and function of these support organizations are explained, many still view them as unfamiliar or impersonal (Sharifzadeh, 2004). Even the use of extended family terms utilized by people of Jewish and Middle Eastern descent show the stark differences. For example, there is only one term in the United States, "cousin," to denote various types of kin relationships. On the other hand, there are, in the Middle East, *eight* different categories of cousins with each having its own unique position and status (Mindel, Habenstein, and Wright, 1988).

In examining the extended family influence from an Irish or Italian perspective, early immigrants to the United States often had to leave their families and extended families to make a new start. Once in the United States, they typically migrated to areas where others of similar backgrounds lived. Cities were often divided into racial or religious groups with very distinct boundaries separating each. These groups there-fore served as a surrogate extended family for many individuals. The extended family networks found in the early years of the country have not been as common in recent decades, and the primary focus in many Irish and Italian American families is on the nuclear family members (Hanson, 2004).

Issues of Cultural Identity and Inequality

The cultural identity issues of white ethnic children and youth may be in discord in much the same manner as those experienced by children and youth of color. Additionally, they have historically derived the same sense of affirmation and belong-ing through membership in a particular ethnic group similar to people of color (Casey Family Programs, 2000). This is true even for those who at first glance may appear "white" and highly assimilated. Diller (2004) notes that it is "important to realize that, even if an individual has been spared the direct experience of racial hatred and discrimination, its emotional consequences can be passed on from previous genera-tions through family dynamics" (p. 238). Casey Family Programs (2000) cautions that the experience of being white and the process of white cultural identity for these children and youth is not comparable with the experiences of groups of color for a number of reasons:

> First, ethnic identity for members of these groups is often heightened by location in ethnic enclaves. Once White ethnics leave these enclaves, the process of integrating into the larger White European society is easier because they share greater similarities in appearance and a common European background. The same cannot be said for people of color. Similarly, members of these groups have not experienced the persistent individual and institutional racism that people of color have. (p. 25)

Over the past few decades, the "white" racial category in the United States has expanded to include groups previously considered "non-white" (Warren and Twine, 1997). The fact that many white ethnic children and youth can so easily assimilate into the majority culture, thus seemingly escaping their collective past, creates a somewhat different identity picture. In comparison to children and youth of color, who are reminded constantly of their ethnicity, white ethnics can bury their conflicts much deeper and further out of awareness. Here again, as in the case of children and youth of color, the rejection of such an important part of identity as one's ethnicity cannot help but cause deep inner conflicts that eventually affect behavior. Therefore, it is not uncommon to find instances of conflict, identity rejection, and self-hatred among white ethnic children and youth (Diller, 2004).

The advantages of being identified with the "white" majority for many white ethnic children and youth in overcoming discrimination in America can be found in the resources shared by white ethnics today. They oftentimes can secure better jobs, earn more money, attain more education, and live in less segregated neighborhoods than many non-European ethnics. Thus, while the persistence of negative stereotyping and discrimination are still evident, these forces have not prevented many white ethnic youth from taking advantage of the resources available in America (Aguirre and Turner, 1998). By simply adopting the culture, speech, values, and other characteristics of the majority, white ethnic children and youth can blend with the general population and move up the educational and occupational ladder (Aguirre and Turner, 1998). Thus, these youth exist in a kind of "psychological demilitarized zone" (Diller, 2004, p. 237). Being identified as white in America, they share the privilege of whiteness. But at the same time, as ethnic group members from cultures who have experienced long histories of oppression, they carry within them many of the internal conflicts that are similar to those of people of color. Human service providers working with these groups face the task of helping them integrate and deal with these two very different psychological realities—that of the oppressor and the oppressed (Diller, 2004).

Other white ethnic children and youth, because of their darker physical features and appearance, have been viewed as non-white by the majority culture. Since 9/11, immigrants and Americans of Middle Eastern descent (as well as other white ethnics with darker physical features—particularly of Arab and Muslim backgrounds) have seen increased prejudice and hostility. With the passage of the USA Patriot Act of 2002, many have been experiencing discrimination and racial profiling at the hands of the U.S. government agencies, public schools, and other institutions (Sharifzadeh, 2004). Here, the "white" classification has served the purpose of denying the Middle Easterners the status of a minority group, hence limiting their opportunity, power and influence. At the same time, white classification has not protected members of Middle Eastern communities from racial profiling and discrimination (Hassan, 2002). Just as early Irish were discriminated against because they were poor and early Italians because of their religion, today many white ethnic children and youth face issues of inequality resulting from their religious beliefs and skin color. As a result, they face an inner conflict with cultural teachings that leads either to conflict within the family or to assimilation and a loss of cultural values and identity (Nadir and Dziegielewski, 2001).

Child Maltreatment Issues and Child-Rearing Practices

The desire for larger families and a strong preference for male children are often characteristic among many white ethnic families, particularly those of Italian and Middle Eastern descent. Sharifzadeh (2004) states that "the birth of a boy has always been a reason for great celebration in a traditional Middle Eastern family. One possible reason could be the loss of men to wars, leaving villages and towns populated only by women" (p. 391). The ramifications of this preference have at times led to abandonment and abortion of some female babies. Others have been abused or neglected. While most Middle Eastern societies have strict laws against abortion, this practice continues in most large cities resulting in an overrepresentation of females in orphanages and child welfare systems (Sharifzadeh, 2004).

Regarding child maltreatment generally, the problem of defining child maltreatment within white ethnic families stems from the variability of perceiving particular children's rights and needs within the culture. While there are laws that define exactly what constitutes abuse and neglect, differences among and between white ethnic groups make the enforcement of such laws (and subsequent treatment) more difficult. This same perception and sensitivity creates the main criteria for establishing effective "best practices" within each of these groups. Further, the variability in perceptions of child maltreatment and the limitations placed upon such perceptions by the relative paucity of public resources and the extensive ideological, religious, and cultural influences (e.g., the Roman Catholic Church, Islam) make each case one that deserves culturally sensitive attention. Finally, a review of the way child maltreatment has been defined over time and across various systems discloses patterns that may or may not be effective when working with a particular family (Harder and Pringle, 1997). For most white ethnics, family privacy is a highly valued right to be protected. It is expected that the family will be left to its own pursuits (which may or may not include extended family) and allowed to raise its children as the parents see fit. Only when parents abuse or fail to provide for their children is family stability in question. Even then, some critics of current child welfare practices feel that agencies are too quick to intervene with these families without the necessary knowledge and training (Crosson-Tower, 2001).

Out-of-Home Care and Adoption Issues

White ethnic children have had a prominent role in the historical development of out-of-home care and adoption policies in the United States. Evidence of family foster care and other forms of out-of-home placements, practiced on a limited basis, have been traced back to the ancient Jewish laws and customs of placing orphaned children in the households of other relatives (Everett, 1995). In the United States in the 1800s, children were often "informally" adopted by relatives, or lived with other families as apprentices, but even in the 1900s when increased urban and rural poverty led to more official adoptions, those adoptions were usually arranged with families needing extra help at home or on the farm (Ruark, 2002). The most prominent example of this is Charles Loring Brace and his out-of-home placement program with the Children's Aid Society that resulted in roughly 10,000 children from 1854 to 1929 being transported for placement, usually to the Midwest (Everett, 1995).

As Charles Loring Brace practiced it, this out-of-home placement program began as an effort to rescue children in New York City whose parents were inadequate, on charity, or had abandoned their children for a variety of reasons. These orphans, known as "the dangerous class" were mainly U.S.-born, but the children of Irish, Italian, and German immigrants (Brace, 1872). Brace began the practice of transporting needy and homeless children by train (becoming known as the "orphan train") from large cities to rural areas in the South and Midwest, where they were adopted or placed in the homes of farmers or tradespeople to be cared for and were expected to work in exchange for this care (Everett, 1995). Many rural people viewed the orphan train children with suspicion and as the incorrigible offspring of drunkards and prostitutes. The children spoke with the accents of Ireland, Germany, and Italy; and unlike most Midwesterners who were Protestant, many of the children were Catholic (Everett, 1995). Although the New York Children's Aid Society retained custody of the children and could remove them at any time, resources provided for very limited follow-up after placement. Although the success of Brace's "orphan train" program has been called into question, it did open up dialog that later set the stage for many of our current foster care and adoption policies. Further, Catholic, Protestant, and Jewish organizations, as well as white ethnic enclaves and society in general, were forced to begin to address where in society white ethnics and their children belonged.

Today, although official statistics on white ethnic children in out-of-home care are unavailable, each year almost 3 million children in the United States are alleged to be abused or neglected (Fernando, 2001). In 2002 for example, there were 896,000 children who were the documented victims of child abuse or neglect nationwide. Although statistics do not distinguish who among the "white" race/ethnicity category are white ethnics, during that same time 54 percent of child victims of maltreatment were identified as white and 38 percent of children in foster care were white (Fernando, 2001). Although child abuse and neglect are not problems unique to white ethnics, there continues to be a great need to address child abuse and neglect issues in white ethnic communities and society at large.

In shifting from out-of-home care issues to adoption practices that have impacted white ethnics, historically, white ethnic children were seen as the least desirable option when mainstream society began allowing open adoptions. As noted previously, white ethnic children available for adoption in the early 1900s were often seen as incorrigible offspring of drunkards and prostitutes. A number of psychological theories at the time (e.g., early studies on genetic determinism, eugenic and IQ testing) also promoted the idea that many of these children's genetic makeup would lead them down the path to destruction—they were predestined to a life of drunkenness and prostitution. Others, including Charles Loring Brace, saw helping these children as a chance to "save" them from a life of poverty, crime and/or religious degradation. As a result, many religious organizations stepped forward to see that these children were adopted by "good Catholic homes" or "a strong Jewish family" (see Maguire 2002 for examples). Even today, the idea of "sharing" ones religious background with a child in need continues to influence whether or not a couple considers adoption.

In the United States, adoptions of white ethnic children has gained greater and greater acceptance. In many cases these children are even preferred because of their lighter skin. Although official adoption statistics on white ethnic children are unavailable, there were 131,000 children in foster care waiting to be adopted in 2000 (Fernando, 2001). As noted previously, although statistics do not distinguish who among the "white" race/ethnicity category are white ethnics, during that same time 34 percent of children waiting to be adopted were identified as white and 43 percent of children in foster care who were adopted were white (Fernando, 2001). Although the recent adoption policy debate has focused on issues involving groups of color, the views and preferences of white ethnic groups also need to be considered as mainstream society moves forward.

As white ethnics have become more and more incorporated into mainstream society, much of the recent adoption discussion involving white ethnics has shifted to international adoptions. Historically, international adoption have been promoted and succeeded in the aftermath of wars. After World War II, American families adopted European orphans, chiefly from Germany, Italy, and Greece. In 2003, three of the top 10 countries of international adoptions in the United States were Russia (5,209) (second only to China), Kazakhstan (825), and Ukraine (702). Further, although no Russian child was adopted abroad prior to 1990 (with the collapse of the Soviet Union), Russia is now the world's second largest country that parents in the United States choose to adopt from (ACCEPT, 2004; Kapstein, 2003). Similarly, Romania, which was once one of the leading countries in international adoptions, has imposed moratoriums on adoptions from Romania. In 2001, Romania placed 782 children in the United States, and the following year the number dropped to 168. During the same period, adoptions in the United States of children from Russia increased by about 700 (Kapstein, 2003). As international adoptions continue to broaden and increase, people adopting children from white ethnic countries need to understand the dynamics and potential consequences involved with adopting a white ethnic child.

One example is that as international adoptions continue to increase, with many of these involving white ethnic children, the social service and health delivery systems are also impacted. With costs associated with international adoptions also rising, more and more parents in the Unites States are considering adopting children with special needs as fees and process time for such children are dramatically reduced. While many parents know exactly what the special needs of these children will be and are willing to make the necessary arrangements for these children, many children, because of lack of adequate medical information, bring with them special needs that require long-term social service and medical attention. This issue continues to be one that both adoption agencies and social/health service delivery systems will monitor closely.

Importance of Education

Traditionally and even today, education has been the major institutional mechanism for assimilation into the majority culture; yet early on, many white ethnics were excluded from many educational opportunities. For example, universities such as Columbia University and New York University had long-standing restrictions on Jewish admissions (Guzzetta, 1995). Other schools simply did not allow white ethnics of a particular religious or cultural background to be accepted. As a result, upon arrival to the United States, many Italian Catholics and Jewish immigrants sought to maintain their own religious practices and teachings by sending their children to religious-based schools, thereby ensuring that their children would retain their culture and religion (Inglehart and Becerra, 1995). In spite of the great variation in language, religion, and social and political systems, most white ethnic families share similar values pertaining to the importance of education in achieving a better life for their children (Sharifzadeh, 2004). Whereas many early Irish and Italian immigrants had little education upon arriving in the United States, establishment of schools and emphasis on education has enabled many subsequent youth to rise up the socioeconomic ladder. Today, in many cities across the United States, these religious-based schools hold high esteem in the academic arena and further promote the ideals of these white ethnic groups.

Regarding people of Middle Eastern descent, many children and families in the United States came with educated backgrounds, and almost all of the Middle Eastern people who came to live here before the 1980s can speak English. Although the knowledge of English and the educational level of the more recent immigrants have been lower than their predecessors, a great majority of them have at least a high-school degree (Sharifzadeh, 2004). Further, the so-called "brain drain" of the 1990s and 2000s, where the United States has recruited many of the most talented and educated from around the world, continues to impact white ethnic culture and immigration to the United States. Here, many white ethnics in these countries have entered the United States not from lower socioeconomic statisus as was the case historically, but these individuals and families are coming to the United states already well educated and in a high socioeconomic category. The future impact of this group on the overall culture of the United States, as well as their impact on child welfare and adoption policies, is yet to be determined. But, they will have a great impact.

PART III: THERAPEUTIC INTERVENTIONS FOR SOCIAL WORK PRACTICE

Child welfare interventions focus on the protection of children from maltreatment, and are increasingly concerned with ensuring both safety and permanence for children (CWLA, 2004). The success of these interventions depends on a perspective that is sensitive to "the full context of the client's identity, emotions, thought, and history" (Walker and Staton, 2000, p. 453). This perspective has been called a guiding value for social work; indeed, empathy for the client demands an appreciation of the client's culture, the social worker's culture, as well as the nexus of person and culture (Walker and Staton, p. 459).

Some of the mandates for child welfare present particular challenges for culturally appropriate child welfare practice with white ethnic families. Among these challenges are (1) ensuring a safe continuum of care for children which is based on age appropriate expectations and discipline; (2) involvement of fathers; (3) preserving families and ensuring permanence for children through the use of kinship care or out-of-home placement; and (4) involvement of the community, including participation in child and family team collaboration. While each of these four challenges exists across cultures, the family's level of acculturation may have a significant influence on all four. Allegiance to family and country, experiences of hostility towards immigrants, and the poor conditions and hardships encountered all have an influence on families who immigrate (Balgopal, 2000). The racial and ethnic disproportionality in child welfare has been well documented (Courtney and Skyles, 2003), and white ethnic families may not escape this phenomenon. There is further recognition of the impact of family structure, poverty, substance abuse, domestic violence, welfare reform, and juvenile delinquency on child welfare (Courtney and Skyles, 2003; Crosson-Tower, 2001). White ethnic families may also experience these risk factors. Gender biases have been found to be pervasive in child welfare, with little attention to fathers (Risley-Curtiss and Heffernan, 2003). For many white ethnic families, the role of the father is central. The recognition of culture, the meaning of family and belonging, and partnerships with families have all been positively associated with permanency (Ernst, 2001). Yet, developing effective approaches specifically sensitive to white ethnic families have not been well established. Child and family team collaboration is resource intensive (Sieppert, Hudson, and Unrau, 2000), yet child welfare agencies are struggling to meet increased demands with limited staffing (CWLA, 2004).

Child welfare practice requires a set of knowledge, skills, and values for appropriate intervention. Essential learning is both experiential and contextual (Walker and Staton, 2000), so no description of distinct groups can provide an absolute blueprint for intervention. The social worker in child welfare may be well served by respecting both the general and the unique aspects of each individual and family encountered, within the context of the community (Hutchison, 2000). Nevertheless, social workers in child welfare draw on knowledge, skills, and values essential to their practice. The knowledge base for culturally appropriate child welfare practice includes the recognition of the cultural variants for coping strategies, values, and attitudes toward discipline, child rearing, age of accountability, sexual norms, caregiving responsibilities, help seeking, self disclosure, and the role of children (Kane and Houston-Vega, 2004). The quality of the worker/client relationship remains an essential skill associated with positive client outcomes (Smithgall, 2003). Harper and Lantz (1996) offer an approach which is rooted in naturalistic research process, a plan for gathering data in the field. The manner of uncovering cross-cultural factors suggests a manner in which one might approach ethnically diverse clients. Recognizing and appropriately applying Harper and Lantz's (1996) eight cross-cultural curative factors represents sound, ethical practice. These factors include a respect for the client's worldview, firmly rooted in the social work value of dignity and respect for the individual; recognizing the need for hope, which is provided in part through the worker's integrity and empathy; helper attractiveness through demonstration of worker competence; providing a sense of control through empowerment; utilizing rites of initiation, such as celebrating or honoring change and loss; and cleansing experiences, including the need for making amends or restitution; supporting existential realization, a sense of meaning making. All of these curative factors exist along with physical interventions or concrete helping, which has formed the basis of social work interventions (Harper and Lantz, 1996). Case studies presented at the end of this section will offer an opportunity to apply these factors. Social workers also need skills in affirming diversity, reducing defensiveness, identifying barriers to effective collaboration, and recovering when communication goes awry (Kavanaugh and Kennedy, 1992).

In short, social work interventions in child welfare require recognition that family, respect, harmony, cooperation, and spirituality are all valued differently among diverse groups (Lum, 2003). We have common human needs, with uncommon ways of meeting them (Harper and Lantz, 1996). The work of Harper and Lantz (1996) is particularly useful with white ethnic families, as it is based on naturalistic research and a "grounded" theory approach, and allows the social worker to use a similar approach in intervening with families from diverse backgrounds.

Child welfare intervention also is based on the generalist practice model, which recognizes the steps of engagement, assessment, intervention, and evaluation throughout the process, and that this may be focused at the individual (micro), family, and group (mezzo), or community and organizational (macro) levels (Kirst-Ashman, 2003). For white ethnics, the model of social justice may be a useful organizing background to the child protection foreground. The organizing framework for "just practice" requires attention to context, history, power, meaning, and possibility (Finn and Jacobson, 2003).

Four cases will be presented to illustrate opportunities for "just practice" in child welfare. Each case presents opportunities for culturally appropriate child welfare practice, from engagement, through assessment, intervention, and evaluation/termination. Each family scenario is presented to afford the opportunity to apply specific knowledge, skills, and values to the four child welfare issues and challenges presented. It is suggested that you may wish to use each scenario as the basis for a role play, adapting and embellishing the family scenario throughout the process of investigation and risk assessment, treatment plan development, ongoing intervention and monitoring, and evaluation and termination. Following the scenarios, questions are provided. These questions are intended to guide your planning for culturally appropriate child welfare interventions with white ethnic families.

CASE STUDY 1   RUSSIAN JEWISH FAMILY

The Kozakov family immigrated to the United States in 1996. Zvi and Olga, their son Oleg, his wife Luda, and their two children, Sasha (11) and Katya (8) lived together in a two-bedroom apartment, which houses several immigrant families from different countries. The family left Russia for many reasons, but Zvi and Olga were most happy to be able to exercise their religious practices without fear. Oleg and Luda were not involved in religious practices, but were beginning to encourage Sasha and Katya to attend the synagogue, after pressure from Zvi. Shortly after arriving in the United States, Zvi became ill; he had 6 years of limited mobility and increasing dementia before his death a few months ago. His wife, Olga, is blind. She is always at home, and does much of the cooking for the family. Oleg worked as an engineer in Russia, but has had difficulty learning English. He works as the groundskeeper at a local cemetery. Luda is trained as a physician; she is presently working as a physician's assistant at the state hospital for the seriously mentally ill. Three nights a week she takes classes: a medical review class and an English class. She is hoping to take examinations to become licensed as a physician.

The Kozakov family has developed a small circle of friends, also Russian immigrants. They regularly enjoy evenings together, sharing food, drink, music, and dancing in each other's homes. Oleg is very handy with tools, and is often called upon by friends to assist them with minor repairs. The family has some conflicts within their apartment complex. Twice the police have been called to the Kozakov apartment due to complaints from the neighbors about noise, yelling, and fighting.

Sasha is in the sixth grade. He takes violin lessons and is on the soccer team. He is big for his age and, at home, spends more time with his grandmother than with friends. Family friends of Oleg and Luda rely on Sasha to babysit after school two girls, aged 3 and 4. Sasha was very close to his grandfather, Zvi, who also played the violin. Sasha has been failing in mathematics at school, and his parents are trying to find a tutor for him. Twice they have scheduled appointments with the teacher to address their concerns about his school performance.

Katya is in third grade, and calls herself "Katie." She has many friends at school, and speaks English very well. At home, she often answers her grandmother twice: once in Russian, once in English. She is talkative and active, and takes gymnastics classes at the local YWCA. She helps her grandmother in all the family meal preparation and laundry.

On the same day, two separate child protective service referrals were received: the first, reported by Sasha's teacher, that Sasha had fallen asleep at his desk, and smelled of alcohol. He was sent home early. The teacher reported that his father, when he came to pick up Sasha, appeared "not at all concerned" about the alcohol, but was angry about his falling asleep, and chided him vociferously for being lazy. The teacher reported that Oleg "dragged the boy by the arm, as Sasha let out a yell." The second call, late in the afternoon, came from the gymnastics coach. He reported that Katie had several visible bruises, as well as a nasty-looking burn on her leg. He reported that Katie's explanation was she fell off a stool in the kitchen, while helping her grandmother fix dinner.

A referral was made for a child protective service investigation.

CASE STUDY 2 PALESTINIAN MUSLIM FAMILY

Mahmoud Al-Ma'ad and his wife Leila came to the United States six months before September 11, 2002. They had been trying for several years to immigrate, since Mahmoud's brother Ahmed had moved to the United States several years before. Mahmoud and Leila have two children: Samira (13), and Ahmed (10). Mahmoud works long hours at the gas station owned by his brother, and has been able to provide a nice apartment for his family across the street from an excellent elementary school and just a few blocks from the high school. He recently purchased a computer for his son Ahmed, and has made it clear that he expects Ahmed to focus on his studies so he can get into a good university. Their community has a very small Muslim population, and Mahmoud's

(continued)

■ ■ ■ ■ ■ ▬▬▬▬▬▬▬▬▬▬▬▬▬▬▬▬▬▬▬▬▬▬▬▬▬▬▬▬

CASE STUDY 2   Continued

great disappointment is that he cannot afford to send his children to a private school. Ahmed is a good student, very shy, and often is ridiculed at school. Both children were kept home from school for several weeks after the September 11 event. A school counselor visited and insisted that it would be safe for the children to return to school. Samira has few friends. She has a very poor attendance record at school. Attempts to contact the parents about this have been difficult, since they have no telephone. Leila will not let anyone enter her home when her husband is not present, and he returns home late at night.

Leila has become increasingly fearful. She often paces the floor at night, and when Samira or Ahmed returns home, she questions them repeatedly about whom they have talked to. Samira notices that her mother is not eating, and has lost a lot of weight. She often stays home to try to reassure her mother that she will be all right, and tries to encourage her to go out.

Child welfare authorities received a referral from the school counselor, who has been unsuccessful in determining any legitimate reason for Samira's excessive absences, and unable to engage the parents. She made the report after another student, who has tried to befriend Samira, told the counselor that Samira had said her mother is very ill and that she often has to take care of her.

■ ■ ■ ■ ■ ▬▬▬▬▬▬▬▬▬▬▬▬▬▬▬▬▬▬▬▬▬▬▬▬▬▬▬▬

CASE STUDY 3   ITALIAN CATHOLIC FAMILY

Roberto and Maria Aversano have a large extended family. Roberto works in his father's restaurant, and enjoys the company of his brothers, sisters, and their children. The family has been a lot of help with Tonio, Roberto and Maria's only son. He was born when Maria was using drugs, and is a "cocaine baby." Maria has been in rehab four times for her addiction, and is presently serving time in prison for a crime she committed. Tonio is a special needs child, but has been "catching up," according to Roberto. He is now 5 years old, and has spent much of his life in kinship care with Roberto's sister, Anna. Anna and her husband Michael have no children of their own, and were the first to step forward to provide care for Tonio. Roberto was upset when authorities officially removed Tonio from his care, but reluctantly accepted it.

Maria has been working hard in prison to complete her program. She is determined to maintain sobriety, and get her child back. Her counselor has strongly encouraged her to relocate to another community when she is released, to avoid the people and places associated with her addiction. Roberto is ambivalent about the move, since he depends on his father for his employment, and his sister for childcare. He thinks a move would leave the family with no support at all. Roberto's mother has never cared for Maria, and thinks that Anna should raise Tonio.

In preparation for Maria's prerelease training, the foster care worker has been asked to set up a family meeting.

CASE STUDY 4   IRISH PROTESTANT FAMILY

The O'Bryans moved to the United States reluctantly, but convinced that the violence in Northern Ireland placed them at risk. Sean and Kathleen had seen the murder of Sean's brother, and Kathleen's parents had also perished in a suspicious fire. Their three children, Margaret, Michael, and Mallory, were adjusting to their new environment. Margaret, 15, was a source of concern to both her parents. She was sexually active, and became pregnant at the age of 14. Mallory, aged 1, was being raised to believe that Sean and Kathleen were her parents, rather than grandparents, and her biological mother was called her sister. The family believed that it was shameful for Margaret to have had a child out of wedlock, and they continually reminded her of the embarrassment she had brought to the family. Sean and Kathleen have few friends, and no family. Michael, aged 13, was thought by his parents to be a good boy. However, he has recently become involved with a group of boys who have been arrested numerous times for vandalism. Recently Michael was caught, along with four other boys, breaking into a storage facility. He is scheduled to go to juvenile court in two weeks, and it will be his second appearance in two months. Michael has also had two curfew violations, and tested positive for drugs.

When approached by the police, Sean said he expected they were there about Margaret, and was surprised to learn Michael was in trouble. He reportedly told the officer, "Well, boys will have a little fun, won't they? It's no big deal." The officer indicated that it was a big enough deal to demand their appearance in court.

Michael and Kathleen have scheduled an appointment with the legal aid attorney. They are very concerned about keeping the matter private, and don't think their son has done anything wrong. The attorney has heard that the juvenile court and child protection are using "child and family teams," and has called to request a team meeting.

For each case, attention should be given to the following questions.

ENGAGEMENT ISSUES

1. What aspects of resistance might be present for this case?
2. What cultural considerations may assist you in developing a relationship?
3. How does the status of the family within the larger community have an impact on engagement?
4. What fears (considering context and history for the family) might interfere with your communication with this family? How might these be communicated?
5. How will you communicate hope and possibility from your first encounter?
6. What verbal and nonverbal behaviors will assist you in demonstrating respect for the client's worldview?
7. How will you use your initial encounter to empower the clients to draw on their strengths?
8. What strategies will assist you in engaging the father? Why will it be important to engage the father? What barriers to father involvement may be present with the family, with yourself, with the agency?
9. Are there other family worldviews that you do not understand? How might you come to understand them, and demonstrate respect for the differences from your own worldviews?

ASSESSMENT ISSUES

1. What coping strategies have assisted the family in surviving other risks or threats?
2. How does this family connect with kin, friends, and community? What alliances or threats exist? How does the family view its place in the larger social system?
3. What unique duties and obligations exist for each family member? How are these determined?
4. How does this family exercise power? What historical and cultural factors influence this? How do they address competing individual and collective needs?
5. What does this family value? What are its goals? How important is education?
6. How does the family describe or view itself in its new context? What identities are supported, what identities are discouraged?
7. How will you assess the risk and safety factors for vulnerable family members?
8. What differences exist in age appropriate expectations for the children? Are there generational differences in expectations? How does the family's culture influence these expectations?
9. What are the risks of acculturation for each family member?
10. What special needs for this family (poverty, substance abuse, mental illness, health concerns, juvenile delinquency, domestic violence, teen pregnancy, etc.) need further assessment and exploration?

INTERVENTION ISSUES

1. How will safety and permanence best be assured for the children? Are there historical and contextual issues which influence your selection of interventions?
2. If needed, how will family traditions, meanings, and context be provided in out-of-home care?
3. Are there family rituals or experiences that need to be understood in order to intervene more effectively?
4. What strategies will assist you in identifying and evaluating appropriate kinship resources?
5. How will the family's sense of connection to their community assist or resist collaboration with the child/family team?
6. What resources exist within the community to support the level of acculturation of this family? How will this family view itself in relationship to these resources?

EVALUATION/TERMINATION ISSUES

1. What indicators will you look for to determine if your communication with the family is appropriate and well received?
2. What evidence will you rely on to evaluate your level of engagement with the family throughout the process?
3. How will you prepare the family for the boundaries of your relationship with them, and plan for termination?
4. How will you monitor your own reactions and responses to the differences you observe?
5. What community and organizational/agency barriers exist to prevent the family from meeting its needs? How might you advocate for change?

6. What steps can you take to ensure that your helping relationship has not fostered dependence or undermined the unique values of the family?

7. What are the most positive or hopeful aspects of the case? How will you ensure that the family's strengths are used effectively?

8. What have you done to promote hope in the family, and how is it linked to the family's worldview?

9. What elements of control have been supported in the family? How might you proceed differently to enhance the family's sense of control?

10. Are there aspects of ritual, healing, or restitution that the family may wish to incorporate? How have you effectively explored these deeper meanings within the family's worldview?

Application of intervention strategies to each case will reveal the complexities of culture. For child welfare workers, the challenge in providing safety, involving fathers, fostering permanency, and involving the community is complicated by the cultural components of social work's major tools: communication, relationship, and hope. A discussion of these tools in respect to each case will be examined.

■ ■ ■ ■ ■

CASE STUDY 1   RUSSIAN JEWISH FAMILY

Communicating with the Korsakov family may require some adjustment in style. A cultural component of communication is the value placed on correct thought. In families where communication is terse, direct, and forceful, and personal space is very narrow, there is a risk of assuming argumentativeness and aggression where it does not exist. The child welfare worker may have to take into account the family's experience with authority and power, and its emphasis on what is good for the whole family, rather than just the individual. Multigenerational families are often structured differently from nuclear families, and the cross-generational relationships may be much more intense. The high value placed on education will need to be considered. In addition, cultural differences regarding the use of alcohol by children in family gatherings will need to be explored. Reponses to stress, grief, and loss across multiple domains in this family will also have cultural components. The child welfare worker will need to attend to these concerns. In families where friendships are valued as well as intense, there is a particular challenge in building relationship. Gift-giving and sharing food and drink in the context of relationship may be at odds with professional boundaries. A key issue for the Korsakov family is the safety of the two children. Investigative efforts will need to address strategies for discipline that do not erode family structure and support. Availability of community resources, such as Jewish Family Services or Community Centers, may provide a resource for culturally appropriate support. In some areas, Jewish Children's Bureaus may offer culturally relevant family preservation services and an array of connections. Russian immigrant resettlement programs may also offer resources in language proficiency and job services, as well as bereavement programming. Acculturation may be further supported by community involvement in culturally relevant programs. Contextually, the Korsakov family appears to be working very hard to insure the future for themselves and their children. Acknowledging the considerable strengths and resiliency displayed by Korsakov family is an essential component of relationship building, and fostering hope.

CASE STUDY 2   PALESTINIAN MUSLIM FAMILY

The Al-Mead family presents significant challenges to relationship building and communication. In families where the gender roles are very different, involving the father will be crucial. However, the gender of the worker will also need to be considered. Developing relationships without intrusiveness into the family will also require special preparation. Even routine gestures, such as extending a hand, may be received as offensive. Respecting the differing expectations of girls and boys within a cultural context may be very challenging as well. The larger community issues in post-9/11 America create another level of barrier to developing relationship. The role of guardedness and suspiciousness will need to be assessed within the context of the Muslim reality. Cultural taboos and stigma may also create difficulties for the child welfare worker. Assessment of mental status across cultures requires significant sensitivity and awareness. Values are critical for the Al-Ma'ad family. The child welfare worker will need to validate the strengths of the family's capacity to work and support its members, and its desire to maintain cultural identity within a new environment. Involving Islamic Social Services Associations may be challenging in smaller communities, but the resources may be accessed through existing groups, such as schools or mosques, and some may be accessed through the Internet. In larger communities, resettlement efforts and other social services, which support and respect religious beliefs with Muslim families may be particularly helpful. Within Muslim communities, service is a valued obligation. Child welfare workers may need to familiarize themselves with informal networks to assist families such as the Al-Ma'ad's.

CASE STUDY 3   ITALIAN CATHOLIC FAMILY

Kinship care and adoption within an extended family always requires careful relationship building. Family loyalties and connections may have strong cultural components. For the Aversano family, divided loyalties and conflicts present a very enmeshed picture; yet the centrality of family and the interconnection of family and work may also demonstrate a significant strength and resource, particularly for Tonio. Ensuring that Maria's effort toward recovery are maintained within a family structure that may minimize her accomplishments will require relationship building with various subunits within the family, while carefully ensuring that the communication and alliances are clear. Efforts to reinforce Roberto and Maria as parents may put them at risk of losing the considerable support and connections that they rely on and that they may continue to need. Identifying culturally appropriate resources outside of the family, such as Catholic Social Services, may offer the unique set of services to both support Roberto and Maria, and maintain the social and family networks which create both support and conflict for them. Some multiservice agencies assist with adoption, prison reentry, and multiple family counseling issues, within a context which acknowledges cultural and religious beliefs. In addition, Italian American Brotherhood Clubs may also offer resources to families such as the Aversanos. Tonio's placement needs may ultimately reflect the centrality of family, the considerable involvement of parents of adult children, and the shared responsibility within the family for parenting.

■ ■ ■ ■ ■

CASE STUDY 4   IRISH PROTESTANT FAMILY

The O'Bryan family presents challenges to teamwork and appropriate planning for the various needs presented. While it may appear that communication will be difficult, styles do vary within families and across culture. A rich cultural tradition of expressive storytelling and metaphor may be present for the O'Bryans, along with the inability to reflect on and express personal feelings within the family. The subtleties of magical thinking, which may permeate culture, can include embellishments of the truth and verbal ambiguity. The challenge of effective teamwork with the O'Bryans will need to allow for privacy in accommodating the public nature of their problems. Engaging the family will include acknowledgement of the considerable strengths and effort involved in maintaining privacy, and to use stories and metaphors to encourage hopefulness regarding change. Team meetings, which review lots of information from the past, may not be as effective as focusing on the present, and making plans for the future. The child welfare worker would be well served by avoiding power struggles and insisting on acknowledgement of responsibility, and focusing instead on expectations and goals for the future. Accessing culturally specific resources, such as the Irish Immigration Center in Boston, may provide additional services to address the needs of the O'Bryan family.

In summary, a multidimensional approach to understanding the interplay of culture within white ethnic families, across multiple child welfare issues, through the mechanisms of generalist practice model and with a strong focus on communication, relationship, and hope may provide the child welfare worker with assistance in negotiating the various aspects of child welfare practice. Attention to acculturation, and the worker's ability to examine his or her own values will also provide an effective basis for engaging white ethnic families in the problem solving process.

PART IV: SUMMARY

Part I of this chapter has provided an overview of demographic and cultural information and how it may relate to family relationships and child welfare issues among several white ethnic and Middle Eastern groups in America. A historical account of immigration challenges and the process of acculturation has provided a basic understanding of cultural similarities and differences between and among the various groups and how this may affect the adjustment and well-being of the offspring. Racial identity, religious diversity, the American Catholic Church, the Protestant work ethic and establishment, Muslims, Christians, multiculturalism, multigeneration, behavioral problems, enmeshment, poverty, education, employment, and resourcefulness are but a few of the more prevalent themes that have been discussed. Theoretical perspectives pertaining to ethnic minorities in general such as assimilation, cultural pluralism, multiculturalism, and acculturation, along with theories of personality and child development have been highlighted to assist in clarifying the relationship between cultural and religious values and traditions, child welfare, and social work practice.

Part II has addressed specific child welfare issues and problems such as the impact of the extended family, kinship care, cultural inequality, child maltreatment issues, out-of-home care and adoption isssues, and child-rearing practices. We have suggested that while many similarities persist in maintaining cultural and religious traditions among all groups of European and Middle Eastern immigrants, many of these groups show unique differences in family relationships values and parenting of their children. For those white ethnic groups that immigrated with their entire family, the extended family has provided considerable support and resources. For those groups who immigrated without their families, the distinct and new communities that were developed after immigrating to this country were often seen as a surrogate family. Cultural identity of children and youth and the benefits and challenges it presents to preserving tradition or assimilation need to be considered. Concerning out-of-home care and adoption, recent discussions have shifted to international adoptions. For children of white ethnics, access to education and the consequences of 9/11, continue to impact development and service utilization. Nevertheless, challenges remain in child welfare service delivery for the social worker that is working with individuals from these backgrounds.

Part III has presented therapeutic interventions, which may be used as guidelines for culturally competent child welfare practice. Four important considerations for work with white ethnic families are addressed, including (1) ensuring a safe continuum of care for children which is based on age appropriate expectations and discipline; (2) involvement of fathers; (3) preserving families, and ensuring permanence for children through the use of kinship care or out-of-home placement; and (4) involvement of the community, including participation in child and family team collaboration. Four case scenarios are presented, with accompanying questions to guide the processes of engagement, assessment, intervention, and evaluation. The case examples are not intended to be stereotypical generalizations of all families; yet they offer a learning laboratory to critically examine the relevant issues and concerns in working with white ethnic families. Finally, specific resources and services are suggested to provide background information as to the possible directions for referrals addressing the needs of the various groups.

It is difficult to describe white ethnics as assimilation into American society has occurred at different rates and times; however, diversity in religions such as the strong Catholic identity and Protestant work ethic remains. European as well as Middle Eastern groups vary in terms of language, religion, social class, levels of education, reasons for immigration, and ways of assimilating into society (Healy, 1996). The "pathways to integration by the European groups are generally not available to racial minority groups today" (Healey, 1996, p. 260). Most European American groups are multigenerational, yet for most groups religious and cultural values have been dominant over time. Child-rearing values and parenting styles range from the more egalitarian in Russian Jewish families to the enmeshment and/or emotional indirectness of Irish families. The patriarchal image among Italian families, and the focus among Middle Eastern families on integrating their children into American society represent a continued sense of cultural pluralism. The unique and specific needs of these families based on religious practices among Muslim and Christian Arabs and their concern over their children in school and the community due to harassment and blame for terrorism are important issues in child welfare services and practice today.

TRANSCULTURAL APPROACHES IN WORKING WITH TRAUMATIZED REFUGEE AND ASYLUM-SEEKING CHILDREN, YOUTH, AND THEIR FAMILIES

S. MEGAN BERTHOLD, PH.D., LCSW, CTS
Program for Torture Victims, Los Angeles, California

*Refugee family
(India/Pakistan).*

OVERVIEW

This chapter provides a brief overview of some of the central issues confronting traumatized refugee and asylum-seeking children, youth, and their families in the United States. Key challenges are explored and suggestions provided for clinicians and social service providers approaching assessment and intervention with these children, youth, and their families. Part I of this chapter addresses issues and concerns within and across refugee and asylum-seeking families with a focus on transcultural and trauma issues. The experiences of organized violence and other traumas are described, including traumas experienced in the United States and the impact of the events of 9/11, along with the common associated physical, psychosocial, and developmental consequences. The inequities in available services depending on legal status will be explored. Part II highlights assessment and treatment issues with this population. Attention is given to special issues such as principles of transcultural and trauma-oriented assessment and intervention, suggestions related to child protective services, and the characteristics of resilient youth and families, and a theoretical framework for work with traumatized refugee and asylum-seeking children, youth, and families is provided. Part III includes several case vignettes, providing an opportunity to apply the assessment and intervention principles to typical cases practitioners may encounter. Examples of how narrative and solutions-focused approaches to therapy can be used with refugee and asylum-seeking families are highlighted.

INTRODUCTION

Since the time of the early nonindigenous settlers, waves of immigrants have come to what is now known as the United States of America. The patterns of and reasons for immigration have shifted over the years in response to complex historical, social, economic, political, and legal factors. Not all of these newcomers had a choice about whether to leave their home countries. Refugees and asylum seekers were forced to flee their countries, often at great risk, due to persecution or fear of future persecution.

The definition of who is a refugee has been hotly debated around the world perhaps, in part, because it prescribes obligations for governments and intergovernmental organizations. The definition of refugee which has been generally accepted as the standard, and which most Western governments derive their asylum decisions from, is based on the *1951 United Nations Convention Relating to the Status of Refugees*, and later modified in the *1967 Protocol Relating to the Status of Refugees* (Lawyers Committee for Human Rights, 1991; UNHCR, 2002). International law narrowly defines the term "refugee" to refer to someone who is outside his or her nation and is unwilling or unable to return due to a well-founded fear of persecution based on one of five grounds: race, religion, nationality, membership in a social group, or political opinion. The United States relies, in part, on this definition of refugee when determining whether to grant asylum. This definition has been criticized, as the meaning of persecution and social group are vague and gender is excluded as one of the recognized grounds. Asylum seekers differ from refugees in that refugees obtain this designation prior to arriving in the United States, often through interviews in a refugee camp, while asylum seekers apply for protection after they arrive in the United States.

Refugees and asylum seekers typically come into contact with multiple international, national, and regional public and private organizations (e.g., the United Nations High Commission for Refugees, United Nations Children's Fund (UNICEF), the Department of Homeland Security, the Office of Refugee Resettlement (ORR), voluntary agencies working overseas and in the United States, such as the International Rescue Committee, the International Committee of the Red Cross, refugee resettlement and social services agencies in the United States, school systems, and nonprofit health and mental health providers). Although there were sixteen National Child Traumatic Stress Network (NCTSN) sites in nine states in the United States in 2002 that offered mental health services for refugee children (Lustig et al., 2002), many refugees do not come into contact with these providers. Many service providers in the United States are likely to be ill equipped to appropriately assess and intervene with these families who may present with challenges different from other clients, due to their unique life experiences, trauma histories, and/or culture.

This chapter will explore key challenges and provide suggestions to clinicians and social service providers for approaching assessment and interventions with these children, youth, and their families. Part I of this chapter will address issues and concerns within and across refugee and asylum-seeking families with a focus on transcultural and trauma issues. The experiences of organized violence and other traumas will be described, including traumas experienced in the United States and the impact of the events of 9/11, along with the common associated physical, psychosocial, and developmental consequences. The challenges in finding adequate transitional housing and the inequities in available services depending on legal status will be explored. Part II will highlight assessment and treatment issues with this population. Attention will be given to special issues such as principles of transcultural and trauma-oriented assessment and intervention, suggestions related to child protective services and the characteristics of resilient youth and families, and provide a theoretical framework for work with traumatized refugee and asylum-seeking children, youth, and families. Part III will include several case vignettes, providing for an opportunity to apply the assessment and intervention principles to typical cases practitioners may encounter.

Throughout the chapter, the term "immigrant" is used to encompass immigrants, refugees, and asylum seekers who are residing in the United States, unless otherwise specified. There is enormous diversity within the experience of refugees and asylum seekers, even among those from a given country or ethnic group. While generalizations will be drawn in places in this chapter, those working with this vulnerable population are cautioned to be alert for assumptions they may make and to take great care to assess how relevant or accurate these generalizations are for any given individual, family, or community.

PART I: ISSUES AND CONCERNS WITHIN AND ACROSS REFUGEE AND ASYLUM-SEEKING FAMILIES

Organized Violence and Other Traumatic Experiences

Overview of Experiences.   There are a wide range of experiences that lead children, youth, and their families to leave their homelands and come to the United States to live. The continuum of experiences includes individual economic reasons (e.g., trafficked to work in sweatshops), violence or persecution targeted at the individual (e.g., Female Genital Cutting/Female Circumcision/Female Genital Mutilation (FGC/FC/FGM)[1], state-sponsored torture[2] due to political or religious reasons, violence perpetrated against members of a group (e.g., abduction of children forced to be child soldiers, ethnic cleansing, or massacres), and community violence, war, or terrorism. The fundamental right to safety has been severely compromised for those who were forced to flee as refugees or asylum seekers.

As of January 1, 2003, the United Nations High Commissioner for Refugees (UNHCR, 2003a) estimated that there were 20.6 million refugees, asylum seekers, displaced persons, and other persons of concern to UNHCR around the world. This computes to roughly 1 of every 300 persons on earth. A little over 1 million of these persons of concern were in North America. Children and adolescents under the age of 18 accounted for 45 percent of all the world's refugees (57 percent of all refugees in Central Africa and 20 percent in Central and Eastern Europe), and youth between the ages of 12 and 24 made up 35 percent of all refugees according to the United Nations (Global Network for Justice, 2003). At the end of fiscal year 2002, approximately 638,000 refugees and asylum seekers were in the United States (U.S. Committee for Refugees, 2003a).

The United Nations estimated that 81,100 persons submitted new asylum claims in the United States in 2002, predominantly coming from China, Mexico, Columbia, India, and Haiti, although in smaller numbers from many countries around the world (UNHCR, 2003b). Roughly 20,000 were granted asylum in the United States each year. Approximately 8,500 children sought asylum in the United States each year (U.S. Committee for Refugees, 2003a), of which roughly 5,000 were detained by the Department of Homeland Security (formerly the Immigration and Naturalization Service) during the course of their proceedings, at times in jails with juvenile offenders. Less than half of the children seeking asylum had legal representation according to a 2002 report by the Women's Commission for Refugee Women and Children (Lustig et al., 2002). In the Homeland Security Act of 2002, Congress charged the ORR, part of the Department of Health and Human Services, with taking over the responsibility for the care of these undocumented youth who were in federal custody.

Frequently, asylum seekers and refugees have been exposed to organized violence and a range of other traumatic experiences in their homelands that have left them with little or no choice but to flee in order to protect their lives. Children and adolescents who fled their homelands, and to a far lesser extent youth whose families chose to immigrate to the United States, often have experienced trauma at high rates, either directly or as witnesses. Approximately 70 percent of the 8,500 undocumented children detained by the Immigration and Naturalization Service (INS) in 1990 were unaccompanied minors (Human Rights Watch Children's Rights Project, 1997). Refugee and asylum-seeking youth are particularly vulnerable to abuse, particularly if they are without the protection of family or, for girls, are in areas such as in parts of the Middle East, Africa, or Asia where the social position of women and girls is not strong. Youth and their families who come to the United States as refugees or asylum seekers may have loved ones who have been "disappeared" (been abducted by the authorities with no further trace) or have been imprisoned for political reasons, or as they are perceived as dissidents due to their religious, ethnic, or national backgrounds, or their membership in a social group. Sometimes they lose their lives in the process.

Problems with Statistics on Youth Survivors. It can be hard to ascertain the numbers of youth and other individuals who have experienced various traumatic experiences, as most statistics are drawn from estimates from human rights organizations operating in areas where individuals fear for their lives if they report their experiences, or from small-scale nonprobability studies. Many of the experiences are considered too shameful or painful to report. Often these studies do not include minors, or utilize questionable methodology. Some studies focus on children who survived war but typically do not make distinctions between the widely diverse experiences of these children (e.g., those who witnessed atrocities versus those forced to commit violence as child soldiers).

The Case of Torture. The difficulty in precisely estimating prevalence rates is illustrated by the case of torture. Torture is a widespread, global problem.[3] This social problem cuts across all social, cultural, ethnic, racial, age, sexual orientation, religious, socioeconomic, and regional boundaries. Amnesty International reported in 2000 that 150 nations practiced systematic torture and maltreatment (see Amnesty International website at www.amnesty.org). Torture may be physical, sexual, and/or psychological in nature. All cases of torture have a psychological impact. The prevalence of torture in refugees varies from 5 to 70 percent depending on the composition of the sample in relation to age, sex, nationality, and point in time. The most commonly cited review estimates that from 5 to 35 percent of refugees were tortured (Baker, 1992). A recent study with a nonprobability sample of Somali and Oromo refugees in Minnesota (Jaranson et al., 2004) found torture prevalence rates from 25 to 69 percent by gender and ethnicity, and suggests that the previous estimate of 400,000 torture survivors in the United States (Jaranson, 1995) may be too low.

Of the nearly 26,000 individuals granted asylum in Fiscal Year 2002, approximately 11,000 resided in California, and over 25 percent of all asylum seekers granted asylum in the United States in Fiscal Year 2002 were adjudicated by the U.S. immigration office in Los Angeles (U.S. Department of Homeland Security, 2002). One-third of the nation's asylum cases were registered in the Los Angeles metropolitan area. Not all asylum seekers or asylees have been tortured. Extrapolating from U.S. government statistics, anywhere from 20,000 to 140,500 torture survivors may have settled in California within the last 17 years. It is unclear how many of these may be minors.

What is clear to human rights workers, health and mental health professionals, and attorneys who work with the survivors, however, is that one of the tactics used by torturers or perpetrators of other organized violence is to pick up the children, adolescents, and other loved ones of their perceived opponents. These loved ones may be held hostage, interrogated, tortured, and sometimes killed in order to put pressure on their relative to turn themselves in or stop their opposition work. Additionally, not all targets of torture and other forms of organized violence have actually done anything against the perpetrator or the government. It is not uncommon for individuals to be falsely accused of opposition to the government or other organized powerful groups in a society. Frequently arbitrary and widespread violence is used as a method of instilling fear in the society, with the hopes of preventing dissent and further enhancing or solidifying the perpetrator's power. In some countries where civil unrest is rampant, those on different sides of the conflict, government troops and guerilla or paramilitary forces alike, target individuals. Individuals or communities are often accused of collaborating with or supporting the other faction(s), and may feel that they have nobody to turn to for protection. Indeed, there may be no private or public person, agency, or organization that can provide or is willing to provide protection or recourse.

Child Soldiers.   Some youth are recruited or forced, often under the threat of death, into being child soldiers. The United Nations estimated that 300,000 children, boys and girls, were being forced to fight as child soldiers with government or opposition forces in some of the most violent wars in over thirty countries around the world.[4] These youth were often compelled (sometimes with a death threat) to commit various human rights violations including murdering their families or other youth who refused to fight. Hundreds of thousands more minors were recruited into government military, paramilitary, militia, and armed rebel or other opposition groups in over eighty-five countries (Coalition to Stop the Use of Child Soldiers, 2001).

The Coalition to Stop the Use of Child Soldiers (CSUCS) found that this problem was most prevalent in Africa and Asia; however, countries in Europe, the Americas, and the Middle East also used child soldiers. Approximately 120,000 child soldiers, some only 7 or 8 years old, were fighting in Africa. At the time of CSUCS' report, this was particularly common in Angola, Burundi, Congo-Brazzaville, the Democratic Republic of Congo (DRC), Ethiopia, Liberia, Rwanda, Sierra Leone, Sudan, and Uganda. Some other notable examples of countries that used child soldiers were Iran in the early 1980s during the Iran–Iraq war, Lebanon, Afghanistan, Myanmar, Sri Lanka, Cambodia, Colombia, and Peru. In many parts of Central America, former child soldiers were reintegrated into the armed forces. Some industrialized countries in Europe and North America accepted voluntary military recruits who were 17 years old, and occasionally as young as 16 (Coalition to Stop the Use of Child Soldiers, 2001). During the decade from the early 1990s through the beginning of the twenty-first century, approximately 2 million children died in conflicts, while 6 million were maimed and 1 million were orphaned (Global Network for Justice, 2003). Many of those who escaped death themselves were highly traumatized by the brutality of what they experienced.

Sexual Trauma and Honor Killings.   Youth and their families do not always survive their violent experiences. The perpetrators sometimes kill their victims. In certain cultures and societies, girls and women who survive rape or other sexual trauma may be ostracized by their community, disowned by their family, or even killed by male relatives in what is often referred to as "honor killings." These relatives perceive that the female victim has misused her sexuality, thereby dishonoring the reputation of the family. Women who are accused of infidelity or flirting, or other actions deemed disgracing to the family might also be killed. Killing the girl or woman is done to restore the family's reputation and name in society. The victim is often not given an opportunity to defend herself, even when there is no evidence. The men who murder them are frequently not punished or are given reduced sentences.

Some of the countries where honor killings have occurred are Bangladesh, Brazil, Ecuador, Egypt, India, Israel, Italy, Jordan, Morocco, Pakistan, Sweden, Turkey, Uganda, and the United Kingdom (Women's Issues, 2003). At the turn of the twenty-first century, while honor killings were found to be prevalent mostly in the Middle East and in some countries where the majority of the population was Muslim, honor killings pre-dates Islam. Many Islamic scholars and leaders have condemned honor killings and state that it is not based on Islamic religious doctrine. Again, prevalence statistics are difficult to determine given that many honor killing are not reported. The United Nations Population Fund estimated that, in the early 2000s, approximately 5,000 females might be killed every year (Women's Issues, 2003).

Familial and Other Interpersonal Violence.   Familial and other interpersonal violence, including rape, child abuse, domestic violence, assault, murder, and other traumatic violence, can be found in every society. The societal conditions often found in war zones or repressive societies where organized violence is rampant can lead to high rates of familial and interpersonal violence (Bawa, 1995, as cited in Pynoos, Kinzie, and Gordon, 2001), in part due to untreated posttraumatic stress reactions[5] and chronic societal stress and disruption.

Victims of Trafficking.   The Coalition to Abolish Slavery and Trafficking reported that a woman or child was trafficked into the United States for forced labor every 10 minutes at the end of the twentieth century (H.J. Cho and J. Stanger, personal communication, December 7, 1999). Some were trafficked into servile work in sweatshops or other labor situations, sex work, domestic servitude, or servile marriages. A $9 billion a year global industry, human trafficking was frequently an activity of organized crime. Roughly 27 million people lived in slavery worldwide. The United States enacted the most comprehensive modern-day antislavery legislation in the world in October 2000. The Victims of Trafficking and Violence Protection Act of 2000 (P.L. 106–386) and the Trafficking Victims Protection Reauthorization Act of 2003 (H.R. 2620) provided significant tools to combat trafficking domestically and worldwide and to protect victims.[6] By 2004, the U.S. State Department figures indicated that of the 800,000–900,000 estimated victims trafficked around the world each year, approximately 18,000–20,000 were trafficked to the United States (Administration for Children and Families, 2004).

Victims of Natural Disasters and Temporary Protected Status.   In addition to human-perpetrated violence, some have lived through natural disasters, or serious accidents such as the 2001 earthquake in El Salvador, and Hurricane Mitch in Honduras and Nicaragua in 1998. These types of disasters led many survivors to come to the United States. The INS offered approximately 150,000 Hondurans and Nicaraguans emergency relief in the form of Temporary Protected Status (TPS), a type of temporary amnesty, to stay in the United States while their homelands recovered from Hurricane Mitch. The TPS has also been provided on an annual basis to survivors of other situations who are in the United States when the U.S. government deems that it is temporarily unsafe for them to return to their homelands, such as those from Sudan, Sierra Leone, and Burundi who fled from situations of armed conflict beginning in the late 1990s. Such temporary status may be extended, subject to the review of country conditions on an annual basis.

Serial Trauma.   Refugee and asylum-seeking youth and their families have frequently been exposed to multiple traumas before they fled their homelands. Such serial or sequential trauma is common in environments where political violence is widespread (Gibson, 1989; Keilson, 1980; Swartz and Levett, 1989). Having fled from violent and other traumatic situations, many refugees and asylum seekers found that they experienced continued trauma during their migration. Some spent considerable time in dangerous refugee camps or camps for displaced persons. Some of these camps were at the edge of war zones, such as Site 2 and other camps for displaced Khmer at the Thai–Cambodian border throughout the 1980s and beginning of the 1990s (Mollica et al., 1993), and border camps in Thailand for more than 100,000 ethnic minority refugees from Burma who fled from forced labor and relocation, rape, and a variety of human rights violations committed against them by the military dictatorship in Burma (U.S. Committee for Refugees, 2003b). Residents of some of these camps were exposed to shelling or other fighting between warring factions, particularly because some camps harbored or were seen as harboring combatants. Conditions in these camps also sometimes led to widespread exploitation, bandit attacks, forced prostitution, or the resolution of interpersonal conflicts by threats or the use of hand grenades or other heavy weaponry that were abundantly available. In 1990, international medical personnel on the Thai–Cambodian border reported every month approximately 1,000 cases of loss of life, limbs, or mutilation due to individuals stepping on landmines surrounding the displaced persons' camps on the border, sometimes when they went out to gather firewood to cook their meals.[7] Some of these victims were children, who faced lifetimes ahead of them as disabled individuals in cultures where the loss of a limb or eyesight is generally stigmatizing and may limit one's options for marriage and gainful employment.

Continued Trauma in the United States and the Impact of "9/11".   For those who eventually come to the United States or other countries, many hope to find a place of refuge, safety, and opportunity. Instead, often they find themselves initially living in dangerous inner-city neighborhoods where there can be high rates of community violence (Berthold, 1999, 2000). They also do not always find themselves welcomed by their neighbors or society at large. There has been an increasing call to deal with the "problem of illegal aliens" in the United States in the past several years, particularly following the terrorist attacks in the United States on September 11, 2001 (otherwise known as "9/11"). Immigration laws periodically evolve, reflecting changes in society and the shifting political pressures and opinions of the times. A number of anti-immigrant pieces of legislation were proposed, with some passed, in the United States post 9/11, including legislation that significantly affected asylum and the civil rights of detainees held by the U.S. government. Some prominent examples are the Real ID Act and the Patriot Acts I and II.[8]

In 2004, widespread media attention was paid to the use of torture and other degrading and humiliating abusive treatment by members of the U.S. military on detainees in Iraq, including vivid photographic images of the atrocities on television and in newspapers. Clinicians working with survivors of state-sponsored torture from other countries who had fled to the United States found that these reports and images triggered memories in many survivors of their own torture.[9] The impact of the involvement of U.S. service personnel in these atrocities, as well as the initial response of the U.S. government, on survivors of torture who fled to the United States looking for safety has been mixed. Some have expressed dismay and an increased sense of fear and insecurity, as their prior view of the United States as a champion of human rights and justice was called into question.[10] Others took comfort in the U.S. government's official statements denouncing the atrocities and calling for an investigation and adjudication of those involved (some of these survivors who were in asylum proceedings in the United States appeared to have powerful psychological motivations for continuing to perceive the United States as a country committed to upholding justice and protecting those who were persecuted). At the time of this writing, these investigations were underway and the extent and role of the higher authorities as well as the range of reactions among torture survivors in the United States remained to be determined.[11]

What is important to recognize, however, is that the implication of the U.S. government's involvement in human rights abuses and torture is not new. The U.S. government established the U.S. Army School of the Americas (SOA) in 1946 and for decades since has been implicated in training numerous members of the military from around Latin America in counterinsurgency tactics and interrogation techniques, including psychological manipulation and maltreatment, and techniques that could amount to torture (Amnesty International, 2002).[12] Graduates of the SOA have been responsible for a number of Latin America's worst human rights abuses.[13] The Pentagon was forced to release some of the SOA's training manuals in 1996 that advocated practices such as execution, extortion, kidnapping, and torture (Amnesty International, 2002). Amnesty International (2002) argues that the secrecy surrounding such training contributes to the risk that the United States may be training individuals or forces that commit human rights abuses.

Common Consequences of Traumatic Experiences

The consequences of the traumatic experiences faced by immigrant, refugee, and asylum-seeking youth and families are varied, including impact on their physical and mental health, academic and occupational performance, moral and social development, and behavior (Pynoos, Kinzie, and Gordon, 2001). The physical consequences depend to a large extent on the type of abuse they have experienced (Randall and Lutz, 1991), as well as their access to appropriate health care and the resources available to them. Many youth who came from impoverished circumstances, areas without affordable health care, or from war-torn regions may arrive in the United States having had little or no physical or mental health care throughout their lives, even after their violent experiences.

Physical Consequences.   There are a wide array of possible physical consequences of torture, physical abuse, and other violence including pain (e.g., headaches, back pain, and other pain including psychosomatic pain), scars, deformities, chronic disabilities, fractures, damaged teeth, punctured eardrums, impaired hearing and/or vision, cardiovascular disorders, respiratory disorders, gastrointestinal disorders, nutritional disorders, urologic disorders, genital disorders, musculoskeletal disorders, and neurologic disorders (Goldfeld et al., 1988; Goldman and Goldston, 1985 as cited in Basoglu et al., 2001; Holtan, 1998; Randall and Lutz, 1991; Rasmussen, 1990; Skylv, 1992). Survivors of torture and others who have been subjected to lengthy detention have been found to have an elevated risk of malignancies, infectious disease, heart disease, and cerebrovascular accidents (Goldman and Goldston, 1985, as cited in Basoglu et al., 2001). Head trauma may result in neurological damage (Lustig et al., 2002). Trauma to the head can lead to brain hemorrhage resulting in traumatic stroke, and can also produce brain edema and dementia (Quiroga and Berthold, 2004). Women who have been raped or sexually tortured may become pregnant or experience miscarriage, contract sexually transmitted diseases, become infertile, or have their genitalia mutilated, while men have reported sexual dysfunction and testicular atrophy (Goldfeld et al., 1988). Given the widespread epidemic of HIV and AIDS, male and female torture survivors who are raped are at risk of contracting the HIV virus. Rape and other forms of sexual abuse can have profound impact on the psychosexual functioning of both genders, an impact that can be further compounded by the stigma and shame associated with sex outside of marriage in many cultures.

Psychosocial Consequences.   Numerous factors appear to be associated with the psychosocial impact of trauma on youth and their families, including age and developmental stage, dose of exposure to the original trauma, type of trauma, severity, chronicity, type of exposure (direct, witness, hear about, or forced participation in perpetration), extent of injury, individual vulnerability prior to trauma exposure, resettlement stress, and access to parental or family support networks (Ahearn and Athey, 1991; Almqvist and Broberg, 1999; Gerrity, Keane, and Tuma, 2001; Sack, Clarke, and Seeley, 1996). Repeated or sequential traumatization, frequently found in situations of political or community violence, can further affect the traumatic reactions of youth (Boothby, 1994; Kilpatrick et al., 1995).

Culture is another important factor that influences the outcome, and a child's relationship to their culture may affect their adjustment on resettlement in another country (Lustig et al., 2002). Youth and their families from diverse cultural backgrounds may react to trauma differently. In a study of 156 school-aged Central American and Southeast Asian refugee children, Rousseau, Drapeau, and Corin

(1998) found differences in the role of premigration and postmigration factors. Family trauma history was most closely correlated with symptoms in the Central American children, while family variables (e.g., family conflict and parental depression) were more highly correlated with symptomatology in the Southeast Asian youth.

A study of children and adolescents in the former Yugoslavia exposed to war-related traumas found that those who had been tortured had the most severe Posttraumatic Stress Disorder (PTSD) and comorbid depression (UNICEF, 1995, as cited in Pynoos, Kinzie, and Gordon, 2001).[14] Other studies found that refugee children affected by war experience depression and anxiety, psychic numbing, paranoia, anger and violence, a heightened awareness of death, and insomnia (Garbarino and Kostelny, 1996; Jablensky et al., 1994). A positive dose–effects association between exposure to trauma and symptoms of distress was found in a study of Cambodian adolescents living on the edge of a war zone on the Thai–Cambodian border (Mollica et al., 1997), with the most frequent symptoms being anxiety, depression, social withdrawal, somatic complaints, and attention problems. Children and youth exposed to extreme violence suffer from high levels of hypervigilance, startle reactions, and sleep disturbances (Eth and Pynoos, 1994; Kirsten et al., 1980). Persistent sleep disturbances have been found in children who have been physically abused (Glod et al., 1997). Children with chronic sleep problems who had survived a sniper attack at their school were found to experience learning difficulties (Pynoos et al., 1987). The normal maturation of a variety of biological systems may be altered by disturbances in arousal found among traumatized children and adolescents (Pynoos, Kinzie, and Gordon, 2001), and overall developmental and biological maturation can be affected (Pynoos, Steinberg, and Wraith, 1995). Youth who have been exposed to traumatic bereavement and severe threats to their life have frequently been found to suffer from comorbid chronic PTSD and depression. Among youth whose bodily integrity has been threatened or violated, such as in sexual trauma, dissociative reactions are often found (Putnam and Trickett, 1993). Long-lasting posttraumatic stress reactions spanning many years have been found in longitudinal studies of Cambodian child survivors of the Khmer Rouge regime (Kinzie et al., 1989; Kinzie et al., 1986; Sabin et al., 1996), Armenian child survivors of the 1988 earthquake (Goenjian et al., 1995, 1997; Pynoos et al., 1993), children kidnapped and buried alive in a bus (Terr, 1983), and children traumatized by terrorism (Dreman and Cohen, 1990).

Chronic intrusive symptoms of the trauma(s), such as traumatic memories, as well as ongoing and current stress and difficulties appear to be factors increasing the risk that youth with PTSD will also suffer from concurrent depression (Goenjian et al., 1996; Sack, Clarke, and Seeley, 1996). Intrusive PTSD symptoms have been found to wax and wane over many years in Cambodian refugees (Kinzie et al., 1989; Sack et al., 1993) and other trauma survivors, suggesting that chronic PTSD symptoms sometimes follow a fluctuating course. Individuals who may have been in remission or partial remission can go through periods of exacerbation or reemergence of their symptoms in the face of traumatic reminders many years after the original trauma. New traumatic experiences or stresses can also prompt the rekindling of posttraumatic stress symptoms.

Multiple Losses and Bereavement.   Children and adolescents need not be directly targeted with violence to experience detrimental psychological and developmental consequences. Those who witness their family members or neighbors being beaten, threatened, raped, killed, or subjected to other atrocities, or who have relatives who have been tortured, "disappeared," or killed, may be deeply affected as well. Loss is typically pervasive in the lives of immigrant youth and families, often at multiple levels. Loss of homeland, culture, loved ones, support networks, cultural identity, trust in the humanity of others, and one's sense of safety and security in the world are just some of the many losses experienced by immigrants, refugees, and asylum seekers. It is not surprising, therefore, that grief is a pervasive experience faced by many immigrants. Depending on the context in which the losses occur, the grief reactions can often be complicated, such as when a loved one has "disappeared" and relatives and friends are unable to learn their fate.

Ahearn and Athey (1991) hold that while bereavement and loss is difficult for most children, these experiences can be even more complicated for refugee youth. They found that among eleven vulnerability factors identified in various studies of bereavement in children that point to increased risk for psychological problems, five are common to the experience of being a refugee. These five factors are sudden or unexpected deaths; deaths involving violence or other trauma; lack of community or family support systems; an inconsistent and unstable environment; and a surviving parent's own vulnerability and increased dependence on their child or children (Ahearn and Athey, 1991). For children who have experienced both significant trauma and loss, it may be even more difficult to successfully work through the trauma and adequately grieve their losses (Ahearn and Athey, 1991; Pynoos and Eth, 1985).

Family-Related Issues (Role Reversals, Interaction with Child Protective Services System).   Clinicians who work with immigrant, refugee, and asylum-seeking youth and their families frequently see role reversals in the family system, particularly during the early years in the new country. In the United States, for example, children often learn English more quickly than their parents, and often are called on to interpret for their parents with social service providers, health providers, school personnel, and law enforcement personnel. This can put them in very vulnerable, distressing, and inappropriate situations, such as when a child is asked to interpret for their mother when she sees an OB-GYN regarding family practice issues, or when discussing with a social service provider how all their benefits are expiring putting them at risk of homelessness. Advocacy is needed to ensure adequate resources are available for appropriate interpreter services. In addition, the authority of the parents can be compromised when parents must depend on benefits in the United States. Marital power dynamics may also be affected in cases where the wife finds it easier to get employment in the United States, particularly when the husband is traditionally the breadwinner of the family.

In many parts of the world, child-rearing and disciplining traditions and practices are very different from that in the United States. For example, in some countries parents and extended members of the family (and in some communal societies, trusted community members) are observed to utilize corporal punishment techniques with children. There are different conceptions of what is considered child abuse, and some immigrant families settling in the United States come in contact with child protective services or law enforcement for allegations of child abuse. Indeed, some immigrant youth have even threatened their parents that they will call the authorities and report them for child abuse (whether or not it was occurring) in order to pressure their parents into allowing them to go out with their friends or do other things they want.[15] The impact of being separated again from family by authorities can be devastating and traumatic for children and parents alike, particularly if they have lost other loved ones in the past, and this new separation may feel like further abuse. This experience may even trigger memories of earlier traumatic losses and situations where they felt abused by authorities or where their rights were violated. It can exacerbate their distrust of the system and authorities.

In general, there may be profound cultural difference between the immigrant family and the public child welfare system and law enforcement personnel. The reasons for the involvement of child protective services or law enforcement may seem incomprehensible to the family. The resulting clash of cultures may compromise the ability of the system to effectively serve these families, unless the interventions are tailored to the individual families.[16]

Some parents who have developed PTSD as a result of torture or other traumas may have increased irritability or anger outbursts subsequent to their traumatic experiences. If they are accused of child abuse, they may be reluctant to reveal their trauma history and psychological condition to others, for fear that this information will negatively influence the perception of the child protective service or law enforcement personnel toward them (e.g., labeling them as a danger to others, or at risk of acting out violently). Suggestions for practitioners who come into contact with newly arrived immigrant families at risk of becoming involved with child protective services will be provided later in this chapter.

Developmental Issues. Immigrant youth may find themselves facing incompatible values, expectations, and responsibilities from their parents and American peers and the larger society that may compromise their abilities to adjust and experience normal development. In addition, traumatic experiences suffered by children and adolescents have been found to have far-reaching developmental consequences that may influence the later development of psychopathology and the impairment of functioning (Pynoos, Kinzie, and Gordon, 2001). Two key aspects of development that may be affected by trauma are (1) developmental delays that occur when the child's negotiation of developmental tasks are disrupted or altered as a result of the trauma; and (2) delayed developmental effects. When traumatized youth go through new developmental stages, issues associated with the earlier trauma may be experienced in new ways. For example, an adolescent girl who was raped years before, prior to puberty, by soldiers looking for her politically active father may experience significant issues surrounding her sexuality as she enters adolescence. Just as the types of traumatic experiences fall on a continuum, so too do the consequences.

The age of the traumatized youth often influences the way posttraumatic stress is manifested, although somatic symptoms are common in refugees and asylum seekers of all ages. According to the American Psychiatric Association's criteria for PTSD in its Fourth Edition of the *Diagnostic and Statistical Manual of Mental Disorders* (DSM-IV-TR) (American Psychiatric Association, 2000), children may express their fear, helplessness, or sense of horror through agitated or disorganized behavior. Young children's intrusive memories of the traumatic events may be acted out in repetitive traumatic play, using themes or aspects from their traumatic experience. Children may have nightmares without readily identifiable content, and young children may engage in traumatic reenactment of their experiences. Separation anxiety and attachment issues may be prominent in preschool-aged children. Strong internalizing and externalizing behaviors such as withdrawal, inhibitions, disturbance in attention, and disruptive behaviors are commonly seen among school-aged youth. These youth may become more argumentative or distant, and their academic performance may deteriorate.

Reactions frequently found in adults, such as PTSD, depression, antisocial behavior, and substance use or abuse, may be more likely in traumatized adolescents (Pynoos, Kinzie, and Gordon, 2001). School truancy and delinquency, precocious sexual behavior, or risky reenactment behavior that can endanger the adolescent have been observed. Conversely, other traumatized adolescents may react by becoming withdrawn or passive, and may develop pessimistic or constricted views of their future possibilities that can influence their subsequent development. Cultural and socioenvironmental factors may influence the rates of some of these reactions, as studies of Cambodian refugee youth and other youth have found (Dinicola, 1996; Sack et al., 1986).

It can be extremely challenging to adapt to life in a radically different country. In the transition period, immigrant youth may experience what feels like a series of "failures," which can have a negative impact on their developing self-esteem. Newly arrived immigrant school children may fall behind in their schoolwork as they learn a new language, have identity issues, and find it difficult to make new friends and alliances with their peers (Anderson, 2001). Their self-confidence and sense of efficacy can be compromised if they do not have success experiences (Ahearn and Athey, 1991). In addition, studies have found powerful feelings of guilt and revenge fantasies among traumatized school-aged and adolescent youth (Pynoos et al., 1993; van der Kolk, 1985; Yule, 1992). This guilt may be related to the youth's feelings or beliefs that they were a coward, were ineffective in their responses to the trauma, or that their actions or failure to act resulted in the injury, incarceration, or the death of a loved one.

Research conducted with youth in war zones has found a number of prominent symptoms of distress. These symptoms include numbness, helplessness, difficulty concentrating, anxiety, desensitization to threat, high levels of risk taking and engagement in dangerous activities, and a sense of "futurelessness" (Garbarino et al., 1992; Lorion and Saltzman, 1993). In a study of 480 youth in Croatia during the Bosnia–Herzegovina war, Zivic (1993) found high rates of depressive symptoms. The rates were particularly high among those children who fled as refugees from the war zones. Psychological distress was common in Palestinian children exposed to political violence (Baker, 1991; Khamis, 1993; Mahjoub et al., 1989; Punamaki, 1989).

Children in Beirut who were repetitively exposed to violence were more likely to be traumatized (Macksoud, 1992). This effect was additive. Research that examined the impact of risk factors on developmental difficulties suggests that children who have only one risk factor have no greater chance of developing problems than children with no risk factors (Rutter, 1987). The level of problems increased, however, with each additional risk factor. The risk of experiencing developmental damage may be ten times higher for children with four or more risk factors.

Macksoud and Aber (1996) found that the number of war traumas experienced by 10- to 16-year-old youth in Lebanon accounted for 16 percent of the variance in their PTSD symptoms. Those youth who experienced combat or shelling, witnessed violence, were exposed to multiple war traumas, were victims of violent acts, or were bereaved were significantly more likely to have symptoms of PTSD. Those with symptoms of depression were significantly more likely to have been separated from their parents than those who were exposed to other war traumas. Kinzie et al. (1986) found that half the Cambodian children they studied had symptoms of PTSD 4 years after they left Cambodia, but those who were with families fared better than unaccompanied youth.[17]

In addition to the numerous traumatic experiences noted above, refugee and asylum-seeking children and their families frequently have been in situations of extreme deprivation prior to coming to the United States, such as malnutrition or starvation. Over time, extreme deprivation can lead to children failing to reach normal developmental landmarks. Children may experience physical consequences (e.g., failure to reach the norms for height and weight for their age), learning problems and compromised mental development, and/or psychological and behavioral problems as a result of developmental attrition (Eisenberg, 2000 as cited in Murad, 2003).

Refugee and asylum-seeking children and adults may have faced similar types of traumas and losses. Children, however, are not as equipped developmentally to understand fully the reasons why they are in the situation they find themselves in (James, 1995 as cited in Murad, 2003). Existential issues frequently rise to the forefront for survivors of organized and other human-perpetrated violence, particularly for adolescents and adults. Questions such as "Why me?" and "What did I do to deserve this?" can trouble many youth, even those who are quite young. Older youth may begin to grapple with questions such as "What is the meaning of life?" and "How could one human do this to another?" One's cognitive abilities at different developmental stages can have an impact on the coping mechanisms utilized. Children and their family members who live through years of political and social violence and unrest, along with insufficient or ineffective efforts at community recovery, may experience changes in their moral development and consciences, according to findings from South Africa and other studies (Goenjian et al., 1999; Straker, 1993 as cited in Pynoos, Kinzie, and Gordon, 2001; Tudin, Straker, and Mendolsohn, 1994). Although such experiences may lead to some beneficial changes in moral judgment, ongoing symptoms and hardships can increase the survivor's negative views of self and negative expectations toward others and the social contract (Pynoos, Kinzie, and Gordon, 2001). One's perspective on the world and oneself may be profoundly altered by the experiences that lead refugees and asylum seekers to flee their homelands.

Some children grow up never having known their parent or other extended relatives due to organized violence, and may have lingering seething anger and thoughts of revenge as a consequence. Other youth may gain a sense of meaning and purpose in their lives by internalizing the values and principles for which their parent or other loved one died fighting for. Adolescents are seen to be at particular risk of acting out impulsively on their revenge fantasies or rage (van der Kolk, 1985). War-related trauma and postwar stresses have been found to negatively influence adolescent ambition, motivation, and adaptation and in turn compromise their successful adjustment to adulthood (Pynoos, Kinzie, and Gordon, 2001).

Transitional Housing Issues.   One of the most pressing initial concerns that immigrant families often have to contend with when they arrive in the United States is finding adequate housing, or sometimes any housing at all. Not all arriving immigrants are sponsored by organizations or have individual sponsors including immediate or extended family members in the United States or friends who are able or willing to provide them with housing and/or other assistance. Some of the family or friends already in the United States may be struggling to meet their own needs. Some may live in overcrowded situations that cannot appropriately accommodate anyone else, and lengthy separations or family conflicts may make living together stressful or untenable. Some may have given distorted or exaggerated impressions to their relatives and friends back home of their standard of living in the United States, often for reasons of not wanting to alarm or concern them. This frequently can contribute to an inaccurate, overly rosy picture that many newly arriving immigrants have that life is easy and everyone is well off in the United States. The realities of life in the United States can leave the new immigrant in shock when they encounter homeless individuals and families, the high cost of housing and food, difficulties in obtaining work (particularly for the undocumented and those without work authorization), and the overall high cost of living in many areas of the United States.[18] Unaccompanied minors can face unique challenges on arrival in the United States. They may be taken in by unrelated adults, and can be at risk of exploitation. Some enter the child welfare system and may be placed in foster care or other residential placements. Factors that contribute to involvement with the child welfare system are discussed elsewhere in this chapter.

While some immigrants may have been able to bring modest savings or, in some cases, rather substantial assets with them to help them get started in their new life in the United States, many others do not have any financial assets at all when they arrive. This is particularly common for those who had to suddenly flee their homeland due to war, torture, and other forms of persecution in order to protect their lives. They may have had to pay substantial bribes to get out of prison, to be allowed to leave the country, or to individuals to smuggle them to the United States. They may not have the money to pay for rent, not to mention the first and last month's rent and security deposits that many landlords require. It is common for newly arriving immigrants to initially reside in inner-city neighborhoods where rents are relatively low, and in some cases they can find concentrations of others from their homeland that speak their language and share their culture. While there can be many benefits associated with more affordable housing and ethnic community networks in some of these areas, one common risk is that these inner-city neighborhoods may also have high rates of community violence.

Exposure to significant levels of community violence, on top of their prior exposure to multiple traumatic events, sometimes spanning many years, can further compromise the well-being of immigrant children and their families (Berthold, 1999, 2000; see also Garbarino et al., 1992). Parental concerns about their children's exposure to violence and involvement or risk of involvement in gangs in inner-city areas, along with the higher cost of living in some cities, can contribute to secondary migration away from costly urban areas. By the end of the twentieth century, immigrant families were increasingly relocating to rural, suburban, and urban areas throughout the United States where the cost of living was more modest and work often easier to obtain. Some of these areas had not been home to certain populations of immigrants for long, and thus the communities and health and social service providers often did not have much experience in meeting the special needs of some of these immigrants that arose.

While refugees have sponsors, including nonprofit refugee service organizations, to assist them with finding housing and with transitional benefits to help them get established and find jobs, asylum seekers and some immigrants may not have anyone to help them. On arriving in the United States, asylum seekers and immigrants may not know anyone they can stay with. Some have found very supportive and nurturing temporary living situations with individuals or families by making contact with religious organizations or ethnic community associations or individuals from their home country or region.[19] These "host" families often welcome them to stay for free for varying lengths of time, typically in exchange for childcare or other household tasks. Many more established asylees, refugees, or immigrants remember how others helped them when they first arrived in the United States and are eager or willing to similarly assist newly arrived immigrants during their transition. This is not always the case, however, particularly when the regional economy is performing poorly and more and more households are struggling to make ends meet. Some new arrivals find themselves reluctantly entering into varying degrees of exploitive living situations, out of a feeling that there is no other option. In some areas, organizations that fight against such exploitation exist. For example, the Korean Immigrant Workers Advocate (KIWA) in Los Angeles, California, is one such example of an organization devoted to empowering low-wage immigrant workers. The KIWA also seeks to build a progressive leadership and constituency amongst these low-wage immigrant workers.[20]

Immigrant children and youth, asylum seekers, and other immigrants who do not have legal status in the United States are particularly vulnerable to situations of economic, physical, sexual, and/or psychological exploitation in the United States in order to meet their needs for housing, food, and other basic necessities. The increased attention in recent years to the phenomenon of human trafficking is one such example. Other new arrivals to the United States may find themselves in exploitive living situations that can mirror aspects of prior exploitation they may have experienced in the past. For example, a number of teenage and young adult women from countries such as Ethiopia, Eritrea, and Sudan who came to the United States in the late twentieth and early twenty-first centuries left their countries to find work in such countries as Saudi Arabia, Yemen, or other neighboring countries primarily due to economic necessity or in order to flee war, torture, or other human rights abuses in their homelands. Some of these young females experienced physical or sexual violence (at times gang rape over extended periods of time) in their country, only to find themselves in similar situations at the hands of their new employer.

Clinicians at the Program for Torture Victims in Los Angeles, and the Coalition to Abolish Slavery and Trafficking and similar programs around the United States, have encountered such women, for example, after they ran away from their Saudi Arabian employers who brought them to be their servants while they were in the United States for a visit. Trafficked individuals and others in exploitive living situations in the United States may be kept isolated from the outside community by their traffickers, employers, or those they live with, further enhancing the conditions of exploitation and limiting their opportunities to extricate themselves from the situation. The dependency and additional traumatization that can result in these situations can further complicate their well-being, similar to other survivors who have been chronically exposed to multiple and repeated traumas, compounded over many years. They may feel dependent on their exploiters, unable to navigate their needs alone in the United States given their isolation from the larger society and forced dependency on the perpetrator to meet these needs, and hopeless about escaping this situation.

Some immigrants find themselves homeless at some point in the United States. Asylum seekers and others without legal status in the United States are particularly at risk of being homeless, as long as they are without work authorization. Many either live on the streets or in shelters or hotels in areas where drugs and violence are rampant. Shelters often have a long waiting list, and the person must call daily to see if there is space available. When an opening is available, it may be only for a few days or weeks. Some of these facilities are not appropriate for or do not accommodate youth and families. Longer-term transitional housing for homeless youth and families are in short supply, although there are some programs, albeit with limited beds.[21]

Even after they are approved for asylum, some must wait to get the documents needed for employment such as a photo I.D. from the Department of Motor Vehicles and a social security number. Until an individual has a permanent address, it can be hard to obtain these types of documents, further prolonging their delay in being able to get legal work (International Rescue Committee Los Angeles, 2003). While typically eager to work to support themselves, those without legal status can jeopardize their future chances of legalizing their status if they are caught working illegally or "under the table."

Inequities in Services Depending on Legal Status and Associated Implications. Many traumatized refugees and asylum seekers do not inform their health care providers or other social service providers of the realities of what they have experienced. A cross-sectional survey study of 638 Latino immigrants who presented at three primary health care clinics in Los Angeles, California, found that 54 percent had experienced political violence in their home countries, and 8 percent had been tortured (Eisenman et al., 2003). Only 3 percent had told their health care provider about their experience with organized violence and none were asked about torture.

Clinical experience with these populations reveals that a number of factors may contribute to this lack of disclosure. The ability to trust in others is frequently shattered by traumatic experiences, particularly in cases of human-perpetrated violence where betrayal occurred. Some may fear telling people they perceive to be in authority, particularly if they were abused or attacked by authority figures in their homeland. They may also fear that the health or social service provider will turn them in to immigration authorities if they learn that they do not have legal status in the United States, and in turn fear the consequences of being deported, including further violence, detention, torture, or even death. In addition, one of the hallmarks of PTSD commonly experienced by trauma survivors is avoidance of thinking or talking about their traumas, or being in situations that trigger memories of their traumatic experiences. The environment in many clinics and social service agencies in the United States can trigger such memories. For example, the long waits common in agencies that provide free or low-cost services may bring back frightening memories of waiting to be interrogated or tortured. For all of these reasons, it is perhaps to be expected that many traumatized immigrants, refugees, or asylum seekers would not reveal their traumatic experiences to service providers initially, compromising the ability of the provider to appropriately assess their needs.

Eisenman and his colleagues' (2003) study indicates that the population of torture survivors and other traumatized immigrants seeking health care in Los Angeles is large, but unidentified. Many other large U.S. cities probably experience a similar scenario. Refugees and immigrants do not generally report themselves as survivors of torture and related traumas and knowledge about screening and treating these survivors is scarce among health professionals. This is a public health problem, and the costs of not addressing it are enormous. If left untreated or inappropriately treated, survivors may end up with more severe or acute health problems and increased visits to emergency rooms, with a corresponding increased financial and social cost to society. Efforts to train health and mental health professionals, teachers, and others who interact with immigrant children about the unique needs of this population and transcultural approaches to intervention are essential.

At the time of this writing in 2004, asylum seekers are not eligible for refugee benefits, are excluded from many public social services, and are generally not eligible to apply for work authorization until at least 150 days after they submit their asylum application. It can take an additional 90–180 days to receive a work permit after applying. Depending on the status of their asylum application (e.g., whether their case is in front of an Immigration Judge, if they requested a continuance in their case, or if their case is on appeal), they may not be eligible for a work authorization until or unless they are granted asylum or another form of relief.[22] While some free or sliding scale dental, physical, and mental health care services exist, typically there can be long waits for services and the providers may lack appropriate training or knowledge to effectively address some of the needs of the new arrivals who may have extensive trauma histories. This may be especially challenging for providers in rural areas who may have less experience with traumatized refugee and asylum-seeking populations (Markstrom et al., 2003).

Once granted asylum, asylees become eligible for the same set of benefits and services that refugees are entitled to; however, these benefits can vary considerably from state to state.[23] It is important to keep in mind that asylum law and related regulations are ever evolving, and these policies are subject to change. In 2004, for example, refugees received benefits, including cash and medical, starting in their first month of arrival to the United States through their first 8 months in the country. They were eligible for refugee social services for 5 years. Until Fiscal Year 2000, asylees (those granted asylum) were in essence left without government benefits, given that they could not receive any benefits until granted asylum, the fact that it generally took longer than 8 months to be granted asylum, and by then their 8-month eligibility for benefits had expired as their 8-month period started from the date they entered the country. This discrepancy in how refugees and asylum seekers were treated continued for many years, despite the fact that the main difference between a refugee and an asylee is that a refugee makes their claim for protection abroad while an asylee makes their claim once in the United States. By the start of the 2000s, once granted asylum, an asylee was eligible for cash benefits and medical assistance for a period up to 8 months from the date asylum was granted and was eligible for other social services for 5 years. Generally they qualified for food stamps and, in some cases, training or job club programs. This policy change had a tremendous impact on the quality of life for asylees who often struggled in their first few years in the United States, sometimes without a work authorization, to become self-sufficient, adapt to a new culture and society, sponsor family members whose lives may be in danger back home, reestablish their lives, and, for some, regain their health and well-being.

PART II: ASSESSMENT AND INTERVENTION

Some General Considerations

Conducting effective assessments and interventions with immigrant youth and their families can be extremely challenging. Normalizing their reactions in order to prevent misinterpretations and reduce anxiety and fear (Dyregrov and Raundalen, 2000 as cited in Murad, 2003), explaining your role, remaining ever attentive to the verbal and nonverbal cues provided by the children and their family members (Gibbs and Huang, 2003), and adapting one's approach to be culturally attuned and appropriate are important basics to keep in mind. Maintaining confidentiality and providing a context of safety and trust for one's clients are essential for any effective therapeutic work. This is doubly essential with traumatized refugee and asylum-seeking youth and their families, and care must be taken to avoid or minimize retraumatizing them. In general, encouraging such traumatized clients to be in control of as many aspects of the setting and session as possible can help in maintaining their sense of security and facilitating a therapeutic relationship. For example, some clients who have been detained and tortured in small cells may not be able to tolerate having the door to your office shut.

In working transculturally, it is vital for the clinician to continually challenge their own prejudices, assumptions, and attitudes, particularly with clients who are unfamiliar with Western forms of intervention and treatment. Assessing their knowledge and past history of treatment, as well as what they consider to be helpful or healing, are important first steps. Collaborating with a cultural consultant or indigenous healer, while empowering the client as the expert, is often extremely useful. Restoring agency and meaning to the survivor's life, as well as restoring social connections that may have been lost when they left their country, can be very therapeutic. A general approach that focuses on "undoing" the trauma[24]—including counteracting the messages of the perpetrator or torturer, validating the client's experience and reality, and acknowledging their courage, achievements, hopes, strengths, and resilience—is recommended.

Assessment of Children

Adolescents and school-aged children have been found to be capable of providing reliable and valid accounts of their own traumatic experiences and related distress (Pynoos, Kinzie, and Gordon, 2001). As in the case of adults, the memory of children may be somewhat distorted when they are under pressure (Perlman, 1999). Age-appropriate screening instruments have been developed to assess a variety of emotional and behavioral reactions in youth. Most of these instruments, however, were developed with Western youth. Some of these instruments may not be valid for youth from different cultural backgrounds, and ethical issues have been raised (Bracken, 1997). It is recommended that collateral information from other sources such as parents, other caretakers, and teachers be gathered in addition to the youth's own self-report when possible. Pynoos and his colleagues (2001) recommend that the following areas are necessary in a comprehensive assessment: frequency and nature of traumatic reminders; level of physiological and psychological reactivity; other traumas and losses; medical conditions and treatment; secondary adversities and stresses; and a host of developmental consequences including those that affect peer, academic, and family functioning.[25] For adolescents, the assessment should also screen for reckless and delinquent behavior, and substance abuse.

Diagnostic Issues and Transcultural Concerns

In the United States, mental health professionals utilize the American Psychiatric Association's Fourth Edition of the *Diagnostic and Statistical Manual of Mental Disorders*, otherwise known as the DSM-IV, to classify psychiatric conditions (American Psychiatric Association, 2000). Some of the most common DSM-IV conditions diagnosed in traumatized refugee and asylee youth and their families are PTSD, acute stress disorder, panic attacks, and other anxiety disorders; Major Depressive Disorder; bereavement; abuse of or dependence on alcohol and other substances; somatoform disorders; dissociative disorders (although sometimes episodes of dissociation may be part of a PTSD reaction); Separation Anxiety Disorder in younger children; and behavioral or attentional disturbances in adolescents and older children (see Pynoos, Kinzie, and Gordon, 2001).

Many clinicians and researchers have found that conditions such as PTSD, depression, and panic cross cultural and regional boundaries (Beiser, Cargo, and Woodbury, 1994; Marsella et al., 1996; Sack, Seeley, and Clarke, 1997). Others hold that PTSD symptoms may have diverse meanings in different cultures (Bracken, Giller, and Summerfield, 1995). There has been lively debate as to whether these classifications are appropriate for individuals from non-Western cultures (see Bracken, Giller, and Summerfield, 1995; Chakraborty, 1991; Friedman and Jaranson, 1994; and Marsella et al., 1996 for further discussion). Traumatized non-Western individuals may not experience the requisite number of avoidant/numbing symptoms to be classified as having PTSD, for example, and survivors from many cultures may have significant somatic or dissociative symptoms that accompany classic PTSD symptoms (Marsella et al., 1996). Mollica (2004) holds that despite the popular emphasis on PTSD, depression is the most common mental illness diagnosed in torture survivors. Further, he states that these survivors' somatic symptoms are frequently signs of an underlying depression and typically are culture-specific expressions of their emotional distress.

The DSM-IV (American Psychiatric Association, 2000) includes a brief section on cultural formulation and culture-bound syndromes that outlines some of the issues.[26] Culture-bound syndromes are recurrent patterns of behavior and distressing experiences specific to a region or locality that are considered by the indigenous people of that area to be an "illness" or affliction. These syndromes generally have a local name (e.g., Zar, Attaques de Nervios, Pruoy Cet) and may or may not correspond to a DSM-IV diagnostic category. PTSD may also be considered a culture-bound diagnosis that is probably most applicable to individuals from English-speaking countries (Briere, 2004). While PTSD has been found in survivors from many different societies, the symptoms and expression of posttraumatic stress may indeed differ according to the survivor's culture. Eisenbruch (1992) has proposed that Cultural Bereavement is a more appropriate and less stigmatizing classification for the response of many Cambodian survivors of the Khmer Rouge regime than PTSD. Often, what Western trained mental health professionals view as signs of mental illness are considered in other cultures to be moral and religious problems (Kleinman, 1995).

It is important for clinicians to understand the framework in which they evaluate symptoms and the causal explanations implied in their cultural framework (Lee and Lu, 1989). There are cultural differences in the causes people ascribe to illnesses (van der Veer, 1998). For example, illness in traditional Cambodian culture is commonly viewed as the consequence of coming into contact with dangerous spirits, witchcraft, or sorcery (Eisenbruch and Handelman, 1989; van de Put, 1997 as cited in van der Veer, 1998). There are similar beliefs in certain parts of India, the Caribbean, and Africa. Similarly, there can be cultural differences in ideas regarding the cause of traumatic experiences. Mollica and Son (1988, cited in van der Veer, 1998) found that Cambodian refugees who were tortured relate their torture to the concept of "karma," feeling in some way responsible for their suffering. This is very different from the Western concept that torture is done to an individual by the government or other entity to persecute them, typically for political, religious, or other reasons to preserve their own position of power or authority.

Practitioners need to understand the worldview and system of meaning of the person, and their explanation for their distress in order to be effective.[27] Harvard psychiatrist and medical anthropologist Arthur Kleinman (1980, 1988, 1995) advocates an approach to cross-cultural medicine that is very different from the approach used by most Western practitioners. He has identified eight key questions that practitioners working with individuals from different cultural backgrounds should ask. These questions are meant to elicit the patient's "explanatory model": (1) What do you call the problem? (2) What do you think has caused the problem? (3) Why do you think it started when it did? (4) What do you think the sickness does and how does it work? (5) How severe is the sickness, and will it have a short or long course? (6) What kind of treatment do you think the patient should receive, and what are the most important results you hope he/she receives from this treatment? (7) What are the chief problems the sickness has caused? and (8) What do you fear most about the sickness? Kleinman further recommends the use of a model of mediation that includes negotiation and compromise with the patient. He cautions that the Western practitioner must be aware of their own interests, emotions, and biases in their own culture of biomedicine. While developed for physicians and other health workers, these guidelines are very appropriate for social workers, psychologists, and other mental health practitioners.[28]

It is essential for mental health practitioners in the United States to keep in mind that the Western concept of mental health may be utterly foreign and strange to immigrant children and their families from culturally diverse backgrounds and they may feel fearful to see a therapist (Gibbs and Huang, 2003), particularly if they have been hurt or betrayed by someone in authority. It should not be assumed that a Western approach to therapy/treatment will work, particularly given that more than three-fourths of the world's population live in non-Western cultures, and more than 90 percent are not familiar with Western psychotherapeutic constructions (Elsass, 1997). Indeed, they may have never even heard of a social worker or therapist before. There may be no similar professionals in their homeland, or they may not have access to those that exist for financial or geographic reasons. It may be highly stigmatizing to seek professional help. Further it may be against tradition or considered shameful or taboo to discuss one's problems or private matters with someone outside the family (Gibbs and Huang, 2003) or who is not a respected elder or spiritual leader. This prescription against seeking outside help can be particularly strong when the problems involve issues such as FGC/FC/FGM or sexual trauma.

Recommendations to Prevent Involvement with Child Protective Services

As discussed previously, some traumatized refugee and asylum-seeking families are at risk of becoming involved with child protective services, frequently with a resulting clash of cultures that can have detrimental effects on the family and the society. It is important for child protective service workers who come into contact with immigrant youth and families not to assume that they understand the system or the laws in the United States. Many come from societies where the state rarely, if ever, gets involved in such family matters. The laws and policies in the United States may in fact seem incomprehensible and be perceived as threatening to the family. The family may not understand why the system has become involved with their family, why their child(ren) was(were) removed from the home, nor what is required for them to get their child(ren) back. Clear and ongoing communication, along with respect for the immigrant's culture and traditions, is essential if there is to be an effective working relationship and in order for the services to be responsive to the needs of all families.

Adopting a preventive approach is recommended with newly arriving immigrant, refugee, and asylum-seeking families or, better yet, prior to their arrival in the United States if possible (e.g., in refugee camps). Social service practitioners, health and mental health care providers, refugee resettlement workers, and other individuals who come into contact with these families can look for opportunities to connect with their intentions to promote the well-being of their children and family while integrating discussions about different traditions of educating and disciplining children and the child abuse laws in the United States as part of their services. In this way, newly arriving families can obtain important cultural orientation information that may help prevent their becoming involved with child protective services or law enforcement to begin with. It will generally be most effective if such education is provided without judging the immigrant's traditions or cultural attitudes or approach to rearing their children. Instead, it is recommended to work with the family in a positive proactive way, showing genuine empathy and desire to see them have a successful transition to life in the United States.

Waiting to intervene until a situation rises to the level deemed to be child abuse could have seriously damaging consequences. These issues should be explored early in a nonthreatening manner. Given the common intergenerational conflicts that arise in many new immigrant homes, it may be valuable for those assisting newly arriving parents to help them anticipate some of the stressors that may emerge as their children seek to integrate into the new society, such as becoming heavily influenced by the values and behavior of their American peers and society that may conflict with the views and expectations of the parents. Identifying which of their traditional strategies of child discipline may continue to be successful in the new environment, those that may put them at risk for becoming involved with child protective services, and teaching new strategies that they can experiment with and that may achieve their desired result without risking legal problems are encouraged. Those who work directly or indirectly with public-school systems may be uniquely placed to provide such preventive services given their access to newly arriving families (e.g., immigrant resource center personnel, teachers, school counselors, and health workers who give children immunizations in preparation for school); however, many school districts lack adequate resources to do so. Community activism and public policy efforts directed at obtaining or allocating adequate resources to appropriately assess and provide for the needs of newly arriving refugee and asylum-seeking children and their families are needed.

Those who work with refugee and asylum-seeking families need to be aware that much of the world's population has a communal rather than an individual orientation (Elsass, 1997). When keeping family units in tact or when family reunification is the goal, immigrant families may need assistance in identifying and building a new support system as they may be without the natural or traditional supportive figures and community that may have assisted with child-rearing duties back home. The absence of such support may be a key stressor that jeopardizes the preservation of the family unit. Seeking out the expertise of cultural consultants, and enhancing one's knowledge of the experience and impact of trauma common among refugee and asylum-seeking families, will further increase the chances of effective intervention.

Intervention Approaches with Children and Families

A three-tiered approach to intervention with children who have experienced political violence, war, and catastrophic disasters has been advocated (Pynoos, Goenjian, and Steinberg, 1998). This approach can be modified and used with refugee and asylum-seeking youth in the United States as well: (1) general support to affected children through their religious organizations, community-based agencies, and their schools (e.g., psychoeducational forums, peer support, conflict resolution, mentorship, and afterschool programs); (2) interventions targeted toward youth who have personally experienced severe trauma with ongoing posttraumatic distress symptoms, depression, and grief; and (3) referral for those youth identified as needing more in-depth mental health assessment and services for a wider range of psychiatric conditions. Individual, family, group, or classroom-based psychotherapy focused on trauma and grief (a two-tiered intervention) and psychotropic medication have been found to alleviate PTSD and depression symptoms among traumatized youth (Goenjian et al., 1997; Murphy, Pynoos, and James, 1997; Yule and Canterbury, 1994).

Therapeutic interventions focusing on grief and trauma are often paramount, and include the following key components identified by Pynoos and his colleagues (2001) in their work with traumatized youth and their families affected by political violence, war, and other traumas: (a) reconstructing traumatic events using an appropriately timed, culturally informed, and developmentally sensitive approach; (b) enhancing recognition, cognitive discrimination, and recovery from powerful reactions to traumatic reminders; (c) improving problem-solving and coping skills in relation to secondary adversities and stresses; (d) facilitating bereavement appropriate to the survivor's age, family, and culture, less burdened by traumatic images and thoughts; and (e) resuming disrupted or lost opportunities and initiating future planning and prosocial activities to promote normal development.

A variety of approaches have been employed effectively with traumatized youth, including cognitive-behavioral therapy, psychoeducation, developmental psychodynamic psychotherapy, physical rehabilitation, educational assistance, group therapy, and remedial approaches targeted at developmental disruptions. Art therapy, music therapy, writing, storytelling, sandplay therapy, drama, dance, the use of rituals, and other creative approaches have been found to be therapeutic in the processing of traumatic events and healthy adjustment of refugee and asylum-seeking youth and adults (Dokter, 1998). It is recommended that follow-up interventions be planned at subsequent developmental transition periods, times of additional adversities, and expected future reminders (e.g., anniversary dates). Interventions with youth who have been victimized by violence and have also participated in committing violent acts, such as the case of many child soldiers, require an approach that takes into consideration the complexities involved (see Lustig et al., 2002 for a review of some of the key issues to be considered). Incorporating religious or spiritual practices and altruistic actions to benefit others may also be therapeutic for some, such as survivors of torture (Mollica, 2004) and other severe trauma, and those who perpetrated violence on others.

In addition to working directly with the youth, interventions aimed at the reactions of their parent(s) or caretaker(s) can be vital, particularly for young children. Parents/caretakers can be assisted in learning how to respond effectively to the child's posttraumatic distress. Frequently, due to the nature of the trauma and/or cultural factors, refugee and asylum-seeking youth may have felt they had to keep quiet about what they experienced, in some cases to avoid further persecution. This may promote or aggravate intrusive memories and other symptoms commonly found in PTSD. Dyregrov and Raundalen (2000, as cited in Murad, 2003) recommend drawing out and documenting the child's feelings in order to better shape appropriate interventions. Care must be taken to avoid retraumatizing the youth in the process.

One common intervention issue for those youth and families who have come to the United States from countries where disappearances are common is helping survivors to grieve the loss of their loved ones when they have no evidence of where their loved one is or if they are dead or alive. Survivors may presume that their loved one has been murdered or died under torture or captivity if this is a common occurrence in their homeland. Some do not give up hope of finding their relative alive one day. Some must live with powerful feelings of guilt associated with giving up the search for their loved one, or for feeling responsible for their disappearance or death. In some cultures and societies, it is considered important to have a body to bury in order to properly conduct burial and mourning rituals. Some survivors are far from home and do not have their traditional support systems available to them or have a body to bury. The grieving process for these survivors may be facilitated by helping them develop or plan meaningful rites, rituals and prayers in keeping with their religious beliefs. With those from communal cultures, or cultures where the healing process is public, involving others in this process may be healing.

Interventions at Level of Social Institutions

With youth exposed to community violence, war, torture, or other forms of human-perpetrated trauma, interventions at the level of social institutions or organizations can be critical in helping to restore the traumatized youth's belief in the larger social contract. For example, societal and legal interventions aimed at fighting impunity can be helpful for children, family members, and their friends who may fixate on the traumatic context and circumstances surrounding the death of loved ones and issues of human accountability (Clark, Pynoos, and Goebel, 1996). These issues, if not addressed or left unresolved, can further complicate the survivors' process of bereavement. In many countries, impunity is rampant in situations of state-sponsored or state-perpetrated human rights violations. Some efforts to combat impunity have been made around the world, such as the prosecution of war crimes and other human rights abuses by the International Military Tribunal after World War II, the International Criminal Tribunal for the former Yugoslavia, the Inter-American Human Rights Court, The International Criminal Court, and civil prosecutions of torturers from around the world who are in the United States by the Center for Justice and Accountability in California. Precautions should be taken to protect youth involved in legal hearings from being unnecessarily exposed to traumatic details of events that they did not know about or experience in order to prevent an exacerbation of their symptoms or the development of new symptoms (Nader et al., 1993). In addition, emotional support and psychological preparation for preventing or minimizing the retraumatizing impact of testifying should be provided before, during, and after the legal proceedings.

Intervening with Secondary Hardships

Many immigrant, refugee, and asylum-seeking youth and their families experience a host of secondary hardships that can further compromise their functioning, such as displacement and relocation, parental under employment or unemployment and economic stresses, physical disabilities, overcrowding or homelessness, disrupted community and social networks/supports, secondary community violence, and domestic violence. Under these circumstances, youth may be at risk of engaging in gang or other delinquent behavior. Interventions aimed at ameliorating these secondary hardships can be important in promoting the effective healing and recovery of immigrant youth and their families and enabling the youth to become productive and healthy adults.[29] The caregivers and other family members may need therapeutic interventions as well, to optimize the functioning of the child's family system (Dyregrov and Raundalen, 2000 as cited in Murad, 2003). They may need assistance in gaining access to health care, or in obtaining shelter and benefits. Given the strength and cohesion of extended family units in many cultures, and the fact that their parents may be dead or not with them, some youth may arrive in the United States under the care of grandparents, uncles or aunts, an older cousin, or other extended family members. In some cases, they may be with official or unofficial adopted families, or with fictive family members.[30] The basic safety and survival needs of the child and the family should be met first before engaging in other psychosocial interventions. The child should be helped to reestablish normal routines to restore a sense of order and familiarity in their lives (James, 1995 as cited in Murad, 2003) while protecting them from further unnecessary exposure to traumatic sensory material.

Resilient Youth and Their Families

Despite the disruptions, numerous traumas, and the serious consequences commonly experienced by immigrant, refugee, and asylum-seeking youth and their families in the United States, they typically have enormous strengths as well. There are numerous examples of resilient youth and families who have experienced trauma—individuals who have been exposed to severe risks yet have bounced back successfully and are functioning well. Many view themselves as survivors rather than victims. Child development specialists estimate that as many as 80 percent of all youth who have experienced significant stressors do not develop developmental damage, and some grow stronger through the challenges these situations present (Fish-Murray, 1990; Garbarino et al., 1992; Rutter, 1979; Werner, 1990 cited in Garbarino et al., 1992). A number of factors have been identified that seem to contribute to resilience in children, often in combination, including intelligence, positive early relationships, robust temperament, community support and encouragement, role models for active coping, altruistic activities and future-oriented plans, coping strategies, social competence, autonomy, effective problem-solving skills, belief systems, ideological commitment, and a sense of purpose and future (Benard, 1995, 1997; Garbarino et al., 1992; Losel and Bliesener, 1990; Lustig et al., 2002; Macksoud and Aber, 1996; McWhirter et al., 1998; Servan-Schreiber, Lin, and Birmaher, 1998). The importance of context is apparent for some coping strategies, in that some strategies may have worked well during the trauma or flight but no longer are effective in a refugee camp or the country of resettlement (Farwell, 2001).

Garbarino et al. (1992) have broken down childhood resiliency factors into various categories: character traits found in infancy (e.g., cuddly, affectionate, active, and easy to deal with), additional character traits (e.g., realistic, flexible, positive self-esteem, popular with adults and peers, competence beyond their developmental level, ability to shape and manipulate the environment, good natured, humorous, ability to exercise self-control, and ability to make sense of threatening experiences), protective factors in the environment (e.g., social support outside the family, a stable emotional relationship with at least one parent or other caretaker, and a secure attachment relationship between the infant and the primary caregiver), the parent(s) level of resiliency (e.g., parents who are themselves "models of resiliency" tend to have resilient children), stable environment (e.g., children who stay with a parent or caregiver in a stable routine and environment), other family members (e.g., the presence of other family members who lessen stress, encourage coping behavior, and provide additional adult nurturance), community social support (e.g., social support in the community that help children believe that they are secure and cared for), and neurobiological factors (our heredity and development can have a lasting impact on our ability to adapt and cope in the face of trauma; resilience appears to be dependent on reenforcement, including consistent nurturance from caregivers during key developmental periods). Garbarino and his colleagues hold that children who can develop the ability to calm themselves down, distance themselves and maintain appropriate boundaries, and know that they will be all right with time tend to fare better when they experience trauma. Frequently, however, they need help in developing these capacities.

Some situations are so traumatic and overwhelming, however, that these positive factors cannot effectively buffer the youth from experiencing a variety of posttraumatic stress reactions (Garbarino et al., 1992). Some youth fare better developmentally and psychologically than others despite facing overwhelming circumstances. Interventions that draw on the strengths of these youth and families, and the communities in which they live, often have a better chance of success, particularly given the limited resources available in most agencies. Clinicians operating from an empowerment and strengths-based perspective start with and build on the strengths of these survivors.

Theoretical Framework Based on Narrative and Solution-Focused Approaches

In addition to a strong empowerment and strengths-based foundation (described elsewhere in this book, including in the chapter by Rhee and Huynh-Hohnbaum), a theoretical framework that draws on the narrative and solution-focused approaches to assessment and intervention is well suited to work with refugee and asylum-seeking children, youth, and families. Narrative and solution-oriented therapies assume that people already inherently have the ability to effectively respond to their difficult situations (Wade, 1997). Not only are these approaches nonpathologizing and appropriate for use with culturally diverse families, but they emphasize working with individuals to recognize their existing resourcefulness and strengths. These approaches can be very empowering when they are used to build on the creative everyday strategies to resist violence and oppression (Wade, 1997) that many refugees and asylum seekers have used in order to survive. While space does not permit a full description of these approaches here, some of the core principles of each that are relevant to work with refugees and asylum seekers are presented below.

A narrative approach to therapy views problems as being conceptualized and embedded in cultural, social, and political contexts and that we develop the meaning of our own lives out of the stories available to us in these contexts (Monk et al., 1997). The pioneers of narrative therapy were Australia's Michael White and New Zealand's David Epston. Narrative therapists utilize the metaphors of narrative and social construction. They work collaboratively with people to draw out their stories and to engage in reconstructing the stories so that they might experience their lives in fulfilling and meaningful ways. At the same time, attention is given to the ways in which a person's interactions with others and institutions serve to construct their interpersonal realities and how social realities help to shape the meaning of their lives (Freedman and Combs, 1996). Therapists work jointly with people to unearth their resources, talents, competencies, and abilities in the process of transforming their description of themselves. This approach facilitates the deconstruction of pathologizing stories, and as such is well suited to work with refugee and asylum seekers from other countries and cultural backgrounds who too often have experienced their culturally syntonic expressions of distress and healing to be misunderstood, labeled, and pathologized. Narrative therapists do not view the person as a victim, but rather look for their life stories that highlight their struggles against injustice. Many refugees and asylum seekers indeed have abundant stories of such struggles, and these very struggles often are what propelled them to flee. Drawing out these stories, amplifying their meaning, and making sense and meaning of their struggles and experiences has long been recognized as a key task for trauma survivors.

Solution-focused brief therapy, codeveloped by Insoo Kim Berg and Steve de Shazer, strives to find efficient and effective means for people to reach their preferred state of being. It views the client as competent and focuses on facilitating the process of people generating their own solutions instead of emphasizing and targeting their problems (De Jong and Berg, 2002). Solution-focused therapists maintain an optimistic, respectful, and "not-knowing" stance as they reinforce their clients' strengths, assist them to visualize the changes they desire, identify the exceptions to their problems (when the problem could have happened but did not), and build on what they are already doing that is working. In the process the clients uncover their own hidden resources and heal themselves. Clients develop specific, measurable, concrete plans to achieve and sustain their solutions. In the context of child welfare practice, solution-focused workers engage respectfully with their clients, encourage their clients' sense of control over what happens to them and encourage them to make choices, while holding the parent accountable for ensuring their child's safety (see Berg and Kelly, 2000; Berg, De Jong, and Gonzales, 2005).

A solution-focused approach appears well suited to work with refugees and asylum seekers for whom Western psychotherapy may be foreign and incompatible with their culture, worldview, and pathways to healing. Refugees and asylum seekers are generally quite resilient and have proven themselves highly capable of generating solutions to and overcoming enormous challenges. They may come into contact with a child welfare practitioner in the United States at a time when they need immediate support and practical solutions in the face of a new destabilizing situation in a foreign environment where their natural support networks and external resources are absent. One of the strengths of applying such an approach in transcultural practice with this population is that it is empowering and respectful of the wisdom and capabilities of survivors to find their own solutions rather than having them imposed by an outside "expert."

PART III: CASE VIGNETTES AND PRACTICE GUIDELINES

The case vignettes included below are designed to introduce the reader to some of the multiple challenges and possibilities involved in working with traumatized refugee and asylum-seeking children, youth, and families.[31] By their very nature, the life situations presented here tend to be complex, given the realities and multiple layers of trauma, loss, and adaptation such families typically face as a result of the factors that led them to flee their countries along with the challenges inherent in transitioning into a new, sometimes radically different, society. A competent practitioner working with the population must be well versed in transcultural and trauma-specific approaches to assessment and intervention, as well as have a solid foundation in relevant theoretical frameworks. Given the space limitations of this chapter, the practice guidelines presented here are not intended to be comprehensive or address all aspects of the cases. The guidelines will illustrate some of the early interventions to be considered in addressing a few of the key issues involved. Alternative starting points and approaches may also be effective.

The following case study demonstrates the complexity and multiple traumas that many refugee and asylum-seeking youth have experienced, as well as how narrative approaches to therapy may be integrated into the overall treatment approach. Space constraints prohibit the presentation of the full treatment plan. Emphasis will be placed on some of the salient issues.

■ ■ ■ ■ ■ ▬▬▬

CASE STUDY 1   UNACCOMPANIED REFUGEE MINOR RUNS AWAY

Mary is a 13-year-old refugee girl from a rural village in the Democratic Republic of Congo (hereafter referred to as the DRC) who came to the United States 1 year ago as an unaccompanied minor after fleeing her war-torn village. Mary is living with her foster parents Sheila and John Anderson and their two children (Steve, aged 16, and Sally, aged 12), in a crime-ridden inner-city neighborhood. Although Mary has gained increased mastery of English and is starting to get good grades in school, her teachers have noticed that she appears socially withdrawn, particularly around males, and seems to have diffi- culty adjusting to the social norms of her peers. An attractive girl, Mary has begun to go through puberty and has been receiving unwanted attention from her male classmates. The Andersons recently requested help from a child guidance agency, stating that Mary recently ran away from their home one night when Mr. and Mrs. Anderson were in a verbally heated argument with her after she refused to have a routine medical checkup. Mary stayed away overnight at her friend's house without informing the Andersons where she was. This was particularly concerning to the Andersons as there had been several teens shot in their neighborhood in recent months.

At the initial appointment at the child guidance clinic, Mr. and Mrs. Anderson told the therapist that they are concerned about Mary but do not understand why she is so different from their children and they do not know how to handle her anymore. Mary is initially quite guarded toward the therapist. Over the course of several weeks of therapy, Mary gradually reveals to her therapist some details about her life back in the DRC, how strange things seem to her in the United States, and how lonely she feels. Eventually, bits and pieces of the story of her escape from the DRC emerge. Mary shares that for several years before she escaped, her village was the site of periodic clashes between government soldiers and rebel forces. Her father, an elementary school teacher, was suspected by both sides of spying for the other. One night, a group of armed rebels barged into their home and interrogated her father at gunpoint. Mary and her siblings were restrained by rebels and forced to watch as her father was beaten and her mother was raped in front of them. When her father pleaded with the rebels not to harm his wife, they shot him in the head and he died. The rebels took Mary's mother and younger brother and sister with them when they left, but not before they raped

(continued)

. . . . . ▬▬▬▬▬▬▬▬▬▬▬▬▬▬▬▬▬▬▬▬▬▬▬▬▬▬

CASE STUDY 1   Continued

Mary, cutting her stomach with a knife as she resisted. Mary was advised by her neighbors to flee before the rebels or government forces returned and, after a hasty burial of her father, a family friend helped her to escape.

Mary expresses that she has had no contact with her family since, and does not know if her mother and siblings are dead or alive. She is Christian and has been going to church, but is deeply troubled that she was not able to perform the proper communal rituals and prayers for her father when they buried him. She also blames herself for not staying in the DRC to look for her mother and siblings. Images of what she experienced in the DRC haunt her during the day and invade her sleep at night, and she tries to avoid thinking or talking about her traumatic past. When asked why she ran away, Mary expressed the fear she felt at the prospect of being examined by the doctor, as she didn't want the doctor to see the scar on her stomach and ask how it happened, and she didn't want anyone to touch or examine her private parts given the taboo associated with this and the memories of her rape. She indicated that she was terrified that she might have "gotten AIDS" when she was raped as she has seen others in her community die from it. Furthermore, when her foster parents yelled at her, she was reminded of the interrogation of her father by the rebels and was flooded with memories of what they did to her and her family.

SELECTED PRACTICE GUIDELINES

- *Individual therapy* is recommended for Mary to address the impact of her multiple traumatic experiences, the complicated grief, and loss she is experiencing, and focus on addressing the current factors in her life that are triggering reminders of the violence in the DRC that she fled from (such as her reactions to her foster parents' yelling at her and the community violence in her neighborhood). Exploration of how the rape is perceived in her culture and how she views the experience, and exploration of the meaning attached to her avoidance symptoms related to the medical examination may be helpful. It is likely that Mary has never had a gynecological exam and may need psychological preparation to undergo one. Appropriate pretest counseling should be conducted that incorporates the realities of Mary's life before any STD testing is considered. It is possible that Mary may consider an HIV positive status as a death sentence given the high incidence of AIDS in her country, exacerbated by the conditions of war and the inadequate state of treatment options available in her country. Specifically, drawing on principles from narrative therapy, the therapist may incorporate the following:

  - Ask questions and draw out Mary's stories in order to gain a more complete account of her experience of the situation, the history of the problem, and the factors that have influenced its development. Create an environment conducive to Mary's exploration of the difficulties and meaning for her own life, as well as the range of approaches to healing and health she may have utilized in her country of origin.
  - Collaborate with Mary to help her uncover her competencies, talents, abilities, and resources (recognizing and building on her enormous strengths and resilience, including what helped her survive the civil war, enabled her to

escape, and eased her initial adjustment to a radically different culture). Facilitate Mary's reconnection with her pretrauma self.

■ Deconstruct the problem and examine the unstated cultural assumptions being made. Transform the label and description given to Mary by herself and by others (e.g., maybe she has been labeled as a loner and/or defiant). Mary can be encouraged to redescribe herself and come up with a new name for the problem. Validate the new story she elaborates about her life.

■ Use externalizing conversations with Mary in order to shift her focus away from self-blame, attack, judgment, and recrimination that typically serve to inhibit positive therapeutic outcomes.

■ *Family therapy* may help Mary's foster parents and foster siblings better understand her culture, life experiences, and traumas. Regarding their insistence that she have a medical evaluation, work to increase their understanding of the meaning of that experience for her while protecting her privacy and control over what she discloses to the Andersons. Engage Mary as the expert on her life and, if relevant and if Mary is open to this, include a cultural broker/consultant. As part of the family therapy, work to deconstruct the problem and give Mary and her foster family the opportunity to examine unstated cultural assumptions that appear to be perpetuating the conflict and lack of understanding in the family system and explore new ways of relating to one another. Invite her family and friends into a healing circle of support to validate Mary's experiences and her strength as well as to support her in her new story.

■ Given that Mary is from a communal society, *seek to engage the Congolese and/or broader community* as a support for Mary and as consultants for the therapist. In exploring what would feel healing to Mary, the therapist might ask whether she would like to involve local community leaders and/or healers (assuming there are some in your community) to explore the possibility of a communal ceremony or ritual to grieve and pray for her loved ones. Such rituals may be meaningful for Mary and provide her with support to cope with the death of her father and the traumatic disappearance of her other family members. There may also be opportunities for Mary to connect with other Congolese teens and adults through community events and activities, enabling her to feel less alienated and ease her transition to the new country. The therapist can facilitate this link. Care should be taken, however, to ensure that Mary feels comfortable with the community members (recognizing that she may not feel safe and may have difficultly trusting others from her refugee community, particularly if she perceives that members of the community may have links to the DRC government or the rebels). If there are no other Congolese nearby, consultations from and links to the Congolese community elsewhere in the United States may be provided by contacting torture treatment or refugee resettlement agencies. Alternatively or in conjunction, Mary's local church may be invited to participate and support Mary in her grieving process.

This next case study illustrates the application of solution-focused procedures and questions to a situation involving an Albanian family's difficulties in adjusting to forced exile.

CASE STUDY 2   FORCED EXILE AFTER TORTURE

Marina, her husband Gazmend, and their son Edmond (aged 9) moved to the community 6 months ago. Gazmend is working long hours at the local factory during the day and as a security guard at night in order to support the family and send money home to Marina's ailing parents. Marina, a full-time worker in Albania, does not work outside of the home currently. She attends English as a Second Language course at the local community center several days a week, but has made little progress in learning English and has begun to skip many of her classes. She appears distracted in class. She regularly takes Edmond out of school in order to interpret for her when she goes to the doctor for her chronic health problems or to help her with other errands. Edmond sometimes appears disheveled and dirty in school, and some of his classmates have complained that he smells.

Edmond's frequent school absences and the complaints of his classmates are brought to the attention of the school psychologist and she meets with Edmond and later with his mother to assess the situation. The school psychologist learns that Edmond arrived in the United States 3 years ago from Albania. Edmond shares with her that he is often needed at home because his father is always at work and his mother can't take care of things herself and needs him to help her talk to the doctor. Marina appears quite depressed to the psychologist, and with Edmond interpreting, she learns that Marina often stays in bed all day and Edmond takes care of the cooking, shopping, and other household chores on a regular basis. Often he is too tired at night to do his homework or bathe and sometimes there isn't enough food in the house for dinner. Edmond reluctantly shares that his father and mother often "fight" and that this scares him and makes it hard for him to sleep. Marina confirms this, but indicates that she thought Edmond was asleep and didn't hear their arguments. Marina reveals that Gazmend used to be very gentle and loving, but that he changed since he was released from prison in Albania where he was tortured. She explains that the police arrested Gazmend at their home one night due to his vocal political activism and opposition to the government, beating him up in front of her and Edmond, before taking him off to prison for several months. Gazmend fled the country shortly after he was released, and Marina and Edmond followed a year later, leaving behind her elderly sick parents whom she was taking care of. Edmond cries as he supplies some additional details about the incident when the police beat and arrested his father in front of him, and Marina seems surprised, stating that she had always believed Edmond was too young to remember or be affected by the incident.

SELECTED PRACTICE GUIDELINES

- Each of the members of this family has undergone significant life changing and traumatic events, and would benefit from further assessment before deciding on the appropriate course of treatment. A combination of individual, marital, and family therapy may be warranted as well as connecting them to community support as they navigate and adjust to living in a new society and culture. The extent and factors influencing Marina's apparent depression need to be fully assessed and treated, including, for example, the meaning and impact of having to leave her ailing parents behind, the significant changes in her marriage, and the multiple losses she has experienced. Her condition and the absence of Gazmend from the household for most of each day appear to be contributing to an environment of neglect of some of Edmond's basic needs, and a corrective plan needs to be implemented to prevent further neglect and harm, and enhance the well-being and functioning of the family and its members. A determination will need to be reached as to whether a report needs to be made to child welfare authorities. It is unclear to what extent Gazmend's experiences of torture and forced exile have contributed to his reported change in behavior and what his needs may be. Edmond's witnessing of his father's beating and arrest, his experience of his father's absences from home from the time of his imprisonment to the present, the impact of his parents "fighting," and his sudden loss of country and the presence of his extended family need to be explored, acknowledged by his parents, and addressed. Marital therapy focusing on the marital conflict and possible domestic violence may be helpful in conjunction with family therapy to address the changed roles and functions within the family and establish healthy patterns in the family that support culturally appropriate roles and boundaries between Edmond and his parents.

- The following solution-building questions (from the Brief Family Therapy Center's website at www.brief-therapy.org/docs/Solution-building_procedures.pdf) can be utilized as part of the work with this family. These questions can facilitate the negotiation of goals, the finding of exceptions, and the process of *scaling* as Marina, Gazmend, and Edmond assess their own perceptions and understandings of the problem, its seriousness, their motivation and level of hopefulness, and the progress they have made toward the goals they set for themselves:

    1. What needs to be different with your situation?
    2. What do you know about your situation that tells you that this can happen?
    3. When was the most recent time this happened?
    4. Tell me about the times when this problem we have been talking about is just a little bit better or it is gone even for a short time. What is different for you during those times?
    5. How close to your goals have you moved so far?
    6. What is the next small step you need to take toward your goal?
    7. How confident are you that you can maintain the level of success achieved so far?

Utilizing a solutions-focused brief therapy model, incorporating the procedures and questions noted above, the clinician(s) involved can facilitate the process such that Marina, Gazmend, and Edmond draw on their strengths and capabilities to find their own solutions to their situation, and are empowered to take the steps needed to ensure that Edmond is protected.

The final case study illustrates some strategies of working with an asylum-seeking family affected by FGC to provide respectful and appropriate services while preparing them psychologically for their asylum hearing.

■ ■ ■ ■ ■

CASE STUDY 3   PREPARING FOR AN ASYLUM HEARING

Kamau came to the United States on a student visa 2 years ago from Kenya, accompanied by his wife Aisha and their two children (Fausia, aged 7, and Njau, aged 4). The family applied for political asylum and they must appear before an Immigration Judge in a couple of months. Their attorney referred Aisha and Fausia to a therapist for evaluation of the impact of Aisha's infibulation (the most severe form of FGC) on her, and her daughter's feelings about the possibility of being subjected to FGC if deported to Kenya. The therapist may be called on to write a forensic psychological report and provide expert witness testimony in court. Although Aisha and Kamau do not want Fausia to undergo FGC and there is legislation in Kenya that officially bans FGC for girls as well as other types of violence against children (the Children's Act, passed by parliament in 2001 and put into effect in 2002), they are aware that the widespread practice of FGC continues and that they may be unable to prevent others from subjecting Fausia to FGC. Fausia, usually an outgoing and vivacious girl, has become increasingly withdrawn, irritable, and subdued as the date of their court-hearing approaches.

The therapist initially meets with Aisha and her daughter Fausia separately, obtaining Aisha's permission to assess Fausia and discuss their asylum case with her. Aisha, in describing why she and her children left Kenya with her husband when he came to study in the United States said, "Before we left Kenya some relatives tried to kidnap my daughter to cut her when I was at the market. I came home just in time. I know that it is the custom, but it would kill me to have my daughter go through what I've gone through. It hurts so much and it is hard to feel desire. It affects my marriage." Aisha informs the therapist that FGC is considered a taboo subject in her culture, and that one is not supposed to talk about it. The only reason she revealed her FGC in her asylum application is that she was told she had to if she and her family were going to have a chance at being granted asylum and in order to protect her daughter from being "forcibly circumcised." She further reveals that there is intense shame about the topic, and stigma arises for any girl and her family if the girl goes against the wishes of their tribe and extended relatives and does not undergo the procedure. Aisha comments that FGC is considered a very important and significant rite of passage to adulthood that enhances the tribe's cohesion, increases the marital chances of the girl, and prevents promiscuity. Families that do not circumcise their girls, she continues, are considered irresponsible and immoral. Fausia, reluctant to talk at first, gradually shares with the therapist her feelings regarding FGC. "I don't want it. I'm so afraid that if I have to go back to Africa the older women or some of my relatives would force me to be cut. Even my mom and dad couldn't protect me. I've heard some girls die from it."

SELECTED PRACTICE GUIDELINES

These guidelines are not meant to be comprehensive and the clinician(s) involved are encouraged to access the reference material on FGC listed in the endnotes as well as clinicians experienced in this area for more information, recommendations, and ongoing consultation as needed.

- Clinicians conducting forensic psychological evaluations or providing therapeutic services to females and their families who have experienced FGC or may be at risk of experiencing FGC in the future are cautioned to be very aware of their own individual and cultural values, assumptions, and stereotypes regarding the practice of FGC and the experience of those affected by it. There is a wide range of experiences of, beliefs about, and reactions to FGC, including those who view their own experience of FGC as normal and desirable. Some women may not think it is an appropriate or relevant issue to discuss with a therapist, and even express shock that what they view as a natural and normal part of their life would even be an issue of concern or be considered persecution and a valid ground for seeking asylum.

- In order to work successfully with a person who has experienced FGC (or who may experience it), it is important to have good communication skills and cultural competency. Some basic guidelines to communicating with Aisha and Fausia would include inquiring about the FGC in a casual nonjudgmental tone, as part of the general history taking, and using the term they use to refer to it (often *circumcision* or a local phrase rather than *genital mutilation*). Assure confidentiality and that you will care for them in a private and respectful way, making sure to clarify any limits to confidentiality, including those related to your possible report and testimony in their asylum case. If an interpreter is needed, use a trained, culturally and linguistically competent interpreter who is supervised and bound to confidentiality and is acceptable to the clients. Avoid using family to interpret, especially children.

- The asylum process can be intensely retraumatizing for those subjected to FGC. For those who believe that they or their children will be forcibly subjected to FGC if they are ordered to be deported, or face repercussions from those in their tribe or others for opposing the practice, the fear can be enormous. Clinicians working with asylum seekers can play a valuable role in preparing them psychologically for their testimony in their asylum interview or in court, so that they will have a better chance of testifying effectively and not having to face deportation. Clarifying in advance what will happen if they apply for asylum based on FGC, and the extent of details and evidence needed, is vital so that they can make an informed choice as to whether they are prepared to reveal their FGC experience or not. In this case, the therapist can work with Aisha and Fausia to develop individualized coping plans to manage and prevent symptoms of distress so they do not interfere with their ability to undergo the evaluations needed to document their situation, effectively testify and endure the commonly retraumatizing process of seeking asylum.

- Despite their reluctance to discuss FGC, this family's asylum case is based on Aisha's own FGC experience and the fear that Fausia will undergo a similar procedure against her and her parents' will if deported. In asylum cases involving persons who have undergone FGC, medical evidence of the FGC is generally required. Undergoing a forensic gynecological exam and having one's genitalia discussed in detail in public along with the impact of the FGC on one's health, psychological and sexual functioning (either in an asylum interview or in Immigration Court) are usually very distressing for the asylum applicant and their loved ones. This distress is often exacerbated by the intense shame associated with and the taboo against discussing sexual matters in public. Undergoing a pelvic exam, sometimes for the first time in one's live, can trigger overwhelming and frightening traumatic memories of the FGC as well as go against cultural norms. Many physicians have never encountered a female who has experienced FGC and may exhibit shock and other reactions that can have a negative impact on the female being examined. Providing support to the female and education to the physician, or locating a physician with relevant experience and sensitivity in your area to conduct

(continued)

CASE STUDY 3   Continued

the exam, can be helpful. If the female perceives that the therapist or physician is judging them or they feel they are being gawked at as "abnormal or weird," the therapeutic relationship and services can be jeopardized. Sensitivity and flexibility to whether they have a gender preference in therapist, medical personnel, and/or interpreter are also recommended.

■ It is recommend to discuss with Aisha, Kamau, and their daughter in advance of the court hearing their wishes regarding requesting a closed hearing. Although the hearing is open to the public, they have the right to request a closed hearing where the judge clears the courtroom of everyone not directly involved in the case. The common practice is that all family members on the asylum petition are to be present in court for the entire hearing. Often, however, the judge will permit selected family members to wait outside the courtroom during testimony or at other times while sensitive matters are discussed. In this case, Aisha may prefer to have her husband, son, and daughter out of the courtroom during testimony regarding her FGC and the impact on her life. Fausia can be brought in for her own testimony if it is needed. The clinician evaluating the family may play an important advocacy role to ensure that the well-being of each family member is protected during the hearing. When possible, the applicants' attorney can advocate to have limited oral testimony about FGC. Follow-up services to the family may be indicated following the hearing, regardless of the outcome, but particularly if the asylum request is denied. Some recent case law, including a 2005 decision in the 9th Circuit Court of Appeals,[32] provides some legal precedent for girls and women obtaining asylum based on cases of FGC, finding the procedure to be persecution and those subjected to it to be eligible for asylum in the United States.

CONCLUSION

This chapter has provided a brief overview of some of the key issues confronting traumatized refugee and asylum-seeking children, youth, and their families in the United States. Those who work with these individuals and families need to be well versed in multicultural and transcultural approaches to assessment and intervention at multiple levels as well as have a solid foundation in trauma theory and practice. Examples of how narrative and solutions-focused approaches to therapy can be used with refugee and asylum-seeking families were highlighted. Care must be taken to not pathologize refugee and asylum-seeking children, youth, and their families and avoid overemphasizing their trauma and its negative consequences (Summerfield, 1999, 2000; Watters, 2001). Instead, focus should be placed on their strengths and resilience, and the benefits gained from their life experiences (Rousseau, 1993–1994; Rousseau et al., 1998; Watters, 2001). Summerfield (1999) draws on social constructionist theory and advocates framing refugee youth's experiences from a culturally relativist viewpoint rather than exclusively in terms of the hardships and losses they have faced.

For any intervention to be successful, it is essential to first establish trust. As van der Veer (1998) points out, different cultures have different criteria for determining who is an expert and who is trustworthy. These are critical issues for those who have been highly traumatized. For clinicians working with immigrant, refugee, and asylum-seeking youth and their families it is important to become credible in the eyes of one's client. To do so, Zane and Sue (1991) recommend that (a) the conceptualization of problems must be congruent with the client's belief systems; (b) the means for problem resolution must be culturally compatible and acceptable to the client; and (c) the client and the therapist must agree on the goals for treatment. Frequently, immediate safety and survival issues must be addressed first, in keeping with Maslow's (1970) concept of the hierarchy of needs.

These recommendations are applicable to transcultural work with children, youth, and families from diverse backgrounds. Rather than routinely utilizing specific therapeutic interventions or modalities of treatment, a multidisciplinary approach drawing on a solid foundation in the principles of working transculturally and with trauma survivors, coupled with a strengths- and empowerment-based perspective and a flexible and creative attitude will prove invaluable for clinicians serving immigrant populations. Techniques drawn from narrative and solutions-focused therapies may prove effective and appropriate.

In addition, it is important to be familiar with the traditional approaches to healing in the culture of one's client, as well as assessing to what extent the client believes in these approaches. One's own knowledge of the client's culture, as well as the expertise gained from cultural consultants, can be helpful in assessing the appropriateness of various approaches and in identifying possible effective modifications. Ultimately, the therapeutic services need to be tailored to the particular client(s), remaining ever aware of diversity within immigrant groups, and safeguards must be taken to ensure that the clinician does no harm.[33] For example, respecting a traumatized client's own pace in addressing the trauma is highly recommended. Cultural and individual differences have been found in traumatized refugees' need to directly focus on and work through their traumatic experiences. Compared to Indo-Chinese refugees, those from South America appeared more receptive to recounting their trauma histories (Morris and Silove, 1992).

A long-term approach with severely traumatized refugees is recommended (Boehnlein and Kinzie, 1996; Jaranson et al., 2001). A key therapeutic ingredient in treatment is the relationship between the client and the clinician (Kinzie, 2001). Time must be given for the therapeutic relationship and treatment to develop before some key issues can be addressed. This long-term approach is particularly relevant for refugee and asylum-seeking youth and their families, who frequently have had their trust in others shattered, and may experience chronic or recurrent episodes of psychological distress. Refugee and asylum-seeking youth and their families typically have encountered violations of their rights and injustices perpetrated by people in power before they fled their countries. Ensuring one's respect for the client and recognizing the client as the expert on their own life, history, and healing process can be instrumental in reversing traditional power dynamics between professional and client that often mirror traumatic experiences from the client's past.

Clinicians working with traumatized immigrant youth and their families also need to be attentive to their own needs, limitations, and the impact of vicarious or secondary trauma on their own well-being.[34] If not attended to appropriately, it can have a negative impact on their immigrant clients as well. While working with traumatized immigrant, refugee and asylum-seeking populations can be challenging, such work can be enormously meaningful as well.

There is a need for involvement at all levels in order to ensure a better future for traumatized refugee and asylum-seeking children, youth, and their families who resettle in the United States: clinical interventions and case management, community activism and advocacy to safeguard the protection of human and civil rights and ensure adequate resources and organizational responsiveness, public policy efforts, public and professional education, research to document the extent and nature of the problems and challenges and to inform interventions, and judicial and legal efforts to combat impunity. These efforts must not just be reactive and national in focus, but must be international and preventive in scope if there is to be any chance of transforming the conditions that propel individuals and families to flee their countries in the first place.

NOTES

1. For information about Female Genital Cutting/Female Circumcision/Female Genital Mutilation (FGC/FC/FGM) visit the following websites: AMANITARE (www.amanitare.org); Center for Reproductive Law and Policy (http://crlp.org); Equality Now (www.equalitynow.org); FGM Education and Networking Project (www.fgmnetwork.org); RAINBOW African Immigrant Program (www.rainbq.org); and the World Health Organization (www.who.int/frh-whd/topics/fgm.htm). One place to find specialized gynecological care and clinical information for women who have experienced Female Genital Cutting is provided at: The African Women's Health Clinic at the Brigham and Women's Hospital, 75 Francis Street, Boston, MA 02115, Tel: 617-732-4740, e-mail: africanwomen@partners.org, Director: Nawal Nour, M.D., MPH, www.brighamandwomens.org/africanwomenscenter/.
2. For further information on torture visit these online resources: The Program for Torture Victims (www.ptvla.org); The International Rehabilitation Council for Torture Victims (www.irct.org/usr/irct/home.nsf); and for an online course about caring for survivors of torture visit Boston Center for Refugee Health and Human Rights' site at www.glphr.org/refugee/ed.htm. Additional information is found in the following sources: Gurr, R. and Quiroga, J. (2001) and Gerrity, Keane, and Tuma (2001).
3. There are several different definitions of torture. In its *1984 Convention Against Torture and Other Cruel, Inhuman or Degrading Treatment or Punishment* the United Nations defined torture as: "For the purpose of this Convention, the term 'torture' means any act by which severe pain or suffering, whether physical or mental, is intentionally inflicted on a person for such purpose as obtaining from him or a third person information or a confession, punishing him for an act he or a third person has committed, or is suspected of having committed, or intimidating or coercing him or a third person, or for any reason based on discrimination of any kind, when such pain or suffering is inflicted by, or at the instigation of, or with the consent or acquiescence of, a public official or other person acting in an official capacity. It does not include pain or suffering arising only from, inherent in, or incidental to lawful sanctions" (United Nations, 1995). *Note: This legal definition by the United Nations was applicable only to nations and restricted the definition of torture to government-sponsored torture. Not included in the definition are cases of mutilation, whipping, or caning, which are practiced in some countries as lawful punishment. Also not included are acts of torture practiced by gangs or hate groups.*

4. This 300,000 figure comes from a series of twenty-six country case studies, conducted by the UN and several members of the advocacy community. United Nations, Report of the Expert of the Secretary-General, Graça Machel, on the "Impact of Armed Conflict on Children," Document A/51/306 & Add 1, August 26, 1996, as cited by the Coalition to Stop the Use of Child Soldiers (2001).

5. There is a wide range of posttraumatic stress reactions or responses, one of the most common being PTSD. In the Diagnostic and Statistical Manual of Mental Disorders-Fourth Edition, test revision (DSM-IV-TR), a person must meet six criteria in order to be diagnosed with PTSD. In general terms, these six criteria involve (1) exposure to a major stressor that the person responded to with intense fear, helplessness, or horror (for children, responded with disorganized or agitated behavior); (2) at least 1 of 5 possible reexperiencing symptoms; (3) at least 3 of 7 possible symptoms of avoidance and numbing; (3) at least 2 of 5 possible hyperarousal symptoms; (4) duration of disturbance being at least 1 month; and (6) clinically significant distress or impairment in social, occupational, or other important areas of functioning (see American Psychiatric Association, 2000 for complete diagnostic criteria).

6. For online information about human trafficking, visit the U.S. Department of Health and Human Services website on trafficking at www.acf.hhs.gov/trafficking/, the U.S. Department of State site at http://usinfo.state.gov/gi/global_issues/human_trafficking.html, the 2004 Trafficking in Persons Report at www.state.gov/g/tip/rls/tiprpt/2004/, the Coalition to Abolish Slavery and Trafficking's (CAST) website at www.castla.org/, and the U.S. *Congressional Research Institute's 2002 Report for Congress on Trafficking in Women in Children: The U.S. and International Response* at http://fpc.state.gov/documents/organization/9107.pdf. For information about state-specific victims' assistance programs contact the HHS Refugee Coordinator for that state at www.acf.hhs.gov/programs/orr/partners/coordina.htm or call the Trafficking Information and Referral Hotline at: 1 (888) 373–7888.

7. The author learned about these situations when she worked for the Catholic Office for Emergency Relief for Refugees (COERR) in Site 2, a camp for displaced Cambodians at the Thai–Cambodian border. In her work at the Program for Torture Victims (PTV) and other nonprofits in Los Angeles, California, the author encountered many who had faced similar dangers in other refugee camps around the world.

8. Further information on these issues can be found on the American Civil Liberties Union website at www.aclu.org/legislative/legislativemain.cfm or on the U.S. Justice Department website at www.usdoj.gov/immigrationinfo.htm, or at the U.S. Department of Homeland Security website at www.dhs.gov/dhspublic/.

9. The author encountered this phenomenon in her work at the Program for Torture Victims, and other clinicians working with torture survivors around the country reported similar findings.

10. It is important to note that Article 2 of the Convention Against Torture states that "no exceptional circumstances whatsoever, whether a state of war or a threat of war, internal political instability or any other public emergency, may be invoked as a justification of torture" (UNHCR, 1995, p. 294).

11. On June 29, 2004, in the case of *Sosa v. Alvarez-Machain*, the U.S. Supreme Court again ruled against the Bush Administration and upheld the rights of victims of torture, genocide, crimes against humanity, and other egregious human rights violations to pursue cases against the perpetrators under the Alien Tort Claims Act, as long as the perpetrators are within the U.S.' jurisdiction.

12. These acts include those condemned by the Geneva Convention (see UNHCR, 1949a and 1949b).

13. The School of the Americas was legally closed in 2001, and its name was changed to the Western Hemisphere Institute for Security Cooperation (WHINSEC) in Fort Benning, Georgia. The WHINSEC is the U.S. government's main facility for training Latin American military personnel, and while there have been some changes in the curriculum, nobody had been held accountable at the time of this writing for the unlawful training manuals or the conduct of the SOA graduates. The SOA/WHINSEC students are only a small number of foreign military and police personnel trained by the U.S. government. In 2002 Amnesty International reported that each year the United States trained approximately 100,000 foreign

military and police from 150 countries in approximately 275 different schools in the United States, with more being trained in their own countries.

14. See Note 5 for the DSM-IV-TR definition of PTSD. Many traumatized refugees suffer from depression at the same time as PTSD, such that their conditions are comorbid. In order to be diagnosed with Major Depressive Disorder the DSM-IV-TR states that an individual must have five or more of nine specified symptoms. These symptoms include depressed mood most of the day, nearly every day; markedly diminished interest or pleasure in all or almost all activities; significant weight loss or gain; insomnia or hypersomnia nearly every day; psychomotor agitation or retardation observable by others; fatigue or loss of energy nearly every day; worthlessness or excessive or inappropriate guilt; problems concentrating or indecisiveness; and/or recurrent thoughts of death, suicidal ideation, or a suicide plan or attempt. The individual must have at least five of these symptoms during the same 2-week period that cause clinically significant distress or impairment in their functioning, and represent a change from the person's previous level of functioning. The symptoms must also not meet the criteria for any psychotic disorder, manic, mixed, or hypomanic episodes, and not be better explained by bereavement or be due to a general medical condition or the physiological effects of a substance (see American Psychiatric Association, 2000 for complete diagnostic criteria).

15. The author has encountered this in her work at a variety of nonprofit organizations serving immigrant, refugee, and asylum-seeking youth and families in the United States, and has heard similar reports from her colleagues.

16. Throughout the 1980s and 1990s, charges of child abuse were brought against some Southeast Asian parents who utilized the traditional healing techniques of "cupping" and "coining" with their ill children (Look and Look, 1997; Wong, 1999). In order to alleviate pain, cups or coins are topically applied to create pressure, draw blood to the surface of the skin, and draw out fever and illness (Ackerman, 1997; Diversity resources, 2000). Efforts were made to educate child protective service workers, health care providers, and law enforcement personnel that these were traditional healing practices designed to promote the health of individuals, rather than harm them (see Child Abuse Prevention Council, 2005). Such educational efforts resulted in a decrease in such charges in California but further education is needed.

17. See Lustig et al. (2002) for a discussion of the particular vulnerabilities of unaccompanied minors.

18. This has been the professional experience of the author in providing services since the late 1980s. In addition, many organizations such as Little Tokyo Service Center (LTSC), Korean Immigrant Workers Advocate (KIWA), Central American Resource Center (CARECEN in Los Angeles: www.carecen-la.org/), and Clergy and Laity United for Economic Justice (CLUE) have had similar experiences in addressing these issues.

19. One caution is that some refugees or asylum seekers who experienced human-perpetrated violence before fleeing their home country, such as those who experienced state-sponsored torture, may not feel safe interacting with others from their country in the United States or community groups for fear that they may be associated with those in power back home or with those who harmed them. This should be carefully assessed.

20. See: www.kiwa.org/ for more information on KIWA.

21. For readers interested in exploring how such programs have been set up, one such example (at the time of this writing) can be found at St. Vincent's Cardinal Manning Center, 231 Winston Street, Los Angeles, CA 90013, Tel: 213-229-9963.

22. A flow chart outlining the process of applying for asylum in the United States as of the early twenty-first century can be found at: www.asylumlaw.org/docs/united_states/us_flow_chart.htm. As asylum law has changed over the years, this process may be subject to change as well and is provided here for informational purposes only. With the passage of the Real ID Act in 2005, asylum regulations and policies have tightened such that eligibility for asylum will likely be affected and the appeal process further limited.

23. Persons who have recently been granted asylum can call the Office for Refugee Resettlement (ORR) Asylee Hotline at 1-800-354-0365 for information on services in their state.

24. The concept of "undoing" the trauma was developed by Ana C. Deutsch, Clinical Director and cofounder of the Program for Torture Victims in Los Angeles, California. She has

presented this concept in many conferences and public forums, including Deutsch, A.C. and Berthold, S.M. (October 24, 2003). "Women as Survivors." *Invited Speakers. Violence Against Women Conference*, California Hospital Medical Center, Los Angeles, California.

25. See also Nader (2004) for more information about the assessment of traumatized children, and Briere (2004) regarding the assessment of posttraumatic states in adults.

26. See also Dinicola, V. F. (1996). *Ethnocultural Aspects of PTSD and Related Disorders Among Children and Adolescents* (pp. 389–414). In Marsella, A.J., Friedman, M.J., Gerrity, E.T., and Scurfield, R.M. (1996) (Eds.), *Ethnocultural Aspects of Posttraumatic Stress Disorder: Issues, Research, and Clinical Applications*. Washington, DC: American Psychological Association.

27. For an example, see Berthold (1989) for discussion of recommendations for social workers that work with clients who believe in Spiritism.

28. The author had the opportunity to work alongside traditional healers at two holistic healing centers in the Site Two camp for displaced Khmer on the Thai–Cambodian border in 1990–1991 as part of an interdisciplinary team. The Khmer name for one of these centers translates as "The Center for Healing of the Heart and Spirit." This and other programs that combine Western and traditional indigenous approaches to healing have been well-received and provide effective models of working transculturally with displaced refugee and asylum-seeking individuals. Efforts to build and sustain capacity in traumatized refugee communities and culturally competent community-based interventions, such as those developed by the Transcultural Psychosocial Organization (TPO) in fifteen countries in Africa, Asia, and Europe, may be beneficial (Eisenbruch, de Jong, and van de Put, 2004). See also Higson-Smith (2002) for lessons learned from South Africa about working with communities affected by violence.

29. A helpful guide to planning appropriate interventions with refugee children is UNHCR's (1994) *Refugee Children: Guidelines on Protection and Care* that can be downloaded online from UNHCR's website at www.unhcr.ch/cgi-bin/texis/vtx/home?page=search (search: "Refugee Children").

30. For example, some Amerasian youth were sold to unrelated adults by their impoverished Vietnamese mothers to pose as their children, in order for the fake parents and other family members to qualify for resettlement to the United States under the Orderly Departure Program for Amerasians and their families. These youth came to be known as "Gold Kids" by relief workers in the Philippine Refugee Processing Center (PRPC) where they were sent for 6 months of English language training and cultural orientation prior to resettlement in the United States (Author, personal experience).

31. Identifying information has been altered, including names, and key characteristics have been compiled from different cases in each of the vignettes presented here in order to protect the identities of the survivors.

32. See *Mohammed* v. *Gonzales*, No. 03-70803 (U.S. Court of Appeals for the Ninth Circuit filed March 10, 2005).

33. For a fuller discussion of some of the ethical issues and recommendations involved for clinicians and other service providers working with refugee youth, see Lustig et al. (2002). For example, they may not be aware of their rights in the United States and may benefit from advocacy to ensure their rights are protected.

34. For more information about vicarious or secondary trauma, visit www.isu.edu/~bhstamm/ts.htm. The Traumatic Stress Institute's Center for Adult and Adolescent Psychotherapy also has a program designed to train clinicians working with trauma survivors to address their vicarious trauma. See "Risking Connections" at www.riskingconnection.com/.

CHAPTER NINE

ADMINISTRATIVE ISSUES IN DIVERSITY

EILEEN MAYERS PASZTOR, DSW

Associate Professor, Assistant Director, and Coordinator of Field Education, Department of Social Work, California State University, Long Beach

PAUL ABELS, PH.D.

Professor Emeritus, Department of Social Work, California State University, Long Beach

TERESA DECRESCENZO, MSW

Executive Director, Gay and Lesbian Adolescent Social Services (GLASS)

VERNON MCFARLAND-BROWN, MPA

Chief Executive Officer, Moss Beach Homes, Inc.

Agency staff discusses how administrative interventions require an integration of best policy, practice, leadership, and advocacy from a multi-cultural perspective.

OVERVIEW

Service delivery does not occur in a vacuum. There must be attention to administrative issues that not only affect ethnic diversity, but impact sexual minority youth and families as well. The premise of this chapter is that many, if not most, students assigned to read this chapter may not do so eagerly. They may not visualize themselves as ever being administrators. But even if they never become managers, it is imperative to understand that the issues facing administrators and the decisions they make profoundly affect the lives of clients and staff on a daily basis.

Just as children have histories that help us understand their current functioning, best practice also has roots. The chapter begins with an historical perspective on administrative theories that are used to drive managerial practices, after providing definitions for key terms. Basic administrative principles that every practitioner or aspiring administrator should know are described with examples of outside forces or "change-drivers" that affect agencies and organizations on a macrolevel but have direct impact on client services and human resources. The chapter identifies agency dynamics that influence services and staff, and considers issues that form the framework for an ethical approach to diversity for both clients and staff. Finally, the chapter provides case examples of challenges in administrative diversity that require an integration of best practice, agency policy, leadership, and advocacy, all of which provide an opportunity to consider appropriate administrative interventions.

INTRODUCTION

Social services typically are provided through agencies and organizations, and this chapter addresses the elements of administration that facilitate service delivery, with an emphasis on implications regarding diversity. If you do not intend to be a supervisor, manager, or administrator—and even if you believe you will be a clinician or a direct service social worker throughout your entire career—it is essential to be knowledgeable about administrative issues. That is because the decisions administrators make, and the actions they take, profoundly affect both clients and staff. Practitioners can better serve clients while making their own workplace more effective and pleasant if they understand some basic issues about administration, especially as it impacts services for children and families who may be cultural, ethnic, religious, or sexual minorities. The purpose of this chapter is to:

1. Provide basic administrative principles that every practitioner or aspiring administrator should know.
2. Describe outside forces or "change-drivers" that affect agencies and organizations on a macrolevel and have direct impact on client services and personnel issues.
3. Identify dynamics inside an agency that influence services and staff.
4. Consider issues that form the framework for an ethical approach to diversity for both the clients and the staff who serve them.

5. Give readers case examples of challenges in administrative diversity that require an integration of best practice, agency policy, leadership, and advocacy; and provide the opportunity to consider appropriate administrative interventions.

The following definitions are used in this chapter:

Diversity: Diversity is the ways in which individuals and groups differ from each other, especially in two categories: primary and secondary (Loden and Rosenor, 1991). Primary diversity encompasses characteristics that cannot be changed, such as age and ethnicity. Secondary diversity includes characteristics that may reflect some kind of choice, such as marital status, religion/spirituality, and cultural expression. According to Weinbach (1998), there are "overlapping categories of primary and secondary diversity" so "today's workplace is characterized by cultural differences, value differences, and behavioral differences" (p. 120). Nationality, for example, may be both a primary and a secondary characteristic. Some would argue whether sexual orientation is primary or secondary. Nonetheless,

> Social workers generally understand diversity and its importance in understanding human behavior. In our professional education we have been taught to appreciate and value diversity . . . however, like any change . . . increased diversity within an organization bring some potential problems. The social worker as manager needs to anticipate these and to be able to shape the work environment so that it will at least minimize them. (Weinbach, 1998, p. 120)

At-risk Children and Families: Jansson (1999) proposed that social welfare policy is organized and delivered to address seven major deprivations. When just a few people suffer deprivation, it may be largely ignored. But when classes of individuals have a specific need, often it is addressed through legislation. For example, the Americans with Disabilities Law assures that public places, such as lavatories and sidewalks, must be wheelchair accessible. In this way, private problems become public issues. Jansson's seven deprivations include material resources such as food, clothing, and shelter; cognitive challenges such as mental retardation; physical handicapping conditions; mental illness; interpersonal problems such as child, partner, or elder abuse or neglect; lack of opportunities such as the need for special education; and discrimination. The term "at-risk" encompasses children, youth, individuals, and families that have experienced one or more of these deprivations.

Agencies and Organizations: Sometimes these words are used interchangeably. If you go to a meeting, you may be asked to give your name and the agency you work for, or the organization you are representing. But there are subtle differences. An *agency* provides direct services for human service clients, that is child and adult protective services, counseling, shelters, financial aid, adoptions, and mental health or drug treatment. An *organization* tends to have more of a macrofocus and typically provides assistance to direct service agencies. There are national and state advocacy organizations such as Child Welfare League of America, National Association of Social Workers, and National Alliance for the Mentally Ill; and these organizations may have local affiliates. Or there may be local organizations with no state or national affiliates, such as a

Coalition for the Homeless or AIDS advocacy associations. Agencies may be public or private. If private, they may be for profit, such as a nursing home or hospital. Or they may be not-for-profit, such as a mental health clinic or foster care agency. In this chapter, agency and organization will be used interchangeably because the administrative dynamics are similar.

National Association of Social Workers (NASW) Code of Ethics: Administrative decisions, like casework decisions, must be made to reflect and respect the Code of Ethics promulgated by the NASW (1999): competence, dignity of individuals, importance of human relationships, integrity, service, and social justice (p. 1).

ADMINISTRATIVE PRINCIPLES

Overview

Agencies and organizations are tools that have been created by people to help them accomplish a goal or serve their needs. The prime movers of an organization, whether a family service agency, a settlement house, or a welfare department, take pride in their accomplishments and trust that their agency will continue to serve at a high level. Board members, managers, and staff alike—not to mention clients—want their agencies to do a good job, but the assumption that the organization, new or long established, will continue to operate as planned does not always hold true.

Administration is the process of organizing the efforts of a number of people in order to accomplish the mission, goals, and tasks of the agency in an effective and responsible manner. "Administration" is also a term used to refer to those in the organization who are in authority and/or policy-making positions. According to Weinbach (1998), "management" is another term that is used arbitrarily and interchangeably with "administration." In his text, *The Social Worker as Manager,* Weinbach proposed that "management consists of certain functions performed by social workers at all administrative levels within human service organizations which are designed to facilitate the accomplishment of organizational goals" (p. 5).

In the past decade, our country has seen some of our largest businesses destroyed by poor management. There also have been national news reports of welfare agencies admitting to having lost track of the children they were mandated to serve. There has been media documentation of the recent warehousing of mentally ill persons, leading to abuse, rape, and the unnecessary suffering and even death of those in the agency's care. In addition, administrations of hospitals and even the time-honored United Way charity have been charged with the misuse of funds. While some of these illegal and immoral actions are the result of greed, many other administrative problems in the social services arena are due to a lack of funds, lack of skill, and a lack of societal awareness and concern. All organizations are shaped by both history and the social context of their current surroundings. The context includes the technology available to them, their resources, the knowledge and skills of the staff, and, in the case of child welfare organizations, the nature of the clients they serve. When clients are children, agencies are obligated to follow laws and regulations related to minors.

If agencies operate under private funding, they may be selective of the clients they serve within the limits of their incorporation. If they are funded by the state or receive federal support, they are most often obligated to serve all clients of the particular category for whom they are responsible. For example, a private residential treatment or family foster care agency can select which children it wants to accept from referrals; but the public child protection agency must have a "no reject/no eject" policy. It must assess all referrals for potential service, and it cannot close a case until it is appropriate to do so.

Faith-based groups can, under certain circumstances, set the criteria for the clients they will serve. Historically, private agencies at least could be exclusive in their services, but increasingly the culture and morays of our society are demanding a more open service policy. At the same time, services are becoming more open, groups previously denied services are establishing or pushing for services under their own auspices. There is a belief (not documented sufficiently at this time) that mainstream agencies are not sufficiently sensitive or skilled in working with ethnic, cultural, spiritual, or sexual minority groups.

Literature about organizational behavior has evolved over many decades highlighted by Goffman's *Asylums* (1961), Polsky's *Cottage Six* (1977), Foucault's (1975) *The Birth of the Clinic*, and Weick's *The Collapse of Sensemaking in Organizations* (1993). Perrow (1978) suggested that while organizational analysts find an agency's goals to be rational, why are we puzzled with that same agency's inability to reach its goals? Were an agency's goals not met because of external factors in the environment, as indicated regarding "change-drivers?" Or were there knowing violations which created additional hardships for those entrusted to the agency's care? Such behavior is unconscionable, as all decisions made with clients have implications, and must reflect the NASW Code of Ethics.

The course of an organization's mission is set by those directed by and affiliated with the organization, and how they fit in. The need to understand one's place and "who one is" as a human service administrator is understood by many professionals. Private agencies are comprised of a board of directors that sets the policy and ultimately is responsible to keep the agency operating legally, ethically, financially, and according to best practice. Administrators and staff implement policies set by their boards. The actions of the staff are in a strong sense controlled by the board. These actions are mitigated somewhat by the ability of administration to help train board members and educate them on the agency vision, their roles, and the mandate of the profession. Public agencies, however, typically are directed locally by county commissioners or a board of supervisors. On the state level, they may report to a member of the governor's cabinet.

A social service agency's mandate is related to the concept of social justice and a society in which its citizens are treated with dignity and respect. By placing its trust in welfare and caregiving institutions, society needs to be assured that its trust is well founded. While the organization is a design in which the patterns of work have been set, the administrator has the option of being either a manager who follows the design no matter what and imposes its restrictions, or one who works with the board (or other officials) and staff to improve that grand design as the needs and means are identified. Client input, while sometimes challenging to obtain without appearance of coercion, is always essential. The administrator is constantly in an inquiry mode, seeking the best possible means of helping the agency/client. The social agency and its network of community resources represent a powerful force in society. More than 50 years ago, scholars recognized that early social workers were certain of their ability to modify social forces by developing settlements, charitable societies, mental health services, and policies aimed at bringing desired changes to support the American dream of religious freedom, democratic processes, and respect for the dignity of persons. Sometimes these prime movers were the agency executives, but often they were citizens who saw themselves as "community housekeepers." An interesting narrative of these efforts is presented in *How Women Saved the City* (Spain, 2002).

An organization's structure, rules, norms, policies, human interactions, and common goals will be influenced not only by the people in the organization, but also by that agency's ecology. Administrators, by their actions, attempt to understand and impact the environment so that its influence tends to support the behavior of staff toward the desired design. When the administration ignores the agency and its community history and culture, both the agency and the community it is mandated to serve can suffer the consequences.

Historical Perspectives

Administrative practice in the human services has unique qualities that are grounded in the histories, experience, values, sanctions, skills, and goals of the organizations and people involved in that field. The nineteenth-century pioneer work of Jane Addams in her experiences at Hull House and Mary Richmond's works as well were instrumental in influencing social work administrators for many years. These factors have merged to create basic structural frameworks, communication patterns, and a philosophical context unlike other organizations. The climate created by a professional sense of mission was often a guideline for what made sense to agency administrators. These patterns have consequently been influenced by the interpersonal and reciprocal relations of the clients and the staff, and their mutual visions of what life might be. Thus, the administrative processes of the community-oriented settlement houses were usually less formal in their status relations than administration in the Charity Organization Societies that preceded them historically, but which did not have the same community ties.

Attention to diversity, as we know it today, was not a particular component of policies and practices in the early years of services for children and families. This is evidenced, for example, in the evolution of the foster care system. Historically, foster care was seen as a service for Anglo children. Prior to World War II, black children were "virtually excluded" from child welfare services (Roberts, 2001, p. 7). African American children were typically cared for by kin. If children were not taken in by relatives, they might be labeled *delinquent* and thus imprisoned (Roberts, 2001). Diversity had more to do with nationality of origin than religion or ethnicity. The children sent West by the Children's Aid Society orphan trains program were predominantly of Irish, German, and Italian descent, and they were Catholic. Their integration into the Protestant families of British descent found in the farm communities of Illinois, Indiana, and points West was documented as administratively challenging because of nationality and class differences, not ethnicity. Any issues regarding gay, lesbian, bisexual, transgender, and questioning youth (GLBTQ) were not addressed. The 1960s Civil Rights movement led to the women's movement that, in turn, sparked more attention to the needs of *all* children in the child welfare system (Pasztor, McNitt, and McFadden, 2005).

Administration in the public human service agencies tends to be even more formal due to legally mandated regulations, hierarchical positions, and policies. Other factors such as the 1960s "War on Poverty" forced agencies to increase the involvement of client and community in the operations of the private agency. During the past two decades, most agencies have been influenced by both governmental and insurance-mandated regulations that have tended to formalize agency administrations more strictly and have come into conflict with the traditional visions and less-formal bureaucratic processes of the human service professions. To maintain the vision of the social work profession, it is imperative that the actions of administrative leadership parallel the underlying motifs of the profession's heritage.

Most of our Western-oriented organizations are modeled after a traditional bureaucratic model put forth by the sociologist Max Weber in the early 1900s. Through observation of the organizations of his time, Weber proposed that a certain "ideal type" of organization seemed to be emerging that would eventually become ubiquitous. He did not invent bureaucracies, he only conceptualized their properties, studied, and wrote about them. He did view the bureaucratic structure as the most expedient and practical way to run complex organizations. Four elements made up the heart of his organizational structuring of the bureaucratic paradigm, related to division of labor and considerable specialization, with specific roles assigned to specific people:

- The people in the assigned roles were well trained, reaching a high level of expertise within their specializations.
- Often these people were technicians and/or professionals. Roles were assigned on the basis of merit.
- A formal hierarchy existed which stratified these roles in some way—rejecting superior and subordinate roles.
- Emphasis was placed on formal, written communications, and rules which applied to all (Weber, 1970).

Bureaucracy seemed to be a rational development within a rapidly industrializing society. Governmental intervention was growing, along with expanding organizations and corporations, surpassing the "family run" business. Over 40 years ago, Blau (1962) pointed out that the degree of complexity of administrative tasks was important to the development of bureaucratization.

While there were numerous theorists formulating ideas of management and administration, here are a few who made important contributions to administrative theory. The attempt to make management theory more reliable and structured led to Frederick Taylor's influential work, *Management* (1911). Some of his ideas included the importance of worker selection and training, time studies, the provision of short work breaks (he discovered the worker would start to be less productive after a certain period of work), and required that each worker be supervised by only one person. His ideas riled many people in the country by the way he spoke of workers, but his views remain in the forefront of some management approaches. His book has been reissued hundred times and translated into numerous languages, thereby implying that it has cross-cultural benefit.

In contrast to what was seen as his authoritarian orientation to management, a number of researchers looked toward a more "human relations-oriented" approach to management. A series of studies showed the willingness of staff to produce when they were treated in a way that led them to believe management cared about them. Other research demonstrated the power of the work group to influence productivity. This endeavor came to be known as the Hawthorne Studies (Roethlisberger and Dickson, 1939). Another theorist, Douglas McGregor (1960), in his book, *The Human Side of Enterprise*, introduced the idea of X and Y managers, the latter being more worker oriented and the X managers more authoritarian. Many of these more humanistic approaches were adopted by the Japanese in their industries and led to small group ideas being used both to increase productivity and to maintain worker morale. One of the most well known is "quality circles," in which work groups meet on company time to discuss and suggest improvements.

Note should be taken of Mary Parker Follet, a social worker whose contributions grew out of her experiences in service and politics over 70 years ago. She introduced the idea of "constructive conflict," explaining that it was important for disagreements to be openly examined and worked to a mutually accepted resolution. Other more current theories include the use of systems thinking, cybernetics, and "management by objectives." This approach maintained that issues should be looked at and discussed by all levels of staff and worked through the entire organization, informing the administration prior to decisions for action (Drucker, 1954). Drucker saw this as differing from management by control, and he also has done some important work regarding management of nonprofit agencies.

Basic Administrative Principles

The evolving administrative theory has led to some principles generally accepted in organizations. These include the following.

- A worker should be responsible to only one supervisor.
- A supervisor should not have to directly supervise more than five persons. Boards hire their agency executive directors or chief administrators, who are then accountable directly to the board. Board members make policy; the administrator sees that it gets carried out. (Inputs from the administrator are obligatory and vital.) Both work on preparing the budget.
- Administrators and their managers supervise the staff.

- Administrators should help educate their boards and boards should educate themselves, especially new members.
- Organizational goals need to be clear, and evaluated frequently, and objectives should be observable and measurable.
- There is a cycle of management involving planning, motivating, organizing, and controlling—all of which involves calling for decisions that lead to further decision making, continuing the cycle (Abels and Murphy, 1981).
- Supervision and staff development are vital for organizational growth.

If these principles are the same for all organizations and agencies, how is social welfare administration different? This question seems simple enough, and a range of immediate responses might include "getting the work of the agency done," "helping the worker do a better job," or "to be more effective," or "more efficient," "insuring accountable services," and so on. But why accomplish these tasks? Why do a better job? Why serve the client? All the activities of an agency—including the staff, management, and board—must reflect the purposes for which all social welfare organizations are created. It must reflect the profession from which it evolved and to which it gives shape. The commitment and tasks of administration ought to be to increase the agency's ability to function in a manner that helps lead to a more "just society."

These values are reflected by the tentative principles suggested below.

- Helping people and institutions arrive at sound sense-making judgments regarding what ought to be;
- Developing people's individual competence in keeping with those judgments; and
- Developing the agency's capacity to secure the services and social arrangements that support those judgments.

Principle #1: Administrative actions should lead to "just" consequences. The goals of the administrative process are closely related to what the functions and purposes of the social agency "ought to be." In general terms, these include: (a) helping people arrive at sound judgments regarding what ought to be; and (b) securing social arrangements and individual competence in conformity with such judgments. Agencies should be interested in evolving.

Principle #2: The agency structure ought to insure a democratic, minimally stratified environment. The structure and the pattern of the interactions within the agency, as well as its relations with other agencies, should be structured within a framework of democratic processes and moral behavior that insures dignity and respect for all people involved. It should also permit and encourage minimizing the role of the supervisor as an "expert," while promoting the concept of the agency as a "just" community.

Principle #3: Decisions and practice need to be based on rational inquiry and evidence. The major mode for the gathering of knowledge to be used in practice needs to be based on scientific inquiry—regardless of whether that practice is counseling, social change, supervision, or administration. The knowledge base must be grounded in human services practice, utilizing social science–management research. Decisions need to be based on available information, and the level of practice should be the "current state of the art." Power and status should not be the catalyst for a decision. Where there seems to be contradictory evidence, consultation is required.

Principle #4: Interactions within and among agencies need to be synergistic. Synergy is the melding of two elements into a greater unit. The establishment of a pattern of symmetrical, synergistic relationships, such as administrator–board, administrator–supervisor, supervisor–worker, and worker–client, permits mutual problem-solving without contest strategies. Attitudinal change alone is not enough to improve system effectiveness. The interaction between people and technology, and among people themselves, is what makes the organization more than just an aggregate of individual efforts. These interactions determine the degree of synergy, and hence the effectiveness the organization will achieve.

Principle #5: Administration should foster independence for staff and clients through mutual support and growth. The administration has a continuing responsibility to encourage staff autonomy and to permit clients to develop their own self-help resources. Administration can promote these values by developing and disseminating materials that can be used by the community in either self-help or worker-supported groups. Within the agency this would mean: (a) a flattening of hierarchical administrative practices and shared decision making; (b) ongoing staff development programs, including administrative leadership development; and (c) the development and support of interagency and community social networks. Support groups provide added social capital by increasing the number of people available to help the client. The worker's social capital and that of the administrators provide added contacts when needed.

Principle #6: The administrator promotes mutual accountability to insure the highest ethical level of practice. This view suggests that accountability is not necessarily to a hierarchical structure, but to peers, clients, and the moral community within which one functions. One must also evaluate one's work and give feedback to the broader professional community. The optimal result of this can be an ethical approach to practice, where any techniques not grounded in solid evidence are identified as such to the community. The major thrust for accountability is to provide the highest level of professional practice, reflecting the current state of the art.

The development of administrative practice also has implications for accountability in social work. Its development makes accountability a more ordinary part of practice through the collective investigation of consequences, and builds it into the development of professional knowledge. As a consequence there will be less dependence on a hierarchical structure of authority for accountability. Just as the individual scientist is generally accountable to the scientific community, so too, individual administrators will come to be generally accountable to their peers through responsibility to contribute knowledge of consequences. The major thrust for accountability is to provide state-of-the-art professional practice, or "best practice."

Principle #7: The administrator is a guide. The administrator not only carries out, in a respectful manner, some of the traditional enabling administrative and development tasks long associated with the manager's role, but also assumes the task of architect and reconstructor. In this way, just consequences can result within the agency and for the clients served, and the agency can evolve toward higher levels of functioning. Where the policies or practices of the agency or funding sources prevent practice which leads to "just consequences," the administrator must undertake reconstruction efforts to alter these procedures.

The questions facing administrators include:

- What modes of practice will bring out the best in staff's ability to work with people?
- What practice promotes good consequences?
- How can administrative behavior demonstrate the values of the agency and still offer high-quality service?
- What does it take to establish the contextual climate that brings out the best in the entire agency?

The actions of any administrator impact the total staff and, sooner or later, the clients. This systems view is an important part of understanding administration. It recognizes the interrelatedness of actions and the idea that actions also may have unanticipated consequences. This outcome may be especially true when there is diversity among and between the leadership of the agency, the staff who deliver services, and the clients themselves.

Pasztor, Goodman, Potts, Santana and Runnels (2002) refer to the "Double D" dynamic, or the "Demographic Diversity" among clients and their caseworkers or other decision makers. Consider, for example, a foster care case that goes before a judge. What kind of educational, socioeconomic, and ethnic differences might be there among the child and the family, the social worker, the foster parents, the attorneys, and the judge? Consider age diversity alone. If the judge, for example, was born in 1946 and is 59 years old, he was born before television, penicillin, polio shots, frozen foods, cell phones, and contact lenses were invented. Presidential speeches were heard on the radio. "Grass" was mowed, "coke" was a cold drink, and "pot" was a cooking utensil. The HIV/Aids and "crack" were unheard of, and "software" was not yet a word. How are emotionally charged issues decided when all participants may have multiculturally different views of the world?

In summary, an effective administrative approach stresses the interrelatedness of agency and community, worker and client, administrator and staff, and their impact on each other. It holds that each person is due respect and dignity as an individual, by having their ideas acknowledged. In a democratic society, the statuses and stratification and subsequent alienation that hierarchical organization often creates must be minimized. This objective can be accomplished if people are treated with respect within the agency, and synergetic processes that emphasize the just consequences of actions are used. For an administrator, following the NASW Code of Ethics helps insure that these principles are being addressed.

FORCES AFFECTING ADMINISTRATORS AND THEIR AGENCIES: CHANGE-DRIVERS

Introduction

Several years ago, the television show *Frontline* showed a three part series titled *"Failure to Protect: The Taking of Logan Marr."* This was a documentary of a white teenage mother of two young children in a semirural New England community. Because of alleged lack of supervision, first the older child, a pre-schooler, and then her little sister born a few years later were placed in foster care. The foster parent was a former child welfare worker with that same child protection agency, a mother herself of sons and admittedly eager to adopt girls into her family. While the birth mother client was endeavoring to have her daughters returned to her, the agency was working toward termination of parental rights, with the goal of having the former employee adopt. Psychosocial assessments showed that Logan, the older child, was deeply attached to her birth mother. But an unskilled caseworker, flawed agency policy, and a demanding worker-turned-foster parent were just some of the factors that came together to cause the death of Logan and conviction of the worker/foster parent for murder. The younger daughter ultimately was returned to the birth mother.

In a large city in a border state, a Latina mother of three girls became involved with child protective services because of child sexual abuse by her husband. If the father went to prison, the mother—undocumented—had no means of supporting herself and her children. The mother forced her daughters to recant. The public agency child welfare worker, with a decade of experience and an MSW degree, understood the dynamics. She would have liked to intervene on the mother's behalf to help her obtain services for her daughters and herself. But she had a caseload of seventy children, including some who lived with parent(s), some in kinship care, and some in foster care with reunification as the casework plan. She just could not get to it.

In California, the state chapter of the NASW has twice endeavored and failed to get title or consumer protection legislation passed. In California, the title "social worker" can be used by anyone who provides social services so, for example, an eligibility worker with a high-school diploma may be called a "social worker." Child welfare workers are called "social workers," no matter what degree they hold. The legislation was opposed primarily by public social service agency administrators and labor union representatives, believing that the term "social worker" is important for staff recruitment and retention. And it would cost money to reclassify positions. Although veterinarians, attorneys, real estate agents, and registered nurses hold claim to their professional titles by virtue of specific educational and licensing credentials, clients of social services do not have the same consumer protection.

Consider the connections between these three scenarios and the administration of a child welfare agency. What is the relevance to you as a social work student, an intern, or an employee of an agency? What if your primary aim is to become a licensed clinical social worker in private practice? Each of these examples illustrates that issues affecting the management of an agency impact the personal lives of clients as well as the professional lives of staff. But in these instances, the problems had more to do with factors outside the agency's control than internal issues. The following section of this chapter addresses these types of issues that affect administrative decisions, rather than the consequences of decisions made by administrators. These macroevents, also known as "change-drivers," are prompted by outside forces and can positively or negatively affect delivery of services for children and families. Here are eight typical change-drivers.

The Community's View and Value of Its Public and Private Child Welfare Agencies

> Samantha is an intern at a private agency that provides family preservation services, under contract to a public child welfare agency. This past year, three children died from physical abuse while under the jurisdiction of the public child welfare agency, although none of the children were clients of Samantha's organization. The area's major newspaper ran a series of articles about the value of family preservation, titled "Are Some Families NOT Worth Preserving?" As a result of community and political pressure, the public agency decided to cut back family preservation services and canceled contracts with its private providers. Families lost their relationships with their social workers; the intern lost her placement.

- What parts, if any, of this situation were under the control of the private agency director?
- What client needs were addressed by the private agency?
- What were the community's expectations, and did those expectations match the needs?
- How much could the private agency do, at what cost, for whom, and who really paid attention until a child died?
- Were clients valued or devalued, and by whom?
- Was the private agency valued or devalued, and by whom?

To some extent, an agency may be valued according to community perceptions of the status of its clients. For example, agencies that provide assistance to the homeless may be viewed with some ambivalence by their respective communities. On one hand, there may be some public sympathy for the homeless; on the other hand, such clients may be viewed as adults who made poor choices in their lives that resulted in homelessness. Agencies that provide hospice assistance may receive higher esteem, because the need crosses socioeconomic boundaries. While public perception of an agency's services may be an external issue, it should be noted that agencies might have some control over how they and their clients are viewed. According to Rapp and Poertner (1992), the first principle of "client-centered management" is "venerating the people called clients" (p. 17). This expression means that advocacy for the agency's clients—whoever they are and whatever they need—is a constant theme. If agency staff are pro-client, perhaps that perspective permeates through the community and becomes in itself a change-driver.

IMPACT OF STATE AND LOCAL DEMOGRAPHICS ON CURRENT AND PROJECTED CLIENTS

In order to make service delivery effective, agencies need to assess current and future demographic shifts. For example, there can be internal migration such as from inner cities to suburbs, sometimes known as "white flight," or from "rust belt" states to southern and western states. Demographics also reflect immigration, such as individuals and families coming to the United States, both as documented and undocumented citizens. Further, demographics include changes in family composition, such as the number of single-parent households or a change in the number of multigenerational households. Communities can experience shifts in their ethnic or religious/spiritual makeup. There may be increases or decreases in the number of individuals who have conditions causing disabilities. Finally, demographics may show changes in the number of sexual minority individuals and families.

An example of utilizing demographics shifts to develop a service strategy comes from the *Master Plan for Social Work Education*, developed by the California Association of Deans and Directors of the Schools of Social Work (2004) and submitted to the California Assembly. Before spelling out its recommendations to address a shortage of approximately 20,000 social workers statewide (Pasztor, Saint-Germain, and DeCrescenzo, 2002), the report identified demographic change-drivers. These included how California's residents suffer from a range of Jansson's previously mentioned deprivations.

- Poverty afflicts 12 percent of the California's families;
- Homelessness affects 361,000 individuals and families;
- Mental illness drives almost 600,000 individuals to seek services annually, nearly twice as many since 1999;
- Child abuse and neglect referrals in California amount to 21 percent of the country's referrals.

On national, state, and community levels, consider the demographic changes that impact an agency's ability to serve its target group. If a community has an influx of individuals and families that do not speak English, then its workforce must change to include staff able to speak Spanish, Arabic, Russian, or Vietnamese, for example. Demographics have an impact on capacity building, with "professional practice at the community level that encompasses social, economic, and political capacity-building within a value framework of inclusive, demographic participation, respect for diversity, and self-determination" (Daley and Wong, 1994, p. 10).

Economic and Funding Factors

Reductions in city, county, and state funding have a direct impact on service delivery. Sometimes, there can be freezes in hiring. Other times, funding can increase. In California, for example, voters in 2004 passed Proposition 63, which increases funding for mental health services by taxing upper-income individuals. Funding change-drivers can have particular impact on children and families of color. On a federal level, funding was requested for a mentoring program for children of incarcerated parents. With minorities making up a disproportionate share of the population behind bars, this funding may provide resources to agencies that serve this population. According to the National Council of La Raza (2004), Hispanics represented 13 percent of the U.S. population in 2000, but accounted for 31 percent of those incarcerated in federal facilities.

In the case of some minority groups, particularly gays and lesbians, program funding may be directly connected to community values. That explains the historical lag in funding for programs advocating help for AIDS victims. Often, the beneficiaries of services have to organize and create their own programs, hopefully getting help from social workers who are familiar with administrative principles and committed to the NASW Code of Ethics.

With children of color disproportionately represented in the child welfare system, special needs adoption tax credits and educational and training vouchers for children transitioning out of foster care can be beneficial. Conversely, there is a marketplace economy in the delivery of social services for the private sector. States are looking to performance-based contracts, with increasing accountability and requirements for measurable outcomes. There also can be tougher licensing requirements. Mergers and strategic affiliations between agencies may affect service delivery, as the cost of doing business may drive smaller agencies out of certain areas. Competing for service contracts may pit for-profit and not-for-profit agencies against each other, prompting questions about cost-containment versus quality of care. Moreover, a distinction needs to be made between true collaboration and what is known as "collab-petition," when agencies pretend to work together but really are competing for the same contracts and grants.

Federal and State Legislative Mandates

Federal and state legislation has a mandatory influence on the delivery of services, especially in the child welfare arena. Today's social work students write papers about challenges in serving youth transitioning from foster care to independent living. If students had wanted to write about, much less served this population 25 years ago, there would have been little opportunity for research or a specialized caseload. What events made it possible to have this body of knowledge or to carry a caseload solely comprised of older teens in foster care?

The Adoption Assistance and Child Welfare Act of 1980 (P.L. 96-272) was considered one of the most important pieces of child welfare legislation in decades. It endeavored to discourage the use of foster care by creating incentives for public child welfare agencies to make "reasonable efforts" to prevent children from being separated from their parents and, once in the child welfare system, to be reunified or adopted more quickly. In the early 1980s, the foster care population, about 500,000 when the law was passed, dropped below 300,000 children. But the emergence of compelling socioeconomic change-drivers dramatically impacted the promise and hope of P.L. 96-272. These included federal social service budget cuts, and the spread of crackcocaine and HIV/AIDS which brought hundreds of thousands of children into the child welfare system. The number of children in foster care began to climb again, with an increasing number of adolescents growing up in out-of-home care. Then the Independent Living Initiative (P.L. 99-272) of 1986 was passed, with the intent to increase services for this population. Again, funding did not match the need. By the mid-1990s, the foster care population soared to over 500,000 once again. That prompted the passage of the Foster Care Independence Act in 1999, which doubled funding for independent living programs and services, and extended Medicaid coverage for youth in foster care upto the age of 21.

Federal legislation also has been a change-driver for the child welfare program known as "kinship care." In the 1970s, relatives caring for younger family members in Illinois sued the state claiming financial support discrimination. Foster parents, unrelated to the children in their care, could receive more financial assistance than relatives who were caring for younger family members under the Aid to Families with Dependent Children (AFDC) program. The suit reached the Supreme Court which ruled, in *Miller* v. *Youakim*, 1979, that kin raising children who had been abused or neglected should receive the higher foster care rates if they met state requirements. Families of color, with a long tradition of caring for members of the extended family, have been particularly impacted by this legislative change-driver. In some large urban jurisdictions, there are now more children in kinship care than in family foster care.

Over the past decade, perhaps the most influential legislative change-driver has been the Adoption and Safe Families Act of 1997 (ASFA), P.L. 105-89. It requires that all state departments of social services meet national standards for child safety, well-being, and permanency. These measurable outcomes include specific reductions in the incidence of abuse in foster care, increases in placement stability for children in foster care, decreases in the number of children who enter foster care before the age of 12 and leave for independent living, and increases in the number of children placed adoptively. Through the end of 2004, all states failed their federal audits, putting pressure on administrators to find system-wide solutions to avoid large financial penalties.

The ASFA may have a particular impact on children of color. According to the Child Welfare League of America (2000), since "racism is a fact of life in American society, and racial profiling has been demonstrated to exist in numerous areas, families of color may be subjected to disproportionate scrutiny and be reported more often than other families. Because children of color enter the child welfare system in disproportionate numbers, any unintended consequences of ASFA implementation will fall more heavily on them and their families" (p. ix). Also, since ASFA uses a narrow view of "family," it does not sufficiently accommodate kinship care as a valued resource for children and families.

Hundreds of bills are introduced in state legislatures each year that have an impact on the workload of social workers in a variety of programs and services. In child welfare, these have included extending sibling visiting rights to intercountry adoptions, so social workers must facilitate contact between adopted children and their families of origin. Social workers also have been mandated to identify persons with significant relationships with children in foster care; to maintain those relationships, social workers are required to find these individuals, assess their safety risks to the child, and incorporate them into the child's lives as appropriate. Some also specifically address diversity issues. California, for example, requires special training for child welfare workers and foster parents on sensitivity toward GLBTQ. In many instances, however, these legislative mandates do not come with the funding to increase staff positions or other essential resources. Action may be authorized, but the funding is not appropriated.

MEDIA COVERAGE OF CHILD WELFARE ISSUES

> Marshall was a public agency child welfare worker with an MSW degree who was involved in a case where a group of children lived with foster parents in what the newspaper called, "horrid, filthy conditions." The police raided the house, the foster parents were arrested, and the children were sent to other foster families. Marshall's name was mentioned in the newspaper article. He was devastated; he believed he was doing his job by seeing the foster family monthly as required, and the conditions were not unsafe at the time of his last visit. He believed that the news story did not represent all the facts, and that he should not have been named.

Child welfare stories have become highly publicized and politicized in the last 30 years. Since the passage of The Child Abuse Prevention & Treatment Act of 1974 (CAPTA), P.L. 93-247, dozens of professional groups have become mandated reporters, and public awareness has increased dramatically. Today, 3 million children are reported abused and neglected annually, and about one-third of these cases are substantiated. The Western Child Welfare Law Center documents child abuse cases that are featured in newspapers and magazines, with headlines such as "System Fails to Protect Kids in Group Homes"; "Sex Assaults by Counselors Alleged at Group Homes"; "Cost of Foster Care Abuse—$3.5 Million in 13 Months"; "Case of Child Abuse, Death Tells Tale of Official Neglect"; and "Judge Says Worker Lied in Court."

When these stories appear, as tragic as they are, social workers ought to flood the media with letters and stories about the positive outcomes that occur everyday for the hundreds of thousands of children and families cared for in their agencies.

Administrators should take the lead on this, and work in conjunction with their local NASW chapters. Guidelines established by the California chapter of NASW include:

- Have one consistent expert spokesperson for the agency on any case.
- Ensure that the spokesperson has all of the facts for the case, based on input from all available parties, especially the case-carrying workers and supervisors, and caregivers as appropriate.
- Change the language used both within the agency and when talking with media to be strengths based, and child and family friendly. This would include, for example:
  — referring to youngsters as children, not as placements;
  — referring to caregivers as foster parents or foster families as adoptive parents; or adoptive families, not as homes and especially not as caretakers;
  — explaining that children are separated, not removed and, especially, not "pulled"; and
  — clarifying the credentials of staff generically labeled as "social workers," but who hold degrees other than in social work.
- Coordinate with other organizations, including juvenile courts and any private agencies that may be involved, such as foster family agencies, to help ensure that information is consistent and proactive.
- Refrain from publicly identifying staff, foster parents, adoptive parents, and kinship caregivers pending ongoing investigations; if they are named, provide them with the opportunity to formally rebut any allegations.
- Provide a public apology process for staff and foster parent, kinship caregivers, or adoptive parents when they are inappropriately or wrongly charged.
- Hold the entire agency and the community responsible when services are not appropriately delivered, rather than "blaming" individual staff. Agencies that do not meet national standards regarding caseload size, staff credentials, and so on should inform their communities that there is a gap between the resources that are needed, and those that exist. Advocate for taxpayers and policy makers to take responsibility for the resulting service delivery system failure, not individual staff and caregivers, unless, of course, there is an individual ethical, professional, or legal breach of duty (Pasztor and Pederson, 2004).

In some jurisdictions, child welfare case tragedies may be used for political gain. Candidates may run for a state office with an election goal of "cleaning up" the system. Public child welfare agencies have historically been run by political appointees. On a state level, they may report to cabinet officials appointed by the governor, or they may be appointed by the governor without holding a cabinet position. On a county level, they may be appointed by county administrators—perhaps boards of supervisors or county commissioners. In any case, it behooves politically appointed administrators to maintain two major wishes of their "bosses" who hold elected positions: keep the agency out of the newspaper because of child harm or, worse, death; and do not ask for more money to run the program which might require raising taxes. Child welfare advocates know that as long as child welfare agencies are directed by political appointees, it is difficult to get children on the political radar screen.

Class Action Lawsuits

National, regional, and local advocacy groups have taken legal measures to address structural problems in agencies' delivery of child welfare services, usually following a high-profile death of a child or children. The intervention may be a class action lawsuit that results in a consent decree. This means that the agency promises the court that it will take specific measures to rectify problems, avoiding judicial penalties or even a court-imposed administrator, commonly known as "receivership." At the end of 2004, fourteen states had active consent decrees or settlement agreements, and seven states/localities no longer had to operate under consent decrees or settlement agreements (Wingfield, 2004). Therefore, almost half of the states in the country have had to invest resources to address legal issues regarding alleged or confirmed malpractice. Increasingly, agencies face risks with smaller margins for error, greater potential liability, and enormous fiscal and human costs for making bad personnel decisions. A preferred alternative would be investing adequate resources to create a higher-quality service delivery system that could avoid such protracted litigation.

Several jurisdictions are doing just that. A decade ago, the Illinois Department of Children and Family Services was an agency in crisis, with problems that were all too common for many large public child welfare agencies: caseloads that were too large, children who were growing up in numerous foster families, poor staff morale, and commensurately low public confidence. A number of child deaths and dozens of lawsuits led the agency's director to seek national accreditation as a problem-solving approach. Accreditation means that an agency not only meets the highest program standards recognized nationally, but it can document compliance. The agency chose to pursue accreditation through the Council on Accreditation for Children and Family Services (COA).

In 2000, Illinois's Department of Children and Family Services (DCFS) achieved national accreditation, and a *Chicago Tribune* editorial headline proclaimed the "Resurrection of DCFS." The agency documented improved foster care outcomes, smaller caseloads across all services, and all supervisors having a master's degree in social work (the agency actually sent 200 supervisors back to school to get those degrees). According to the line staff and administrators, "We wouldn't have gone through the pain of doing this if we weren't totally convinced we were taking the best step we've ever made. We've made the commitment to providing quality services every day of the year" (Blassingame, 2001, p. 33). Currently, only a dozen or so public state and county child welfare agencies and several hundred private agencies have invested in national accreditation with either COA or Joint Commission on the Accreditation of Healthcare Organizations (JCAHO). Most of us would not attend a school of social work that was not accredited, or go to a hospital that was not accredited, says a former longtime regional administrator of one of the oldest accredited public agencies in the county (Daniel, 2004).

Technology

In addressing the impact of change on an organization, the issue of technology and, especially, computerization merits "special attention" (Weinbach, 1998, p. 294). Social service agencies—whether using the most basic technology or striving for a "paperless" workplace—find that there are both possibilities and problems. The transition may be especially hard for staff whose original work experience was with typewriters, "snail mail," and a receptionist who actually answered the main number for an agency and took handwritten messages for staff. Most networking was done with colleagues across town and, at the most, perhaps across the state for a conference. National contacts focused mostly around interstate contacts regarding the placement of a child out-of-state. International contacts were rare.

Now computerization affects the daily practice of all social service providers. New hires right out of college or graduate school grew up with computers and cell phones. They are typically willing and able to manage the demands of new technology. However, there are also risks with computerized data. And access to the Internet requires new workplace guidelines regarding the use of the worldwide web for personal communication and confidentiality on the job.

Perhaps the greatest risks are to the clients themselves. According to Weaver, Furman, Moses, Lindsey, and Cherin (1999):

> It is clear that the current system, which mandates the investigation and processing of a multitude of cases in a resource-poor environment, generates an overwhelming amount of paperwork. For each report of abuse or neglect, a file is created by a caseworker detailing the allegations, and describing the child and family. This file will eventually include an ever-growing mountain of facts, details, opinions, testimony, and judgments, all of which will be appended at regular intervals over the next several years, while the child moves through the bureaucratic and legal system . . . The information collected on paper forms often contains timely and critical data that is lost in static storage. The limitations of paper storage are obvious . . . How many human-hours are wasted, or how many lives of children and families are disrupted, due to the inability of caseworkers to efficiently process the mountain of paper with which they are confronted? (p. 3)

As agencies move toward new technologies, studies have been conducted on how computerization and technology impact employees. Research has looked at staff responses to computer systems, demographic characteristics, attitudes toward proficiency, work environment and change, job satisfaction, implementation issues, social interaction and technological change, and use of time (Weaver et al., 1999). Findings indicate that there is no link between ethnicity and response to technological change, and little connection between gender and acceptance of new technologies. According to Weaver et al. (1999), "Perhaps the most important overall insight from the literature is that attitudes toward technological change and workers' consequent adaptations are embedded in their attitudes toward their job and the workplace" (p. 37). In other words, it is not the technology itself, but rather the overall way an agency addresses change with its staff that is critical.

Administrators should be aware that computerization and technology can be another aspect of addressing age diversity. Younger clerical staff may become especially valued when they are more technology proficient than the professional staff; in turn, older staff with decades of practice experience may suddenly feel out of touch. The use of e-mail and teleconferencing may inspire agencies to diversify services and sites, creating regional offices across town, the state, or the country. Directors, especially those without "people skills," may find it more comfortable to deal with staff by e-mail, avoiding essential in-person contact.

The social work administrator can build on the benefits of technology advances and computerization by implementing the following strategies:

- Provide assurances about continuity of service when staff are afraid that a computer will replace a person in making social diagnoses;
- Compensate for individual losses regarding status when staff might lose their jobs;
- Use functional authority to balance the computer skills of younger staff with the work expertise of older staff;
- Ensure adequate in-person communication between management and staff, and among staff; and
- Balance technology with human intervention (Weinbach, 1998, p. 298).

Workforce Shortage and Impending Leadership Crisis

The Field Guide to Child Welfare (Rycus and Hughes, 1998), a four-volume text that addresses all aspects of child welfare practice, describes "Species: The Child Welfare Caseworker":

> Environmental Alert: The child welfare casework is an endangered species. Child welfare caseworkers have historically been under-supported, and have recently suffered significant political assault. Their physical, social, and economic environments need to be made safe, nurturing, and supported if we are to prevent their extinction. (Volume I, p. ix)

The demand for social workers has been documented on national and state levels, a concern because necessary services may go unprovided, may be provided by staff with lesser qualifications, or may be assigned to qualified staff already carrying full caseloads, exacerbating turnover (Pasztor, Saint-Germain, and DeCrescenzo, 2002). Studies conducted by The Urban Institute (Malm, Bess, Leos-Urbel, Geen, and Markowitz, 2001). The Annie E. Casey Foundation (2003), and the Alliance for Children and Families/American Public Human Services Association/Child Welfare League of America (2001) all document the shortage and turnover of staff in the child welfare field.

No more studies on the workforce shortage are necessary. There are sufficient recommendations on how to address the problem, including the following.

- Positions that do not require formal coursework in social work should not have a "social work" job title.

- Candidates for jobs requiring a social worker can be increased by expanded opportunities for social work education, including distance education; accelerated BSW–MSW degrees; internships; tuition assistance; and certificates or associate degrees to help entry-level staff advance in the field.
- Retention and recruitment of social workers can be enhanced by creating a more positive public image for social workers;
- Improving working conditions, including smaller caseloads, flexible work schedules, and increased support staff; and
- Making compensation and benefits commensurate with the demands of the job (Pasztor, Saint-Germain, and DeCrescenzo, 2002).

At this point, what seems to be lacking is the "political will" to make the changes. It is easier to commission studies that give the illusion of action than to implement recommendations. Policy makers must provide the increased levels of support necessary to comprehensively and effectively address the long-standing problem of the shortage of professional child welfare social workers across the country.

In addition to a systemic problem in the development and support of line staff, there is also an impending "leadership deficit" with the aging of baby-boomer administrators. Experienced social workers, the first of the "baby-boom" generation, will start to retire in the next 5–10 years. Younger human service workers, according to national studies, are not making a long-term professional commitment to social work. National and state studies indicate that unrealistic workloads, poor supervision, administrative turnover, and lack of public support and understanding increase the turnover rate and thus affect the demand for social workers.

The Urban Institute's report, aptly named *Running to Keep in Place*, highlighted turnover in public sector administrators as a critical factor (Malm et al., 2001). In the 3 years in which the study was underway in twelve states and multiple local jurisdictions, the directors of the agencies changed in half of the states. Line staff in particular noted that leadership changes precipitate changes in other management staff, which creates instability. These changes also create shifts in agency vision and priorities as well as the administration's ability to understand and work with staff. A key concern was the ability of constantly shifting management to respond to problems in the community. Likewise, turnover in line staff and supervisors restricts the universe of social work professionals who eventually may be promoted to management and administrative positions. Human services agencies often go outside the field of social work, such as law or business, to appoint administrators. While these credentials are significant, there is a message to the social work field that its experience and education are not valuable.

According to Shay Bilchik, President/Chief Executive Officer of the Child Welfare League of America:

> An estimated 50 percent of today's child welfare leaders will be retiring during the next decade, creating what many have called a "crisis in child welfare leadership." To avert this crisis, the field must act now to develop and support the next

generation of leaders, people capable of meeting the expanding demands of our communities and the needs of our most vulnerable children, youth, and families. Tomorrow's leaders will have to possess the skills to address significant challenges, including: (a) meeting the increasingly complex needs of children and families with stable or declining resources; (b) managing multiple and complex funding mechanisms; (c) meeting increased demands for accountability and proof of program impact; (d) competing for economic and political support in a context of heightened security concerns; and (e) supporting and recruiting quality child welfare professional staff. (2004)

INTERNAL DYNAMICS IMPACTING SERVICES AND STAFF: LEADERSHIP, VISION, MISSION, AND MANAGEMENT

Introduction

In addition to external forces or change-drivers outside the agency, organizational policies, staff practices, and client outcomes also are profoundly affected by the management or leadership style and skill of the agency's chief administrator. In most not-for-profit, private settings, these individuals are typically known as "directors." In the case of large agencies where there may be various program directors, they may be called "executive directors." In other settings, especially organizations which use more of a corporate model, administrative leaders may be known as the "president" and/or "chief executive officer." Whatever the title, leadership is essential, and it includes a number of critical tasks:

- Keeping the vision, mission, and values of the agency in the forefront of stakeholders (community, clients, staff, and board);
- Overseeing the development of fiscal resources, and managing the annual and projected budget;
- Developing and maintaining programs that meet the mission of the agency with measurable goals, objectives, and outcomes;
- Ensuring that human resources (i.e., personnel and staffing) are appropriate for the agency's programs;
- Overseeing resource development, both human and fiscal;
- Being accountable for cost-effective service delivery;
- Ensuring that the agency has a quality assurance/risk management program;
- Promoting advocacy on behalf of the agency's clients; and
- Being a leader in the community to facilitate community support, from public relations to budget allocations or donor contributions.

The size of the agency (whether 50 employees, 500, or 5,000), the auspices of the agency (public or private, for-profit or not-for-profit), and kind of services provided (i.e., child protection or adult day care) will direct the specific scope of the administrator's work. Nonetheless, because these tasks are common to all administrators, the previously mentioned Council on Accreditation mandates that all agencies meet the same generic standards in each of these areas.

No matter what size the organization is or what services it provides, it is not uncommon to hear the following statements about directors: "She is a good leader, but a poor manager." Or, "He is a good manager, but a poor leader." "She talks the talk, but doesn't walk the walk." New hires entering a child and family services agency will immediately hear from peers exactly what type of "leader" or "manager" their administrators are perceived to be. David Liederman, a former executive director of the Child Welfare League of America who held a master's degree in social work and also served as an elected state representative, described the characteristics of effective leaders:

- They have a vision.
- They can articulate their vision.
- They have integrity, meaning what they say and saying what they mean.
- They have the authority to fulfill their agencies' vision and mission.

Unfortunately, there are leaders who have a vision for their agencies, but cannot explain it. Or perhaps they have a vision and can explain it, but they lack integrity. Others may have vision and integrity, but they do not use their authority to make decisions or address conflicts. And perhaps the most ineffective administrators are those who have no articulated vision or integrity, but just use their authority in a heavy-handed way.

Whether the agency director works for a private or public sector organization, leadership and management skills must be demonstrated. An agency's approach to diversity, whether regarding services for clients or supports for staff, will be modeled by the administrator.

Attention to diversity in terms of an agency's policies and practices will be affected by a number of critical leadership tasks. These include:

- Having an organizational definition of the agency's mission and vision, commensurate with values and goals;
- Providing meaning and context for the agency's services;
- Recognizing that change is constant;
- Improving business processes; and
- Achieving outcomes.

The actions that child welfare administrators take in response to the myriad of issues that confront them will in large part determine how their message of organizational effectiveness and competency is shared among staff and the community. Supervisory staff also take their cue from the initiatives that administrative leadership chooses to prioritize.

Whereas the public sector administrator has to provide justification for expenditure of public funds in support of the community's social services programs to elected officials, the private sector administrator has to provide justification for expenditure of funds to the organization's board of directors. The political and organizational processes in which these choices and decisions are made can be fundamentally different. Focus of mission, complexity of systems, delivery of services, funding streams, organizational structure, and community responsiveness impact the type of leadership and management skills. The ability to "act" on both leadership and management is the "art" of being a successful administrator.

Organizational Definition: Vision, Mission, Values, and Goals

How directors define their organizations both internally and externally is critical. Without the definition that leadership can provide, organizations can drift. To avoid a lack of focus, staff must be engaged at every level—support, service, supervisory, and management—in creating an organization that is in alignment with its vision, mission, values, and goals.

Though the field of organizational development gives guidance in approaching this fundamental challenge, many times organizations have difficulty in meeting the vision, mission, and core values that are imbedded in their public trust. Many organizations simply "redo" or periodically "revisit" their vision, mission, core values, and goals at organizational retreats, but fail to harness the power of the messages contained in those statements. The concepts are many times crafted in such a way to maximize their presentation value to constituency groups. They become nothing more than politically correct statements of what the organization might become. In high-functioning organizations, time is dedicated to focus on how vision, mission, values, and goals can be drivers of organizational change and definition. To begin, it might be more effective to call these events—if not strategic planning efforts—at least "advances" in organizational definition instead of "retreats."

A learning environment helps to create an organizational culture in which work product is evaluated, enriched, and shared. A set of shared organizational core values can create a work environment that provides clear guidelines to help evaluate day-to-day relationships among clients, staff, and the public. Organizations tend to make value statements that do not challenge the manner in which individual interactions are defined. Therefore, shared core values have to be available and present in a meaningful way to all staff in the organization.

Meaning and Context

The professional choice of becoming a social worker comes with the orientation of wanting to impact society. The career choice to become a social worker is a statement of one's belief system. A leader who is capable of connecting the desire that motivates individual social workers to devote themselves to their profession, with the vision and mission of the organization, has recognized an important tenet of organizational development. Commitment to the desired outcomes of the organization is a powerful motivator. So much of social services today is proscriptive and compliance driven that many lose sight of why they came to this "good" work in the first place. Social work focused only on compliance issues loses the depth of the commitment that defines meaningful work.

Organizational meaning can be defined by vision. If leadership can hold the vision that defines the organization, there is an opportunity to engage with all staff regarding what is meaningful about the work they perform. Vision is what the future is hoped to be. A shared vision of what type of future the organization wishes to create is a powerful tool that an administrator can utilize to engage staff and constituency groups. If social services become driven by a collective vision of what the future could be for children, youth, and families, as well as older adults and families, the outcomes for at-risk populations might improve. An example of a forward-looking statement is, "Our vision is to take collective action to support families and communities as they love and care for their children."

Commitment to meaningful work creates a backdrop from which a social services administrator can drive the discussion within the organization about practice and performance standards. If commitment to the vision has been established, commitment to the context within which the work is performed is of equal value to a social worker. In complex organizations, a discussion of context can be framed by the mission statement. Mission is how the agency is going to accomplish its vision, or the way in which the work is to be done. Mission connected to practice and performance standards allows an administrator to create a shared view of the desired future for at-risk children and families in their communities. An example of a mission statement is "to meet the need for quality human services for children, individuals, and families in their communities."

Administrators may find that by inspiring all agency members with the vision and mission, they will find staff more willing to deliver quality services because of a passion for the service and the outcome, rather than fear of being noncompliant. Also, leaders who fail to provide organizational meaning and context for their staff may find that employees will impose their own meaning and context for the organization. If the director continuously defines the agency's vision and mission, and continuously demonstrates the agency's core values (for example, respect, integrity, courage, and hope), then staff may be more likely to adopt these guidelines. Further, if the administrator values diversity as an integral component of giving meaning and context to the agency's work, then it is more likely the staff may follow. Surely staff, as a group, will not practice core values related to diversity unless the organization's leadership models the behavior.

Change as a Constant

Social service administrators are faced with one constant, and that is change. It is "so common within human service organizations that it almost does not seem like a special situation" (Weinbach, 1998, p. 286). If change is a constant that must be attended to, then agency directors and their organizations' ability to learn and assimilate change must be equal to or greater than the rate of change, a concept proposed over 70 years ago by English physicist Reg Revins. The creation of a learning environment throughout the organization is a first-order task. Learning environments within complex organizations take time and effort to develop. The first step of a director in creating a learning environment is to establish a team-learning approach at the senior leadership level. The time dedicated to identifying the elements of such an environment will go far in starting the transformation that team-building can accomplish within the organization. It is the standard from which a new social worker entering a child welfare organization will discover how important adherence to the professional practice and performance standards established by their profession will be met. It sets the stage for staff orientation.

Business Process Improvement

Social services administrators have to be vigilant about the "business-side" of their agencies. The impact that leadership can have on business process improvement is substantial. Improvements in reimbursement or claiming formulas can translate into millions of extra dollars of revenue. Business process improvements, when they are combined with other changes within an organization, sometimes can have unexpected practice impacts. Numerous studies have chronicled the need to address the problem of paperwork processing. Paperwork and documentation issues have tremendous impact on how social workers view their work environment. Administrators must value the benefits of applying new technologies at the line level. An administrator who cannot address the management needs of the organization through business process improvement is missing an important opportunity to demonstrate commitment to practice improvement. As emphasized at a Child Welfare League of America conference for executive directors, "Run your agency like a business, but remember the business you are in."

Outcome-Driven Administration

Outcomes are essential. Clients respond when they are being helped. Staff perceive the value of their interventions. Formal outcome measures indicate "whether a program has achieved its intended effects, realizing the goals that service staff members have set for their clients. It answers the question, does this service make a difference?" (Kluger and Baker, 1994, p. 47).

For example, how a child welfare administrator directs social work practice has become vitally important with the establishment of federal reporting through the mandated ASFA outcomes. Just as public schools are being evaluated through the federal "No Child Left Behind Act," now child welfare agencies are accountable through a set of national criteria. Constituency groups have a standard to judge the effectiveness of child welfare administrations, at least in the public sector. Measurable outcomes in child safety, well-being, and permanency also can be used to provide insight into the challenges inherent in delivering child and family services.

In the public sector, how administrators respond to the standards set by elected policy makers has a significant impact on the success of their endeavors. The appointment of public sector administrators is an important choice of the community's leadership, especially in large urban areas. Highly publicized failures to protect children in care have forced out a succession of agency directors, giving the appearance of "cleaning house." However, new administrators with the same old resources typically perpetuates a cycle of administrative turnover.

Risk management occupies a central role in all social service organizations to guard against tragic outcomes for clients and staff, along with protocols for interventions when crises occur. Defining a risk management strategy also impacts the method administrators choose to address practice and performance standards. Such standards not only contribute to outcomes, but also become key measures in how social workers understand their role within the organization. They help new social workers discover the importance of adhering to professional standards. In addition, standards provide the foundation for staff orientation and ongoing staff development. Quality assurance is an essential component of risk management. It provides a quarterly and then annual feedback loop, as recommended by the Council on Accreditation, to keep track of incidents, accidents, and grievances, listed by their frequency, nature, and severity.

Private or voluntary agency administrators are facing increased pressure from public sector organizations to meet contracted outcomes for service. Yet case management responsibilities between the public and the private sectors are not always well defined. The range of factors that influence the delivery of service has created an upsurge of interest in evidence-based practice. The private sector administrator is faced with the prospect of not being able to meet outcomes due to definitional and public policy factors, which often are difficult to translate into activities and performance standards that can be quantified.

Upon assuming administrative responsibility, a new director has to immediately demonstrate commitment to the agency's vision, mission, values, and goals while beginning to assess the organization's capacity. A review of the organization's current policies, procedures, and practices offers a starting point. Assessing the organization's capacity to perform is an important first step in any new administrator's tenure. A competent administrator also will assess the organization's planning and budgeting process, structure, internal and external communication systems, technology, union relations, staff training, human resource services, and employment practices. Attention to how management respects staff diversity and how staff, in turn, embrace client diversity is essential. An assessment of managerial and organizational capacity to meet the ASFA standards is now a primary responsibility of every child welfare administrator.

Planning and organizational structures abound within the array of social services. Variations on planning processes and organizational structure are diverse and varied. Public sector planning and organizational structures reflect the demands of the political and governmental entities that provide oversight and funding. Private sector planning and organizational structures generally operate on a smaller scale, and they have to take into account broader external factors that dictate service delivery. All of these processes and structures are subject to management and business process improvement initiatives. The "latest" management technique or business process improvement can catapult child welfare administrators into a spiral of change upon change, and the process also can seem "never ending" to social workers on the line. In this regard, consistency of planning and organizational stability are significant factors that shape staff perceptions regarding the effectiveness of administrators.

On a daily basis, administrators communicate with their social work and support staff in many ways and on various levels. How communication with staff is managed and utilized has an important impact on the effectiveness of the organization. Managerial communication is generally perceived as compliance driven. Social workers are provided with policy and procedural process updates. Legal and regulatory responsibilities drive reporting and work load issues. The time demands to complete documentation to maintain fiduciary compliance can be difficult. Administrators, for their part, have no choice but to address compliance issues in order to meet legal, contractual, regulatory, and procedural requirements. Compliance-driven administration can lead to dissonance, complicated by demographic diversity among management and staff. These inherent challenges can create rifts between administrative and practice staff unless the organization has a common vision of how its work impacts the lives of the children, families, and communities it serves.

FRAMEWORK FOR AN ETHICAL APPROACH TO DIVERSITY FOR CLIENTS AND THE STAFF WHO SERVE THEM

In the dozen years between The Hudson Institute's report (Johnston and Packer, 1987) which astonished corporate America with its revelation that the workforce was no longer predominately white and male, and Allison's (1999) conclusion that "The very success or failure of community programs in the next millennium will be determined to a high degree by the ability of agencies to comfortably, sensitively, and successfully deal with diverse populations" (p. 98), much has been written about managing the new multicultural workplace. Diversity training programs abound, and most human services agencies report that they value diversity and pluralism, that they recruit volunteers and staff from diverse populations, and that they both tolerate and value multiple cultures and groups. Yet, few indicate that staff diversity is *critical* to their efforts in serving diverse client populations, including children, youth, and families (Peterson, Betts, and Richmond, 2002).

Further, U.S. census data confirms changing demographics regarding ethnic diversity. "Over the last decade, immigrants and refugees from Central and South America, Africa, Eastern Europe, and the former Soviet Union—including thousands of children, youth, and families—have come to the United States seeking refuge, asylum, and opportunity. Their arrival has brought increased cultural diversity—and with that has come, in some cases, cultural misunderstandings and confusion" (Malik and Velazquez, Jr., 2002, p. 24). Cultural competence is essential. The Child Welfare League of America (2002) defines it as the ability of individuals and systems to respond respectfully and effectively to people of all cultures, races, ethnic backgrounds, sexual orientations, and faiths or religions in a manner that recognizes, affirms, and values the worth of individuals, families, tribes, and communities, and protects the dignity of each.

There is a dearth of literature addressing multicultural workplace issues as they relate to the GLBT population, either as staff or as consumers of services. Among the reasons to support the need for diversity in human services agencies are (a) to foster better morale, (b) to promote heightened creativity, (c) to improve decision making, and (d) to accomplish social justice (Esty, Griffin, and Hirsch, 1995, p. 21). It has also long been recognized that while many people do not feel comfortable dealing with people who differ from them, that difference can actually add value to an organization. That is because agencies—including the managers, supervisors, and line staff—tend to react to culturally different people in the same way as their peers, colleagues, and friends. As a result, prejudices found in communities are mirrored and acted out in the workplace (Henderson, 1994).

There is also the matter of acculturation. In considering GLBT acculturation, the concept itself must be modified. Usually acculturation is seen as the movement of a minority or "inferior" group into membership in a larger, dominant group. The GLBT people have the peculiar experience of moving *from* the dominant culture to a subculture. According to Goodwin (1989), GLBT acculturation is somewhat voluntary, sought rather than imposed, and GLBT people almost always retain membership in the dominant culture. Since neither prestige nor financial benefits are associated with affiliation with the subculture, it is inferred that the need to be with like-minded others is stronger than the stigma. Also, during acculturation, a process occurs in which one learns and internalizes folklore. When people are under stress, as GLBT people historically have been due to discrimination, folklore comes into consciousness as an accessible and acceptable coping mechanism. The reason for adapting this coping mechanism is that folklore is used to define territory by inhibiting outsiders' understanding of information, so that nonmembers are excluded and the community is protected (Kirshenblatt-Gimblett, 1983).

A cultural sea change relative to GLBT citizens is taking place in America. The Vermont legislature legalized same-gender civil unions in 2000 and the U.S. Supreme Court struck down sodomy laws in *Lawrence* v. *Texas* in 2003. Further, there have been predictions that Constitutional questions about same gender marriage eventually will be decided in favor of GLBT people (Wolfson, 2004). Simultaneously, GLBT professionals, who have always been present in human services agencies, are now part of the drive to ensure that efforts to achieve cultural diversity in agencies serving children, youth, and families are successful and effective. Yet the recent failure of legislation to support same-sex marriage in all eleven states where the legislation was proposed shows the mood of the country regarding equal opportunity for all citizens, and certainly undermines the "social justice" principles of the NASW Code of Ethics.

Statistics dominate discussions of GLBT-inclusion in organizational life, whether related to diversity training content, or to a Gay Pride Month celebration. Data point to the expectation that by 2005, white males will represent only an estimated 40 percent of all workers (Coile, 1999). Additionally, data are reported on the percentages of African Americans, Asians, women, and Hispanics in the work force (Cejka, 1993). The tendency to identify diversity as being only about gender or skin color has created a narrow perspective on diversity management (Ivancevich and Gilbert, 2000). This has resulted in an incomplete transformation of organizational culture (JobCircle.com, 1999). A typical narrow definition of diversity management is "the commitment on the part of the organization to recruit, retain, reward and promote minority and female employees" (Ivancevich and Gilbert, 2000, p. 76). Diversity management *must* be defined in a broader sense as "the commitment on the part of organizations to recruit, retain, reward, and promote a heterogeneous mix of productive, motivated and committed workers, including people of color, whites, females, and the physically challenged" (Ivancevich and Gilbert, 2000, p. 77). Such a definition is the first step toward improving organizational culture with respect to diversity. It understands and seeks to effectively deal with barriers in language, culture, age, ethnicity, marital status, religion, sexual orientation, and gender identity, abilities, and disabilities—in short, any characteristic that differentiates one individual from another.

Gaps in earnings between people of color and women have been well documented elsewhere (deAnda, Dolan, Lee-Eddie, Ellison, and Honkawa, 1998). However, it was only in the 2000 Census that *any* effort was made to actually quantify the numbers of same-sex couples and single households comprised of GLBT people in the United States. One study which emerged from that Census data shows that black lesbian couples are raising children at almost the same rate as black married couples, and that black same-sex couples raise children at twice the rate of white same-sex couples (National Black Justice Coalition, 2004).

Gathers (2003) recommended that, as part of a concerted effort to reduce the gaps between groups—whether in earnings, promotions, mentoring, or other aspects of organizational life—managers should raise certain basic questions:

- Do I treat all people with respect regardless of age, race, religion, sexual orientation, or gender identity?
- Do I encourage people of different backgrounds to work together to create unity?
- Am I sensitive to cultural differences?
- Do I believe that all people are created equal?
- Do I pay equal attention to each ethnic group's work performance?
- Do I value opportunities to learn more about people of other ethnic backgrounds?
- Am I more critical of one ethnic group than another?
- Do I believe that people need people, regardless of ethnicity?
- Am I now more fearful of one ethnic group than another?
- Do I support efforts to promote diversity?

An excellent exercise for students, staff, and administrators might be to see how many questions can be adapted to this checklist addressing sexual orientation, gender identity, and expression, and whether they identify sexual orientation as primary or secondary diversity. Administrators also should look at comparable job descriptions to ensure that there are no "glass ceilings" or "sticky floors" for GLBT employees, or any other minority group.

Another question for consideration is what impact diversity—or lack of it—in our work environments has on organizational operations and service delivery. An endless stream of academic and popular literature touts the benefits of diversity in the workplace. The set of activities recommended to achieve these benefits come under the heading of "diversity management," a voluntary organizational program designed to create greater inclusion of all individuals into informal workplace social networks and formal company programs (Gilbert, Stead, and Ivancevich, 1999). Sessa (1992) stated that "To manage diversity effectively, an organization must value diversity; it must have diversity, and it must change the organization to accommodate diversity and make it an *integral* part of the organization" (p. 37). Cox and Blake (1991) argued that proper management of cultural diversity could achieve the following benefits:

- Cost-cutting—reducing turnover and absenteeism;
- Resource acquisition—attracting the best personnel as the labor pool shrinks and changes;
- Marketing—bringing insight and cultural sensitivity to marketing efforts;
- Creativity—increasing creativity and innovation;
- Problem-solving—bringing a wider range of perspectives and more thorough critical analysis; and
- System flexibility—reacting to environmental changes faster and at less cost.

A number of these benefits have been cited by organizations as among the reasons they instituted same-gender partner health benefits and Family Medical Leave Act (FMLA) benefits to GLBT employees. It just made good business sense not to lose valuable employees to companies that were offering such benefits.

Over 25 years ago, social identity theory predicted that an individual's identity derives from memberships in cultural groups. It is important to honor differences that result from group memberships and equitably reward employees for dissimilar contributions (Tajfel and Turner, 1979). An "Ethical Decision Making Checklist" (Murphy, 1988) may encompass

- Identifying facts relevant to each decision;
- Assigning responsibility;
- Articulating benefits, rights, and justice implications;
- Analyzing available solutions;
- Identifying the solutions that would do the most to maximize benefits, reduce harm, respect rights, and increase fairness;
- Communicating to those involved;
- Assuring that decisions will have the intended outcome;
- Implementing the decision; and
- Evaluating whether the decision maximized benefits, reduced harm, respected rights, and treated all people fairly.

Administrators have special responsibilities to create a workplace free of harassment, as they set the tone for and model culturally competent behavior. Guidelines include

- Be attuned to intercultural program management;
- Assess your organization's level of cultural competence;
- Lead the way by arranging for continuous staff training in cultural competence and participate;
- Develop or update your cultural competence policies, involving your board if you have one;
- Require all members of your organization—from the receptionist to the CEO—to take continuing education in cultural competence; and
- Hire and retain a qualified, but diverse staff. Consider building an "international team" to assist with culturally specific care. At the least, designate one person as a diversity resource contact or for referrals (Malik and Velazquez, Jr., 2002, p. 25).

ADMINISTRATIVE CASE VIGNETTES AND PRACTICE GUIDELINES

Listed below are four case examples of challenges in administrative diversity that require an integration of best practice, agency policy, leadership, and advocacy, and administrative interventions are suggested. These interventions are based on the previously described NASW Code of Ethics (NASW, 1999)—competence, dignity, importance of human relationships, service, and social justice—as well as Murphy's (1988) "An Ethical Decision Making Checklist": identifying facts relevant to each decision; assigning responsibility; articulating benefits, rights, and justice implications; analyzing available solutions; identifying the solutions that would do the most to maximize benefits, reduce harm, respect rights, and increase fairness; communicating to those involved; assuring that decisions will have the intended outcome; implementing the decision; and evaluating whether the decision maximized benefits, reduced harm, respected rights, and treated all people fairly.

■ ■ ■ ■ ■

CASE STUDY 1   PATRICE

Patrice is a 16-year-old female who has grown up in the foster care system and is now living in a group home. Through neighbors, Patrice found her mother whom she had not seen for many years. Now living with a husband and children by him, Patrice's mother again rejected her. Patrice believes this rejection is because she told her mother that she is a lesbian. Patrice has threatened suicide with detailed descriptions of various plans, including hanging herself, jumping off an overpass, and getting herself shot by the police. As the group home administrator, what actions would you take?

PRACTICE GUIDELINES

Convening the management or administrative team to develop a culturally competent, strengths/needs assessment, oversee the interventions, and conduct a policy and program evaluation of the circumstances that led to this challenge as well as its resolution. The focus should be on how to integrate casework practice with Patrice to ensure her safety, well-being, and permanency (being connected to a safe relationship with at least one caring adult), as well as administrative practices to support the staff and ensure that the agency is minimizing risk to all. Specific interventions may include the following steps.

1. Providing round-the-clock shadowing for Patrice until a skilled clinician assesses that she is no longer at suicide risk, and this may include appropriate use of medication as prescribed by a psychiatrist.
2. Informing the agency's board of directors, as well as the public agency that placed her, of the risk and the extra funds that must be incurred to provide her with 24-hour protection; however, hospitalization should not be ruled out if clinically deemed essential.
3. Ensuring that both the child care and social work staff are trained/skilled in protecting and working with depressed young people, finding ways to help them grieve their rejections, and build their self-esteem while continuously keeping them safe.
4. Knowing that GLBTQ youth in the foster care system are at a high risk (Mallon, 2001); therefore, putting into place programs and services that have staff and caregivers (childcare workers, foster parents, caseworkers, managers) trained to be nonjudgmental, committed to being a safe haven, and able to work with birth parents to help address homophobia and improved relationships with their children (Sullivan, Sommer, and Moff, 2001).
5. Helping Patrice, when she is more stable, plan for her eventual transition from the group home, probably at the age of 18 when her "independent living" clock starts ticking. The intervention should include helping her begin to develop the protective and coping skills she mostly likely will need. Connecting Patrice to one caring, nurturing adult is essential, otherwise she may be destined to high-risk life on the streets.
6. Working with the agency's board of directors, public agency administration, and the community to ensure services and supports for young people like Patrice and, for prevention, work to reduce the number of youth who actually have to grow up in a child welfare system.

CASE STUDY 2   BABY S.

An 18-year-old gives birth prematurely to an infant with low birth weight, requiring an Apnea machine because of the irregular heartbeat. The mother leaves the hospital and returns to live with her own mother, aged 34, who also has some history of alcohol and other drug abuse. A caseworker is assigned to the baby and the mother. The baby is placed with a foster family on discharge from the hospital. The caseworker sets up an appointment to meet with the baby's mother to begin the case assessment and service plan. The night before the meeting, the baby dies. The police report indicates that the baby died from Sudden Infant Death

(continued)

346 CHAPTER NINE

CASE STUDY 2 Continued

Syndrome (SIDS), so no criminal charges were filed. However, the baby's mother and grandmother claim the baby died because the foster parents were of a different ethnicity from the baby, and did not care about the baby. They hired an attorney to file a civil suit against the agency and the foster parents, alleging negligence. Although the birth father had discontinued his relationship with the mother when she became pregnant, nonetheless joined in the suit. The agency serves a semirural community and the media picked up on the story, resulting in local news coverage. As the director of your agency, what actions would you take?

PRACTICE GUIDELINES
Convening the management or administrative team to develop a culturally competent, strengths/needs assessment, oversee the interventions, and conduct a policy and program evaluation of the circumstances that led to this challenge as well as its resolution. The focus should be on how to offer grief counseling and support for the birth family, and provide counseling and support for the foster family and staff, with special attention to the complexity of the tragedy raised by the adversarial nature of the law suit. Specific interventions should include the following steps.

1. Working with the agency's Communications Director, or using the Executive Director specifically if the agency is not large enough to have its own Communications or Public Relations staff member to give a statement to and work as appropriate with the media (Only one person in an agency should be designated and have the expertise to talk with any media representatives and every agency should have a policy to this effect.). Information shared with the media should include the expression of sympathy; the agency's internal process for investigating child deaths, the process of training caregivers and staff; and information about the dynamics of SIDS. It may be helpful to inform the media of how rare the occasion of a child death is in the agency, using the formula of multiplying the number of children in care by the number of days in the year in which children were safe. For example, if an agency has 20,000 infants and toddlers in care and this tragedy has not occurred in 5 years, then the agency has provided 36,500,000 days of care in which a child has not died from SIDS.
2. Offering to connect the birth family with resources for grief counseling, using a mental health agency that would support the NASW Code of Ethics.
3. Arranging grief counseling for the foster family and staff involved, ensuring that the counseling adheres to the NASW Code of Ethics.
4. Meeting with other foster parents and staff who are distressed about the media coverage and the issues. Some foster parents and staff may be angry with the birth family, feeling that they have no right to press charges when it was the birth mother's behavior that resulted in the baby being born so medically fragile; the birth father did not claim responsibility; and the paternal family did not step forward to offer kinship care.
5. Reviewing the agency's policies on the training and supervision that foster parents and staff must have when caring for and working with medically fragile babies.
6. Reporting back to the media and to the agency's governing body (i.e, a county board of supervisors) the outcomes of the case, that is exonerating the foster parents and using this tragedy as an example to inform the community about SIDS and foster care for medically fragile babies.

■ ■ ■ ■ ■

CASE STUDY 3   DERRICK

Derrick, aged 24, worked for 3 years as a childcare worker in a residential treatment facility in a community in which he was a minority. When he moved with friends to a large urban area, he immediately got another childcare worker job in residential treatment facility where most of the adolescents in care and many of the staff, including the executive director, were of his ethnicity. Derrick had excellent references including that he was a role model for the young people of all ethnicities, and he was an all-around solid childcare worker. Within a month or so after joining the new agency, Derrick's behavior began to change. Although other staff did not, he started to wear clothing that was too casual. He began to treat the children of his ethnicity differently, excusing or overlooking bad behavior. He was rude toward colleagues who were not of his ethnicity. As the residential treatment center administrator, what actions would you take?

PRACTICE GUIDELINES

Convening the management or administrative team to develop a culturally competent, strengths/needs assessment, oversee the interventions, and conduct a policy and program evaluation of the circumstances that led to this challenge as well as its resolution. The focus should be on how to integrate Kadushin's (1976) classic three components of supervision—administrative, educative, and supportive—with Derrick while ensuring appropriate care for the children on his watch and professional relationships with his colleagues. Specific tasks should include the following.

1. Fulfilling *administrative* responsibilities for the children in care, Derrick, and other staff, which could include
   - Having Derrick's supervisor meet with him to identify the agency's specific concerns, with documentation regarding time, place, circumstance, and behavior, and discuss Derrick's perspectives. If Derrick acknowledges a problem, move directly to educative/supportive responsibilities; if he does not, restate the terms of his probationary period and inform him of the behavior that is needed, the behavior that must change, the time frames, and the consequences.
   - Having a plan to intervene with a specific child or staff member should Derrick be observed treating them inappropriately.
2. Fulfilling *educative* responsibilities for Derrick, which could include clarifying the risks of his actions to the well-being of the children in his care, and to his working relationships with his colleagues.
3. Fulfilling *supportive* responsibilities for Derrick, which could include explaining surprise at his new behaviors, compared to the excellent references he had received in his previous childcare work; expressing concern over his behavior; asking him—without being intrusive—to consider if might be a connection between his change of professional behavior and his change of work, community, and so on. It may also be that Derrick has found a group with whom to identify and he may have pent-up feelings from quietly suffering discrimination in a previous setting. However, Derrick's supervisor is not his counselor or therapist so one of the ways the supervisor can be supportive is by referring Derrick to a mental health agency that supports the NASW Code of Ethics.

■ ■ ■ ■ ■

CASE STUDY 4   JUDY

Judy is an emergency response social worker for a public child welfare agency. She works in a unit that has three male social workers, and two other female social workers. The unit supervisor is male. The unit seems to work well together, and all six coworkers are friendly. In fact, they often have lunch together or go out together after work; no one in the unit has a significant other. The agency was required to have all staff attend a new sexual harassment training program; because of space limitations, only some staff could participate the first time. The unit supervisor randomly sent one male and two female social workers. When they returned the Monday after the two-day Thursday/Friday training, instead of talking with their other colleagues about their weekend activities (as they had for over a year), they filed sexual harassment charges against the three staff who did not attend, citing sexually explicit questions and discussions as the principal complaint. They also charged the unit supervisor for failure to intervene in the harassment. As the executive director of the agency, what actions will you take?

PRACTICE GUIDELINES

Convening the management or administrative team to develop a culturally competent, strengths/needs assessment, oversee the interventions, and conduct a policy and program evaluation of the circumstances that led to this challenge as well as its resolution. The focus should be on how to investigate the complaints, and review the agency's policies regarding sexual harassment identification, prevention, and intervention. Specific interventions should include the following.

1. Including the agency's human resources or personnel director in the entire process, to obtain consultation and direction. (While smaller agencies may not have a designated "human resources administrator," each agency must have one individual who holds a personnel management position.) That person must be experienced with sexual harassment regulations.
2. Including the agency's attorney in the entire process, to obtain consultation and direction. (While smaller agencies may not have a staff attorney, they must have at least a contractual attorney. That person must be experienced with legal proceedings regarding sexual harassment charges.)
3. Working diligently to have a timely investigation.
4. Determining an intervention plan based on the findings. Allegations may be founded because the unit supervisor was aware of sexual discussions in the workplace and failed to stop them; or they may unfounded because the unit supervisor was unaware and, further, the complainants were definitively complicit in discussions.
5. Determining a process for confidentiality regarding the issues of this specific case.
6. Providing up-to-date sexual harassment training for all staff, in which they sign that they are aware of and can adhere to their responsibilities.
7. Working with the unit supervisor and staff involved regarding conflict resolution and reassignment of duties as appropriate.
8. Ensuring that services to clients are maintained and not compromised through the entire investigation and resolution process.

CONCLUSION

If you read this chapter as a practitioner, hopefully you are more aware of the range of issues that affect the decisions of your administrators. Perhaps you have become intrigued by the challenges and are willing to explore taking on a supervisory or management position. If you are currently an administrator, perhaps you have been able to find information that validates your management approach, or you are now considering some new perspectives.

Administrators are ethically and professionally mandated to help their staff, boards, and financial backers—all the stakeholders, including clients—respect if not appreciate the mission of the agency and of any desired project. Rather than force a proposal's acceptance, the vision of what it can offer the people served should be emphasized. Instead of saying "Do as I tell you," the administrator should persuade with "Behold what might be!"

Administrators must be concerned with goal achievement, but need to go beyond the goals to their consequences. For example, the goal to find adoptive families for all children needing them is not really effective unless the consequences for the children and adoptive families are positive. Decision making is always a risk. According to Pecora, Whittaker, Maluccio, Barth, and Plotnik (2000), despite the proliferation of statutes, policies, and legal procedures, decision making is heavily influenced by availability of prevention and placement resources, values and biases of service providers, presence of advocates, attitudes of judges, ambiguities in abuse and neglect definitions, the imprecise nature of information about human behavior, and the impossibility of predicting the future.

Administrators must be self-aware, concerned, and proactive in order to help their clients, agencies, and communities. An important concept is that "Environment shapes behavior." A workplace that is friendly, helpful, and respectful of its staff sets the stage for staff respecting clients, colleagues, and the administration. But competent administrators cannot lead without a competent staff. So whatever one's role in service to others may be, it is hoped that this chapter has provided administrative basics for effective practice with diverse groups. This impact is essential since diversity is an integral part of services not only for at-risk children and families, but for all individuals and groups with whom we work.

CHAPTER TEN

SUMMARY AND CLOSING REMARKS

NEIL A. COHEN
School of Social Work, California State University, Los Angeles

THANH V. TRAN
Boston College, Chestnut Hill

SIYON Y. RHEE
School of Social Work, California State University, Los Angeles

Our book has endeavored to add to the body of child welfare practice knowledge by blending contemporary child issues with emphasis on practice skill enhancement. The authors have focused on serving communities, child welfare organizations, and families of different racial, ethnic, religious, economic, and structural backgrounds. Throughout, each chapter has emphasized the importance of utilizing a proactive, strengths-based practice strategy to maximize the quality, timeliness, and scope of the social services intervention.

Dale Weaver's chapter entitled "The Boundaries of Child Welfare" sets a tone for the book. The chapter walks the readers and students through the historical development of child welfare as social concerns, social problems, and a field of professional practice. This chapter presents a comprehensive overview of the history of child welfare in the United States and the developments of child welfare services and interventions. The readers learn how this nation's history has shaped the scopes and boundaries of child welfare public policies and services. Weaver carefully organized the developments of child welfare according to significant historical periods. He has discussed how economic and political conditions in each historical period influence social policies within the social welfare system and the directions of child welfare services. More importantly, Weaver's chapter helps the readers and students of child welfare appreciate the interconnections among historical, economic, political, and social changes that determine the nature of our child welfare systems. Finally, Weaver also has given the readers a concise review of child welfare policies, services, and interventions from both historical and multicultural perspectives.

The next chapter, "Fairness and Multicultural Competence in the Child Welfare System," coauthored by Clark and Gilman, has addressed fairness as one of the fundamental issues in Child Welfare practice. Although we all agree with the idea that all children should be treated equally, the reality often does not confirm our belief. In this chapter, the readers and students are introduced to the concept of "fairness" in child welfare from theoretical, practical, legal, policy, and political perspectives. For readers and students who are not familiar with sociological and legal theories of fairness and equity, the authors have offered a comprehensive explanation of social exchange theory, distributive justice, and procedural justice as they relate to child welfare system and practice. Furthermore, the chapter has highlighted problems with the child welfare system and services concerning ethnic/minority populations, such as African American children in foster care system nationwide, and how child welfare systems treat children differently because of their racial/ethnic identity. The students can learn from this chapter that fairness has to be the golden standard for all aspects of the child welfare system. To achieve this, child welfare workers and the child welfare system have to be culturally knowledgeable about diversity and have the right attitudes and values toward children and their needs in appropriate cultural and ethnic contexts.

When working with historically oppressed groups of children and their families at any levels of practice, child welfare workers' understanding of their experience, including their historical background and enduring episodes of discrimination and racism, is essential for effective service delivery. Additionally, given the enormously diverse groups of children, youth, and families served in the child welfare system, "knowledge among human service professionals of the cultural determinants of behavior is a first step toward enabling those who, for historical reasons, have not been full participants in mainstream culture" (Leigh, 1999, p. xi). It is our conviction that cultural awareness and competence in cross-cultural practice can enable child welfare professionals to provide more effective services and promote the cause of social justice in multicultural settings. However, it is not an easy task for the practitioners to determine which interventions are culturally appropriate and ethnic sensitive. Furthermore, the term "cultural competence" is not well defined and lacks consensus among human service practitioners over the years.

To become a culturally competent worker, our authors throughout this book have emphasized the importance of the workers' recognition of and openness to the others' cultures and self-awareness of their own values, prejudices, and racist attitudes. It has been discussed throughout the book that knowledge of other cultures and culturally competent practice skills, which are vital in transcultural work, can be acquired through a variety of sources including genuine interest in other cultures, ongoing practice experience with multicultural clients, written materials, and consultation with ethnic community leaders.

Our authors draw attention to the importance of linking culturally competent practice with relevant theoretical perspectives through which theory and cross-cultural practice reinforce each other. Among numerous perspectives, the Generalist,

Strengths, and Empowerment approaches are highlighted as overarching perspectives for multicultural child welfare practice with children, youth, and families. Throughout the book, our authors have focused extensively on the interaction between individual systems and their broader environments such as families, groups, organizations, and communities as a key component of generalist practice. To bring about positive changes in ethnically diverse children and families, special attention was given to their strengths, capacities, resources, and empowerment, which are consistent with the Educational Policy and Accreditation Standards adopted by the Council on Social Work Education in 2004 (CSWE, 2004).

Within the holistic framework of theoretical perspectives, a variety of ethnic-sensitive intervention strategies have been introduced, which can be successfully applied by child welfare practitioners and students in working with diverse populations in many different settings. For example, many African American youth are confronted with the challenges of poverty, lack of quality education, negative stereotypes, racial discrimination, and involvement in delinquent acts. Coach's chapter "Child Welfare Perspectives and Approaches with African American Children, Youth and Families" has presented an Afrocentric approach as an effective intervention model that can significantly promote African American children's sense of self-worth and inner strengths. According to Coach, through this approach, child welfare practitioners can successfully explore their aspirations, build on their strengths, and thus empower them to become socially responsible individuals.

Ledesma's chapter entitled "American Indian and Alaska Native Children: A Legacy of Suffering, Survival and Strength" has also revealed that the present circumstance of American Indians and Alaska Native (AI/AN) children and families is directly related to histories of American colonialism and atrocious experiences of trauma and multiple losses. As highlighted in other chapters, this author has emphasized that to engage in effective working relationships with the AI/AN clients, it is crucial for child welfare practitioners to develop knowledge about their historical, cultural, social, and political backgrounds. It is important to understand that their presenting problem which brings them to the attention of practitioners, help-seeking behaviors, treatment expectations, and possible solutions are drastically affected by these macrosystems. Especially, according to the author, knowledge about the history and provisions of the Indian Child Welfare Act (P.L. 95-608) is helpful in working with AI/AN children, youth, and families in their communities. Among a variety of treatment models, Ledesma suggests that "attachment theory" and "basic understanding of their unresolved grief and loss experiences" will help the practitioner make comprehensive assessments and enhance successful intervention outcomes.

Rhee and Huynh-Hohnmaum's chapter entitled "Multicultural Child Welfare Practice with Asian and Pacific American Children, Youth, and Families" has offered the readers an overview of research findings and practice issues concerning this ethnically and culturally diverse population. The authors address the myths and reality concerning child welfare issues within this population. The chapter points out that contrary to their general stereotype of an intact family, immigrant Asian and Pacific Islander (API) families were reported to experience a variety of problems ranging from domestic violence, divorce, parent–child conflict, substance abuse, juvenile delinquency, unemployment, and discrimination, all of which have a significant bearing on API children's psychological well-being.

Underutilization of formal services in proportion to their population size among API families has been identified as one of the major service delivery issues. Rhee and Huynh-Hohnbaum in this chapter have cautioned that this underutilization of service should not lead to the false assumption that there is no need for services in this population. It is highly probable that the low utilization of services has more to do with the lack of appropriate services and barriers to service than the lack of service need in this population. There are four broad categories of barriers to seeking and maintaining services among API families—cognitive, affective, value orientation, and physical and structural barriers. The authors provide guidelines for culturally relevant and appropriate practice in multidisciplinary child welfare settings within an overarching framework of generalist, empowerment, and strengths perspectives with a special emphasis on the client's problem-solving process. When working with API children and families, according to Rhee and Huynh-Hohnbaum, the knowledge of indigenous interventions and a constructive critique of Western interventions that contradict the traditional API values are crucial for successful treatment outcomes. For example, it is important for child welfare practitioners to understand that deeply ingrained in the Eastern culture is the significance of the family, which often goes against the individualism of Western culture. Western professionals, sometimes, may view a family's involvement as unnecessary, intrusive, and even pathological in working with API youth and adolescents. However, when working with API children, the practitioner should be sensitive to the child's fear of isolation from the family and understand the need to treat API children with their families conjointly.

Negroni-Rodríguez and DeLa Cruz-Quiróz in "Multicultural Child Welfare Practice with Latino Children, Youth, and Families" have emphasized that many problems experienced by Latino children, youth, and their families are attributed to external sources. The authors have suggested that, when working with this population, child welfare workers must explore the family's experiences of poverty, availability of adequate resources and natural support systems, immigration/migration-related hardships as well as levels of acculturation, and experiences of racial discrimination and oppressive treatment. Generalist interventions at different levels involving individual, family, group, community, and the society in general through the development and implementation of ethnic-sensitive policies and direct services have been highlighted by the authors to help Latino children, youth, and their families effectively. The two authors have demonstrated that their histories of being victimized by racial discrimination and the bureaucratic nature of the systems have contributed to lack of trust in formal services and service providers among Latino families. It is crucial, therefore, for child welfare workers to take into consideration their values, belief systems, unique experiences, help-seeking behaviors and coping mechanisms when conducting multidimensional assessments and implementing change-oriented intervention strategies. Among many useful strategies, it is particularly important to utilize the support of extended/blended family members, and/or compadres/padrinos (godfather), and comadres/madrinas (godmother) when working with Latino children, youth, and their families.

Fitzpatrick, Limb, and Bushfield in "Social Services among White Ethnic and Middle Eastern Children, Youth, and Families" have insightfully pointed out that the continued influx of Middle Easterners and other white ethnic groups to America in the 1990s has shaped non-Hispanic white populations increasingly diverse. And yet, the amount of literature focusing on child welfare issues and practice targeting these groups is extremely scarce. This chapter presents effective child welfare intervention strategies as they specifically relate to the Irish, Italians, Russian Jews, Jewish and Palestinian immigrants, and Arab Americans. The authors highlight that their multi-generational families are often structured differently from other white American nuclear families, and that their intergenerational relationships are much more likely to be intense. As such, when working with children, youth, and families with these ethnic backgrounds, child welfare workers need to take into account the family's expectation with authority and power, and its emphasis on the importance of the whole family, rather than just the individual. Additionally, in families where the gender roles are very hierarchical, it is crucial to involve the father in the intervention process.

Refugees are consequences of war, calamities, political and religious persecutions, and other types of human exploitations. From the birth of this nation, refugees of all types from all over the globe have arrived here to seek asylum. During the twentieth century, the United States has opened her arms to receiving refugees fleeing from the Nazi regime, from communist countries, and from natural and man-made calamities in almost every continent. Refugee children and youth arriving here by themselves or with families often bring with them multiple physical, emotional, and social problems that require special attention from the child welfare institutions. A wide range of experiences in organized violence, torture, trafficking, and other traumatic events among refugee and asylum-seeking children and their families make this population particularly vulnerable to various health and mental health problems such as PTSD and contracting the HIV virus as a result of rape and sexual abuse.

In general, very little is known about the key issues facing refugee and asylum-seeking children and their families throughout the world. Berthold's chapter entitled "Transcultural Approaches in Working with Traumatized Refugee and Asylum-Seeking Children, Youth and Their Families" is one of the rare-published materials in human service practice fields. Berthold's chapter helps readers learn valuable information about the challenges confronting refugee children and their families in the United States, such as physical and psychological trauma, economic hardships, and the breakdown of their support systems. This chapter has also emphasized the needs for child welfare professionals to understand the refugees' experiences and their cultures and value systems in order to plan and implement meaningful interventions. Berthold has provided useful suggestions and guidelines for clinicians and social service providers seeking assessments and interventions with this growing population. Special attention is given to such principles as transcultural and trauma-oriented assessments and interventions.

Berthold finds that a theoretical framework based on narrative and solution-focused approaches is well suited to work with this population. The author informatively describes a narrative therapy, pioneered by Michael White and David Epston, as being relevantly conceptualized and embedded in cultural, social, and political contexts in which the meaning of our own lives out of the stories available to us can be developed. According to Berthold, solution-focused brief therapy developed by Peter De Jong, Insoo Berg, and Steve de Shazer can competently address the issues experienced by immigrant refugee children and their families by facilitating the process of people's generating their own solutions instead of overemphasizing their problems.

Ethnic diversity among clients affects not only direct practice with children and families, but administration of various child welfare agencies and organizations. As Allison (1999) noted in her article, "Organizational Barriers to Diversity in the Workplace," the success of community-based programs in the future largely depends on how proactively they respond to the needs of diverse populations. Yet, the current organizational culture is not very responsive to diversity issues, and the premises underlying organizational functioning are predominantly monocultural. "Organizations, then, must critically evaluate their nature and understand the prominence of the status quo in the continuation of inequitable practices and policies" (Allison, 1999, p. 96).

Pasztor et al.'s chapter entitled "Administrative Issues in Diversity" has addressed a wide range of issues facing administrators as well as staff and clients in multiethnic child welfare settings. This chapter has provided an overview of the core elements of administrative principles that facilitate effective service delivery to racially/ethnically diverse client groups. The authors highlight that, fundamentally, the administrative commitment and tasks of all child welfare organizations ought to aim to increase their function that helps lead to a more "just society." With this overarching organizational goal in mind, the authors provide seven essential administrative principles for child welfare administrators and other decision makers. Some of those principles include "Administrative actions should lead to just consequences," "The agency structure ought to insure a democratic, minimally stratified environment," and "The administrator promotes mutual accountability to insure the highest ethical level of practice." The authors have envisioned that an effective as well as ethical administrative approach acknowledges the interrelatedness of agency and community, worker and client, administrator and staff, and their mutual support and influence on each other.

This truly is a challenging time to examine and discuss issues of diversity relating to the delivery of quality social services to children, youth, and families and making them culturally accessible in this country. A few examples that illustrate this challenge are the increasing efforts to thwart affirmative action policies; to restrict and more closely monitor immigration from Mexico, Central America, and the Middle East; to reduce or otherwise make more punitive welfare benefits; and to reduce financial aid for needy college students, the majority of whom are students of color. As well, we can readily observe the deepening schism between the haves and the have-nots, and between liberal and conservative political camps. These forms of polarization add to the challenge human service professionals encounter in their everyday work with clients of diverse backgrounds.

Our authors, cognizant of these challenges, rather than viewing diversity as a liability, through discussion and illustration, have consistently conceptualized diversity as a strength and resource. For what is this country if it hasn't always been a complex mosaic of diversity? New arrivals, fifth-generation inhabitants, speakers of many languages (at our university, California State University, Los Angeles, there are no fewer than 150 languages spoken), different cultures, values, interests, and family structure, to name but a few, all characterize present-day living in the United States.

We should note that regardless of a family's characteristics and background, all families, to varying degrees, seek the opportunities of prosperity, freedom, and security offered in this country. Diversity in this country, as has been discussed throughout, should be seen through the multifaceted prisms of class, oppression, privilege, opportunity, race, ethnicity, religion, age, education, gender preference, sexual preference, state of health and mental health, urban or rural background, length of time in the United States, or any combination of the aforementioned. None of these variables are mutually exclusive and some, including race, class, education, opportunity, privilege and oppression, are often mutually reinforcing. This understanding, sensitivity to diversity, tolerance of differences, and ability to put this knowledge into effective practice are salient features that should inform social services work with children, youth, and families.

Authors of this book have taken on the challenging task of operationalizing how these multicultural variables influence and shape the social contract which takes place between social work professionals and their child welfare clients. We have endeavored to provide a clearly presented, in-depth overview of the history, growth, and development of the child welfare movement in this country. Specific emphasis has been focused on working with African American, American Indian and Alaska Native, Asian Pacific Islander, Latino, white, and refugee and asylum-seeking children, youth, and families. Throughout, the authors have noted that there are distinct differences within culturally different groups. There is no "modal type" Asian Pacific Islander, African American, Latino, American Indian, and whites. Examined closely, the reader will quickly discern that there are some 50–80 distinct cultures within the API group alone. The term "Latino" covers a broad range of distinct nationalities and cultures ranging from Central Americans, Puerto Ricans, Latin Americans, Mexicans, and so on. Furthermore, Rita Ledesma's chapter indicates that there are 562 federally recognized tribal nations and Alaska Native villages. Tanya Fitzpatrick et al. in their chapter on white ethnics have noted that it is difficult to describe white Americans as many can trace their ancestry to the following groups: English, German, Irish, French, Scottish, Polish, Dutch, Swedish, Norwegian, Russian, Czech, Slovakian, Hungarian, Welsh, Danish, and Portuguese.

Our authors have presented new and important material concerning work with torture victims, the issues surrounding equity and fairness in the child welfare system, and administrative, policy practices and their interface with multicultural dynamics in the arena of child welfare. Writers of this book, both male and female, come from many different racial, ethnic, and religious backgrounds. As well, their life experiences include different international birthplaces, enriched by differing cultural lifestyles and growth and development opportunities. Yet, they are of one voice in sharing their concern, dedication, and expertise in clarifying and providing quality practice with multicultural children, youth, and families.

Throughout, emphasis has been on providing an informed, strengths-based perspective in working with multicultural clients. "Front-loading" of social services in child welfare has been discussed throughout this book as the provision of timely, relevant interventions that can significantly reduce the many problems and issues occurring in working with children, youth, and families. Too often policies and practices reflect a reactive, money-chasing problems approach in child welfare. What for-profit company could stay in business if they spent $60,000–80,000 per child in a residential treatment facility when this could have been avoided by providing the child's family up-front, timely, resource-rich, expert intervention for 1/10th the cost?

Moreover, while sensitive, effective culturally competent social work practice is desirable, it is not always sufficient to bring about the positive changes sought in working with children, youth, and families. Fellin (2000) among others has noted that "the historical trend in our knowledge base has moved from an emphasis on cultural sensitivity, through cultural competence, to critical consciousness regarding oppression, status differences and structures of inequality" (as quoted in Anderson and Carter, 2003). Budding social work professionals and students need to fully understand that practice takes place in a politically charged, policy-driven arena. Far too often, the vicissitudes of this country's collective political will can have, and have had, negative consequences for decent housing, education, employment, and health and safety especially for minority families and their children. Human service professionals spend too much of their time trying to remediate questionable policy decisions that have placed their clients at a distinct disadvantage. As Michael Lipsky (1980) pointed out in his seminal book, *Street-Level Bureaucracy* over two decades ago, finding resources and making them culturally sensitive are still daunting tasks that can be attested to by human service workers on the front lines.

Our future rests with our children and their children's children. How we prepare them for their future is a daunting task for which all of us are responsible—family, neighborhood, community, region, nation, and the world. Human service professionals will continue to provide quality care to children, youth, and families to the extent that they enhance their sensitivity to differences and reach out to build linkages across and among peoples, places, and organizations. We trust that this book will add in that journey.

REFERENCES

■ ■ ■ ■ ■ ▬▬▬▬▬▬▬▬▬▬▬▬▬▬▬▬▬▬▬▬▬▬▬▬▬▬▬▬

CHAPTER 1

Abramovitz, Mimi. (1996). *Regulating the Lives of Women: Social Welfare Policy from Colonial Times to the Present.* Revised Edition. Boston, MA: South End Press.

Archard, David William. (2003). *Children, Family and the State.* Burlington, VT: Ashland Publishing Company.

Aries, Philippe. (1962). *Centuries of Childhood: A Social History of Family Life.* Robert Baldick, translator. New York, NY: Vintage Books.

Besharov, Douglas J. (Ed.) (2003). *Family and Child Well-Being After Welfare Reform.* New Brunswick, NJ: Transaction Publishers.

Billingsley, Andrew and Giovannoni, Jeanne M. (1972). *Children of the Storm: Black Children and American Child Welfare.* New York, NY: Harcourt Brace Jovanovich.

Brogan, Hugh. (1999). *The Penguin History of the USA.* New York: Penguin Books.

Campbell, Bruce A. and Trilling, Richard J. (Eds.) (1980). *Realignment in American Politics: Toward A Theory.* Austin, TX: University of Texas Press.

Children's Bureau. (2004). Native American Community-Based Family Resource and Support Program. *Children's Bureau Express.* Author. Available from: http://cbexpress.acf.hhs.gov.

Cook, Jeanne F. (1996). A history of placing-out: The orphan trains. *Child Welfare,* 74(1).

Cunningham, Hugh. (1995). *Children & Childhood in Western Society since 1500.* London: Longman.

Davis, Allen F. (2000). *American Heroine: The Life and Legend of Jane Addams.* Chicago, IL: Ivan R. Dee.

Day, Phyllis J. (2003). *A New History of Social Welfare.* 4th Edition. New York, NY: Allyn and Bacon.

Deloria, Jr., Vine and Lytle, Clifford M. (1983). *American Indians, American Justice.* Austin, TX: University of Texas Press.

Downs, Susan Whitelaw, Moore, Ernestine, McFadden, Emily Jean, Michaud, Susan M., and Costin, Lela B. (2004). *Child Welfare and Family Services: Policies and Practices.* 7th Edition. Boston, MA: Allyn and Bacon.

Epstein, William M. (1999). *Children Who Could Have Been: The Legacy of Child Welfare in Wealthy America.* The University of Wisconsin Press.

Foner, Eric. (1988). *Reconstruction: America's Unfinished Revolution.* 1st Perennial Classics Edition, 2002. New York, NY: Harper and Row.

Golden, Renny. (1997). *Disposable Children: America's Child Welfare System.* Belmont, CA: Wadsworth Publishing.

Gordon, Linda. (1994). *Pitied but not Entitled: Single Mothers and the History of Welfare.* New York, NY: The Free Press.

Gordon, Linda. (1999). *The Great Arizona Orphan Abduction.* Cambridge, MA: Harvard University Press.

Handler, Joel and Hasenfeld, Yeheskel. (1991). *The Moral Construction of Poverty: Welfare Reform in America.* Newbury Park, CA: Sage Publications.

Heywood, Colin. (2001). *A History of Childhood: Children and Childhood in the West from Medieval to Modern Times.* Cambridge: Polity Press.

Hogan, Patricia Turner and Siu, Sau-Fong. (1988). Minority children and the child welfare system: An historical perspective. *Social Work,* November–December, 493–498.

Iglehart, Alfreda P. and Becerra, Rosina M. (1995). *Social Services and the Ethnic Community.* Project Heights, IL: Waveland Press.

Johnson, Paul. (1997). *A History of the American People.* New York, NY: HarperPerennial.

Jones, Jacqueline. (1992). *The Dispossessed: America's Underclass From the Civil War to the Present.* New York, NY: Basic Books.

Kahn, Alfred J. (1979). *Social Policy and Social Services.* 2nd Edition. New York, NY: Random House.

Katz, Michael B. (1986). *In the Shadow of the Poorhouse: A Social History of Welfare in America.* New York, NY: Basic Books.

Kolko, Gabriel. (1984). *Main Currents in Modern American History.* New York, NY: Pantheon Books.

Lindsey, Duncan. (2004). *The Welfare of Children.* 2nd Edition. Oxford University Press.

Lubove, Roy. (1965). *The Professional Altruist: The Emergence of Social Work as a Career.* Cambridge, MA: Harvard University Press.

Mannes, Marc. (1995). Factors and events leading to the passage of the Indian Child Welfare Act. *Child Welfare,* 74(1).

McPhatter, Anna R. (1997). Cultural competence in child welfare: What is it? How do we achieve it? What happens without it? *Child Welfare,* 76(1), 255–278.

National Association of Social Workers. (2001). *NASW Standards for Cultural Competence in Social Work Practice.* Washington, DC: Author.

Nelson, Barbara J. (1984). *Making an Issue of Child Abuse: Political Agenda Setting for Social Problems.* Chicago, IL: The University of Chicago Press.

Olson, James S. and Wilson, Raymond. (1984). *Native Americans in the Twentieth Century.* Urbana and Chicago, IL: University of Illinois Press.

Pardeck, John T. (2002). *Children's Rights: Policy and Practice.* New York, NY: The Haworth Social Work Practice Press.

Pecora, Peter J., Whittaker, James K., Maluccio, Anthony N., and Barth, Richard P. (2000). *The Child Welfare Challenge: Policy, Practice, and Research.* 2nd Edition. New York, NY: Aldine de Gruyter.

Piven, Frances Fox and Cloward, Richarad A. (1971). *Regulating the Poor: The Functions of Public Welfare.* New York, NY: Vintage Books.

Platt, Anthony M. (1977). *The Child Savers: The Invention of Delinquency.* 2nd Edition. Chicago, IL: University of Chicago Press.

Quadagno, Jill. (1994). *The Color of Welfare: How Racism Undermined the War on Poverty.* New York, NY: Oxford University Press.

Reisch, Michael and Andrews, Janice. (2002). *The Road Not Taken: A History of Radical Social Work in the United States.* New York, NY: Brunner-Routledge.

Roberts, Dorothy. (2002). *Shattered Bonds: The Color of Child Welfare.* New York, NY: Basic Books.

Scott, W. Richard and Meyer, John W. (1994). *Institutional Environments and Organizations: Structural Complexity and Individualism.* Thousand Oaks, CA: Sage Publications.

Sealander, Judith. (2003). *The Failed Century of the Child: Governing America's Young in the Twentieth Century.* Cambridge: Cambridge University Press.

Skocpol, Theda. (1989). Sociology's historical imagination, pp. 1–21 in Theda Skocpol (Ed.), *Vision and Method in Historical Sociology.* Cambridge: Cambridge University Press.

Skocpol, Theda. (1992). *Protecting Soldiers and Mothers: The Political Origins of Social Policy in the United States.* Cambridge, MA: Harvard University Press.

Stein, Theodore J. (1991). *Child Welfare and the Law.* White Plains, NY: Longman Publishing.

U.S. Census Bureau. (2003). Poverty in the United States: 2002. Author. Available from www.census.gov/prod/2003pubs/p60–222.pdf.

Veronico, Anthony J. (1983). One Church, One Child: Placing children with special needs. *Children Today, 12,* 6–10.

Weaver, Hillary N. and White, Barry J. (1999). Protecting the future of indigenous children and nations: An examination of the Indian Child Welfare Act. *Journal of Health and Social Policy, 10*(4), 35–50.

Wilensky, Harold and Lebeaux, Charles. (1965). *Industrial Society and Social Welfare.* 2nd Edition. New York, NY: Russell Sage Foundation.

Zelizer, Viviana A. (1985). *Pricing the Priceless Child: The Changing Social Value of Children.* New York, NY: Basic Books.

Zinn, Howard. (2003). *A People's History of the United States: 1492–Present.* New York: HarperCollins.

CHAPTER 2

Adams, J.S. (1965). Inequity in social exchange. In Berkowitz, L. (Ed.), *Advances in Experimental Social Psychology Volume 2* (pp. 267–299). New York: Academic Press.

Annie E. Casey Foundation. (2001). *Family to Family: Tools for Rebuilding Foster Care.* Baltimore, MD: Author.

Ards, S., Chung, C. et al. (1998). The effects of sample selection bias on racial differences in child abuse reporting. *Child Abuse & Neglect, 22*(2), 103–115.

Ards, S. and Harrell, A. (1993). Reporting of child maltreatment: A secondary analysis of the National Incidence surveys. *Child Abuse & Neglect, 17*(3), 337–344.

Ards, S., Myers, S., Malkis, A., Sugrue, E., and Zhou, L. (2003). Racial disproportionality in reported and substantiated child abuse and neglect: An examination of systematic bias. [Special Double Issue: The overrepresentation of children of color in the child welfare system]. *Children and Youth Services Review, 25*(5/6), 375–392.

Baird, C., Ereth, J., and Wagner, D. (1999). *Research-based Risk Assessment: Adding Equity to CPS Decision Making.* Madison, WI: Children's Research Center.

Berger, P.L. and Luckmann, T. (1966). *The Social Construction of Reality.* Garden City, NY: Doubleday & Co.

Berger, J., Zelditch, M., Anderson, B., and Cohen, B. (Eds.) (1972). Structural aspects of distributive justice: A status value formulation. *Sociological Theories in Progress.* Boston MA: Houghton-Mifflin.

Berns, D. (2001). Addressing poverty and child welfare issues. In A. Sallee, H., Lawson, and K. Briar-Lawson (Eds.), *Innovative Practice with Vulnerable Children and Families.* Dubuque, IA: eddie bowers publishing.

Berns, D. and Drake, B. (1999). Combining child welfare and welfare reform at a local level. *Policy and Practice. The Journal of the American Public Human Services Association, 57*(1), 26–34.

Boas, F. (1967). *Kwakiutl Ethnography.* Helen Codere (Ed.). Chicago, IL: Prentice Hall.

Brooks, D. and James, S. (2003). Willingness to adopt black foster children: Implications for child welfare policy and recruitment of adoptive families. [Special Double Issue: The overrepresentation of children of color in the child welfare system]. *Children and Youth Services Review, 25*(5/6), 463–489.

Center on an Aging Society. (2004). Cultural competence in health care. *Issue Brief on Challenges for the 21st Century: Chronic and Disabling Conditions,* No. 5. Washington, DC: Georgetown University Health Policy Institute.

Child Welfare League of America. (2000). *Demographic Fact Sheet.*

Clark, S.J. and McCormick, K. (2000). Linking a competency-based public child welfare curriculum with field work: Achieving agreement about who is responsible for teaching what. In G. Kenyon and R. Power (Eds.), *No Magic: Readings in Social Work Field Education,* 129–147. Toronto Canada: Canadian Scholars' Press.

Cook, K. and Hegvedt, K. (1983). Distributive justice, equity and equality. *Annual Review of Sociology, 9,* 217–241.

Courtney, M., Barth, R., Berrick, J., Brooks, D., Needell, B., and Park, L. (1996). Race and child welfare services: Past research and future directions. *Child Welfare, 75*(2).

Cross, T.L., Bazron, R.J., Dennis K.W., and Issacs, M.R. (1989). *Towards a Culturally Competent System of Care,* volume 1. Washington, DC: Georgetown University Child Development Center.

Denby, R., Curtis, C., and Alford, K. (1998, January–February). Family preservation services and special populations: The invisible target. *Families in Society: The Journal of Contemporary Human Services, 79.*

De Panfilis, D. (2002). Report to the California Stakeholders' Early Intervention Workgroup. Sacramento CA: California Department of Social Services.

Derezotes, D.M., Testa, M.F., and Poertner J. (Eds.) (2005). *Race Matters: Examining the Overrepresentation of African Americans in the Child Welfare System.* Washington, DC: Child Welfare League of America.

Dworkin, R. (1978). *Taking Rights Seriously.* Cambridge, MA: Harvard University Press.

Emerson, R. (1981). Social Exchange. In M. Rosenberg and R. Turner (Eds.), *Social Psychology.* New York: Basic Books.

Fadiman, A. (1997). *The Spirit Catches You and You Fall Down.* New York: Farrar, Strauss and Giroux.

Finkelstein, M., Wamsley, M., and Miranda, D. (2002). What keeps children in foster care from succeeding in school? *Views of Early Adolescents and the Adults in Their Lives.* New York, NY: Vera Institute of Justice.

Fluke, J., Yuan, Y., Hedderson, J., and Curtis, P. (2003). Disproportionate representation of race and ethnicity in child maltreatment: Investigation and victimization. *Children and Youth Services Review, 25*(5/6), 359–373. (Special Double Issue: The overrepresentation of children of color in the child welfare system).

Garland, D.R. and Escobar, D. (1988). Education for cross-cultural social work practice. *Journal of Social Work Education, 3,* 229–241.

Garland, A.F., Landsverk, J.A., and Lau A.S. (2003, May). Racial/ethnic disparities in mental health service use among children in foster care. *Children and Youth Services Review, 5*(5), 491–507.

Garrett, M.T., Borders, L.D., Crutchfield, L.B., Torres-Rivera, E., Brotherton, D., and Curtis, R. (2001). Multicultural supervision: A paradigm of cultural responsiveness for supervisors. *Multicultural Counseling and Development, 29,* 147–158.

Gatmon, D., Jackson, D., Koshkarian, L., Martos-Perry, N., Molina, A., Patel, N., and Rodolfa, E. (2001). Exploring ethnic, gender, and sexual orientation variables in supervision. Do they really matter? *Journal of Multicultural Counseling and Development, 29*(2), 102–113.

Geroski, A. and Knauss, L. (2000). Addressing the needs of foster children with a school counseling program. *ACSA Professional School Counseling, 3*(3), 152–161.

Green, M.Y. (2001). Balancing the scales: Targeting disproportionality in child welfare and juvenile justice. *Children's Voice.* Washington DC: Child Welfare League of America.

Haj-Yahia, M. (1997). Culturally sensitive supervision of Arab social work students in western universities. *Social Work, 42*(2), 166–175.

Hardy-Desmond, S., Langston, E.J., Pierce, D., and Reilly, T. (2001). Competent practice: Diversity, racism, and heterosexism. In A.L. Sallee, H. Lawson, and K. Briar-Lawson (Eds.), *Innovative Practices with Vulnerable Children and Families,* pp. 145–163. Dubuque, Iowa: eddie bowers publishing, inc.

Harris, M. and Courtney, M. (2003). Interaction of race ethnicity and family structure with respect to the timing of family reunification. [Special Double Issue: The overrepresentation of children of color in the child welfare system]. *Children and Youth Services Review, 25*(5/6), 409–429.

Hird, J.S., Cavalieri, C.E., Dulko, J.P., Felice, A.A.D., and Ho, T.A. (2001). Visions and realities: Supervisee perspectives on multicultural supervision. *Journal of Multicultural Counseling and Development, 29,* 114–130.

Hochschild, J. (1981). *What's Fair? American Beliefs about Distributive Justice.* Cambridge, MA: Harvard University Press.

Homans, G. (1958). Social behavior as exchange. *The American Journal of Sociology, 63,* 597–606.

Jackson, V. (2003, Summer). 12 steps to lessen disproportionality in child welfare. *Best Practices/Next Practices Newsletter* [Special Issue on mental health in child welfare: A focus on children and families]. Washington DC: National Child Welfare Resource Center for Family Centered Practice, Learning System Group.

Johnson, L.B. (1965). *Public Papers of the Presidents of the United States: Lyndon B. Johnson, 1965.* Volume II, entry 301, 635–640. Washington, DC: Government Printing Office, 1966.

Lomawaima, K.T. (1994). *They Called it Prairie Light: The Story of Chilocco Indian School.* Lincoln: University of Nebraska Press.

Lowenthal, B. (1999). Effects of maltreatment and ways to promote children's resiliency. *Childhood Education, 75*(4), 204–210.

Lum, D. (1999). *Social Work Practice and People of Color: A Process-Stage Approach*. Pacific Grove, CA: Brooks-Cole.

McLagan, P.A. (1997). Competencies: The next generation. *Training and Development*, *51*(5), 40–48.

National Association of Social Workers. (2000). *NASW Code of Ethics*. Washington, DC: Author.

National Association of Social Workers, National Committee on Racial and Ethnic Diversity. (2001). *NASW Standards for Cultural Competence in Social Work Practice*. Washington, DC: Author. Approved by NASW Board of Directors June 23, 2001.

Needell, B., Webster, D., Cuccaro-Alamin, S., Armijo, M., Lee, S., Brookhart, A., and Lery, B. (2003). *Performance Indicators for Child Welfare in California*. Available at: http://cssr.berkeley.edu/PIReports/index.html.

Pew Commission on Children in Foster Care. (2004). *Fostering the Future: Safety, Permanence, and Well-Being for Children in Foster Care*. Washington, DC: Pew Charitable Trusts.

Purtilo, R. and Cassel, C.K. (1981). *Ethical Dimensions in the Health Professions*. Philadelphia, PA: W.B. Saunders.

Rawls, J. (1971). *A Theory of Justice*. Cambridge, MA: Harvard University Press.

Rescher, N. (1966). *Distributive Justice*. Indianapolis IN: Bobbs-Merrill.

Roberts, D. (2002). *Shattered Bonds: The Color of Child Welfare*. New York: Basic Books.

Sue, D.W. (2003). Cultural competence in the treatment of ethnic minority populations. In Council of National Psychological Associations for the Advancement of Ethnic Minority Interests (Eds.), *Psychological Treatment of Ethnic Minority Populations*, 4–7. Washington, DC: Association of Black Psychologists.

Thibaut, J. and Kelley, H. (1959). *The Social Psychology of Groups*. New York: Wiley.

Trennert, Robert A., Jr. (1988). *The Phoenix Indian School: Forced Assimilation in Arizona 1891–1935*. Norman: University of Oklahoma Press.

Tummala-Narra, P. (2004). Dynamics of race and culture in the supervisory encounter. *Psychoanalytic Psychology*, *21*(2), 300–311.

United States Department of Health and Human Services, OPHS, Office of Minority Health. (2001, March). *National Standards for Culturally and Linguistically Appropriate Services in Health Care, Final Report*. Washington, DC: Author.

Vonk, M.E. (2001). Cultural competence for transracial adoptive parents. *Social Work*, *46*(3), 246–255.

Yelaja, S.A. (1984). Teaching professional values and ethics: A survey. In C. Guetta, A.J. Katz, and R.A. English (Eds.), *Education for Social Work Practice: Selected International Models*. New York: Council on Social Work Education.

CHAPTER 3

Annie E. Casey Foundation. (2004). Kids Count PRB Report. www.kidscount.org.

Appleby, G. A., Colon, E., and Hamilton, J. (2001). *Diversity, Oppression and Social Functioning: Person-in-Environment Assessment and Intervention*. Needham Heights, MA: Allyn and Bacon.

Belenko, S., Peugh, J., Califano, J. A., Usdansky, M., and Foster, S. E. (1998). Substance abuse and the prison population: A three year study by Columbia University Reveals widespread substance abuse among offender population. *Corrections Today*, 60, 82–90.

Berrick, J. D., Barth, R. P., and Needell, B. (1994). A comparison of kinship foster homes and foster family homes: implications for kinship foster care as family preservation. *Children and Youth Services Review*, 16(1–2), 33–63.

Berrick, J. D., Needell, B., Barth, R. P., and Jonson-Reid, M. (1998). *The Tender Years: Toward Developmentally Sensitive Child Welfare Services for Very Young Children*. New York, NY: Oxford University Press.

Billingsley, A. and Giovannoni, J. M. (1972). *Children of the Storm: Black Children and American Child Welfare*. New York: Harcourt, Brace and Jovanovich.

Bowen, W. G. and Bok, D. (1998). *The Shape of the River: Long-term Consequences of Considering Race in College and University Admissions*. Princeton, NJ: Princeton University Press.

Bremner, R. H., Barnard, J., Hareven, T. K., and Mennel, R. M. (Eds.) (1974). *Children and Youth in America: A Documentary History*. Cambridge, MA: Harvard University Press.

Browne, A. and Bassuk, S. S. (1997). Intimate violence in the lives of homeless and poor housed women: Prevalence and patterns in an ethnically diverse sample. *American Journal of Orthopsychiatry*, 67(2), 261–278.

Brunswick (1999), as cited in De La Rosa, Segal and Lopez, *Conducting Drug Abuse Research With Minority Populations*. New York: The Hawthorn Press, Inc.

Butler, S. K. (2003). Helping Urban African American High School Students to Excel Academically: The Roles of School Counselors. *The High School Journal*, October/November, 51–56.

Canino, I. A. and Spurlock, J. (1994). *Culturally Diverse Children and Adolescents: Assessments, Diagnosis and Treatment*. New York: The Guilford Press.

Cazenave, N. A. and Straus, M. A. (1979). Race, class, network embeddedness and family violence: A Search for Potent Systems. *Journal of Comparative Family Studies*, 10, 280–300.

Child Welfare League of America. (2002). Juvenile Justice Division, Fact and Figures 2002. (retrieved 2/3/04 from www.cwla.org/programs/juvenilejustice/jjdfacts.2002.htm).

Children's Defense Fund. (2002). Education and Youth Development. (retrieved from www.childrensdefense.org/education/prevention/factsheets/blackyouth.aspx).

Children's Defense Fund. (2003). Family Income and Jobs. (retrieved 12/29/05 from www.childrensdefense.org/pressreleases/2003/031024.aspx).

Cole, E. R. and Omari, S. R. (2003). Race, Class and the dilemmas of Upward Mobility for African Americans. *Journal of Social Issues*, 59, 785–802.

Courtney, M. and Wong, Y. (1996). Comparing the timing of exits from substitute care. *Children and Youth Services Review*, 18(4/5), 307–334.

Curtis, C. M. (1996). The adoption of African American children by Whites: A renewed conflict. *Families in Society*, 77(3), 156–165.

Davis, F. J. (1991). *Who Is Black?* University Park: Pennsylvania State University Press.

De La Rosa, M. R., Segal, B., and Lopez, R. (1999). *Conducting Drug Abuse Research with Minority Populations*. New York: The Hawthorn Press, Inc.

Denby, R., Curtis, C., and Alford, K. (1998). Family preservation services and Special Populations: The Invisible Target. Families in Society. *The Journal of Contemporary Human Services*, 79(1), 21–35.

Devore, W. and Schlesinger, E. G. (1999). *Ethnic–Sensitive Social Work Practice*. Needham Heights, MA: Allyn and Bacon.

Diller, J. V. (2004). *Cultural Diversity: A Primer for Human Services* (2nd ed.). Belmont, CA: Brooke/Cole-Thompson Learning.

Dillion, D. (1994). Understanding and assessment of inter-group dynamics in family foster care: African American families. *Child Welfare*, 73(2), 129–139.

Downs, S. W., Moore, E., McFadden, E. J., Michaud, S. M., and Costin, L. B. (2004). *Child Welfare and Family Services: Policies and Practice*. Needham Heights, MA: Allyn and Bacon.

Ellis, R. A. and Sowers, K. M. (2001). *Juvenile Justice Practice: A Cross-Disciplinary Approach to Intervention*. Belmont, CA: Wadsworth.

Encyclopedia of Social Work. (1997). Silver Springs, MD: National Association of Social Workers Press.

Fenster, J. (2002). Transracial adoption in Black and White: A survey of social work attitudes. *Adoption Quarterly*, 5(4), 33–58.

Gil, A. G., Vega, W. A., and Turner, R. J. (2002). Early and mid-adolescence risk factors for later substance abuse by African Americans and European Americans. *Health Reports*, 117, S15–S29.

Gutman, H. G. (1976). *The Black Family in Slavery and Freedom*. New York: Vintage Books, pp. 1750–1925.

Hacsi, T. (1997). *Second Home: Orphan Asylums and Poor Families in America*. Cambridge: Harvard University Press.

Hairston, C. F. and Williams, V. G. (1989). Black adoptive parents: How they view agency adoption practices. *Social Casework*, 70(9), 534–538.

Harvey, A. R. (1997). Group work with African-American youth in the criminal justice system: A culturally competent model, in G. L. Greif and P. H. Ephross (Eds.), *Group Work with Populations at Risk*. New York: Oxford University Press, pp. 160–174.

Harvey, A. R. and Hill, R. B. (2004). Africentric youth and family rites of passage Program: Promoting resilience among at-risk African American Youths. *Social Work*, 49, 65–74.

Hegar, R. L. and Scannapieco, M. (1995). From family duty to family policy: The evolution of Kinship Care. *Child Welfare*, 4, 200–216.

Hill, R. B. (1971). *The Strengths of Black Families*. New York: Emerson Hall.

Hill, R. B. (1998). Understanding black family functioning: A holistic perspective. Special Issue: Comparative perspectives on Black family life. *Journal of Comparative Studies*, 29, 15–26.

Hope, J. F. and Moss, A. (2000). *From Slavery to Freedom, A History of African Americans* (8th ed.). New York: Alfred A. Knopf.

Hyde, C. A. (2004). Multicultural development in human services agencies: Challenges and solutions. *Social Work*, 49, 7–16.

Juszkiewics, J. and Schindler, M. (2001). Youth crime/adult time: Is justice served? *Corrections Today*, February, 102–107.

Kaplan, C. (1997). Job Protection Act of 1996 (P.I. 104–188): Implications for social work Practice. NASW Homepage: www.naswdc.org/practice/adopt.htm.

Karenga, M. (1988). *The Book of Coming Forth By Day*. University of Sankore Press.

Kilpatrick, A. C. and Holland, T. P. (1999). *Working with Families: An Integrative Model by Level of Need*. Needham Heights, MA: Allyn and Bacon.

Kirst-Ashman, K. K. (2000). *Human Behavior, Communities, Organizations & Groups in the Macro Social Environment: An Empowerment Approach*. Pacific Grove, CA: Brooks/Cole.

Lacy, D. (1972). *The White Use of Blacks in America*. New York: McGraw-Hill.

Ladner, J. (1978). *Mixed Families: Adopting Across Racial Boundaries*. Garden City, NY: Anchor Press.

Locke, D. C. and Ciechalski, J. C. (1995). *Psychological Techniques for Teachers* (2nd ed.). Washington, DC: Accelerated Development 1995.

Lott, B. and Bullock, H. E. (2001). Who are the poor? *Journal of Social Issues*, 57, 1–12.

Lum, D. (Ed.) (2003). *Culturally Competent Practice: A Framework for Understanding Diverse Groups and Justice Issues* (2nd ed.). Pacific Grove, CA: Brooks/Cole–Thomson Learning.

Manning, M. C., Cornelius, L. J., and Okundaye, J. N. (2004). Empowering African Americans through social work practice: Integrating an Afrocentric perspective, ego psychology, and Spirituality. *Families in Society*, 85, 229–234.

McCray, J. (1994). Challenges to diversity from an African-American perspective. *Journal of Extension*, 32, www.joe.org/joe/1994june/a3.html.

McDonald, W. R. and Associates/American Humane. (2004). Child Maltreatment 2002. US Department of Health and Human Services, Administration for Children and Families.

McRoy, R. G. (1990). A historical view of black families, in S. M. L. Logan, E. M. Freeman, and R. G. McRoy, *Social Work Practice with Black Families: A Culturally Specific Perspective*. New York: Longman, pp. 3–17.

National Center for Children in Poverty. (2003). (retrieved, July 29, 2004, www.policyalmanac.org/social_welfare/poverty.shtml).

National Low Income Housing Coalition. (2003). Out of reach 2003. (retrieved July 23, 2004, www.nlihc.org/oor_current/introduction.htm).

National Research Council. (1993). *Losing Generations: Adolescents in High-risk Settings*. Washington, DC: National Academy Press.

O'Donnell, J. M. (1999). Casework practices with fathers in kinship foster care, in P. Gleeson, C. F. Hairston, *Kinship Care, Improving Practice Through Research*. Child Welfare League of America, pp. 167–188.

Office of Democratic Leader Nancy Pelosi, 6/9/03; Associated Press, 2/24/03. No child left behind, two years later: Empty promises, empty rhetoric, Every child left behind: Three years of unfunded mandates. (retrieved 7/26/04 from www.democrats.org/special/reports/nclb).

Palacios, M. and Franco, J. N. (1986). Counseling Mexican-American women, in *Journal of Multicultural Counseling and Development*, 14, 124–131.

Pardeck, J. T. (1984). A profile of the child likely to experience unstable foster care. *Adolescence*, 20(79), 689–696.

Pinderhughes, E. (1982). Afro-American families and the victim system, in M. McGoldrick, J. K. Pearce, and J. Giordano (Eds.), *Ethnicity and Family Therapy*. New York: The Guilford Press, pp. 108–122.

Pinderhughes, E. (1997). Developing diversity competence in child welfare and permanency. *Journal of Multicultural Social Work*, 5(1/2), 19–38.

Pollard, L. (1996). *Complaint to the Lord: Historical Perspectives on the African American Elderly*. Selingsgrove, PA: Susquehanna University Press.

Pryor, A. (1999). *Domestic Violence and African Americans*. San Jose Mercury News, Wednesday, August 4, 1999, p. 3B.

Quadagno, J. (1994). *The Color of Welfare: How Racism Undermined the War on Poverty*. NY: Oxford University Press.

Queralt, M. (1996). *The Social Environment and Human Behavior: A Diversity Perspective*. Boston: Allyn and Bacon.

Roberts, D. E. (2002). *Racial Disproportionality in the U.S. Child Welfare System: Documentation, Research on Causes and Promising Practices*. Washington, DC: Annie E. Casey Foundation. [PDF Electronic version].

Silverman, A. R. (1993). Outcomes of transracial adoption. *The Future of Children*, 3(1), 104–118.

Smith, C. J., and Devore, W. (2004). African American children in the child welfare and kinship system: From exclusion to over inclusion. *Children and Youth Services Review*, 26, 427–446.

Smith, D. K., Stormshak, E., Chamberlain, P., and Whaley, R. B. (2001). Placement disruption in treatment foster care. *Journal of Emotional and Behavioral Disorders*, 9(3), 200–205.

Stehno, S. M. (1990). The elusive continuum of child welfare services: Implication for Minority Children and Youth. *Child Welfare*, 69: 551.

Stewart, P. E. (2004). Afrocentric approaches to working with African American families. *Families in Society*, 85, 217–224.

Takaki, R. (1993). *A Different Mirror: A History of Multicultural America*. Boston, MA: Little, Brown and Company.

Taylor, R. J., Chatters, L. M., and Celious, A. K. (2003). Extended households among Black Americans. *African American Research Perspectives*, 9, 133–151.

Taylor, R. J., Ellison, C. G., Chatters, L. M., Levin, J. S., and Lincoln, K. D. (2000). Mental health services in Faith Communities: The role of clergy in Black churches. *Social Work*, 45, 73–87.

Tjaden, P. and Thoenns, N. (1998). *Prevalence, Incidence, and Consequences of Violence Against Women: Findings from the National Violence Against Women (NVAW) Survey*. Washington, DC: U.S. Department of Justice, National Justice Programs. (retrieved 7/22/04 from www.ncjrs.org/txtfiles/172837.txt).

Tjaden, P. and Thoenns, N. (2000). *Extent, Nature, and Consequences of Intimate Partner Violence*. Washington, DC: National Institute of Justice and the Centers for Disease Control and Prevention. (retrieved 7/22/04 from www.ncjrs.org/txtfiles/172837.txt).

Tucker, C. M., Herman, K. C., Pedersen, T., Vogel, D., and Reinke, W. M. (2000). Student generated solutions to enhance the academic success of African American youth. *Child Study Journal*, 30, 205–221.

U.S. Census Bureau. (2001). *Statistical Abstract of the United States 2001* (121st ed.). Washington, DC: U.S. Census Bureau.

U.S. Census Bureau. (2004). American Community Survey. Washington, DC: U.S. Census Bureau.

U.S. Department of Education. (2003). *No Child Left Behind Act of 2001*. Washington, DC: U.S. Department of Education.

U.S. Department of Health and Human Services, Administration for Children and families, Administration on Children, Youth, and Families–Children's Bureau. (2004). *The Adoption and Foster Care Analysis and*

Reporting System (AFCARS) Report. (retrieved 3/21/05 fromwww.acf.hhs.gov/programs/cb/publications/afcars/report9.htm).

U.S. Department of Health and Human Services, Administration for Children and families, Administration on Children, Youth, and Families–Children's Bureau. Report to Congress on kinship foster care. (2000). (retrieved 12/18/04 from http://aspe.hhs.gov/hsp/kinr2c00/full.pdf).

U.S. Department of Health and Human Services, Children's Bureau. (1996) *The Third National Incidence Study of Child Abuse and Neglect.* Washington, DC: U.S. Government Printing Office.

U.S. Department of Health and Human Services, Children's Bureau. (1997a). *Foster Care and Adoption Statistics Current Reports (AFCARS).* (retrieved on 7/22/04 from www.acf.dhhs.gov/programs/cb/stats/afcars/).

U.S. Department of Health and Human Services, Children's Bureau. (1997b). *National Study of Protective, Preventive and Reunification Services to Children and Their Families.* Washington, DC: U.S. Government Printing Office.

Washington, J. A. (2003). Literacy Skills in African American Students: The Legacy of the Achievement Gap? *African American Research Perspectives,* 9, 1–6.

Wolfner, G. D. and Gelles, R. J. (1993). A profile of violence toward children: A national study. *Child Abuse and Neglect,* 17, 197–212.

Zedlewski, S. R. (2000). 1999 Snapshots of America's Families II: Family Economic Well-Being, National Survey of America's Families. Washington, DC: *Urban Institute.*

CHAPTER 4

Annie E. Casey Foundation. (2000). *Kids Count Data Book 2000: State Profiles of Child Well-Being.* Baltimore, MD: Author.

Blanchard, E.L. (1983). "The growth and development of American Indian and Alaska Native children," in Powell, G.J. (Ed.) *The Psychosocial Development of Minority Group Children.* Brunner/Mazel. New York, 115–130.

Cassidy, Jude and Shaver, Phillip R. (1999). *Handbook of Attachment: Theory, Research and Clinical Applications.* New York: Guilford Press.

Champagne, Duane. (Ed.) (1994). *Chronology of Native North American History, From Pre-Columbian Times to the Present.* Detroit: Gale Research Inc.

Dorris, Michael. (1989). *The Broken Cord.* New York: Harper and Row.

Duran, B. and Duran, E. (1995). *Native American Post-Colonial Psychology.* New York: State University of New York.

Green, Bonnie L. (2000). Traumatic loss: Conceptual and empirical links between trauma and bereavement in *Journal of Personal & Interpersonal Loss,* 5:1.

Green, James W. (1999). *Cultural Awareness in the Human Services, A Multi-Ethnic Approach (Third Edition)* Boston: Allyn and Bacon.

Guilmet, George and Whited, David (1989). The people who give more: Health and mental health among the contemporary Puyallup Indian tribal community, *American Indian and Alaska Native Mental Health Research.* Monograph 2.

Indian Health Service. (1997). *Regional Differences in Indian Health.* U.S. Department of Health and Human Services, Indian Health Service, Office of Public Health. Washington.

LaFromboise, T.D. and Bigfoot, D.S. (1988). Cultural and cognitive considerations in the prevention of American Indian suicide. *Journal of Adolescence,* 11, 139–153.

Leigh, James W. (1998). *Communicating for Cultural Competence.* Boston: Allyn & Bacon.

Locust, Carol. (1988). Wounding the spirit: Discrimination and traditional American Indian belief systems. *Harvard Educational Review,* 58:3, 315–330.

May, Philip. (1988). The health status of Indian children: Problems and prevention in early life. *American Indian and Alaska Native Mental Health Research,* 1, 244–289.

McLuhan, T.C. (1971). *Touch the Earth, A Self Portrait of Indian Existence.* New York: Touchstone Books.

McShane, Damian. (1988). An analysis of mental health research with American Indian youth. *Journal of Adolescence,* 11, 87116.

Moncher, M.S., Holden, G.W., and Trimble, J.E. (1990). Substance Abuse Among Native American Youth. *Journal of Counseling and Clinical Psychology,* 58:4, 408–415.

Moyers, B. (1991). *The Faithkeeper, A Conversation with Oren Lyons.* Public Broadcasting Service.

Ogunwole, Stella. (2002). *The American Indian and Alaska Native Population: 2000.* Census 2000 Brief, U.S. Department of Commerce, Economics and Statistics Administration, U.S. Census Bureau, Washington DC.

Ong, Paul with Hyun-Gun Sung, and Heintz-Mackoff, Julia. (2004). *American Indian Children in Los Angeles, California & the U.S.* Policy Brief, University of California at Los Angeles: The Ralph & Goldy Lewis Center for Regional Policy Studies and the Los Angeles American Indian Children's Council.

Pollard, Kelvin M. and O' Hare, William P. (1999). *America's Racial and Ethnic Minorities. Population Bulletin.* Washington DC: Population Reference Bureau.

Price, Monore. (1973). *Law and the American Indian: Readings, Notes and Cases.* Indianapolis: The Bobbs-Merrill Company, Inc.

Red Horse, J. (1983). Indian family values and experiences, in Powell, G. (Ed.) *The Psychosocial Development of Minority Group Children.* Brunner/Mazel, New York, 258–271.

Sage, G.P. (1991). Counseling American Indian adults in Lee, C. and Richardson, B. (Eds) *Multicultural Issues in Counseling: New Approaches to Diversity.* Alexandra, AACD.

Saleebey, Denis. (2002). *The Strengths Perspective in Social Work Practice (Third Edition).* Boston: Allyn and Bacon.

Schriver, Joe. (1995). *Human Behavior and the Social Environment: Shifting Paradigms in Essential Knowledge for Social Work Practice.* Allyn and Bacon, Massachusetts.

Standing Bear, Luther. (1975). *My People the Sioux.* Lincoln: University of Nebraska Press.

Standing Bear, Luther. (1978). *Land of the Spotted Eagle.* Lincoln: University of Nebraska Press.

Standing Bear, Luther. (1988). *My Indian Boyhood.* Lincoln: University of Nebraska Press.

Tafoya, Terry. (1989). Circles and Cedar: Native American and family therapy. *Journal of Psychotherapy and the Family*, 6, 71–98.

U.S. Department of Commerce, Economics, and Statistics Administration. (1995). "Bureau of the Census, Statistical Brief, Housing of American Indians on Reservations–Plumbing"; "Bureau of the Census, Statistical Brief, Housing of American Indians on Reservations–Structural Characteristics".

CHAPTER 5

Abe, J.S. and Zane, N.W. (1990). Psychological maladjustment among Asian and White American college students: Controlling for confounds. *Journal of Counseling Psychology*, 37(4), 437–444.

Abe-Kim, J., Takeuchi, D., and Hwang, W. (2002). Predictors of help seeking for emotional distress among Chinese Americans: Family matters. *Journal of Consulting & Clinical Psychology*, 70(5), 1186–1190.

Agbayani-Siewert, P. and Revilla, L. (1995). Filipino Americans. In P.G. Min (Ed.), *Asian Americans: Contemporary Trends and Issues.* Thousand Oaks, CA: SAGE Publications, pp. 134–168.

Akutsu, P.D. (1997). Mental health care delivery to Asian Americans: A review of the literature. In E. Lee (Ed.), *Working with Asian Americans: A Guide for Clinicians.* New York, NY: Guilford Press, pp. 464–476.

Akutsu, P.D., Snowden, L.R., and Organista, K.C. (1996). Referral patterns in ethnic-specific and mainstream programs for ethnic minorities and Whites. *Journal of Counseling Psychology*, 43, 56–64.

Ambrosino, R., Heffernan, J., Shuttlesworth, G., and Ambrosino, R. (2001). *Social Work and Social Welfare* (4th ed.). Belmont, CA: Thomson Learning.

Asaman, J. and Berry, G. (1987). Self-concept, alienation, and perceived prejudice: Implications for counseling Asian Americans. *Journal of Multicultural Counseling and Development*, 15(4), 146–161.

Asian Pacific American Legal Center of Southern California. (2004). *The Diverse Face of Asians and Pacific Islanders in Los Angeles County.* (retrieved July 12, 2004 from www.unitedwayla.org/pages/rpts_resource/ethnic_profiles/ASP_Report.pdf).

Atkinson, D.R. and Gim, R.H. (1989). Asian-American cultural identity and attitudes toward mental health services. *Journal of Counseling Psychology*, 36(2), 209–212.

Atkinson, D.R., Lowe, S., and Matthews, L. (1995). Asian-American acculturation, gender, and willingness to seek counseling. *Journal of Multicultural Counseling & Development*, 23(3), 130–138.

Bauer, H.M., Rodriguez, M.A., Quiroga, S.S., and Flores-Ortiz, Y.G. (2000). Barriers to health care for abused Latina and Asian immigrant women. *Journal of Health Care for the Poor and Underserved*, 11(1), 33–44.

Baumrind, D. (1991). Parenting styles and adolescent development. In J. Brooks-Gunn, R.M. Lerner, and A.C. Petersen (Eds.), *The Encyclopedia on Adolescence.* New York: Garland Publishing, pp. 746–758.

Baumrind, D. (1994). The social context of child maltreatment. *Family Relations*, 43(4), 360–369.

Berry, J.W. (1980). Acculturation as varieties of adaptation. In A.M. Padilla (Ed.), *Acculturation: Theory, Model, and Some New Findings.* Boulder, CO: Westview, pp. 9–25.

Berry, J.W., Trimble, J., and Olmedo, E. (1986). Assessment of acculturation. In W. Lonner and J.W. Berry (Eds.), *Field Methods in Cross-Cultural Research.* Newbury Park, CA: Sage, pp. 297–324.

Bui, K.T. and Takeuchi, D.T. (1992). Ethnic minority adolescents and the use of community mental health care services. *American Journal of Community Psychology*, 20(4), 403–418.

Center for Mental Health Services. (1999). *Annual Report to Congress on the Evaluation of the Comprehensive Community Mental Health Services for Children and Their Families Program, 1999.* Atlanta, GA: ORC Macro.

Chae, K.M. (1990). *Korean American Juvenile Delinquency in Relation to Acculturation Differences Between Parents and Children.* Doctoral dissertation, Illinois Institute of Technology.

Chang, J., Rhee, S., and Weaver, D. (in press) Characteristics of child abuse in immigrant Korean families and correlates of placement decisions. *Child Abuse & Neglect.*

Chen, C. and Stevenson, H.W. (1995). Motivation and mathematics Achievement: A comparative study of Asian-American, Caucasian-American, and East Asian high school students. *Child Development, 66*(4), 1215–1234.

Chen, C.L. and Yang, D.C.Y. (1986). The self-image of Chinese-American adolescents: A cross-cultural comparison. *International Journal of Social Psychiatry, 32* (4), 19–26.

Chen, S., Sullivan, N.Y., Lu, Y.E., and Shibusawa, T. (2003). Asian Americans and mental health services: A study of utilization patterns in the 1990s. *Journal of Ethnic Cultural Diversity in Social Work, 12*(2), 19–42.

Cheung, F.K. and Snowden, L.R. (1990). Community mental health and ethnic minority populations. *Community Mental Health Journal, 26*(3), 277–291.

Children's Defense Fund (2004). *The State of America's Children, Yearbook.* Boston, MA: Beacon Press.

Cho, P.J. (1998). Awareness and utilization: A Comment. *Gerontologist, 38*(3), 317–319.

Chung, H., Teresi, J., Guarnaccia, P., Meyers, B.S., Holmes, D., Bobrowitz, T., Eimick, J.P., and Ferran, E.J. (2003). Depressive symptoms and psychiatric distress in low income Asian and Latino primary care patients: Prevalence and recognition. *Community Mental Health Journal, 39*(1), 33–46.

Chuong, C.H. and Ta, M.H. (2003). Vietnamese: Overcoming the past and building a future. In E. Lai and D. Arguelles (Eds.), *The New Face of Asian Pacific America: Numbers, Diversity & Change in the 21st Century.* Los Angeles, CA: UCLA Asian American Studies Center Press, pp. 67–72.

Cowger, C.D. and Snively, C.A. (2002). Assessing client strengths: Individual, family, and Community empowerment. In D. Saleeby (Ed.), *The Strengths Perspective in Social Work Practice.* Boston, MA: Allyn & Bacon, pp. 106–123.

Crosson-Tower, C. (1998). *Exploring Child Welfare: A Practice Perspective.* Needham Heights, MA: Allyn & Bacon.

de Anda, D. (1984). Bicultural socialization: Factors affecting the minority experience. *Social Work, 29*(2), 101–107.

Dean, R.G. (2001). The myth of cross-cultural competence. *Families in Society, 82*(6), 623–630.

Dela Cruz, M. and Agbayani-Siewert, P. (2003). Filipinos: Swimming with and against the tide. In E. Lai and D. Arguelles (Eds.), *The New Face of Asian Pacific America: Numbers, Diversity & Change in the 21st Century.* Los Angeles, CA: UCLA Asian American Studies Center Press, pp. 45–50.

Delucchi, M. and Do, H.D. (1996). The model minority myth and perceptions of Asian-Americans as victims of racial harassment. *College Student Journal, 30*(3), 411–414.

Derezotes, D.S. (2000). *Advanced Generalist Social Work Practice.* Thousand Oaks, CA: Sage.

Devore, W. and Schlesinger, E.G. (1999). *Ethnic-Sensitive Social Work Practice* (5th ed.). Boston, MA: Allyn and Bacon.

Dhooper, S.S. (1997). *Social Work in Health Care in the 21st Century.* Thousand Oaks, CA: Sage.

Dhooper, S.S. and Moore, S.E. (2001). *Social Work Practice with Culturally Diverse People.* Thousand Oaks, CA: Sage.

Diaz, T.P. (2002). Group work from an Asian Pacific Island perspectives: Making connections between group worker ethnicity and practice. *Social Work with Groups, 25*(3), 43–60.

Do, P.V. (2002). Between two cultures: Struggles of Vietnamese American adolescents. *Review of Vietnamese Studies, 2*(1), 1–19.

Durvasula, R. and Sue, S. (1996). Severity of Disturbance Among Asian American Outpatients. *Cultural Diversity & Mental Health, 2*(1), 43–51.

Early, T.J. and GlenMaye, L.E. (2000). Valuing families: Social work practice with families from a strengths perspective. *Social Work, 45,* 118–130.

Erickson D'Avanzo, C. (1997). Southeast Asians: Asian-Pacific Americans at Risk for substance Misuse. *Substance Use & Misuse, 32*(7–8), 829–848.

Erikson, E.H. (1963). *Childhood and Society* (2nd ed.). New York: Norton.

Farver, J.A.M., Narang, S.K., and Bhadha, B.R. (2002). East meets West: Ethnic identity, acculturation, and conflict in Asian Indian families. *Journal of Family Psychology, 16*(3), 338–350.

Feliciano, C. (2001). The benefits of biculturalism: Exposure to immigrant culture and dropping out of school among Asian and Hispanic youths. *Social Science Quarterly, 82*(4), 865–879.

Florsheim, P. (1997). Chinese adolescent immigrants: Factors related to psychosocial adjustment. *Journal of Youth and Adolescence, 26*(2), 143–163.

Fong, R. (2003). Cultural competence with Asian Americans. In D. Lum (Ed.), *Culturally Competent Practice: A Framework for Understanding Diverse Groups and Justice Issues.* Belmont, CA: Thomson, Brooks/Cole, pp. 261–286.

Freeman, J.M. (1989). *Hearts of Sorrow: Vietnamese-American Lives.* Stanford, CA: Stanford University Press.

Fu, M. (2002). *Acculturation, Ethnic Identity, and Family Conflict Among First- and Second-Generation Chinese Americans.* Doctoral dissertation submitted to Alliant International University, U.S.A.

Fugita, S.S. and O'Brien, K.J. (1991). *Japanese American Ethnicity: The Persistence of Community.* Seattle: University of Washington Press.

Furuto, S.M. (1991). Family violence among Pacific Islanders. In N. Mokuau (Ed.), *Handbook of Social Services for Asian and Pacific Islanders.* Westport, CT: Greenwood Press, pp. 203–215.

Furuto, S.M. and Murase, K. (1992). Asian Americans in the future. In S.M. Furuto, R. Biswas, D.K. Chung, K. Murase, and F. Ross-Sheriff (Eds.), *Social Work Practice with Asian Americans.* Newbury Park, CA: Sage Publications, pp. 240–253.

Futa, K.T., Hsu, E., and Hansen, D.J. (2001). Child sexual abuse in Asian American families: An examination of cultural factors that influence prevalence, identification, and treatment. *Clinical Psychology: Science & Practice, 8*(2), 189–209.

Gim, R.H., Atkinson, D.R., and Kim, S.J. (1991). Asian-American acculturation, counselor ethnicity and cultural sensitivity, and ratings of counselors. *Journal of Counseling Psychology, 38*(1), 57–62.

Goto, S.G., Gee, G.C., and Takeuchi, D.T. (2002). Strangers still? The experience of discrimination among Chinese Americans. *Journal of Community Psychology, 30*(2), 211–224.

Graves, T.D. (1967). Psychological Acculturation in a tri-ethnic community. *Southwestern Journal of Anthropology, 23*, 337–350.

Green, J.W. (1982). *Cultural Awareness in the Human Services.* Englewood Cliffs, NJ: Prentice Hall.

Green, J.W. (1999). *Cultural Awareness in the Human Services: A Multiethnic Approach.* Boston: Allyn & Bacon.

Gutierrez, L.M. (1990). Working with women of color: An empowerment perspective. *Social Work, 35*(2), 149–153.

Hahm, H.C., Lahiff, M., and Guterman, N.B. (2003). Acculturation and parental attachment in Asian-American adolescents' alcohol use. *Journal of Adolescent Health, 33*(2), 119–129.

Herrick, C.A. and Brown, H.N. (1998). Underutilization of mental health services by Asian-Americans residing in the United States. *Issues in Mental Health Nursing, 19*(3), 225–240.

Hmong Studies Internet Resource Center. (2004). *U.S. Census 2000: Cambodian Residential Distribution.* (retrieved July 12, 2004 from www.hmongstudies.org/uscen20camre.html).

Ho, C.K. (1990). An analysis of domestic violence in Asian American communities: A multicultural approach to counseling. *Women & Therapy, 9*(1–2), 129–150.

Ho, M.K. (1992). *Minority Children and Adolescents in Therapy.* Newbury Park, CA: Sage Publications.

Hong, G.K. and Hong, L.K. (1991). Comparative perspective on child abuse and neglect: Chinese versus Hispanics and whites. *Child Welfare, 70*(4), 463–475.

Hopkins, M. (1996). *Braving a New World: Cambodian (Khmer) Refugees in an American City.* Westport, CT: Bergin & Barvey.

Hsu, J. (1983). Asian family interaction patterns and their therapeutic implications. *International Journal of Family Psychiatry, 4*(4), 307–320.

Hune, S. and Chan, K.S. (1997). Special focus: Asian Pacific American demographic and educational trends. In D.J. Carter and R. Wilson (Eds.), *Minorities in Higher Education: Fifteenth Annual Status Report.* Washington, DC: American Council on Education, pp. 39–67.

Hurh, W.M. and Kim, K.C. (1990). Correlates of Asian Immigrants' mental health. *Journal of Nervous and Mental Disease, 178*(11), 703–711.

Ima, K. and Hohm, C.F. (1991). Child maltreatment among Asian and Pacific Islander refugees and immigrants: The San Diego case. *Journal of Interpersonal Violence, 6*(3), 267–285.

Israel, B.A., Checkoway, B., Schulz, A., and Zimmerman, M. (1994). Health education and community empowerment: Conceptualizing and measuring perceptions of individuals, organizational, and community control. *Health Education Quarterly, 21*(2), 149–170.

Ito, K.L. and Maramba, G.G. (2002). Therapeutic beliefs of Asian American therapists: Views from an ethnic-specific clinic. *Transcultural Psychiatry, 39*(1), 33–73.

Ja, D. and Yuen, F.K. (1997). Substance abuse treatment among Asian Americans. In E. Lee (Ed.), *Working with Asian Americans.* New York: Guilford Press, pp. 295–308.

James, S. and Prilleltensky, I. (2001). Cultural diversity and mental health. Towards integrative practice. *Clinical Psychology Review, 22*(8), 1133–1154.

James, W.H., Kim, G.K., and Moore, D.D. (1997). Examining racial and ethnic differences in Asian adolescent drug use: The contributions of culture, background and lifestyle. *Drugs: Education, Prevention & Policy, 4*(1), 39–51.

Johnson, L.C. (1992). *Social Work Practice: A Generalist Approach* (4th ed.). Boston: Allyn & Bacon.

Kahn, R.L. and Juster, F.T. (2002). Well-Being: Concepts and Measures. *Journal of Social Issues, 58*(4), 627–644.

Kim, H. (2004). *Relationship Between Parenting Styles and Self-Perception—Academic Competence, Morality, and Self-Reliance—Among Korean American College Students.* Doctoral dissertation submitted to University of Southern California, U.S.A.

Kim, B.S.K., Atkinson, D.R., and Yang, P.H. (1999). The Asian values scale: Development, factor analysis, validation, and reliability. *Journal of Counseling Psychology, 46*, 342–352.

Kim, B.S.K. and Omizo, M.M. (2003). Asian cultural values, attitudes toward seeking professional psychological help, and willingness to see a counselor. *Counseling Psychologist, 31*(3), 343–361.

Kim, T.E. and Goto, S.G. (2000). Peer delinquency and parental social support as predictors of Asian American adolescent delinquency. *Deviant Behavior, 21*(4), 331–347.

Kitano, H.H.L. (1997). *Race Relations* (5th ed.). Upper Saddle River, NJ: Prentice Hall.

Kitano, H.H.L. and Daniels, R. (2001). *Asian Americans: Emerging Minorities* (3rd ed.). Upper Saddle River, NJ: Prentice Hall.

Kitano, H.H.L. and Nakaoka (2001). Asian Americans in the twentieth century. *Journal of Human Behavior in the Social Environment, 3*(3/4), 7–17.

Korean American Family Service Center. (2004). *Annual Statistics.* Los Angeles, CA.

Krishnan, S., Baig-Amin, M., Gilbert, L., El-Bassel, N., and Waters, A. (1998). Lifting the veil of secrecy: Domestic violence against South Asian women in the United States. In S. Dasgupta (Ed.), *A Patchwork Shawl: Chronicles of South Asian Womanhood in America*. New Brunswick, NJ: Rutgers University Press, pp. 145–159.

Lai, E. and Arguelles, D. (2003). *The New Face of Asian Pacific America: Numbers, Diversity & Change in the 21st Century* (Eds.). Los Angeles, CA: UCLA Asian American Studies Center Press.

Lau, A. and Zane, N. (2000). Examining the effects of ethnic-specific services: An analysis of cost-utilization and treatment outcomes for Asian American clients. *Journal of Community Psychology, 28,* 63–77.

Lee, E. (Ed.) (1997). *Working with Asian Americans: A Guide for Clinicians.* New York: Guilford Press.

Lee, J.A.B. (1996). The Empowerment approach to social work practice. In F. J. Turner (Ed.), *Social Work Treatment: Interlocking Theoretical Approaches* (4th ed.). New York, NY: Free Press, pp. 218–249.

Lee, L.C. and Zane, N.W.S. (Eds.) (1998). *Handbook of Asian American Psychology.* Thousand Oaks, CA: Sage.

Lee, R.M., Choe, J., Kim, G., and Ngo, V. (2000). Construction of the Asian American family conflicts scale. *Journal of Counseling Psychology, 47*(2), 211–222.

Lee, S. (1994). Behind the model-minority stereotype: Voices of high- and low-achieving Asian American students. *Anthropology & Educational Quarterly, 25*(4), 413–429.

Leong, F.T. (1986). Counseling and psychotherapy with Asian-Americans: Review of the literature. *Journal of Counseling Psychology, 33*(2), 196–206.

Leong, F.T.L. and Lau, A.S.L. (2001). Barriers to providing effective mental health services to Asian Americans. *Mental Health Services Research, 3*(4), 201–214.

Leong, F.T.L., Wagner, N.S., and Kim, H.H. (1995). Group counseling expectations among Asian American students: The role of culture-specific factors. *Journal of Counseling Psychology, 51*(2), 103–114.

Lim, S.L. (2002). *Acculturation Consonance and Dissonance: Effect on Parenting Style, Parent–Adolescent Relationship, and Adolescent Psychological Well-Being in Immigrant Chinese-American Families.* Doctoral dissertation submitted to Texas Tech University, U.S.A.

Lin, C. and Liu, W.T. (1999). Intergenerational relationships among Chinese immigrant families from Taiwan. In H.P. McAdoo (Ed.), *Family Ethnicity: Strength in Diversity.* Thousand Oaks, CA: Sage Publications.

Lin, K.M. and Cheung, F. (1999). Mental health issues for Asian Americans. *Psychiatric Services, 50*(6), 774–780.

Lin, K.M., Inui, T.S., Kleinman, A.M, and Womack, W.M. (1982). Sociocultural determinants of the help-seeking behavior of patients with mental illness. *Journal of Nervous & Mental Disease, 170*(2), 78–85.

Lin, T. (1985). Mental disorders and psychiatry in Chinese culture: Characteristic features and major issues. In W.S. Tseng and D.Y.H.Wu (Eds.), *Chinese Culture and Mental Health.* Orlando, FL: Academic Press, pp. 369–393.

Lindsey, D. (1994). Family preservation and child protection: Striking a balance. *Children and Youth Services Review, 16*(5/6), 279–294.

Liu, W.T., Yu, E.H., Chang, C.F., and Fernandez, M. (1990). The mental health of Asian American teenagers: A research challenge. In A.R. Stiffman and L.E. Davis (Eds.), *Ethnic Issues in Adolescent Mental Health.* Beverly Hills, CA: Sage, pp. 92–112.

Lum, D. (2003). *Culturally Competent Practice* (2nd ed.). Pacific Grove, CA: Brooks/Cole.

Markus, H.R. and Kitayama, S. (1991). Culture and the self: Implications for cognition, emotion, and motivation. *Psychological Review, 98*(2), 224–253.

Masaki, B. and Wong, L. (1997). Domestic violence in the Asian Community. In E. Lee (Ed.), *Working with Asian Americans: A Guide for Clinicians.* New York, New York: Guilford Press, pp. 439–451.

Mass, A.I. and Geaga-Rosenthal, J. (2000). Child Welfare: Asian and Pacific Islander families. In N.A. Cohen (Ed.), *Child Welfare: A Multicultural Focus* (2nd ed.). Needham Heights, MA: Allyn and Bacon, pp. 145–164.

Matsuoka, J.K., Breaux, C., and Ryujin, D.H. (1997). National utilization of mental health services by Asian Americans/Pacific Islanders. *Journal of Community Psychology, 25*(2), 141–145.

McGregor, D. (2003). Seeking recognition and the return of Aloha. In E. Lai and D. Arguelles (Eds.), *The New Face of Asian Pacific America: Numbers, Diversity & Change in the 21st Century.* Los Angeles, CA: UCLA Asian American Studies Center Press, pp. 79–84.

McKelvey, R.S., Baldassar, L.V., Sang, D.L., and Roberts, L. (1999). Vietnamese parental perceptions of child and adolescent mental illness. *Journal of the American Academy of Child & Adolescent Psychiatry, 38*(10), 1302–1309.

McKelvey, R.S. and Webb, J.A. (1995). A pilot study of abuse among Vietnamese Amerasians. *Child Abuse & Neglect, 19*(5), 545–553.

Mercado, M.M. (2000). The invisible family: Counseling Asian American substance abusers and their families. *Family Journal: Counseling and Therapy for Couples and Families, 8*(3), 267–272.

Miley, K.K., O'Melia, M., and DuBois, B.I. (2004). *Generalist Social Work Practice: An Empowering Approach* (4th ed.). Boston, MA: Allyn & Bacon.

Min, P.G. (1995). An overview of Asian Americans. In P.G. Min (Ed.), *Asian Americans: Contemporary Trends and Issues.* Thousand Oaks, CA: Sage, pp. 10–37.

Min, P.G. (1998). *Changes and Conflicts: Asian Immigrant Families in New York.* Needham Heights, MA: Allyn and Bacon.

Minuchin, S. (1974). *Families and Family Therapy*. Boston, MA: Harvard University Press.

Modarres, A. (2003). Immigration: From gold mountain to globalization. In E. Lai and D. Arguelles (Eds.), *The New Face of Asian Pacific America: Numbers, Diversity & Change in the 21st Century*. Los Angeles, CA: UCLA Asian American Studies Center Press, pp. 23–28.

Montero, D. (1979). *Vietnamese Americans: Patterns of Resettlement and Socioeconomic Adaptation in the United States*. Boulder, CO: Westview Press.

Moy, E. (2003). Recognizing identity beyond the categories. In E. Lai and D. Arguelles (Eds.), *The New Face of Asian Pacific America: Numbers, Diversity & Change in the 21st Century*. Los Angeles, CA: UCLA Asian American Studies Center Press, pp. 85–92.

Murase, K. (1977). Delivery of social services to Asian Americans. In National Association of Social Workers (Ed.), *The Encyclopedia of Social Work*. New York: NASW, pp. 953–960.

Narikiyo, T.A. and Kameoka, V.A. (1992). Attributions of mental illness and judgments about help seeking among Japanese-American and White American students. *Journal of Counseling Psychology*, 39(3), 363–369.

Nguyen, L. and Peterson, C. (1993). Depressive symptoms among Vietnamese-American college students. *Journal of Social Psychology*, 133(1), 65–71.

Nishioka, J. (2003). Socioeconomics: The model minority? In E. Lai and D. Arguelles (Eds.), *The New Face of Asian Pacific America: Numbers, Diversity & Change in the 21st Century*. Los Angeles, CA: UCLA Asian American Studies Center Press, pp. 29–35.

Okamura, A., Heras, P., and Wong-Kerberg, L. (1995). Asian, Pacific Island, and Filipino Americans and sexual child abuse. In L.A. Fontes (Ed.), *Sexual Abuse in Nine North American Cultures: Treatment and Prevention*. Thousand Oaks, CA: Sage, pp. 67–96.

Omi, M. (1993). Out of the melting pot and into the fire: Race relations policy. In *The State of Asian Pacific America: Policy Issues to the Year 2020*. Los Angeles: LEAP Asian Pacific American Public Policy Institute and UCLA Asian American Studies Center, pp. 199–214.

Ong, P.M. and Leung, L. (2003). Diversified growth. In E. Lai and D. Arguelles (Eds.), *The New Face of Asian Pacific America: Numbers, Diversity & Change in the 21st Century*. Los Angeles, CA: UCLA Asian American Studies Center Press, pp. 7–16.

Padilla, A.M., Wagatsuma, Y., and Lindholm, K.J. (1985). Acculturation and personality as predictors of stress in Japanese and Japanese Americans. *The Journal of Social Psychology*, 125, 295–305.

Park, H. (2002). Parenting practices, ethnicity, socioeconomic status and academic achievement in adolescents. *School Psychology International*, 23(4), 386–395.

Pfeifer, M.E. (2001). U.S. census 2000: An overview of national and regional trends in Vietnamese residential distribution. *Review of Vietnamese Studies*, 1(1), 1–9.

Phinney, J.S. (1989). Stages of ethnic identity development in minority group adolescents. *Journal of Early Adolescence*, 9(1/2), 34–49.

Phinney, J.S. and Alipuria, L. (1990). Ethnic identity in college students from four ethnic groups. *Journal of Adolescence*, 13, 171–184.

Phinney, J.S. and Kohatsu, E. (1997). Ethnic and racial identity development and mental health. In J. Schulenberg, J.L. Maggs, and K. Herrelmann (Eds.), *Health Risks and Developmental Transitions During Adolescence*. Cambridge, MA: Cambridge University Press, pp. 420–443.

Pinderhughes, E. (1982). Afro-American families and the victim system. In M. McGoldrick, J.K. Pearce, and J. Giordana (Eds.), *Ethnicity and Family Therapy*. New York: Guilford, pp. 108–122.

Prater, G. (2000). Child welfare and African-American families. In N.A. Cohen (Ed.), *Child Welfare: A Multicultural Focus* (2nd ed.). Needham Heights, MA: Allyn & Beacon, pp. 87–115.

Querimit, D.S. and Conner, L.C. (2003). Empowerment psychotherapy with adolescent females of color. *Journal of Clinical Psychology*, 59(11), 1215–1224.

Rao, K.V. (2003). Instant identity: The emergence of Asian Indian America. In E. Lai and D. Arguelles (Eds.), *The New Face of Asian Pacific America: Numbers, Diversity & Change in the 21st Century*. Los Angeles, CA: UCLA Asian American Studies Center Press, pp. 51–56.

Rhee, S. (1996). Effective social work practice with Korean immigrant families. *Journal of Multicultural Social Work*, 4(1), 49–61.

Rhee, S. (1997). Domestic violence in the Korean immigrant Families. *Journal of Sociology and Social Welfare*, 24(1), 63–77.

Rhee, S. and Chang, J. (2004). *Child Maltreatment Among Immigrant Asian families: Characteristics and Implications for Practice: Final Report*. A final report submitted to the California Social Work Education Center, Title IV-E, University of California, Berkeley.

Rhee, S., Chang, J., and Rhee, J. (2003). Acculturation, communication patterns, and self-esteem among Asian and Caucasian American adolescents. *Adolescence*, 38(152), 749–768.

Riger, S. (1993). What's wrong with empowerment. *American Journal of Community Psychology*, 21(3), 279–292.

Rosenbloom, S.R. and Way, N. (2004). Experiences of discrimination among African American, Asian American, and Latino adolescents in an urban high school. *Youth Society*, 35(4), 420–451.

Saleeby, D. (2002). Introduction: Power in the people. In D. Saleeby (Ed.), *The Strengths Perspective in Social Work Practice*. Boston, MA: Allyn & Bacon, pp. 1–22.

Schaefer, R.T. (2002). *Racial and Ethnic Groups* (8th ed.). Upper Saddle River, NJ: Prentice-Hall.

Schrodt, G.R. and Fitzgerald, B.A. (1987). Cognitive therapy with adolescents. *American Journal of Psychotherapy*, *41*(3), 402–408.

Segal, U.A. (2000). Exploring child abuse among Vietnamese refugees. *Journal of Multicultural Social Work*, *8*(3/4), 159–191.

Shin, J.K. (2002). Help-seeking behaviors by Korean immigrants for depression. *Issues in Mental Health Nursing*, *23*(5), 461–476.

Shinagawa, L.H. and Pang, G.Y. (1996). Asian American panethnicity and intermarriage. *Amerasia Journal*, *22*(2), 127–142.

Shrake, E.K. and Rhee, S. (2004). Ethnic identity as a predictor of problem behaviors among Korean American adolescents. *Adolescence*, *39*(155), 601–622.

Simon, B. (1994). *The Empowerment Tradition in American Social Work: A History*. New York: Columbia University Press.

Smith, C. and Krohn, M.D. (1995). Delinquency and family life among male adolescents: The role of ethnicity. *Journal of Youth and Adolescence*, *24*(1), 69–94.

Solomon, B.B. (1976). *Black Empowerment: Social Work in Oppressed Communities*. New York: Columbia University Press.

Spencer, M.B. and Dornbusch, S.M. (1990). *At the Threshold: The Developing Adolescent*. Cambridge, MA: Harvard University Press.

Stevensen, H.W. and Lee, S. (1990). Contexts of achievement: A study of American, Chinese, and Japanese children. *Monograph of the Society for Research in Child Development*, *55* (1–2, Serial no. 221).

Strand, P.J. and Jones, W. (1985). *Indochinese Refugees in America*. Durham, NC: Duke University Press.

Suan, L.V. and Tyler, J.D. (1990). Mental health values and preference for mental health resources of Japanese-American and Caucasian-American students. *Professional Psychology: Research & Practice*, *21*(4), 291–296.

Sue, D. (2005). Asian American/Pacific Islander families in conflict. In K.H. Barrett and W.H. George (Eds.), *Race, Culture, Psychology, and Law*. Thousand Oaks, CA: Sage, pp. 257–268.

Sue, D.W. and Sue, D. (1990). *Counseling the Culturally Different: Theory and Practice* (3rd ed.). New York: Wiley.

Sue, S. and Morishima, J.K. (1982). *The Mental Health of Asian Americans*. San Francisco: Jossey-Bass.

Sue, S. and Okazaki, S. (1990). Asian-American educational achievements: A phenomenon in search of an explanation. *American Psychologist*, *45*(8), 913–920.

Sue, S. and Zane, N. (1985). Academic achievement and socioemotional adjustment among Chinese university student. *Journal of Counseling Psychology*, *32*, 570–579.

Sue, S., Fujino, D., Hu, L., Takeuchi, D., and Zane, N. (1991). Community mental health services for ethnic minority groups: A test of the cultural responsiveness hypothesis. *Journal of Consulting and Clinical Psychology*, *59*(4), 533–540.

Suinn, R.M., Ahuna, C., and Khoo, G. (1992). The Suinn-Lew Asian self-identity Acculturation Scale: Concurrent and factorial validation. *Educational and Psychological Measurement*, *52*(4), 1041–1046.

Suinn, R.M., Rickard-Figueroa, K., Lew, S., and Vigil, P. (1987). The Suinn-Lew Asian self-identity acculturation scale: An initial report. *Educational and Psychological Measurement*, *47*, 401–407.

Takaki, R. (1989). *Strangers from a Different Shore: A History of Asian Americans*. Boston, MA: Little, Brown and Company.

Takaki, R. (1995). *From Exiles to Immigrants: The Refugees from Southeast Asia*. New York: Chelsea House Publishers.

Takeuchi, D.T., Sue, S., and Yeh, M. (1995). Return rates and outcomes from ethnicity-specific mental health programs in Los Angeles. *American Journal of Public Health*, *85*, 638–643.

Tang, N.M. (1997). Psychoanalytic psychotherapy with Chinese Americans. In E. Lee (Ed.). *Working with Asian Americans: A Guide for Clinicians*. New York: Guilford Press, pp. 323–341.

Tenhula, J. (1991). *Voices from Southeast Asia: The Refugee Experience in the United States*. New York, NY: Holmes & Meier Publishers.

Thornberry, T.P., Lizotte, A.J., Krohn, A., Farnworth, M., and Jang, S.J. (1994). Delinquent peers, beliefs, and Delinquent Behavior: A longitudinal test of interactional theory. *Criminology*, *32*, 47–84.

Toji, D.S. (2003). The rise of a Nikkei generation, In E. Lai and D. Arguelles (Eds.), *The New Face of Asian Pacific America: Numbers, Diversity & Change in the 21st Century*. Los Angeles, CA: UCLA Asian American Studies Center Press, pp. 73–78.

Torsch, V.L. and Xueqin Ma, G. (2000). Cross-cultural comparison of health perceptions, concerns, and coping strategies among Asian and Pacific Islander American Elders. *Qualitative Health Research*, *10*(4), 471–489.

Toy, C. (1992). Coming out to play: Reasons to join and participate in Asian gangs. *Journal of Gang Research*, *1*(1), 13–29.

Tracey, T.J., Leong, F.T., and Glidden, C. (1986). Help seeking and problem perception among Asian Americans. *Journal of Counseling Psychology*, *33*(3), 331–336.

Turner, F.J. (1974). Some considerations on the place of theory in current social work practice. In J. Turner (Ed.), *Social Work Treatment: Interlocking Theoretical Approaches* (4th ed.). New York: The Free Press, pp. 3–19.

Uba, L. (1994). *Asian Americans: Personality Patterns, Identity, and Mental Health*. New York: Guilford Press.

Uba, L. and Sue, S. (1991). Nature and scope of services for Asian and Pacific Islander. In N. Mokuau (Ed.), *Handbook of Social Services for Asian and Pacific Islanders*. Westport, CT: Greenwood Press, pp. 3–19.

U.S. Census Bureau. (1973a). *1970 Census of the Population: Population by Sex and Race, 1790–1970.* Series A 91–104. Washington, DC: Government Printing Office.

U.S. Census Bureau. (1973b). *1970 Census of the Population: Subject Reports: Japanese, Chinese, and Filipinos in the United States.* Washington, DC: Government Printing Office.

U.S. Census Bureau. (1981). *1980 Census of the Population: The United States Summary.* PC80-S1-3. Part 1, Chapter C. Washington, DC: Government Printing Office.

U.S. Census Bureau. (1993a). *We the American Asians.* Washington, DC: Government Printing Office.

U.S. Census Bureau. (1993b). *1990 Census of the Population: Asians and Pacific Islanders in the United.* CP-3-5. Washington, DC: Government Printing Office.

U.S. Census Bureau. (1995). *Statistical Brief: The Nation's Asian and Pacific Islander Population, 1994.* SB/95-24. Washington, DC: Government Printing Office.

U.S. Census Bureau. (2000). *U.S. Census 2000: SF2* (Table PCT1). Washington, DC: Government Printing Office.

U.S. Census Bureau. (February, 2002). *The Asian Population 2000: Census 2000 Brief.* www.census.gov/prod/2002pubs/c2kbr01-16.pdf.

U.S. Census Bureau. (August, 2002). *Profile of the Foreign-Born Population in the United States, 2000.* www.census.gov/population/www/socdemo/foreign/ppl-145.html.

U.S. Census Bureau. (September, 2002). *Poverty in the United States: 2001.* www.census.gov/prod/ 2002pubs/p60-219.pdf.

U.S. Census Bureau. (2003a). *Selected Historical Decennial Census and Housing Counts.* www.census.gov/population/www.censusdata/hiscendata.html.

U.S. Census Bureau. (2003b). *Facts for features Asian American Heritage Month: May 2003.* www.census.gov/Press-Release/www/2003/cb03-ff05.html.

Warr, M. and Stafford, M. (1991). The influence of delinquent peers: What they think or what they do? *Criminology, 29*(4), 851–866.

Way, N. and Chen, L. (2000). Close and general friendships among African Americans, Latino, and Asian American adolescents from low income families. *Journal of Adolescent Research, 15*(2), 274–301.

Weaver, H.N. (2005). *Exploration in Cultural Competence: Journeys to the Four Directions.* Belmont, CA: Thompson Brooks/Cole.

Weisz, J.R., Weiss, B., Wasserman, A.A., and Rintoul, B. (1987). Control-related beliefs and depression among clinic-referred children and adolescents. *Journal of Abnormal Psychology, 96*, 58–63.

Wong, D. (1987). Preventing child sexual assault among Southeast Asian refugee families. *Child Today, 16*(6), 18–22.

Woods, M.E. and Robinson, H. (1996). Psychosocial theory and social work treatment. In F. J. Turner (Ed.), *Social Work Treatment: Interlocking Theoretical Approaches* (4th ed.). New York: The Free Press, pp. 555–580.

World FactBook (2004). *American Samoa.* www.cia.gov/cia/publications/factbook/geos/aq.html#People.

Yee, B.W.K., Huang, L.N., and Lew, A. (1998). Families: Life-span socialization in a cultural context. In L.C. Lee and N.W.S. Zane (Eds.), *Handbook of Asian American Psychology.* Thousand Oaks, CA: Sage Publications, pp. 83–135.

Yeh, M., McCabe, K., Hough, R.L., Dupuis, D., and Hazen, A. (2003). Racial/ethnic differences in parental endorsement of barriers to mental health services for youth. *Mental Health Services Research, 5*(2), 65–77.

Yeh, M., Takeuchi, D.T., and Sue, S. (1994). Asian-American children treated in the mental health system: A comparison of parallel and mainstream outpatient service centers. *Journal of Clinical Child Psychology, 23*(1), 5–12.

Yick, A.G. (2001). Feminist theory and status inconsistency theory: Application to Domestic Violence in Chinese Immigrant Families. *Violence Against Women, 7*(5), 545–562.

Yick, A.G., Shibusawa, T., and Agbayani-Siewert, P. (2003). Partner violence, depression, and practice implications with families of Chinese descent. *Journal of Cultural Diversity, 10* (3), 96–104.

Ying, Y.W. (1990). Explanatory models of major depression and implications for help-seeking among immigrant Chinese—American Women. *Culture, Medicine, and Psychiatry, 14*(3), 393–408.

Ying, Y.W. (1994). Chinese American adults' relationship with their parents. *International Journal of Social Psychiatry, 40*(1), 35–45.

Ying, Y.W. (1998). Educational program for families on intergenerational conflict. In E. Kramer, S. Ivey, and Y. Ying (Eds.), *Immigrant Women's Health: Problems and Solutions.* San Francisco, CA: Jossey-Bass, pp. 282–294.

Ying, Y.W. and Miller, L.S. (1992). Help-seeking behavior and attitude of Chinese Americans regarding psychological problems. *American Journal of Community Psychology, 20*(4), 549–556.

Ying, Y.W., Allen Lee, P., Tsai, J.L., Lee, Y.J., and Tsang, M. (2001). Relationship of young adult Chinese Americans with their parents: Variation by migratory status and cultural orientation. *American Journal of Orthopsychiatry, 71*(3), 342–349.

Yoshioka, M.R., Dinoia, J., and Ullah, K. (2001). Attitudes toward marital violence: An examination of four Asian communities. *Violence Against Women, 7*(8), 900–927.

Yu, E.Y., Choe, P. and Han, S.I. (2002). Korean population in the United States, 2002: Demographic Characteristics and socio-economic Status. *International Journal of Korean Studies, 6*(1), 71–107.

Zhang, N. and Dixon, D.N. (2003). Acculturation and attitudes of Asian international students toward seeking psychological help. *Journal of Multicultural Counseling & Development, 31*(3), 205–222.

Zhang, A.Y., Snowden, L.R., and Sue, S. (1998). Differences between Asian and White Americans' help seeking and utilization patterns in the Los Angeles area. *Journal of Community Psychology, 26*(4), 317–326.

Zhou, M. (2003). Chinese: Once excluded, now ascendant. In E. Lai and D. Arguelles (Eds.), *The New Face of Asian Pacific America: Numbers, Diversity & Change in the 21st Century.* Los Angeles, CA: UCLA Asian American Studies Center Press, pp. 37–44.

Zimmerman, M. A. and Rappaport, J. (1988). Citizen participation, perceived control, and psychological empowerment. *American Journal of Community Psychology, 16*(5), 725–750.

CHAPTER 6

Abney, V.D. and Priest, R. (1995). African Americans and child abuse. In L.A. Fontes (Ed.), *Sexual Abuse in the North American Cultures* (pp. 11–30). California: Sage Publications, Inc.

Alegría, M., Canino, G., Ríos, R., Vera, M., Calderón, J., Rusch, D., and Ortega, A.N. (December, 2002). Mental health care for Latinos: Inequalities in use of specialty mental health services among Latinos, African-Americans, and Non-Latino Whites. *Psychiatric Services, 53,* 1547–1555.

Annie E. Casey Foundation. (2003). *Latino Children: State Level Measures of Child Well-Being from the 2000 Census.* KIDS Count Pocket Guide.

Armas, G.C. (December 6, 2002). Census admits it missed minority kids. CBSNEWS.com. Retrieved from http://cbsnews.com/stories/2002/12/06/national/printable532079.shtml.

Bauermeister, J.J., Canino, G., Bravo, M., Ramírez, R., Jensen, P.S., Chavez, L., Martínez, A., Ribera, J., Alegría, M., and García, P. (2003). Stimulant psychosocial treatment of ADHD in Latino/Hispanic Children. *Journal of the American Academy of Child and Adolescent Psychiatry, 42*(7), 851–856.

Bernal, G. and Shapiro E. (1996). Cubans Families. In M. McGoldrick, J. Giordano, and J.K. Pearce (Eds.), *Ethnicity and Family Therapy* (pp. 155–168). New York: The Guilford Press.

Black, L. (1996). Families of African Origin: An Overview. In M. McGoldrick, J. Giordano, and J.K. Pearce (Eds.), *Ethnicity and Family Therapy* (pp. 57–65). New York: The Guilford Press.

Bornstein, M.H. (1991). *Cultural Approaches to Parenting.* New Jersey: Lawrence Erlbaum Associates.

Buriel, R. and Hurtado, M.T. (1998). *Child Care in the Latino Community: Needs, Preferences and Access* (Research Report). California: The Tomás Rivera Policy Institute.

Cazenave, N.A. and Neubeck, K.J. (March/April 2001). Fighting welfare racism. *Poverty and Race Research Action Council Newsletter, 10*(2), 1–7.

Center for Disease Prevention and Control (2005). Hispanic or Latino Populations. Retrieved from www.cdc.gov/omh/Populations/HL/HL.htm.

Coalition for Juvenile Justice. (2005). Latino youth and the juvenile court. Retrieved from www.juvjustice.org/resources/fs009.html.

Culler, T. (January/February 2004). *Children's Voice Article, Many Efforts, One Vision.* Washington, DC: The Child Welfare League of America.

Delaker, J. (September 2001). *Poverty in the United States 2000.* Current Population Reports Consumer Income (pp. 60–214). Washington, DC: U.S. Census Bureau.

De Anda, D. (2002). The GIG: An innovative intervention to prevent adolescent pregnancy and sexually transmitted infection in a Latino community. In D. De Anda (Ed.), *Social Work with Multicultural Youth* (pp. 251–277). New York: The Haworth Press.

De-Navas-Watts, C., Proctor, B.D., and Mills, R.J. (August 2004). Income, poverty and health insurance coverage in the United States: 2003. *Current Population Report: Consumer Income.* Washington, DC: U.S. Census Bureau.

Devore, W. and Schlesinger, E.G. (1996). *Ethnic-Sensitive Social Work Practice* (4th ed.). Boston: Allyn and Bacon.

Díaz-Royo, A. (1983). Cultural themes in the enculturation of children from the Puerto Rican highlands. In R.J. Duncan, R.L. Ramírez, E. Seda-Bonilla, C. Buitrago-Ortíz, J. Wessman, M. Valdés-Pizzini, M. Morris, A. Díaz-Royo, and E. Jacob (Eds.), *Social Research in Puerto Rico: Science, Humanism and Society* (pp. 149–165). Puerto Rico: InterAmerican University Press.

Domínguez de Ramírez, R. and Shapiro, E.S. (1998). Teacher ratings of attention deficit hyperactivity disorder symptoms in Hispanic children. *Journal of Psychopathology and Behavioral Assessment, 20*(4), 275–293.

Driscoll, A.K., Biggs, M.A., Brindis, C.D., and Yankah, E. (2001). Adolescent Latino reproductive health: A review of the literature. *Hispanic Journal of Behavioral Sciences, 23,* 255–326.

Falicov, C.J. (1996). Mexican families. In M. McGoldrick, J. Giordano, and J.K. Pearce (Eds.), *Ethnicity and Family Therapy* (pp. 169–182). New York: The Guilford Press.

Falicov, C.J. (1998). *Latino Families in Therapy*. New York: The Guilford Press.

Flores, G., Fuentes-Afflick, E., Barbot, O., Carter-Pokras, O., Claudio, L., Lara, M., McLaurin, J.A., Patcher, L., Ramos-Gómez, F., Mendoza, F., Valdez, R.B., Villaruel, A., Zambrana, R.E., Greenberg, R., and Weitzman, M. (July 3, 2002). The health of Latino children: Urgent priorities, unanswered questions, and a research agenda. *The Journal of the American Medical Association, 288*, 82–91.

Fluke, J.D., Yuan, Y.-Y. T., Hedderson, J., and Curtis, P.A. (2003). Disproportionate representation of race and ethnicity in child maltreatment: Investigation and victimization. *Children and Youth Services Review, 25*(5/6), 359–373.

García-Prieto, N. (1996). Latino families: An Overview. In M. McGoldrick, J. Giordano, and J.K. Pearce (Eds.), *Ethnicity and Family Therapy* (pp. 141–154). New York: The Guilford Press.

Garland, A.F., Landsverk, J.A., and Lau, A.S. (2003). Racial/ethnic disparities in mental health service use among children in foster care. *Children and Youth Services Review, 25*(5/6), 491–507.

Green, J.W. (1999). *Cultural Awareness in the Human Services: A Multi-Ethnic Approach*. Massachusetts: Allyn and Bacon.

Halfon, N., Berkowitz, G., and Klee, L. (1992). Mental health service utilization by children in foster care in California. *Pediatrics, 89*, 1238–1244.

Harris, M.S. and Courtney, M.E. (2003). The interaction of race, ethnicity, and family structured with respect to timing of family reunification. *Children and Youth Services Review, 25*(5/6), 409–429.

Hayes-Bautista, D.E. (2004). *La Nueva California: Latinos in the Golden State*. Berkeley: University of California Press.

Hesselbrock, M., Negroni-Rodríguez, L.K., and Grube-Chartier, K. (2003). *Evaluation Report of the Latino Family Connection Program* (Unpublished Research Report). Connecticut: Department of Mental Health and Addiction Services. Federal Grant Funded by the Center for Substance Abuse Prevention of the Substance Abuse and Mental Health Services Administration.

Hines, A.M., Lemon, K., Wyatt, P., and Merdinger, J. (2004). Factors related to the disproportionate involvement of children of color in the child welfare system: A review an emerging themes. *Children and Youth Services Review, 24*(1), 507–527.

Iglehart, A.P. and Becerra, R.M. (2003). Hispanic and African American youth: Life after foster care emancipation. In D. De Anda (Ed.), *Social Work with Multicultural Youth* (pp. 79–107). New York: Haworth Social Work Practice Press, Inc.

Johansen, P. (November 2002). Discrimination in metropolitan housing markets 1989–2000 report (News Release). Washington, DC: U.S. Department of Housing and Urban Development. Retrieved from www.hud.gov.

Kaiser Permanente. (2001). *A Provider's Handbook on Culturally Competent Care: Latino Population*. Oakland, CA: Kaiser Permanente National Diversity Council.

Kolko, D.J., Selelyo, J., and Brown, E.J. (1999). The treatment histories and service involvement of physically and sexually abusive families: Description, correspondence, and clinical correlates. *Child Abuse & Neglect, 23*, 459–476.

Landale, N. and Litcher, D.T. (1996). Latino poverty has its own diversity. Retrieved from www.personal.psu.edu/dept/ur/NEWS/LIFESTYLE/Latino.html.

Landon, P.S. (1999). Generalist and advanced generalist practice. In R.L. Edwards and J.E. Hopps (Eds.), *Encyclopedia of Social Work* (pp. 1101–1108). Washington, DC: NASW Press.

Laureano, M. and Poliandro, E. (1991). Understanding cultural values of Latino male alcoholics and their families: A culturally sensitive model. *Journal of Chemical Dependency Treatment, 4*(1), 137–155.

Lecca, P.J., Quervalú, I., Nunes, J.V., and González, H.F. (1998). *Cultural Competency in Health, Social and Human Services: Directions for the Twenty-First Century*. New York: Garland Publishers.

Lee, E. (1996). Asian American families: An overview. In M. McGoldrick, J. Giordano, and J.K. Pearce (Eds.), *Ethnicity and Family Therapy* (pp. 227–248). New York: The Guilford Press.

Lillas, C.M., Lester-Langer, J., and Drinane, M. (Spring, 2004). Addressing infant and toddler Issues in Juvenile Court: Challenges for the 21st Century. *Juvenile and Family Court, 22*(5), 26–32.

Marsiglia, F.F., Miles, B.W., Dustman, P., and Sills, S. (2003). Ties that project: An ecological perspective on Latino/a urban pre-adolescent drug use. In D. De Anda (Ed.), *Social Work with Multicultural Youth* (pp. 191–220). New York: Haworth Social Work Practice Press, Inc.

National Center on Child Abuse and Neglect. (2003). *Foster Care National Statistics*. Washington, DC: National Clearinghouse on Child Abuse and Neglect Information. Retrieved from www.calib.com/nccanch.

National Latina Health Network. (February 4, 2005). *Latina Leaders for Health*. Western Regional Symposium celebrated at the University of Southern California Davidson Executive Conference Center. Los Angeles, California.

Negroni-Rodríguez, L.K. (1998). *Puerto Rican Mothers' Beliefs and Attitudes About Child Discipline and Child Abuse; Their Expectations and Attributions of Children* (Doctoral dissertation, Boston College). Dissertation Abstracts #9905884.

Negroni-Rodríguez, L.K. (2003). Puerto Rican abusive and non-abusive mothers' beliefs about appropriate and inappropriate child discipline. *Journal of Ethnic and Cultural Diversity in Social Work, 12*(4), 65–90.

Negroni-Rodríguez, L.K. and Morales, J. (2002). Individual and family assessment skills with Latino/ Hispanic-Americans. In R. Fong and S. Furuto (Eds.), *Cultural Competent Social Work Practice: Practice Skills, Interventions, and Evaluation* (pp. 132–146). Massachusetts: Allyn and Bacon.

Nine, C.J. (August 1984). *Contrastive Analysis of Cultural Values Between Puerto Ricans and Anglos.* Unpublished manuscript.

Novas, H. (1994). *Everything You Need to Know About Latino History.* New York: Peguin Books.

Ortega, R.M. (September 2000). *Latino Children and Well-Being: Implications from Child Welfare.* Paper presented at the Research Symposium on child well-being, University of Illinois: Urbana-Champaign.

Ortega, R.M., Guillean, C., and Gutierrez-Najera, L. (1996). *Latinos and Child Welfare/Latinos y el bienestar del niño: Voces de la comunidad.* The University of Michigan School of Social Work.

Osofsky, J.D. (October 2001). Addressing youth victimization. *Coordinating Council on Juvenile Justice and Delinquency Prevention Action Plan Update.* U.S. Department of Justice, Office of Justice Programs, Office of Juvenile Justice and Delinquency Prevention. Retrieved from www.ncjrs.org/html/ojjdp/action_plan_update_2001_10/index.html.

Pabón, A. and Pabón, E. (2004). *The Circles of Care Initiative: The Use of Informal Natural Helpers in Latino Communities.* (Unpublished manuscript available from Marywood University School of Social Work, Allentown, Pennsylvania.)

Peacock, M.J., McClure, F., and Agars, M.D. (2003). Predictors of delinquent behaviors among Latino youth. *The Urban Review, 35*(1), 59–72.

Pecora, P.J., Whittaker, J.K., Maluccio, A.N., and Barth, R.P. (2000). *The Child Welfare Challenge.* New York: Aldine De Gruyter.

Ramírez, R.R. and De La Cruz, G.P. (June 2003). The Hispanic population in the United States: March 2002, Population Characteristics. *Current Population Report, P20–545.* Washington, DC: U.S. Census Bureau.

Rivera, P.J. (1995). *Parenting Values and Practices of Puerto Rican Families.* Utah: Family Development Resources.

Saleebey, D. (2003). *The Strengths Perspective in Social Work Practice* (3rd ed., pp. 9–130). Boston: Allyn & Bacon.

Samantrai, K. (2004). *Culturally Competent Public Child Welfare Practice.* California: Brooks and Cole, Inc.

Spiegel, J. (1982). An ecological model of ethnic families. In M. McGoldrick, J.K. Pearce, and J. Giordano (Eds.), *Ethnicity and Family Therapy* (pp. 31–54). New York: The Guilford Press.

Sue, D.W. (1973). Ethnic identity: The impact of two cultures in the psychological development of Asian Americans (Chapter 15). In S. Sue and N. Wagner (Eds.), *Asian Americans: Psychological Perspectives.* California: Palo Alto Science and Behavior Books.

Sue, D.W. and Sue, D. (1990). *Counseling the Culturally Different: Theory and Practice.* New York: John Wiley & Sons.

Suleiman, L.P. (2003). *Creating a Latino Child Welfare Agenda: A Strategic Framework for Change.* New York: Committee for Hispanic Children and Families, Inc.

Talvi, Silja, J.A. (2002). *Guilty of Being Brown* (Press Coverage). Retrieved from www.building- blocksforyouth.org/latino_rpt/pr_cov_alternet.html.

Therrien, M. and Ramírez, R. (2000). The Hispanic population in the United States: March 2000. *Current Population Reports* (pp. 20–535). Washington, DC: U.S. Census Bureau.

Tingus, K.D., Heger, A.H., Foy, D.W., and Leskin, G.A. (1996). Factors associated with entry into therapy in children evaluated for sexual abuse. *Child Abuse and Neglect, 20*(1), 63–68.

U.S. Department of Health and Human Services, Administration on Children, Youth and Families. (2001a). *Child Maltreatment 1999: Reports From the States to the National Child Abuse and Neglect Data System.* Washington, DC: U.S. Government Printing Office.

U.S. Department of Health and Human Services, Public Health Service, Office of the Surgeon General. (2001b). *Mental Health: Culture, Race, and Ethnicity—A Supplement to Mental Health: A Report of the Surgeon General.* Rockville (pp. 141–142). Maryland: U.S. Department of Health and Human Services.

U.S. Department of Health and Human Services, Administration on Children, Youth and Families. (2004). *Child Maltreatment 2002.* Washington, DC: U.S. Government Printing Office.

Vigil, J.D. (Ed.) (2002). Mexican-Americans in the Barrio of Los Angeles (Chapter 3), *Street Cultures in the Mega City: A Rainbow of Gangs.* Houston: University of Texas Press.

Villarruel, F.A. and Walker, N.E. (2002). *¿Dónde está la justicia? A Call to Action on Behalf of Latino and Latina Youth in the U.S. System: Executive Summary.* The Building Blocks Initiative. Retrieved from www.buildingb-locksforyouth.org/.

Wagenheim, K. and Jiménez, O. (1994). *The Puerto Ricans: A Documentary History.* New York: Marcus Wiener Publishers.

Weinberg, D.H. (August 26, 2004). *2003 Income and Poverty Estimates from the Current Population Survey* (press briefing). Washington, DC: U.S. Census Bureau. Retrieved from www.census.gov/hhes/www/income/income03/prs04asc.html.

Williams, S. and Robinson, J. (March 2001). Trends among Hispanic children, youth and families. *Child Trends.* Washington, DC: U.S. Census Bureau.

Yancey, A.K. (1998). Building positive self-image in adolescents in foster care: The use of role models in an interactive group approach. *Adolescence, 33*(130), 253–267.

Zambrana, R.E. (October 15, 1999). *Promoting Latino Family and Child Social Welfare: A Call for Transformation of the Child Welfare System.* Unpublished paper presented at the Conference on Los Niños de los Barrios, New York: Manhattan Borough Community College.

Zambrana, R.E. and Zoppi, I.M. (2003). Latina students: Translating cultural wealth into social capital to improve academic success. In D. de Anda (Ed.), *Social Work with Multicultural Youth* (pp. 33–53). New York: Haworth Social Work Practice Press, Inc.

Zayas, L.H. (1994). Hispanic family ecology and early childhood socializations: Health care implications. *Family Systems Medicine, 12*(3), 315–325.

CHAPTER 7

Abudabbeh, N. (2001). Advice to Arab-American parents: Helping children cope. In Action Alert (ed.), *The Montgomery County, Maryland, Gazette,* September 14, 2001.

ACCEPT. (2004). *Useful Facts About International Adoption.* Retrieved 9/23/04 from www.acceptadoptions.org/info.html.

Aguirre, A. and Turner, J. (1998). *American Ethnicity* (2nd ed.). New York: McGraw-Hill.

Alemán, S., Fitzpatrick, T.R., Tran, T.V., and Gonzalez, E. (Eds.) (2001). *Therapeutic Interventions with Ethnic Elders: Health and Social Issues.* New York, London: Haworth Press, Inc.

Althausen, L. (1993). Adult day care: A developing concept. *Journal of Gerontological Social Work, 5,* 35–47.

Bahira, S. (1999). Islamic family ideals and their relevance to American Muslim families. In H.O. McAdoo (2nd ed.), *Family Ethnicity: Strength and Diversity* (pp. 203–212). Thousand Oaks, CA: Sage Publications.

Balgopal, P.R. (Ed.) (2000). *Social Work Practice with Immigrants and Refugees.* New York: Columbia University Press.

Bowlby, J. (1969). *Attachment and Loss. Volume 1 & 2.* New York: Basic Books.

Brace, C.L. (1872). *The Dangerous Classes of New York and Twenty Years' Work Among Them.* New York: Wynkoop & Hallenbeck, 1872; reprinted, Washington, DC: National Association of Social Workers, 1973.

Camarota, S.A. (2002). Immigrants for the Middle East: A profile of the foreign-born U.S. population from Pakistan to Morocco. *The Journal of Social, Political, and Economic Studies, 27,* 315–340.

Carlson, V.J. and Harwood, R.L. (2003). Attachment, culture, and the caregiving system: The cultural patterning of everyday experiences among Anglo and Puerto Rican mother-infant pairs. *Infant Mental Health Journal, 24,* 53–73.

Casey Family Programs. (2000). *A Conceptual Framework of Identity Formation in a Society of Multiple Cultures: Applying Theory to Practice.* Seattle, WA: Author.

Cohen, Y. and Tryee, A. (1994). Palestinian and Jewish Israeli-born immigrants in the Unites States. *International Migration Review, 28,* 243–254.

Courtney, M. and Skyles, A. (2003). Racial disproportionality in the child welfare system. *Children and Youth Services Review, 25*(5/6), 355–358.

Crosson-Tower, C. (2001). *Exploring Child Welfare* (2nd ed.). Boston: Allyn and Bacon.

CWLA. (2004) Child Welfare League of America Best Practice guidelines for child maltreatment in Foster Care. *In Partnership with Casey Family Programs* (pp. 73–75). Washington, DC; Child Welfare league of America, C2003.

Diller, J. (2004). *Cultural Diversity: A Primer for the Human Services.* Belmont, CA: Brooks/Cole-Thompson.

Ernst, J.S. (2001). Culture and child welfare: Insights from New Zealand. *International Social Work, 44*(2), 163–178.

Everett, J.E. (1995). Child foster care. In the *Encyclopedia of Social Work* (19th ed.), (Vol. 1, pp. 375–389). Washington, DC: National Association of Social Workers.

Faragallah, M.H., Schumm, W.R., and Webb, F.J. (1997). Acculturation of Arab American immigrants. *Journal of Comparative Family Studies, 28*(3), 182–203.

Farley, J.E. (2000). *Majority-Minority Relations* (4th ed.). Upper Saddle River, New Jersey: Prentice Hall.

Fernando, J.L. (2001). Children's Rights. *Annals of the American Academy of Political & Social Science, 0002–7162, v. 575.* Thousand Oaks, CA: Sage Publications.

Finn, J., and Jacobson, M. (2003). Just practice: Steps towards a new social paradigm. *Journal of Social Work Education, 39,* 57–78.

Fitzpatrick, J. (1969). *The Role of the White Ethnic Communities in the Urban Adjustment of Newcomers.* Paper presented at the Chicago Consultation on Ethnicity.

Fitzpatrick, T.R. (2001). Elderly Russian immigrants. In S. Alemán, T.R. Fitzpatrick, T.V. Tran, and E. Gonzalez (Eds.), *Therapeutic Interventions with Ethnic Elders: Health and Social Issues.* New York, London: Haworth Press, Inc.

Germain, C. (1994). Human behavior and the social environment. In R. Reemer (Ed.), *The Foundations of Social Work Knowledge* (pp. 88–121). New York: Columbia University Press.

Germain, C. and Gitterman, A. (1980). *The Life Model of Social Work Practice.* New York: Columbia University Press.

Giordano, J. and McGoldrick, M. (1996). European families: An overview. In M. McGoldrick, J. Giordano, and J.K. Pearce (Eds.), *Ethnicity and Family Therapy* (pp. 427–441). New York: The Guilford Press.

Gold, S. (1991). *Soviet Jewish émigrés in the U.S.: What We Know and What We Don't Know.* Paper presented at the Wilstein Institute Conference, Stanford University, June.

Goldstein, E. (1979). Psychological adaptations of Soviet immigrants. *The American Journal of Psychoanalysis, 39,* 219–234.

Guadalupe, K.L. and Lum, D. (2005). *Multidimensional Contextual Practice: Diversity and Transcendence.* Australia, Canada: Thompson, Brooks/Cole.

Guzzetta, C. (1995). White ethnic groups. In the *Encyclopedia of Social Work* (19th ed.), (Vol. 1, pp. 2508–2517). Washington, DC: National Association of Social Workers.

Hanson, M. (2004). Families with Anglo-European roots. In E. Lynch and M. Hanson (Eds.), *Developing Cross-Cultural Competence* (pp. 81–108). Baltimore, MD: Brooks.

Harder, M. and Pringle, K. (Eds.) (1997). *Protecting Children in Europe: Towards a New Millennium.* Denmark: Aalborg University Press.

Harper, K. and Lantz, J. (1996). *Cross Cultural Practice: Social Work with Diverse Populations.* New York: Lyceum Books.

Hassan, S.D. (2002). *Arabs, Race and the Post September 11 National Security State.* Retrieved 8/4/04 from www.merip.org/mer/mer224/224_hassan.html.

Healey, J.F. (Ed.) (1996). *Race, Ethnicity, and Gender in the United States.* Thousand Oaks, CA: Pine Forge Press.

Heinrich, J. (2004). *Marriage, A Test of Love, Romance and Religion.* In *The Gazette,* Saturday, July 24, 2004.

Hutchison, E.D. (1999). *Dimensions of Human Behavior: Person and Environment.* Thousand Oaks, CA: Pine Forge Press.

Inglehart, A. and Becerra, R. (1995). *Social Services and the Ethnic Community.* New York: Allyn and Bacon.

Kane, M. and Houston-Vega, M.K. (2004). Maximizing content on elders with dementia while teaching multicultural diversity. *Journal of Social Work Education, 40*(2), 285–303.

Kapstein, E.B. (2003). The baby trade. *Foreign Affairs, 82*(6), 115–125.

Karger, H.J. and Levine, J. (2000). Social work practice with European immigrants. In P.R. Balgopal (Ed.), *Social Work Practice with Immigrants and Refugees* (p. 167). New York: Columbia University Press.

Kavanaugh, K. and Kennedy, P. (1992). *Promoting Cultural Diversity: Strategies for Health Care Professionals.* Newbury Park, CA: Sage.

Kirst-Ashman, K. (2003). *Introduction to Social Work and Social Welfare: Cultural Thinking Perspectives.* Pacific Grove, CA: Brooks/Cole—Thomson Learning.

Kulczycki, A., Aguirre, B., and Fernandez, M. (2002). Patterns, determinants and implications of intermarriage among Arab Americans. *Journal of Marriage and Family, Feb. 2002.* In the National Council on Family Relations entitled "Arab Americans and the Melting Pot."

Lum, D. (Ed.) (2003). *Culturally Competent Practice.* Pacific Cove, CA: Brooks/Cole-Thompson Learning.

Maguire, M.J. (2002). Foreign adoptions and the evolution of Irish adoption policy. *Journal of Social History, 36*(2), 387–404.

Markides, K.S. and Mindel, C.H. (1987). *Aging and Ethnicity.* Newbury Park, CA: Sage Publications.

Mather, J.H. and Lager, P.B. (2000). *Child Welfare.* Australia, Canada: Brooks/Cole.

McCaffrey, L.J. (1976). *The Irish Diaspora in America.* London: Indiana University Press.

McGoldrick, M. (2005). Irish families. In M. McGoldrick, J.K. Pearce, and J. Giordano (Eds.), *Ethnicity and Family Therapy (2nd Ed),* (pp. 544–566). New York, London: The Guilford Press.

McGoldrick, M., Pearce, J.K., and Giordano, J. (Eds.) (1982). *Ethnicity and Family Therapy.* New York, London: The Guilford Press.

Mindel, C., Habenstein, R., and Wright, R. (Eds.) (1988). *Ethnic Families in America* (3rd ed.). New York: Elsevier.

Nadir, A. and Dziegielewski, S. (2001). Islam. In M.V. Hook, B. Hugen, and M. Aguilar (Eds.), *Spirituality Within Religious Traditions in Social Work Practice* (pp. 146–162). Pacific Grove, CA: Brooks/Cole.

Risley-Curtiss, C. and Heffernan, K. (2003). Gender biases in child welfare. *Affilia: Journal of Women and Social Work,* 18(4), 395–410.

Rothstein, R. (2000). And so just what good were the good old days? In *The New York Times,* February 2, 2000.

Ruark, J. (2002). What makes a family? *The Chronicle of Higher Education,* 49(9), A12.

Saleebey, D. (1992). *The Strengths Perspective in Social Work Practice.* New York: Adison-Wesley.

Samantrai, K. (2004). *Culturally Competent Public Child Welfare Practice.* Australia, Canada: Brooks/Cole.

Schaefer, R.T. (2000). *Racial and Ethnic Groups* (8th ed.). Upper Saddle River, New Jersey: Prentice-Hall, Inc.

Schwartz, W. (1999). Arab American students in public schools. *ERIC Clearing House on Urban Education, ERIC Digest,* Number 142. New York, NY.

Sharifzadeh, V.S. (2004). Families with middle eastern roots. In E. Lynch, and M. Hanson (Eds.), *Developing Cross-Cultural Competence* (pp. 373–414). Baltimore, MD: Brooks.

Sieppert, J.D., Hudson, J., and Unrau, Y. (2000). Family group conferencing in child welfare: Lessons from a demonstration projects. *Families in Society,* 81(4), 382–391.

Smith, T. (Ed.) (2004). *Practicing Multiculturalism.* New York: Allyn and Bacon.

Smithgall, C.D. (2003). Assessing the worker–client relationship in child welfare and family preservation services. *Social Work Abstracts, 39*(4), No. 1526.

Tran, T.V., Fitzpatrick, T.R., Berg, W.R., and Roosevelt Wright, Jr. (1996). Acculturation, health, stress and psychological distress among elderly Hispanics. *Journal of Cross-Cultural Gerontology, 11*, 149–165.

Tyyaka, V. (2002). *Immigrant Adjustment and Parenting: A Study of Newcomer Groups in Toronto, Canada.* Department of Sociology, Ryerson University, Toronto, Canada.

U.S. Bureau of Census. (1994). *Statistical Abstracts of the United States 1994.* Washington, DC: Sage Publications.

U.S. Bureau of Census. (2000). *Statistical Abstracts of the United States 2000.* Washington, DC: Sage Publications.

Valpy, Michael. (2003). Dinner dance. *The Globe and Mail*, June 21, 2003.

Walker, R. and Staton, M. (2000). Multiculturalism in social work ethics. *Journal of Social Work Education, 36*(3), 449–462.

Warren, J. and Twine, F. (1997). White Americans, the new minority? Non-blacks and the ever-expanding boundaries of whiteness. *Journal of Black Studies, 28*(2), 200–218.

Zaki, K., Sinno, J., and Johnson, D. (2001). Muslim immigrants: Social, cultural and religious issues of youth, families and schools in greater Lansing. In *Families and Communities Together* (2001). Retrieved 8/5/04 from www.fact.msu.edu/Projects/grants2001muslim_immigrants.htm.

Zeidner, R.F. (1976). From Babylon to Babylon: Immigrants from the Middle East. In Helen Zeese Papanikolas (Ed.), *The Peoples of Utah* (1st ed.). Salt Lake City: Utah State Historical Society.

Zoll, R. (2004). Clergy sexual abuse crisis. *Associated Press.* February 27, 2004.

CHAPTER 8

Ackerman, L.K. (1997). Health problems of refugees. *Journal of the American Board of Family Practice, 10*, 337–348.

Administration for Children and Families. (2004). Fact sheet: Human trafficking. [On-line]. Available: www.acf.hhs.gov/trafficking/about/fact_human.html. Washington, DC: U.S. Department of Health and Human Services.

Ahearn, F.L. and Athey, J.L. (1991). *Refugee Children. Theory, Research and Services.* Baltimore, MD: Johns Hopkins University Press.

Almqvist, K. and Broberg, A.G. (1999). Mental health and social adjustment in young refugee children 3¹/₂ years after their arrival in Sweden. *Journal of the American Academy of Child and Adolescent Psychiatry, 38*, 723–730.

American Psychiatric Association. (2000). *Diagnostic and Statistical Manual of Mental Disorders* (4th ed., text rev.). Washington, DC: Author.

Amnesty International. (2002). *Unmatched Power, Unmatched Principles: The Human Rights Dimensions of US Training of Foreign Military and Police Forces.* Washington, DC: Amnesty International USA Publications.

Anderson, P. (March 2001). You don't belong here in Germany. On the social situation of refugee children in Germany. *Journal of Refugee Studies, 14*(2), 187–199.

Baker, A. (1991). The psychological impact of he Intifada on Palestinian children in the occupied West Bank and Gaza: An exploratory story. *American Journal of Orthopsychiatry, 60*, 496–504.

Baker, R. (1992). Psychological consequences for tortured refugees seeking asylum and refugee status in Europe. In M. Basoglu (Ed.), *Torture and Its Consequences: Current Treatment Approaches* (pp. 83–101). Cambridge, England: Cambridge University Press.

Basoglu, M., Jaranson, J.M., Mollica, R., and Kastrup, M. (2001). Torture and mental health: A research overview. In E. Gerrity, T.M. Keane, and F. Tuma (Eds.), *The Mental Health Consequences of Torture.* New York: Kluwer Academic/Plenum Publishers.

Beiser, M., Cargo, M., and Woodbury, M.A. (1994). A comparison of psychiatric disorder in different cultures: Depressive typologies in Southeast Asian refugees and resident Canadians. *International Journal of Methods in Psychiatric Research, 4*, 157–172.

Benard, B. (1995). Fostering Resilience in Children. In B. Cesarone, (Ed.), *Resilience Guide: A Collection of Resources on Resilience in Children and Families.* Champaign, Ill: ERIC Clearinghouse on Elementary and Early Childhood Education. EDO-PS-95-9 (Also available online, accessed February 3, 2004) http://resilnet.uiuc.edu/library/benard95.html.

Benard, B. (1997). Fostering resiliency in children and youth: Promoting protective factors in the school. In D. Saleebey, (Ed.), *The Strengths Perspective in Social Work Practice* (pp. 167–182). New York: Longman.

Berg, I.K. and Kelly, S. (2000). *Building Solutions in Child Protective Services.* New York, NY: W. W. Norton.

Berg, I.K., De Jong, P., and Gonzales, J. (Eds.) (2005). *Safety Planning in Children's Protective Services: Building Solutions with Clients* [Video]. (Available from Brief Family Therapy Center, P.O. Box 13736, Milwaukee, WI, 53213, www.brief-therapy.org.)

Berthold, S.M. (1989). Spiritism as a form of psychotherapy: Implications for social work practice. *Social Casework, 70*(8), 502–509.

Berthold, S.M. (1999). The effects of exposure to community violence on Khmer refugee adolescents. *Journal of Traumatic Stress Studies, 12*(3), 455–471.

Berthold, S.M. (2000). War traumas and community violence: Psychological, behavioral, and academic outcomes among Khmer refugee adolescents. *Journal of Multicultural Social Work, 8*(1/2), 15–46. Co-published simultaneously in D. de Anda and R.M. Becerra (Eds.), *Violence: Diverse Populations and Communities*. New York: Haworth Press.

Boehnlein, J.K. and Kinzie, J.D. (1996 Winter). Psychiatric treatment of Southeast Asian refugees. *NCP Clinical Quarterly, 6*(1), 19–22.

Boothby, N. (1994). Trauma and violence among refugee children. In A.J. Marsella, T. P. Bornemann, E. Solvig, and J. Orley (Eds.), *Amidst Peril and Pain: The Mental Health and Well-Being of the World's Refugees*. Washington, DC: American Psychological Association Press.

Bracken, P. (December 1997). Rethinking mental health work with survivors of wartime violence and refugees. *The Journal of Refugee Studies, 19*(4), 431–442.

Bracken, P.J., Giller, J.E., and Summerfield, D. (1995). Psychological responses to war and atrocity: The limitations of current concepts. *Social Science and Medicine, 40*(8), 1073–1082.

Briere, J. (2004). *Psychological Assessment of Adult Posttraumatic States: Phenomenology, Diagnosis, and Measurement* (2nd ed.). Washington, DC: American Psychological Association.

Chakraborty, A. (1991). Culture, colonialism, and psychiatry. *Lancet, 337*, 1204–1207.

Child Abuse Prevention Council. (2005). About child abuse: Cultural customs. www.capcsac.org/childabuse/customs.html (accessed from the web on 1–4–05). Child Abuse Prevention Council of Sacramento, Inc.

Clark, D.C., Pynoos, R.S., and Goebel, A.E. (1996). Mechanisms and processes of adolescent bereavement. In R.J. Haggerty, L.R. Sherrod, N. Garmezy, and M. Rutter (Eds.), *Stress, Risk, and Resilience in Children and Adolescents: Processes, Mechanisms, and Interventions* (pp. 100–146). New York: Cambridge University Press.

Coalition to Stop the Use of Child Soldiers. (2001). *Child Soldiers: Global Report 2001. The Impact of Soldiering on Children*. www.eldis.org/static/DOC8815.htm.

De Jong, P. and Berg, I.K. (2002). *Interviewing for Solutions* (2nd ed.). Pacific Grove, CA: Brooks/Cole.

Dinicola, V.F. (1996). *Ethnocultural Aspects of PTSD and Related Disorders Among Children and Adolescents*. In A.J. Marsella, M.J. Friedman, E.T. Gerrity, and Scurfield, R.M. (1996) (Eds.), *Ethnocultural Aspects of Posttraumatic Stress Disorder: Issues, Research, and Clinical Applications* (pp. 389–414). Washington, DC: American Psychological Association.

Diversity Resources, Inc. (2000). Culture-sensitive health care: Asian. *What Language Does Your Patient Hurt In? A Practical Guide to Culturally Competent Care*. Amherst, MA: Author.

Dokter, D. (Ed.) (1998). *Arts Therapists, Refugees and Migrants: Reaching Across Borders*. London and Philadelphia, PA: Jessica Kingsley Publishers.

Dreman, S. and Cohen, E. (1990). Children of victims of terrorism revisited: Integrating individual and family treatment approaches. *American Journal of Orthopsychiatry, 60*(2), 204–209.

Eisenbruch, M. (1992). Commentary: Toward a culturally sensitive DSM: Cultural bereavement in Cambodian refugees and the traditional healer as taxonomist. *The Journal of Nervous and Mental Disease, 180*(1), 8–10.

Eisenbruch, M. and Handelman, L. (1989). Development of an explanatory model of illness schedule for Cambodian refugee patients. *Journal of Refugee Studies, 2*, 243–256.

Eisenbruch, M., de Jong, J., and van de Put, W. (April 2004). Bringing order out of chaos: A culturally competent approach to managing the problems of refugees and victims of organized violence. *Journal of Traumatic Stress, 17*(2), 123–131.

Eisenman, D.P., Gelberg, L., Liu, Honghu, and Shapiro, M.F. (2003). Mental health and health related quality of life among adult Latino primary care patients living in the United States with previous exposure to political violence. *JAMA, 290*, 627–634.

Elsass, P. (1997). *Treating Victims of Torture and Violence: Theoretical, Cross-Cultural, and Clinical Implications*. New York: New York University Press.

Eth, S. and Pynoos, R.S. (1994). Children who witness the homicide of a parent. *Psychiatry, 57*, 287–305.

Farwell, N. (2001). Onward through strength: Coping and psychological support among refugee youth returning to Eritrea from Sudan. *Journal of Refugee Studies, 14*, 1–69.

Freedman, J. and Combs, G. (1996). *Narrative Therapy: The Social Construction of Preferred Realities*. New York: W. W. Norton & Company.

Friedman, M.J. and Jaranson, J.M. (1994). The applicability of the PTSD concept to refugees. In A.J. Marsella, T.H. Borneman, S. Ekblad, and J. Orley (Eds.), *Amid Peril and Pain: The Mental Health and Well-Being of the World's Refugees* (pp. 207–228). Washington, DC: American Psychological Association.

Garbarino, K. (1996). What do we need to know to understand children in war and community violence? In R.J. Apfel and B. Simon (Eds.), *Minefields in Their Hearts: The Mental Health of Children in War and Communal Violence* (pp. 33–51). New Haven, CT: Yale University Press.

Garbarino, J., Dubrow, N., Kostelny, K., and Pardo, C. (1992). *Children in Danger: Coping with the Consequences of Community Violence*. San Francisco, CA: Jossey-Bass Publishers.

Gerrity, E., Keane, T.M., and Tuma, F. (Eds.) (2001). *The Mental Health Consequences of Torture*. New York: Kluwer Academic/Plenum Publishers.

Gibbs, J.T. and Huang, L.N. (Eds.) (2003). *Children of Color: Psychological Interventions with Culturally Diverse Youth* (2nd rev. ed.). San Francisco, CA: Jossey-Bass.

Gibson, K. (1989). Children in political violence. *Social Science in Medicine, 28,* 659–667.

Global Network for Justice. (2003). www.globalnetwork4justice.org/story.php?c_id=78.

Glod, C.A., Teicher, M.H., Martin, H., Hartman, C., and Harakal, T. (1997). Increased nocturnal activity and impaired sleep maintenance in abused children. *Journal of the American Academy of Child and Adolescent Psychiatry, 36*(9), 1236–1243.

Goenjian, A.K., Pynoos, R.S., Karayan, I., Minassian, D., Najarian, L.M., Steinberg, A.M., and Fairbanks, L.A. (1997). Outcome of psychotherapy among pre-adolescents after the 1988 earthquake in Armenia. *American Journal of Psychiatry, 154,* 536–542.

Goenjian, A.K., Pynoos, R.S., Steinberg, A.M., Najarian, L.M., Asarnow, J.R., Karayan, I., Ghurabi, M., and Fairbanks, L.A. (1995). Psychiatric co-morbidity in children after the 1988 earthquake in Armenia. *Journal of the American Academy of Child and Adolescent Psychiatry, 34*(9), 1174–1184.

Goenjian, A.K., Stilwell, B.M., Steinberg, A.M., Fairbanks, L.A., Galvin, M., Karayan, I., and Pynoos, R.S. (1999). Moral development and psychopathological interference with conscience functioning in adolescents after trauma. *Journal of the American Academy of Child and Adolescent Psychiatry, 38*(4), 376–384.

Goenjian, A.K., Yehuda, R., Pynoos, R.S., Steinberg, A.M., Tashjian, M., Yang, R.K., Najarian, L.M., and Fairbanks, L.A. (1996). Basal cortisol and dexamethasone suppression of cortisol and MHPG among adolescents after the 1988 earthquake in Armenia. *American Journal of Psychiatry, 153,* 929–934.

Goldfeld, A.E., Mollica, R.F., Pesavento, B.H., and Faraone, S.V. (1988). The physical and psychological sequelae of torture: Symptomatology and diagnosis. *Journal of the American Medical Association, 259,* 2725–2729.

Gurr, R. and Quiroga, J. (2001). Approaches to torture rehabilitation: A desk study covering effects, cost-effectiveness, participation, and sustainability (Supplementum No. 1). *Torture, 11*(1a), 5–35.

Higson-Smith, C. (2002). *Supporting Communities Affected by Violence: A Casebook from South Africa.* Oxford: Oxfam Publications. ISBN 0 85598 477 5.

Holtan, N.R. (1998). How medical assessment of victims of torture relates to psychiatric care. In J.M. Jaranson and M.K. Popkin (Eds.), *Caring for Victims of Torture.* Washington, DC: American Psychiatric Press.

Human Rights Watch Children's Rights Project. (1997). *Slipping Through the Cracks: Unaccompanied Children Detained by the U.S. Immigration and Naturalization Service.* Library of Congress Catalog Card Number 97–71373. www.hrw.org/reports/1997/uscrcks/, Human Rights Watch.

The International Rescue Committee Los Angeles. (Spring 2003). Less than homeless, more than capable. *NewStart, 5*(1), 1–2.

Jablensky, A., Marsella, A.J., Ekblad, S., Jansson, B., Levi, L., and Bornemann, T. (1994). Refugee mental health and well-being: Conclusions and recommendations. In A. J. Marsella, T. Bornemann, S. Ekblad, and J. Orley (Eds.), *Amidst Peril and Pain: The Mental Health and Well-Being of the World's Refugees* (pp. 327–339). Washington, DC: American Psychological Association.

Jaranson, J.M. (1995). Government-sanctioned torture: Status of the rehabilitation movement. *Transcultural Psychiatric Research Review, 32,* 253–286.

Jaranson, J.M., Butcher, J., Halcon, L., Johnson, D.R., Robertson, C., Savik, K., Spring, M., and Westermeyer, J. (2004). Somali and Oromo refugees: Correlates of torture and trauma history. *American Journal of Public Health, 94,* 591–598.

Jaranson, J.M., Kinzie, J.D., Friedman, M., Ortiz, D., Friedman, M.J., Southwick, S., Kastrup, M., and Mollica, R. (2001). Assessment, diagnosis, and intervention. In E. Gerrity, T.M. Keane, and F. Tuma (Eds.), *The Mental Health Consequences of Torture* (pp. 249–275). New York: Kluwer Academic/Plenum Publishers.

Keilson, H. (1980). Sequential traumatization of children. *Danish Medical Bulletin, 27,* 235–237.

Khamis, V. (1993). Post-traumatic stress disorder among the injured of the Intifada. *Journal of Traumatic Stress, 6,* 555–560.

Kilpatrick, D.G., Saunders, B.E., Resnick, H.S., and Smith, D.W. (1995). *The National Survey of Adolescents: Preliminary Findings on Lifetime Prevalence of Traumatic Events and Mental Health Correlates.* Charleston, SC: National Crime Victims Research and Treatment Center, Medical University of South Carolina.

Kinzie, J.D. (2001). Psychotherapy for massively traumatized refugees: The therapist variable. *Journal of Psychotherapy, 55,* 475–490.

Kinzie, J.D., Sack, W., Angell, R., Clarke, G., and Binn, R. (1989). A three-year follow-up of Cambodian young people traumatized as children. *Journal of the American Academy of Child and Adolescent Psychiatry, 28*(4), 501–504.

Kinzie, J.D., Sack, W.H., Angell, R.H., Manson, S., and Rath B. (1986). The psychiatric effects of massive trauma on Cambodian children: I. The children. *Journal of the American Academy of Child and Adolescent Psychiatry, 25*(3), 370–376.

Kirsten, J.C., Holzer, I.M., Koch, L., and Severin, B. (1980). Children and torture. *Danish Medical Bulletin, 27,* 238–239.

Kleinman, A. (1980). *Patients and Healers in the Context of Culture.* Berkeley, CA: University of California Press.

Kleinman, A. (1988). *The Illness Narratives: Suffering, Healing, and the Human Condition.* New York: Basic Books.

Kleinman, A. (1995). Violence, culture, and the politics of trauma. In A. Kleinman (Ed.), *Writing at the Margin: Discourse Between Anthropology and Medicine* (pp. 173–189). Berkeley, CA: University of California Press.

Lawyers Committee for Human Rights. (February, 1991). *The UNHCR at 40: Refugee Protection at the Crossroads.* New York: Author.

Lee, E. and Lu, F. (1989). Assessment and treatment of Asian-American survivors of mass violence. *Journal of Traumatic Stress, 2*, 93–120.

Look, K.M. and Look, R.M. (1997). Skin scraping, cupping, and moxibustion that may mimic physical abuse. *Journal of Forensic Science, 42*(1), 103–105.

Lorion, R.P. and Saltzman, W. (1993). Children's exposure to community violence: Following a path from concern to research to action. *Psychiatry, 56*, 55–65.

Losel, F. and Bliesener, T. (1990). Resilience in adolescence: A study on the generalizability of protective factors. In K. Hurrelmann and F. Losel (Eds.), *Health Hazards in Adolescence.* New York: Walter de Gruyter.

Lustig, S.L., Kia-Keating, M., Knight, W.G., Geltman, P., Ellis, H., Keane, T., and Saxe, G.N. (2002). *White Paper: Child and Adolescent Refugee Mental Health.* National Child Traumatic Stress Network. Boston, MA: Center for Medical and Refugee Trauma.

Macksoud, M. (1992). Assessing war trauma in children: A case study of Lebanese children. *Journal of Refugee Studies, 5*, 1–15.

Macksoud, M. and Aber, L. (1996). The war experiences and psychosocial development of children in Lebanon. *Child Development, 67*, 70–88.

Mahjoub, A., Leyens, J., Yzerby, V., and Di Giacomo, J. (1989). War stress and coping modes: Representations of self-identity and time perspective among Palestinian children. *International Journal of Mental Health, 18*, 44–62.

Markstrom, C.A., Stamm, B.H., Stamm, H.E., Berthold, S.M., and Running Wolf, P. (2003). Ethnicity and rural status in behavioral healthcare. In B.H. Stamm (Ed.), *Behavioral Healthcare in Rural and Frontier Areas: An Interdisciplinary Handbook.* A Publication of the American Psychological Association Committee on Rural Health.

Marsella, A.J., Friedman, M.J., Gerrity, E.T., and Scurfield, R.M. (Eds.) (1996) . *Ethnocultural Aspects of Posttraumatic Stress Disorder: Issues, Research, and Clinical Applications.* Washington, DC: American Psychological Association.

Maslow, A. (1970). *Motivation and Personality* (2nd ed.). New York: Harper & Row.

McWhirter, J.J., McWhirter, B.T., McWhirter, A.M., and McWhirter, E.H. (1998). *At-Risk Youth: A Comprehensive Response.* Pacific Grove, CA: Brooks-Cole Publishing.

Mollica, R.F. (July 1, 2004). Global health: Surviving torture. *New England Journal of Medicine, 351*(1), 5–7.

Mollica, R.F., Donelan, K., Tor, S., Lavelle, J., Elias, C., Frankel, M., and Blendon, R.J. (1993). The effect of trauma and confinement on functional health and mental health status of Cambodians living in Thailand-Cambodian border camps. *Journal of the American Medical Association, 270*, 581–586.

Mollica, R.F., Poole, C., Son, L., Murray, C., and Tor, S. (1997). Effects of war trauma on Cambodian refugee adolescents' functional health and mental health status. *Journal of American Child and Adolescent Psychiatry, 36*, 1098–1106.

Monk, G., Winslade, J., Crocket, K., and Epston, D. (Eds.) (1997). *Narrative Therapy in Practice: The Archaeology of Hope.* San Francisco, CA: Jossey-Bass Inc.

Morris, P. and Silove, D. (1992). Cultural influence in psychotherapy with refugee survivors of torture and trauma. *Hospital and Community Psychiatry, 43*, 820–824.

Murad, Z. (June 2003). Refugee children: A world beyond pain. *NIPA Karachi, 8*(2), 1–13. On-line at: www.nipa-khi.edu.pk/Refujee percent 20Children-june2003.pdf.

Murphy, L., Pynoos, R. S., and James, C.B. (1997). The trauma/grief focused group psychotherapy module of an elementary school-based violence prevention/intervention program. In J.D. Osofsky (Ed.), *Children in a Violent Society* (pp. 223–255). New York: Guilford Press.

Nader, K.O. (2004). Assessing traumatic experiences in children and adolescents: Self-reports of RSM PTSO Criteria B-D Symptom. In J.P. Wilson and T.M. Keane (Eds.), *Assessing Psychological Trauma and PTSD: A Practitioner's Handbook* (pp. 513–537) (2nd ed.). New York: Guilford Press.

Nader, K., Pynoos, R.S., Fairbanks, L.A., Al-Ajeel, M., and Al-Asfour, A. (1993). A preliminary study of PTSD and grief among the children of Kuwait following the Gulf crisis. *British Journal of Clinical Psychology, 32*, 407–416.

Perlman, S.D. (1999). *The Therapist's Emotional Survival: Dealing with the Pain of Exploring Trauma.* Northvale, NJ: Jason Aronson.

Punamaki, R. (1989). Factors affecting the mental health of Palestinian children exposed to political violence. *International Journal of Mental Health, 18*, 63–79.

Putman, F.W. and Trickett, P.K. (1993). Child sexual abuse: A model of chronic trauma. *Psychiatry, 56*, 82–95.

Pynoos, R., Goenjian, A.K., Tashjian, M., Karakashian, M., Manjikian, R., Manoukian, G., Steinberg, A.M., and Fairbanks, L. (1993). Posttraumatic stress reactions in children after the 1988 Armenian earthquake. *British Journal of Psychiatry, 163*, 239–247.

Pynoos, R.S. and Eth, S. (1985). Children traumatized by witnessing personal violence: Homicide, rape, or suicide behavior. In S. Eth and R. Pynoos (Eds.), *Posttraumatic Stress Disorder in Children.* Washington, DC: American Psychiatric Press.

Pynoos, R.S., Frederick, C., Nader, K., Arroyo, W., Steinberg, A.M., Eth, S., Nunez, F., and Fairbanks, L. (1987). Life threat and posttraumatic stress in school-age children. *Archives of General Psychiatry, 44*, 1057–1063.

Pynoos, R.S., Goenjian, A.K., and Steinberg, A.M. (1998). A public mental health approach to the postdisaster treatment of children and adolescents. *Child and Adolescent Psychiatric Clinics of North America, 7*(1), 195–210.

Pynoos, R.S., Kinzie, J.D., and Gordon, M. (2001). Children, adolescents, and families exposed to torture and related trauma. In E. Gerrity, T.M. Keane, and F. Tuma (Eds.), *The Mental Health Consequences of Torture* (pp. 211–225). New York: Kluwer Academic/Plenum Publishers.

Pynoos, R.S., Steinberg, A.M., and Wraith, R. (1995). A developmental model of childhood traumatic stress. In D. Cicchetti and D.J. Cohen (Eds.), *Manual of Developmental Psychopathology: Vol. 2. Risk, Disorder, and Adaptation* (pp. 72–95). New York: Wiley.

Quiroga, J. and Berthold, S.M. (March/April 2004). Torture survivors: Unique health and mental health issues. *Refugee Reports, 25*(2), 5–8. A News Service of Immigration and Refugee Services of America.

Randall, G.R. and Lutz, E.L. (1991). *Serving Survivors of Torture.* American Association for the Advancement of Science: Washington, DC.

Rasmussen, O.V. (1990). Medical aspects of torture. *Danish Medical Bulletin, 37*, 1–88.

Rousseau, C. (1993–1994). The place of the unexpressed: Ethics and methodology for research with refugee children. *Canada's Mental Health, 41*, 12–16.

Rousseau, C., Drapeau, A., and Corin, E. (1998). Risk and protective factors in Central American and Southeast Asian refugee children. *The Journal of Refugee Studies, 11*(1), 20–37.

Rousseau, C., Said, T., Gagne, M-J., and Bibeau, G. (1998). Resilience in unaccompanied minors from the north of Somalia. *Psychoanalytic Review, 85*, 615–637.

Rutter, M. (1979). Protective factors in children's responses to stress and disadvantage. In M.W. Kent and J.E. Rolf (Eds.), *Primary Prevention of Psychopathology.* Vol. 3. Hanover, NH: University Press of New England.

Rutter, M. (1987). Continuities and discontinuities from infancy. In J. Osofsky (Ed.), *Handbook of Infant Development* (2nd ed.). New York: Wiley.

Sabin, D., Sack, W.H., Clarke, C.N., Meas, N., and Richart, I. (1996). The Khmer Adolescent Project: 3. A study of the trauma from Thailand Site Two Refugee Camp. *Journal of the American Academy of Child and Adolescent Psychiatry, 35*(3), 384–391.

Sack, W.H., Angell, R.H., Kinzie, J.D., and Rath, B. (1986). The psychiatric effects of massive trauma on Cambodian children: II. The family, the home, and the school. *Journal of the American Academy of Child and Adolescent Psychiatry, 25*(3), 377–383.

Sack, W.H., Clarke, G.N., and Seeley, J. (1996). Multiple forms of stress in Cambodian adolescent refugees. *Child Development, 67*(11), 107–116.

Sack, W.H., Clarke, G., Him, C., Dickason, D., Goff, B., Lanham, K., and Kinzie, J.D. (1993). A 6-year follow-up study of Cambodian refugee adolescents traumatized as children. *Journal of the American Academy of Child and Adolescent Psychiatry, 32*(2), 431–437.

Sack, W.H., Seeley, J., and Clarke, G.N. (1997). Does PTSD transcend cultural barriers: A look from the Khmer Adolescent Refugee Project. *Journal of the American Academy of Child and Adolescent Psychiatry, 36*(1), 49–54.

Servan-Schreiber, D., Lin, B.L., and Birmaher, B. (1998). Prevalence of posttraumatic stress disorder and major depressive disorder in Tibetan refugee children. *Journal of the American Academy of Child and Adolescent Psychiatry, 37*, 874–879.

Skylv, G. (1992). The physical sequelae of torture. In M. Basoglu (Ed.), *Torture and Its Consequences: Current Treatment Approaches* (pp. 38–55). Cambridge: Cambridge University Press.

Summerfield, D. (1999). A critique of seven assumptions behind psychological trauma programmes in war-affected areas. *Social Science and Medicine, 48*, 1449–1462.

Summerfield, D. (2000). Childhood, war, refugeedom and "Trauma": Three core questions for mental health professionals. *Transcultural Psychiatry, 37*, 417–433.

Swartz, L. and Levett, A. (1989). Political repression and children in South Africa: The social construction of damaging effects. *Social Science in Medicine, 28*, 741–750.

Terr, L.C. (1983). Chowchilla revisited: The effects of psychic trauma four years after a school bus kidnapping. *American Journal of Psychiatry, 140*, 1543–1550.

Tudin, P., Straker, G., and Mendolsohn, M. (1994). Social and political complexity and moral development. *South Africa Journal of Psychology, 24*(3), 163–168.

UNHCR. (1949a). Geneva convention relative to the protection of civilian persons in time of War. Adopted on August 12, 1949. Entry into force October 21, 1950. Geneva, Switzerland: Author. [On-line]. Available: www.unhchr.ch/html/menu3/b/92.htm.

UNHCR. (1949b). Geneva Convention Relative to the Treatment Of Prisoners Of War of August 12, 1949 (Geneva Convention III). Entry into force October 21, 1950. Geneva, Switzerland: Author. [On-line]. Available: http://fletcher.tufts.edu/multi/texts/BH240.txt.

UNHCR. (1994). Refugee Children: Guidelines on Protection and Care. www.unher.ch/cgi-bin/ exis/vtx/home?page=search (search: "Refugee Children").

UNHCR. (2002). Special feature on the 50th anniversary of the convention. www.unhcr.org/1951convention index.html.

UNHCR. (2003a). www.unhcr.ch/cgibin/texis/vtx/home/opendoc.pdf?tbl=STATISTICS&id=3d075d374&page= statistics.

UNHCR. (2003b) Refugees by numbers 2003 edition, link to report from www.unhcr.ch/cgi-bin/texis/ vtx/basics.

United Nations. (1995). Convention against torture and other cruel, inhuman or degrading treatment or punishment. (Document 50, A/RES/39/46, December 10, 1984). In *The United Nations and Human Rights: 1945–1995.* (The United Nations Blue Book Series, Volume VII, pp. 294–300.) United Nations, New York: Department of Public Information.

U.S. Committee for Refugees. (2003a). *World Refugee Survey 2003.* www.refugees.org/world/articles/ wrs03_americas2.cfm.htm#unitedstates.

U.S. Committee for Refugees. (2003b). www.refugees.org/news/crisis/BURMESE2003.cfm.

U.S. Department of Homeland Security. (2002). *2002 Yearbook of Immigration Statistics.* Table 21. On-line at http://uscis.gov/graphics/shared/aboutus/statistics/RA2002yrbk/RA2002list.htm.

van der Kolk, B.A. (1985). Adolescent vulnerability to post-traumatic stress. *Psychiatry, 48,* 365–370.

van der Veer, G. (1998). *Counseling and Therapy with Refugees and Victims of Trauma: Psychological Problems of Victims of War, Torture and Repression* (2nd ed.). Chichester, England: John Wiley & Sons.

Wade, A. (March 1997). Small acts of living: Everyday resistance to violence and other forms of oppression. *Contemporary Family Therapy, 19*(1), 23–39.

Watters, C. (2001). Emerging paradigms in the mental health care of refugees. *Social Science and Medicine, 52,* 1709–1718.

Werner, E.E. (1990). Protective factors and individual resilience. In S.J. Meisels and J.P. Shonkoff (Eds.), *Handbook of Early Childhood Education.* Cambridge, England: Cambridge University Press.

Women's Issues. (2003). On-line at womensissues.about.com/cs/honorkillings/a/honorkillings.htm.

Wong, H.C.G. (1999). Signs of physical abuse or evidence of moxibustion, cupping, or coining? *Canadian Medical Association Journal, 160,* 785.

Yule, W. (1992). Post-traumatic stress disorder in child survivors of shipping disasters: The sinking of the Jupiter. *Psychotherapy and Psychosomatics, 57,* 200–205.

Yule, W. and Canterbury, R. (1994). The treatment of posttraumatic stress disorder in children and adolescents. *International Review of Psychiatry, 6,* 141–151.

Zane, N. and Sue, S. (1991). Culturally-responsive mental health services for Asian Americans: Treatment and training issues. In H. Myers, P. Wohlford, and P. Guzman (Eds.), *Ethnic Minority Perspectives on Clinical Training and Services in Psychology* (pp. 49–58). Washington DC: American Psychological Association.

Zivic, I. (1993). Emotional reactions of children to war stress in Croatia. *Journal of American Academy of Child and Adolescent Psychiatry, 32,* 709–713.

CHAPTER 9

Abels, P. and Murphy, M. (1981). *Administration in the Human Services: A Normative Systems Approach.* Englewood Cliffs: Prentice Hall.

Alliance for Children and Families, American Public Human Services Association, and Child Welfare League of America. (May 2001). *The Child Welfare Workforce Challenge: Results from a Preliminary Study.* Washington, DC: Child Welfare League of America.

Allison, M.T. (1999). Organizational barriers to diversity in the workplace. *Journal of Leisure Research, 31*(1), 78–101.

Bilchik, S. (2004—November 3). Personal communication. (Mr. Bilchik, JD, is the President/Chief Executive Officer of the Child Welfare League of America.)

Blassingame, K. (2001). An agency renewed, a commitment revived. *Children's Voice, 10*(1), 32–35.

Blau, P.M. (1962). *Bureaucracy in Modern Society.* New York: Random House.

California Association of Deans and Directors of Schools of Social Work. (2004). *Master Plan for Social Work Education in the State of California.* Berkeley, CA: California Social Work Education Center (Cal.SWEC), School of Social Welfare, University of California at Berkeley.

Cejka, S. (1993). The changing healthcare workforce: A call for managing diversity. *Healthcare Executive, 8*(2), 23.

Child Welfare League of America. (2000). *Standards for Cultural Competence.* Available online at www.cwla.org/ prorgrams/cultural competence.

Child Welfare League of America. (2002). *The Impact of ASFA on Children and Families of Color* (Proceedings of a Forum). Washington, DC: CWLA.

Coile, R.C. Jr. (1999). Millennium management: New rules for 21st century healthcare organizations. *Healthcare Executive, 14*(1), 11.

Cox, T.H. and Blake, S. (1991). Managing cultural diversity: Implications for organizational competitiveness. *Academy of Management Executive, 5,* 45–56.

Daley, J.M. and Wong, P. (1994). Community development with emerging ethnic communities. *Journal of Community Practice, 1*(1), 9–24.

Daniel, G. (2004—June 22). Personal Communication. (Mr. Daniel, MSW, is a former Regional Administrator for Texas Child Protective Services, Department of Protective and Regulatory Services, serving a 13-county area including Houston/Harris County; and is a consultant to agencies in social services administration, as well as those seeking to achieve accreditation through the Council on Accreditation.)

deAnda, J., Dolan, T.C., Lee-Eddie, D., Ellison, C., and Honkawa, Y. (1998). A race/ethnic comparison of career attainment in healthcare management. *Healthcare Executive, 13*(3), 28–33.

Drucker, P. (1954). *The Practice of Management.* NY: Harper.

Esty, K., Griffin, R., and Hirsch, M. (1995). A manager's guide to solving problems and turning diversity into a competitive advantage. *Workplace Diversity,* 7–12. Holbrook, MA: Adams Media.

Foucault, M. (1975). *The Birth of the Clinic.* NY: Vintage Books.

Gathers, D. (2003). Diversity Management: An Imperative for Healthcare Organizations. *Hospital Topics,* 81(3), 14.

Gilbert, J.A., Stead, B.A., and Ivancevich, J.M. (1999). Diversity management: a new organizational paradigm. *Journal of Business Ethics,* 21(1), 61.

Goffman, I. (1961). *Asylums.* NY: Anchor Books.

Goodwin, J.P. (1989). *More Man Than You'll Ever Be: Gay Folklore and Acculturation in Middle America.* Bloomington & Indianapolis: Indiana University Press.

Henderson, G. (1994). *Cultural Diversity in the Workplace: Issues and Strategies.* Westport, CN: Quorum.

Ivancevich, J.M. and Gilbert, J.A. (2000). Diversity management: Time for a new approach. *Public Personnel Management,* 29(1), 75–77, 84–87.

Jansson, B. (1999). *Becoming an Effective Policy Advocate.* Pacific Grove, CA: Brooks/Cole.

JobCircle.com. (1999). Breaking through: How minorities can break-or bend-corporate barriers. Available at www.jobcircle.com/career/articles/2862.html.

Johnson, W.B. and Packer, A.E. (1987). *Workforce 2000: Gaining the Diversity Advantage.* San Francisco: Jossey-Bass.

Kadushin, A. (1976). *Supervision in Social Work.* New York: Columbia University Press.

Kirshenblatt-Gimblett, B. (1983). Studying immigrant and ethnic folklore. *Handbook of American Folklore.* E. Dorson (Ed.), Bloomington, IN: Indiana University Press, pp. 43–44.

Kluger, M. and Baker, W. (1994). *Innovative Leadership in the Nonprofit Organization.* Washington, DC: Child Welfare League of America.

Loden, M. and Rosenor, J.B. (1991). *Workforce America! Managing Employee Diversity as a Vital Resource.* Homewood, IL: Irwin.

Malik, S. and Velazquez, J. Jr. (2002). Cultural competence and the new Americans. *Children's Voice, 11*(4), 23–25.

Mallon, G. (2001). Sticks and stones can break your bones: Verbal harassment and physical violence in the lives of gay and lesbian youths in child welfare settings. *Journal of Gay & Lesbian Social Services,* 13(1/2), 63–81.

Malm, K., Bess, R., Leos-Urbel, J., Geen, R., and Markowitz, T. (2001). Running to keep in place: The continuing evolution of our nation's child welfare system. *Assessing the New Federalism,* Occasional Paper Number 54. Washington, DC: The Urban Institute.

McGregor, D. (1960). *The Human Side of Enterprise.* New York: McGraw Hill Book Company.

Murphy, P.E. (1988). Implementing Business Ethics. *Journal of Business Ethics,* 7, 907–915.

National Association of Social Workers. (1999 revised). *Code of Ethics.* Washington, DC: National Association of Social Workers.

National Black Justice Coalition. (2004). Black Couples Have the Most at Stake in Marriage Debate. *Los Angeles Magazine,* November 1, 2004.

National Council of La Raza (NCLR). (2004). *Lost Opportunities: The Reality of Latinos in the U.S. Criminal Justice System.* www.nclr.org/.

Pasztor, E.M., Saint-Germain, M., and DeCrescenzo, T. (2002). *The Demand for Social Workers in the California.* Retrieved February 14, 2004, from www.csus/edu/calst/Government_Affairs/faculty_fellows_program. html.

Pasztor, E.M., Goodman, C.C., Potts, M., Santana, M.I., and Runnels, R.A. (2002). *Kinship Caregivers and Social Workers: The Challenge of Collaboration (An Evidence-based Research to Practice Curriculum).* Berkeley: California Social Work Education Center (CalSWEC), School of Social Welfare, University of California at Berkeley.

Pasztor, E.M. and Pederson, T. (2004). Image of social workers in the media. *NASW California News.* Sacramento, CA: National Association of Social Workers, California Chapter.

Pasztor, E.M., McNitt, M., and McFadden, E.J. (2005). Foster parent recruitment, development, support and retention: Strategies for the 21st century. In G. Mallon and P. Hess (Eds.), *Handbook of Children, Youth, and Family Services: Practices, Policies, and Programs.* New York: Columbia University Press, 2005.

Pecora, P., Whittaker, J., Maluccio, A.N., Barth, R., and Plotnik, R. (2000). *The Child Welfare Challenge: Policy, Research, and Practice.* New York: Aldine De Gruyter.

Perrow, C. (1978). Demystifying Organizations. In R. Sari and Y. Hasenfeld (Eds.), *The Management of Human Services.* New York: Columbia University Press.

Peterson, D.J., Betts, S.C., and Richmond, L.S. (2002). Diversity in children, youth, and family programs: Cooperative extension. *Journal of Family and Consumer Sciences,* 94(2), 58.

Polsky, H. (1977). *Cottage Six.* New York: Kreiger Publishing.

Rapp, C.A. and Poertner, J. (1992). *Social Administration: A Client-Centered Approach*. New York: Longman Publishing Group.

Roberts, D. (2001). *Shattered Bonds: The Color of Child Welfare*. New York: Basic Books.

Roethlisberger, F.J. and Dickson, W.J. (1939). *Management and the Worker*. Cambridge, MA: Harvard University Press.

Rycus, J. and Hughes, R. (1998). *Field Guide to Child Welfare*. Washington, DC: CWLA Press.

Sessa, V.I. (1992). Managing Diversity at the Xerox Corporation: Balanced work force goals and Caucus groups. *Diversity in the Workplace*. The Guilford Press: New York.

Spain, D. (2002). *How Women Saved the City*. Minneapolis, MN: University of Minnesota Press.

Sullivan, C., Sommer, S., and Moff, J. (2001). *Youth in the Margins: A Report on the Unmet Needs of Lesbian, Gayu, Bisexual, and Transgender Adolescents in Foster Care*. New York: Lambda Legal Defense and Education Fund.

Tajfel, H. and Turner, J. (1979). An integrative theory of intergroup conflict in W.G. Austin and S. Worchel (Eds.), *The Social Psychology of Intergroup Relations*, 33–47. Monterey, CA: Brooks/Cole Publishing Company.

Taylor, F. (1911). *Scientific Management*. New York: Harper & Row.

The Annie E. Casey Foundation. (2003). *The Unsolved Challenge of System Reform: The Condition of the Frontline Human Services Workforce*. Baltimore, Maryland: Author.

Weaver, D., Furman, W., Moses, T., Lindsey, D., and Cherin, D. (1999). *The Effects of Computerization on Public Child Welfare Practice*. Long Beach, CA: California Child Welfare Resource Library, Department of Social Work, California State University, Long Beach.

Weber, M. (1970). Bureaucracy. In O. Grusky and G. Miller (Eds.), *The Sociology of Organizations*. New York: The Free Press.

Weick, K.E. (1993). The Collapse of Sensemaking in Organizations: The Mann Gulch Disaster. *Administrative Science Quartery*, 38, 628–652.

Weinbach, R. (1998). *The Social Worker as Manager*. Boston, MA: Allyn and Bacon.

Wingfield, K. (2004—November 5). Personnal communication. (Ms. Wingfield, MSW, is Senior Advisor to the President/CEO of the Child Welfare League of America.)

Wolfson, E. (2004). *Why Marriage Matters: America, Equality, and Gay People's Right to Marry*. New York: Simon & Schuster.

CHAPTER 10

Allison, M.T. (1999). Organizational barriers to diversity in the workplace. *Journal of Leisure Research*, *31*(1), 78–101.

Anderson, J.A. and Carter, R.W. (Eds.) (2003). *Diversity Perspectives for Social Work Practice*. Boston, MA: Allyn & Bacon.

CSWE. (2004). The educational policy and accreditation standards. Retrieved July 22, 2005, from www.cswe.org.

Fellin, P. (2000). Revisiting multiculturalism in social work. *Journal of Social Work Education*, *36*, 261–278.

Leigh, J.W. (1999). Forward. In J.W. Green. *Cultural Awareness in the Human Services: A Multicultural Approach* (pp. xi–xii). Boston, MA: Allyn & Bacon.

Lipsky, M. (1980). *Street-Level Bureaucracy: Dilemmas of the Individual in Public Services*. New York: Russell Sage Foundation.